Luke Bissell

THE ENCYCLOPEDIA OF THE
MOTORCYCLE

THE ENCYCLOPEDIA OF THE
MOTORCYCLE

HUGO WILSON

PHOTOGRAPHY BY DAVE KING

DORLING KINDERSLEY

LONDON • NEW YORK • STUTTGART • MOSCOW

A DORLING KINDERSLEY BOOK

First published in Great Britain in 1995
by Dorling Kindersley Limited,
9 Henrietta Street, London WC2E 8PS
Reprinted 1996

Art editor Claire Pegrum
Senior editor Janice Lacock
Editors Jo Evans, Laurence Henderson, Jacky Jackson
Assistant designers Carla De Abreu, Stephen Croucher
Assistant editors David T. Walton, David Williams
Senior art editor Tracy Hambleton-Miles

Deputy art director Tina Vaughan
Managing editor Sean Moore
DTP designer Zirrinia Austin
Production controller Stephen Stuart

A CIP catalogue record for this book is
available from the British Library

ISBN 0 7513 0206 6

Reproduced by Colourscan, Singapore
Printed and bound in Italy by A. Mondadori, Verona

NOTE ON SPECIFICATIONS
*Every effort has been made to ensure that the motorcycle specification
information is accurate. In some cases only estimated values were
available and, in a very few cases, no relevant information existed.
Measurements of individual components and of the motorcycle's weight,
speed, capacity, etc., are quoted according to the convention of the country
of origin. In the United States, for example, the capacity of motorcycles
was given in cubic inches until the 1950s and 1960s. More modern
machines are measured in cubic centimetres. In addition, motorcycling
convention dictates that engine measurements be given in metric only.*

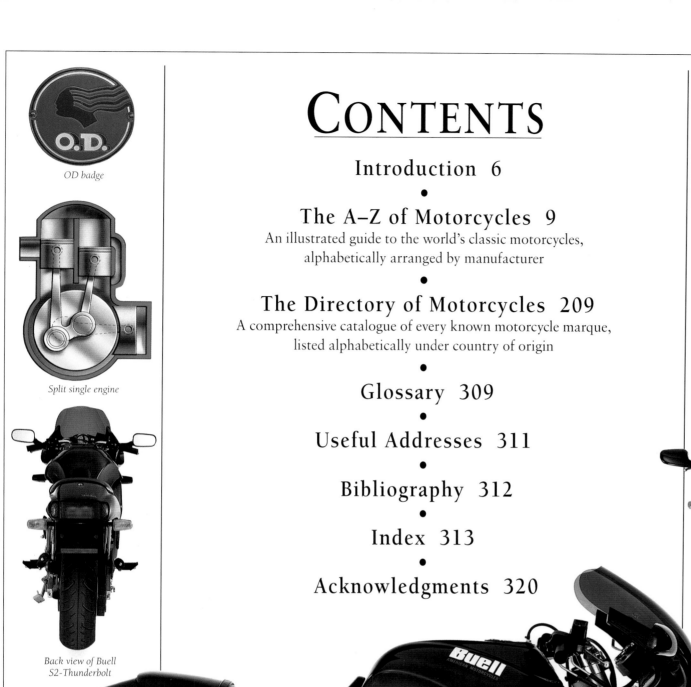

OD badge

Split single engine

Back view of Buell S2-Thunderbolt

CONTENTS

Harley-Davidson badge

Early Motor Cycling *magazine*

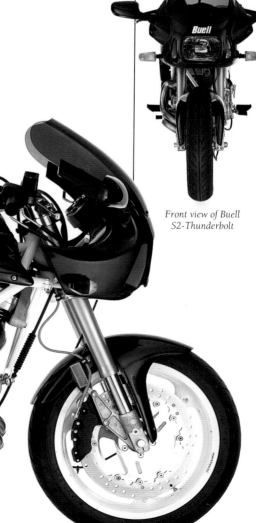

Front view of Buell S2-Thunderbolt

Buell S2-Thunderbolt

INTRODUCTION

THE FIRST MOTORCYCLE
was the work of Gottlieb Daimler and his associates. But it was not a practical means of transport.

THIS BOOK is about more than motorcycles. It is the story of the designers and factory workers who made the motorcycles, the competitors who raced the motorcycles, the people who bought and rode the motorcycles, and the mechanics and enthusiasts who fixed the motorcycles. It shows how the particular circumstances, culture, climate, and terrain of countries have affected the marketing and manufacture of these machines. Politics, economics, and two World Wars have had a bigger effect on motorcycle production and sales than radical designs and racing success.

National Influences

The vast size and rugged terrain of the United States called for a rugged machine as the motorcycle replaced the horse in the American mid-West at the turn of the 20th century. Harley-Davidson and Indian established themselves as the top American manufacturers because they made tough bikes that could be ridden by farmhands and fixed by blacksmiths.

Restrictions on the German aircraft industry imposed by the victors of World War I forced several aircraft and engine makers into motorcycle production. BMW was among them. Its background led the company to build an innovative and advanced machine superior to most others of the period.

The demand for cheap, efficient transport in the chaos of post-World War II Japan resulted in Soichiro Honda creating the Honda Cub, the world's most successful motorcycle and the basis of the huge Honda corporation of today.

A similar response in war-torn Italy led to the rejuvenation of the Italian industry. But there, where style and sporting heritage mean more than mundane practicalities, companies like MV Agusta and Ducati raised the motorcycle to an art form.

Conversely, in the United Kingdom, the industrial malaise of the 1950s and 1960s is reflected in the collapse of its once-dominant industry in the 1960s and 1970s.

A selection of the world's best machines from all these countries is featured in the A–Z of motorcyles (see pp.9–208).

THE INTRODUCTION
of the "new" Werner in 1901 provided a pattern that many early manufacturers copied.

IN THE MID-1920S MANY MANUFACTURERS
were producing similar machines. The 1926 Diamant from Germany has a typical diamond-pattern frame and girder forks. The engine and gearbox are proprietary components. A similar machine could have been made by many companies.

The Inventors and the Early Days

Individuals like William Harley, Soichiro Honda, Carlo Guzzi, and James Norton left their mark on the machines that bear their names. But many other designers, racers, and entrepreneurs have also left their two-wheeled tracks since 1869 when French cycle maker Michaux first attached a steam engine to a bone-shaker bicycle.

Compact engines and the bicycle both underwent intensive development in the second half of the 19th century. The motorcycle was inevitable as soon as someone realized that a bicycle that moved without the rider's physical exertion had to be a good idea. Unfortunately the performance and reliability of early engines ensured that pioneer motorcyclists spent much of their time pushing or pedalling their crude machines. It was not until the second decade of the 20th century that motorcycle makers felt confident enough in the capabilities of their machines to dispense with the bicycle chain and pedalling gear.

BRITISH MOTORCYCLE MAKERS
lost touch with the needs of the market in the years after this 1948 BSA Star Twin was produced.

The first petrol-engined motorcycle is credited to Gottlieb Daimler, who built his Einspur in 1885. It was built to test his new engine design and he did not show much interest in the motorcycle once his engine had proved its mettle. The maiden journey of the Einspur was a trip of six miles (ten kilometres) during which it apparently set fire to the rider's seat. It was a long way from being a practical vehicle.

In 1894 Messrs Hildebrand & Wolfmüller offered production versions of their new design for sale to the general public. Interest in motor vehicles was sufficient to create a brief flurry of orders. But the machine was undeveloped, unreliable, and uneconomic.

Albert DeDion and Georges Bouton took the next leap forward. Their faster running petrol engine produced sufficient power and was reliable enough to make the DeDion tricycle an (almost) practical motor vehicle. Once it was in production in the late 1890s it was widely copied.

With the availability of engines and a ready market for the new machines, blacksmiths and bicycle makers began to set themselves up as motorcycle manufacturers. This was the cutting edge of new technology and the birth of a new industry.

The Manufacturers

Lots of individuals and small firms started making motorcycles in the early 1900s. In Britain, France, and Germany it was (comparatively) easy. Budding manufacturers bought an engine, a frame, and a bag full of miscellaneous components. Each bolted his pieces together to create his own motorcycle, then gave it a name and created his own marque. Some of these machines were good, others bad. Some sold, others did not. All that remains of many embryonic motorcycle marques is an advert or a paragraph in a period

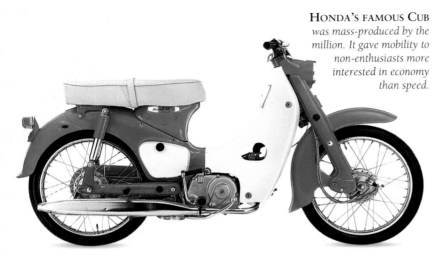

HONDA'S FAMOUS CUB *was mass-produced by the million. It gave mobility to non-enthusiasts more interested in economy than speed.*

publication. Most are listed in the directory of motorcycles in this book (see pp.209–308). Others have vanished forever. Small-scale motorcycle manufacturing was common until the 1920s, especially in Britain and Germany, where hundreds of small makers appeared.

Soon, established companies began making large numbers of machines. Many had their roots in the bicycle industry – Triumph and BSA in the United Kingdom, Peugeot in France, Indian in the United States, Victoria and NSU in Germany, and Bianchi in Italy.

The biggest industries were established in the countries with the largest markets. The United States, United Kingdom, France, Germany, and Italy rapidly emerged as the major motorcycle producing nations. Import restrictions and taxation classes ensured the viability of some producers and made particular-sized machines popular in different places. Manufacturers also emerged in smaller countries though these were often reliant on engines and other components supplied from Britain, Germany, or elsewhere.

The motorcycle industry provided mobility. While racing machines and expensive prestige models were coveted by enthusiasts, money was made by producing cheap, bread and butter motorcycles that transported people to work. And when a family needed to move, it hitched a sidecar to its machine.

But the arrival of the cheap car changed all that. Henry Ford's mass-produced Model T was

MANY LARGE-CAPACITY MACHINES, *like this 1994 Kawasaki ZX-11, are sold more for their image, performance, and riding pleasure than as a means of transport. The popularity of prestige models depends on the whims of the buying public rather than value for money or practicality.*

cheaper than most motorcycles and it effectively killed off the American motorcycle industry between 1910 and 1920. In France and Germany a similar effect was felt in the late 1950s.

At that time the emerging Japanese industry moved swiftly towards mass production of motorcycles. Its machines were sold to a world market interested in economy of use and traffic-beating manoeuvrability.

Full Circle

The motorcycle market has since changed again. A bike is still a good way to get to work, but it is also a prestige plaything – a leisure product like a windsurfer or a mountain bicycle. Marques like BMW, Harley-Davidson, and Triumph do not just produce motorcycles, they make status symbols for image-conscious customers.

But while Western markets move further towards the idea of the motorcycle as a toy, volume production of utilitarian motorcycles is increasing in developing nations like China, India, and Korea. There, manufacturers are filling the transportation needs of huge domestic markets while making export inroads elsewhere.

While mainstream motorcycle manufacture is now dominated by large companies dealing in huge numbers of machines, there is still room for small concerns that produce remarkable machines in very small numbers. They include Patrick Barigo in France, Arturo Magni in Italy, and John Britten in New Zealand. These individuals have made a minuscule number of bikes compared to Suzuki or BSA, but have still played a significant role in the history of the motorcycle. They, and another three thousand motorcycle makers, past and present, from around the world, appear in this book.

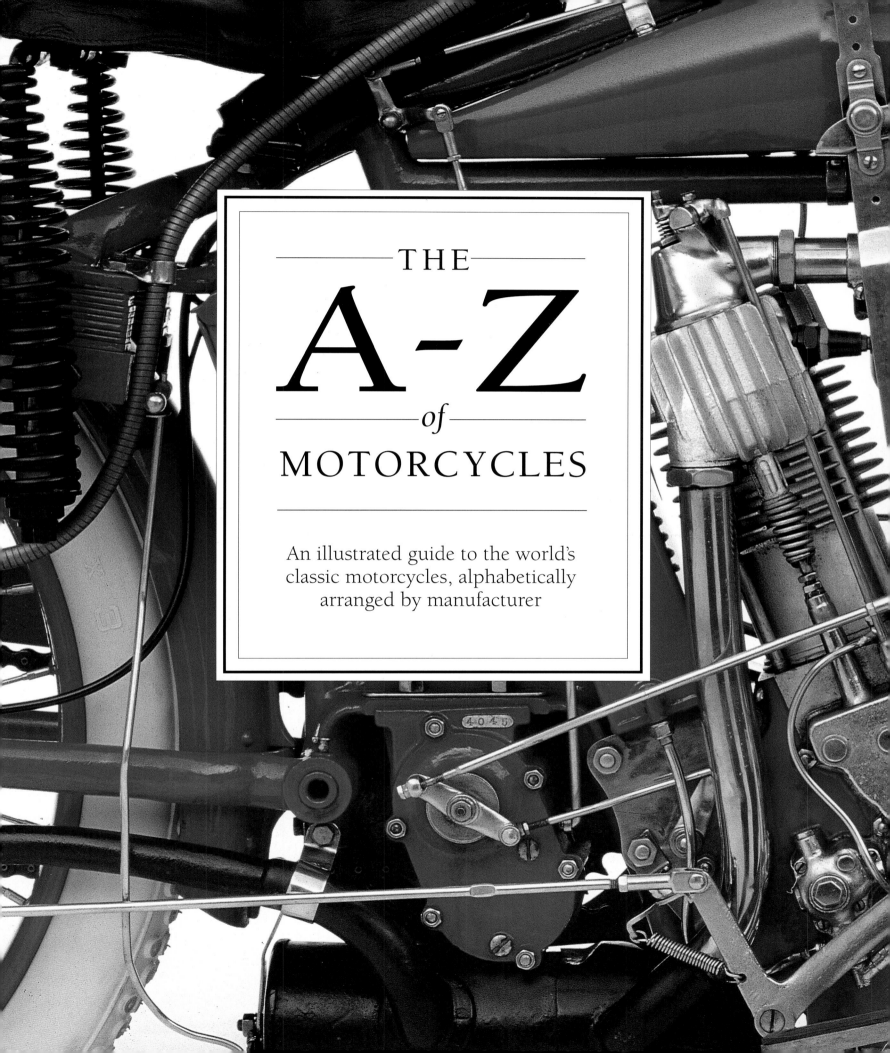

THE
A-Z
of
MOTORCYCLES

An illustrated guide to the world's
classic motorcycles, alphabetically
arranged by manufacturer

ABC

Capacity 398cc • Power output not known • Weight 243lb (110kg) • Top speed 60mph (97km/h) (estimated)

W**HEN THE PROTOTYPES** of the ABC first appeared in 1919 they featured one of the most advanced specifications of any motorcycle up to that date. The ABC was fitted with front and rear suspension, front and rear drum brakes, a four-speed gearbox, a multi-plate clutch unit, and a tubular cradle frame. The 398cc flat-twin engine was mounted transversely in the frame and had overhead valves. In many ways the ABC was a forerunner of the BMW transverse twin that appeared in Germany in 1923 (see p.26)

though because it was fitted with rear suspension the British machine had chain drive. The rigid-framed BMW used a shaft. The light weight of the ABC promised good performance despite the small-capacity engine. Front and rear springing promised a comfortable ride. On both counts the ABC delivered. The ABC illustrated is a 1921 model. Originally made in England, the bikes were made under licence in France by aircraft engine-makers Gnome & Rhône (see p.65) between 1920 and 1924.

F**RONT** VIEW

C**YLINDER DAMAGE** was a risk if a transverse flat twin was dropped, especially when the valve gear was exposed. On the ABC the cylinders are protected by the very widely splayed downtubes of the cradle frame. This also allows the fitting of an apron, giving some weather protection for the rider's legs. Footboards are also mounted within the frame's perimeter.

Leg shields are fitted within the frame rails

•DESIGN PROBLEMS•

D**espite** its high price, there were plenty of orders when the ABC was launched. The machine was designed by Granville Bradshaw and built by the Sopwith Aircraft company, which was looking to diversify after World War I. Unfortunately by the time the new machine reached the market in any quantity the price had risen dramatically. And there were problems, particularly with the valve gear and kickstarter. These factors turned customers away and Sopwith was soon in trouble, although the ABC was still available in 1923.

An ABC photographed in 1921

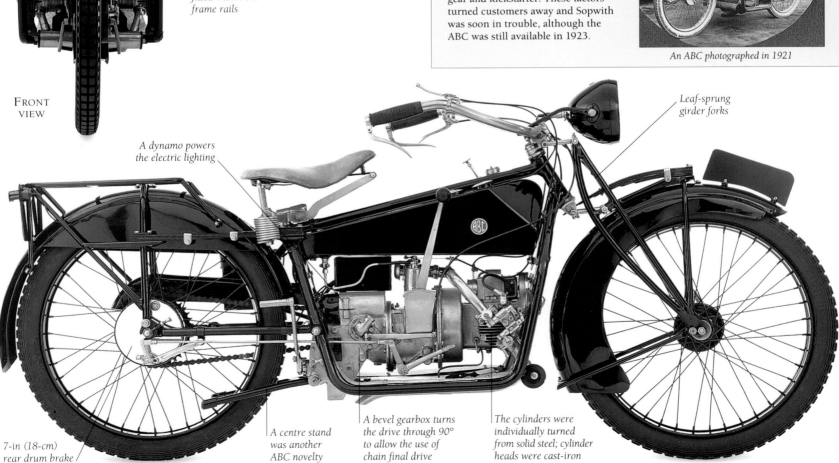

Leaf-sprung girder forks

A dynamo powers the electric lighting

7-in (18-cm) rear drum brake

A centre stand was another ABC novelty

A bevel gearbox turns the drive through 90° to allow the use of chain final drive

The cylinders were individually turned from solid steel; cylinder heads were cast-iron

ACE

Capacity 1229cc • Power output not known • Weight 365lb (166kg) • Top speed not known

THE ACE WAS DESIGNED by William G. Henderson after he parted company with the Henderson marque in 1919 (see p.80). The new machine followed the style of the Henderson, with the i.o.e. engine mounted in line with the wheels. There was a three-speed, hand-operated gearbox, and final drive was by chain. The front forks were a typical leading-link construction. But the Ace design achieved a considerable weight saving over its opposition. It was 60lb (27kg) lighter than the Chicago-built Henderson machine with a resulting increase in performance. Production models became available for 1920. Tragically, William Henderson was killed in an accident in 1922 while testing a new model. He was succeeded as designer by Arthur O. Lemon. Unfortunately Ace's management was less talented than its designers and production came to a stop late in 1924 when the firm experienced financial difficulties. Ownership of the firm changed at least twice before Indian bought the stock, tools, and rights in 1927. Indian marketed an Indian Ace until 1928.

THE MOTORCYCLE pictured here is one of the machines built by the Michigan Motors Corporation in 1926 before Indian acquired the manufacturing rights and production moved to Springfield, Massachusetts. Indian marketed the Indian Ace for one year only before it introduced revised machines designed by Arthur O. Lemon. Indian continued to produce an in-line four until 1942.

Blue and cream paint finish was used on all Ace machines

FRONT VIEW

•RACING ACES•

The Ace was a popular mount for competition riders in hill climbs and endurance runs. In September 1922, "Cannonball" Baker set a new transcontinental speed record with a time of six days, 22 hours, and six minutes to cover the 3,332 miles (5,365km) from Los Angeles to New York. In 1924 Red Wolverton set a new world speed record of 129mph (208km/h) on a specially prepared Ace. This picture shows Charlie Cole taking on liquid refreshment at a 1922 Pennsylvania endurance race.

1922 endurance race

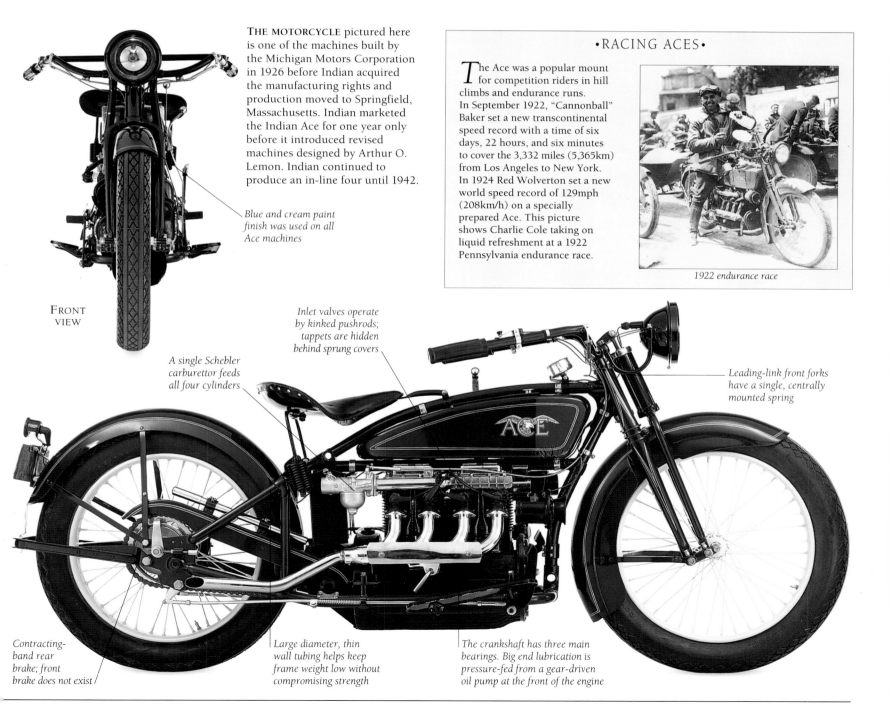

Inlet valves operate by kinked pushrods; tappets are hidden behind sprung covers

A single Schebler carburettor feeds all four cylinders

Leading-link front forks have a single, centrally mounted spring

Contracting-band rear brake; front brake does not exist

Large diameter, thin wall tubing helps keep frame weight low without compromising strength

The crankshaft has three main bearings. Big end lubrication is pressure-fed from a gear-driven oil pump at the front of the engine

ADLER MB200

Capacity 195cc • Power output 16bhp @ 5,590rpm • Weight 135kg (297lb) • Top speed 95km/h (59mph)

Adler re-entered the motorcycle market in 1949 after a gap of over forty years. The new machines were lightweight, two-stroke singles. In 1951 a 195cc twin was added to its expanding range. The new model was the M200; the machine pictured here is a 1954 example. A 250 version was also produced from 1952. To achieve the 247cc capacity, the bore was expanded to 54mm, which resulted in the classic two-stroke dimensions of 54 x 54mm. Despite the excellent quality and reputation of Adler machines, the German motorcycle market was in a severe depression during the late 1950s. Adler was taken over by Grundig, makers of televisions and radios, and subsequently the company concentrated on making typewriters. Although Adler disappeared, its twin-cylinder design had a significant effect on motorcycle development. Designers in Britain and Japan were heavily influenced by the design. The first two-stroke twins made by two emerging Japanese producers, Suzuki and Yamaha, were based on the German machine.

The twin had a 180° crankshaft with the clutch mounted on the left-hand end of the crank. Primary drive was by helical gear to a four-speed gearbox. The engine was mounted in a duplex cradle frame with plunger rear suspension. Front suspension was by leading-link forks with "clock" springs. The final drive chain was fully enclosed.

Racing versions of the Adler M250 competed with some success in German domestic race meetings. In 1954 the factory offered a production race machine, the RS250, for sale. Lack of development, probably caused by the factory's imminent demise, meant that it never achieved notable results.

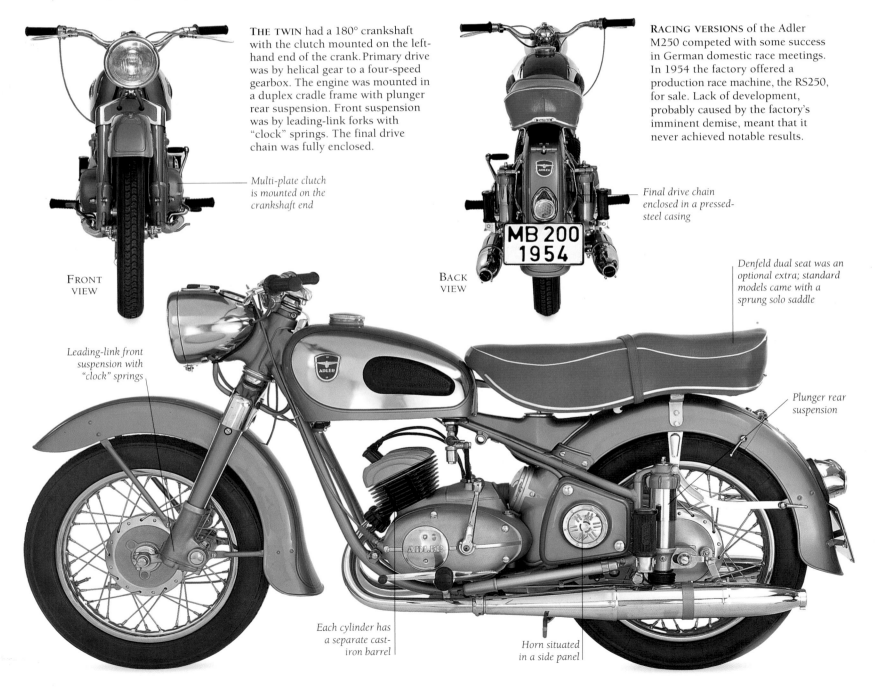

Multi-plate clutch is mounted on the crankshaft end

Front view

Final drive chain enclosed in a pressed-steel casing

Back view

MB 200 1954

Denfeld dual seat was an optional extra; standard models came with a sprung solo saddle

Leading-link front suspension with "clock" springs

Plunger rear suspension

Each cylinder has a separate cast-iron barrel

Horn situated in a side panel

AJS Model D

Capacity 748cc • Power output not known • Weight 276lb (125kg) • Top speed not known

Launched in 1912, the Model D was the first of a series of AJS V-twins that ended with the 1000cc Model 2 of 1940. The 698cc machine had detachable cylinder heads, chain drive, and a three-speed countershaft gearbox. By 1915 the capacity had risen to 748cc and the heads were non-detachable. Fitted with a magneto and an automatic carburettor, the 74 x 87-mm side-valve engine relied on a total-loss oiling system. The 1915 model pictured here has been equipped with acetylene lighting.

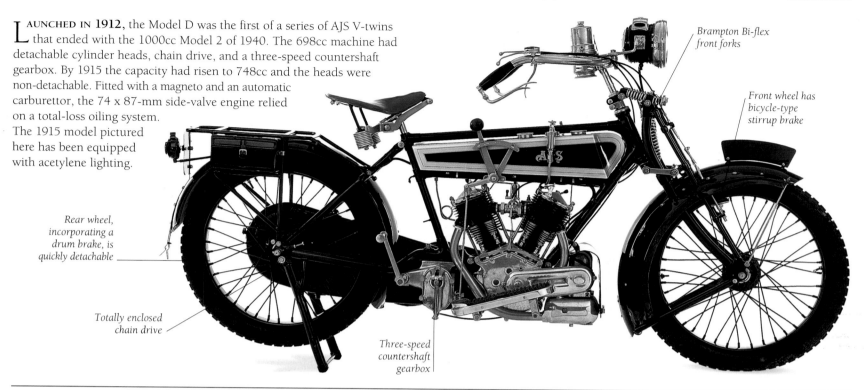

Brampton Bi-flex front forks

Front wheel has bicycle-type stirrup brake

Rear wheel, incorporating a drum brake, is quickly detachable

Totally enclosed chain drive

Three-speed countershaft gearbox

AJS 350 G6

Capacity 349cc • Power output not known • Weight 210lb (95kg) • Top speed 75mph (121km/h) (estimated)

In the early 1920s AJS achieved legendary sporting success with its o.h.v. 350s, winning the Junior TT for four straight years from 1920. It also won the Senior in 1921, despite the 150cc capacity advantage of the opposition. The factory racing machines of 1922 were nicknamed "big ports" because of the exceptional size of the bike's exhaust port and the 2¼-in (57-mm) diameter exhaust pipe. Production models followed in 1923. The dimensions of the ports shrank for 1925 and 1926, as on this 1926 model, but returned to full size in 1927. This engine was probably the first truly successful British o.h.v. design.

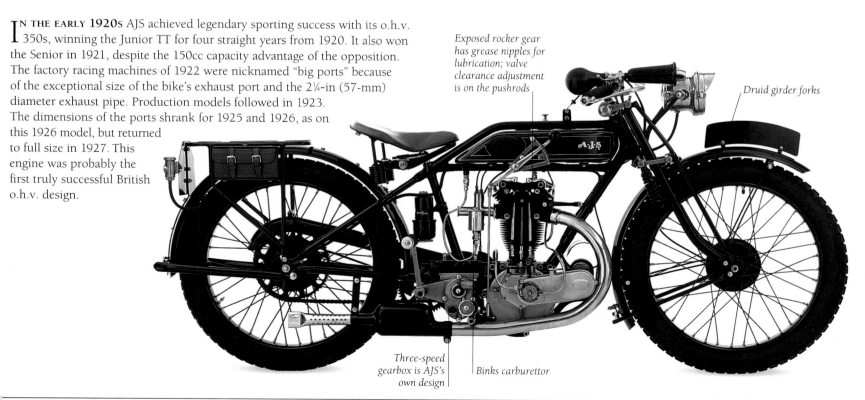

Exposed rocker gear has grease nipples for lubrication; valve clearance adjustment is on the pushrods

Druid girder forks

Three-speed gearbox is AJS's own design

Binks carburettor

AJS R7 (30/7)

Capacity 346cc • Power output not known • Weight 290lb (132kg) • Top speed not known

Iн **1927 AJS FOLLOWED THE LEAD** of Velocette and Norton and produced its own overhead camshaft sporting singles. Production versions appeared the following year. They were available in 350cc and 500cc versions. By the time the R7 (the letter indicated the model year 1930, the 7 indicated a 350) shown here was produced, the design had been uprated with a new frame and revised engine internals. This bike is a factory racing machine, but production models were very similar. Matchless took over AJS in 1931, and it is probable that no o.h.c. machines were built in the following two years.

Girder forks have friction damping

21-in (53.3-cm) front wheel

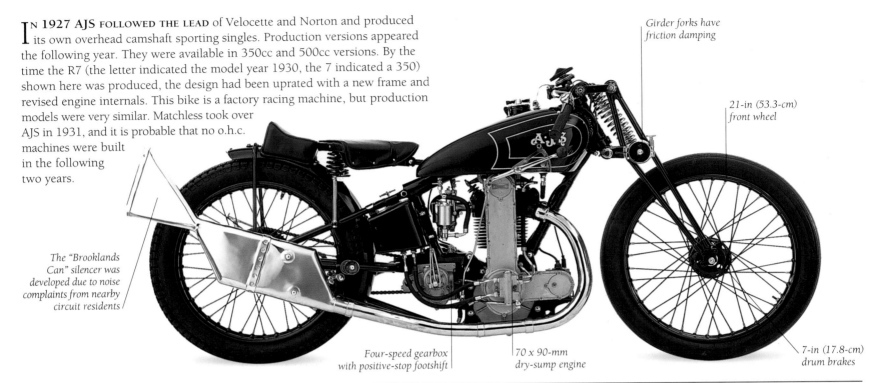

The "Brooklands Can" silencer was developed due to noise complaints from nearby circuit residents

Four-speed gearbox with positive-stop footshift

70 x 90-mm dry-sump engine

7-in (17.8-cm) drum brakes

AJS S3

Capacity 498cc • Power output not known
Weight 353lb (160kg) • Top speed not known

ANNOUNCED IN **APRIL 1931** shortly before the firm's buy-out by Matchless, the S3 was a novelty design aimed at boosting sales and public awareness of the AJS name. Very few were made before it was dropped by AJS's new owners. Set across the frame, the avant-garde 50° side-valve V-twin engine had chain-driven camshafts that ran outside the V. Apart from the duplex frame, the rolling chassis and cycle parts were standard AJS, although the front mudguard was so wide that the fork tubes had to pass through it. The bike came with a full lighting and horn set.

Three-speed gearbox is shaft driven by the 65 x 75-mm engine

AJS SUPERCHARGED V4

Capacity 495cc • Power output 80bhp (estimated)
Weight 405lb (184kg) • Top speed 135mph (217km/h)

DEVELOPED BY THE **AMC RACE SHOP** for the 1939 Senior TT, the formidable supercharged V4 was built to respond to the super-charged Italian and German factory racers dominating the TT and Grand Prix circuits at the time. It was the first machine to lap a Grand Prix course at over 100mph (161km/h). The parallel-twin blocks were arranged in a 50° V-layout with chain-driven single overhead camshafts. The supercharger lay across the front of the magnesium crankcases. The outbreak of war prevented racing victory in 1940, and supercharging was banned in 1946 by the Auto Cycle Union (ACU).

Seat-pad is positioned on rear mudguard due to length of fuel tank

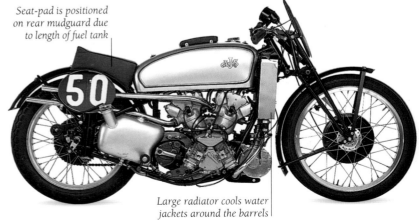

Large radiator cools water jackets around the barrels

AJS 7R/3A

Capacity 350cc • Power output 40bhp @ 8,000rpm • Weight not known • Top speed not known

F OR THE **1954 JUNIOR TT,** race-shop development chief Ike Hatch developed a three-valve version of the 348cc 7R. As well as changes to the cylinder head and cam box, the bore and stroke dimensions were revised to a near-square 75.5 x 78mm. The 7R/3A, or "Triple Knocker", so called because of its three cam lobes, used the frame and running gear developed for the firm's Porcupine racers (see below). Hatch went on to develop a shaft and bevel drive for the machine's triple-camshaft top end but the project was shelved by the firm's accountants.

Fly screen

Pannier-style fuel tank was originally developed for the Porcupine (see below)

Light alloy brake drums

Exposed primary chain drives a four-speed gearbox

Two exhaust pipes run from the twin-port cylinder head

AJS PORCUPINE

Capacity 500cc • Power output 55bhp @ 7,600rpm
Weight 143lb (65kg) • Top speed not known

T HE **D.O.H.C., PARALLEL-TWIN PORCUPINE** first appeared in 1947. The nickname derived from the quill-like cylinder head finning between the twin cam boxes, although this feature had been deleted by 1954. Initial plans to cast the cylinder heads in silver for good thermal conductivity were abandoned due to impracticability and cost. It should have had a supercharged engine, but the post-war ban on superchargers prevented this. Fed by twin carburettors with a single, remote-float chamber, the engine never realized its potential.

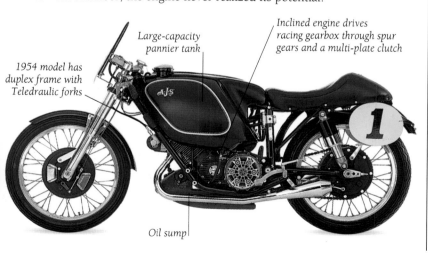

1954 model has duplex frame with Teledraulic forks

Large-capacity pannier tank

Inclined engine drives racing gearbox through spur gears and a multi-plate clutch

Oil sump

ALLRIGHT

Capacity 320cc • Power output 2.25bhp
Weight not known • Top speed 40km/h (25mph)

A LLRIGHT WAS ONE OF THE TRADEMARKS used by the Köln-Lindenthaler Metallwerke company. This 1903 machine is typical of the period. It used a vertically mounted single-cylinder Kelecom engine. The exhaust valve was controlled by a camshaft mounted in front of the cylinder, but the inlet valve was automatic. It was held shut by a weak spring; the vacuum created in the cylinder by the falling piston caused the valve to open under atmospheric pressure.

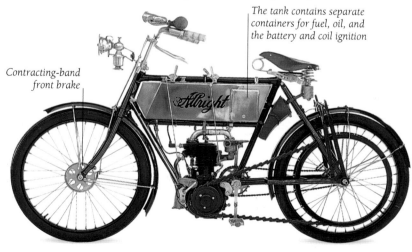

The tank contains separate containers for fuel, oil, and the battery and coil ignition

Contracting-band front brake

ALLSTATE COMPACT

Capacity 59cc • Power output not known
Weight not known • Top speed 42mph (68km/h) (estimated)

U.S.A.

ALLSTATE 250

Capacity 248cc • Power output 16.5bhp @ 5,800rpm
Weight 360lb (163kg) • Top speed 72mph (116km/h)

U.S.A.

THE SEARS DEPARTMENT STORE and mail order chain (see p.168) began selling American-built Cushman scooters under its Allstate badge from 1951. Austrian-made Puch motorcycles were added in 1954 and for two years from 1961, the Puch-built Compact was part of its range, bridging the gap between a conventional lightweight and a scooter. The fuel tank was in the conventional motorcycle position and the gap between the seat and tank was so small that the "step-thru" advantages of the scooter were lost.

SOLD AS AN ALLSTATE IN THE U.S., this machine was actually an Austrian-built Puch. It used the unusual, split-single cylinder two-stroke engine layout that Puch had used from 1923. The first of the 248cc models on which this 1965 Allstate is based appeared in 1949. The design was revised in 1953 when the pressed-steel frame was introduced. When it first appeared, the 250 was considered a good performer. But in time the conventional two-stroke caught up and then overtook the modest 16.5bhp output of the Puch engine. By the mid-1960s the design was considered sedate and solid.

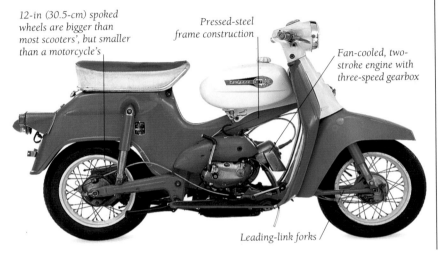

12-in (30.5-cm) spoked wheels are bigger than most scooters', but smaller than a motorcycle's

Pressed-steel frame construction

Fan-cooled, two-stroke engine with three-speed gearbox

Leading-link forks

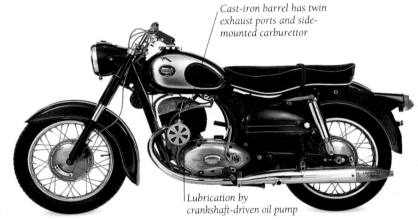

Cast-iron barrel has twin exhaust ports and side-mounted carburettor

Lubrication by crankshaft-driven oil pump

APRILIA RSV 250

ITALY

Capacity 249cc • Power output 84bhp @ 12,500rpm • Weight 91kg (200lb) • Top speed 250km/h (155mph) (estimated)

THE YOUNG APRILIA COMPANY recognized competition success as an important way to enhance its image. Originally the firm produced motocross machines, but in the mid-1980s it began a campaign for Grand Prix success in the 250, and later 125 classes. The early racers used a Rotax tandem, twin-cylinder, disc-valve, two-stroke engine, but 1989's new machine had a V-formation engine layout. As well as being campaigned by the factory's riders, these bikes were also sold to private competitors. Max Biaggi won Aprilia's first 250 World Championship in 1994. The bike shown dates from 1990.

Steering damper

Brembo brakes

Marvic wheels

Upside-down forks

"Banana" swingarm allows the expansion chamber exhaust to be tucked closer to the wheel for increased cornering clearance

APRILIA PEGASO 650

Capacity 652cc • Power output 49bhp @ 7,000rpm
Weight 156kg (345lb) • Top speed 175km/h (109mph)

CLOSE CO-OPERATION between Aprilia and Austrian engine makers Rotax resulted, in 1993, in this high-tech trail bike. The engine has a five-valve cylinder head, with the valves arranged radially around a central spark plug. The valves are controlled by twin, chain-driven, overhead camshafts. The combination of technology, looks, price, and performance have made the Pegaso serious competition to Japanese domination of the trail bike market.

Advanced single-cylinder water-cooled engine

A smaller than usual, 48-cm (19-in) front wheel improves road handling

Alloy frame with rising-rate rear suspension

Upside-down forks

ARDIE 3PS

Capacity 305cc • Power output 3hp @ 2,000rpm
Weight not known • Top speed not known

ARNO DIETRICH BEGAN BUILDING his own motorcycles in 1919, having previously worked for the Premier company. His early machines were two-stroke singles of 305cc and 348cc with deflector piston engines. This bike is one of the smaller capacity machines dating from 1923. It uses a vertical cylinder with both the carburettor inlet and the exhaust port positioned at the front of the cylinder. In 1922 Dietrich was killed in a racing accident and the company changed hands. The two-strokes continued in production for a short time before the new owners adopted a policy of using proprietary engines.

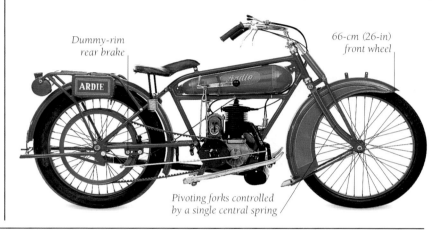

Dummy-rim rear brake

66-cm (26-in) front wheel

Pivoting forks controlled by a single central spring

ARDIE TM500

Capacity 498cc • Power output 11bhp @ 3,400rpm • Weight not known • Top speed 90km/h (56mph) (estimated)

FOLLOWING THE DEATH of Arno Dietrich, the firm was taken over by the Bendit family, who began making more orthodox machines using JAP engines. The model shown here is a 1927 TM500. It uses a 498cc JAP side-valve, single-cylinder engine mounted in a typical diamond frame of the period. Other Ardie machines used single-cylinder and V-twin JAP engines of 248cc to 996cc. The three-speed gearbox was made by Hurth but was a copy of the British Burman box. This machine was equipped with typical period accessories, including a pillion seat on the luggage rack.

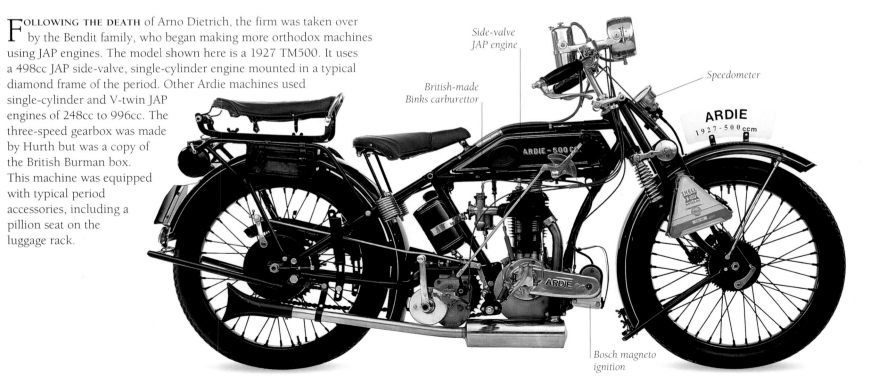

Side-valve JAP engine

Speedometer

British-made Binks carburettor

ARDIE 1927-500 ccm

Bosch magneto ignition

ARIEL SQUARE-FOUR

Capacity 597cc • Power output 24bhp @ 6,000rpm • Weight 413lb (187kg) • Top speed 85mph (137km/h)

AFTER TWO YEARS OF DEVELOPMENT the Edward Turner designed Square-Four was ready for production for the 1931 season. The new engine layout offered the advantages of four-cylinder power and smoothness in an exceptionally compact unit. The engine was put into a frame that differed little from that used on Ariel's 500cc single-cylinder model. The disadvantages included high production costs and inadequate cooling. The engine layout was essentially two parallel-twins sharing a common crankcase, cylinder block, and cylinder head with the overhung crankshafts geared together by central coupling gears. In the original design the coupling gear of the rear crankshaft also drove the three-speed gearbox which was built into the unit with the engine. The production machine used a chain primary drive taken from the rear left-hand cylinder to a four-speed Burman gearbox. Space in the extended and horizontally split crankcases, which had presumably been intended for the gearbox, was used as an integral oil reservoir. Shown here is a 1932 model.

THE OVERHEAD CAMSHAFT, magdyno, and double-gear oil pump were all driven via a half-speed shaft driven from the front crankshaft, and the end of the camshaft carried a distributor for the ignition system. Within the cylinder head casting and beneath the separate cambox, an X-shaped manifold, fed at its centre from the front-mounted carburettor, distributed the fuel mixture via equal-length paths to the four cylinders.

FRONT VIEW

Mudguard stay

• SHOW SENSATION •

The Ariel Square-Four caused a sensation when it was launched at the Olympia Motorcycle Show in 1930 where this picture was taken. The first production models were 497cc but the following year capacity was increased to 597cc, presumably with sidecar use in mind. The 500 was listed for 1932 but was made in very limited numbers and dropped the following year.

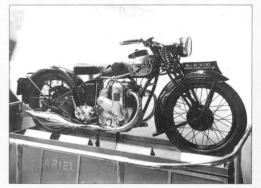

Ariel Square-Four at the 1930 Olympia Motorcycle Show

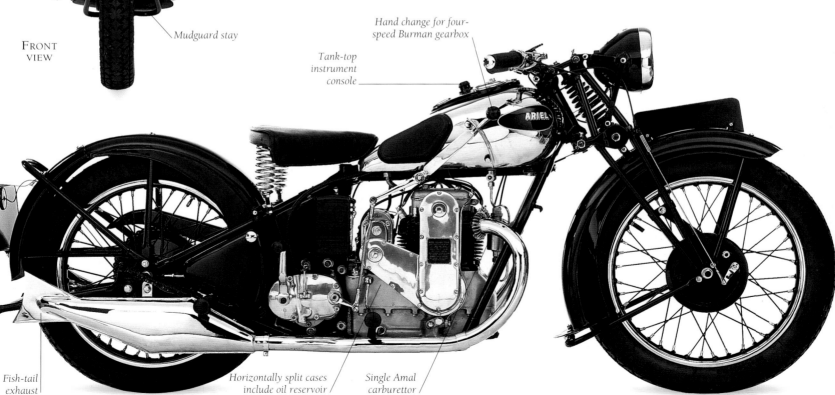

Hand change for four-speed Burman gearbox

Tank-top instrument console

Fish-tail exhaust

Horizontally split cases include oil reservoir

Single Amal carburettor

ARIEL RED HUNTER

Capacity 347cc • Power output 17bhp @ 5,600rpm • Weight 320lb (145kg) • Top speed 80mph (129km/h)

THE PEDIGREE OF THE RED HUNTER goes back to designs produced by Val Page in 1926. The Red Hunter name was first used in 1932 on a Sporting version of Ariel's o.h.v. 500 single. The Red Hunter range was soon expanded to include 250cc and 350cc models. From the start, the machine's merits were recognized by trials and grass-track riders but it was not until Edward Turner embarked on a styling exercise that involved brighter colours and more chromium plating that it became popular with the general public. By the late 1930s, it was well established with a loyal following until production ceased in 1959. The bike shown is a 350 model from 1937.

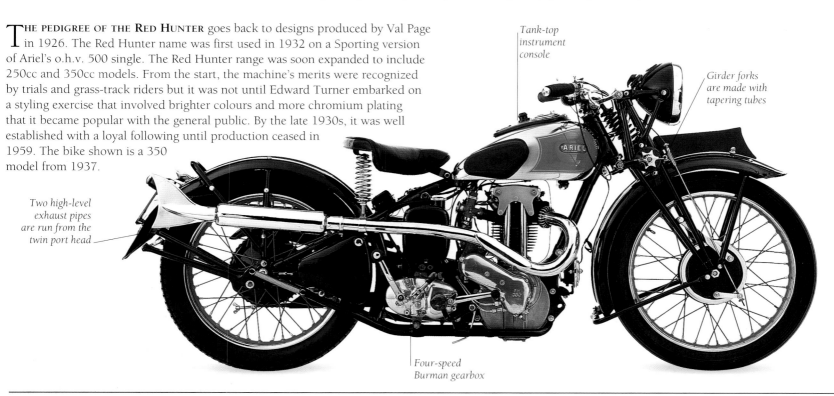

Tank-top instrument console

Girder forks are made with tapering tubes

Two high-level exhaust pipes are run from the twin port head

Four-speed Burman gearbox

ARIEL SQUARE-FOUR

Capacity 997cc • Power output 40bhp @ 5,600rpm • Weight 425lb (193kg) • Top speed 102mph (164km/h)

THE SQUARE-FOUR OF 1955, like the machine shown here, represented almost the final development of the o.h.v. machine introduced in 1937. Over the years the machine had adopted rear suspension, telescopic forks, an all-alloy engine, and a four-pipe exhaust outlet from the head. In this form, it represented the ultimate touring machine of the day with a performance equal to that of many sports machines. The engine was large and flexible, making the four-speed gearbox more of a luxury than a necessity. Production finished in 1960.

Single SU carburettor

Telescopic forks

Compensated-link rear suspension

All-alloy engine has four separate exhaust ports

Single leading-shoe drum brake in 19-in (48-cm) front wheel

ARIEL LEADER

Capacity 247cc • Power output 17.5bhp @ 6,750rpm • Weight 300lb (136kg) • Top speed 70mph (113km/h)

THE INCREASING POPULARITY OF SCOOTERS throughout the 1950s led many motorcycle manufacturers to introduce machines offering a degree of weather protection comparable to the scooter, while retaining the handling characteristics of a motorcycle. Among the most successful of such designs was the 247cc Ariel Leader. When introduced in 1958, the Leader broke new ground with its pressed-steel, beam-type frame clothed in attractive bodywork incorporating a windscreen and leg shields. The cycle shown here is a 1964 model.

MANY EXTRAS WERE AVAILABLE for the Leader, such as pannier boxes to supplement the storage space incorporated into the dummy fuel tank. Other extras included flashing indicators, a prop stand, and a clock to fit in the instrument panel. The Leader lived up to Ariel's slogan "The Modern Motorcycle".

Matching pannier boxes were an option

Indicators mounted in the fairing

16-in (40-cm) wheels have Dunlop whitewall tyres

Pressed-steel panels conceal the bike's mechanicals

Trailing-link forks

FRONT VIEW

ARIEL ARROW SUPER SPORTS

Capacity 247cc • Power output 20bhp @ 6,650rpm • Weight 285lb (129kg) • Top speed 80mph (129km/h)

OFTEN KNOWN AS THE GOLDEN ARROW, the Arrow Super Sports was introduced in 1961, the second sports derivative of the 1958 Leader design. It was inspired by Mike O'Rourke's performance in the 1960 Lightweight TT race: riding a modified version of the normal Arrow, he averaged a speed of 80mph (129km/h) and finished seventh. The Leader/Arrow family had always displayed excellent handling properties and, with only mild engine tuning and minor cosmetic and equipment changes, it captured the hearts of a generation. The bike shown dates from 1963.

Pressed-steel beam frame contains the fuel tank

Dummy fuel tank conceals a storage compartment

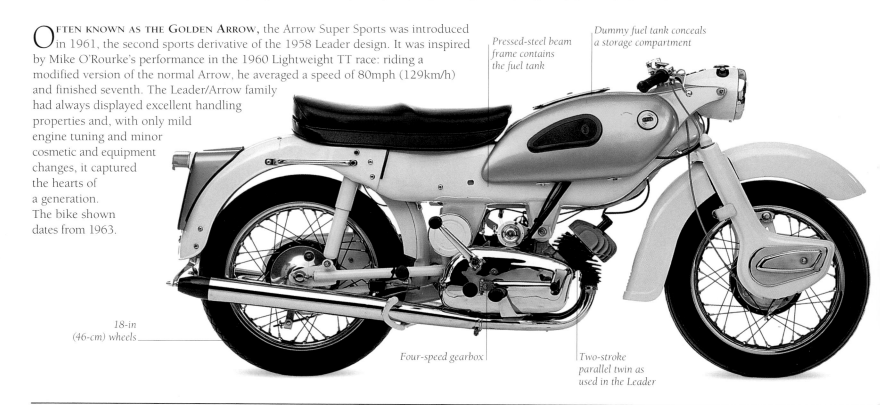

18-in (46-cm) wheels

Four-speed gearbox

Two-stroke parallel twin as used in the Leader

ARMSTRONG MT500

ARMSTRONG, components supplier to the motor trade, moved into motorcycles in 1980, establishing a base by buying the Cotton and CCM marques. Off-road specialists CCM provided the expertise and knowledge used in this military machine. The result was a very functional motorcycle with good on- and off-road capabilities.

THE POWER UNIT was supplied by Rotax in Austria, but the rest of the machine was British. When Armstrong withdrew from the motorcycle business, manufacturing rights were acquired by Harley-Davidson. The model shown here is from c.1985.

Oil tank is part of the frame

Luggage frames

Plastic front mudguard

Drum front brake

Four-valve o.h.c. Rotax engine

Box-section steel swingarm

FRONT VIEW

ASCOT-PULLIN 500cc

THIS WAS A MACHINE embodying every worthwhile feature and lacking only one thing – success. The pressed-steel frame housed a unit-construction engine and gearbox, with the cylinder lying horizontally and the gearbox above the crankcase. All working parts, including the drive chain, were fully enclosed, making the machine clean to ride. The civilized image was enhanced by a neat instrument panel incorporated into the handlebar assembly as well as optional leg shields and windscreen, with wiper if required. Unfortunately, Britain was entering a recession at the time and the bike did not survive. The 500 illustrated here is a 1929 machine.

Pressed-steel frame contains petrol and oil tanks

Pressed-steel girder forks

Chain is hidden by a pressed-steel enclosure

Two exhaust pipes run from the twin port head

Coupled brakes hydraulically operated from foot pedal

AUTOPED

U.S.A.

Capacity 155cc • Power output 1.5hp (estimated)
Weight not known • Top speed 20mph (32km/h) (estimated)

THE AUTOPED – little more than a motorized version of a child's scooter – was built in the U.S. from 1915 to 1921; in Germany, Krupp was licenced to produce the same design. Its engine was mounted beside the front wheel and the fuel tank was above the mudguard. The handlebar column controlled the clutch and brake: pushed forward to engage the drive, pulled back to brake. A lever controlled the throttle. The rider would control all this and steer at the same time from a standing position.

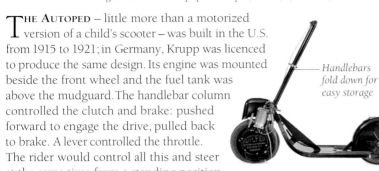

Handlebars fold down for easy storage

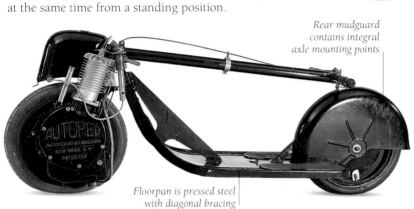

Rear mudguard contains integral axle mounting points

Floorpan is pressed steel with diagonal bracing

BARIGO

FRANCE

Capacity 599cc • Power output 61bhp @ 8,000rpm
Weight not known • Top speed 110mph (177km/h) (estimated)

PATRICK BARIGO BUILDS LIMITED NUMBERS of motorcycles using single-cylinder, four-stroke engines supplied by the Austrian Rotax company. This 1992 road bike is based on Barigo's Super Motard competition machines. Premium-quality suspension and brake components are used, and low weight, good handling, and a tractable engine offer impressive performance. Proven in the gruelling Paris-Dakar rally and other testing events, Barigo was the only motorcycle manufacturer operating in France in the early 1990s.

Alloy frame

Upside-down forks

Four-valve, twin-cam Rotax engine

BAT

UNITED KINGDOM

Capacity 500cc (estimated) • Power output not known • Weight not known • Top speed 25mph (40km/h) (estimated)

THE FIRST BAT MOTORCYCLES were built by S. R. Batson in south London, England, in 1902, but by the time this machine was built around 1904 the company was run by T. H. Tessier. He coined the slogan "Best after Test" to advertise the proven ability of his machines. This bike uses an a.i.v. engine produced by Harry Lawson's Motor Manufacturing Company (MMC) but DeDion engines were also used in early machines.

THE VERTICALLY MOUNTED power unit is bolted in the "new" Werner position and the frame has additional stays running from the back-axle mounting lugs. For 1909, a sprung seat assembly was offered. Bat regarded the fitting of pedals as an admission that engines were not powerful enough to climb hills. Bat riders had to dismount and push.

Strengthened frame features extra bracing

Bicycle-style forks have additional bracing tubes

BACK VIEW

Benelli

BENELLI 750 SEI

Capacity 748cc • Power output 71bhp @ 8,900rpm • Weight 220kg (485lb) • Top speed 190km/h (118mph)

THE SEI WAS AN ATTEMPT BY BENELLI'S NEW OWNER, Alessandro De Tomaso, to better high Japanese standards. Ironically, the engine was an almost-perfect copy of a four-cylinder, 500cc, Honda power unit, but with two extra cylinders grafted on. The alternator was mounted behind the cylinders in a rather futile attempt to reduce the engine's width. Although prototypes appeared as early as 1972, production models did not reach the market until 1974. This is a 1976 model.

Squared instruments were another 1970s' style statement

The unusual six-pipe exhaust system was dropped on the 900cc versions that followed

Three 24-mm (1-in) Dell'Orto carburettors

S.o.h.c. engine is based on the Honda layout

Bianchi

BIANCHI ES250/1

Capacity 248cc • Power output 10bhp @ 4,800rpm • Weight 148kg (326lb) • Top speed 105km/h (65mph)

THIS 1937 ES250/1 MODEL was typical of the quality machines produced by Bianchi. The firm was one of Italy's longest-lasting motorcycle companies, building machines from the turn of the 20th century until 1967. It still exists as a bicycle manufacturer. This machine featured a shaft-driven overhead camshaft with exposed hairpin-valve springs. The cast-iron cylinder head had two exhaust ports with the pipes running down either side of the bike. The bottom of the engine featured an integral oil reservoir.

O.h.c. engine with iron barrel and cylinder head

Sky blue paint work was a Bianchi trademark

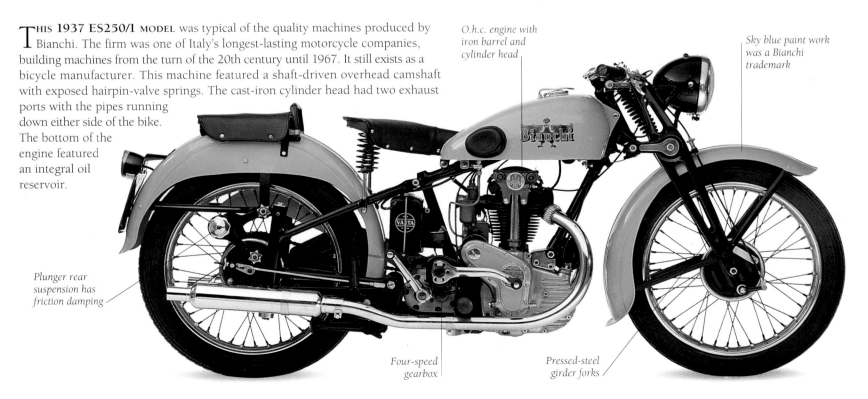

Plunger rear suspension has friction damping

Four-speed gearbox

Pressed-steel girder forks

BIMOTA TESI 1D

Capacity 904cc • Power output 118bhp @ 9,000rpm • Weight 188kg (414lb) • Top speed 266km/h (165mph)

THE TINY ITALIAN BIMOTA COMPANY occupies an extraordinary position in the motorcycle marketplace. It builds superlative sporting machines in very limited numbers and to very high standards, using the best available materials and components. This is reflected in the equally impressive price tags. The designs are innovative, and Bimota has always been at the forefront of chassis technology and development. As a small company it is reliant on engines supplied by other manufacturers for its road-going machines. Bimota was the first manufacturer to offer an alternative to the conventional telescopic front fork on a modern sporting motorcycle.

The Tesi (Thesis) was first shown in prototype form at the Milan Show in 1982, and a racing prototype appeared in 1984. Early versions used V4 Honda engines in a carbon fibre frame with the steering controlled by hydraulics. By the time production versions became available in 1990, the design had progressed. The "frame" now comprised two machined alloy plates that bolted around a Ducati V-twin engine. The seat, fuel tank, fairing, and handlebar pivot were mounted on a subframe made from small diameter tubing. The swingarms were alloy with front and rear shock absorbers operated by linkages. This is a 1992 Tesi 1D.

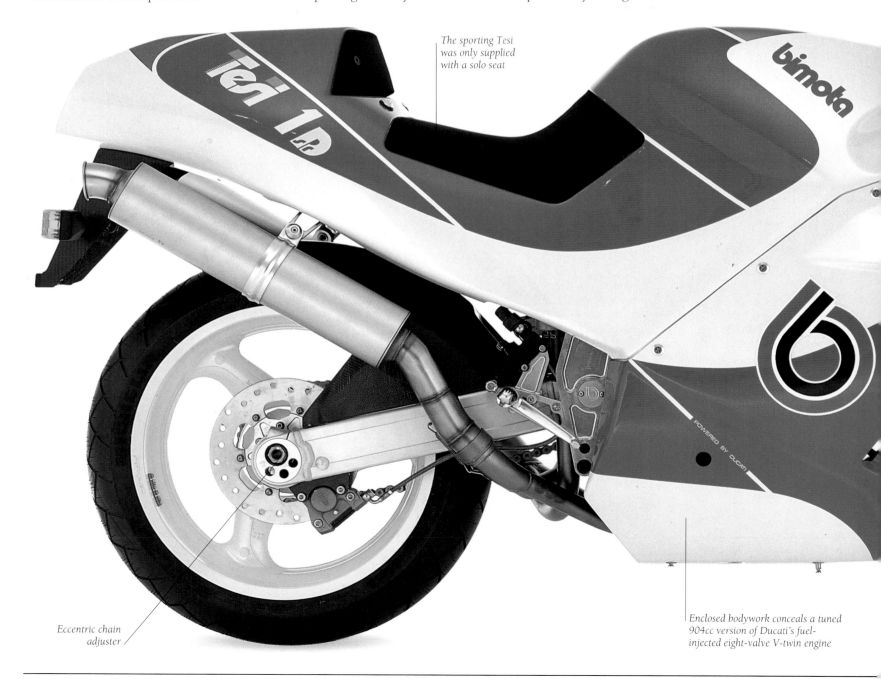

The sporting Tesi was only supplied with a solo seat

Eccentric chain adjuster

Enclosed bodywork conceals a tuned 904cc version of Ducati's fuel-injected eight-valve V-twin engine

WHEN BRAKING, A TELESCOPIC FORK compresses. This means that road shocks cannot be absorbed and that the steering geometry changes as the bike's attitude alters (although some argue that this is a good thing). The high steering head necessary with telescopic forks means that severe braking forces are transmitted high up in the frame. On the Tesi the forces are passed backwards directly to the frame which, as it does not have to deal with severe loads, can be a minimalist structure.

Shock absorber

Alloy swingarm

Machined alloy frame plate

THE FRONT WHEEL rotates around a large diameter hollow hub. Passing inside the hub is a spindle that is attached to the swingarm at either side. A vertical pin fixed to the centre of the spindle is attached to the hub by bearings that allow steering movement. This is controlled by an arm projecting from the hub, which connects to the handlebars by a system of rods and pivots.

Steering rod

Wheel hub

Brake torque arm

Steering arm on the front hub is connected to the handlebars by linkage

Width of fork restricts steering lock

FRONT VIEW

Wheel spindle

BMW R32

Capacity 494cc • Power output 8.5bhp @ 3,300rpm • Weight 122kg (269lb) • Top speed 85km/h (53mph)

THE FLAT-TWIN ENGINE was common in 1920s motorcycles and many manufacturers around the world used the power unit in the fore-and-aft position. The Bavarian Motor Works at Munich introduced its M2 B15 flat-twin engine in 1922. These were supplied to Victoria and other manufacturers; BMW also used the engine in the Helios motorcycle. The following year, designer Max Friz produced a remarkable new design for a completely integrated motorcycle. The R32 was launched at the 1923 Paris Show. The side-valve 494cc engine was turned through 90° so that its cylinder projected into the cooling air. A three-speed car-type gearbox and clutch were bolted to the back of the engine. This layout had been used earlier on the British ABC machine (see p.10). But unlike ABC, BMW chose to use shaft drive to the rear wheel. It has retained this

engine layout and transmission system ever since, proving the worth of the original design. The engine and gearbox unit of the R32 were put into a duplex tubular frame. Front suspension was provided by a leaf-sprung trailing-link fork. The use of shaft drive precluded the provision of rear suspension but it did allow the rear wheel to be removed without disturbing the transmission. The front brake was a drum while a dummy rim brake was added at the rear. The advanced specification included a centre stand, enclosed valve gear, automatic lubrication, and electric lighting. The valanced mudguards, raised fronts to the footboards, and the absence of an oil chain made the BMW an exceptionally clean and practical machine, especially for routine maintenance. The bike shown below is a 1923 R32 from the first year of production.

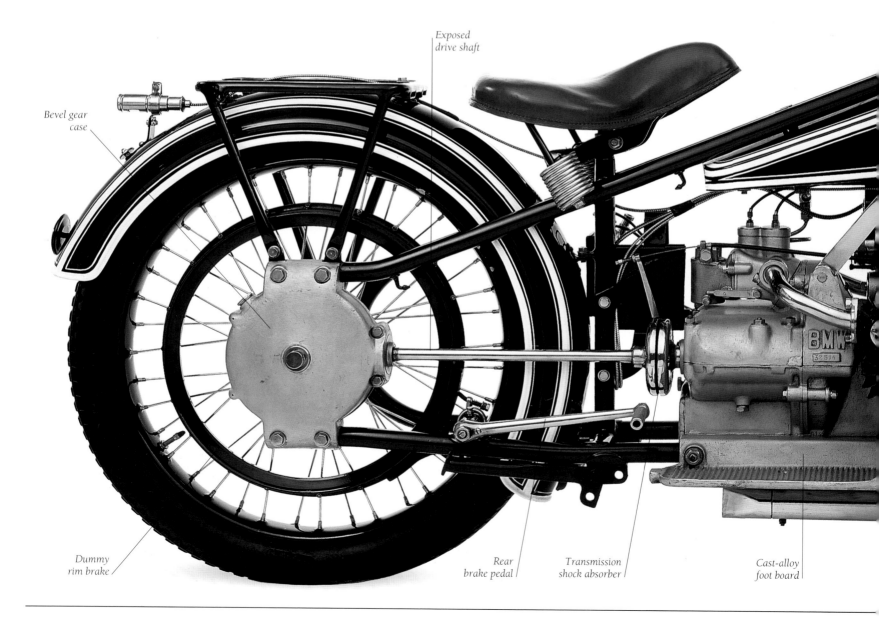

Exposed drive shaft

Bevel gear case

Dummy rim brake

Rear brake pedal

Transmission shock absorber

Cast-alloy foot board

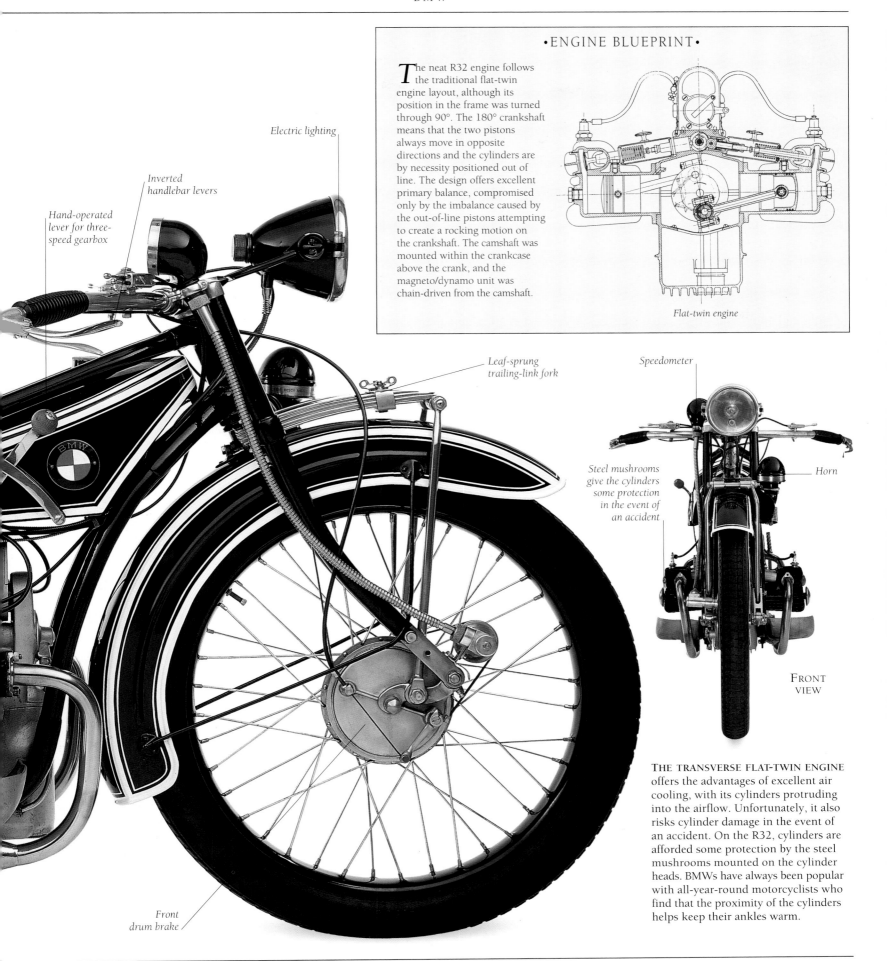

•ENGINE BLUEPRINT•

*T*he neat R32 engine follows the traditional flat-twin engine layout, although its position in the frame was turned through 90°. The 180° crankshaft means that the two pistons always move in opposite directions and the cylinders are by necessity positioned out of line. The design offers excellent primary balance, compromised only by the imbalance caused by the out-of-line pistons attempting to create a rocking motion on the crankshaft. The camshaft was mounted within the crankcase above the crank, and the magneto/dynamo unit was chain-driven from the camshaft.

Flat-twin engine

Electric lighting

Inverted handlebar levers

Hand-operated lever for three-speed gearbox

Leaf-sprung trailing-link fork

Speedometer

Horn

Steel mushrooms give the cylinders some protection in the event of an accident

Front drum brake

Front View

THE TRANSVERSE FLAT-TWIN ENGINE offers the advantages of excellent air cooling, with its cylinders protruding into the airflow. Unfortunately, it also risks cylinder damage in the event of an accident. On the R32, cylinders are afforded some protection by the steel mushrooms mounted on the cylinder heads. BMWs have always been popular with all-year-round motorcyclists who find that the proximity of the cylinders helps keep their ankles warm.

BMW R63

Capacity 734cc • Power output 24bhp @ 4,000rpm
Weight 155kg (342lb) • Top speed 120km/h (75mph)

GERMANY

This first o.h.v. 750 from BMW in 1928 was effectively a development of the 500cc R57, and its oversquare, 83 x 68mm engine provided an exhilarating performance by the standards of its day. The valve gear was completely enclosed, and although the three-speed gearbox and the cycle parts were similar to those introduced on the R32 five years earlier, everything was stronger. The front brake was bigger and the rear brake was now a heel-operated device contracting around a drum at the front end of the driveshaft.

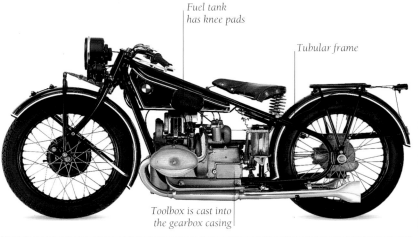

Fuel tank has knee pads

Tubular frame

Toolbox is cast into the gearbox casing

BMW R2

Capacity 198cc • Power output 6bhp @ 3,500rpm
Weight 110kg (242lb) • Top speed 95km/h (59mph)

GERMANY

The R2, with its 198cc single-cylinder o.h.v. engine, was a machine designed to suit the economic conditions of its time. During the world recession of the early 1930s, BMW's answer was to produce in 1931 a *Volksmotorrad* (people's motorcycle). Its size was chosen to comply with tax laws in many European countries, which favoured machines of less than 200cc. With so little power available, the designer minimized losses through the use of a straight drive line in top gear, resulting in the engine being offset to the right of the pressed-steel duplex frame.

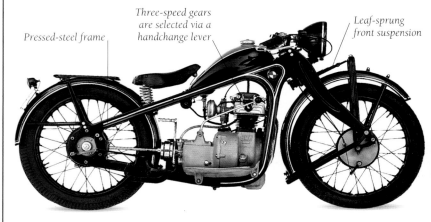

Three-speed gears are selected via a handchange lever

Leaf-sprung front suspension

Pressed-steel frame

BMW R12

Capacity 745cc • Power output 18bhp @ 3,400rpm
Weight 185kg (408lb) • Top speed 110km/h (68mph)

GERMANY

The s.v. R12 and its o.h.v. stablemate, the R17, built in 1935, were notable for being the first machines fitted with the BMW hydraulically damped telescopic fork, a leap forward that the rest of the world simply had to follow. Among the different types of front suspension offered over the preceding 30 years there had been a few telescopic types, but this was the first one to incorporate hydraulic damping as part of the design. Other new features included a four-speed gearbox controlled via a handchange lever, and interchangeable wheels.

Gear-change lever operates in a gate built into the right knee pad

Telescopic front forks

Four-speed gearbox

BMW KOMPRESSOR

Capacity 494cc • Power output 68bhp @ 8,000rpm
Weight 138kg (304lb) • Top speed 225km/h (140mph)

GERMANY

Until 1935 BMW had concentrated on trials, hill climbs, and the solo speed record, which Ernst Henne and his 750cc twin had monopolized since 1929. In 1935 it produced a new design of 500cc twin that had an overhead camshaft and a supercharger driven directly from the crankshaft. Meier won the European Championship in 1938, but in 1939 (the year that this machine was built), BMW was beaten by the supercharged four-cylinder Gilera. The four would ultimately oust the twin, just as the twin had the single.

Hydraulically damped telescopic forks

Plunger rear suspension

Supercharger

BMW Rennsport

AFTER WORLD WAR II, supercharging was banned, and when Germany was readmitted to the international racing scene in 1951, BMW fielded a revised version of the pre-war twin, but this was outclassed by its better-developed rivals. A replacement machine, the Rennsport, appeared in 1954, and although the general layout of the engine was similar to that of the pre-war machine, with its unusual d.o.h.c.s and rockers, it was in fact a new design. The improved engine/gearbox unit was mounted in a frame with pivoted fork suspension front and rear; the drive shaft was enclosed in the right-hand arm of the rear fork. A twin leading-shoe front brake was provided, various types of fairing were tried, and eventually a five-speed gearbox was used. Despite all this, various permutations of bore and stroke, and experiments with both low-pressure fuel injection into the induction tracts and high-pressure injection into the combustion chambers, the machine achieved only limited success against the four-cylinder opposition in the solo class.

Rev counter

This machine is equipped with Dell'Orto carburettors, although the factory also experimented with fuel injection

•STURDY COMPETITOR•

Although the Rennsport never actually won a solo Grand Prix event, consistently solid finishes by Walter Zeller in 1956 gave him the runner-up position on the 500cc championship table, while Dickie Dale achieved third place two years later. The machine dominated sidecar racing until the early 1970s.

A Rennsport in action

BACK VIEW

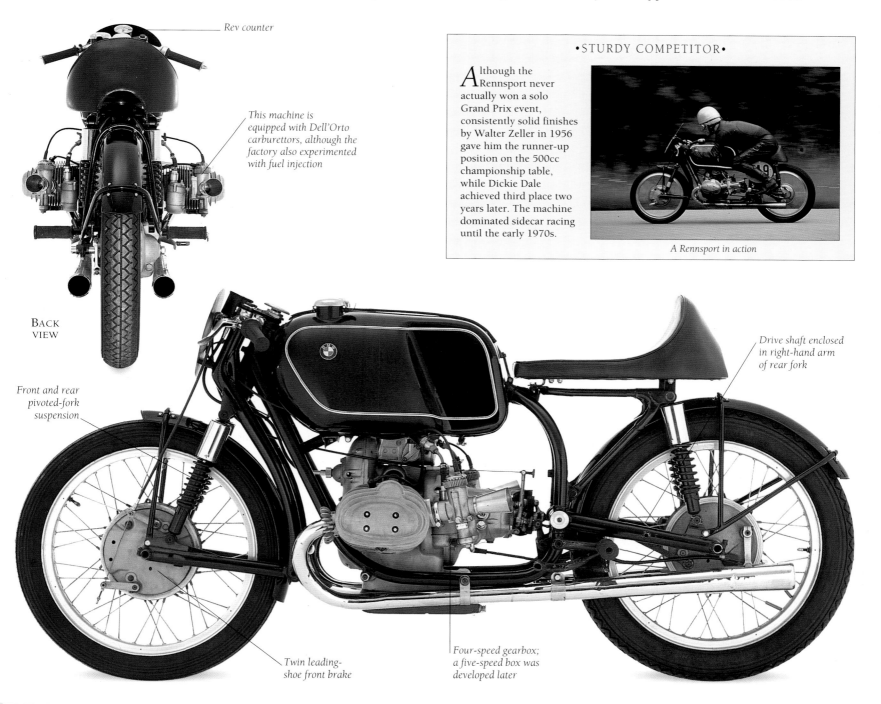

Front and rear pivoted-fork suspension

Drive shaft enclosed in right-hand arm of rear fork

Twin leading-shoe front brake

Four-speed gearbox; a five-speed box was developed later

BMW R26

Capacity 247cc • Power output 15bhp @ 6,400rpm • Weight 158kg (348lb) • Top speed 115km/h (71mph)

Half an **R50** in terms of engine specification and 90 per cent of one in terms of weight, the R26 was nonetheless deemed suitable by BMW for light sidecar duty, and a lower-geared final drive was offered for such use. The Earles type of fork was enjoying a brief spell of popularity in the late 1950s, particularly in Germany, and with pivoted forks at each end, the R26 was the luxury end of the 250cc market. This machine dates from 1958.

The sidecar fittings on the R26 were really there only because many of the cycle parts were borrowed from the larger twins. This resulted in the machine being more renowned for its comfort and than for its performance.

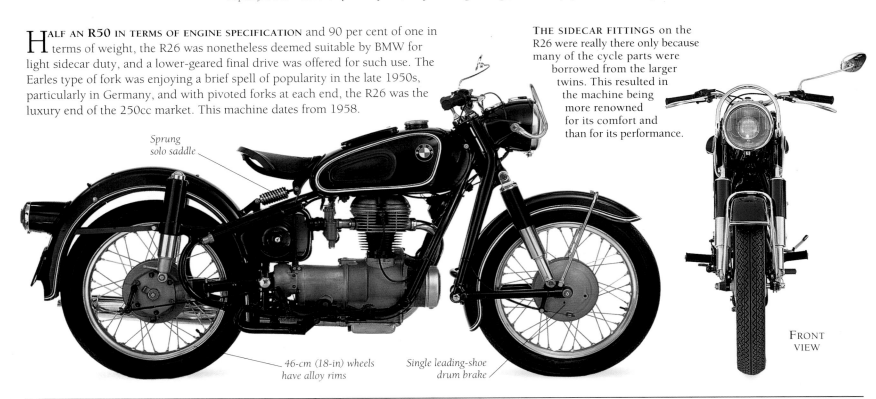

Sprung solo saddle

46-cm (18-in) wheels have alloy rims

Single leading-shoe drum brake

Front View

BMW R60

Capacity 590cc • Power output 28bhp @ 5,600rpm • Weight 195kg (430lb) • Top speed 145km/h (90mph)

The **R60** series was in production from 1955 to 1967 with very few changes. The machine it superseded was similar to its pre-war counterpart and, although the new engine had a familiar look to it, the cycle parts were entirely new. Telescopic front forks had been replaced by a long leading-link (Earles) type, more beneficial to the sidecar rider than the soloist, but the adoption of a pivoted rear fork instead of the old plunger system reversed the benefits. By the mid-1960s BMW twins looked dated and dull, but change was around the corner. This machine dates from 1967.

Indicators positioned on handlebars

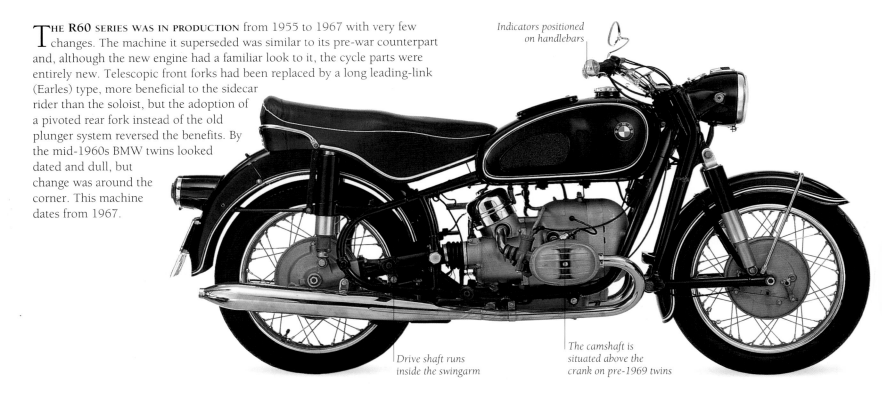

Drive shaft runs inside the swingarm

The camshaft is situated above the crank on pre-1969 twins

BMW R90S

Capacity 898cc • Power output 67bhp @ 7,000rpm • Weight 205kg (452lb) • Top speed 200km/h (124mph)

By **1973 THE R50/5, R60/5, AND R75/5** had evolved into the R60/6, R75/6, and the R90 in both /6 and S variants. All had five-speed gearboxes while the R90S, still regarded by many as the ultimate sporting BMW, had double-disc front brakes, cockpit fairing with instrument panel, and an attractive air-brushed paint job. Depicted is a 1975 R90S.

THE MACHINES that replaced the Earles-forked BMWs in 1969 had an altogether sportier and more modern appearance and were new in practically every respect. The stylist was now becoming as important as the engineer.

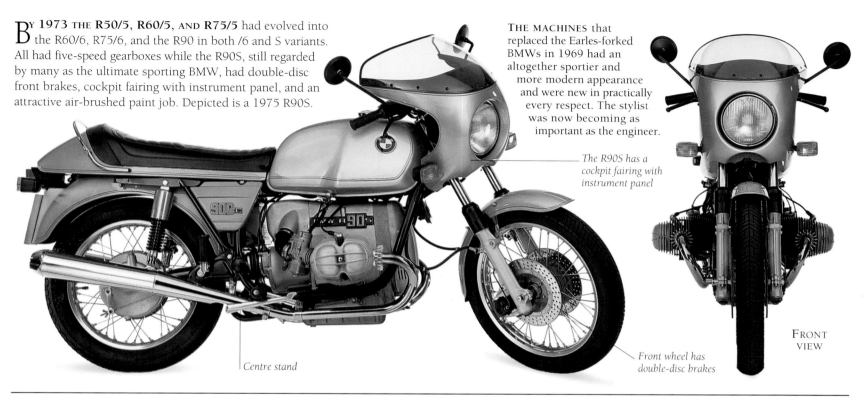

The R90S has a cockpit fairing with instrument panel

FRONT VIEW

Centre stand

Front wheel has double-disc brakes

BMW K1

Capacity 987cc • Power output 100bhp @ 8,000rpm • Weight 258kg (569lb) • Top speed 238km/h (148mph)

THE REVOLUTIONARY-LOOKING K1 was offered to an unsuspecting public in 1990 with some real engineering advances beneath its bodywork. "Paralever" rear suspension improved handling and comfort, and an electronic anti-lock braking system added to rider safety. The engine had four valves per cylinder and digital electronic control of the fuel and ignition systems. Once again, BMW was forging the way ahead in motorcycle design. This K1 is a 1992 model.

Radiator cooling vents

Removable tail piece conceals a pillion seat

The electronic anti-lock braking system was, at the time, exclusive to BMW

Stainless steel exhaust system

BMW R1100GS

Capacity 1085cc • Power output 80bhp @ 6,750rpm • Weight 209kg (460lb) • Top speed 214km/h (133mph)

EVER SINCE **BMW** BUILT ITS FIRST MOTORCYCLE in 1923, the firm has been associated with the flat-twin engine and shaft-drive layout. Although it produced in-line, three- and four-cylinder, water-cooled machines in the 1980s, the company returned to the flat-twin layout for new machines developed to take its motorcycle range into the 21st century. First unveiled in 1993, the new machines followed the traditional layout but were radically different to anything seen before. The engine had a high-camshaft design which kept cylinder width minimal but gave the advantages of overhead cams. Fuel injection and a catalytic converter were used to keep emissions to a minimum. The front suspension was controlled by a single shock absorber, which was mounted vertically from the wishbone. The forks provided steering. Other novel details included adjustable seat height and ABS braking. The new machine was first launched as the R1100RS, but the GS trail-bike version, like the model shown here, followed in 1994. This machine dates from that year.

Front suspension wishbone

Rear shock absorber

THE FRAME ITSELF is almost non-existent, comprising two minimalist subframes that bolt to the engine unit and do little more than provide mounting points for the steering and other components.

Windscreen

Four-valve cylinder head

FRONT VIEW

ALTHOUGH THE ENGINE bristles with technological innovation, the radical part of the machine is the chassis. This features "Telelever" front suspension with a pressed-steel wishbone that pivots from a mounting above the cylinders. It connects with a bridge on the front fork above the wheel.

Seat height is adjustable

Offset spokes allow the use of tubeless tyres

Bosch fuel injection

Engine protectors

Shaft final drive

48-cm (19-in) front wheel with alloy rim

BMW F650

Capacity 652cc • Power output 48bhp @ 6,500rpm • Weight 189kg (417lb) • Top speed 163km/h (101mph)

THE FIRST SINGLE-CYLINDER BMW SINCE 1967, the F650 is also the first BMW to use a chain instead of a shaft drive between the engine and the rear wheel. The 652cc water-cooled engine and five-speed gearbox unit is made under BMW control by Rotax in Austria and features a four-valve cylinder head fitted with two carburettors. It is assembled, again under BMW control, at the Aprilia factory in Italy. The "F" in the model designation stands for "Funduro", suggesting the market sector it is aimed at. Not strictly for competition, the F650 is more an enduro-style bike equally at home on motorways or tracks.

Sculpted plastic bodywork conceals a 17.5-litre (3⅞-gallon) fuel tank

Stainless steel exhaust system

THE F650 STRIPPED DOWN to the frame, engine, and cycle parts. This view shows the vertical Rotax engine, a departure from BMW's 50-year commitment to horizontally opposed twins.

Rear suspension adjustment control knob for single shock absorber

BÖHMERLAND

Capacity 603cc • Power output 16bhp @ 3,000rpm • Weight 227kg (500lb) • Top speed 95km/h (59mph)

DESIGNED BY ALBIN LIEBISCH and built from 1925 until 1939, the long wheelbase Böhmerland was one of the strangest motorcycles ever made. Seating was provided for three people; a short wheelbase two-seater version was also made. The extraordinary frame design suggested a bridge rather than a motorcycle. The front fork springs operated in tension not compression, and the wheels were made of cast-alloy. Liebisch's long-stroke engine retained exposed valve gear until production ended. Without the protection of a normal fuel tank, riders hoped that the engine did not eject its pushrods. This is a 1927 model.

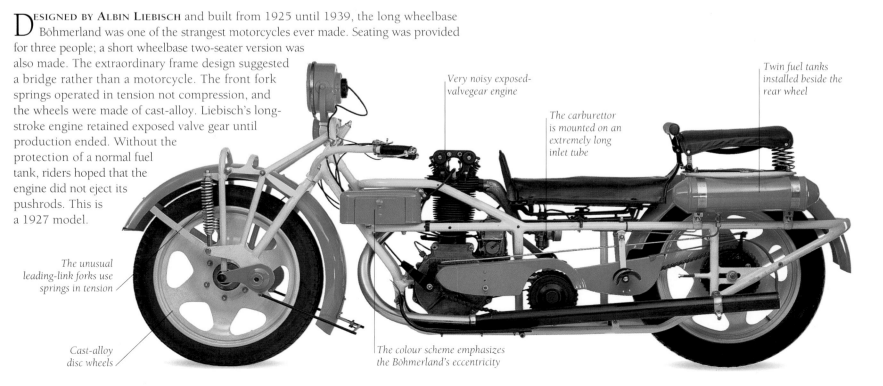

Very noisy exposed-valvegear engine

Twin fuel tanks installed beside the rear wheel

The carburettor is mounted on an extremely long inlet tube

The unusual leading-link forks use springs in tension

Cast-alloy disc wheels

The colour scheme emphasizes the Böhmerland's eccentricity

BRIDGESTONE HURRICANE

Capacity 177cc • Power output 20bhp @ 8,000rpm • Weight 123kg (271lb) • Top speed 126km/h (78mph)

JAPAN

THE HURRICANE WAS INTRODUCED in 1968 – taking advantage of interest in so-called "fun bikes" – and won immediate praise for both its performance and build. Dubbed a scrambler, it was really a dual-purpose machine that was more at home on the road than on the dirt. An unusual feature of the Hurricane was its gearbox: in one mode it had four speeds arranged in rotary sequence, so when in top gear one notch down was neutral, then another took you into bottom. This was not too popular with riders, but a conventional five-speed arrangement was available at the flick of a switch. The pictured Hurricane hails from 1968.

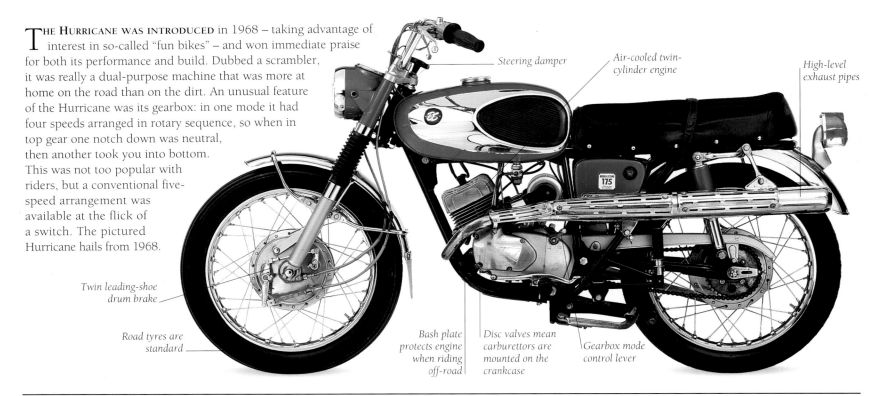

Steering damper

Air-cooled twin-cylinder engine

High-level exhaust pipes

Twin leading-shoe drum brake

Road tyres are standard

Bash plate protects engine when riding off-road

Disc valves mean carburettors are mounted on the crankcase

Gearbox mode control lever

BROUGH SUPERIOR SS100

Capacity 996cc • Power output 45bhp @ 4,800rpm • Weight 400lb (181kg) • Top speed 100mph (161km/h) (estimated)

UNITED KINGDOM

BROUGH SUPERIORS were made in limited numbers for discerning and wealthy customers. Many of the components used were bought from outside suppliers, and others were copied from established designs, but the total was greater than the sum of the parts. Styling, finish, engineering, and performance were superb. Like the sprung-frame 1930 Alpine Grand Sport model shown here, they were almost all V-twins, using engines supplied by JAP, Matchless, and MAG.

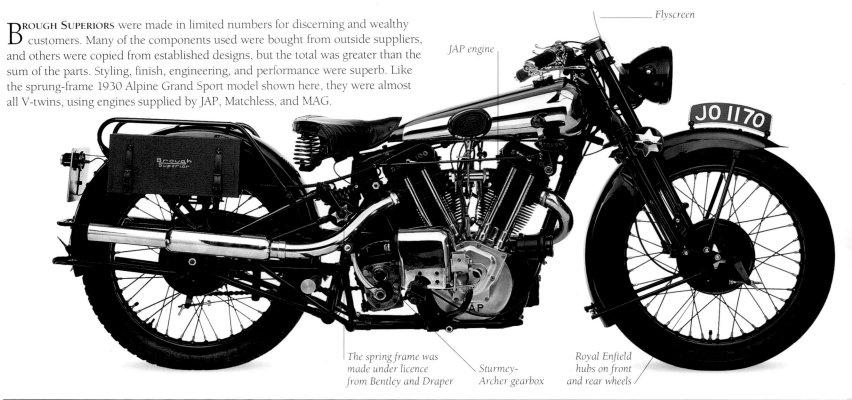

Flyscreen

JAP engine

The spring frame was made under licence from Bentley and Draper

Sturmey-Archer gearbox

Royal Enfield hubs on front and rear wheels

BROUGH SUPERIOR DREAM

Capacity 998cc • Power output not known • Weight not known • Top speed not known

MASTER PUBLICIST GEORGE BROUGH repeatedly stunned visitors to Britain's annual motorcycle show with a series of innovative four-cylinder machines. In 1927 there was a 994cc side-valve V4, which never went beyond prototype form. The following year a MAG-engined in-line four was exhibited. Again, it did not reach production. In 1931, an extraordinary device with twin rear wheels, which was based on an Austin Seven car engine was shown. Ten were built. Seven years later Brough exhibited his most remarkable creation. The Brough Superior Dream was, in essence, two flat twins mounted one above the other. They shared a common crankcase and both crankshafts were geared together. The gearbox bolted to the rear of the engine and drove the rear wheel by shaft. The engine was put into a duplex tubular cradle frame with plunger rear suspension and Brough's own Castle leading-link forks. Two or three prototypes, all slightly different, were reputedly built before World War II ended the project. Even by Brough's standards that hardly counts as production.

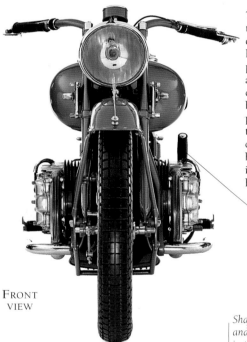

FRONT VIEW

THE DREAM inherited many of the traditional advantages and disadvantages of the flat-twin layout. The cylinders were perfectly positioned for air cooling and accident damage. The twin camshafts ran between the cylinder bores, operating the valves by pushrods situated fore and aft of the barrels. On early versions the camshafts were gear driven, but by the time this version was built in 1939, chain drive to the cams had been adopted.

Lever operates centre stand

•SMOOTH AS A DREAM•

The Dream had two 360° crankshafts mounted one above the other. The pistons on each side of the engine reach t.d.c. together while those on the other side are at b.d.c. The crankshafts were geared to turn in opposite directions, cancelling out the undesirable balance forces and gyroscopic forces and making the engine perfectly smooth.

The Dream's 998cc engine

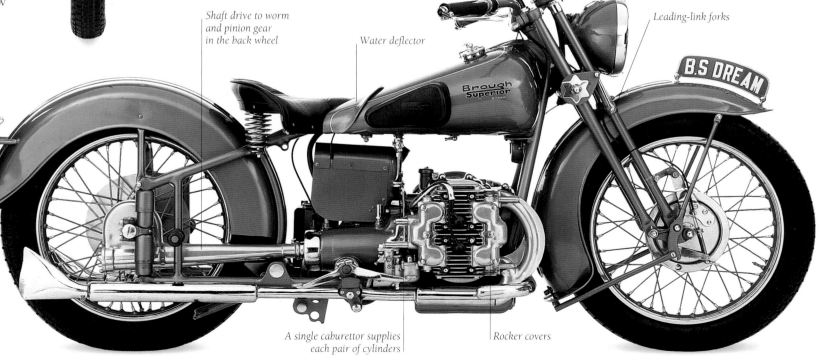

Shaft drive to worm and pinion gear in the back wheel

Water deflector

Leading-link forks

A single caburettor supplies each pair of cylinders

Rocker covers

BSA Model E

Capacity 770cc • Power output 6hp
Weight 336lb (153kg) • Top speed 55mph (88km/h) (estimated) UNITED KINGDOM

THE MODEL E appeared at the Olympia Show in 1919 for the 1920 season and was the first of a series of side-valve V-twins that were built by BSA between World Wars. The 1920 machine illustrated here had a three-speed gearbox, primary and final drive chains enclosed in a cast-aluminium case, a 50° V-twin engine, and a tubular, diamond-pattern frame. Although the design was unremarkable, the machines were cheap and reliable, so they became very popular. The Model E was primarily intended for pulling sidecars.

Girder forks
Flat-sided tank design
Tool bag

BSA Model B

Capacity 249cc • Power output 35bhp @ 6,000rpm
Weight 143lb (65kg) • Top speed 43mph (69km/h) UNITED KINGDOM

IN 1924 THE MOTOR CYCLE proclaimed, "So well proportioned is the new model that it is difficult to believe that it has only 24-in (61-cm) wheels". The object of envy was BSA's new 250cc bike with simple two-speed gearbox and side-valve engine. Its cylindrical 1½-gallon (6.8-litre) fuel tank gave the little machine the nickname, Round Tank. Retailing at a low price, this lightweight, 1924 bike sold extremely well as a basic, no-frills machine. In total, 35,000 were made.

Handchange gear lever was criticized for being too far forward

BSA Sloper

Capacity 493cc • Power output 20bhp (estimated)
Weight 337lb (153kg) • Top speed 70–75mph (113–120km/h) UNITED KINGDOM

THE SPORTING BSA Sloper MACHINES launched in 1926 were so named to reflect the foward tilt of the engines in their frames. Six models were produced in all, in 350cc, 500cc, and 600cc sizes. The first model was called the S27 o.h.v. and was housed in a twin downtube frame. The 493cc single had wet-sump lubrication, a gear-driven magneto in front of the cylinder, and a single port head with two valves. By 1929 the Sloper came with a twin-exhaust port head and a 349cc model was available, but it was only marginally cheaper than the 500cc. This is a 1930 model.

Chrome saddle-tank
Three-speed, handchange gearbox

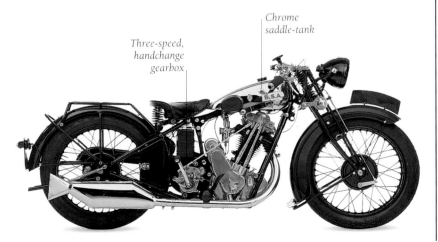

BSA Star Twin

Capacity 495cc • Power output 29bhp @ 6,000rpm
Weight 375lb (170kg) • Top speed 86mph (138km/h) UNITED KINGDOM

THE LAUNCH OF TRIUMPH'S INNOVATIVE Speed Twin in 1937 (see pp.182–83) set British manufacturers in fierce competition with each other to produce similar twin-cylinder bikes. World War II prevented BSA launching its entry until 1946. It was a 495cc o.h.v. twin that produced 25bhp at 5,800rpm. The Star Twin is a sports model of the original A7. An increased compression ratio and twin carburettors boosted performance by 4bhp. The Star Twin only lasted until 1950 when the 650cc A10 took its place. Shown here is a 1948 model.

Cast-iron cylinder head and engine block
Plunger rear suspension
Telescopic forks

BSA BANTAM

Capacity 123cc • Power output 4.5bhp @ 5,000rpm • Weight 170lb (77kg) • Top speed 53mph (85km/h)

THE BANTAM PROVED TO BE a simple, reliable design that earned BSA a huge amount of revenue. It was copied from the pre-World War II German DKW RT125, a two-stroke single offered as part of German war reparations. The 123cc Bantam was launched in June 1946. Many parts of the bike were painted mist green, including the wheel rims. A poor top speed on the early models was compensated for by miserly fuel consumption of around 120mpg (42.5km/l). In addition, widely spaced gear ratios meant that power dropped rapidly on hills, but the lightweight Bantam was inexpensive to buy and maintain, endearing it to the consumer. The British General Post Office bought a fleet of Bantams for telegram delivery service, adding leg shields, crash bars, and its bright red livery. Later models were slightly more sophisticated: rear suspension arrived in 1950 and a four-speed gearbox in the 1960s. BSA dropped the much-loved Bantam in 1971 after decades of use and abuse from novice riders, commuters, trials riders, and even road racers.

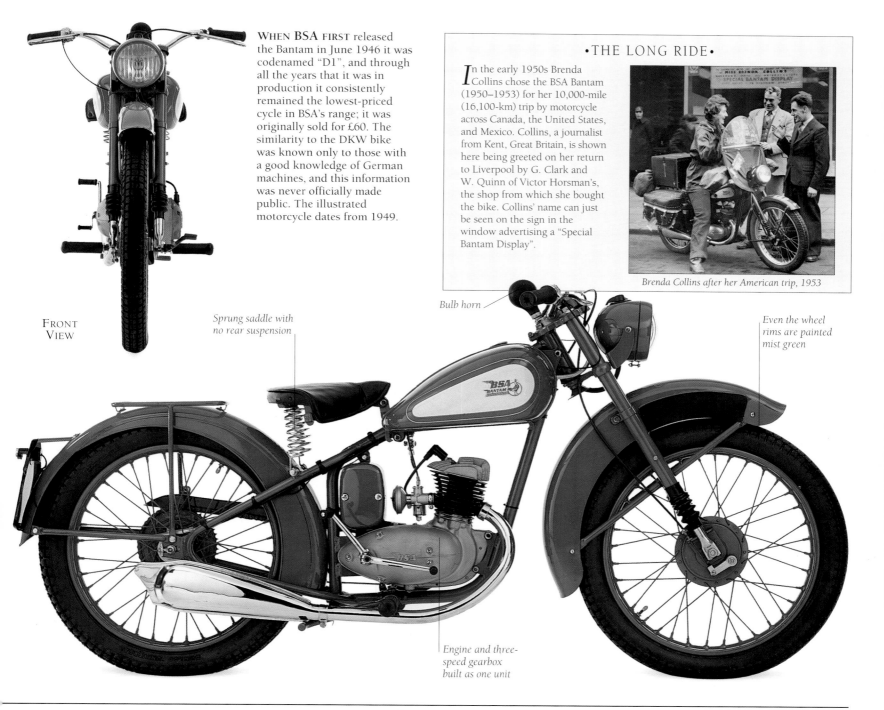

WHEN BSA FIRST released the Bantam in June 1946 it was codenamed "D1", and through all the years that it was in production it consistently remained the lowest-priced cycle in BSA's range; it was originally sold for £60. The similarity to the DKW bike was known only to those with a good knowledge of German machines, and this information was never officially made public. The illustrated motorcycle dates from 1949.

FRONT VIEW

•THE LONG RIDE•

*I*n the early 1950s Brenda Collins chose the BSA Bantam (1950–1953) for her 10,000-mile (16,100-km) trip by motorcycle across Canada, the United States, and Mexico. Collins, a journalist from Kent, Great Britain, is shown here being greeted on her return to Liverpool by G. Clark and W. Quinn of Victor Horsman's, the shop from which she bought the bike. Collins' name can just be seen on the sign in the window advertising a "Special Bantam Display".

Brenda Collins after her American trip, 1953

Bulb horn

Sprung saddle with no rear suspension

Even the wheel rims are painted mist green

Engine and three-speed gearbox built as one unit

BSA Gold Star DBD34

Capacity 499cc • Power output 40bhp @ 7,000rpm • Weight 308lb (140kg) • Top speed 110mph (177km/h)

ARGUABLY THE MOST EVOCATIVE NAME in motorcycle history, the Gold Star took its name from a lapel badge awarded to riders who completed a race lap at Brooklands in England of over 100mph (161km/h). This was in the 1930s and the first Gold Star was an o.h.v., all-alloy, 500cc single. It soon became known for its versatility, being equally competitive on and off road, and its sporting reputation led to the Gold Star becoming the chosen mount for racing riders by 1960. They demanded essential modifications that

were all the rage outside the coffee bars of the period, so clip-on handlebars and a swept-back exhaust pipe were fitted to the top-of-the-range Clubman model, giving the popular café-racer look. Other classic Gold Star fitments included an RRT2 close-ratio gearbox, an Amal 1½-in (38-mm) Grand Prix carburettor, a distinctive – and noisy – silencer, and a 7½-in (19-cm) front drum brake. A 350cc version was also available in 1960, but only built to order. The 500cc machine remained in production until 1963. This is a 1960 model.

A RIDE ON A TYPICAL Gold Star is characterized by tall gearing, which means awkward getaways and slipping the clutch at slow speeds. But once on the move, a speed of nearly 90mph (145km/h) in second gear should be possible. Today genuine Gold Stars are valuable collectors' items, but parts are still being manufactured to keep BSA's sporting single going strong.

•WHAT'S IN A NAME?•

*T*he origin of the BSA Gold Star dates back to 1937. Riding a 500cc Empire Star – the model recently redesigned by Val Page – Wal Handley won a Brooklands Gold Star badge for his best lap speed of 105.5mph (170km/h). BSA promptly changed the cycle's name to Gold Star for the 1938 revamped version. The bike was dropped in 1939 and did not reappear until 1948.

Eddie Dow in the 1955 Senior Clubmans TT

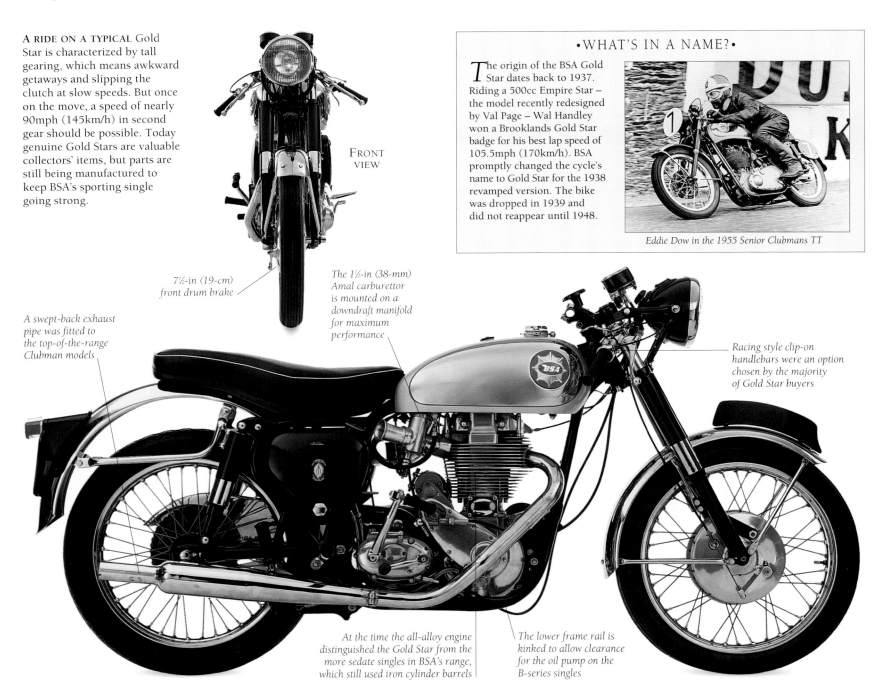

FRONT VIEW

7½-in (19-cm) front drum brake

The 1½-in (38-mm) Amal carburettor is mounted on a downdraft manifold for maximum performance

A swept-back exhaust pipe was fitted to the top-of-the-range Clubman models

Racing style clip-on handlebars were an option chosen by the majority of Gold Star buyers

At the time the all-alloy engine distinguished the Gold Star from the more sedate singles in BSA's range, which still used iron cylinder barrels

The lower frame rail is kinked to allow clearance for the oil pump on the B-series singles

BSA C15

Capacity 249cc • Power output 15bhp @ 7,000rpm
Weight 143lb (65kg) • Top speed 68mph (109km/h) UNITED KINGDOM

Launched in **1958**, the C15 was one of a line of utilitarian BSA 250s stretching back to the round tank of 1924 (see p.36). The most striking feature of the new design was the unit construction of the engine and gearbox. The 250cc single is a plodder and early examples suffered engine main-bearing failure. Also on early models the distributor was mounted behind the cylinder. However, trials and scramble versions proved successful, unsurprising since former trials ace Bert Perigo was chief development engineer of the C15.

Capacity of the unit-construction o.h.v. BSA single eventually reached 499cc

BSA A65L

Capacity 654cc • Power output 53bhp @ 7,000rpm
Weight 421lb (191kg) • Top speed 115mph (185km/h) UNITED KINGDOM

Unit construction was adopted for BSA's 499cc (A50) and 654cc (A65) twins in 1962. A hump-backed seat, twin carburettors, and rev counter put the Lightning Clubman version of the A65 firmly in the sports class. Unfortunately for BSA, Triumph's 650cc Bonneville (see p.185) and Norton's 650SS (see p.146) had the performance edge, but the A65 was still a fine bike. Its smooth lines were reflected in the oval cases of the unit-construction engine and gearbox. Before production ceased, the Lightning was made into a 750cc version – the U.S.-only A70L – by lengthening the stroke to 85mm. The 1962–63 original A65 was known as the Star. This bike is from 1966.

BSA's "crinkle hub" wheel is quickly detached

Unit-construction engine and gearbox

Single leading shoe drum brake

"Siamese" two-into-one exhaust pipe

BSA Rocket 3

Capacity 740cc • Power output 60bhp @ 7,250rpm UNITED KINGDOM
Weight 490lb (222kg) • Top speed 122mph (196km/h)

The three-cylindered Rocket 3 – or A75 – was launched in Britain in 1969. The BSA/Triumph group had to act quickly to catch up with Honda which was known to be developing a four. The Rocket 3 and Triumph Trident (see p.186) were similar, though BSA's engine design had its cylinder block tilted forward where the Triumph's was vertical. Styling was radical, with raygun silencers and slab-sided bodywork over a duplex frame. Ground clearance was poor and the triple cost more than Honda's new CB750 four. This Rocket 3 is from 1970; BSA ceased production the following year.

Inclined cylinders distinguish BSA's 740cc triple from Triumph's version

"Raygun" silencers indicate an attempt at futuristic styling

BSA
ROCKET 3 RACER

Capacity 740cc • Power output 69bhp @ 8,500rpm UNITED KINGDOM
Weight 380lb (172kg) • Top speed 152mph (245km/h)

Despite the short life of the Rocket 3 road bike, the racing version was a success, outpacing bikes such as Honda's 750 four on the track. Its high point came at Mallory Park's "Race of the Year" in 1971 when British rider John Cooper beat the world champion Giacomo Agostini, who was riding an MV. Good performances in America and Britain by riders like Mike Hailwood, Percy Tait, and Ray Pickrell bolstered the Rocket's reputation. Part of the racer's success was due to the excellent handling given by the frames, which were specially built by Rob North for the Rocket 3 and Triumph Trident racers.

Specially designed racing frame

Letterbox fairing – so called because of the front air slot for the oil cooler

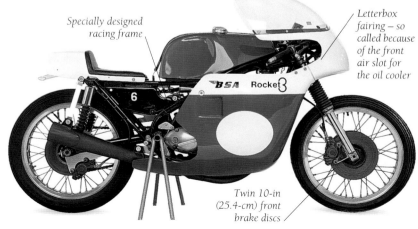

Twin 10-in (25.4-cm) front brake discs

BUELL S2-THUNDERBOLT

Capacity 1203cc • Power output 76bhp • Weight 450lb (204kg) • Top speed 110mph (177km/h)

U.S.A.

ERIC BUELL HAD BEEN a Harley-Davidson employee before setting up on his own in the early 1980s to make sporting machines with Harley power units. Early Buells used a multi-tubular frame with high-quality suspension, wheels, and brakes. The engine was a Harley Sportster unit, and the whole machine was clothed in bulbous fibreglass bodywork that concealed the engine and a large part of the front wheel. The demand for a sports bike with a Harley engine was minimal; Buell machines were hand-built in limited numbers and sold for a high price. In early 1993, a new company was formed, with Harley-Davidson itself taking a significant stake. A new Buell bike was developed for production in 1994. The production run was intended to be 700 in the first year – a vast number compared to the early Buell. The new bikes were distributed through Harley-Davidson dealers and offered with a Harley-Davidson warranty and back-up. Harley's intention was to extend into new markets without alienating its traditional customers. Pictured here is a 1994 machine.

THE THUNDERBOLT uses premium-quality chassis components and a neat tubular frame, but the engine and belt final-drive system are taken from Harley-Davidson's 1200 Sportster. The 45° o.h.v. V-twin engine does not really produce sufficient power to tax the Buell chassis.

Sculpted fuel tank with cut outs for riders knees

BACK VIEW

•FINE HANDLING•

Good-quality components, a short wheelbase, a steep steering head angle, and a rigid tubular chassis make the Buell a fine machine to manoeuvre. In contrast the handling of conventional Harley-Davidson motorcycles does not inspire exuberant cornering.

A Thunderbolt in action

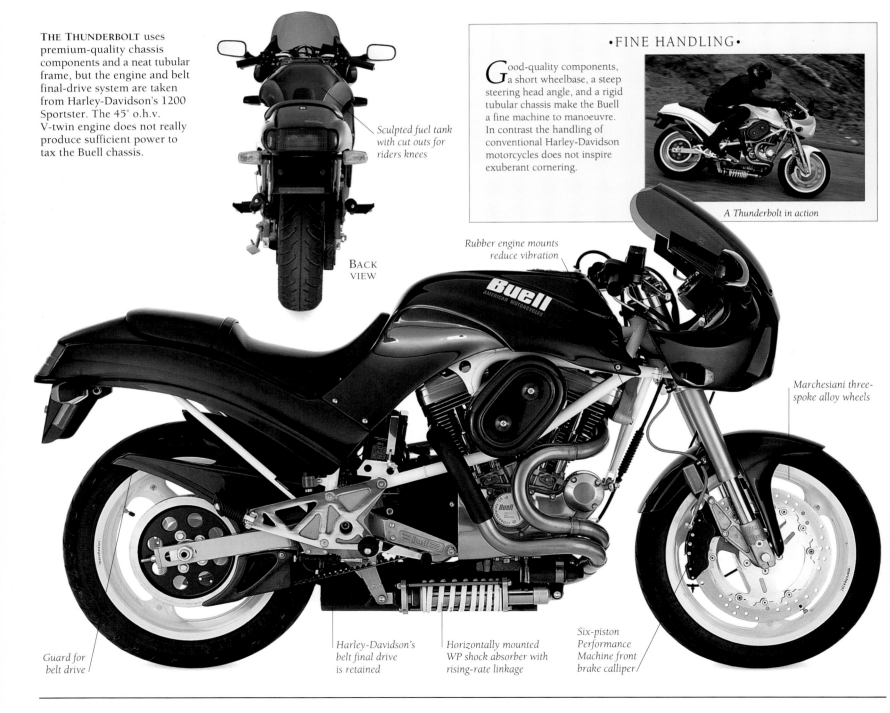

Rubber engine mounts reduce vibration

Marchesiani three-spoke alloy wheels

Guard for belt drive

Harley-Davidson's belt final drive is retained

Horizontally mounted WP shock absorber with rising-rate linkage

Six-piston Performance Machine front brake calliper

BULTACO SHERPA

Capacity 244cc • Power output 18bhp
Weight 93kg (204lb) • Top speed not known

DEVELOPED BY **SAMMY MILLER** and introduced late in 1964, the Sherpa was so successful that most other trials machines were immediately rendered obsolete. Never before had a combination of low-speed pulling power, hill-climbing ability, and instant throttle response allied to docility when required, been available in one machine. Using many existing parts – basic engine, wheels, and forks – it was claimed that the prototype progressed from concept to finished product in just 12 days. The Sherpa shown here is Sammy Miller's development machine from 1964.

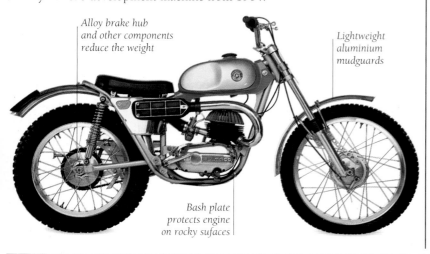

Alloy brake hub and other components reduce the weight

Lightweight aluminium mudguards

Bash plate protects engine on rocky surfaces

BULTACO METRALLA

Capacity 244cc • Power output 25bhp
Weight 123kg (271lb) • Top speed 137km/h (85mph)

IN CONTRAST TO THE SOPHISTICATED 250cc Japanese sports machines, the Spanish lightweight sports roadster was basically a motocross engine fitted into race-bred cycle parts. Its success was amply demonstrated when Metrallas finished in the first three places in the 250cc production class at the 1967 TT. The engine was devoid of performance aids such as reed or rotary valves. A six-speed gearbox, expansion-chamber exhaust, and a twin leading-shoe front brake completed the specification of a well-developed machine. This bike dates from 1975.

Simple, piston-ported, two-stroke engine runs on petrol/oil mixture

Air scoop for twin leading-shoe front drum brake

Enclosed final drive chain

BULTACO ALPINA

Capacity 244cc • Power output 19bhp • Weight 109kg (240lb) • Top speed not known

WHEN INTEREST IN OFF-ROAD MOTORCYCLING rose in the early 1970s, Bultaco had a well-established reputation and a range of trials and motocross machines. The firm was in an excellent position to take advantage of the market with proven products. The Alpina illustrated is a 1975 model.

THE ALPINA probably appealed to the leisure rider who wanted to dabble in competition rather than the serious competitor. More of a trail bike than an enduro machine, it was still pretty good for either usage.

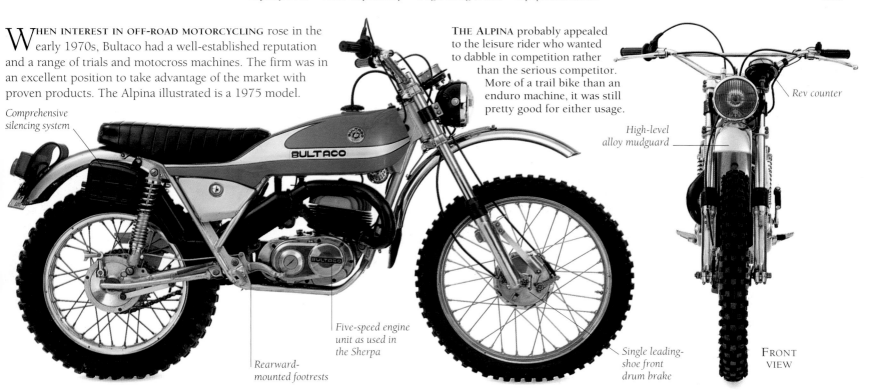

Comprehensive silencing system

Five-speed engine unit as used in the Sherpa

Rearward-mounted footrests

Rev counter

High-level alloy mudguard

Single leading-shoe front drum brake

FRONT VIEW

CAGIVA SST

Capacity 122cc • Power output 14bhp (estimated)
Weight 107kg (236lb) • Top speed 105km/h (65mph)

ITALY

FROM **1960 HARLEY-DAVIDSON** produced lightweight motorcycles at the former Aermacchi factory at Varese in Italy. In 1978 Cagiva took over. The firm's first machines were based on existing Harley models, although there were detail improvements. As well as a new logo on the fuel tank, the 125 model shown here was given cast wheels, improved switchgear, and electronic ignition. It was enough to make Cagiva the biggest-selling manufacturer in the critical Italian 125cc market from 1979 until 1982.

56 x 54-mm piston port, two-stroke engine with five-speed box

Cast-alloy wheels

CAGIVA MITO

Capacity 124cc • Power output 30bhp @ 11,000rpm
Weight 125kg (275lb) • Top speed 169km/h (105mph) (estimated)

ITALY

FIFTEEN YEARS AFTER **CAGIVA'S SST** (see left), the 125 market had moved on. Buyers demanded looks and performance as delivered by bikes like the 1994 Cagiva Mito, shown here. In return, motorcycle manufacturers demanded that buyers have fat wallets. The price for "just" a 125 was high. The comprehensive specification, stunning performance, and superlative handling almost justified it. The Mito was styled to look like the 916 Ducati and had a twin-spar alloy frame.

Ducati 916-inspired twin-headlight fairing

CLEVELAND

Capacity 16.4cu. in. (269cc) • Power output 2.5hp • Weight 167lb (76kg) • Top speed 45mph (72km/h)

U.S.A.

PROBABLY THE MOST SUCCESSFUL TWO-STROKE to be built in America, the Cleveland lightweight was manufactured from 1915 until 1927. Engine capacity started at 13.5cu. in. (222cc), but by the time this 1919 model was built, displacement was 269cc. The engine was mounted with the crankshaft running longitudinally.

Two-speed gearbox operated by hand lever

Chain driven by identically sized sprockets

Horizontally sprung pivoting forks

Single-cylinder engine

Final drive was turned through 90° by a worm and pinion gear

CLEVELAND TORNADO

Capacity 61cu. in. (1000cc) • Power output 31bhp (estimated) • Weight 540lb (245kg) • Top speed 100mph (161km/h)

U.S.A.

THE FIRST CLEVELAND FOUR appeared in 1925 based on a design by L. E. Fowler. The new machine was not a success and was replaced the following season by a completely new four designed by Everitt DeLong. Original capacity was 45cu. in. (737cc), but by the time this improved Tornado model appeared in 1929, capacity had been increased to 61cu. in. (1000cc). The machine used i.o.e. valve gear, and a three-speed gearbox with chain final drive.

I.o.e. engine achieves greater power by using alloy pistons and bigger valves

Leading link forks

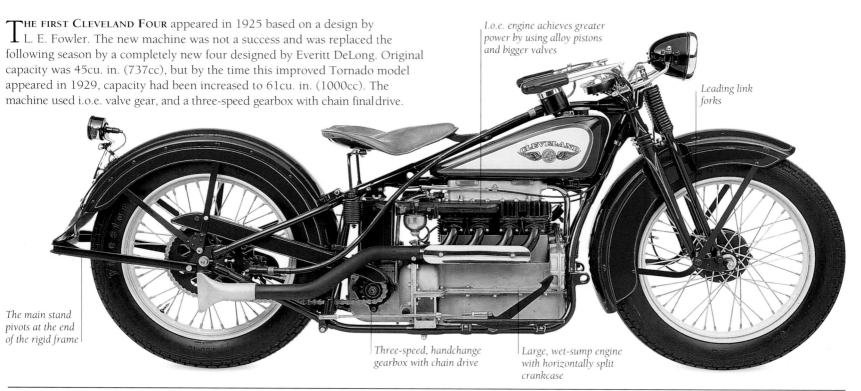

The main stand pivots at the end of the rigid frame

Three-speed, handchange gearbox with chain drive

Large, wet-sump engine with horizontally split crankcase

COTTON 500

Capacity 490cc • Power output not known • Weight 255lb (116kg) • Top speed 75mph (121km/h) (estimated)

UNITED KINGDOM

THE DISTINCTIVE FEATURE of Cotton machines was the triangulated frame developed by Frank Willoughby Cotton. The steering head was connected to the rear axle by four straight tubes. This structure made the frame very rigid, thus endowing Cotton machines with excellent handling. They achieved considerable sporting success in the 1920s. This machine dates from 1937.

Hand lever to operate gearbox

High-level exhaust

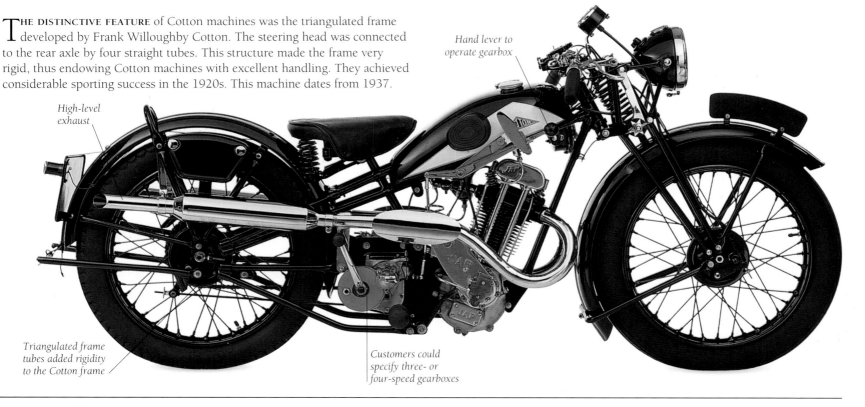

Triangulated frame tubes added rigidity to the Cotton frame

Customers could specify three- or four-speed gearboxes

CUSHMAN
AUTO-GLIDE

Capacity 13.5cu. in. (222cc) • Power output 1.5hp　　U.S.A.
Weight 180lb (82kg) (estimated) • Top speed 30mph (48km/h) (estimated)

Scooters do not get much simpler than the early Cushman. The frame was made of channel-section steel, the engine was a simple industrial power unit, and it had neither suspension nor gearbox. Proper production began in 1937, and this machine was produced in 1938. Cushman's main business was making industrial engines, and the scooter was a good way of selling more of the firm's side-valve "Husky" engines. The throttle was controlled by a twistgrip, and the clutch and brake were foot operated. The bike had no suspension.

Kickstarter

Front wheel is unbraked

CUSHMAN
32 AUTO-GLIDE

Capacity 14.88cu. in. (244cc) • Power output 4hp　　U.S.A.
Weight not known • Top speed not known

Cushman production continued through World War II and although some machines were supplied to the military the bulk of production went to civilians. The 30 series was introduced in 1942, and this 32 model was built in 1945. It was fitted with "Floating Drive", an automatic clutch and transmission system. A luggage compartment was incorporated in the re-styled bodywork, and lighting equipment was standard. The engine capacity of the 34 increased to 15cu. in. (246cc) and led to improved performance. The 50 series replaced the 30s for 1946.

Sprung front fork

Engine concealed behind louvered panel

CUSHMAN HIGHLANDER

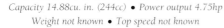

Capacity 14.88cu. in. (244cc) • Power output 4.75hp　　U.S.A.
Weight not known • Top speed not known

Cushman supplied a stripped-down version of its scooter to the military during World War II for use by troops dropped by parachute during airborne invasions. After the war, Cushman continued building these machines for general sale. They were based on the conventional scooter but the bodywork was omitted; instead the seat and fuel tank were mounted on a simple tubular structure. The Highlander name was added in 1949 and the model pictured here dates from 1958. At this time Cushman used a long, leading-link, front fork design.

4.75 x 7.75-in diameter tyres

Steel-channel frame member

CUSHMAN EAGLE

Capacity 19.44cu. in. (319cc) • Power output 8hp　　U.S.A.
Weight not known • Top speed not known

An extension of the craze for conventional scooters that swept America in the 1950s was a fashion for strange, small-wheeled motorcycles. These combined the small wheels and the industrial engines of scooters with styling inspired (loosely) by big Indians and Harley-Davidsons. The Eagle was Cushman's offering in this class in which the other key players were the Mustang and the Powell A-V-8 (see pp.134 and 274). The first Eagle appeared in 1949, and the line continued until the firm's production stopped in 1965. The machine pictured here is a 1958 model.

Tubular frame has no rear suspension

Optional oilbath air cleaner

CYC-AUTO

Capacity 98cc • Power output 2bhp
Weight 110lb (50kg) (estimated) • Top speed 25mph (40km/h) (estimated)

UNITED KINGDOM

T HE CYC-AUTO WAS, IN A SENSE, A REVERSION to the pioneer motorcycle designs since it consisted of an engine mounted in a strengthened bicycle frame. The prototype appeared in 1931 with a 98cc engine; initially the company made its own, but it changed to a Villiers unit in 1938. Financial problems resulted in a take-over by Scott also in 1938, and thereafter Scott engines were used. Subsequent developments included adding a clutch and sprung forks, but by the early 1950s the autocycle's days were numbered – the moped was about to arrive. Shown here is a 1947 Cyc-Auto.

Transmission from the engine via a worm and wheel, then by chain to the rear wheel

CYKLON

Capacity 130cc • Power output 1.5hp @ 2,000rpm
Weight 35kg (77lb) • Top speed 30km/h (19mph)

GERMANY

T HE BERLIN FIRM OF CYKLON took a straightforward route to motorcycle production. It used a bicycle frame with reinforced forks and mounted a belt-driven engine above the front wheel. This layout was pioneered by the Werner brothers in Paris, but they soon realized the deficiencies of the design. It was obvious: placing a heavy engine high up above the front wheel resulted in appalling handling characteristics. The cycle shown here dates from 1901.

Tubing supplies petrol vapour to engine

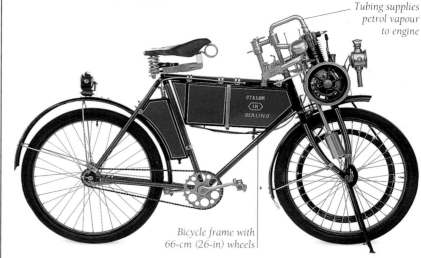

Bicycle frame with 66-cm (26-in) wheels

CZ 175 ENDURO DT

Capacity 172cc • Power output 16bhp @ 4,000rpm
Weight 112kg (247lb) • Top speed 105km/h (65mph)

CZECH REPUBLIC

T HE CZECH STATE-OWNED motorcycle company CZ produced two types of two-stroke motorcycles during the 1960s and 1970s: simple, sturdy, unremarkable utilitarian models and serious off-road competition bikes for motocross and enduro. These were very competitive, winning several Motocross World Championships and numerous enduro awards for the firm. The machine shown here dates from 1974.

Lights, indicators, horn, and mirrors had to be installed to make the machines legal for road use

•GREATER CAPACITY•

T his 1974 CZ Motocrosser uses a 380cc version of the single-cylinder, two-stroke engine. It has an alloy fuel tank and the exhaust system runs beneath the engine.

Braced handlebars

Plastic mudguard

Radially pinned cylinder head

1974 CZ Motocrosser

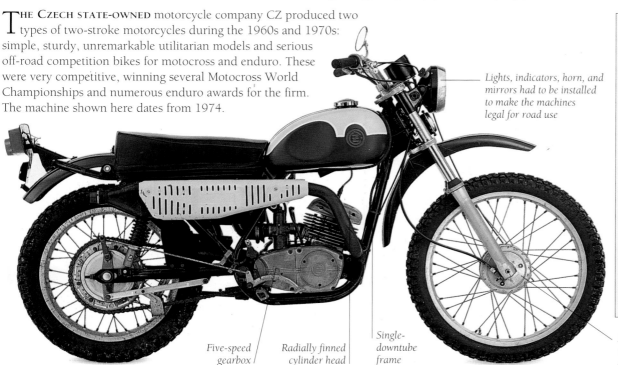

Five-speed gearbox

Radially finned cylinder head

Single-downtube frame

Small alloy brake drums reduce weight but provide adequate off-road braking

DAIMLER EINSPUR

Capacity 264cc • Power output 0.5bhp @ 700rpm • Weight 90kg (198lb) • Top speed 12km/h (7½mph)

THE GERMAN WORD *EINSPURIG* means "single track", an inaccurate description of this early machine, as it was equipped with spring-loaded outrigger wheels to keep it upright; these were necessary because the saddle was so high above the engine that the rider's feet could not reach the ground. The top of the engine projected up between the frame members, and above it was mounted a curved saddle more suited to the back of a horse. On the first machine, the handlebars were attached to a tiller, but this was later replaced by the link arrangement shown here. The engine had an automatic inlet valve fed from a surface carburettor and a mechanically operated exhaust valve. In many ways the engine was ahead of its time. The drive from the engine was by means of a flat belt to a countershaft, on the end of which was a pinion engaging with an internally toothed gear attached to the rear wheel. This was controlled by cords passing around the handlebars, twisting of which simultaneously tightened the belt and released the rear brake.

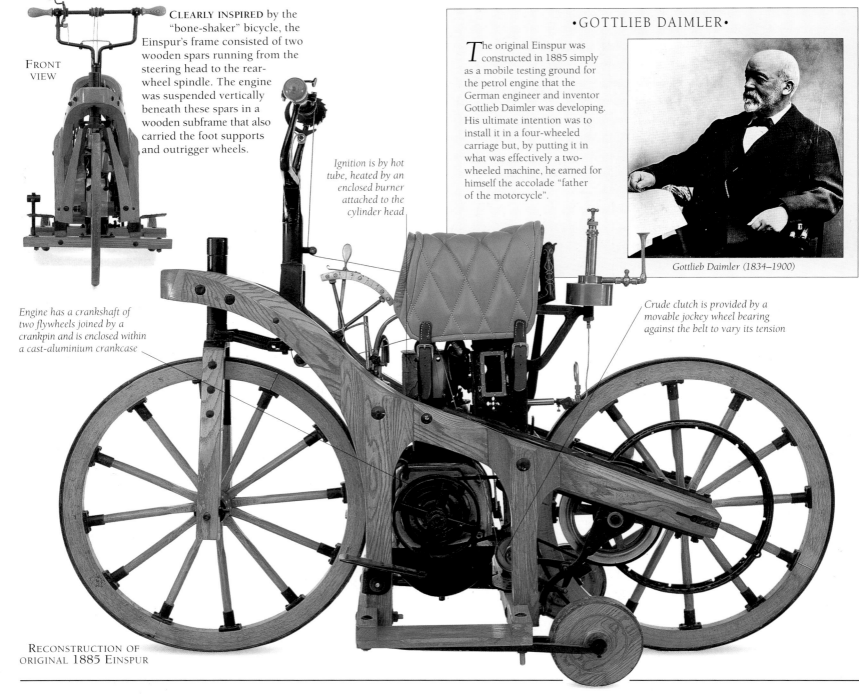

FRONT VIEW

CLEARLY INSPIRED by the "bone-shaker" bicycle, the Einspur's frame consisted of two wooden spars running from the steering head to the rear-wheel spindle. The engine was suspended vertically beneath these spars in a wooden subframe that also carried the foot supports and outrigger wheels.

Ignition is by hot tube, heated by an enclosed burner attached to the cylinder head

• GOTTLIEB DAIMLER •

The original Einspur was constructed in 1885 simply as a mobile testing ground for the petrol engine that the German engineer and inventor Gottlieb Daimler was developing. His ultimate intention was to install it in a four-wheeled carriage but, by putting it in what was effectively a two-wheeled machine, he earned for himself the accolade "father of the motorcycle".

Gottlieb Daimler (1834–1900)

Engine has a crankshaft of two flywheels joined by a crankpin and is enclosed within a cast-aluminium crankcase

Crude clutch is provided by a movable jockey wheel bearing against the belt to vary its tension

RECONSTRUCTION OF ORIGINAL 1885 EINSPUR

DeDion

Capacity 211cc • Power output not known   FRANCE
Weight not known • Top speed not known

ALBERT **C**OMTE **D**E**D**ION and his partner Georges Bouton built their first petrol-engined tricycles in 1895, having previously experimented with steam-powered three wheelers. The tricycle allowed easier engine mounting than a bicycle and also removed the risk of "sideslip", which troubled early motorcyclists. The quality of their new engine and the machine it powered made the vehicle a great success. It was built by DeDion in France and was also widely copied, legitimately and illegitimately.

Braced forks for additional strength

A.i.v. engine mounted vertically behind the rear axle

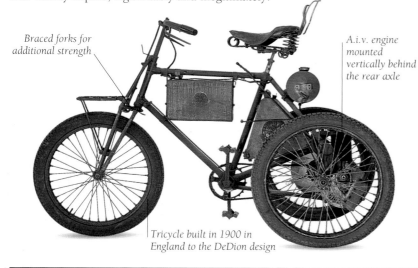

Tricycle built in 1900 in England to the DeDion design

Derbi
TRICAMPEONA SE

Capacity 49cc • Power output 4.5bhp @ 5,700rpm   SPAIN
Weight 54kg (119lb) • Top speed 75km/h (47mph)

ALTHOUGH **D**ERBI did make some larger capacity machines, the company has always specialized in small-capacity mopeds and motorcycles. The model shown here is a 1974 Tricampeona, presumably named to celebrate Derbi's three World Championships in the 50cc class in 1969, 1970, and 1972. It was a typical machine of its period. The pressed-steel frame was equipped with a motorcycle-style seat and fuel tank. The engine was a 49cc two-stroke with a 14-mm (½-in) carburettor. Transmission was by three-speed foot-operated gearbox and enclosed chain final drive. Pedals were used to comply with the legal definition of a moped.

Pressed-steel frame

2.25 x 18-in tyres

DERONZIERE

Capacity 282cc • Power output not known   FRANCE
Weight 45kg (100lb) (estimated) • Top speed 32km/h (20mph) (estimated)

DERONZIERE BUILT MOTORCYCLES in Lyon, France from 1903 until 1914. Some of its machines used engines supplied by Zédel and Peugeot, but the 1907 model shown here is fitted with the company's own 282cc power unit. The a.i.v. engine is installed in the loop frame using clamps rather than lugs. The cylinder is inclined though the cooling fins are horizontal for maximum cooling effect. Final drive is by belt with an idler clutch operated by the left-hand twistgrip. The whole machine is very compact, and the wheels are 51cm (20in) in diameter.

Leading-link front forks with extending springs mounted within polished covers

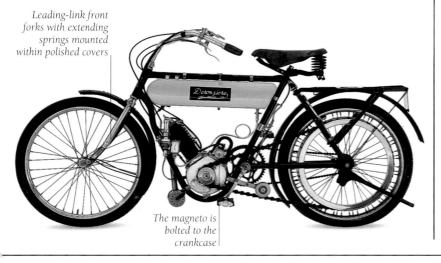

The magneto is bolted to the crankcase

DIAMANT

Capacity 343cc • Power output 17bhp   GERMANY
Weight 130kg (286lb) • Top speed 120km/h (75mph)

DIAMANT HAD BEEN a pioneer motorcycle manufacturer in Germany but stopped production in 1908 to concentrate on cars. The firm re-entered the motorcycle market in 1926 with machines designed by Franz Gnädig. The bike shown here was built in 1926. These new machines used Kühne o.h.v. single-cylinder engines and three-speed Sturmey-Archer gearboxes in tubular frames. In 1927 Diamant merged with Elite; the following year it was taken over by Opel, which produced the Opel Motoclub (see p.153) at the Elite-Diamant factory.

A 496cc version of the Kühne o.h.v. engine was also available

Deep, valanced mudguards

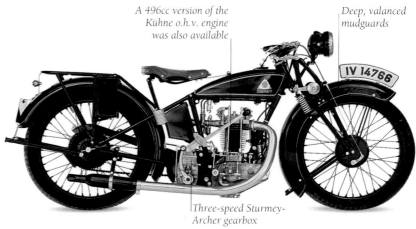

IV 14766

Three-speed Sturmey-Archer gearbox

DKW HILFSMOTOR

Capacity 118cc • Power output 1bhp
Weight (engine) 14kg (31lb) • Top speed 60km/h (37mph)

GERMANY

THIS **1920 ENGINE UNIT** was designed to be attached to a conventional bicycle. It was mounted above the rear wheel, driving it via a belt from a third-speed countershaft built into the crankcase. To advertise the Hilfsmotor, DKW used the slogan *das kleine Wunder* – "the little wonder". DKW is an abbreviation of *Dampf Kraft Wagen*, meaning "steam-powered carriage".

Compact, unobtrusive engine

FRONT VIEW

The Hilfsmotor was simply bolted onto a standard bicycle

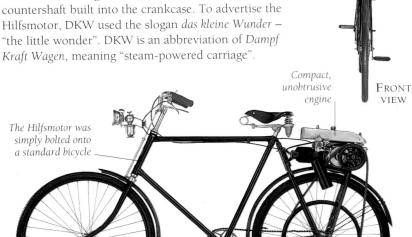

A special pulley was added to the rear wheel

DKW LOMOS

Capacity 142cc • Power output 1.5bhp
Weight 52kg (115lb) • Top speed 60km/h (37mph)

GERMANY

LIKE MANY MANUFACTURERS during the 1920s, DKW experimented with scooter design; this 1922 Lomos was the result. It followed the firm's 1921 attempt, the Golem, a crude and unsuccessful adaptation of the Hilfsmotor (see left). The "step-thru" frame housed a fan-cooled engine beneath a bucket seat that also incorporated the fuel tank. The Lomos was later produced under license by other companies.

FRONT VIEW

An adjustable inner pulley flange acted as clutch and variable transmission

Fuel tank

Leading-link forks

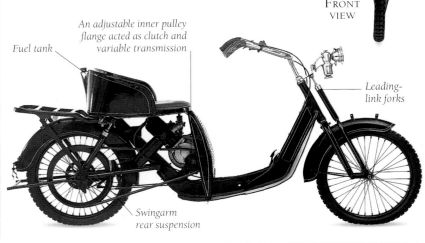

Swingarm rear suspension

DKW ZSW500

Capacity 494cc • Power output 14bhp @ 4,000rpm
Weight 150kg (330lb) • Top speed 105km/h (65mph)

GERMANY

BY THE LATE **1920s, DKW** was the biggest motorcycle manufacturer in the world. It offered a wide range of two-stroke machines from lightweight singles to large water-cooled twins. The ZSW500, with its flat tank design and separate gearbox, appealed to buyers suspicious of fashionable innovations of the time, such as pressed-steel frames. The water-cooled engine coped well when, as was common, the bike was used with a sidecar.

This 1929 model has no rear suspension: a sprung saddle is fitted to the rigid frame

Radiator for water-cooling system

FRONT VIEW

Separate three-speed gearbox

DKW LUXUS

Capacity 198/208cc • Power output 4.5bhp @ 3,500rpm
Weight 85kg (187lb) • Top speed 70km/h (43mph)

GERMANY

THE LUXUS WAS COMMONLY known as the *Blutblase*, meaning "blood blister", because of its bright red saddle tank. The engine on this 1931 model was a fan-cooled two-stroke with a two-speed gearbox. Economies of scale allowed DKW to change rapidly to constructing pressed-steel frames: the Luxus was its first machine to have one. Tax laws differed in the various countries that DKW exported to, hence the minor variations in capacity.

Saddle fuel tank

FRONT VIEW

Rigid pressed-steel frame

Cowling for fan-cooling system

DKW SS250

Capacity 243cc • Power output 21bhp @ 5,000rpm • Weight 141kg (310lb) • Top speed 145km/h (90mph)

ALTHOUGH THIS **1939 PRODUCTION RACER** was inspired by specially built works bikes, the SS250 lacked the sophistication of those machines. To reduce production costs the commercially available SS250 was fitted with a horizontal displacer piston (see inset) to replace cylindrical rotary or reed valves. Works bikes also tried various engine designs, but the SS250 used only a split single. The combination of the limited braking effect available from the

SS250's two-stroke engine and its substantial weight resulted in DKW paying particular attention to brake design. Wide and well-constructed alloy wheel hubs housed similarly generous brake linings. Motorcycles with assisted induction engines of this type were not allowed to compete in international races after World War II: this meant that until Germany was readmitted to the FIM in 1951, the SS250 was confined to national racing. As a result few have survived.

THE ADDITIONAL charge drawn into the SS250's engine by the displacer piston did not produce the intended increase in power output. Peak revolutions were severely limited due to the long and irregular path of combustion gases through the engine. In an effort to overcome this, factory racers eventually adopted rotary superchargers to force the mixture through.

FRONT VIEW

Specially designed, wide, alloy brake drums

The engine is mounted in a duplex frame with swingarm rear suspension linked to plunger spring boxes to control movement

Water-cooled cylinder jacket maintains optimum operating temperature

A large-capacity fuel (and oil) tank was essential on a machine that achieved as little as 5km/l (15mpg)

• THE SPLIT SINGLE ENGINE •

Efficient induction and transfer of gases around a two-stroke engine is vital. To achieve this DKW used a "split single" engine: two pistons run in separate cylinders but share one combustion chamber. Exhaust and induction timing are optimized as each operation is controlled by a separate piston. A third large-diameter piston, operating horizontally with a very short stroke, was used to increase the swept volume of the crankcase. Although complex, power gain was minimal.

Combustion chamber

Linked pistons run in a pair of parallel cylinders

Exhaust port

Displacer piston

Crankshaft runs clockwise

Connecting rods are eccentrically linked

DKW Split Single

As it was only sold in racing specification, the SS250 was not fitted with any accessories

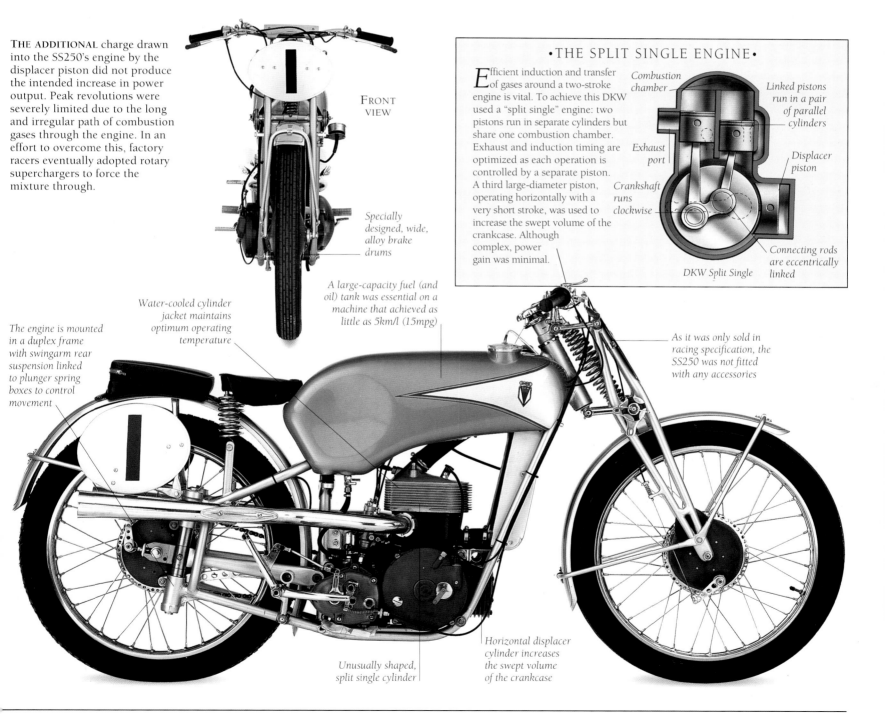

Unusually shaped, split single cylinder

Horizontal displacer cylinder increases the swept volume of the crankcase

DKW RT175VS

Capacity 174cc • Power output 9.6bhp @ 5,000rpm
Weight 130kg (286lb) • Top speed 101km/h (63mph)

GERMANY

THE **RT175VS, AND ITS 200 AND 250 VERSIONS,** was the last DKW model based on the 1939 RT125. The basic layout was the same apart from a gearbox modified to four speeds and the addition of fashionable "streamlined" fairings. The VS suffix stood for *voll Schwing*, meaning "full swing" – a reference to the swingarm suspension at front and rear. Earles forks, as used on this 1957 model, were popular at the time, particularly in Germany. As with the DKW Luxus (see p.48), the RT175VS was produced in various capacities to suit particular markets.

174cc versions were supplied with a single seat; larger capacity versions had a pillion

Earles forks

DKW HUMMEL

Capacity 48cc • Power output 2.4bhp @ 6,600rpm
Weight 78kg (172lb) • Top speed 70km/h (43mph)

GERMANY

THE **GERMAN WORD** *HUMMEL* means "bumble bee"; it was an appropriate name for this stylish and reliable moped. The model shown here was produced in 1965, by which time DKW had merged with Victoria (see p.191) and Express to form the Zweirad Union. The Hummel had excellent features for a bike of its class. It had a fan-cooled, two-stroke engine and a three-speed gearbox. Unusually for a moped, it was fitted with a foot-operated gearchange rather than a twistgrip, swingarm suspension front and rear, and an enclosed chain.

Integral headlight cowl and fuel tank

Fairing design was inspired by science fiction and U.S. cars

Earles forks

Chain housing

DOT SUPERSPORTS

UNITED KINGDOM

Capacity 349cc • Power output 2.75hp • Weight not known • Top speed not known

THE **DOT COMPANY** was founded in 1902 by pioneer racing motorcyclist Harry Reed. Like many British manufacturers, Dot relied on bought-in engines throughout its 60-year history. During the 1920s JAP and Blackburn were its major suppliers of four-stroke engines; however, this Supersports model of 1923 has an o.h.v. Bradshaw engine with oil cooling. This feature was nicknamed "the Oilboiler". The otherwise orthodox Bradshaw-engined model remained in the Dot catalogue for five years.

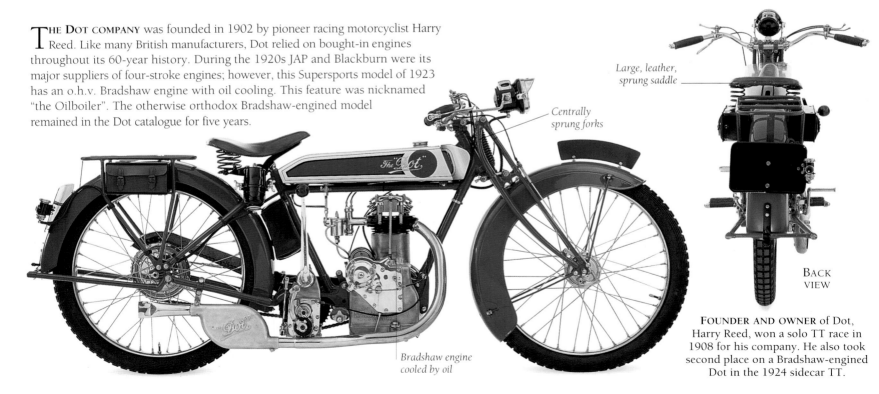

Large, leather, sprung saddle

Centrally sprung forks

Bradshaw engine cooled by oil

BACK VIEW

FOUNDER AND OWNER of Dot, Harry Reed, won a solo TT race in 1908 for his company. He also took second place on a Bradshaw-engined Dot in the 1924 sidecar TT.

DOUGLAS MODEL D

Capacity 340cc • Power output not known • Weight 140lb (64kg) • Top speed 35mph (56km/h) (estimated)

THE FIRST DOUGLAS MOTORCYCLE had a two-cylinder, 340cc engine with automatic inlet valves. By 1910 – the date of the bike illustrated – the frame had been lengthened, the engine lowered, and a thoroughly satisfactory motorcycle resulted, as shown by Eli Clarke's 900-mile (1,448-km) journey down the length of Great Britain in 39 hours 40 minutes. The gearbox also appeared in 1910, though the machine shown here is single-speed.

THE DOUGLAS COMPANY started in 1882, soon developing into a general engineering firm. Joseph Barter's "Fairy" engine castings were from this concern. When Barter's own firm became insolvent in 1907, he moved to Douglas and set up a motorcycle department.

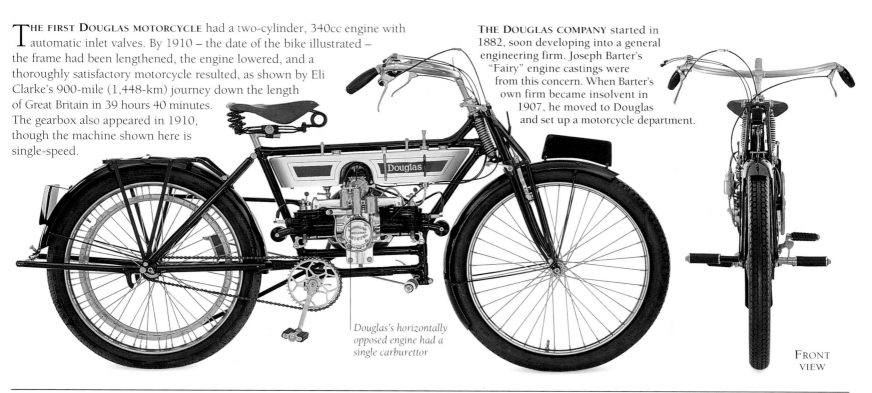

Douglas's horizontally opposed engine had a single carburettor

FRONT VIEW

DOUGLAS DT5

Capacity 494cc • Power output 27bhp
Weight not known • Top speed not known

SPEEDWAY RACING, OR "DIRT TRACK" as it was then known (hence "DT"), came to England from Australia in 1928, although its roots were probably in U.S. The top Australian riders used machines based on the Douglas RA, and before long Douglas produced a specialized speedway bike – the DT5. The standard engine produced 27bhp but a 32bhp engine was available at an extra cost. Long and low, the machine was ideal for the tracks and riding styles of the day, but things were changing, and the shorter Rudge- and JAP-engined machines had rendered the Douglas obsolete by 1931.

DT5 has no clutch because rolling starts were used and the three-speed gearbox remained in top gear throughout

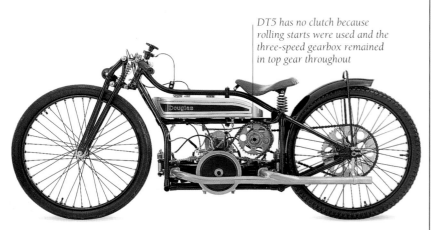

DOUGLAS 80 PLUS

Capacity 348cc • Power output 25bhp @ 7,000rpm
Weight 393lb (178kg) • Top speed 85mph (137km/h)

UNLIKE ALL PREVIOUS DOUGLAS TWINS with the exception of the short-lived Endeavour, the post-war machines had their engines mounted transversely in the frame but did not then use the more logical shaft drive. The frame was fitted with leading-link front forks and pivoted-fork rear suspension using torsion bars in the lower frame tubes, actuated via bell cranks. Two sports variants were announced for 1950: the 90 Plus was built almost to racing standards, while engines that did not meet the 28bhp 90 Plus threshold were put into sports roadsters and designated "80 Plus". The 80 Plus pictured dates from 1953.

The engine drives via a car-type clutch, four-speed gearbox, bevel gears, and a chain to the rear wheel

Chain-driven rear wheel

DRESCH

Capacity 495cc • Power output 18bhp • Weight 141kg (310lb) • Top speed 121km/h (75mph)

LAUNCHED AT THE PARIS SALON IN 1930, the 500 Dresch twin had an impressive specification. The in-line twin-cylinder s.v. engine was mounted in a pressed-steel frame. There was a three-speed hand-operated gearbox and shaft final drive. The instruments – a speedometer, ammeter, and eight-day clock – were set into the fuel tank. Electric lighting and sprung handlebars were standard. In France it was cheaper than most comparable machines. An o.h.v. version was also produced.

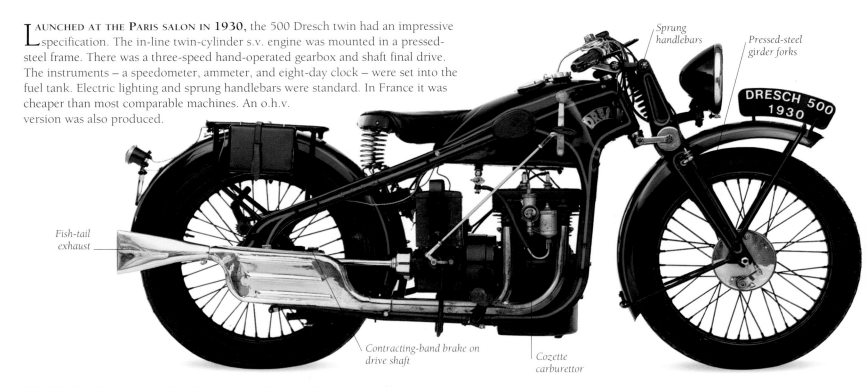

Sprung handlebars

Pressed-steel girder forks

Fish-tail exhaust

Contracting-band brake on drive shaft

Cozette carburettor

DUCATI MACH 1

Capacity 249cc • Power output 26bhp @ 8,500rpm
Weight 116kg (256lb) • Top speed 171km/h (106mph)

ITALY

INTRODUCED IN 1964, the Mach 1 was the fastest 250 road bike available at that time. The new model was based on the earlier Diana model (called the Daytona in the United Kingdom) but was equipped with a five-speed gear cluster, high compression piston, a big carburettor, and other tuning aids. With its high performance and good handling, the Mach 1 was popular for competition use. The model lasted until 1967 when revised "wide-case" engines were introduced. This example dates from 1964. A cheaper and less heavily tuned model was also available.

Rearset footrests were standard

Dell'Orto SS1 carburettor

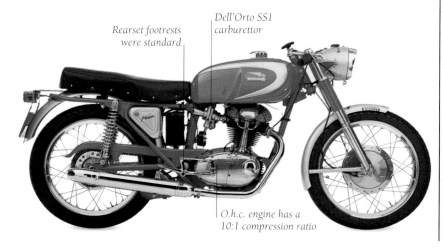

O.h.c. engine has a 10:1 compression ratio

DUCATI 750 SPORT

Capacity 748cc • Power output 55bhp @ 7,900rpm
Weight 219kg (482lb) • Top speed 185km/h (115mph)

ITALY

THE V-TWIN was a logical way for Ducati to enter the big bike class. Two of the company's o.h.c. singles were attached to a common crankshaft to produce a large-capacity machine that relied on existing Ducati technology. The 90° V-twin offered exceptional engine balance at the expense of size; the length of the engine is responsible for the 152-cm (60-in) wheelbase of the 750 Sport. Production versions of the 750 appeared in 1971. The Sport followed in 1972 and a Desmodromic machine the following year. The 90° V-twin became a Ducati trademark.

A dual seat was an option on late model 750 Sports

Leading-axle telescopic forks

Huge sump contains 4.5 litres (1 gallon) of oil

DUCATI

DUCATI 350 DESMO

Capacity 340cc • Power output 38bhp @ 7,500rpm • Weight 128kg (282lb) • Top speed 169km/h (105mph)   ITALY

DESMODROMIC VALVE GEAR had been a feature of Ducati racers since the late 1950s. With this system the valve is closed by the camshaft rather than by a spring. Its accuracy allows high revs to be used without risk of valve bounce. On a road bike with peak power at 7,500rpm its value was debatable, but it became Ducati's unique selling point. The 350 was made from 1971 to 1974. This machine is a 1974 model.

A disc front brake was available on 1974 models

One-piece seat and tail unit

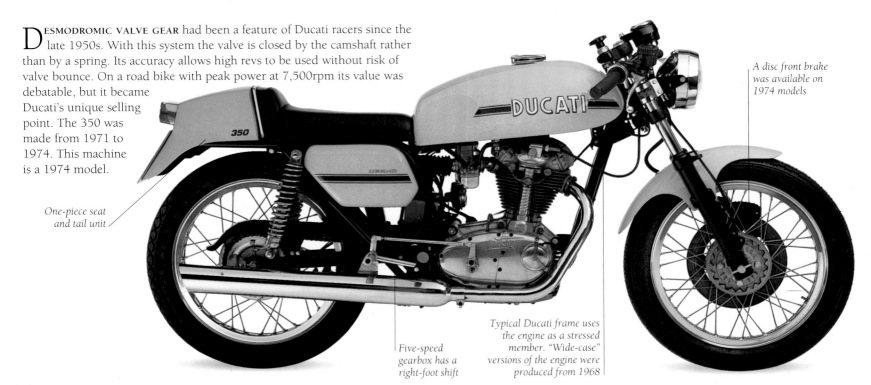

Five-speed gearbox has a right-foot shift

Typical Ducati frame uses the engine as a stressed member. "Wide-case" versions of the engine were produced from 1968

DUCATI
500 SPORT DESMO

Capacity 497cc • Power output 44bhp @ 5,800rpm   ITALY
Weight 191kg (420lb) • Top speed 171km/h (106mph)

THE **500** SPORT was the result of a miscalculation by Ducati's management in the 1970s. Instead of concentrating on its excellent and original V-twin designs, it chose to produce a middleweight parallel twin. The 500 GTL model appeared in 1975 alongside a 350 version. They did not sell well and, despite their good looks, neither did the Desmo versions that appeared in 1977. However, Ducati continued to sell the parallel twins in Spanish and Italian markets until the early 1980s.

The Sport was styled by Leo Tartarini of Italjet

Parallel-twin engine has a 180° crankshaft

DUCATI DARMAH

Capacity 864cc • Power output 53bhp @ 6,250rpm   ITALY
Weight 225kg (496lb) • Top speed 187km/h (116mph)

THE DARMAH WAS AN ATTEMPT to produce a sporting machine for people who would otherwise have bought Japanese or German bikes. Instruments and switchgear were Japanese, electrics were German Bosch components, and styling was by Leo Tartarini of Italjet. The good-looking Darmah, whose name derives from a legendary man-eating tiger, was first introduced in 1977. The final version, like the machine pictured here, appeared in 1979. Its redesigned seat lacked the original stylish duck-tail.

Headlight and other electrical components made by Bosch

Cast-iron five spoke wheel

Shallow steering angle and 155-cm (61-in) wheelbase give the Darmah exceptional stability

Engine is a detuned version of the Desmodromic 900SS power unit

DUCATI PANTAH

Capacity 499cc • Power output 46bhp @ 8,500rpm • Weight 190kg (418lb) • Top speed 190km/h (118mph)

THE PANTAH FIRST APPEARED IN 1977, but only hit the market in 1980. Smaller and lighter than Ducati's earlier road-going 90° V-twins, the new machine had belt-driven overhead camshafts. The hallmark desmodromic valve gear was retained. The engine was an integral part of the frame, with the swingarm pivot situated on special mountings cast in the engine cases behind the gearbox. The machine's performance and handling were exceptional, further reinforcing Ducati's reputation for real sporting motorcycles. The Pantah was revised for 1982 with a new fairing and a 583cc capacity. This engine provided the basis for a new range of air-cooled machines.

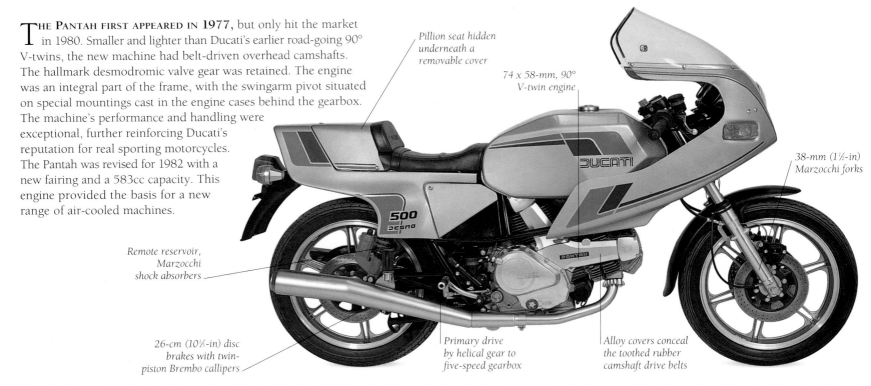

Pillion seat hidden underneath a removable cover

74 x 58-mm, 90° V-twin engine

38-mm (1½-in) Marzocchi forks

Remote reservoir, Marzocchi shock absorbers

26-cm (10⅕-in) disc brakes with twin-piston Brembo callipers

Primary drive by helical gear to five-speed gearbox

Alloy covers conceal the toothed rubber camshaft drive belts

DUCATI MHR 1000

Capacity 973cc • Power output 83bhp • Weight not known • Top speed 221km/h (137mph)

THE MIKE HAILWOOD REPLICA was built to commemorate Hailwood's victory in the 1978 Formula One TT. Introduced in 1980 and based on the 900SS, the body and paintwork were revised to echo Hailwood's bike. This was one of Ducati's biggest sellers in the early 1980s but was gradually overshadowed by smaller machines with belt-driven camshafts. The MHR was axed in 1986, after Cagiva took over Ducati.

THE MHR "MILLE" was introduced in 1985, its capacity was increased to 973cc, and the engine's bottom end was stronger with improved lubrication. This finally ended the machine's crankshaft reliability problems.

Sculpted fuel tank

New cast wheels used on the Mille

Seeley-pattern, threaded-block chain adjuster

Three-piece fairing

BACK VIEW

DUCATI 851

Capacity 851cc • Power output 100bhp @ 9,250rpm • Weight 180kg (396lb) • Top speed 241km/h (150mph) (estimated)

ORIGINALLY INTRODUCED FOR **1988,** the 851 broke new ground for Ducati. It was still a 90° V-twin and it still had Desmodromic valve operation but it had water cooling, four-valve cylinder heads, and fuel injection. These features were introduced to meet increasingly strict emissions and noise legislation, and to meet World Superbike race rules. Ducati 851s were produced for both road (Strada) and track (Superbike). The Superbike, like this 1989 model, was faster and more expensive than the Strada and was instantly competitive in World Superbike racing.

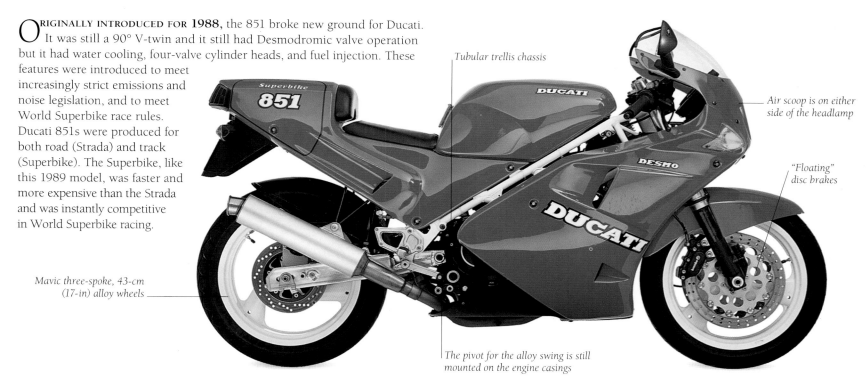

Tubular trellis chassis

Air scoop is on either side of the headlamp

"Floating" disc brakes

Mavic three-spoke, 43-cm (17-in) alloy wheels

The pivot for the alloy swing is still mounted on the engine casings

DUCATI M900 MONSTER

Capacity 904cc • Power output 73bhp @ 7,000rpm • Weight 185kg (408lb) • Top speed 192km/h (119mph)

RECOGNIZING A MARKET TREND towards unfaired bikes, Ducati introduced the Monster in 1994. Unlike much of the opposition in this category, Ducati did not compromise the technology in the new model. The tubular trellis frame had rising-rate rear suspension and was derived from Ducati's Superbike machinery. Brakes and suspension components were all premium quality.

Instrument console does not include a rev counter

THE ENGINE was a four-valve V-twin taken from the 900SS. The combination of torquey motor and a lightweight chassis produced an exceptional fun bike, though the lack of fairing compromised high-speed ability.

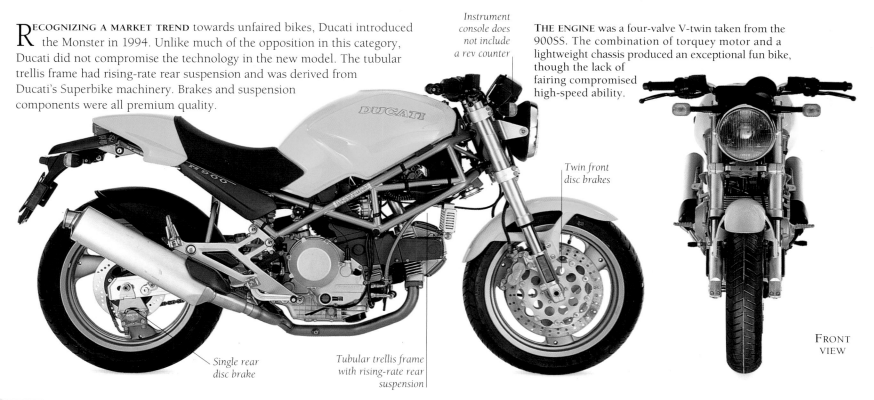

Twin front disc brakes

Single rear disc brake

Tubular trellis frame with rising-rate rear suspension

FRONT VIEW

DUNELT MODEL K

Capacity 250cc • Power output 7bhp (estimated) • Weight 260lb (118kg) • Top speed 50mph (80km/h)

SHEFFIELD STEEL MAKER DUNFORD AND ELLIOT made its first motorcycles in 1919. Its innovative design was a two-stroke single with a double-diameter piston shaped like a top hat. This increased crankcase pumping and gave a supercharging effect as the larger swept volume of the crankcases was forced into the smaller capacity cylinder. Originally it had a 500cc cylinder, but in 1925 a smaller version was produced. This 250cc Model K dates from that year.

The double-diameter piston engine requires an exceptionally long barrel

Tubular frame is conventional diamond pattern

26-in (66-cm) wheels with drum brakes

Cylinder has two exhaust ports

Three-speed Sturmey-Archer gearbox

EMBLEM

Capacity 38.5cu. in. (631cc) • Power output 4hp • Weight 170lb (77kg) • Top speed 40mph (64km/h) (estimated)

THE EMBLEM COMPANY of Angola, New York, produced typical period U.S. motorcycles. At the time that this model was produced, around 1910, it used its own single-cylinder and V-twin engines with a.i.v., although earlier machines used Thor power units. Both engine layouts had the same loop frame. A Heitger carburettor was part of its equipment, but the Ruthardt magneto was optional.

Recessed fuel/oil tank channel fits around the top tube

Unusual fork design was Emblem's own

102 x 89-mm single-cylinder engine has an automatic inlet valve

Contracting-band rear brake

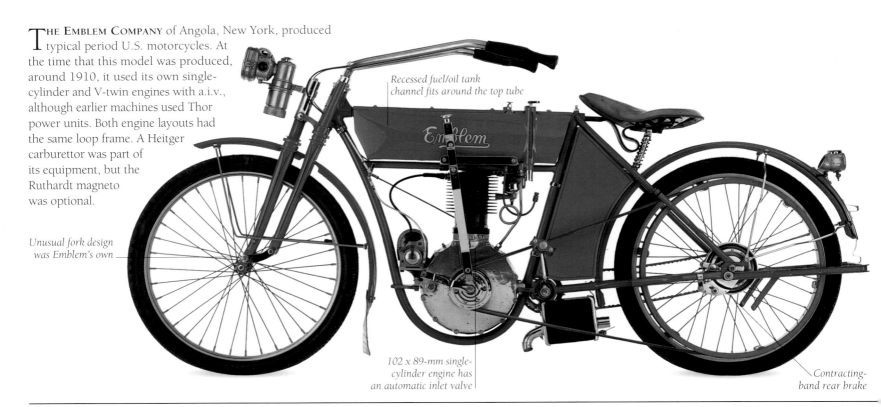

ENFIELD INDIA BULLET

Capacity 346cc • Power output 18bhp @ 5,625rpm • Weight 359lb (163kg) • Top speed 70mph (113km/h)

THE ROYAL ENFIELD BULLET was completely up to date when introduced for 1949, and many were exported all over the world. The Indian government was so impressed that it made arrangements in the 1950s to produce the 350cc machine in Madras for military and civil purposes. The same machine (substantially) is still produced there today and, ironically, it is now exported from India to Great Britain.

Mikuni
carburettor

Indicators; the
original Bullet
was not equipped
with them

7-in (18-cm) twin
leading-shoe drum brake

Primary chain drives
four-speed gearbox

ESO SPEEDWAY

Capacity 497cc • Power output 50bhp @ 8,000rpm • Weight 83kg (182lb) • Top speed not known

WHEN SPEEDWAY RACING FIRST BECAME POPULAR the Douglas was pre-eminent, but as tracks and riding styles changed there was a swing towards shorter machines such as the Rudge, which provided faster – if less spectacular – racing. After the introduction of the speedway JAP engine in 1931, machines changed little until the Eso started to be seen outside its native Czechoslovakia in the late 1950s. The bike shown here dates from 1966.

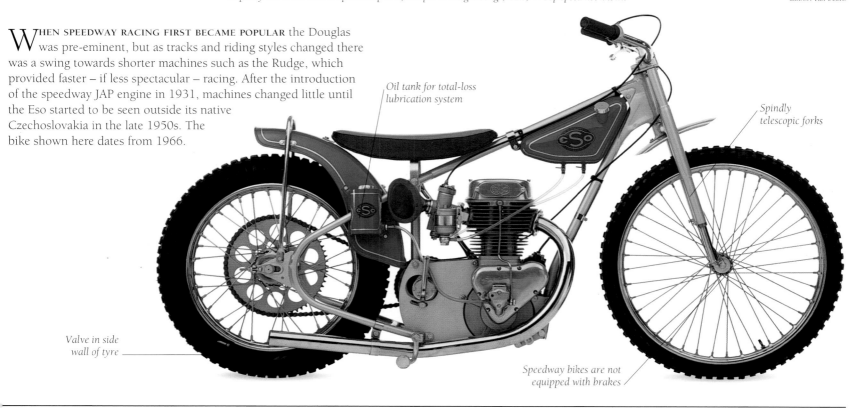

Oil tank for total-loss
lubrication system

Spindly
telescopic forks

Valve in side
wall of tyre

Speedway bikes are not
equipped with brakes

EXCELSIOR AUTO-CYCLE MODEL K

Capacity 30.5cu. in. (500cc) • Power output 4hp • Weight 180lb (82kg) • Top speed 40mph (64km/h) (estimated)

THE FIRST AMERICAN-BUILT EXCELSIOR motorcycles appeared in 1907. Produced by the Excelsior Supply Company of Randolph Street, Chicago, the new 3.25hp Excelsior Auto-Cycle had a vertically mounted, a.i.v. engine of 26.74cu. in. (438cc). The engine was mounted in the gap between the downtube and the bottom bracket of a frame that incorporated a second horizontal bracing tube. The 1911 model shown here is based on the original design though the frame was revised to allow a lower seat height. The

engine capacity was increased to 30.5 cu. in. (500cc). Nickel-plated leading-link front forks were used and the only rear suspension was via the sprung seat, which could be adjusted via the horizontal seat-post. The machine's coaster brake was operated by back pressure on the pedals. The company was taken over by bicycle maker Ignatz Schwinn in 1912 and he remained in control until Excelsior production ended in 1931. The single was dropped from the range in 1913 in favour of V-twin models.

EXCELSIOR CUSTOMERS could specify either drop handlebars or more conventional, extra long, upright versions. The Model K was the base model of the firm's range, while the more expensive KM was equipped with gear-driven magneto ignition.

Twistgrip controls used rod linkages

Pedals were a feature of many early motorcycles

•POCKET VALVES•

The Auto-Cycle followed conventional period practice in having a mechanical exhaust valve and an atmospheric inlet valve. The inlet valve was held shut by a weak spring and opened as the falling piston created a vacuum in the cylinder and sucked in the explosive charge from the carburettor. Both valves were mounted in a pocket beside the cylinder. This layout was said to improve cooling and remained a feature of Excelsior machines for some years, even after mechanical operation of the inlet valves was adopted.

Exhaust cam and ignition mechanism

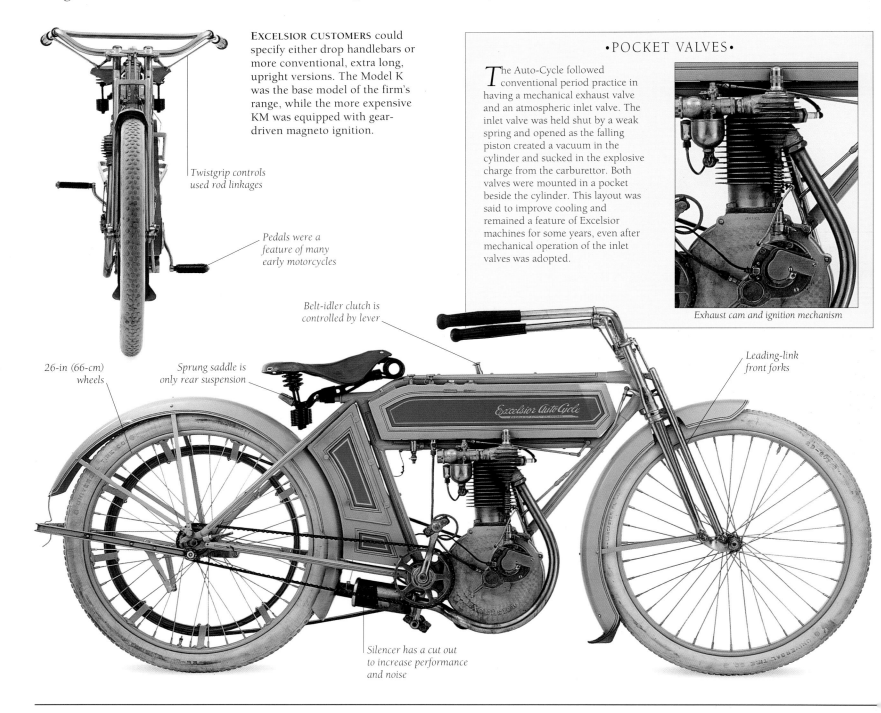

Belt-idler clutch is controlled by lever

26-in (66-cm) wheels

Sprung saddle is only rear suspension

Leading-link front forks

Silencer has a cut out to increase performance and noise

EXCELSIOR 20R

Capacity 61cu. in. (1000cc) • Power output 20bhp (estimated) • Weight 500lb (227kg) (estimated) • Top speed 100mph (161km/h)

U.S.A.

EXCELSIOR FOLLOWED THE EXAMPLE of other American manufacturers and introduced a V-twin model in 1910. It had cylinders spaced at 45° and had a mechanical i.o.e. valve layout. Capacity of the first machines was 50cu. in. (819cc), but in 1912 it grew to 61cu. in. Excellent publicity for the revised model was created when a 61cu. in. Excelsior became the first bike to officially break the 100-mph (161-km/h) barrier. The machine shown here is a three-speed version from 1920. The 61cu. in. model was dropped when the Super X was introduced.

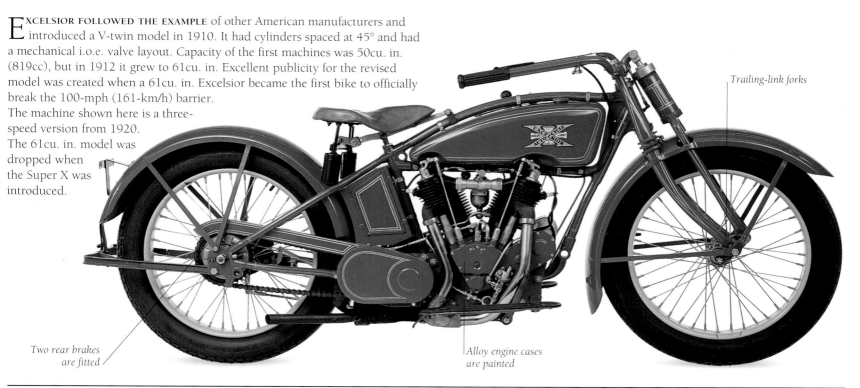

Trailing-link forks

Two rear brakes are fitted

Alloy engine cases are painted

EXCELSIOR SUPER X

Capacity 45.5cu. in. (746cc) • Power output 20bhp (estimated) • Weight 450lb (204kg) (estimated) • Top speed 65mph (105km/h)

U.S.A.

INTRODUCED IN **1925**, the Super X was the first of a new class of American 45cu. in. machines. It was quickly followed into the marketplace by Indian and Harley-Davidson forty-fives. The new model featured a neat unit-construction engine/gearbox. Primary drive to the three-speed gearbox was by helical gear, and the engine was mounted in a duplex cradle frame with leading-link forks. The Super X had exceptional performance and earned an enviable reputation. The design was re-styled for 1929, receiving the "Streamline" look. The bike shown dates from 1930, the year before it was dropped.

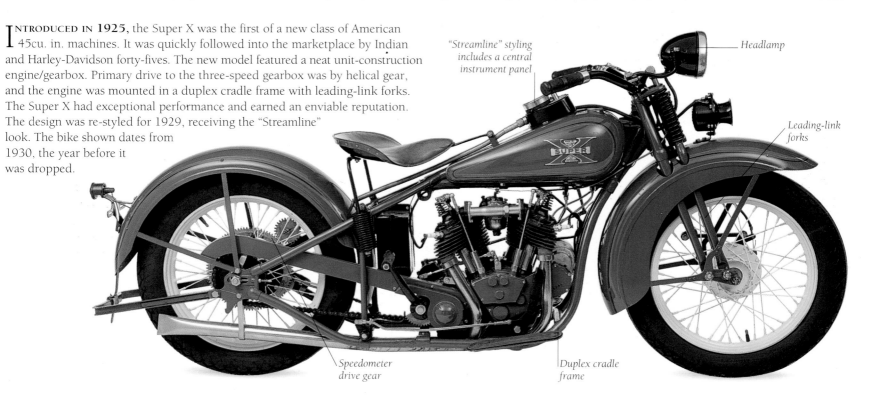

"Streamline" styling includes a central instrument panel

Headlamp

Leading-link forks

Speedometer drive gear

Duplex cradle frame

EXCELSIOR

Capacity 411cc • Power output 2.75hp
Weight not known • Top speed 45mph (72km/h)

BAYLISS, **THOMAS & CO.**, maker of Excelsior bicycles, is credited with having been the first manufacturer to produce and sell a motorcycle in Britain: the firm marketed a Minerva-engined machine in 1896. By 1902 – the year from which this machine dates – the 2.75hp MMC engine was being used. This was a Coventry-built version of the DeDion unit with an atmospheric inlet valve, a surface carburettor, trembler coil ignition, and manual lubrication. It drove the rear wheel directly via a belt.

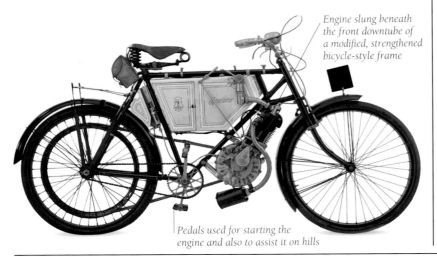

Engine slung beneath the front downtube of a modified, strengthened bicycle-style frame

Pedals used for starting the engine and also to assist it on hills

EXCELSIOR
MECHANICAL MARVEL

Capacity 246cc • Power output 25bhp
Weight not known • Top speed not known

FOLLOWING THE TREND set by aeroplane engine designers in the quest for more power, many motorcycle manufacturers experimented with four-valve designs. Excelsior, which until then had raced machines with JAP or Blackburne engines, sprung a surprise for the 1933 TT races with a new machine featuring an engine designed and made by Blackburne. This had four valves radially disposed in the cylinder head, each pair being operated via a single pushrod and paired rockers. Despite winning the TT at a record speed, the bike proved difficult to maintain. This bike dates from 1933.

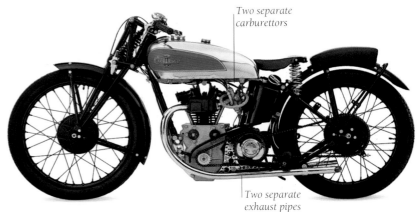

Two separate carburettors

Two separate exhaust pipes

EXCELSIOR MANXMAN

Capacity 349cc • Power output 23bhp @ 6,000rpm • Weight 335lb (152kg) • Top speed 85mph (137km/h)

INTRODUCED IN **1935**, the Manxman was a sporting machine offered in road or racing trim that superseded the mechanically complex Mechanical Marvel (see above). A more conventional design than its predecessor, the Manxman had a shaft-driven overhead camshaft, and the bronze cylinder head contained just two valves. Initially produced in 250cc and 350cc forms, a 500cc followed in 1936.

THE MANXMAN was raced successfully by the factory team and by private riders but, despite the name, it never won an Isle of Man TT race. The bike shown here is an FR12 model dating from 1936.

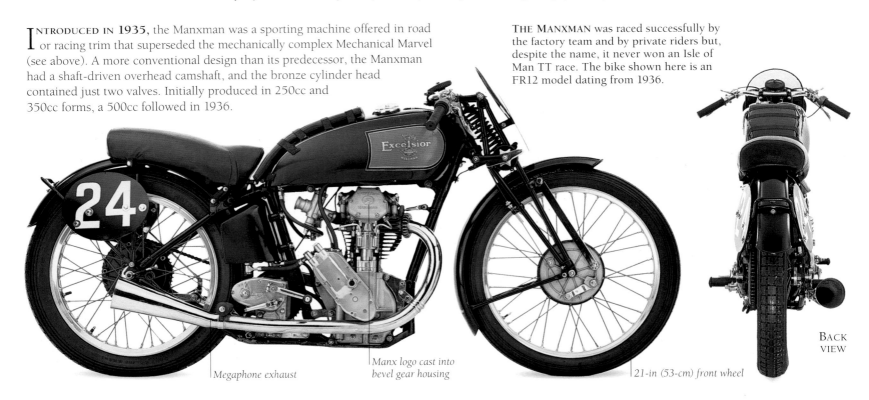

Megaphone exhaust

Manx logo cast into bevel gear housing

21-in (53-cm) front wheel

BACK VIEW

EXCELSIOR
TALISMAN SPORTS

Capacity 244cc • Power output 11bhp @ 4,500rpm
Weight 240lb (109kg) • Top speed 64mph (103km/h)

UNITED KINGDOM

INTRODUCED IN 1952 as a sports version of the Talisman Twin design first seen in 1949, the STT1 improved on the parent machine in both practical and cosmetic respects. Although the engine unit was basically unchanged, its appearance was enhanced by a tidied-up gearbox layout. An adjustable-height dual seat and a more attractive instrument panel added to rider appeal, while the cycle parts were inherited directly from the standard machine. The Talisman Sports probably sold on account of its looks rather than its other merits. The bike shown dates from 1952.

Plunger rear suspension

Twin carburettors

Undamped telescopic forks

FANTIC CHOPPER

ITALY

Capacity 123cc • Power output 13.2bhp @ 6,600rpm
Weight 118kg (260lb) • Top speed 105km/h (65mph)

ONE OF THE WACKIEST BIKES built in the 1970s, the Fantic Chopper was an ideal mount for those aspiring to the wild world of the film *Easy Rider*. But where the actors enjoyed the effortless throb of a large capacity Harley-Davidson V-twin, Fantic riders had to endure the manic wail of a small capacity two-stroke. Surprisingly, the extended forks and weird riding position did not make the Fantic dangerous, even if they did make it uncomfortable. This is a 1977 model.

Backrest height 138cm (54½in)

Ape hanger handlebars

Minarelli single-cylinder, air-cooled, two-stroke engine with five-speed gearbox

40.5 x 12.75-cm (16 x 5-in) rear wheel

FB MONDIAL

ITALY

Capacity 173cc • Power output 10bhp @ 6,700rpm • Weight 120kg (264lb) • Top speed 110km/h (68mph)

FRATELLI BOSELLI MONDIAL chose to advertise its products through racing and won the 125cc World Championship in 1949, 1950, 1951, and 1957. While the racing machines were exotic o.h.c. and d.o.h.c. devices, most production models were orthodox o.h.v. and two-stroke lightweights. The machine shown here is a 1956 sporting model that combines an o.h.c. engine with the cycle parts of its more ordinary stablemates.

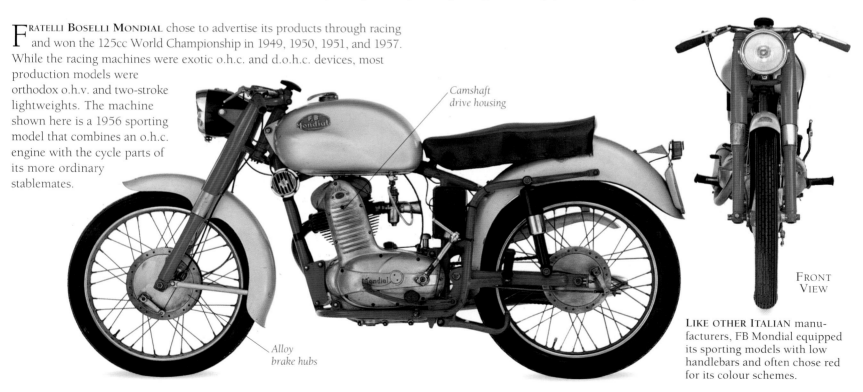

Camshaft drive housing

Alloy brake hubs

FRONT VIEW

LIKE OTHER ITALIAN manufacturers, FB Mondial equipped its sporting models with low handlebars and often chose red for its colour schemes.

FN Four

Capacity 410cc • Power output not known • Weight not known • Top speed 68km/h (42mph) (estimated)

Fɪʀsᴛ ɪɴᴛʀᴏᴅᴜᴄᴇᴅ ɪɴ **1904**, the FN was the first successful four-cylinder motorcycle. Designed by Paul Kelecom, the original design had shaft drive, magneto ignition, splash lubrication, and the benefits of the vibration-free, four-cylinder engine. It was one of the first serious attempts at an integrated design for a motorcycle rather than the usual bicycle-with-engine-style machines of the period. The capacity of the original machine was 362cc but by the time the 1907 model (shown here) was produced, it had increased and there were other detail improvements.

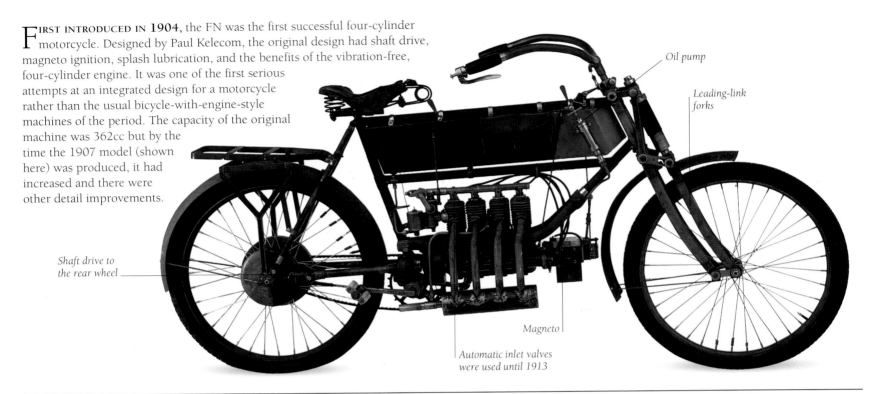

Oil pump

Leading-link forks

Shaft drive to the rear wheel

Magneto

Automatic inlet valves were used until 1913

FN

Capacity 283cc • Power output not known • Weight 80kg (176lb) • Top speed 85km/h (53mph)

Tʜᴇ ғɪʀsᴛ **FN** ᴍᴏᴛᴏʀᴄʏᴄʟᴇs, which were 133cc-engined bicycle-style machines, appeared in 1901. The singles were overshadowed with the introduction of the FN four in 1904. A new 249cc single-cylinder, shaft-drive lightweight appeared in 1909 but featured the same twin-tube engine mounting arrangement of the four with the crankshaft mounted longitudinally in the frame. The FN was updated again in 1912. This bike dates from 1920.

Wɪᴛʜ ɪᴛs ᴍᴜʟᴛɪ-ᴘʟᴀᴛᴇ ᴄʟᴜᴛᴄʜ and two-speed gear, the FN's specification was superior to most machines in the class.

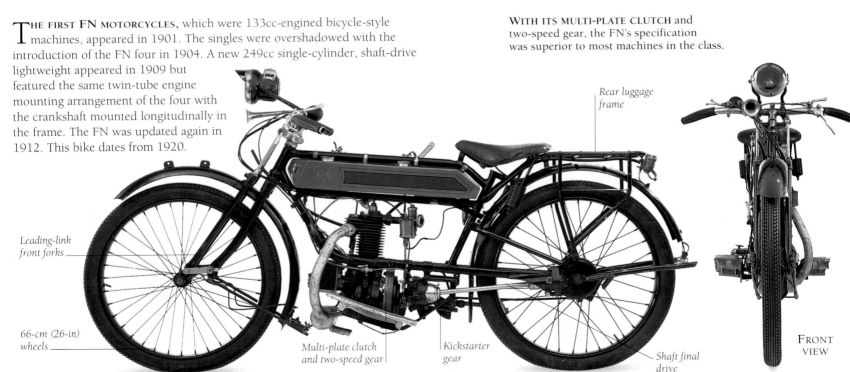

Rear luggage frame

Leading-link front forks

66-cm (26-in) wheels

Multi-plate clutch and two-speed gear

Kickstarter gear

Shaft final drive

Fʀᴏɴᴛ ᴠɪᴇᴡ

FN M13

Capacity 449cc • Power output 11bhp @ 3,500rpm • Weight 136kg (300lb) • Top speed 105km/h (65mph) (estimated)

DESPITE THE SUCCESS OF THE SHAFT-DRIVE FOUR and single-cylinder machines, FN began to develop more conventional chain-driven four-stroke singles in the 1920s. During the 1930s it began producing unit-construction side-valve and o.h.v. single-cylinder machines. The 1948 Model M13 (shown here) had a side-valve engine with wet-sump lubrication, but the most novel feature is its front forks. These were a trailing-link design that tensioned the horizontal springs when the wheel was pushed upwards. From 1953 conventional telescopic forks were used.

Tappet inspection cover

Later versions of the trailing-link fork replaced the springs with rubber bands

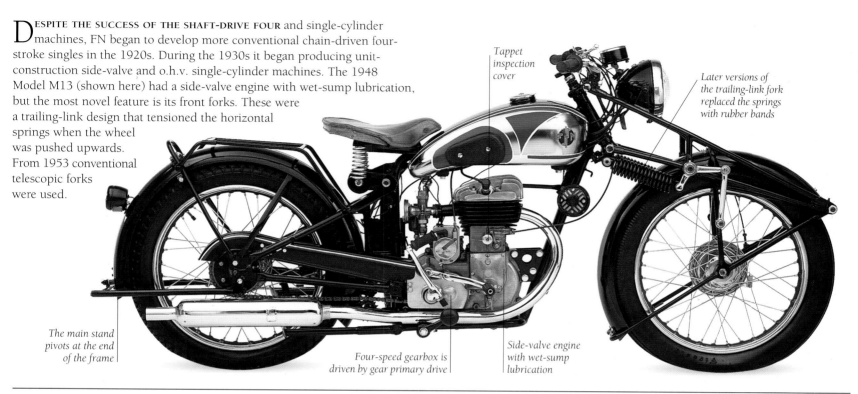

The main stand pivots at the end of the frame

Four-speed gearbox is driven by gear primary drive

Side-valve engine with wet-sump lubrication

FRANCIS-BARNETT PULLMAN

Capacity 344cc • Power output not known • Weight not known • Top speed 55mph (88km/h)

OFFICIALLY KNOWN AS THE MODEL 10 and using an engine that was claimed to be exclusive to Francis-Barnett (although it was also supplied to Monet-Goyen in France), the Pullman was intended for the luxury end of the market. It failed because its performance was the same as machines half its size while its cost was that of machines twice its size. The engine was mounted lengthways in the frame, which had the famous "built like a bridge" design, introduced in 1924. Advertised as "the frame that could be packed into a golf bag", Francis-Barnett never did say where to pack the engine and wheels!

Straight frame tubes have flattened ends and bolt together; the steering head is the only complicated frame component

Gear change lever is connected directly into the gearbox

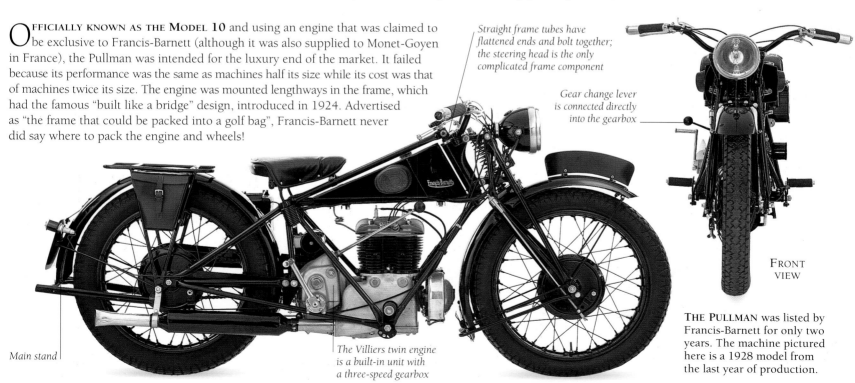

Main stand

The Villiers twin engine is a built-in unit with a three-speed gearbox

FRONT VIEW

THE **P**ULLMAN was listed by Francis-Barnett for only two years. The machine pictured here is a 1928 model from the last year of production.

GILERA SATURNO SANREMO

Capacity 498cc • Power output 38bhp @ 6,000rpm • Weight 128kg (282lb) • Top speed 185km/h (115mph) (estimated)

GILERA'S MOST FAMOUS RACERS were the World Championship-winning four-cylinder machines produced following Gilera's takeover of the Rondine concern in 1937. For use at lesser events and for customers, Gilera produced the single-cylinder San Remo machine, which was based on the Saturno road bike (see below). It had a victorious debut at the 1947 Ospedaletti Grand Prix near San Remo, hence the bike's name. It retained the o.h.v. unit-construction of the road machines but clever modification gave it more power. This is the 1949 model.

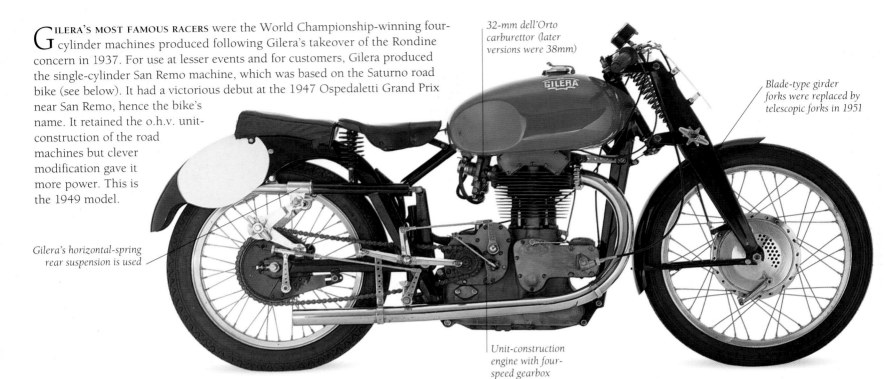

32-mm dell'Orto carburettor (later versions were 38mm)

Blade-type girder forks were replaced by telescopic forks in 1951

Gilera's horizontal-spring rear suspension is used

Unit-construction engine with four-speed gearbox

GILERA SATURNO

Capacity 499cc • Power output 22bhp @ 5,000rpm
Weight 175kg (386lb) • Top speed 129km/h (80mph) (estimated)

BUILT FROM **1940**, the Saturno was a logical development of previous Gilera designs. The 84 x 90-mm engine had overhead valves that were closed by hairpin valve springs. Iron was used for the head and barrel but the engine cases, which also housed the four-speed box, were alloy. Primary drive was by gear. Front forks were centrally sprung girders and rear suspension was provided by Gilera's horizontal-spring system. The machine shown is a 1951 model. Later, uprated "Sports" versions with alloy cylinder heads and telescopic forks were produced.

GILERA
SPECIALE STRADA

Capacity 124cc • Power output 10.5bhp @ 8,500rpm
Weight 93kg (205lb) • Top speed 113km/h (70mph) (estimated)

GILERA INTRODUCED A NEW **125** IN **1959**, and production continued in various forms until 1970. The neat, wet-sump engine unit incorporates a four-speed gearbox with gear primary drive. A single camshaft is gear-driven from the crankshaft and operates the valves via pushrods and conventional tappets with screw and locknut adjustment. Ignition is by battery and coil. A 150cc version of the engine was also produced. The 1966 Speciale Strada model shown here includes chrome mudguards, a rev counter, and a racing saddle.

Front forks are centrally sprung girders

Horizontal-spring rear suspension

Alloy engine cases hide dry clutch and gear primary drive

Racing-style saddle

Instrumentation includes a rev counter

43-cm (17-in) wheels feature alloy rims and brake hubs

GILERA
NUOVO SATURNO

Capacity 492cc • Power output 37bhp @ 7,500rpm
Weight 140kg (309lb) • Top speed 169km/h (105mph) (estimated)

ITALY

ORIGINALLY PRODUCED FOR THE JAPANESE MARKET, the Nuovo Saturno appeared in 1989 and was also sold in Europe. It combined a tubular-steel trellis frame with an excellent four-valve twin-cam water-cooled single-cylinder engine. Its light weight helped to provide excellent handling and also (for a 500 single) performance. Red paint and café-racer styling gave it the desired look. The Gilera badge gave it the correct name. Sadly, it was also very expensive.

The uncompromising Saturno was supplied with a solo seat only

Alloy plates connect engine, swingarm, and frame

GILERA
NORDWEST

Capacity 558cc • Power output 52bhp @ 6,500rpm
Weight 140kg (308lb) • Top speed 187km/h (116mph)

ITALY

GILERA TOOK THE BIG TRAIL BIKE to its logical conclusion with the NordWest. The model was based on the RC600 trail bike, but the compromised trail suspension, and brakes, and wheels were replaced with a pure road set-up. Sticky tyres and sensational brakes combined with a rev-happy engine made the NordWest a stunning road bike. As long as the road was twisting it could stay ahead of genuine sports machines. The model disappeared with the Gilera marque in 1993.

Upside-down telescopic forks

Water-cooled, d.o.h.c., four-valve engine

GNOME & RHONE

Capacity 724cc • Power output 30bhp @ 5,500rpm • Weight not known • Top speed 145km/h (90mph) (estimated)

FRANCE

THE FIRST MOTORCYCLES that were built by aircraft-engine maker Gnome & Rhône were copies of the British ABC flat-twin made under licence. It subsequently made conventional single-cylinder machines before returning to the flat-twin in 1930. The o.h.v. Type X was introduced in 1935. The new machine was one of the largest and most prestigious produced in France at that time. It was also ideal for pulling sidecars and many were put to that use. The model shown here dates from 1939, shortly before production ended.

Girder forks and pressed-steel frame

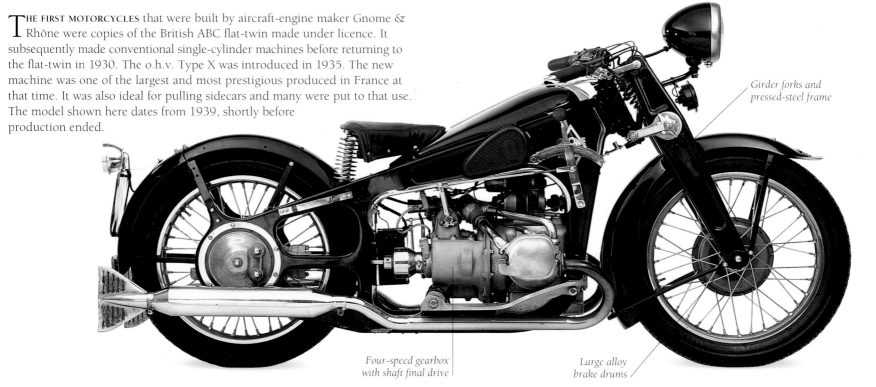

Four-speed gearbox with shaft final drive

Large alloy brake drums

GREEVES 20T

Capacity 197cc • Power output 8.5bhp @ 4,000rpm • Weight 228lb (103kg) • Top speed 50mph (80km/h) (estimated)

UNITED KINGDOM

THE FIRST GREEVES PROTOTYPE motorcycles appeared in 1951; the company also made invalid cars. The first production models, launched in 1953, had novel features such as a distinctive cast-alloy beam in place of a downtube and headstock, and a rubber-in-torsion suspension system. These models included road, scramblers, and trials machines powered by the 197cc Villiers 8E single-cylinder two-stroke engine. This 20T trials model dates from 1955. Later machines had such improvements as new Villiers engines and Girling rear shock absorbers. Greeves later became renowned for its off-road bikes.

Distinctive leading-link forks are a feature of the Greeves

The suspension uses rubber springing – Greeves adopted conventional rear shock absorbers in 1956

Cast-alloy beam frame member

Villiers 197cc engine

GRITZNER MONZA SUPER SPORT

Capacity 50cc • Power output 3hp @ 6,000rpm • Weight 70kg (154lb) • Top speed 60km/h (37mph)

GERMANY

THE MONZA SUPER SPORT was introduced by the long-established Mars motorcycle company in 1957. When Mars folded in 1958 Gritzner took over its production. Sadly, the Monza's good looks and features did not prevent its failure – Gritzner followed Mars and ceased trading in 1962. This model was built in 1960.

Pressed-steel construction frame and fork legs

UNLIKE MANY LIGHTWEIGHTS of the period the Monza Super Sport was built as a true motorcycle: it did not have pedals, and the three-speed gearbox was foot operated rather than the twistgrip type used on other machines.

Flat, narrow, sports style handlebars

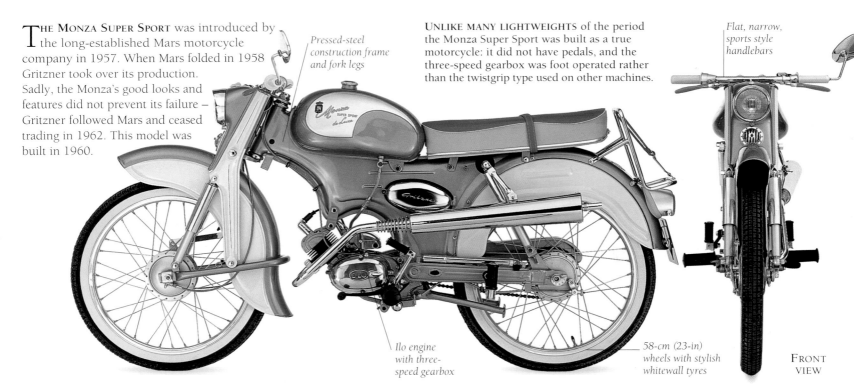

Ilo engine with three-speed gearbox

58-cm (23-in) wheels with stylish whitewall tyres

FRONT VIEW

HARLEY-DAVIDSON SILENT GRAY FELLOW

Capacity 30cu. in. (492cc) • Power output 6.5hp @ 2,700rpm • Weight 195lb (89kg) • Top speed 45mph (72km/h)

U.S.A.

BASED ON **HARLEY-DAVIDSON'S** original prototype machine of 1903, the single-cylinder Silent Gray Fellow remained in production until 1918. The name referred to the efficiency of the exhaust system, the colour scheme, and the model's image of all-round dependability. In 1912 the model shown here was produced with a revised frame and lower sprung seat.

THE SINGLE-CYLINDER ENGINE on this 1912 machine uses an automatic inlet valve. From 1913, mechanical valves were offered. This bike is equipped with battery and coil ignition. A magneto was an optional extra.

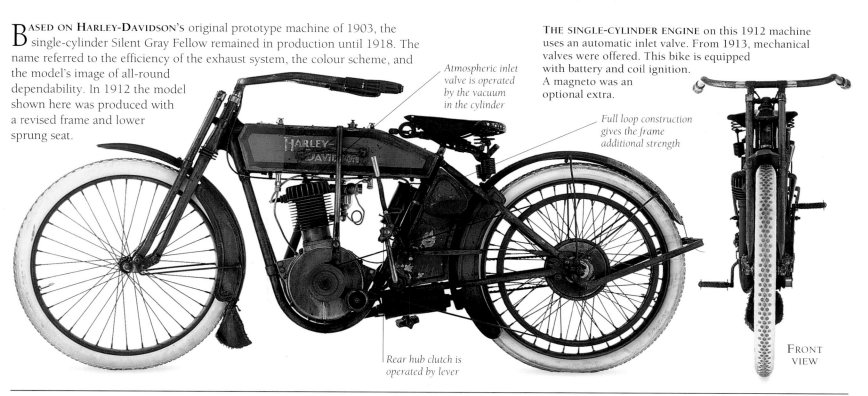

Atmospheric inlet valve is operated by the vacuum in the cylinder

Full loop construction gives the frame additional strength

Rear hub clutch is operated by lever

FRONT VIEW

HARLEY-DAVIDSON J-11

Capacity 61cu. in. (1000cc) • Power output 11hp @ 3,000rpm • Weight 325lb (147kg) • Top speed 60mph (97km/h) (estimated)

U.S.A.

HARLEY **DEVELOPED** its first V-twin machines in 1907. By the time the 1915 model shown here was produced the 45° engine layout was firmly established in its model range. Several significant changes were introduced in 1915, including a three-speed gearbox and a gear-driven oil pump. Pedal starting remained for one more season before a kickstarter was introduced in 1916. The loop frame is similar to that used on the single-cylinder machines.

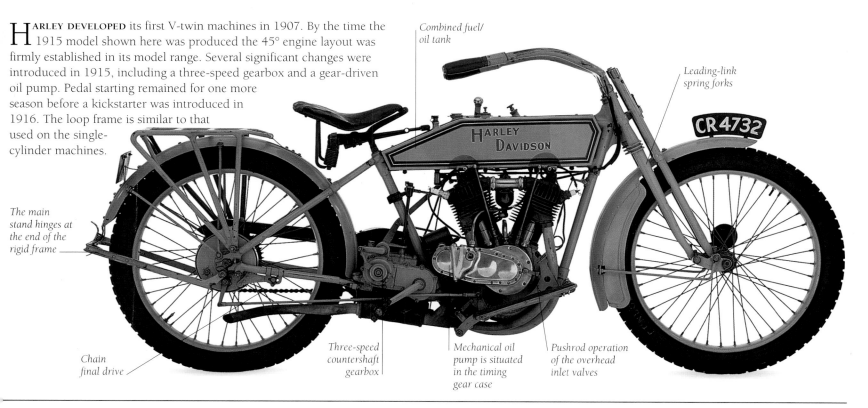

Combined fuel/oil tank

Leading-link spring forks

CR 4732

The main stand hinges at the end of the rigid frame

Chain final drive

Three-speed countershaft gearbox

Mechanical oil pump is situated in the timing gear case

Pushrod operation of the overhead inlet valves

HARLEY-DAVIDSON JD28

Capacity 74cu. in. (1213cc) • Power output 9.5hp @ 4,500rpm • Weight 365lb (166kg) • Top speed 75mph (121km/h)   U.S.A.

THE **JD MODELS** represented the zenith of development of Harley-Davidson's i.o.e. engines. By 1928 the 74cu. in. (1213cc) engine could top 75mph (121km/h). Unlike the two-cam JDH, the JD used the standard, single-camshaft layout. Roller arms bearing on the two-lobe camshaft actuated the inlet valve pushrods and the exhaust valves. Coil ignition was fed by a gear-driven generator that also powered the electric lighting. For this 1928 model a throttle-controlled oil pump was protected by an alloy cover. The finning of the silver-painted iron heads and barrels was improved to aid cooling. An air filter was installed on the carburettor, which necessitated the repositioning of the rear-cylinder priming cup. The rubber cush-drive incorporated into the engine sprocket was uprated while the overall top gear ratio

increased from 6.28:1 to 5.99:1, allowing a slightly higher cruising speed. The three-speed, handshift gearbox was retained, driven by the standard, foot-operated, multi-plate, dry clutch. The rigid frame and springer forks were finished in the distinctive olive-green applied to the rest of the running gear, including the gearbox cases. A front drum brake was introduced on the 18-in (46-cm) wheels. Although not as fast as the two-cam models, the popular JD28 was capable of cruising all day long across the wide expanses of the United States at 60mph (97km/h) or more. Harley-Davidson also offered its own sports and touring sidecars, which had little effect on the JD's speed because of the size of the engine. The firm's annual production figures for 1928 reached 22,000. For 1929, a four-tube silencer made the big twin virtually silent, which was useful from the view-point of the law enforcement agencies that bought seventy-fours.

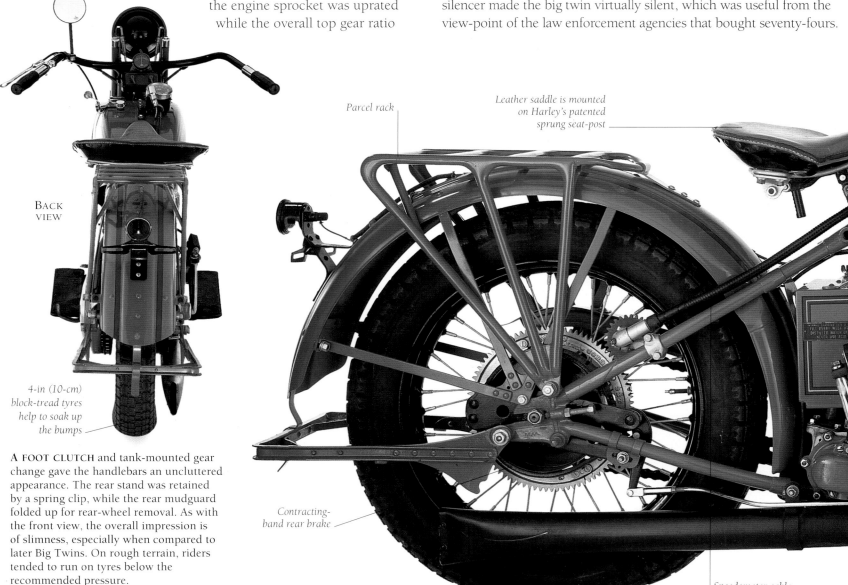

BACK VIEW

4-in (10-cm) block-tread tyres help to soak up the bumps

Parcel rack

Leather saddle is mounted on Harley's patented sprung seat-post

Contracting-band rear brake

Speedometer cable

A FOOT CLUTCH and tank-mounted gear change gave the handlebars an uncluttered appearance. The rear stand was retained by a spring clip, while the rear mudguard folded up for rear-wheel removal. As with the front view, the overall impression is of slimness, especially when compared to later Big Twins. On rough terrain, riders tended to run on tyres below the recommended pressure.

•REAR-WHEEL SPEEDOMETER•

Speedometer running off the rear wheel

The optional, rear-wheel-driven speedometer was fixed to the top of the combined fuel and oil tank, which had cut-outs to accommodate the inlet rockers. The rear wheel was moved to and fro against threaded adjusters to obtain the correct final drive-chain tension. The seat sat on a spring in the rear downtube, and the rear-light housing had a cutaway to illuminate the licence plate. A passenger seat was optional.

VIEWED FROM THE FRONT, the JD28 was an imposing sight – especially if it happened to be ridden by a police officer. An electric air horn below the front light was clearly audible above the various sounds emitted by the engine. The cylindrical case below the horn contained tools as well as the essential puncture repair kit. The rear-view mirror was an optional extra.

Double-sided tank has containers for fuel and lubricating oil

Harley-Davidson's traditional "springer" front forks

Foot clutch

FRONT VIEW

Three-speed gearbox

Silver painted barrels

Front drum brake became standard on U.S. bikes from 1928

HARLEY-DAVIDSON
AA SV PEASHOOTER

Capacity 21cu. in. (346cc) • Power output 8hp @ 4,000rpm
Weight 263lb (119kg) • Top speed 55mph (88km/h) (estimated)

U.S.A.

NICKNAMED THE PEASHOOTER because of its unique exhaust note, this single was introduced in 1926 primarily for export. Also known as the Twenty-one after its capacity, it was equipped with coil ignition and electric lighting. The chassis included a tubular loop frame with springer forks on 20-in (51-cm) wheels with a single rear brake.

FRONT VIEW

The vertical single-cylinder engine has two camshafts actuating the valves

Three-speed handshift gearbox

HARLEY-DAVIDSON
MODEL B RACER

Capacity 21cu. in. (346cc) • Power output 12hp @ 4,000rpm
Weight 240lb (109kg) • Top speed 70mph (113km/h) (estimated)

U.S.A.

A NEW 350CC CLASS IN AMERICAN RACING was instituted on 9 August, 1926, some two months after production of Harley-Davidson's new range of 346cc singles began. In dirt-track trim, the Model B o.h.v. singles entered by the firm did very well. It was lightened by the omission of all non-essentials including gearbox, springer forks, saddle spring, and brakes, and was fast and furious with its abbreviated aircraft-style exhaust header and its 2:1 fixed gearing. The bike shown is from 1926.

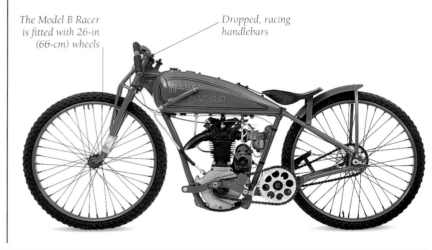

The Model B Racer is fitted with 26-in (66-cm) wheels

Dropped, racing handlebars

HARLEY-DAVIDSON MODEL 61EL KNUCKLEHEAD

Capacity 61cu. in. (988cc) • Power output 40bhp @ 4,800rpm • Weight 515lb (234kg) • Top speed 100mph (161km/h)

U.S.A.

INTRODUCED IN 1936 the 61E was the most important single model Harley ever built; all subsequent "Big Twins" evolved from this machine. It was its first purpose-designed o.h.v. V-twin and its first bike to feature a re-circulating lubrication system, but despite technical advances it was not perfect. There were many detail changes between the first machines and subsequent models, making the 1936 machine, pictured here, rare. The letter L indicates that this model is a sporting version equipped with high-compression pistons.

The two-part fuel tank carries an instrument console

Crash bars

FRONT VIEW

Oil tank sits below the sprung saddle, wrapped around the battery

The 18-in (46-cm) wheels are interchangeable

Carburettor inhales through an air filter on the right-hand side

Knucklehead name derives from shape of alloy rocker boxes

THE 61S were given the duplex, cradle frame originally intended for the V range, but with new, extruded, tubular, springer forks. The Knuckleheads were the first of the modern-day Harley-Davidsons.

HARLEY-DAVIDSON
74FL KNUCKLEHEAD

Capacity 74cu. in. (1213cc) • Power output 48bhp @ 5,000rpm
Weight 535lb (243kg) • Top speed 105mph (169km/h)

U.S.A.

BASED CLOSELY ON THE **61** (see p.70), the 74F was introduced in 1941 in response to police demands for more power. The 74FL was the sporting version with heavier flywheels and strengthened crankcases, while the rolling chassis remained almost unchanged. Only a handful of 1941 74FLs – as shown – were built as the factory was concentrating on military side-valve production.

FRONT VIEW

A new vane-type oil pump replaced the double-gear unit

16-in (41-cm) wheels replaced the 18-in (46-cm) size

Streamlined tool box and rear-light housings designed by Raymond Loewy

HARLEY-DAVIDSON
74FL HYDRA-GLIDE

Capacity 74cu. in. (1213cc) • Power output 55bhp @ 7,200rpm
Weight 590lb (268kg) • Top speed 102mph (164km/h)

U.S.A.

INTRODUCED IN **1949**, the Hydra-Glide was so-called because of the hydraulically damped telescopic forks fitted in place of the springer design. The engine's top end was extensively revised in 1948. Alloy cylinder heads with smooth alloy rocker covers prompted the nickname Panhead. Apart from minor details the transmission, frame, and cycle parts remained essentially unchanged. The Hydra-Glide was aimed primarily at the touring market. The model shown dates from 1949.

Skirted "air-flow" mudguards

Hydraulically damped telescopic forks

Panhead engine

HARLEY-DAVIDSON MODEL 74FLH DUO-GLIDE

Capacity 74cu. in. (1213cc) • Power output 55bhp @ 7,200rpm • Weight 670lb (304kg) • Top speed 100mph (161km/h)

U.S.A.

THE FIRST OF THE "**DRESSERS**", the 1960 Duo-Glide could be ordered with a full complement of touring accessories this example shows. The name Duo-Glide derived from the fact that both ends of the chassis were now fully sprung. FLF versions had a footshift, while sidecar owners could opt for the "three-forward, one-reverse" handshift gearbox. The front half of the Duo-Glide was identical to that of the Hydra-Glide (see above right) apart from the nacelle enclosing the fork tops and headlamp.

Screen, panniers, and other accessories were factory-supplied options

This Duo-Glide features many period accessories such as the elaborate front mudguard detailing

Large rocker covers gave the engine its Panhead nickname

Shock absorbers and swingarm replace the rigid frame of earlier models

Original Harley-Davidson handbook for the Duo-Glide.

Footboards

 HARLEY-DAVIDSON

HARLEY-DAVIDSON WLD

Capacity 45cu. in. (737cc) • Power output 25bhp (estimated) • Weight 530lb (240kg) • Top speed 80mph (129km/h) (estimated)

U.S.A.

THE **WLD SPECIAL SPORT SOLO** was a high-compression version of the WL series, which appeared in 1937. This is a 1941 model. Harley introduced its first 45cu. in. side-valve V-twins, the D series, in 1929, to compete with Excelsior and Indian (see pp.58–60 and pp.101–10). The forty-fives were smaller and lighter than Harley's big twins, but equally rugged, proven by their later success as military motorcycles (see below). Supplying military versions interrupted civilian production from 1942. Forty-fives also provided the basis for Harley's successful Class C racing machines. W models were replaced by K models in 1952.

A new "airplane style" speedometer is fitted to the tank console of 1941 models

The WLD has a rigid frame – suspension is provided by Springer leading-link forks

Paint finish on this model is "Cruiser Green"

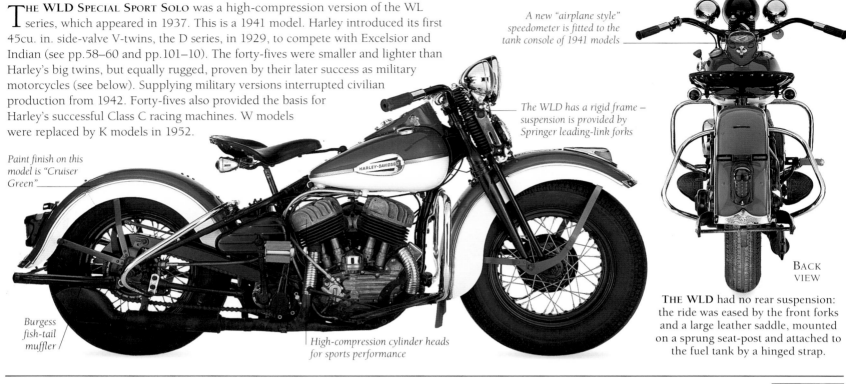

BACK VIEW

THE **WLD** had no rear suspension: the ride was eased by the front forks and a large leather saddle, mounted on a sprung seat-post and attached to the fuel tank by a hinged strap.

Burgess fish-tail muffler

High-compression cylinder heads for sports performance

HARLEY-DAVIDSON WLA

Capacity 45cu. in. (737cc) • Power output 23bhp @ 4,600rpm • Weight 576lb (262kg) • Top speed 65mph (105km/h)

U.S.A.

THIS **VERSION OF THE W SERIES** was produced for the armed forces during World War II. Modifications for military use included a forward-positioned saddle, a full-length bash plate under the engine and gearbox, and improved air filtration. The WLA was also fitted with special lights, gun holders, and windshields. Chrome and other finishes were omitted to keep costs down. The strength, simplicity, and dependability of the forty-five made the WLA an excellent military motorcycle. The only drawback was its weight.

BRITISH FORCES ORDERED the WLA after their motorcycle factories suffered heavy bombing. The Canadian military was supplied with the WLC, a model built to a slightly different specification. Over 80,000 military machines were built during World War II.

Bicycle-type, hand pump for tyres

Special blackou lighting

Slimmed-down mudguards

Specially fitted extra luggage capacity

Protective bash plate

Rifle holster

Crash bars

FRONT VIEW

HARLEY-DAVIDSON 52K

Capacity 45cu. in. (737cc) • *Power output 30bhp (estimated)* • *Weight 400lb (181kg)* • *Top speed 85mph (136km/h) (estimated)*

U.S.A.

THE K SERIES WAS HARLEY'S response to British twins selling in large numbers in post-war America. The British bikes performed and handled better than the domestic product. The K was still a 45cu. in., side-valve V-twin but with right-foot gear-shift and hand clutch operation. The engine and gearbox were one unit and the chassis featured swingarm rear suspension and telescopic forks. This is a 1952 model.

THE 45CU. IN. (737CC) V-TWIN had greater capacity than British twins, but the side-valve layout meant low compression ratios and inefficient cylinder breathing. Lack of power made performance poor. Harley increased the capacity of 1955 KH models to 54cu. in. (883cc).

Handlebar-operated clutch

Updated 4½-gallon (20.5-litre) fuel tank

Swingarm rear suspension

Distinctive "cow horn" handlebars

Telescopic forks with chrome shrouds

Drum brakes

Enclosed primary drive case – the four-speed gearbox was built in unit with the engine

3.25 x 19-in (48-cm) wheels are higher and narrower than previous models

FRONT VIEW

HARLEY-DAVIDSON XL SPORTSTER

Capacity 54cu. in. (883cc) • *Power output 32bhp @ 4,200rpm* • *Weight 463lb (210kg)* • *Top speed 92mph (148km/h) (estimated)*

U.S.A.

THE IMPROVEMENTS THAT HARLEY had put into the K series were insufficient to woo enough buyers away from British bikes. Reliability and performance were still lacking. Harley's solution was to make some cosmetic improvements and to fit overhead valve cylinder heads to the engine to create the Sportster. It was a big success. This model is from 1957, the first year the XL was produced. Nearly forty years later there is still an 883cc Sportster in Harley's range.

COMPARED TO THE previous side-valve models, the XL had a shorter stroke and bigger bore, but capacity remained the same. Engine performance, power, and sales went up. Over the following years power outputs climbed higher as capacity and compression ratios were increased.

Optional luggage rack and panniers

Redesigned fuel tank, livery, and logo

Frame and cycle parts are taken from the earlier K series

Better gas-flow from a redesigned exhaust system

Overhead, rather than side, valves improved the engine

Right-foot gear shift

Optional crash bars are fitted front and rear

FRONT VIEW

HARLEY-DAVIDSON
165 HUMMER

Capacity 165cc • Power output 7bhp @ 5,000rpm
Weight 143lb (65kg) • Top speed 65mph (105km/h) (estimated)

U.S.A.

HARLEY-DAVIDSON introduced a utilitarian 125cc two-stroke motorcycle in 1947. The design was from the German DKW company as part of war reparations. A 165cc version was produced from 1953 to 1959. Pictured is a 1955 model. The three-speed engine unit with its egg-shaped crankcases and iron barrel was almost identical to its German relation.

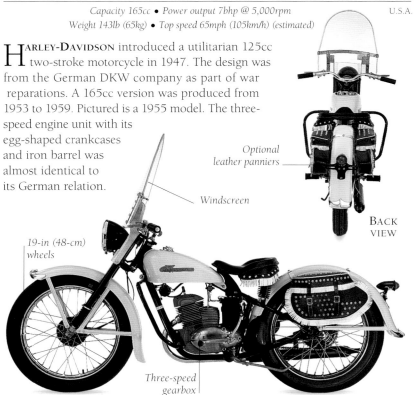

Optional leather panniers

BACK VIEW

Windscreen

19-in (48-cm) wheels

Three-speed gearbox

HARLEY-DAVIDSON
BOBCAT

Capacity 175cc • Power output 10bhp (estimated)
Weight not known • Top speed 65mph (105km/h) (estimated)

U.S.A.

THE BOBCAT WAS REMARKABLE for its one-piece moulded ABS resin bodywork covering the fuel tank and rear wheel, and also for its horizontally sprung rear suspension system. The single-cylinder, two-stroke engine was based on the unit used in the earlier Hummer lightweights. It was available for one year only and was one of Harley's last domestically produced lightweights.

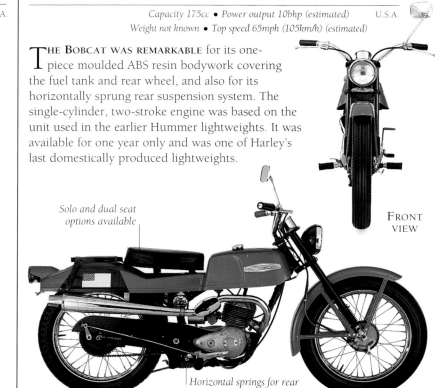

FRONT VIEW

Solo and dual seat options available

Horizontal springs for rear suspension under the engine

HARLEY-DAVIDSON SPRINT H

Capacity 250cc • Power output 28bhp @ 9,500rpm • Weight not known • Top speed 90mph (145km/h) (estimated)

U.S.A.

INTRODUCED FOR 1961 after Harley-Davidson's takeover of the Italian firm of Aeronautica Macchi, thereby establishing the subsidiary Aermacchi Harley-Davidson, the 250cc Sprint was essentially an Italian sports 250 that was sold in Italy as an Aermacchi and in the U.S. as a Harley-Davidson. Aermacchi four-strokes were in production until 1974.

THE SINGLE-CYLINDER o.h.v. Sprint was later offered in 350cc form. Competition versions were also produced.

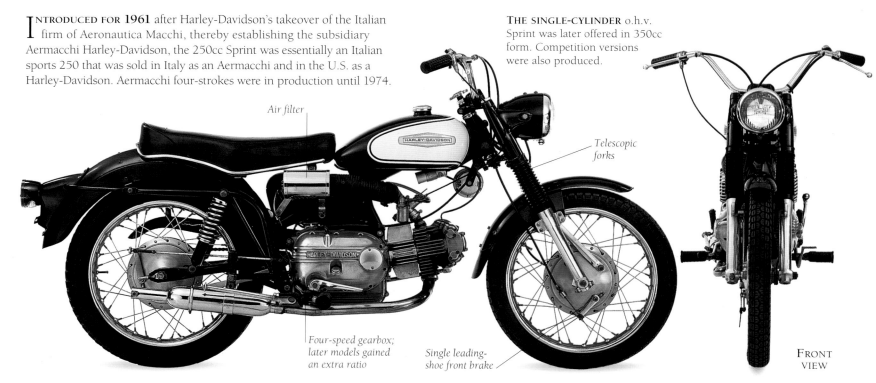

Air filter

Telescopic forks

Four-speed gearbox; later models gained an extra ratio

Single leading-shoe front brake

FRONT VIEW

HARLEY-DAVIDSON
XR-750

Capacity 748cc • Power output 90bhp @ 8,000rpm
Weight 295lb (134kg) • Top speed 115mph (185km/h) (estimated)

U.S.A.

RULE CHANGES FOR **1969** made o.h.v. 750s essential for U.S. racing success. Harley introduced the XR-750 model with iron cylinders and barrels derived from the road-going Sportster model. The iron-engined XR-750 was not a success, and a revised version of the design using alloy cylinders and heads with twin Mikuni carburettors appeared for 1972. The bike shown here won the AMA championship that year, and over 20 years later updated versions remain front runners on U.S. dirt tracks.

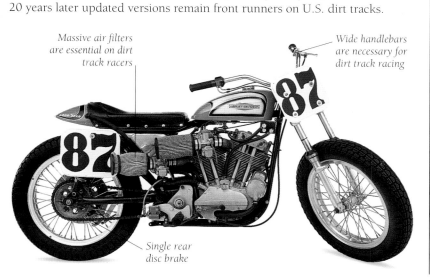

Massive air filters are essential on dirt track racers

Wide handlebars are necessary for dirt track racing

Single rear disc brake

HARLEY-DAVIDSON
XRTT CR TRACK RACER

Capacity 748cc • Power output 90bhp @ 8,000rpm
Weight 324lb (147kg) • Top speed 130mph (209km/h) (estimated)

U.S.A.

THIS WAS THE ROAD-RACING VERSION of Harley's XR dirt track machines. Modifications from the base model included equipping it with appropriate bodywork, such as the fairing and a large-capacity fuel tank. It was also given brakes. The engine was almost identical, except that for road racing the huge air filters could be left off the Mikuni carburettors. This 1972 bike was raced by the great Cal Rayborn.

BACK VIEW

Fairing painted in Harley-Davidson racing colours

Tank pad supports riders when "tucked in"

Rear disc brake

HARLEY-DAVIDSON XR1000

Capacity 998cc • Power output 70bhp @ 6,000rpm • Weight 470lb (213kg) (estimated) • Top speed 120mph (193km/h) (estimated)

U.S.A.

BUILT IN LIMITED NUMBERS, the XR1000 is regarded by some as one of Harley's best bikes. Based on the standard Sportster, the modified engine used cylinder heads from the XR750 racer and also twin Dell'Orto carburettors. In standard form it was 10bph more powerful than a normal Sportster and correspondingly quicker. Despite its performance, it did not sell and was dropped. This machine dates from 1984.

High-level exhaust pipes are mounted on left side

Air filters

Frame and cycle parts were taken from the XLX Sportster

Engine has iron barrels and alloy heads

BACK VIEW

HARLEY-DAVIDSON XLH883 SPORTSTER

Capacity 54cu. in. (883cc) • *Power output 49bhp @ 7,000rpm* • *Weight 470lb (213kg)* • *Top speed 105mph (169km/h)*

U.S.A.

H ARLEY-DAVIDSON INTRODUCED A NEW SPORTSTER for 1986. It retained the appearance of its predecessors, but the revised engine design and improved quality control made it cleaner, quieter, and more reliable. Its reasonable price and appeal to the nostalgia market made it popular with urban riders and commuters, who previously would not have considered buying a Harley-Davidson. Later models used a five-speed gearbox, replacing the earlier four-speed. The bike shown here is the 1987 model.

HARLEY-DAVIDSON naturally retained its trademark, 45° V-twin layout introduced on the 1985 Sportster. But despite the traditional appearance, the Evolution engine and lubrication were vastly improved, with alloy replacing the iron components. A new crankshaft and hydraulic tappets were added.

2½-gallon (10-litre) "peanut" fuel tanks

Both wheels had a single 11½-in (29-cm) disc brake

FRONT VIEW

Oil tank for dry-sump lubrication system

Alloy cylinder head

HARLEY-DAVIDSON
FLHS ELECTRA GLIDE

Capacity 82cu. in. (1344cc) • *Power output 58bhp @ 7,200rpm*
Weight 692lb (314kg) • *Top speed 105mph (169km/h)*

U.S.A.

I N TERMS OF STYLE, THIS **1988 ELECTRA GLIDE** was similar to the original 1960s model, reflecting the firm's retro-marketing strategy, but underneath it was quite different. The all-alloy, o.h.v. Evolution engine introduced in 1984 was superior to the iron-barrelled unit it replaced. Suspension consisted of a conventional twin-shock swingarm and anti-dive, telescopic front forks. The FLHS was equipped with crash bars, panniers, a king-and-queen touring seat, and retro-styled cycle parts and accessories.

Single 1½-in (40-mm) Keihin CV carburettor

Two-into-one exhaust system

45° V-twin engine

16-in (41-cm) cast-alloy wheels

Rubber mountings combat the high level of vibration

HARLEY-DAVIDSON
FXR SUPER GLIDE

Capacity 82cu. in. (1344cc) • *Power output 58bhp @ 7,200rpm*
Weight 570lb (259kg) • *Top speed 115mph (185km/h)*

U.S.A.

T HE SUPER GLIDE WAS ESSENTIALLY an Electra Glide (see left) stripped of its touring accessories. The engine is identical to the rest of the range, but the exhaust system was modelled on the Sportster (see above). The 16-in (41-cm) rear wheel and single disc brake were retained, but a 19-in (48-cm) front wheel was added. Optional extras included spoked wheels, Sportster fuel tanks, twin discs for the front, a solo seat, and tuning kits to boost the restricted output to more than 80bhp.
Shown here is a 1989 model.

Fuel-tank-mounted instrument panel

Duplex cradle frame

Five-speed gearbox

Front disc brake

HARLEY-DAVIDSON EVOLUTION FLTC TOUR GLIDE CLASSIC

Capacity 82cu. in. (1344cc) • Power output 58bhp @ 7,200rpm • Weight 732lb (332kg) • Top speed 110mph (177km/h) (estimated)

U.S.A.

THE **FLTC TOUR GLIDE CLASSIC** was Harley's Full Dresser of the 1980s. Unlike the Electra Glide, it was not an exercise in retro-styling despite its model designation. With two riders and a full load, the FLTC weighed more than half a ton, so the claimed maximum speed was optimistic. Shown here is a 1989 FLTC.

IN TERMS OF ENGINE and chassis, the FLTC was identical to the FLHS but the running gear and touring accessories reflected modern touring riders' requirements.

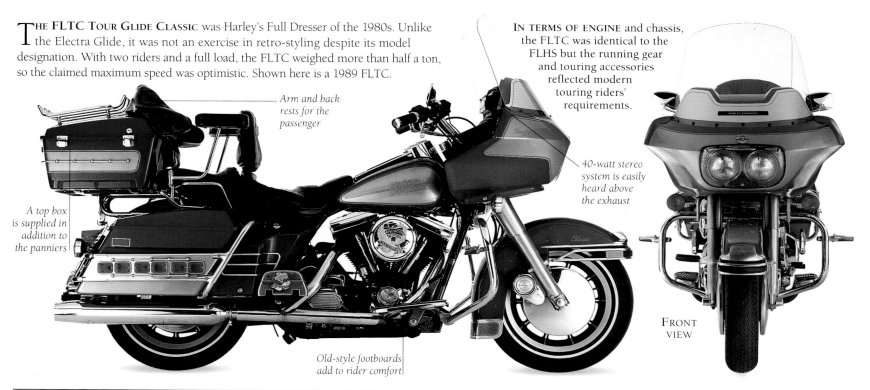

Arm and back rests for the passenger

40-watt stereo system is easily heard above the exhaust

A top box is supplied in addition to the panniers

Old-style footboards add to rider comfort

FRONT VIEW

 ## HEINKEL PERLE

Capacity 49cc • Power output 1.5bhp
Weight not known • Top speed 40km/h (25mph)

GERMANY

AS AN AIRCRAFT MANUFACTURER, Heinkel was able to bring innovative ideas to moped construction when it entered that field. The two-stroke Perle moped appeared in 1954. It had a cast-alloy frame, with the fuel tank situated beneath the seat. All cables and wires from the handlebar controls passed through the tubular structure, giving it a tidy appearance. The drive chain was hidden in a cast-alloy case forming an integral part of the swingarm. The drawback of this high-technology construction was the price, so it did not sell well. This is a 1956 Perle.

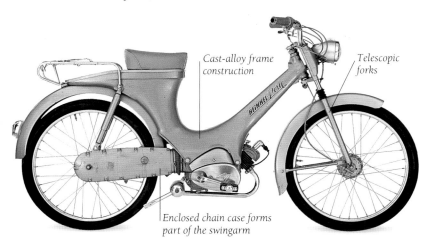

Cast-alloy frame construction

Telescopic forks

Enclosed chain case forms part of the swingarm

 ## HEINKEL TOURIST

Capacity 174cc • Power output 9.5bhp @ 5,500rpm
Weight 145kg (320lb) • Top speed 95km/h (59mph)

GERMANY

HEINKEL FIRST INTRODUCED its Tourist scooter in 1953. It had a 149cc o.h.v. engine mounted under the rider's seat. By 1956, when the machine shown here was built, capacity had increased to 174cc. It had a simple steel tubular chassis and pressed-steel bodywork that covered the front and rear wheels. Unlike other scooters, the Heinkel engine did not move with the rear suspension. Instead, the final drive chain passed through an alloy case, which also formed the swingarm. More than 100,000 Tourist scooters were built before production ended in 1965.

Four-speed gearbox with twistgrip change

Cast-alloy chain case/swingarm

Telescopic forks

HENDERSON

Capacity 56cu. in. (920cc) • *Power output 8hp (estimated)* • *Weight 295lb (134kg)* • *Top speed 60mph (97km/h)*

THE HENDERSON WAS NOT THE FIRST four-cylinder motorcycle made in the U.S., but it was the most famous. Early motorcycle engineers in several countries recognized the advantages of the in-line four-cylinder engine layout with its inherent smoothness and potential for power. In Britain, Charles Binks made a very limited number of in-line fours in the early years of the 20th century. In Belgium, Paul Kelecom designed the far more successful and important FN four at around the same time (see p.62). The Belgian machine, which was widely exported, was influential on U.S. designers. Although the first U.S. production four-cylinder motorcycle was the 1909 Pierce, the figure most identified with the layout in the U.S. was Bill Henderson. Henderson, in partnership with his brother Tom, began motorcycle production at Detroit in 1912, although prototype machines were running the previous year. The motorcycle shown here is a 1912 model from the first production year. Early Henderson machines had a number of bizarre features, including a 65-in (165-cm) wheelbase and an optional passenger seat that mounted on the fuel tank in front of the rider. The valances on the mudguard were there to help keep ladies' skirts out of the wheel. The following year the passenger seat moved to a more conventional position, but there was not a short wheelbase version until 1915. The in-line four-cylinder engine had a four-bearing crankshaft and an i.o.e. valve layout. Drive was turned through 90° behind the engine and final drive was by chain. The motor was started by a crankshaft and there was a clutch in the rear hub. A two-speed hub gear was offered from 1915.

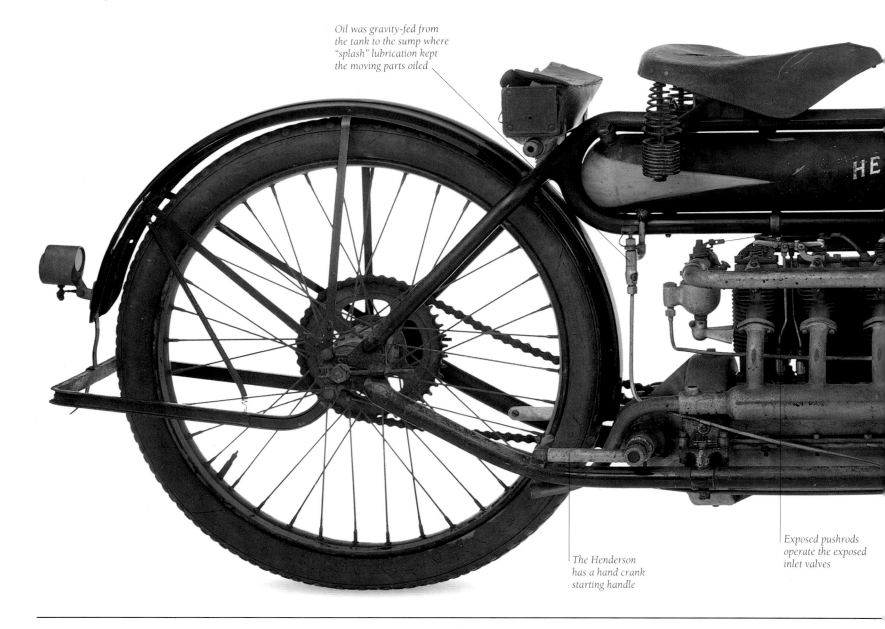

Oil was gravity-fed from the tank to the sump where "splash" lubrication kept the moving parts oiled

The Henderson has a hand crank starting handle

Exposed pushrods operate the exposed inlet valves

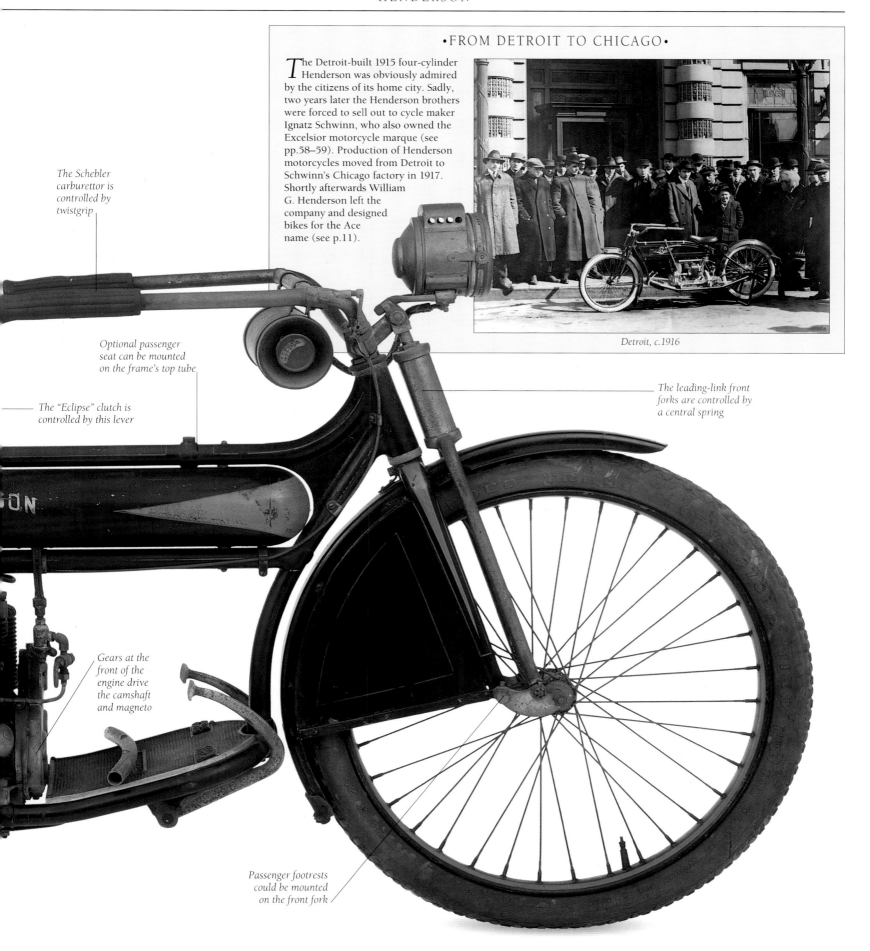

The Schebler carburettor is controlled by twistgrip

Optional passenger seat can be mounted on the frame's top tube

The "Eclipse" clutch is controlled by this lever

Gears at the front of the engine drive the camshaft and magneto

Passenger footrests could be mounted on the front fork

The leading-link front forks are controlled by a central spring

•FROM DETROIT TO CHICAGO•

The Detroit-built 1915 four-cylinder Henderson was obviously admired by the citizens of its home city. Sadly, two years later the Henderson brothers were forced to sell out to cycle maker Ignatz Schwinn, who also owned the Excelsior motorcycle marque (see pp.58–59). Production of Henderson motorcycles moved from Detroit to Schwinn's Chicago factory in 1917. Shortly afterwards William G. Henderson left the company and designed bikes for the Ace name (see p.11).

Detroit, c.1916

HENDERSON MODEL K

Capacity 79cu. in. (1301cc) • *Power output 28bhp @ 3,400rpm* • *Weight 450lb (204kg)* • *Top speed 80mph (129km/h)*   U.S.A.

THE MODEL K, INTRODUCED IN 1920, was the first all-new Henderson produced in Chicago following the company's takeover by Schwinn. It was designed by Arthur O. Lemon. The new 79cu. in. (1301cc) engine used side valves instead of the i.o.e. layout. Crankshaft lubrication was pressure-fed from a gear-driven pump. The chassis was equipped with stronger forks, a twin-downtube frame, an enclosed chaincase, and wider mudguards. The Model K was stronger, more reliable, and more powerful than its predecessors and reinforced Henderson's reputation for quality machines.

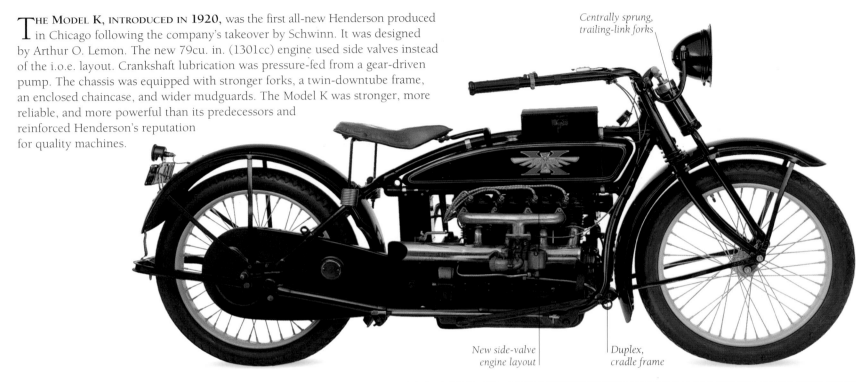

Centrally sprung, trailing-link forks

New side-valve engine layout

Duplex, cradle frame

HENDERSON MODEL KJ

Capacity 79cu. in. (1301cc) • *Power output 40bhp* • *Weight 500lb (227kg) (estimated)* • *Top speed 100mph (161km/h)*   U.S.A.

FOR 1929 HENDERSON INTRODUCED A NEW MACHINE called the KJ. Designed by Arthur Constantine, it retained the 79cu. in. (1301cc) capacity of the earlier K series models. The crankshaft now had five main bearings and alloy pistons were used. Cylinder cooling was improved and a Schebler carburettor was used. New frames allowed lower seats and "streamlined" fuel tanks that included an instrument panel. However, the KJ was short-lived. Schwinn pulled out of the motorcycle business; the last Hendersons were made in 1931.

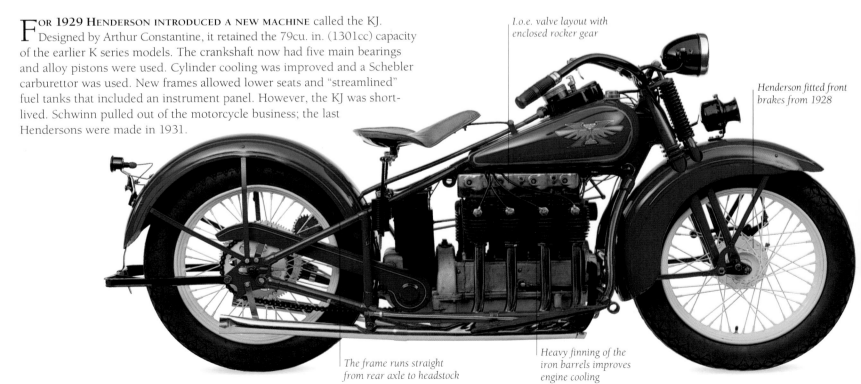

I.o.e. valve layout with enclosed rocker gear

Henderson fitted front brakes from 1928

The frame runs straight from rear axle to headstock

Heavy finning of the iron barrels improves engine cooling

HERCULES W2000

Capacity 294cc • Power output 27bhp @ 6,500rpm • Weight 175kg (386lb) • Top speed 147km/h (91mph)

SEVERAL MOTORCYCLE COMPANIES developed Wankel-engined prototypes in the early 1970s. The Hercules was the first to reach the market, with production versions appearing in late 1974; the W2000 was sold in some markets as a DKW. Its engine was produced by Hercules' parent company, the Fichtel & Sachs group, which had already produced Wankel engines for snowmobiles and as stationary power units. Engine rotation was in-line with the frame, and the drive had to be turned through 90° before it reached the six-speed gearbox. The W2000 was not a success: it was expensive, ugly, and unproven. Less than 2,000 were made.

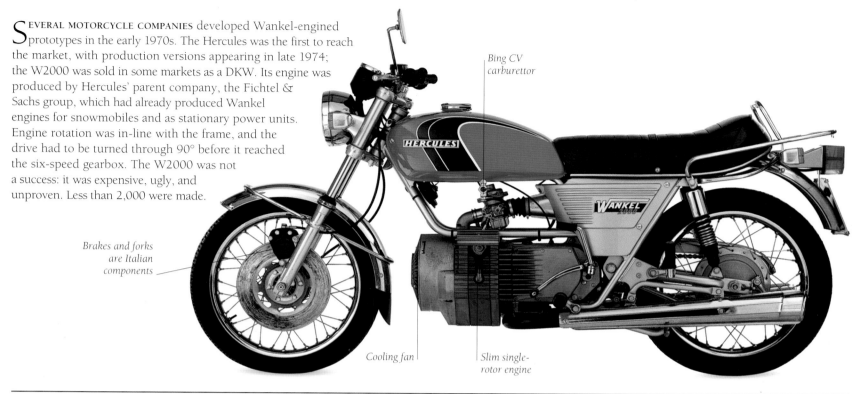

Bing CV carburettor

Brakes and forks are Italian components

Cooling fan

Slim single-rotor engine

HESKETH

Capacity 992cc • Power output 82bhp @ 6,000rpm • Weight 545lb (247kg) • Top speed 120mph (193km/h) (estimated)

ALTHOUGH OFFICIALLY LAUNCHED IN 1980, Hesketh production could not begin until 1982: it took two years to sort out the appalling gearshift, engine noise, and oil leaks. When it finally appeared, the improvements had done nothing to reduce its weight, height, or complexity. Its engine was a 90° V-twin developed by Weslake with four valves and two camshafts on each cylinder. The engine unit alone weighed 220lb (100kg). The original company went bankrupt after just 139 bikes were built. Subsequently, limited production restarted, although probably less than 250 machines were built.

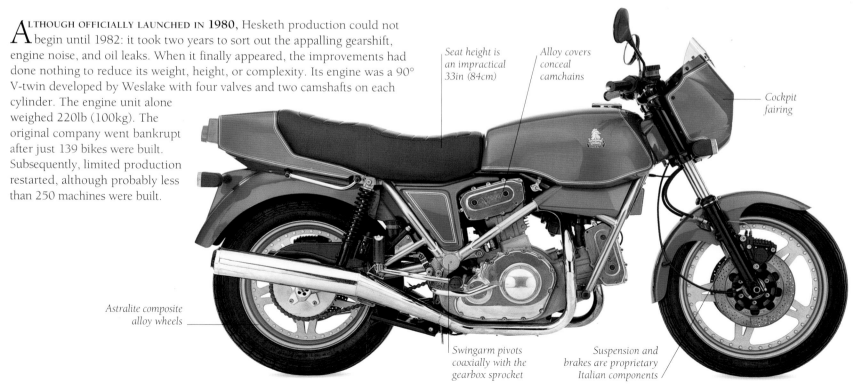

Seat height is an impractical 33in (84cm)

Alloy covers conceal camchains

Cockpit fairing

Astralite composite alloy wheels

Swingarm pivots coaxially with the gearbox sprocket

Suspension and brakes are proprietary Italian components

HILDEBRAND & WOLFMÜLLER

Capacity 1488cc • Power output 2.5bhp @ 240rpm • Weight 87kg (192lb) • Top speed 45km/h (28mph)

DEVELOPED BY THE **H**ILDEBRAND BROTHERS and Alois Wolfmüller, and manufactured from 1894 to 1897, this machine has the distinction of being the first powered, two-wheeled vehicle to be offered to the public on a series production basis. The company also gave us the word "motorcycle" when it registered the word *Motorrad* to describe its new machine. The Hildebrand & Wolfmüller had two horizontal cylinders with both pistons moving in unison and firing on alternate revolutions. The connecting rods were directly attached to cranks on the rear wheel, which therefore also acted as a flywheel. A timing device on the rear wheel controlled the opening of the engine's exhaust valves. The inlet valves were automatic, fed with the fuel/air mixture from a surface carburettor mounted between the frame downtubes. In this arrangement the carburettor and fuel tank are effectively combined, with incoming air moving over the surface

of the fuel before passing, via a regulator valve, to the engine. Water cooling was employed, the water being carried in a curved tank that also served as the rear mudguard. Ignition was by the crude, hot-tube system. The engine was fitted into an open tubular frame in which many of the tubes served additional functions. Despite the several advanced features of the design, the Hildebrand & Wolfmüller was not a practical vehicle, and after an initial burst of enthusiasm the venture soon foundered. Around 2,000 are reputed to have been built. They were also made under licence in Paris by Duncan & Superbie. The machine shown here dates from 1894.

Upper frame tubes contain engine-lubricating oil

Simple pad front brake

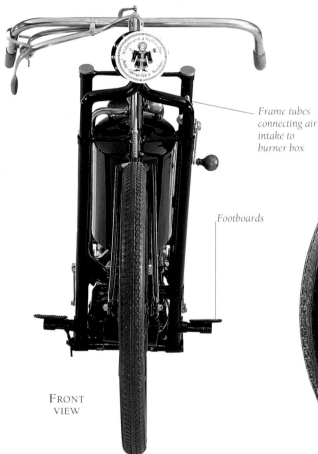

Frame tubes connecting air intake to burner box

Footboards

FRONT VIEW

Fuel tank/surface carburettor

THE DISTINCTIVE BADGE on the front of the machine covers the air intake for and exhaust outlet from the burner for the hot-tube ignition system. Air and exhaust pass through frame tubes to the burner box situated in front of the cylinder. The alcohol-fired burner heated a nickel or platinum tube, the end of which projected into the cylinder to ignite the fuel mixture.

•FROM STEAM TO PETROL•

Hildebrand & Wolfmüller had experimented with steam engines before developing its petrol-engined motorcycle; steam-engine practice is quite evident in its design. The rear wheel assembly served as a crankshaft and flywheel; the connecting rods ran directly from the piston to the cranks mounted on the axle. The direct nature of this connection meant that the wheel had a small diameter to allow a low-gear ratio. The flywheel effect was augmented by rubber straps connected to each connecting rod. These were extended on the outward stroke of the pistons and returned their stored energy on the inward stroke. An eccentric brass ring on the wheel acted as a cam to control the opening of the exhaust valve. A latch mechanism above the cylinders ensured that the valves open on each cylinder alternately, obviating the need for a half engine-speed camshaft.

Stout rubber straps accentuate flywheel effect

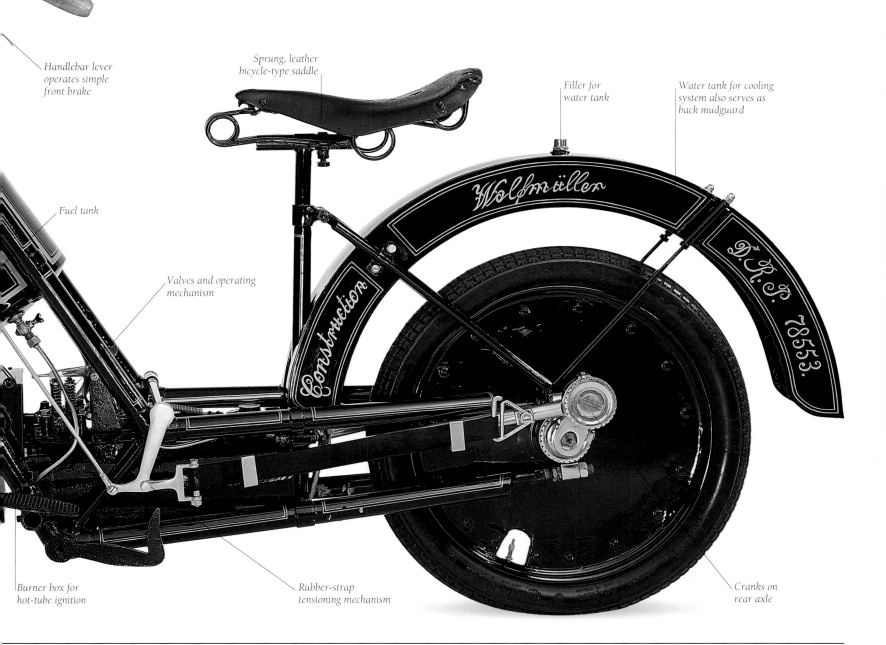

*Wooden
handlebar grips*

*Handlebar lever
operates simple
front brake*

*Sprung, leather
bicycle-type saddle*

*Filler for
water tank*

*Water tank for cooling
system also serves as
back mudguard*

Fuel tank

*Valves and operating
mechanism*

*Burner box for
hot-tube ignition*

*Rubber-strap
tensioning mechanism*

*Cranks on
rear axle*

Wolfmüller

Construction

D.R.P. 78553.

HODAKA SUPER RAT

Capacity 98cc • Power output 16bhp @ 7,250rpm • Weight not known • Top speed not known

HODAKA'S LIGHTWEIGHT off-road motorcycles first appeared in the U.S. in 1964. The original machine was a 90cc two-stroke single; capacity later grew to 100cc and then 125cc. Hodaka motorcycles were simple, rugged, and reliable. During the 1960s, as the American dirt bike market was developing, Hodaka machines proved very popular and gained a cult following.

THE MACHINE SHOWN here is a 1971 Super Rat Motocross, but enduro and trail models were similar and had names like Combat Wombat and Dirt Squirt. Production ended in 1978 when Hodaka was unable to compete with the technology of major Japanese manufacturers.

Wide-braced handlebars give improved handling

High level alloy mudguards

Chrome-plated steel fuel tank

48-cm (19-in) front wheel

Duplex cradle frame

98cc single-cylinder, two-stroke engine

FRONT VIEW

HOFFMANN GOUVERNEUR

Capacity 248cc • Power output 15bhp @ 6,000rpm • Weight 148kg (326lb) • Top speed 112km/h (70mph)

CLEARLY INSPIRED BY the larger capacity BMW flat-twins, Hoffmann introduced the Gouverneur in 1951. The high-quality machine was designed by Richard Küchen, who had designed motorcycles for Victoria and other companies before World War II. A single carburettor hidden in a cowl above the horizontally opposed engine fed the fuel mixture to both cylinders.

THE NOVEL FRAME used a pressed-steel spine that splayed out below the seat. Production lasted only until 1954 when the machine shown here was built.

The steel panels are part of the frame structure

Flat-twin engine

FRONT VIEW

Plunger rear suspension units

Elliptical section tubing unbolts to allow engine removal

Front suspension is provided by inverted telescopic forks

HONDA 50 SUPER CUB

Capacity 49cc • Power output 4bhp @ 9,500rpm • Weight 65kg (143lb) • Top speed 70km/h (43mph)

THE HONDA 50 SUPER CUB was first introduced in 1958. Its descendants are still in production at factories in 11 countries around the world. Over 21 million have been produced worldwide. This is the biggest-selling and most popular motorcycle ever produced. Design changes in 35 years of production have been minimal, proving the worth of the original design. The model shown here is a 1963 version. The Cub used a watch-like 49cc o.h.v. engine

at a time when most small-capacity motorcycles were two-strokes. The Cub was quiet, clean, reliable, and extremely economical. Sales to the U.S. began in 1959, and by 1965 Honda was selling 268,000 a year. This was achieved through a marketing campaign that appealed to a new kind of motorcycle rider: "You meet the nicest people on a Honda," said the slogan. In a 35-year production run the Honda 50 has changed little. In some markets an electric starter is now offered.

THE FRAME was a combination of pressed-steel sections and a single tubular spine. The front forks were a simple leading-link design. An overhead-camshaft engine replaced the o.h.v. power unit in 1966.

Moulded leg shields provide a clean ride

The Cub was one of the first machines to use plastic for leg shields, front mudguard, and side panels

FRONT VIEW

•HONDA'S EASY RIDER•

The Honda 50 Super Cub has always been a basic means of transportation. In fact, in Asia it is a fundamental part of some societies' infrastructures. As well as providing mobility for families (a four-person passenger count is not uncommon), it can also move livestock, including a gaggle of geese.

Livestock being transported by a 50 Super Cub

Pressed-steel leading-link forks

Pressed-steel frame construction

Fuel tank

Enclosed chain

The Cub has a centrifugal clutch and semi-automatic three-speed gearbox

HONDA RC160

Capacity 249cc • Power output 35bhp @ 14,000rpm
Weight 124kg (273lb) • Top speed 201km/h (125mph)

JAPAN

HONDA'S FIRST FOUR-CYLINDER MOTORCYCLE was the 1959 RC160, shown here. It was built in time for the All-Japan Championships of 1959. The spine frame used the engine as a stressed frame member. Early models like this one had a vertically mounted engine with shaft driven cams; later the engine had central gear drive to the twin camshafts and was forward inclined. This helped cooling and lowered the centre of gravity for improved handling.

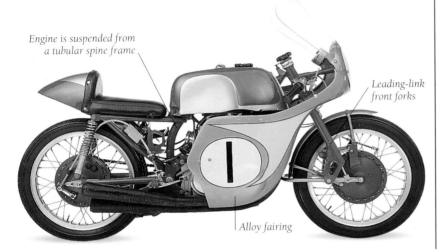

Engine is suspended from a tubular spine frame

Leading-link front forks

Alloy fairing

HONDA DREAM 300

Capacity 305cc • Power output 21bhp @ 7,000rpm
Weight 158kg (348lb) • Top speed 129km/h (80mph)

JAPAN

HONDA ENTERED THE 1960S with a range of four-stroke twins. The Dream 300 was the touring model of the line-up, and included the luxury of electric start and fully enclosed final-drive chain. The chassis was pressed steel with leading-link forks and twin oil-damped rear shocks. The wheels were small – 41cm (16in) front and back – and had 3¼-in tyres. Ultimately, although the Dream offered potential buyers what they wanted – a reliable non-leaking engine with good electrics – it did not handle well.

Deep-valanced front mudguard

Enclosed chain

O.h.c. parallel-twin engine

HONDA CB92 BENLY

Capacity 124cc • Power output 15bhp @ 10,500rpm
Weight 100kg (220lb) • Top speed 113km/h (70mph)

JAPAN

THE CB92 BENLY was perhaps the most radical of the early Hondas that were exported to the West. No other 125cc machines came close to the performance, specification, or quality of construction offered by the Benly. The design was typical period Honda with pressed-steel frame and forks. The twin-cylinder engine featured a single o.h.c., breathing through a single carburettor and driving via a four-speed gearbox. It was equipped with an electric starter, large-diameter drum brakes, and 46-cm (18-in) rims. The machine shown here is a 1960 model.

Flyscreen

Speedometer set in headlamp nacelle

Leading-link forks

Large-diameter drum brakes front and rear

HONDA RC164

Capacity 249cc • Power output 45bhp @ 14,000rpm
Weight 105kg (232lb) • Top speed 225km/h (140mph)

JAPAN

THE 1964 RC164 WAS THE RESULT of five years of development of the earlier RC160 (see above left). It was 10hp more powerful and almost 32km/h (20mph) faster than the earlier machine. The dated leading-link forks were replaced with more modern telescopics. The 1964 250 RC164 was a lighter, lower version of the well-tried four, but still not quick enough to match the fast-improving Yamaha two-stroke twins. A new six-cylinder 250 was introduced at the end of 1964.

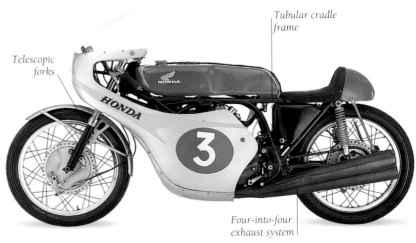

Tubular cradle frame

Telescopic forks

Four-into-four exhaust system

HONDA
CL72 SCRAMBLER

Capacity 249cc • Power output 24bhp @ 9,000rpm
Weight 153kg (337lb) • Top speed 128km/h (80mph)

JAPAN

Honda's sporty **CL72** street scrambler was introduced in 1962. Pictured here is a 1964 model. It had the CB72's 249cc 180°, four-stroke motor, a derivative of the 1960's C70 with recently introduced wet-sump engine. In tune with its street scrambler image, it had twin, high-level exhaust pipes that exited to the left of the engine. The CL72 had a tubular-steel cradle frame with telescopic forks and a hydraulic steering damper. It was the forerunner of the modern trail bike.

Drum brakes front and rear laced to 48-cm (19-in) wheels

Heat shields to protect legs from exhaust pipes

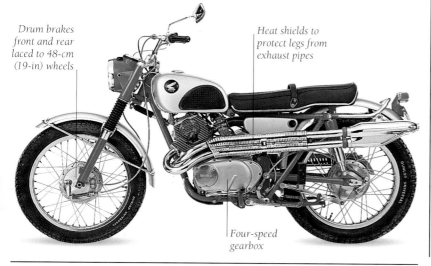

Four-speed gearbox

HONDA
CB77 SUPER HAWK

Capacity 305cc • Power output 27½bhp @ 9,000rpm
Weight 160kg (353lb) • Top speed 166km/h (103mph)

JAPAN

Honda's **CB77 SUPER HAWK** (Super Sport in Britain) was an important model in the 1960s. It proved the Japanese could build stylish, powerful motorcycles – not just small-capacity commuters – and at an affordable price. The 305cc was the biggest bike Honda produced at the time. The tubular frame used the motor as a stressed member. The engine itself was essentially a bored-out 250 motor. Introduced in 1964, the model shown here is a 1966 version. The bike's standard specification included several items that were extras on other machines.

Twin carburettors

Speedo and rev counter are combined in one unit

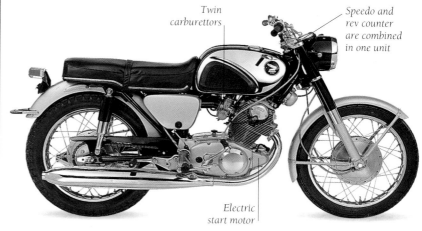

Electric start motor

HONDA CL90

Capacity 89cc • Power output 8bhp @ 9,500rpm
Weight 92kg (202lb) • Top speed not known

JAPAN

Honda's **CL90** was the next stage on from the street scrambler (see above). This small-capacity sportster was fast evolving into a trail bike, with its high-rise handlebars and high-level exhaust. It was based on the CS90 sports road bike, with a four-stroke, two-valve, chain-driven o.h.c. engine. The CL90 had a T-spine pressed-steel frame, 46-cm (18-in) wheels with drum brakes, and a four-speed gearbox. The CL90 represented the leisure side of motorcycle marketing. It offered enough performance to make riding the dry earth tracks in the backwoods fun.

Shortened rear mudguard

Fork gaiters as standard equipment

Single Keihin carburettor

HONDA SUPER 90

Capacity 89cc • Power output 8bhp @ 9,500rpm
Weight 87kg (191lb) • Top speed not known

JAPAN

Honda's **SMALL-CAPACITY SPORTSTERS**, including the Super 90, underwent a number of changes in 1966. Overhead camshafts replaced pushrod-operated valves and there was an alloy head and barrel. What did not change was Honda's familiar four-speed gearbox. The chassis was still spine type, but suspension revisions saw telescopic forks up front and twin shocks at the rear. The model ran until 1969 (1967 version pictured). But fans of the Honda 90 will know that this engine lives on today as the heart of the ever-popular C90 step-thru.

Pressed-steel frame

46-cm (18-in) wheels ran skinny 2½-in section tyres

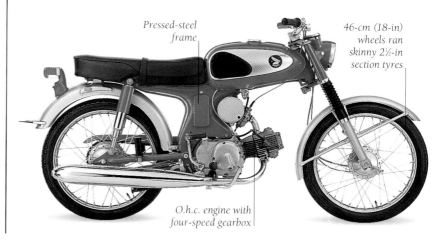

O.h.c. engine with four-speed gearbox

HONDA CB750

Capacity 736cc • Power output 67bhp @ 8,000rpm • Weight 220kg (485lb) • Top speed 200km/h (124mph)

IF ONE MACHINE CHANGED the course of motorcycle development, it was the CB750. Four-cylinder engines are common today, as are disc brakes, electric starters, and 200km/h (124mph) performance. However, when the CB750 was launched in 1969 such a high level of specification was not usually considered by designers of production motorcycles. The CB750 set new standards for performance, practicality, and reliability in the big bike class, heralding the era of the production superbike. Honda had been making small-capacity machines with electric starters since the 1950s. This was the firm's first attempt at a big bike and it was immediately successful. Despite initial criticisms that the CB750 was too big, heavy, and complicated, and that the British-built Triumph Trident (see p.186) was marginally

quicker, consumers preferred the affordable modernity of the Honda design. The CB750 was not revolutionary, but it was well equipped with state-of-the-art technology. The 736cc four-cylinder engine had just two valves per cylinder and a single overhead camshaft, compared to the four-valve, twin-camshaft engines used on Honda's racing machines. The crankshaft used plain bearings and primary drive was by chain. The suspension and chassis were conventional, and in fact the only real innovation was the number of cylinders. The CB750's handling and braking were unimpressive, despite the innovation (for production bikes) of fitting a front disc brake. These problems did not affect the bike's success: it had the engine, performance, and looks that caught the public's imagination.

The engine rev-counter and speedometer are positioned for maximum visibility

Smart candy red livery with gold stripes and plenty of chrome

Indicators

BACK VIEW

THE IMPRESSIVE arrangement of four exhaust pipes – one per cylinder – not only assisted the engine's performance but also made the bike look powerful. No other production bike at the time could match the CB750 for this kind of attention to style and performance details. Honda replaced the eight-valve s.o.h.c. four with a sixteen-valve d.o.h.c. model in 1978.

Expensive four pipe exhaust is a feature of the K series CB750s; the sportier F series, introduced in 1975, used a four-into-one system

THE FOUR VERTICALLY aligned cylinders over wide crankcases give the CB750 a distinctively low-slung, sturdy appearance. This 1969 model had indicators, a hydraulic front disc brake, and two rear-view mirrors fitted as standard. At the time these items were considered to be luxuries for production machines.

Rear-view mirror

Handlebar-mounted hydraulic fluid reservoir for front disc brake

The s.o.h.c. engine has two valves per cylinder

Four 28-mm Keihin carburettors are fitted

The CB750 was the first production bike to be fitted with a hydraulic disc-brake. Unfortunately the sliding calliper's stopping power was unimpressive

FRONT VIEW

Unusually for Honda, it made the 736cc engine under-square at 61mm x 63mm

A five-speed gearbox is fitted; Honda later produced a semi-automatic version

A 210-watt alternator is mounted at the left end of the crankshaft, with the ignition points at this end. An electric starter is situated behind the cylinders

HONDA CT50 TRAIL CUB

Capacity 49.5cc • Power output 4.75bhp @ 10,000rpm
Weight 71kg (157lb) • Top speed 69km/h (43mph)

JAPAN

FOR THE **CT50**, Honda removed the C50's plastic bodywork and added engine crash bars that ran from the steering head to under each side of the motor, a plastic cover over the front-frame downtube, and a dual-range, three-speed gearbox giving three ratios for road use and three lower ratios for off-road riding. A high-level exhaust with heat shields, knobbly tyres, and competition-style mudguards topped off the trail-bike image. Available from 1968 to 1970, this machine dates from 1970.

Large rear rack means single-seat accommodation

Single-cylinder, four-stroke, two-valve engine

43-cm (17-in) wheels with drum brakes

Dual-ratio gearbox

HONDA XR75

Capacity 72cc • Power output 7bhp @ 10,000rpm
Weight 64kg (141lb) • Top speed not known

JAPAN

DURING THE EARLY **1970**S, off-road riding was becoming hugely popular in the U.S. For the young motocross fan, Honda offered the XR75. This 72cc s.o.h.c., four-stroke single was an aggressively styled, yet fun, bike. It took the concept of the street scrambler another step towards the trail/enduro bike. The XR75 had real off-road ability and came well equipped with knobbly tyres and a high-set front mudguard. The XR75 illustrated is a 1973 model.

Overhead camshaft engine

Competition number plates

Single Keihin carburettor

Twin-shock rear suspension

Drum brakes

Four-speed gearbox

Telescopic front forks

HONDA CB350

Capacity 347cc • Power output 32bhp @ 9,500rpm • Weight 169kg (373lb) • Top speed 155km/h (96mph)

JAPAN

THE **CB350** was the smallest of the 1970s' road-going, four-cylinder, s.o.h.c. machines. Never officially imported into Britain and failing to gain support in the U.S., Honda looked to Europe, where some countries' import tax laws favour sub-350cc bikes. Police versions were offered in France and Holland. This bike dates from 1976.

THE **CB350** had a short life. Introduced in 1972, it was replaced in the markets by the CB400F, which appeared in 1974. Capacity of the 400 four was increased to 408cc. It was restyled and given a four-into-one exhaust pipe. The 400 was a big success and was produced until 1979.

Single o.h.c. engine

Four carburettors

Brake master cylinder

Single front disc brake

Four-pipe exhaust system

FRONT VIEW

HONDA GOLDWING GL1000

Capacity 999cc • Power output 80bhp @ 7,500rpm • Weight 259kg (571lb) • Top speed 193km/h (120mph)

Honda's original 1975 Goldwing (shown here) was worlds away from today's heavily accessorized successor. The brief was for it to be "the king of motorcycles", to beat the Z1 (see p.113) and to regain the glory Honda had lost to Kawasaki. When launched, it was Japan's first water-cooled four-stroke; a massive grand tourer that was an immediate hit in the U.S. The British press was less keen. However, its smooth cruising ability made it a favourite with long-distance riders.

BACK VIEW

High, wide handlebars

Dummy tank houses electrics

Twin front disc brakes

Real fuel tank is under seat

Shaft final drive

THE GOLDWING'S chassis was tubular steel with a dummy fuel tank containing a kickstart, some electrics, and storage space. The real fuel tank was under the seat. Many Goldwings were modified with panniers and fairing, which prompted Honda to later supply them as standard.

HONDA ELSINORE

Capacity 247cc • Power output 40bhp • Weight 102kg (224lb) • Top speed not known

THE ELSINORE WAS BUILT in a bid for greater success in American motocross when Honda went against its "four stroke only" policy. Its equipment included upside-down, remote-reservoir rear dampers and electronic ignition. This 1980 model was the first Honda motorcycle built in America.

HONDA EMPLOYEE Soichiro Miyakoshi taught himself everything about two-stroke technology and the air-cooled CR250 Elsinore was the result. Pictured here is a 1980 model, with leading axle, air-assisted front forks, and box-section swing arm.

Aluminium wheels with magnesium front and rear brake hubs

Radial fins help cool the engine

46-cm (18-in) rear wheel has massive (5-in) section rear tyre

Plastic fuel tank reduces weight

BACK VIEW

HONDA CBX1000

Capacity 1047cc • Power output 105bhp @ 9,000rpm • Weight 252kg (556lb) • Top speed 217km/h (135mph)

JAPAN

IN **1968 HONDA CHANGED THE FACE** of motorcycling with the CB750 (see pp.88–89). A decade later, it astounded the world once again with an air-cooled, across-the-frame six. The CBX1000's engine was suspended from a tubular spine frame and canted forward 30° to aid cooling. It had four valves per cylinder and six carburettors. This is a 1980 model; monoshock rear suspension, a full fairing, and more sober styling came later.

EARLY IMPRESSIONS of the awesome six-cylinder stunned journalists. A few were said to have arrived back at the pits at the CBX launch pale, after experiencing high-speed weaves. Handling improved later, when Honda upgraded the swingarm.

Oil cooler

24-valve cylinder head

Carburettors set in a curve to make room for the rider

Six-cylinder, d.o.h.c., four-stroke engine

Ventilated, twin, front disc brakes

FRONT VIEW

HONDA CB900 CUSTOM

Capacity 901cc • Power output 93bhp @ 9,000rpm
Weight 241kg (532lb) • Top speed 213km/h (132mph)

JAPAN

HONDA **REPLACED ITS AGEING S.O.H.C. 750 FOUR** (see p.88) with new 748cc and 901cc 16-valve d.o.h.c. machines, which appeared in 1978. These were produced in a variety of styles, including the sporting F models and custom versions like the 1982 CB900C pictured here. While most models had chain drive, this one uses a shaft. Production of air-cooled 16-valve fours, which evolved from these machines, continues today despite Honda's mid-1980s obsession with the V4 engine.

16-valve, d.o.h.c. motor with four Keihin CV-type carburettors

Twin front disc brakes

Conventional, tubular-steel chassis

HONDA RS500R

Capacity 499cc • Power output 130bhp @ 11,500rpm
Weight 122kg (270lb) • Top speed 282km/h (175mph)

JAPAN

HONDA **HAD FOUND IN THE 1970s** that to stay competitive on the track it had to turn to two-stroke technology. The firm's first two-stroke racer was the NS500 – not only a two-stroke but also a 90° V3. The central cylinders faced forward while the two outer cylinders were more vertical. With its alloy frame and lightweight racing Comstar wheels, the RS500 won the 1983 500cc World Championship. This RS500 was one of a limited number of NS500 replicas sold to non-factory riders in 1983.

Alloy frame

One exhaust exits by the rider's right foot, the other two at the rear of the seat hump

Box-section swingarm and monoshock suspension

HONDA HONDA CX650 TURBO

Capacity 673cc • Power output 100bhp @ 8,000rpm
Weight 235kg (518lb) • Top speed 221km/h (137mph)

JAPAN

Honda started a short craze for turbocharging when it built the CX500 Turbo in 1981. It was based on the humble o.h.v. shaft-drive V-twin CX500. Capacity was increased from 496cc to 673cc in 1983 to create the equally short-lived CX650 Turbo. Both models had electronically controlled fuel injection, a single-shock rear suspension system, and an aerodynamic fairing. Other Japanese manufacturers built turbocharged bikes but based on four-cylinder engines. This is a 1983 model.

Fuel injectors

Anti-dive front forks

O.h.v., transverse twin motor with turbocharger

HONDA CR125

Capacity 125cc • Power output 36bhp @ 11,500rpm
Weight 88kg (193lb) • Top speed not known

JAPAN

Ironically for a company that refused to build two-strokes until the 1970s, by the late 1980s Honda offered a comprehensive line-up of two-stroke motocrossers from 80cc to 500cc. In the hands of such riders as Dave Thorpe, CRs enjoyed many World Motocross Championship race successes. Pictured here is a 1988 CR125. The water-cooled motor featured Honda's ATAC (Auto-control Torque Amplification Chamber) power valve system, and reed valve induction to improve power delivery. It also had a disc rear brake, where earlier models had a drum.

Single Keihin carburettor

Plastic fuel tank

Marginally larger engine than the 1986 model gives the 1988 extra power

HONDA VFR700 INTERCEPTOR

Capacity 700cc • Power output 99bhp @ 10,000rpm Weight 209kg (460lb) • Top speed 245km/h (152mph)

JAPAN

In 1982 Honda introduced the first of a new line of V4 machines that eventually ranged from 400cc to 1000cc in 1982. Early versions proved unreliable, but the problems had been eliminated by 1987 when this VFR700 model appeared. Although excellent, the V4 never threatened the dominance of the conventional four-cylinder layout.

THE VFR700 INTERCEPTOR was on several 700cc versions of Japanese 750s produced in the late 1980s to side-step U.S. import restrictions on bikes over 700cc. In other markets it was sold as the VFR750 with full 750 capacity.

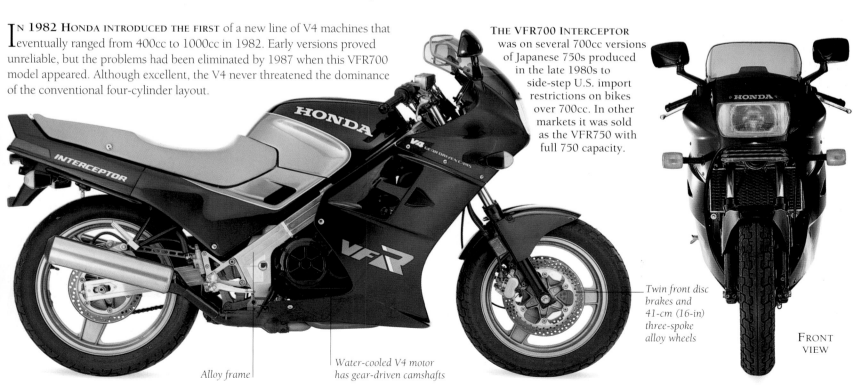

Alloy frame

Water-cooled V4 motor has gear-driven camshafts

Twin front disc brakes and 41-cm (16-in) three-spoke alloy wheels

FRONT VIEW

HONDA GOLDWING GL1500

Capacity 1520cc • Power output 100bhp @ 5,200rpm • Weight 368kg (811lb) • Top speed 187km/h (116mph)

JAPAN

Honda's water-cooled, flat-six – THE GL1500 – is the largest-capacity production bike currently on the market. Launched in 1988, this flagship of Honda's grand tourers was built in Ohio, U.S.A. To some, this large, luxurious, well-equipped motorcycle is the ultimate touring machine. Others just do not understand the appeal of such a large, overweight "armchair on wheels".

BACK VIEW

Cruise control

Adjustable windscreen

Storage pockets

Radio/cassette is mounted on dummy fuel tank

Linked braking systems means only foot control is needed to operate front and rear brakes

Removable panniers for back wheel access

Water-cooled, flat-six engine replaced earlier 1200cc four-cylinder model

THE GL1500 has all the ordinary features one would expect from a tourer as well as a host of other accessories: a digital clock, a radio frequency indicator, and more switches on the handlebars for the radio/cassette than for riding the bike.

HONDA RS125

Capacity 124cc • Power output 36bhp @ 12,000rpm • Weight 70kg (154lb) • Top speed not known

JAPAN

THE HONDA RS125 became the standard machine for the 125cc racing class at national and international level during the late 1980s and into the 1990s. It used a lightweight alloy, twin-spar chassis and a single-cylinder, water-cooled, reed-valve, two-stroke engine. The model has been continually updated since Honda won the 125cc manufacturers' World Championship in 1989. Many other titles followed. Ridden by the German Dirk Raudies, the model shown here won the 1993 World Championship.

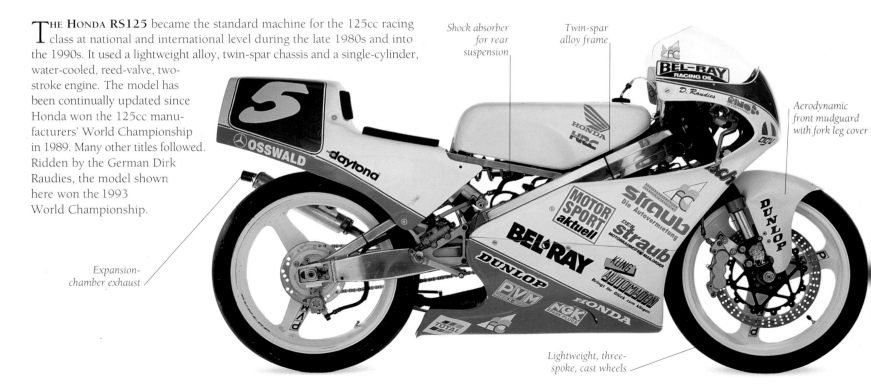

Shock absorber for rear suspension

Twin-spar alloy frame

Aerodynamic front mudguard with fork leg cover

Expansion-chamber exhaust

Lightweight, three-spoke, cast wheels

HONDA CBR600F

Honda took the middleweight field by storm in 1987 with the CBR600F. With its revolutionary bodywork and over 225km/h (140mph) motor, it soon ousted Kawasaki's GPZ600 from the top of the middleweight sales charts. Since then, the CBR600 has been an almost constant best seller in its class. The design was completely revised in 1991 to keep it ahead of the competition. Pictured here is a 1993 model.

There have been numerous changes to the CBR600's specification since the original 83bhp, H model. Engine changes in J and K models saw power output upped to 93bhp. In 1991 power increased to 99bhp and the chassis was redesigned with a smaller frame and other minor refinements.

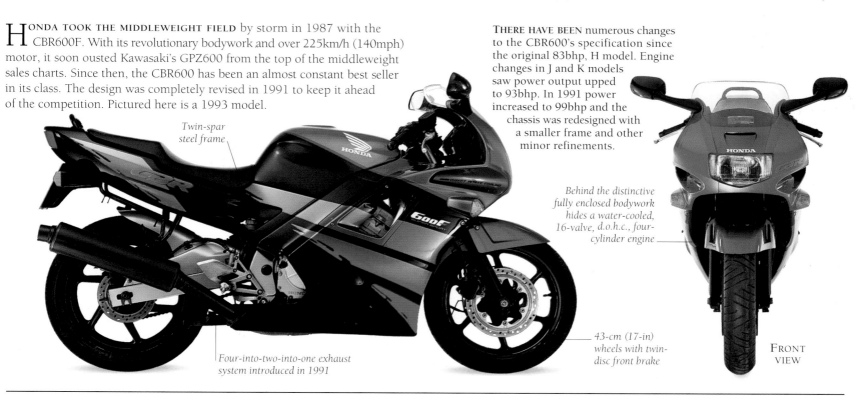

Twin-spar steel frame

Behind the distinctive fully enclosed bodywork hides a water-cooled, 16-valve, d.o.h.c., four-cylinder engine

Four-into-two-into-one exhaust system introduced in 1991

43-cm (17-in) wheels with twin-disc front brake

FRONT VIEW

HONDA RC45

The RC45 is Honda's ultimate V4 production bike. Built to comply with World Superbike racing regulations, the 1994 machine shown here replaced the earlier RC30. Much of the technology for the new machine was developed on the factory's RVF racers. The RC45 had an all-new engine with the gear drive for the camshafts taken from the end of the crank. Electronic fuel injection replaced the RC30's carburettors. Honda's optional race kit increased power to 150bhp but doubled the bike's price.

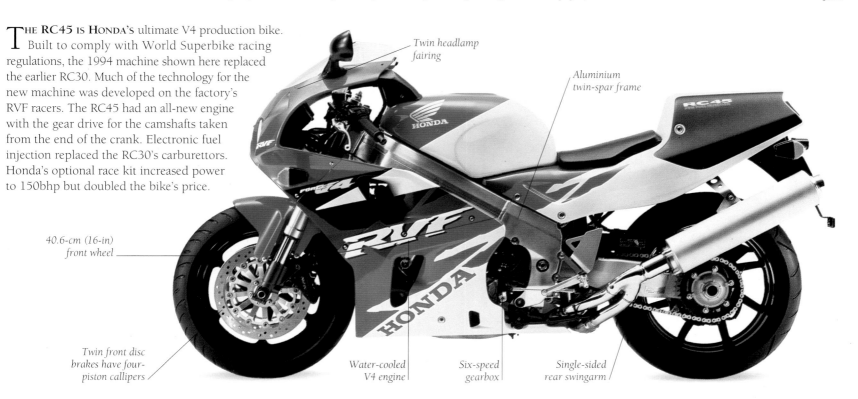

Twin headlamp fairing

Aluminium twin-spar frame

40.6-cm (16-in) front wheel

Twin front disc brakes have four-piston callipers

Water-cooled V4 engine

Six-speed gearbox

Single-sided rear swingarm

HOREX

Capacity 596cc • Power output 10bhp @ 3,500rpm • Weight 130kg (286lb) • Top speed 100km/h (62mph) GERMANY

THE KLEEMAN FAMILY had diverse business interests, including glassware manufacture under the Rex trademark and clip-on engines for bicycles under the Columbus name. They began to make complete motorcycles at Bad Homburg in 1923. The name Horex is an amalgamation of the first two letters of Homburg with the Rex name. The first Horex motorcycles were 248cc o.h.v. singles, but they soon increased in capacity. The 1926 machine illustrated here uses a 596cc side-valve Columbus engine.

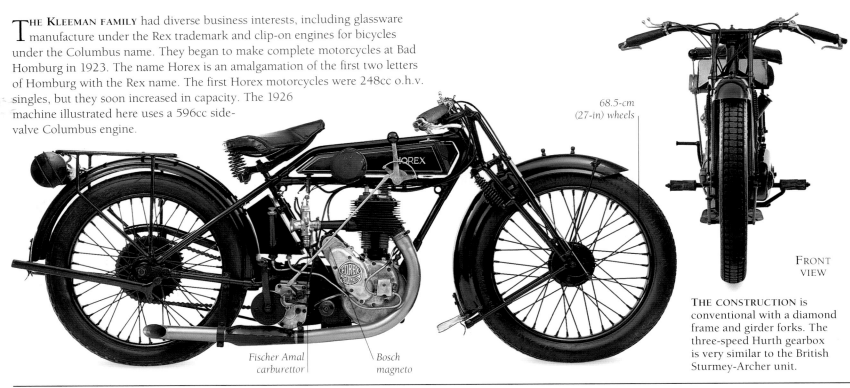

68.5-cm (27-in) wheels

FRONT VIEW

THE CONSTRUCTION is conventional with a diamond frame and girder forks. The three-speed Hurth gearbox is very similar to the British Sturmey-Archer unit.

Fischer Amal carburettor

Bosch magneto

HOREX IMPERATOR

Capacity 398cc • Power output 24bhp @ 5,650rpm • Weight 175kg (386lb) • Top speed 135km/h (84mph) GERMANY

PRODUCTION OF THE NEW IMPERATOR model began in 1954, although twin-cylinder prototypes and racing machines had been produced earlier. The new machine's o.h.c. engine was mounted in a twin-loop cradle frame with swingarm rear suspension. This 1955 model has Schnell front forks; these were once optional but became standard in 1955. But the German market was in steep decline and Horex production ended in 1957.

Single 24-mm (1-in) Bing carburettor

Fully enclosed final-drive chain

Leading-link forks; conventional telescopic units were available in 1954

Unit-construction, four-speed gearbox

HRD

Capacity 344cc • Power output 20bhp (estimated) • Weight 300lb (136kg) (estimated) • Top speed 85mph (137km/h) (estimated)

UNITED KINGDOM

HOWARD DAVIES' FIRST CLAIM TO FAME was as the only person to win the 500cc Senior TT on a 350cc machine, a feat he achieved on an AJS in 1921. His second claim to fame was as one of the few people to have won a TT race on a machine of his own design and manufacture when, on an HRD, he won the 1925 Senior race, having already repeated his 1921 performance of second in the Junior race. The company went into liquidation in 1927, but not before Freddie Dixon gave it another Junior TT victory.

HRD MOTORCYCLES used JAP engines in its own frames, equipped with Druid forks and a Burman three-speed gearbox.

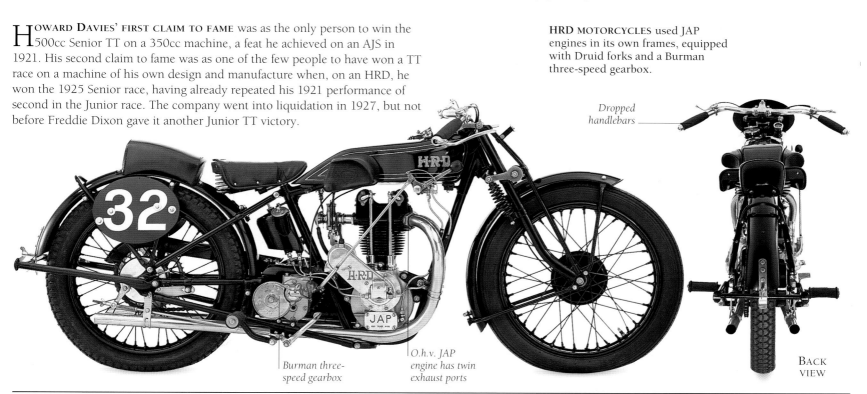

Dropped handlebars

Burman three-speed gearbox

O.h.v. JAP engine has twin exhaust ports

BACK VIEW

HUMBER TRICYCLE

Capacity 239cc • Power output 1bhp (estimated) • Weight 300lb (136kg) • Top speed 15mph (24km/h)

UNITED KINGDOM

HUMBER WAS ONE OF MANY COMPANIES that became involved with H. J. Lawson and his British Motor Syndicate and, until a factory fire caused a change of plan, was scheduled to produce under licence a version of the Léon-Bolée Tricar. Instead, it went on to produce motorized tricycles and then motorcycles. The tricycle shown here is an 1898 model and has a DeDion engine.

IGNITION WAS BY BATTERY and trembler coil while the induction was via a surface carburettor – literally just a fuel container in which the air inlet to the engine wafted over the surface of the fuel. These were common until around 1900 and necessitated a special highly volatile fuel.

Drive gears

Humber-designed frame

FRONT VIEW

DeDion axle assembly

HUSQVARNA V-TWIN RACER

Capacity 498cc • Power output 44bhp @ 6,800rpm • Weight 127kg (280lb) • Top speed 190km/h (118mph)

SWEDEN

Iɴᴛʀᴏᴅᴜᴄᴇᴅ ɪɴ **1932** and steadily developed until the company withdrew from racing after the 1935 season (the year of the model shown), the Husqvarna V-twin never quite made the grade, although it showed the vulnerability of the highly developed single-cylinder opposition to the challenge of a simple twin. High spots during that time were three consecutive victories in the Swedish Grand Prix and Stanley Woods' record lap in the 1934 Senior TT before he ran out of petrol. Extensive use of light alloys kept the weight low, but despite being very fast, the handling of the machine was always something of a handicap.

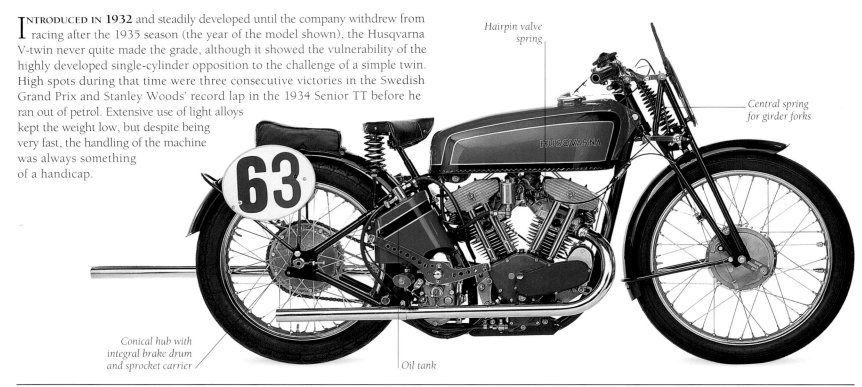

Hairpin valve spring

Central spring for girder forks

Conical hub with integral brake drum and sprocket carrier

Oil tank

HUSQVARNA 250

Capacity 245cc • Power output 22bhp @ 6,000rpm • Weight 94kg (208lb) • Top speed depends on gearing

SWEDEN

Dᴇᴠᴇʟᴏᴘᴇᴅ ꜰʀᴏᴍ ᴀ ᴍɪᴅ-**1950s** 175cc three-speed road model, by 1963 the Husqvarna was the best 250cc motocross machine available, and for a while Torsten Hallman and his "Huskie" were virtually unbeatable in 250cc World Championship events. The engine was a full 250, in-unit with a four-speed gearbox, and combined power with reliability. This is a 1963 model.

Tʜᴇ ᴇɴɢɪɴᴇ ɪs ᴜsᴇᴅ as a stressed member in the simple tubular frame. A single large diameter tube connects the headstock to the swingarm pivot.

Handlebar brace

Heat shield on high-level exhaust pipe

Light alloy, conical brake hubs

Air filter

Fʀᴏɴᴛ ᴠɪᴇᴡ

Norton forks were standard but some owners preferred to use Italian Cerianis

HUSQVARNA 390WR

Capacity 384cc • Power output not known • Weight 113kg (250lb) (estimated) • Top speed depends on gearing

CONTINUED DEVELOPMENT OF HUSQVARNA'S two-stroke off-road machines resulted in bikes such as this 1979 390WR model. The 390 was produced in three versions for motocross, enduro, and desert racing. All were based around the same air-cooled, single-cylinder, two-stroke engine and steel tubular frame. The WR version was equipped with lights to meet the regulations for enduro competitions. Bikes like this were very popular in the large U.S. market for off-road machines.

Fitted with larger fuel tank, lights, and a stand for enduro events

Spark arresting silencer

Gold anodized wheel rims

Radially finned cylinder head

Six-speed engine/ gearbox unit

HUSQVARNA TC610

Capacity 577cc • Power output 50bhp (estimated) • Weight 117kg (258lb) • Top speed depends on gearing

RENEWED INTEREST in the four-stroke single for off-road competition use prompted Husqvarna to develop new machines. This 1992 TC610 uses a typically high-tech engine that features d.o.h.c., four valves, and water cooling. Power is transmitted via a six-speed gearbox. A 349cc version of the machine is also produced.

THE SWEDISH HUSQVARNA COMPANY sold its motorcycle division to the Italian Cagiva group in 1986. All Husqvarna motorcycles are now made in Italy.

Quick action throttle

Tubular steel cradle frame

Upside-down telescopic forks

Alloy swingarm with linkage to shock absorber

BACK VIEW

IFA BK350

Capacity 343cc • Power output 15bhp @ 5,000rpm • Weight 142kg (313lb) • Top speed 109km/h (68mph)

THE POST-WAR PARTITION OF GERMANY left the former DKW works in the zone occupied by the Russians, later to become the German Democratic Republic (East Germany). The state took control of all industry, and the Zschopau factory continued to produce the RT125 DKW, now rebadged as an IFA. The first new model from IFA appeared in 1952 and had very advanced features considering the precarious state of the national economy. Twin carburettors and ignition coils were housed in an enclosure above the engine. Production continued until 1959. The model shown here is from 1956.

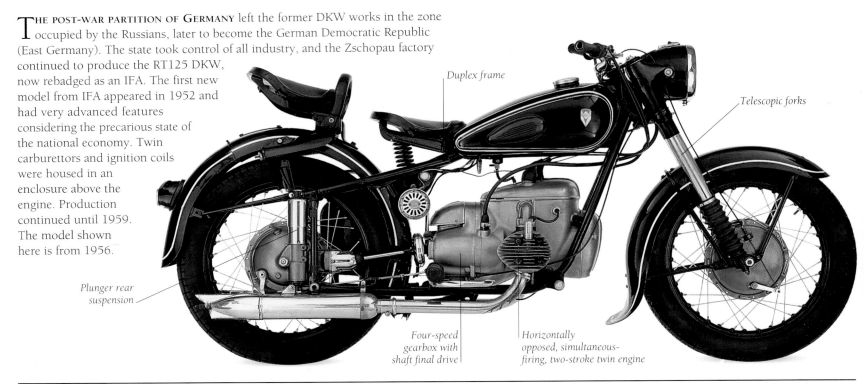

Duplex frame

Telescopic forks

Plunger rear suspension

Four-speed gearbox with shaft final drive

Horizontally opposed, simultaneous-firing, two-stroke twin engine

IMME R100

Capacity 99cc • Power output 4bhp @ 5,800rpm • Weight not known • Top speed not known

BRAINCHILD OF NORBERT RIEDEL, the Imme (so named because it was made in Immenstadt) was unconventional in almost every respect. The combined engine and gearbox was in the form of a "power egg" and mounted on a forward extension of the rear suspension arm, which extended back beyond the rear wheel. It also formed the exhaust system. This arm was pivoted behind the engine to the lower end of the curved backbone-frame tube. This bike dates from 1948.

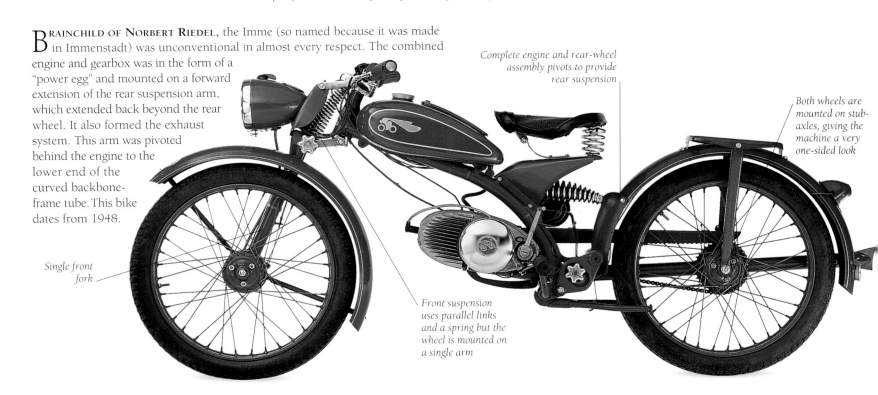

Complete engine and rear-wheel assembly pivots to provide rear suspension

Both wheels are mounted on stub-axles, giving the machine a very one-sided look

Single front fork

Front suspension uses parallel links and a spring but the wheel is mounted on a single arm

INDIAN SINGLE

Capacity 17.59cu.in. (288cc) • *Power output 2hp* • *Weight 115lb (52kg)* • *Top speed 30mph (48km/h)*

INDIAN WAS FOUNDED by George Hendee and Oscar Hedstrom in Springfield, Massachusetts in 1901 to make what they called "motocycles". The early production models established the firm's reputation for quality. The 1904 2hp single shown here is typical of Indians made between 1901 and 1908. Designed by Hedstrom, the 288cc a.i.v. engine formed the saddle downtube of the bicycle-style diamond frame. The exhaust valve was mechanically operated while the automatic inlet valve was actuated by suction. Ignition was total

loss with three rechargeable two-volt dry-cell batteries, housed on a cylindrical case on the front frame downtube, which powered the six-volt ignition coil for 800–2,000 miles (1,288–3,220km) depending on conditions. The engine speed was varied by advancing or retarding the ignition timing with an avant-garde twistgrip control on the right handlebar. This control, consisting of rods and universal joints, often fell apart when the handlebars were turned, thereby jamming the steering; it did not affect the Indian's popularity.

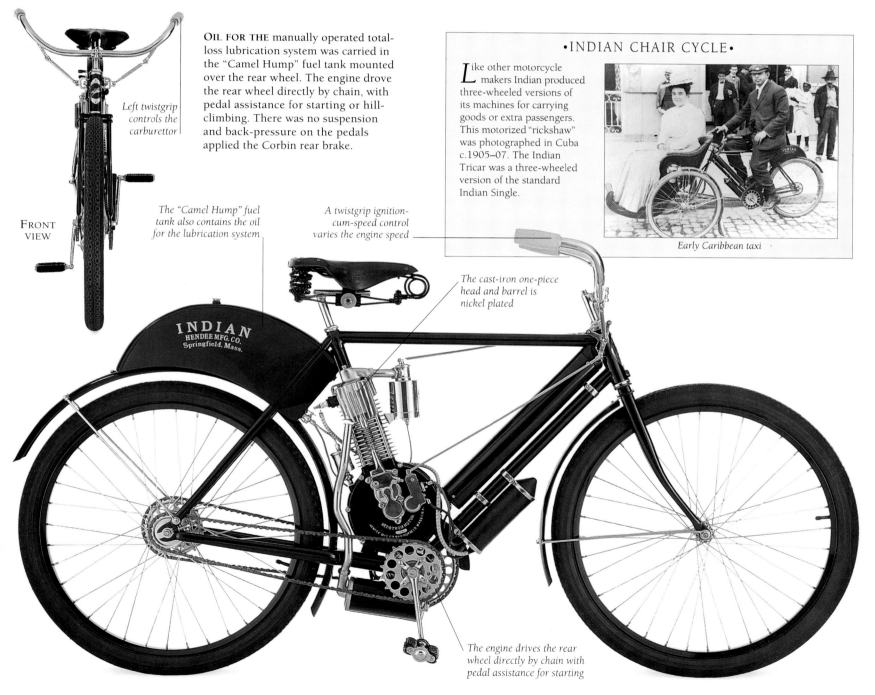

Left twistgrip controls the carburettor

OIL FOR THE manually operated total-loss lubrication system was carried in the "Camel Hump" fuel tank mounted over the rear wheel. The engine drove the rear wheel directly by chain, with pedal assistance for starting or hill-climbing. There was no suspension and back-pressure on the pedals applied the Corbin rear brake.

FRONT VIEW

The "Camel Hump" fuel tank also contains the oil for the lubrication system

A twistgrip ignition-cum-speed control varies the engine speed

•INDIAN CHAIR CYCLE•

*L*ike other motorcycle makers Indian produced three-wheeled versions of its machines for carrying goods or extra passengers. This motorized "rickshaw" was photographed in Cuba c.1905–07. The Indian Tricar was a three-wheeled version of the standard Indian Single.

Early Caribbean taxi

The cast-iron one-piece head and barrel is nickel plated

INDIAN
HENDEE MFG. CO.
Springfield, Mass.

The engine drives the rear wheel directly by chain with pedal assistance for starting

INDIAN 1912 V-TWIN

Capacity 61cu. in. (1000cc) • Power output 7hp • Weight 380lb (172kg) • Top speed 55mph (89km/h)

U.S.A.

ONE OF THE FIRST **A**MERICAN MANUFACTURERS to adopt the V-twin layout, Indian catalogued its first in 1907. Put simply, the design used two of the single's cylinders mounted at 42° on a common crankcase. Mechanical operation of the inlet valves became an option a year later; a single two-lobe camshaft operated the pushrods by means of bellcrank lifters. In 1909 loop frames replaced the bicycle-style structures used earlier. This 1912 model follows the pattern of the 1909 machine, though with minor changes.

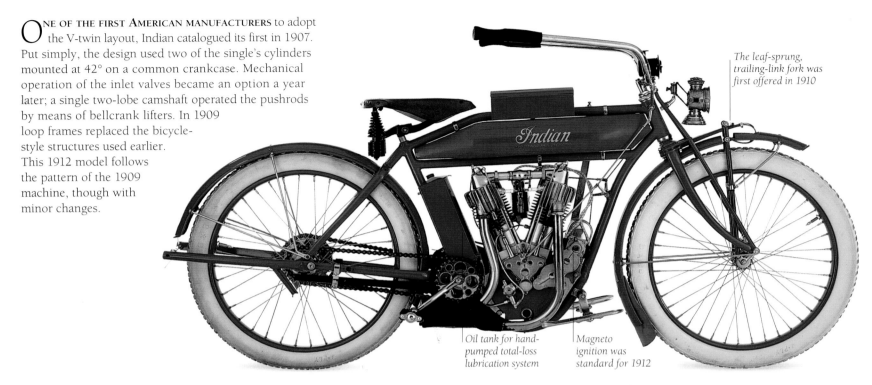

The leaf-sprung, trailing-link fork was first offered in 1910

Oil tank for hand-pumped total-loss lubrication system

Magneto ignition was standard for 1912

INDIAN 1913 SINGLE

Capacity 30cu. in. (492cc) • Power output 4hp • Weight 360lb (163kg) • Top speed 45mph (72km/h)

U.S.A.

INDIAN INTRODUCED the cradle spring frame in 1913, beating the rest of the world by several decades. The frame top tube was lowered while a swingarm pivoted from the saddle downtube. The rigid frame remained an option. Over 90 per cent of Indian production in 1913 focused on V-Twins, making the 1913 single rare.

AS WITH THE **V**-TWIN engine, mechanical inlet valve operation was optional but magneto ignition had replaced the total-loss coil system. Some models used a rotating valve carburettor.

Tank for acetylene lighting system

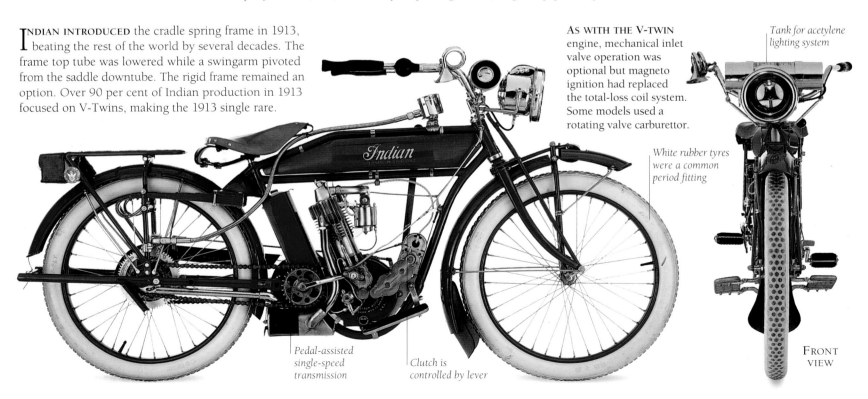

White rubber tyres were a common period fitting

Pedal-assisted single-speed transmission

Clutch is controlled by lever

F RONT
VIEW

INDIAN 1914 V-TWIN

Capacity 61cu. in. (1000cc) • Power output 7bhp • Weight 400lb (181kg) • Top speed 55mph (89km/h)

U.S.A.

THE **1914 1000CC V-TWIN** used the cradle spring frame introduced the previous year with the standard leaf-sprung front forks. There was an electric-start version known as the Hendee Special but only a handful were built as battery technology was not sufficiently developed to make the system reliable. The machine here is equipped with the two-speed gearbox driven through a dry multi-plate clutch. The i.o.e V-twins were superseded by new side-valve engines in 1916.

Electric horn, pillion seat, and speedometer were optional extras

Complex rod linkages were soon to be replaced by cables

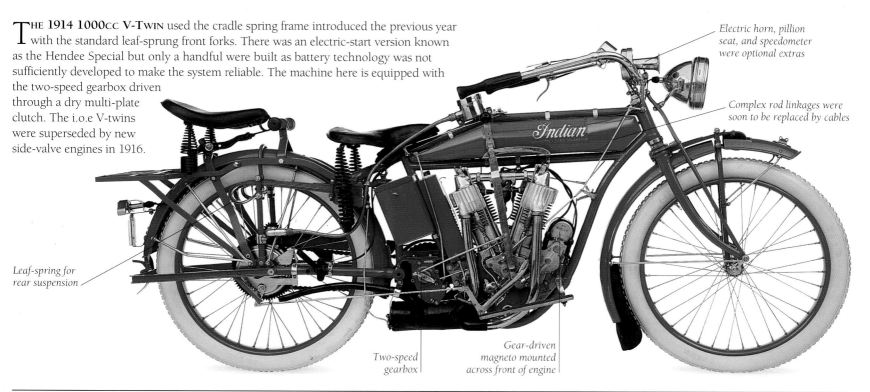

Leaf-spring for rear suspension

Two-speed gearbox

Gear-driven magneto mounted across front of engine

INDIAN SV PRINCE

Capacity 21cu. in. (350cc) • Power output 6hp • Weight 272lb (123kg) • Top speed 60mph (97km/h) (estimated)

U.S.A.

THE **SINGLE-CYLINDER PRINCE** appeared in 1925 and was designed by Charles Franklin, better known for the Scout and Chief models. The Prince uses a diamond frame, with a wedge-shaped fuel tank and a three-speed gearbox built in-unit with the engine. The design was revised in 1926 when a separate gearbox replaced unit construction and a Scout-style fuel tank was used. These changes could not make the bike a success. It was dropped from the range in 1928, when the machine shown here was produced.

INTENDED AS A RIVAL to Harley-Davidson's Peashooters (see p.70), the side-valve Prince was not very successful. Indian and American buyers were more interested in V-twins.

British-style diamond frame

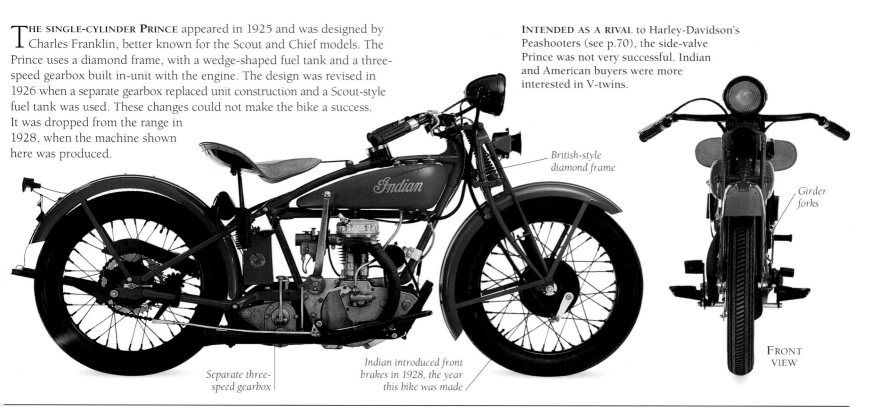

Girder forks

Separate three-speed gearbox

Indian introduced front brakes in 1928, the year this bike was made

FRONT VIEW

INDIAN SCOUT

Capacity 45cu. in. (750cc) • Power output 18bhp • Weight 370lb (168kg) • Top speed 100mph (161km/h)

U.S.A.

THE FIRST OF INDIAN'S FAMOUS SCOUT MODELS appeared in 1920. More popular than its larger sibling, the Chief (see p.106), the Scout was the work of Indian's Irish-born designer Charles B. Franklin. The engine layout followed Indian's traditional 42°, V-twin configuration and, like the larger Powerplus, featured side-valves. The three-speed gearbox was bolted to the back of the engine and driven by an apparently indestructible, if rather noisy, helical-gear primary drive that ran in a cast-aluminium oil bath case. Harley-Davidson afficionados claimed that police models needed no sirens as the sound was built in. A train of gears on the right side of the engine drove two camshafts and the forward-mounted magneto. The generator, clamped to the saddle downtube, is gear- and belt-driven from the clutch. Capacity of the original models was 37cu. in. (606cc). The engine was mounted in a twin-loop cradle frame that

was fitted with Indian's traditional leaf-sprung fork. The design of the Scout engine was such a success that it was scaled up in 1922 to create the Chief. When Excelsior created the 45cu. in. class with the introduction of its Super X model in 1925 (see p.59), Indian responded with a bored and stroked 45cu. in. version of the Scout, introduced alongside the original model in 1927. In 1928, the frame was revised with a longer wheelbase and lower seat height. Front brakes were also introduced on the Indian range that year. The new model was christened the Model 101 Scout. It is widely regarded as the best motorcycle that Indian ever made. The machine shown here is a 1930 model. Sadly, it was withdrawn from the range the following year and replaced by a machine that used the heavier and more cumbersome Chief chassis. The decline of Indian had begun.

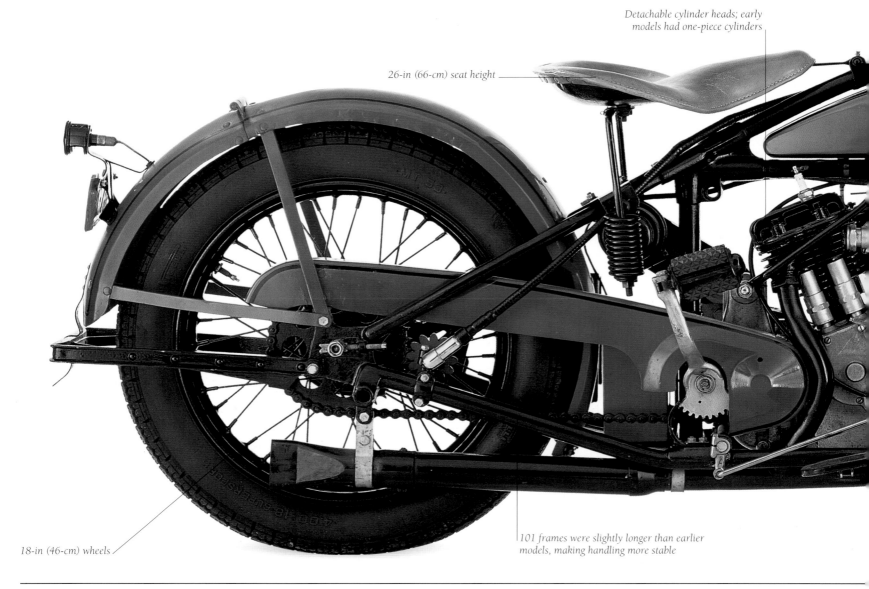

Detachable cylinder heads; early models had one-piece cylinders

26-in (66-cm) seat height

18-in (46-cm) wheels

101 frames were slightly longer than earlier models, making handling more stable

WEIGHING IN AT JUST 370lb (168kg), the stock Model 101 was capable of 75mph (121km/h) and over 100mph (161km/h) with race cams and polished inlet and exhaust ports. Although Scouts were offered with the full complement of optional extras for touring, with their low centre of gravity and excellent handling they were popular with racers, hill climbers, and trick riders.

English-style bars could be specified as an alternative to these conventional pattern handlebars

Sprung leather saddle

BACK VIEW

•EARLY SCOUTS•

Contemporary advertisement for the new Indian Scout

Power, swiftness, stamina, economy claimed the adverts for the 45cu. in. (750cc) Scout. In a rare moment of motorcycle advertising honesty, they spoke the truth. The Scout was one of America's greatest motorcycles. Its early reputation for performance and reliability was enhanced in 1920 when a 37cu. in. (606cc) model set a 24-hour record by covering 1,114 miles (1,793km) over a closed-road course in Australia.

Kickstart pedal

Speedometer mounted on petrol tank

FRONT VIEW

Painted wheel rims

42°, 73 x 89-mm side-valve engine

Front brakes appeared from 1928

INDIAN 402

Capacity 77.21cu. in. (1265cc) • Power output 30bhp
Weight 385lb (175kg) • Top speed 75mph (121km/h)

U.S.A.

INDIAN PURCHASED THE DESIGN and manufacturing rights for the Ace four-cylinder motorcycle (see p.11) in 1927 and produced the Indian Ace based on its original design. It was revised in 1928 by designer Arthur Lemon to create the 401. By the time the 402 model was introduced the following year, the machine was more Indian than Ace. It featured a stronger twin downtube frame and Indian's traditional leaf-sprung forks. The engine now had a five-bearing crankshaft in place of the weaker three-bearing crank on the Ace engine. The 1930 model is shown here.

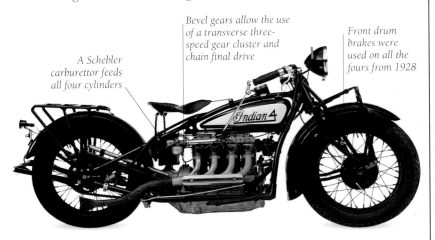

Bevel gears allow the use of a transverse three-speed gear cluster and chain final drive

Front drum brakes were used on all the fours from 1928

A Schebler carburettor feeds all four cylinders

INDIAN CHIEF

Capacity 74 cu. in. (1213cc) • Power output 40bhp
Weight 445lb (202kg) • Top speed 105mph (169km/h)

U.S.A.

THE INDIAN CHIEF OF 1934 traced its origins back to the first Chief, which appeared in 1922. The longstroke 82.5 x 112.5-mm side-valve engine followed Scout lines (see p.104) but generated 40bhp, which pushed the heavy machine up to 85mph (137km/h). Fitted with the optional high performance B motor with racing cams, polished ports, and precision timing, top speed was over 105mph (169km/h). Coil ignition was standard although the magneto was an option.

29-in (74-cm) seat height with optional "Buddy Seat"

Iron cylinder barrels

INDIAN 440

Capacity 77.21cu. in. (1265cc) • Power output 40bhp • Weight 568lb (258kg) • Top speed 90mph (145km/h)

U.S.A.

INDIAN'S FOUR-CYLINDER MACHINES continued to evolve during the 1930s, but were expensive to produce and never really sold in large numbers. Some observers credit Indian's obsession with the layout as contributing to its decline. After an experiment with an exhaust-over-inlet-valve cylinder head in 1936 and 1937, the company reverted to the traditional layout in 1938. For 1940 the fours got Indian's famous skirted mudguards and plunger rear suspension. Production continued until 1942.

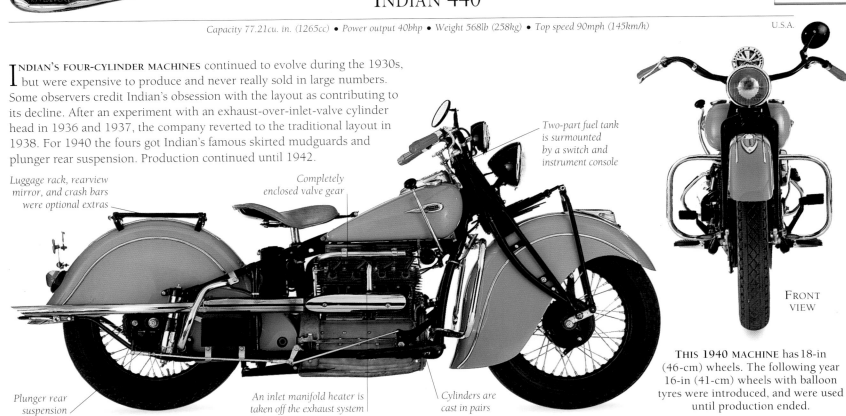

Luggage rack, rearview mirror, and crash bars were optional extras

Completely enclosed valve gear

Two-part fuel tank is surmounted by a switch and instrument console

Plunger rear suspension

An inlet manifold heater is taken off the exhaust system

Cylinders are cast in pairs

FRONT VIEW

THIS 1940 MACHINE has 18-in (46-cm) wheels. The following year 16-in (41-cm) wheels with balloon tyres were introduced, and were used until production ended.

INDIAN
JUNIOR SCOUT

Capacity 30.5cu. in. (500cc) • Power output 15bhp (estimated)   U.S.A.
Weight 340lb (154kg) (estimated) • Top speed 70mph (113km/h) (estimated)

A NEW SMALL-CAPACITY V-TWIN was introduced into the Indian range in 1932. The machine was the cheapest twin on the U.S. market at the time of the Depression. Nicknamed the "Thirty-fifty" to reflect its cylinder capacity, it was sold as a Pony Scout but later became known as the Junior Scout. The new machine had a scaled-down V-twin engine in the frame and the running gear of the single-cylinder Prince. Produced until 1941, the model here dates from 1940.

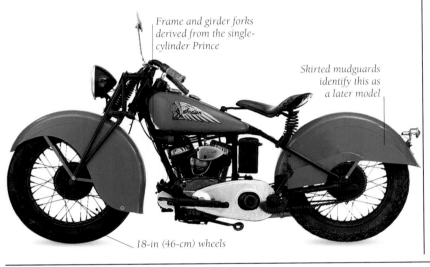

Frame and girder forks derived from the single-cylinder Prince

Skirted mudguards identify this as a later model

18-in (46-cm) wheels

INDIAN
SPORTS SCOUT

Capacity 45.44cu. in. (745cc) • Power output 38bhp   U.S.A.
Weight 380lb (172kg) • Top speed 105mph (169km/h)

INTENDED FOR THE SPORTING MARKET, many machines were converted into racers for use in the production-based Class C. Indian offered a range of tuning parts and racing accessories to the budding private racer. They were equipped with Daytona engines, so named after Ed Kretz's spectacular Daytona 200 win in 1937. The 73 x 89-mm side-valve engine had racing camshafts, high compression pistons, and polished ports generating 38bhp. Coil and distributor ignition was standard.

Oval track racers were not equipped with brakes

Cylinder finning was improved for this 1940 model

Triplex-chain primary drive

INDIAN CHIEF ROADMASTER

Capacity 80cu. in. (1311cc) • Power output 50bhp @ 4,800rpm • Weight 570lb (259kg) • Top speed 85mph (137km/h)   U.S.A.

INDIAN'S FLAGSHIP MODEL underwent various changes in 1950 (the year of the model shown here), the most obvious of which was the use of hydraulically damped telescopic front forks instead of the girders that had replaced the old leaf-spring design after World War II. The 74cu. in. (1213cc) side-valve engine was enlarged to 80cu. in. (1311cc) by increasing the stroke to a massive 4⅞in (122mm).

Post-war models had a distinctive "Indian Head" running light on the mudguard

GENERATING 50BHP at a lazy 4,800rpm, the engine drove a standard three-speed handshift gearbox by triplex chain through a wet, multi-plate clutch. The handshift moved to the left and the throttle to the right, bringing Indian into line with common practice after 49 years.

Models with twin rearview mirrors, a windscreen, and panniers were known as "Full Dressers"

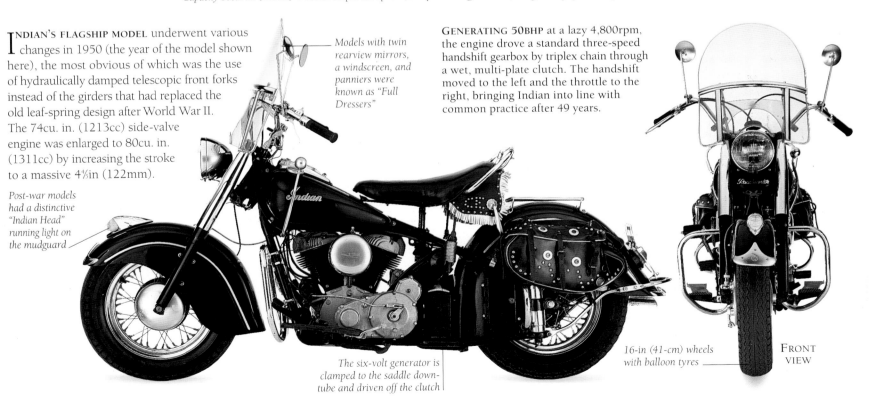

The six-volt generator is clamped to the saddle down-tube and driven off the clutch

16-in (41-cm) wheels with balloon tyres

FRONT VIEW

INDIAN 841

Capacity 45cu. in. (737cc) • Power output 25bhp
Weight not known • Top speed not known

U.S.A.

DEVELOPED SPECIFICALLY FOR MILITARY USE, the 841 was a complete departure from Indian design tradition and was remarkable for various features, including its transverse V-twin layout, shaft drive, and the fact that it was Indian's first footshift model. The 45cu. in. (737cc) side-valve engine employed a lot of Sport Scout internals, which gave bore and stroke dimensions of 73 x 89mm. The 841 was supplied with the usual military accessories but few, if any, ever made it off the U.S. Army's testing grounds into combat service. Moto Guzzi later used the same layout to better effect. This is a 1941 model.

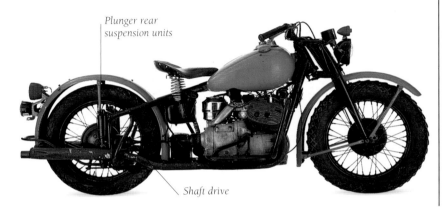

Plunger rear suspension units

Shaft drive

INDIAN 149 ARROW

Capacity 13.3cu. in. (218cc) • Power output 10bhp
Weight 245lb (111kg) • Top speed 60mph (97km/h)

U.S.A.

APPEARING IN 1949, the Arrow 149 was a single-cylinder version of the parallel-twin Scout (see below), hence the 149 designation. In profile, the engine looked virtually identical, although crankcases, cylinder, and head castings were obviously very different. The same 61 x 71mm bore and stroke were employed to give a capacity of 220cc, making this half a twin. Ignition was by magneto and carburation by Amal. Transmission was identical to the Scout, but the engine generated a mere 10bhp, which restricted the Arrow's speed. Several hundred were supplied to the army in olive-drab. The single-cylinder model was available from 1948 to 1950.

Rigid frame; plunger rear suspension was an optional extra

Amal carburettor

Front drum brake

Rear brake lever

INDIAN SUPER SCOUT 249

Capacity 26.6cu. in. (436cc) • Power output 20bhp • Weight 280lb (127kg) • Top speed 85mph (137km/h)

U.S.A.

THE SUPER SCOUT was one of a new range of vertical-engined models that were meant to herald a new dawn for the ailing Indian company in the post-war years. Designed by G. Briggs Weaver, the new models followed the style of British machines. The programme was part of an ultimately doomed attempt by industrialist Ralph B. Rogers to revive the fortunes of the Indian marque. This is a 1949 model.

LIKE THE TRIUMPH ENGINE, the inlet and exhaust camshafts were fore-and-aft of the cylinder block, but the valve pushrods were inclined in the same plane as the valves to minimize stem and guide wear. Ignition was by magneto through a distributor, while a single Amal sidefloat carburettor supplied the fuel mixture.

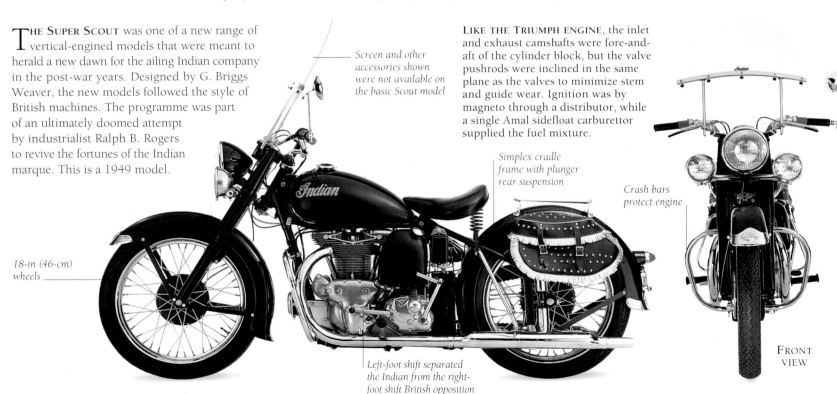

Screen and other accessories shown were not available on the basic Scout model

Simplex cradle frame with plunger rear suspension

Crash bars protect engine

18-in (46-cm) wheels

Left-foot shift separated the Indian from the right-foot shift British opposition

FRONT VIEW

INDIAN 250 WARRIOR

Capacity 500cc • Power output 25bhp • Weight 315lb (143kg) • Top speed 90mph (145km/h)

U.S.A.

INTRODUCED IN 1950, THE MODEL 250 WARRIOR was developed from the Model 249 Scout (see p.108). Increasing the engine's bore from 61mm to 64mm gave an additional 60cc, raising the output to 25 bhp. The gearbox was now clamped to the saddle downtube to eliminate the destructive effects of vertical-twin vibration. Warriors were used by several police forces in the U.S. Illustrated is a 1951 model.

A NUMBER OF MINOR CHANGES to the rolling chassis and cycle parts caused the seat height to increase to 28½in (72cm). The usual leather panniers, crashbars, and rearview mirrors were available as an option. Warriors were made from 1950 until 1953.

Western-style handlebars were standard

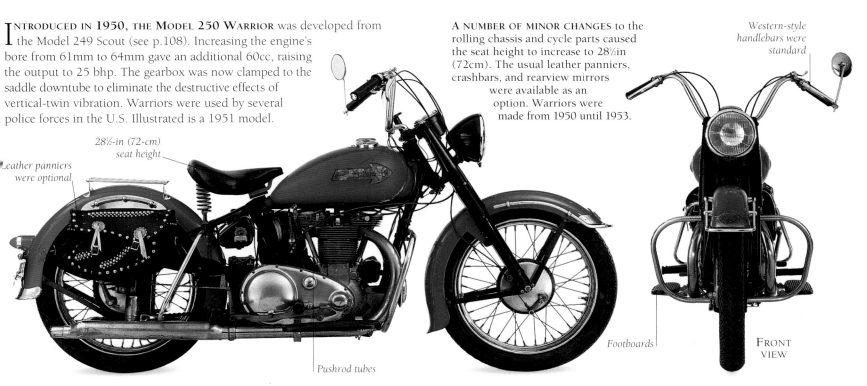

28½-in (72-cm) seat height

Leather panniers were optional

Pushrod tubes

Footboards

FRONT VIEW

INDIAN PAPOOSE

Capacity 98cc • Power output not known
Weight not known • Top speed 35mph (56km/h) (estimated)

U.S.A.

THE BROCKHOUSE CORGI was perhaps the least inspiring of the English models that carried the Indian name from the early 1950s. The Corgi was based on the Welbike, a folding motorcycle designed for paratroops during World War II that used a 98cc two-stroke Villiers engine. With revisions, the Corgi became available to the public in 1948 and, in 1954, was offered as the Papoose with Indian transfers along the fuel tank.

Telescopic front forks running on 12½-in (32-cm) wheels

The saddle mount retracted into the downtube for storage

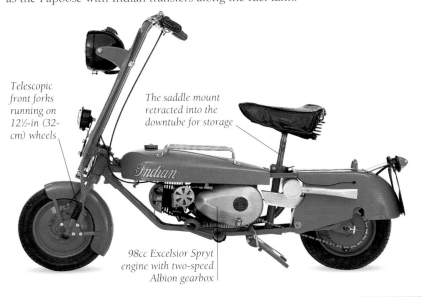

98cc Excelsior Spryt engine with two-speed Albion gearbox

INDIAN CHIEF

Capacity 700cc • Power output 43bhp @ 5,500rpm
Weight 405lb (184kg) • Top speed 106mph (171km/h)

U.S.A.

FROM 1955 UNTIL 1959, Royal Enfield singles and twins sold through Indian outlets in the U.S. were restyled and rebadged as Indians. The reintroduction in 1959 of the Chief as a 700cc Meteor replete with bolt-on Americana was seen as a travesty by fans. The engine was the standard 70 x 90-mm Royal Enfield o.h.v. vertical-twin unit with a four-speed Albion gearbox. The Royal Enfield rolling chassis had 16-in (40-cm) rims laced to the hubs. Fuel tank and mudguards carried Indian badges and the traditional Indian Head running light.

Traditional Indian Head mascot on mudguard

Deep valanced mudguards

Non-standard solo seat and open pipes

Indian

INDIAN VELOCETTE

Capacity 500cc • Power output 37bhp @ 6,200rpm • Weight 345lb (156kg) • Top speed 101mph (163km/h)

A ROUND ONE HUNDRED of these Anglo-Italian hybrids were built during 1969 and 1970. It used an o.h.v. single-cylinder Velocette engine and gearbox in a twin-loop frame, with Italian suspension and brakes. At this time the Velocette company was on the verge of extinction, yet the machine did not enthuse admirers of either marque.

THE MAN RESPONSIBLE for the Indian Velo was former West Coast Indian distributor and motorcycle magazine publisher Floyd Clymer, who dreamed of reviving the famous name. He died in 1970 having succeeded only in attaching the label to a selection of unlikely machines.

Marzocchi front suspension

FRONT VIEW

1⅛-in (30-mm) Amal Concentric carburettor

Ignition and lighting were by Lucas magneto and dynamo

Indian INDIAN MT5A

Capacity 45.5cc • Power output 2.5bhp @ 5,000rpm
Weight 57lb (26kg) • Top speed 25mph (40km/h) (estimated)

T HIS WAS THE SORRY STATE that the Indian name had reached by the early 1970s; reduced from being the biggest bike manufacturer in the world to a label stuck on imported children's bikes. Compare this 1973 "Indian" with the Italjet pictured on the right and the origins of this machine are obvious; it was built by Italjet at Bologna in Italy. There were other models carrying the Indian name also sold at this time, including some made in Taiwan. Fortunately the misconceived venture soon foundered.

10-in (25.4-cm) wheels

ITALJET ITALJET M5B

Capacity 47.5cc • Power output 1.5bhp @ 5,000rpm
Weight 30kg (66lb) • Top speed 32km/h (20mph) (estimated)

D URING THE 1970S AND 1980S, the Italjet company specialized in minibikes for children. This 1973 M5B is a typical example. Its engine was supplied by Franco Morini who supplied power units to many Italian mopeds and motorcycle makers at this time. It has one gear and an automatic clutch, and a smaller version with 20-cm (8-in) wheels was also produced. Brakes and suspension components are scaled-down versions of those supplied to full-size machines.

Seat height is 51cm (20in)

20-cm (8-in) wheels

Air-cooled two-stroke engine

JAMES 600CC

Capacity 599cc • Power output 7bhp (estimated) • Weight not known • Top speed not known

LIKE MANY EARLY MOTORCYCLE MANUFACTURERS, James started out making bicycles, producing its first motorcycle in 1902. Originally, proprietary engines were used but, by 1913, the firm was making its own engines in both two-stroke and four-stroke forms. The four-stroke was a "big single" of 599cc, with the distinctive pineapple-finned cylinder. The model seen here is from 1914.

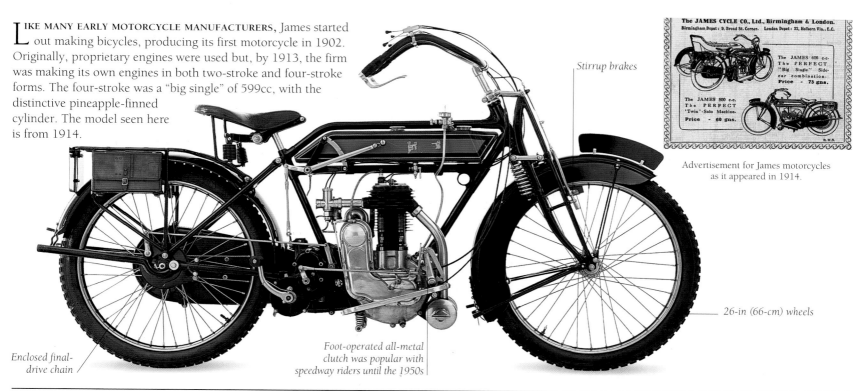

Stirrup brakes

26-in (66-cm) wheels

Foot-operated all-metal clutch was popular with speedway riders until the 1950s

Enclosed final-drive chain

Advertisement for James motorcycles as it appeared in 1914.

JAWA CZ
350 TWIN OILMASTER

Capacity 344cc • Power output 28bhp @ 5,250rpm
Weight 157kg (346lb) • Top speed 135km/h (84mph)

IN 1929 THE CZECH JANACEK ARMAMENTS FACTORY began building the German Wanderer motorcycle; the name Jawa derives from the first two letters of each company's name. In 1949 the company merged with the already nationalized CZ marque and the smoothly styled Jawas gave way to less shapely CZ-inspired products. The 350 Twin Oilmaster was up to date, even including oil injection within its sturdy duplex frame. It represented excellent value but, falling into an unpopular capacity class, it failed to sell. The model seen here is from 1974.

Utilitarian features include enclosed chain

Twin leading-shoe drum brake

A single carburettor feeds both cylinders

KAMASURA

KAMASURA
VRX-250

Capacity 39cc • Power output not known
Weight not known • Top speed 45km/h (28mph) (estimated

THIS MACHINE WAS A BICYCLE equipped with an engine driving the rear wheel by friction roller. It is only of interest for the sales technique used in the U.S. to unload them onto the unsuspecting public. By mail, people were asked to become test riders to help evaluate a new motorcycle. A free motorcycle was promised for just $367 in freight charges; the "revolutionary new motorcycle" that arrived was a motorized bicycle worth around $150. How many were sold like this is unknown. The model shown here is from 1986.

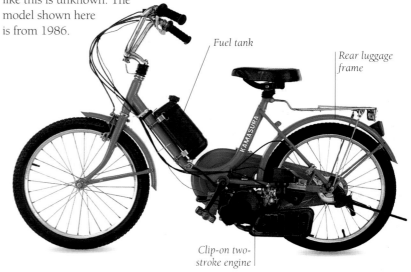

Fuel tank

Rear luggage frame

Clip-on two-stroke engine

KAWASAKI W1

Capacity 624cc • Power output 53bhp @ 7,000rpm
Weight 216kg (476lb) • Top speed 174km/h (108mph)

In 1965 the W1 was the biggest capacity motorcycle built in Japan. Effectively a copy of BSA's 650cc A10, it had a four-stroke, air-cooled parallel-twin engine with valves operated by pushrods. Kawasaki had high hopes for the W1 and expected good sales in the U.S. (where it was known as the Commander). Despite good home sales, the W1 did poorly there because it was often compared to the popular BSAs, a comparison in which the Kawasaki often came off worse. Kawasaki retreated from the U.S. big bike market to rethink its strategy. It was to return four years later with the mighty Mach III (see right and below).

Oil tank for dry-sump lubrication

Instruments incorporated into headlamp unit

Separate gearbox

Right-foot gearchange

KAWASAKI H1 MACH III

Capacity 498cc • Power output 60bhp @ 8,000rpm
Weight 179kg (395lb) • Top speed 193km/h (120mph)

There are few bikes that can compete with the fearsome Kawasaki Mach III's reputation for speed and excitement. Powered by a three-cylinder two-stroke engine, the Mach III (1970 model shown) was a real racer on the road. It could cover 400 metres (¼ mile) in just under 13 seconds and would nudge 193km/h (120mph). Enhancing the Mach III's beast-like reputation was its wild handling that riders either hated or tolerated. The bike heralded the return of Kawasaki to the U.S. market, where it had foundered four years earlier with the W1 (see left).

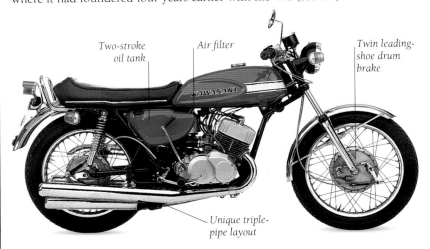

Two-stroke oil tank

Air filter

Twin leading-shoe drum brake

Unique triple-pipe layout

KAWASAKI MACH III

Capacity 498cc • Power output 60bhp @ 8,000rpm • Weight 179kg (395lb) • Top speed 191km/h (119mph)

One of the last incarnations of the 500cc Mach III Kawasaki was this 1973 model. So successful was the 60bhp two-stroke triple engine that minor changes only were made. The capacitor discharge ignition system was replaced by a more conventional battery and coil arrangement. The cycle parts were also modified as Kawasaki fought to contain the power of the triple.

The bike was eventually forced out of production by stringent American emissions laws that Kawasaki could not meet despite a relatively sophisticated lubrication system.

Front brake master cylinder

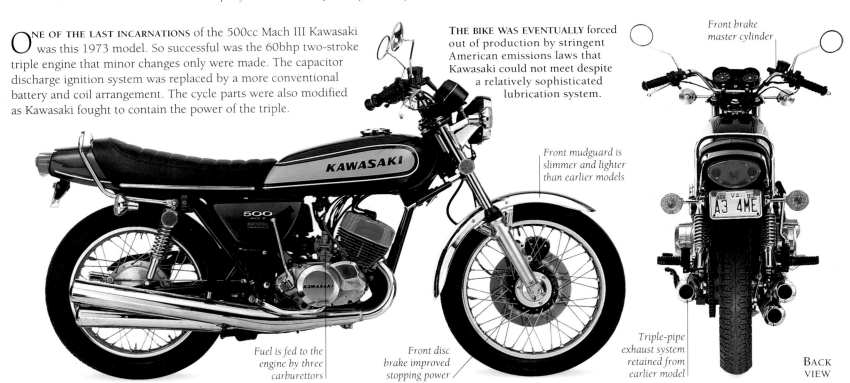

Front mudguard is slimmer and lighter than earlier models

Fuel is fed to the engine by three carburettors

Front disc brake improved stopping power

Triple-pipe exhaust system retained from earlier model

BACK VIEW

KAWASAKI Z1

Capacity 903cc • Power output 82bhp @ 8,500rpm • Weight 230kg (506lb) • Top speed 211km/h (131mph)

I F HONDA'S 750 FOUR created a sensation on its introduction in 1969, then Kawasaki's answer, 1972's 903cc Z1, was a reply worth waiting for. Like the Honda, the Z1 was also an air-cooled, four-stroke in-line four but where the Honda had a single o.h.c., the Z1 had two – a feat that was previously considered too expensive for a production machine. Soon after its introduction, the Z1 was entered in races with great success. In March 1973 the Z1 established a new 24-hour speed and endurance record at Daytona, Florida. Further

endurance success followed at the French Bol d'Or and Tour de France races, prompting Kawasaki to offer a 19,300-km (12,000-mile), 12-month warranty on its production bikes. The Z1 proved extremely popular with those riders looking for out-and-out performance. Often accused of poor handling and being under-braked, it was nevertheless exciting, impressive, and impossible to ignore. The 900 model was replaced by the 1015cc Z1000 in late 1976. The machine illustrated is a 1973 Z1.

•FOUR-STROKE DESIGN•

P roducing 82bhp, the 900cc Kawasaki Z1 was the most powerful production machine of its day, yet it sold for a competitive price. It offered exhilarating performance and handsome, modern styling, and it formed the basis of Kawasaki four-stroke fours for 20 years.

Kawasaki advertisement from 1969

THE Z1'S ENGINE was complex for its day. The nine-piece crankshaft had three gears directly attached, one on the left for primary drive, one in the centre driving the camshafts by chain, and a gear on the right to drive the oil pump. An automatic oiler lubricated the drive chain, fed from a tank behind the left side.

High, wide bars are impractical for a high-performance machine

BACK VIEW

Passenger grab rail

Kickstart as back up to electric start

The co-ordinated tank and tailpiece was a step forward in motorcycle styling

Single front disc brake is barely adequate

The four-pipe exhaust proved too expensive to produce and was discontinued on later models

The d.o.h.c. engine design was later copied by Suzuki for its GS750

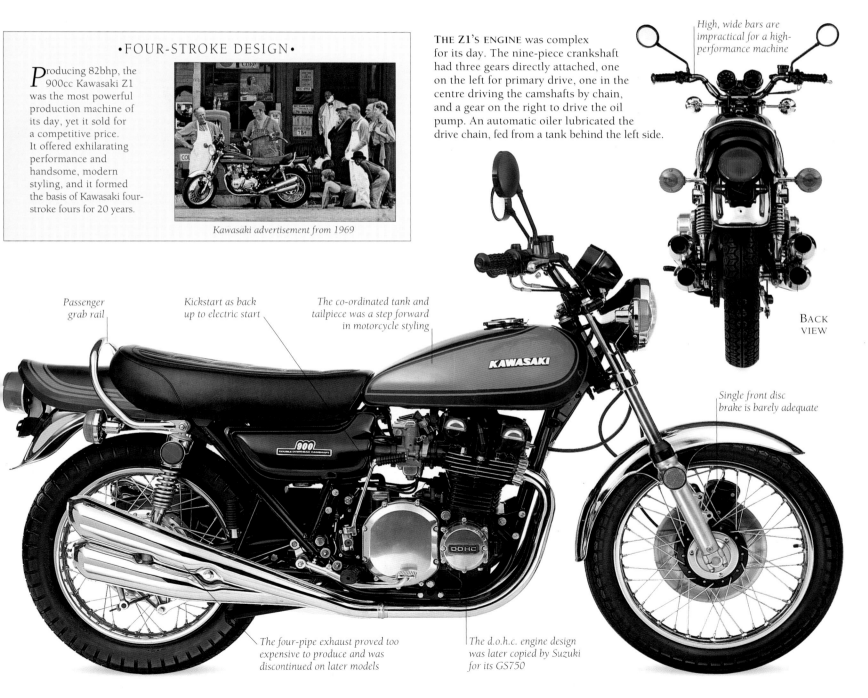

KAWASAKI G3SSD

Capacity 89cc • Power output 10bhp @ 7,500rpm
Weight 84kg (185lb) • Top speed 97km/h (60mph)

JAPAN

Like other Japanese manufacturers, Kawasaki's most successful early efforts in the American market were in the lightweight field. Among the company's first machines were the 82cc models introduced in 1965. These featured a lightweight, two-stroke engine with a single cylinder and rotary-disc valve induction. Later, 89cc and 99cc versions were also produced. This 1974 G3SSD is typical of early Kawasaki lightweights. Trail bike versions were also made and are still sold in some markets.

Air cleaner

Single leading-shoe drum brakes

Duplex, cradle frame

KAWASAKI KZ400

Capacity 398cc • Power output 36bhp @ 8,500rpm
Weight 181kg (398lb) • Top speed 148km/h (92mph)

JAPAN

The KZ400 first appeared in 1974 to a mixed reception. The single o.h.c. parallel-twin was built to take on Honda's CB360 and to provide a practical middleweight motorcycle. Although its acceleration was reasonable, top speed on the road was often no better than 129km/h (80mph) and a head wind could reduce that further. However, the bike had its good points. To avoid typical vibration on a twin with a 360° crank, Kawasaki fitted two counter-balancing weights that spun on the crankshaft opposite the pistons and con-rods.

Simple, reliable parallel-twin engine

Disc front brake

46-cm (18-in) wheels

KAWASAKI KR250

Capacity 249cc • Power output 68bhp • Weight 104kg (229lb) • Top speed 241km/h (150mph)

JAPAN

Although Kawasaki is the smallest of the leading Japanese manufacturers, it has always had a reputation for building powerful innovative machines. This KR250 is no exception. Designed for world-class racing, it is a rotary-valved, two-stroke twin, but instead of having the two cylinders arranged conventionally side by side, and operating a single crankshaft, they are one behind the other and two crankshafts are used. The benefit is a narrower engine, as slim as a single-cylinder machine, with big improvements in aerodynamics.

Recesses in tank allow knees to tuck in out of the wind

Drilled disc reduces weight

Exhaust from rear cylinder

Advanced suspension uses light, aluminium swingarm and single damper unit

Green is the traditional Kawasaki racing colour

KAWASAKI KMX200

Capacity 191cc • Power output 25bhp @ 8,500rpm
Weight 98kg (215lb) • Top speed 132km/h (82mph)

DERIVED FROM ITS **125CC STABLEMATE,** this KMX200, launched in
1988, offered true off-road performance. Powered by a water-
cooled, two-stroke single, part of the bike's off-road success was due to
the frame which, based on that of the KX motocrossers, had a tough,
box-section swingarm and single shock absorber. In this 1991 model,
the engine was effectively an enlarged version
of the KMX125 but the result was an extra
6bhp and a broader spread of torque.

Wide handlebars
enhance steering
on rough terrain

Gaiters protect
fork seals from
dust and mud

Box-section
swingarm

Six-speed
gearbox

KAWASAKI
KX250-K2

Capacity 250cc • Power output not known
Weight 97kg (214lb) • Top speed not known

IN **1994 THE KX250 MOTOCROSS BIKE** underwent a major model
change to produce a bike that offered more refined power delivery and
a stronger low-end. Aimed at both the professional and amateur markets,
it had a liquid-cooled, two-stroke single engine, five-speed gearbox,
chain final drive, a compact lightweight frame, telescopic front fork, and
Uni-Trak rear suspension. The lime green paintwork featured a
chequered flag pattern. The extra-long seat allowed the rider to move
forward for starts and hard cornering.

High-tensile steel tubular
and box section perimeter frame

Narrow front mudguard
gives the rider a clear
view of the race track

Disc brakes
fitted front
and rear

Expansion
chamber

KAWASAKI GPZ900R

Capacity 908cc • Power output 119bhp @ 10,500rpm • Weight 228kg (502lb) • Top speed 248km/h (154mph)

KAWASAKI'S REPUTATION for building ground-breaking sports bikes was
further enhanced with the arrival of the GPZ900R in early 1984. Already
famous for its d.o.h.c. four-cylinder engines, this time it took the concept
a few steps further. Four valves were positioned in each cylinder and water
cooling added. Wet liners (the water flows
directly against the outside of the cylinder
liner rather than in an aluminium block)
meant the cylinders could be positioned
closely together, giving a very slim
profile to the engine. The GPZ's
performance and fine handling made
it an immediate success and a future
classic. It remained in production
for ten years.

Clip-on handlebars
for sporty riding
position

Hydraulic anti-dive system
increases compression
damping as fork
pressure builds

Single rear
disc brake

Alternator is behind
cylinder block and chain
driven from the crankshaft

KAWASAKI ZZ-R1100

Capacity 1052cc • Power output 125bhp @ 9,500rpm • Weight 233kg (513lb) • Top speed 282km/h (175mph)

B<small>Y THE TIME THE</small> **ZZ-R1100** premiered in 1990, Kawasaki had already built a long line of powerful in-line four-stroke fours. The Z1, Z1000, GPZ1100, GPZ900R, ZXR750, and ZX-10 have all been seen as classics of their eras, so the ZZ-R (known as the ZX-11 in the U.S.) had a proud tradition to follow. Neither an out-and-out sportster nor a full tourer, the ZZ-R nevertheless found a niche among lovers of its hugely powerful yet silky-smooth engine that could take the bike from 32km/h (20mph) in top gear right up to 282km/h (175mph) in one strong surge. Riders found the ZZ-R easy to handle despite its weight, much of this being attributed to the huge, aluminium perimeter frame. Basing the engine on the successful ZX-10, Kawasaki increased the bore to 76mm and used shorter-skirted

pistons to save weight. Lighter con-rods were also used, helping to raise the red line to 11,500rpm. A rev limiter automatically interrupted ignition at 12,000rpm to prevent engine damage at the hands of the over-exuberant. Despite the large amount of power at hand, earlier models were decidedly flat below 5,000rpm. Above that, however, the bike would surge forward with a relentless insistence many riders have found irresistible. Everything about the ZZ-R was big and impressive, from its wide 180-section rear tyre to the huge 320-cm (126-in) twin front brake discs. In the early 1990s, as the true sports emphasis turned away from the large-capacity bikes towards the 600cc class, the ZZ-R lost its impact.

Tank is sculpted to accept rider's legs, keeping wind drag to a minimum

Rear subframe is welded to main, twin-beam perimeter frame

Air passes through radiator, collecting heat, then escapes through these vents in the fairing

•UNBEATABLE SPEED•

A power output of 125bhp and a top speed of 282km/h (175mph), made the Kawasaki ZZ-R1100 the fastest production motorcycle of its era. But its extra weight and length meant that the handling was not as agile as some contemporary machines. On twisting roads it was often outclassed by lighter, better handling machines. But as a motorcycle for covering large road distances in staggeringly short times with contemptuous ease, it had no peers. The aerodynamic fairing combines with effortless power delivery to make this a serious tool for high speed use.

Testing the speed of the ZZ-R1100

Forks are adjusted at top for pre-load and rebound damping

Indicators are integral to the design of the fairing

Front mudguard is contoured for aerodynamic efficiency

Instrument console includes a fuel gauge

Silencers are sheathed in sheet aluminium

BACK VIEW

Opposed, four-piston, hydraulic calliper gives powerful, yet predictable braking

THE BIKE SHOWN HERE is a 1994 model. The air intake at the front of the fairing forces cool air into a sealed airbox beneath the fuel tank and then into the semi-downdraught carburettors. It is known as the Ram Air system. Hoses carry water between the engine's cooling water jacket and radiator.

KREIDLER
FLORETT K53M

Capacity 49cc • Power output 1.75bhp @ 4,500rpm
Weight 75kg (165lb) (estimated) • Top speed 40km/h (25mph) (estimated)

GERMANY

IN THIRTY YEARS OF MOTORCYCLE MANUFACTURE, Kreidler only made 50cc machines. This 1959 K53M is typical of Kreidler's machines of the late 1950s. It had a three-speed gearbox with twistgrip change, the final drive chain was enclosed, and the engine was mounted in a pressed-steel frame with swingarm rear suspension. The K53M was a restricted version of the Florett design, which qualified under German law as a moped. Unrestricted models developed almost twice the power and were not supplied with pedals.

Long, leading-link forks

Three-speed gearbox is operated by twistgrip

Fan-cooled two-stroke engine with horizontal cylinder

KREIDLER RENN FLORETT

Capacity 49cc • Power output 14bhp @ 15,000rpm
Weight 59kg (131lb) (estimated) • Top speed 171km/h (106mph)

GERMAN

THE CREATION OF A **50CC RACING CLASS** in the late 1950s was a natural opportunity for Kreidler to develop racing machines. The firm's first racing machines – for the 1961 season – were heavily based on production Florett models. By the time of this 1963 model, the bikes had become more sophisticated. Disc valve induction replaced the piston port and the four-speed gearbox was complemented by an externally mounted three-speed overdrive. When combined, the two sets offered riders 12 gears.

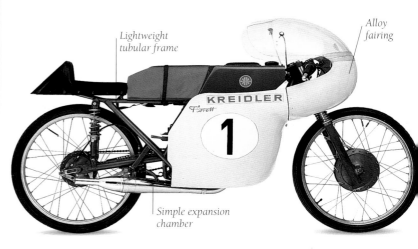

Lightweight tubular frame

Alloy fairing

Simple expansion chamber

KTM 100/4

Capacity 97cc • Power output 8bhp (estimated)
Weight not known • Top speed 88km/h (55mph) (estimated)

AUSTRIA

THE AUSTRIAN COMPANY KTM is most famous for its off-road competition machines, but it has also produced more mundane motorcycles and mopeds. The model shown here is a 1967 100/4. The bike had a two-stroke Sachs engine mounted in a simple, tubular frame. Its gearbox was four-speed and final drive was by an enclosed chain. In the American market these machines were sold under the Hansa name.

Alloy hubs

Passenger grab rail and luggage rack

Sachs two-stroke engine with Bing carburettor

KTM 125 MOTOCROSS

Capacity 125cc • Power output not known
Weight 88kg (193lb) • Top speed not known

AUSTRIA

DURING THE **1970S** KTM became famous for its off-road competition machines and won its first World Championship in 1977 when Soviet rider Gennady Moisseyev took the 250cc title. KTM machines were always at the forefront of technical development and ideas developed on factory bikes were soon adopted on production models. This 1989 125cc model is typical. It features water cooling, upside-down forks, and rising-rate rear suspension.

Radiators hidden behind plastic cowls

Plastic bodywork

Frame constructed of chrome moly tubing

LAMBRETTA LD125

Capacity 123cc • Power output 5bhp @ 4,600rpm • Weight not known • Top speed 72km/h (45mph)

INNOCENTI OF MILAN began building Lambrettas in 1946, and soon the Lambretta and Piaggio's Vespa (see p.190) were established as the two most successful scooters on the market. The Lambretta's two-stroke engine was mounted in front of the rear wheel, which resulted in better weight distribution than the Vespa, and final drive was by shaft. The machine shown here is a 1957 LD125.

THE LAMBRETTA and Vespa designs were very different to each other. From 1950 the Lambretta chassis construction was based on a single, large-diameter tube, and bodywork was an optional extra. In this machine's model name, the letter "L" indicates that it is fitted with bodywork and "D" signifies the fourth series of machines.

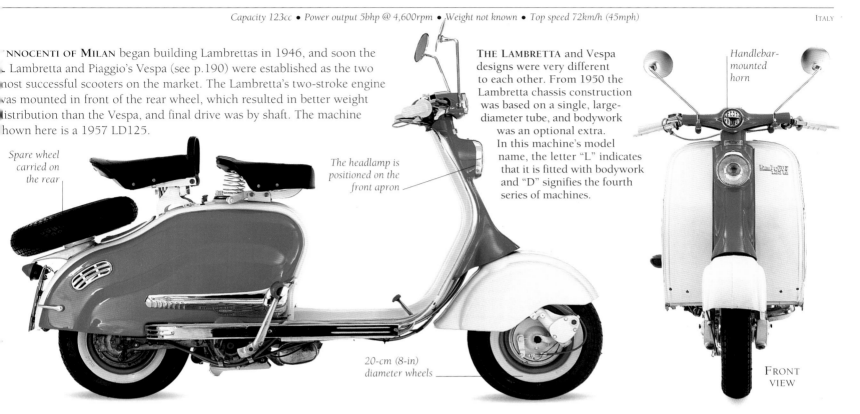

Spare wheel carried on the rear

The headlamp is positioned on the front apron

Handlebar-mounted horn

20-cm (8-in) diameter wheels

FRONT VIEW

LAMBRETTA 150 SPECIAL

Capacity 148cc • Power output 9bhp • Weight not known • Top speed not known

IN 1957 LAMBRETTA introduced the new TV-175 scooter. This was the machine from which the 1960s Lambretta evolved and the styling became sharper and slimmer as the decade progressed. Unfortunately, Innocenti was never as successful as Piaggio, the Vespa producers. Lambretta production in Italy ended in 1971, although the machines remained in production in Spain and India. The machine pictured here is a 150 Special dating from 1967.

REVISED DESIGNS that first appeared in 1957 followed the traditional Lambretta concept, but there was a four-speed gearbox, and final drive was by enclosed duplex chain. The styling had changed too, with a dual seat and the front mudguard mounted on the bodywork rather than on the forks. The pressed-steel body panels were mounted on a tubular-spine frame.

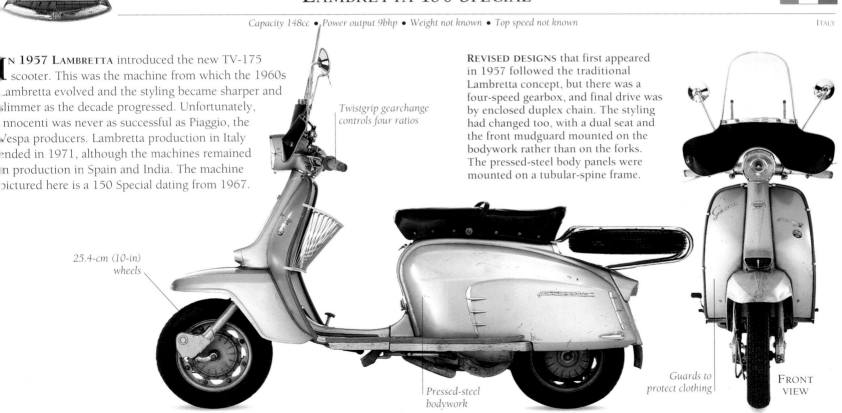

Twistgrip gearchange controls four ratios

25.4-cm (10-in) wheels

Pressed-steel bodywork

Guards to protect clothing

FRONT VIEW

LAURIN & KLEMENT

Capacity 331cc • Power output 2.5bhp • Weight not known • Top speed 50km/h (31mph) (estimated)

CZECH REPUBLIC

BICYCLE MAKER Laurin & Klement built its first motorcycles around 1898. From the start of production its machines contained several advanced features. The engine was placed centrally in a specially constructed frame, while most other machines still used modified bicycle frames. All controls were on the handlebars and final drive was by flat belt. The machine shown here dates from 1903.

LAURIN & KLEMENT was probably the first motorcycle maker to use magneto ignition, which dispensed with the inconvenient and dangerous hot tube system. The magneto was chain driven from the crankshaft and mounted underneath the engine protected by a loop of the frame.

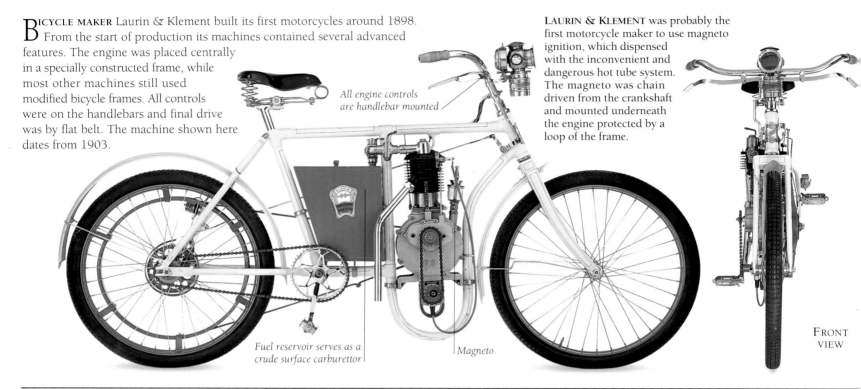

All engine controls are handlebar mounted

FRONT VIEW

Fuel reservoir serves as a crude surface carburettor

Magneto

LAVERDA CHOTT 250

Capacity 247cc • Power output 37bhp @ 7,000rpm

Weight 108kg (237lb) • Top speed 121km/h (75mph) (estimated)

ITALY

LAVERDA INTRODUCED A TWO-STROKE TRAIL BIKE in 1975 alongside its four-stroke models. The Chott used a Laverda-designed engine though later bikes used imported Zündapp and Husqvarna power units. The rolling chassis comprised a duplex, tubular, cradle frame with Ceriani front forks and rear shock units controlling a conventional swingarm. Both wheels had 18-cm (7-in) drum brakes. With magnesium-alloy crankcases and Ceriani suspension, the Chott continued Laverda's tradition of high prices and few sales.

LAVERDA ALPINA 500

Capacity 497cc • Power output 44bhp @ 10,300rpm

Weight 171kg (377lb) • Top speed 192km/h (119mph)

ITALY

THE ALPINA 500 FIRST APPEARED IN 1977 and compared to its famed stablemates was quite reserved in looks. Its conservative appearance, however, masked a thoroughbred motorcycle with excellent performance. Although the 500 was not the lightest of bikes, once on the move its weight was quickly forgotten while its single-loop construction frame was remarkably rigid and able to cope with the power. Braking was by way of three cast-iron Brembo discs that worked well in all weather. This is a 1979 model.

Air-cooled, 68 x 68-mm, single-cylinder engine

32-mm (1¼-in) Dell'Orto carburettor

Full lighting set

Wet, multi-plate clutch drives a five-speed gearbox

Trials-pattern tyres

Two Dell'Orto carburettors

D.o.h.c., parallel-twin engine

Twin Brembo disc brakes

LAVERDA JOTA

Capacity 980cc • Power output 90bhp @ 8,000rpm • Weight 236kg (520lb) • Top speed 224km/h (139mph)

LAVERDA INTRODUCED a new 980cc d.o.h.c. three-cylinder machine in 1973. The Jota, which was to become Laverda's most famous model, was a tuned version of the original triple first produced for the British market in 1976. Limited engine tuning turned the already quick 3CL model into the fastest production bike of its day. A Jota is capable of almost 224km/h (139mph) top speed. Finesse was not a feature of the design; the entire machine is over-engineered. Metal components are high quality and heavy. The controls are leaden and the handling suspect, yet construction quality was better than on many Italian bikes of the period. It had good paintwork and chrome, and many components, especially the instruments and electrics, came from Germany and Japan. Until 1982, Laverda triples had a 180° crankshaft in which the two outer pistons rose and fell together while the central piston did the opposite. It was less expensive to make than the more common 120° crankshaft, but it allowed the engine to vibrate. The bike shown here is a 1982 model.

TOP-HEAVY WEIGHT distribution made the Jota's handling quirky, and yet road tests of the period raved about the machine – which says more about its rivals than it does about the Laverda. The bike's brutal frontal aspect was partly hidden behind a half fairing on later models.

FRONT VIEW

•JOTA PERFORMANCE•

The basic 3CL Laverda triple produced around 80bhp. Jota performance is achieved by liberating another ten bhp. The Jota engine used 10:1 compression pistons and the factory's 4/C high performance camshafts. Gas flow was improved by adding a larger diameter exhaust collector and almost unrestricted "silencers". The resulting noise killed the model after new legislation.

Alloy cambox conceals 4/C cams

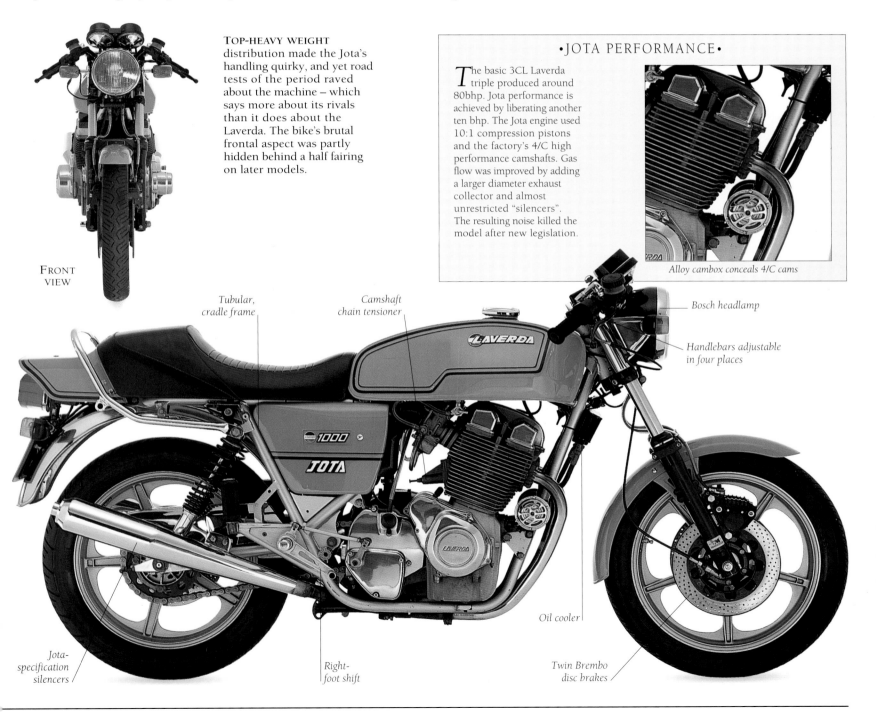

Tubular, cradle frame

Camshaft chain tensioner

Bosch headlamp

Handlebars adjustable in four places

Jota-specification silencers

Right-foot shift

Oil cooler

Twin Brembo disc brakes

LAVERDA F650 SPORT

Capacity 668cc • Power output 70bhp @ 8,900rpm • Weight 180kg (396lb) • Top speed 216km/h (134mph)

AFTER PROTRACTED CONVULSIONS during the late 1980s, Laverda apparently died. A re-formed company introduced a new Laverda machine in 1994. The rolling chassis of the new bike was an up-to-date, twin-spar, alloy frame combined with high-quality suspension and brake components, and clad in race-replica bodywork. Besides the high-tech standards of the chassis, the engine was an anachronism. The eight-valve, air-cooled, d.o.h.c., parallel-twin is based on the engine first used in the 1977 500 (see p.120). For use in the F650, capacity was increased and the lubrication system improved. The machine's high price reflected the quality of the components used.

Airbox for Weber-Marelli fuel injection under dummy fuel tank

The fuel tank is situated under the rider's seat with the filler under the flip-up pillion pad

Upside-down WP forks with Marchesiani alloy wheels and Brembo disc brakes

Alloy frame

MAICO MC350

Capacity 352cc • Power output 28bhp @ 6,500rpm • Weight 113kg (250lb) • Top speed depends on gearing

MAICO STARTED MAKING MOTORCYCLES in the mid-1930s, switched to aircraft parts shortly before World War II, and resumed motorbike production in 1947. The MC350 is typical of the oversized 250s that ousted the big four-strokes in 500cc motocross during the 1960s, being adequately powerful and easier to handle. The bike shown here is a 1969 model.

IN THE LATE 1950s, Maico started producing motocross machines. These have earned Maico the manufacturers' World Championship. It was also runner-up three times in the individual 500cc title.

Braced handlebars

Plastic front mudguard

Long-travel suspension

Four-speed engine/gearbox unit

Sturdy duplex frame

FRONT VIEW

MARS MA1000 SPORT

Capacity 948cc • Power output 7.5bhp @ 3,500rpm • Weight not known • Top speed not known

ALTHOUGH MARS MADE MOTORCYCLES from 1903 to 1957, the company's most famous model was the flat twin introduced in 1920 and produced for a decade. The engine was made specially for Mars by Maybach, better known for its car and aircraft engines. The side-valve engine was mounted lengthways beneath the steel-plate frame, with the three-speed gearbox above the rear cylinder. This 1928 bike's recirculating lubrication system, with the oil being carried in a tank under the engine, was advanced for the time.

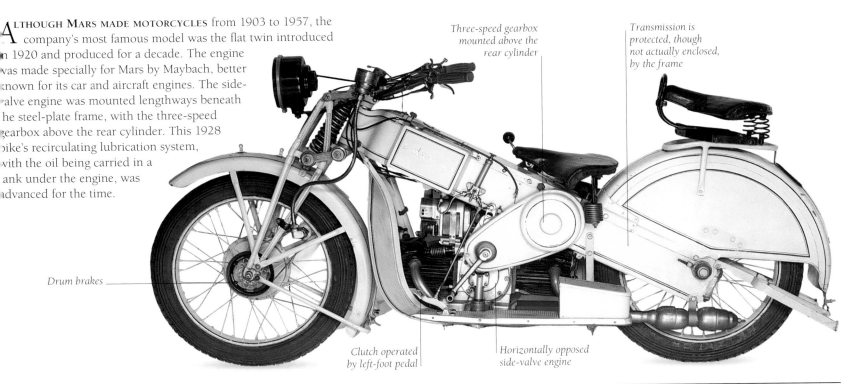

Three-speed gearbox mounted above the rear cylinder

Transmission is protected, though not actually enclosed, by the frame

Drum brakes

Clutch operated by left-foot pedal

Horizontally opposed side-valve engine

SILENT MATCHLESS

Capacity not known • Power output 2.75hp • Weight not known • Top speed not known

THE FIRST MATCHLESS MOTORCYCLES were made in 1901. This 1902 design had the engine underneath the front downtube. The Collier brothers, makers of Matchless bikes, competed in many races on similar machines, including the first 1,000-mile (1,610-km) Reliability Trial.

THIS MACHINE was powered by a DeDion type, single-cylinder engine made under licence in England by H. J. Lawson's Motor Manufacturing Company. It was fitted with coil ignition and Longuemare spray-type carburettor.

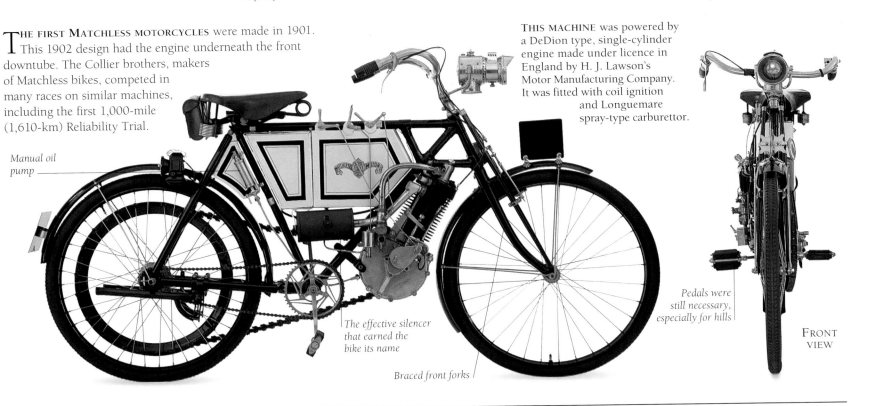

Manual oil pump

The effective silencer that earned the bike its name

Braced front forks

Pedals were still necessary, especially for hills

FRONT VIEW

MATCHLESS
MODEL A SILVER ARROW

Capacity 394cc • Power output not known
Weight 341lb (155kg) • Top speed not known

LAUNCHED IN 1929, the Model A Silver Arrow was an unconventional machine. Although *The Motor Cycle* magazine described it as having "a creditable performance for a side valve of 400cc", it was dropped in 1933 following disappointing sales. The 72° V-twin engine had a single-cylinder block topped by a one-piece cylinder head. A Lucas Magdyno lay along the chassis above the handshift gearbox. The tubular cradle frame had cantilever rear suspension with friction dampers controlling the twin barrel springs. The Silver Arrow had 21-in (53-cm) wheels with 7-in (18-cm) coupled drum brakes. The bike shown here is a 1930 model.

Springs for cantilever rear suspension

Oil tank for dry-sump lubrication

MATCHLESS
MODEL B SILVER HAWK

Capacity 592cc • Power output 26bhp
Weight 380lb (172kg) • Top speed 80mph (129km/h)

UNVEILED AT THE 1931 MOTORCYCLE SHOW, the Silver Hawk engine was essentially two Silver Arrow units side by side, surmounted by a single overhead camshaft. To minimize the effect of fuel surge, the single Amal carburettor was often fitted with twin float chambers. The handshift gearbox was driven by a duplex primary chain with an automatic tensioner allowing the unit to remain fixed. Under pressure the Silver Hawk became noisy and tended to develop cylinder head joint leaks. Only some 500 examples were built, and production ceased in 1935 because the Silver Hawk was too expensive and too problematic for a depressed market.

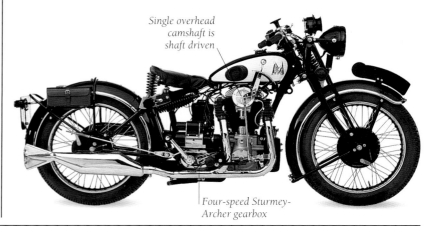

Single overhead camshaft is shaft driven

Four-speed Sturmey-Archer gearbox

MATCHLESS 41/G3L

Capacity 347cc • Power output 16.6bhp • Weight 392lb (134kg) • Top speed 70mph (113km/h) (estimated)

DURING WORLD WAR II, Matchless supplied over 80,000 41/G3Ls to the British War Department. The origins of the o.h.v. G3L can be traced to the G3 Clubman launched in 1935, but the rigid simplex cradle frame planned for the 1940 season was employed as well as the firm's new "Teledraulic" forks. The Lucas magneto and the dynamo were chain-driven. The only criticism of the 1930s and 1940s G3 series was the inaccessibility of the dynamo tucked under the magneto platform; this was later rectified. The G3L was considered vastly superior to other models by many despatch riders.

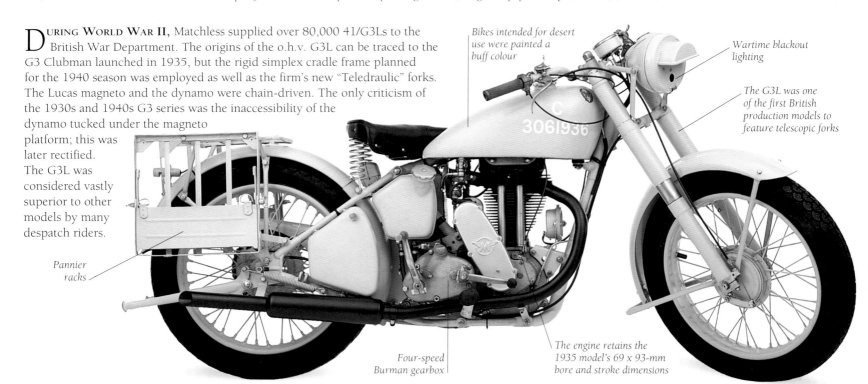

Bikes intended for desert use were painted a buff colour

Wartime blackout lighting

The G3L was one of the first British production models to feature telescopic forks

Pannier racks

Four-speed Burman gearbox

The engine retains the 1935 model's 69 x 93-mm bore and stroke dimensions

MATCHLESS G45

Capacity 498cc • Power output 48bhp @ 7,200rpm
Weight 320lb (145kg) • Top speed 120mph (193km/h) (estimated)

DEVELOPED BY THE **AJS** RACE SHOP for the 1952 season, the G45 was based on the 500cc parallel-twin that came fourth in the 1951 Manx Grand Prix. Twin Amal Grand Prix carburettors, a Lucas racing magneto, and a rev counter drive were standard along with the Burman racing gearbox. Seventeen G45s entered the 1955 Senior race and only ten finished. Although the G45 was not successful compared to other models, it allowed AJS riders to compete in Senior and Junior Clubman TTs. The cycle shown dates from 1957 – the year that production was halted.

The engine includes a one-piece forged steel crank, alloy barrels, and triple valve springs

Friction damper

The G45 is fitted with a 66 x 72.8-mm engine

MATCHLESS G11 CSR

Capacity 593cc • Power output 40bhp @ 6,000rpm
Weight 380lb (172kg) • Top speed not known

INTRODUCED FOR **1958**, the G11 CSR was an early example of the factory custom bike. Developed initially for the American market, it adopted the street-scrambler style. Early CSRs used frames that were lightened versions of the bolt-up, duplex roadster frame. A Lucas alternator was mounted on the driveside crankshaft but magneto ignition was retained. A standard four-speed gearbox was driven by a simplex primary chain through a multi-plate clutch in a new cast-alloy primary chaincase. In 1958 press tests the new model maintained 100mph (161km/h) for one hour.

Twin Amal Monobloc carburettors are fitted along with half-race camshafts

The G11 CSR is fitted with a small fuel tank

The engine has separate iron barrels and alloy cylinder heads

MATCHLESS G50 CSR

Capacity 498cc • Power output 46bhp @ 7,200rpm • Weight 320lb (145kg) • Top speed 115mph (185km/h) (estimated)

JUST FIFTY OF THESE ROADSTERS WERE BUILT in 1961 to make the G50 eligible for competition in America. The G50 CSR combined the rolling chassis of the Matchless CSR twin with the overhead-camshaft, single-cylinder engine from the G50 racer. Many buyers transferred the engine to motocross specials with better frames, hence the rarity of this factory-built hybrid.

FED BY a 1½-in (38-mm) Amal Grand Prix carburettor, the inlet valve was a massive 2in (51mm) in diameter. All steel and tin running parts were finished in either red or blue, with white pinstriping on the scrambles fuel tank.

Standard AMC road silencer

The magnesium and alloy engine has 90 x 78-mm bore and stroke

Rubber fork gaiters

FRONT VIEW

MEGOLA RACING MODEL

Capacity 640cc • Power output 14bhp @ 3,600rpm • Weight not known • Top speed not known

THE MEGOLA PROBABLY RANKS as the world's most unconventional motorcycle ever. Introduced in 1921, approximately 2,000 were built before the factory closed in 1924. This machine dates from 1923. Obviously inspired by the rotary-aero engines of World War I, designer Fritz Cockerell came up with a five-cylinder side-valve radial engine mounted within the front wheel, which it drove via epicyclic gearing. During each forward rotation of the wheel the engine rotated six times in the opposite direction. There was no clutch or gearbox, but different-sized wheels were available to suit the intended use: a track-racing model fitted with a 74-cm (29-in) front wheel was clocked at 148km/h (92mph). The beam-type frame incorporated the fuel tank, which was pressurized by a hand pump feeding fuel to a header tank above the carburettor. This was in a vulnerable position outside the forks at wheel-spindle level. A similar tank on the other side of the forks carried the engine oil, while beneath it, and forward of the wheel spindle, was the magneto.

WITH THE MEGOLA'S rotating engine it was clearly not possible to use a conventional exhaust system, so small individual pipes were mounted on each cylinder. All this complication in the front wheel left no room for a brake, so two brakes were fitted to the rear wheel.

Leaf spring has a leather sheath

Fuel header tank

Magneto

Single carburettor feeds five cylinders

FRONT VIEW

Copper oil tank with hand pump

Main fuel tank is built into box-section frame

A LEAF-SPRUNG, link-type fork carried the front wheel in a substantial looped member, while some machines also had leaf-sprung rear suspension.

Stand

Lower suspension arm

Rear wheel has contracting band and drum brakes

MONTESA COTA 172

Capacity 157.5cc • Power output 9bhp
Weight not known • Top speed not known

FOLLOWING THE LEAD GIVEN BY BULTACO with the Sherpa (see p.41), rival Spanish firm Montesa introduced its 250cc Cota trials machine in 1968. For a while, these two machines dominated the market, and in 1973 Montesa introduced the Cota 172. This designation had more to do with marketing strategy than engine capacity since the machine was simply a large-bore version of the Cota 123. Its power characteristics proved unsuitable for serious trials work but the machine was popular with trail riders. The 172 pictured dates from 1977.

One-piece tank and seat unit

Six-speed gearbox

MONTESA COTA

Capacity 258cc • Power output not known
Weight 83kg (183lb) • Top speed not known

THE MONTESA COMPANY went through a series of upheavals in the early 1980s. It survived because it was associated with Honda, though motorcycle production under its own name all but ended. The remaining Montesa model was a trials machine bearing the famous Cota name. It had front and rear disc brakes, and the rear suspension was by single-shock absorber and rising rate linkage. This 1992 model offered superior performance to its forebears.

Water-cooled single-cylinder, unit construction two-stroke engine with six-speed gearbox

Verlicchi frame composed of welded aluminium forgings and extrusions

Water-cooled cylinder barrel

Upside-down telescopic forks

MORBIDELLI V8

Capacity 847cc • Power output not known • Weight 200kg (441lb) • Top speed 241km/h (150mph)

CONCEIVED BY GIANCARLO MORBIDELLI, a millionaire industrialist and motorcycle enthusiast, the V8 was intended for very limited production. Styled by the car designer Pininfarina, the engine was suspended from the tubular space frame. If prospective buyers were not scared off by its ugly lines and complexity the excessive price tag was highly restrictive, despite including the cost of airfreighting the machine back to the Italian factory for servicing.

THE MORBIDELLI was not the first V8 motorcycle. American pioneer Glenn Curtiss built a V8 in 1912, and Moto Guzzi made a 500cc Grand Prix bike in the late 1950s. This model dates from 1994.

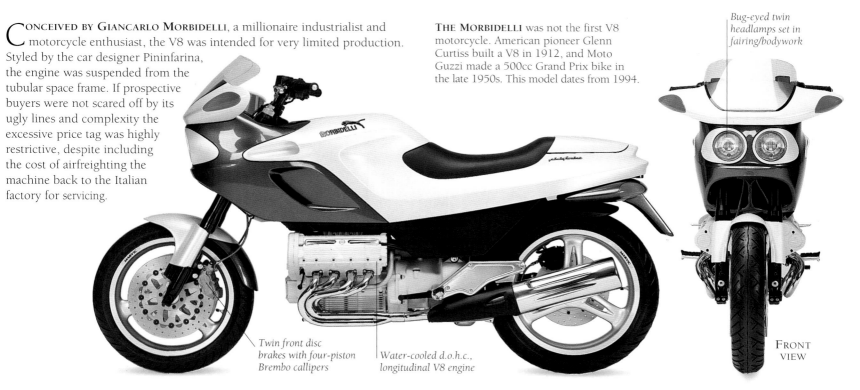

Bug-eyed twin headlamps set in fairing/bodywork

Twin front disc brakes with four-piston Brembo callipers

Water-cooled d.o.h.c., longitudinal V8 engine

FRONT VIEW

MORINI TURISMO 2T

Capacity 123cc • Power output not known • Weight not known • Top speed 88km/h (55mph)

Alfonso Morini began to make motorcycles under his own name in 1946, having been a partner at the MM motorcycle company before World War II. These first motorcycles were two-stroke singles inspired by the German DKW RT125 design (see p.50). They were the basis of Morini racing machines until its four-strokes appeared in 1950.

The Morini engine has distinctive extended engine cases to enhance crankcase cooling. Early versions had pressed-steel girder forks and plunger rear suspension. This 1953 model has switched to telescopic front forks.

Sprung seat

Telescopic front forks

YSU 639

Dell'Orto carburettor

The coil and voltage control unit are fitted into recesses in the fuel tank

FRONT VIEW

MORINI 3½ SPORT

Capacity 344cc • Power output 39bhp @ 8,500rpm • Weight 154kg (340lb) • Top speed 161km/h (100mph)

Introduced in 1972, the 344cc Morini was one of the most innovative machines of the period. Designed for efficiency of performance and manufacture, the 72° V-twin engine used a "Heron" cylinder head design that had parallel valves, a flat cylinder head, and the combustion chamber machined into the crown of the piston. Electronic ignition, rev counter, and fuel tap were supplied. Two models were produced: a Sport version (a 1974 model is shown here), with a more powerful engine and extreme riding position, and the more mundane Strada.

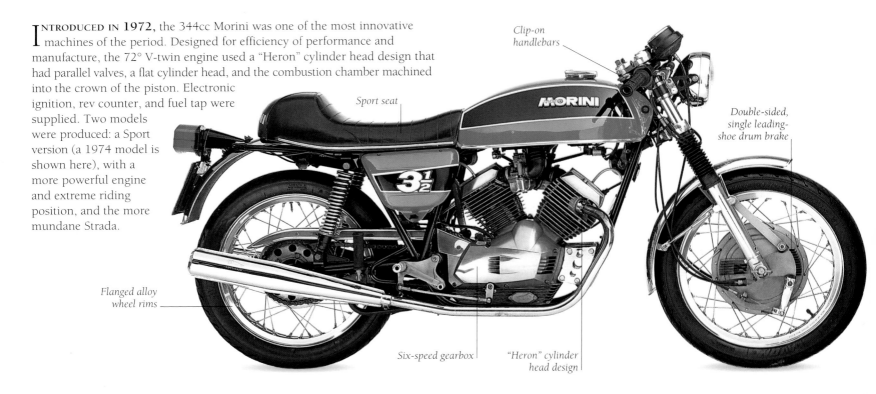

Clip-on handlebars

Sport seat

Double-sided, single leading-shoe drum brake

Flanged alloy wheel rims

Six-speed gearbox

"Heron" cylinder head design

MORINI CAMEL

Capacity 478cc • Power output 42bhp @ 7,400rpm • Weight 140kg (380lb) • Top speed 153km/h (95mph)

MORINI'S V-TWIN ENGINE WAS PRODUCED in three sizes. As well as the original 344cc version, 239cc and 478cc models were also made. Originally, the engine was available only in conventionally styled road bikes, but the fashion for four-stroke trail bikes in the early 1980s encouraged Morini to produce an off-road version. The combination of a flexible and compact engine into a sturdy frame fitted with good-quality suspension produced a surprisingly good off-road machine. Later less attractive versions were biased more heavily towards road use. A 350 version was produced under the unlikely Kangaroo name.

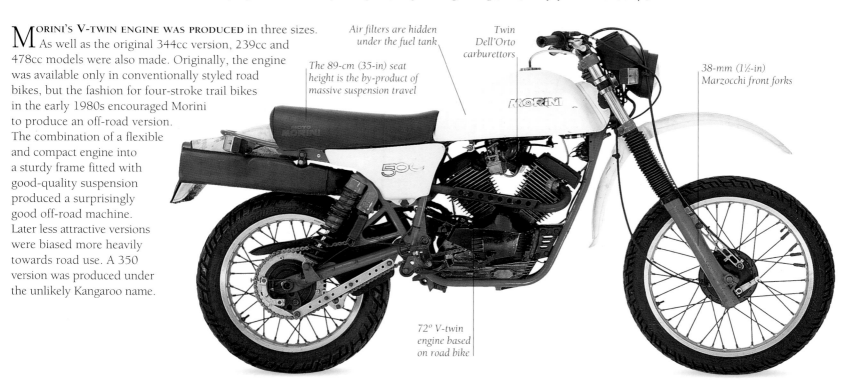

Air filters are hidden under the fuel tank

Twin Dell'Orto carburettors

The 89-cm (35-in) seat height is the by-product of massive suspension travel

38-mm (1½-in) Marzocchi front forks

72° V-twin engine based on road bike

MOTOBÉCANE

Capacity 172cc • Power output 1.75bhp • Weight not known • Top speed 50km/h (31mph)

THE MOTOBÉCANE COMPANY became one of France's major motorcycle manufacturers. Its first machine was this simple lightweight, which sold in large numbers. Introduced in 1923, the Motobécane (meaning "motorbike" in French) was produced by the partnership of Charles Benoit and Abel Bardin. Both these machines date from 1923.

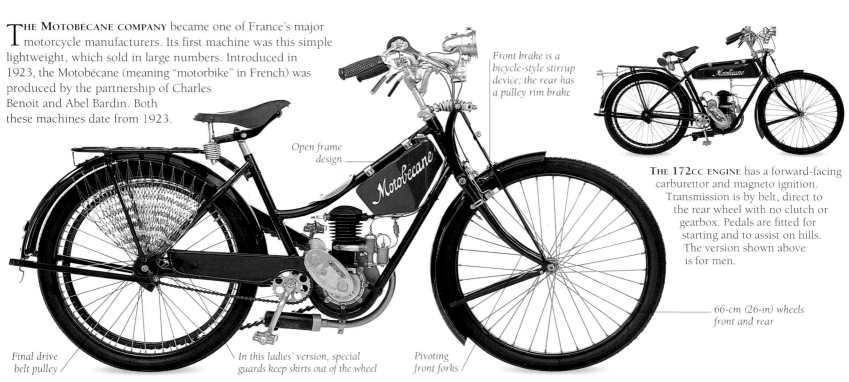

Front brake is a bicycle-style stirrup device; the rear has a pulley rim brake

Open frame design

THE 172CC ENGINE has a forward-facing carburettor and magneto ignition. Transmission is by belt, direct to the rear wheel with no clutch or gearbox. Pedals are fitted for starting and to assist on hills. The version shown above is for men.

66-cm (26-in) wheels front and rear

Final drive belt pulley

In this ladies' version, special guards keep skirts out of the wheel

Pivoting front forks

MOTO GUZZI 500

Capacity 498cc • Power output 18bhp @ 4,000rpm • Weight 130kg (287lb) • Top speed 100km/h (62mph)

AFTER WORLD WAR I, former Italian Air Force pilot Giorgio Parodi set up the Moto Guzzi company with Carlo Guzzi, his former mechanic and driver. Guzzi designed its first prototype in 1920. The design of the single-cylinder machine was so advanced that the company's last horizontal single, built in 1976, had the same bore and stroke dimensions as the original. The "bacon slicer" external flywheel appeared on all models until the late 1960s. Moto Guzzi became one of Italy's biggest manufacturers. The machine shown here dates from 1928.

THE 500's four-stroke motor had an interesting feature for those worried about breaking down. A retaining fork fitted to the combustion chamber made it impossible for the exhaust valve to drop into the engine. Guzzi continued this feature until the 1940s.

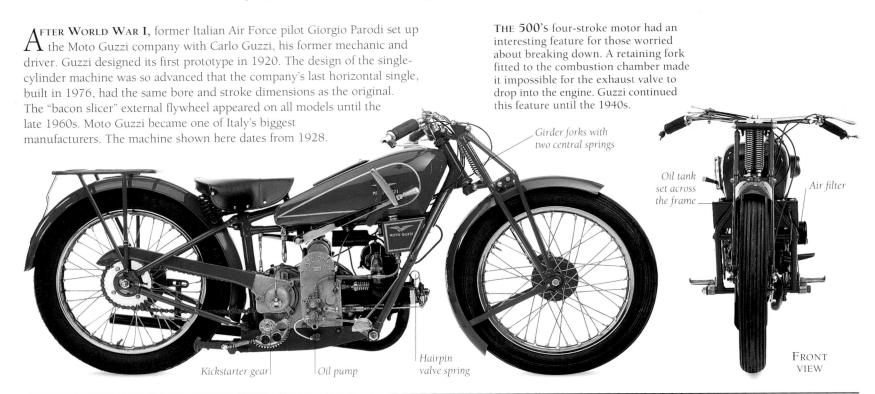

Girder forks with two central springs

Oil tank set across the frame

Air filter

Kickstarter gear

Oil pump

Hairpin valve spring

FRONT VIEW

MOTO GUZZI V7 SPECIAL

Capacity 757cc • Power output 45bhp @ 6,000rpm • Weight 228kg (502lb) • Top speed 164km/h (103mph)

ALTHOUGH MOTO GUZZI FIRST DEVELOPED its V-twin motor in the 1950s, motorcycle interest in Italy was at a low ebb and the motor was used in a three-wheeled military vehicle. The V-twin motorcycle was built to fulfil an order from the Italian police. Overseas interest created a need for a civilian version. The 703cc V7 came out in 1967. In 1969 the bore was enlarged by 3mm and called the V7 Special. It ran until 1971 (the year of this model) and had many features seen on modern Guzzi V-twins.

THE SPECIAL WAS AIMED at the American market, where it sold under various names, such as the Ambassador, Eldorado, and California. It formed the basis of many of the company's successful sports models, including the V7 Sport, S3, and Le Mans.

The screen is an American option

Crash bars

Oil-damped rear shock absorbers with spring pre-load adjustment

Right-foot gearchange

90°, transverse, four-stroke V-twin engine

Front drum brake

FRONT VIEW

MOTO GUZZI STORNELLO 125

Capacity 123cc • Power output 12bhp @ 7,200rpm • Weight 85kg (187lb) • Top speed 110km/h (68mph)

BUILT TO SELL AT A LOW PRICE AND DESIGNED TO APPEAL to the masses, the Stornello 125 was a cheap runabout – and yet was the first road bike designed by Guzzi's race bike designer Guilio Carcano. The four-stroke motor had a two-valve head, wet sump, and direct lighting. Produced from 1960 until 1968 for most markets (the U.S. continued to sell it until 1975), the model shown here is a 1970 version.

THE STORNELLO WAS PRODUCED in many guises during its lifetime, and variations in styling made it the Turismo, Sport, ISDT Trial (1966 only), Scrambler, or Regularita.

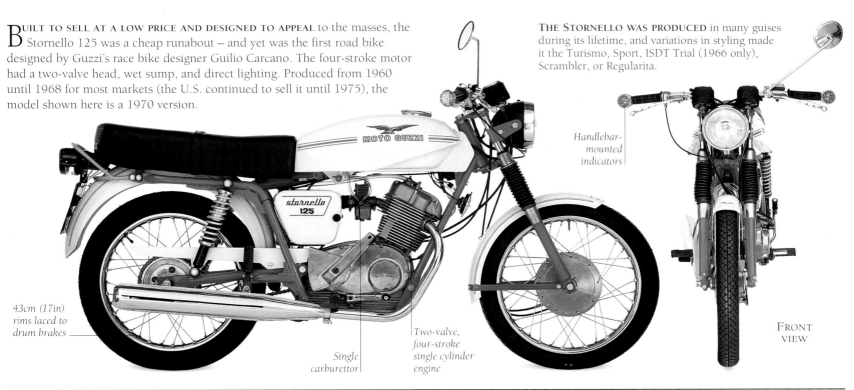

Handlebar-mounted indicators

43cm (17in) rims laced to drum brakes

Single carburettor

Two-valve, four-stroke single cylinder engine

FRONT VIEW

MOTO GUZZI 850 LE MANS 1

Capacity 844cc • Power output 80bhp • Weight 220kg (486lb) • Top speed 216km/h (134mph)

THE LE MANS 1 was one of the fastest of the Moto Guzzi bikes. Low, aggressive, and very stylish, it was always the centre of attention. Its massive, V-twin engine was designed by Giulio Carcano and was developed by Lino Tonti into the shaft-drive model that has since served so well. Much of this 850's weight was quite high in the frame, making it a very responsive bike when cornering. The left-hand front brake disc and the rear disc were pedal-activated, while the right-hand front disc was operated by hand lever. The Le Mans 1 shown here is a 1976 model.

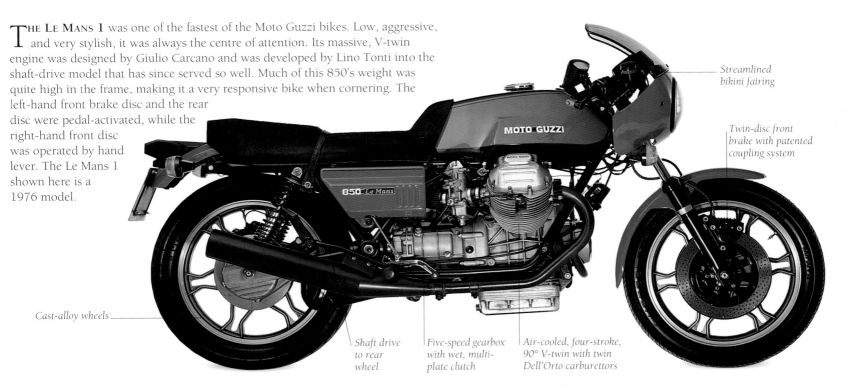

Streamlined bikini fairing

Twin-disc front brake with patented coupling system

Cast-alloy wheels

Shaft drive to rear wheel

Five-speed gearbox with wet, multi-plate clutch

Air-cooled, four-stroke, 90° V-twin with twin Dell'Orto carburettors

MOTO GUZZI V50

*Capacity 490cc • Power output 45bhp @ 7,500rpm
Weight 152kg (334lb) • Top speed 165km/h (103mph)*

ITALY

I N THE 1970S WHEN MOTO GUZZI needed a mid-range model to fill the gap between its small-capacity two-strokes and large four-stroke V-twins, it produced the V50. Although based on the company's larger V-twins, it had a completely redesigned engine and was popular with riders who found the larger models too big. Mass-produced at the old Innocenti plant (the home of Lambretta scooters), it came as well equipped as its peers with electric start, shaft final drive, and Guzzi's linked brake system, where the foot pedal operates both rear and front left-side disc.

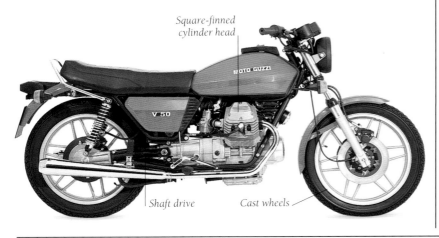

Square-finned
cylinder head

Shaft drive

Cast wheels

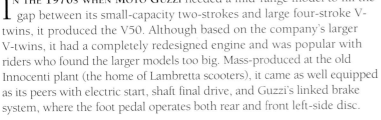

MOTO GUZZI
V1000 G5

*Capacity 949cc • Power output 64bhp @ 6,200rpm
Weight 220kg (484lb) • Top speed 180km/h (112mph)*

ITALY

T HE G5 WAS GUZZI'S MANUAL TOURING MODEL and was manufactured between 1978 and 1983. Developed from the automatic V1000 Convert, a five-speed gearbox was added to appease traditionalists. The pushrod, V-twin engine had 30-mm (1⅛-in) Dell'Orto carburettors and featured a linked braking system. It came with panniers and screen as standard equipment and was sold alongside the sports tourer SP model.

Perspex
windscreen

Factory-supplied
luggage cases

Dual, front
disc brake

Duplex, steel,
tubular frame

MOTOSACOCHE 1913

Capacity 290cc • Power output not known • Weight not known • Top speed 30mph (48km/h) (estimated)

SWITZERLAND

A SIMPLE TRANSLATION of *motosacoche* is "tool-bag engine", and the name was used for the first successful product of the Dufaux brothers of Geneva. This was an auxiliary engine and fuel tank self-contained in a subframe sitting within the frame of a bicycle. By 1913, this had become a fully fledged motorcycle with a larger, more conventional engine in a strong frame with sprung forks. There was still manual lubrication and no clutch, among other things, but the motorcycle as we know it today was beginning to emerge.

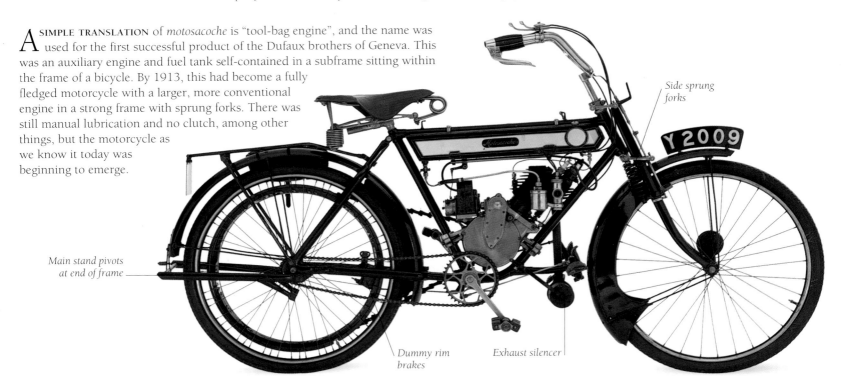

Side sprung
forks

Main stand pivots
at end of frame

Dummy rim
brakes

Exhaust silencer

MOTOSACOCHE JUBILE 424

Capacity 498cc • Power output not known • Weight not known • Top speed 109km/h (68mph) (estimated)

MOTOSACOCHE NOT ONLY MADE MOTORCYCLES but also supplied engines under the MAG name for use in other firms' machines. As a result there was a large variety of engines: side valve, overhead inlet and side exhaust, and full overhead valve were all made in both single and V-twin designs, and all were used in Motosacoche bikes. This 1932 Jubile 424 used a simple, side-valve engine.

BY THE TIME of the Jubile 424's manufacture, battery and coil ignition had been well proven in the car world. Its use on the 424 marked an early application in a motorcycle.

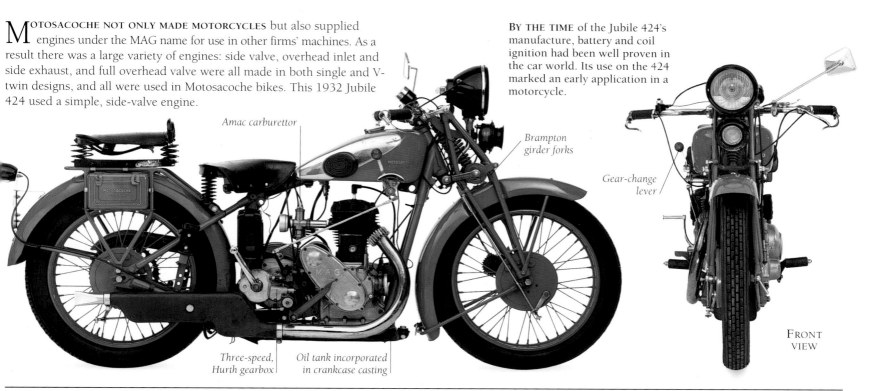

Amac carburettor

Brampton girder forks

Gear-change lever

FRONT VIEW

Three-speed, Hurth gearbox

Oil tank incorporated in crankcase casting

MÜNCH MAMMOTH

Capacity 1177cc • Power output 88bhp @ 6,000rpm • Weight 298kg (656lb) • Top speed 220km/h (137mph)

TAKING AS ITS BASE an engine from an NSU Prinz car, former Horex engineer Friedl Münch created a remarkable motorcycle in the Mammoth. Only produced in limited numbers from 1966 and sold at a price that could have bought three of Norton's heralded Commandos (see p.146), the Mammoth was capable of performance levels that were unequalled at the time. Although its weight made it awkward to manoeuvre at low speed, it was a useful high-speed tourer capable of cruising all day at 177km/h (110mph).

Large-capacity fuel tank

Twin car headlamps provide a high degree of night-time visibility

Airscoop helps to keep the drum-brake cool and efficient

Breather pipe

Although lighter and stronger than steel, Elektron-cast alloys are notoriously prone to corrosion

Four-cylinder, o.h.c. NSU car engine

MUSTANG THOROUGHBRED

Capacity 314cc • Power output 12.5bhp @ 6,000rpm • Weight not known • Top speed 65mph (105km/h) (estimated)

U.S.A.

ONE OF A NUMBER OF aviation companies that diversified into motorcycle production after the war, Gladden Products built the first of its small-wheeled Mustang motorcycles in 1946. Early machines used 197cc Villiers two-stroke engines, but later the firm switched to using its own 314cc side-valve engine, which was originally designed as an industrial power unit.

THE "THOROUGHBRED" model was introduced in 1960 and was the first to feature rear suspension. The example shown here dates from 1962. Sales declined in the 1960s, and Mustang production ended in 1965 when the British Burman company stopped making gearboxes.

Kickstarter

12-in (30-cm) wire wheels

Upside-down telescopic forks

Side-valve engine with camshaft mounted at the front

Carburettor and air filter are positioned at the front of the engine

FRONT VIEW

MV AGUSTA 125 TOURER

Capacity 124cc • Power output 5bhp @ 4,800rpm • Weight 72kg (159lb) • Top speed 85km/h (53mph)

ITALY

AIRCRAFT MAKER AGUSTA had diversified into motorcycle production after World War II. Despite the company's later reputation for racing machines, the first MV motorcycles were crude 98cc two-strokes. The 125 Tourer was a far better machine and was introduced in 1947 (the year of the bike shown here). The model continued in production until 1954 with few changes. The 125 had a four-speed gearbox with gear primary drive. Ignition and lighting were powered by a flywheel magneto.

Girder forks were used on the 125; ironically the earlier 98cc model used telescopics

Fish-tail exhaust

The 53 x 56-mm engine uses a cast-iron barrel

FRONT VIEW

THE COMPANY'S "banana" rear frame members were featured for the first time on the 125 Tourer.

MV Agusta 350 GP

Capacity 347cc • Power output 42bhp @ 11,000rpm • Weight 145kg (320lb) • Top speed 225km/h (140mph) (estimated)

ITALY

THE **1950 SEASON** saw MV build its first four-cylinder racers. They were designed by Piero Remor, who had previously worked for Gilera. Unsurprisingly, the new four had a marked similarity to Gilera's racing machines. The fours were redesigned for 1952 with a five-speed gearbox, chain drive (earlier models had shaft), and many other changes to engine and chassis. These changes made the MV far more competitive, and in September that year the company won its first Grand Prix when team leader Leslie Graham took the chequered flag at the Italian Grand Prix at Monza. A 350 version appeared in 1953. The engine's twin camshafts were driven by a chain of straight-cut gears running from the centre of the six-bearing crankshaft. The same crankshaft gear also provided primary drive to the gearbox. Subsequent evolution of the 350 four design was gradual, changes being made to improve performance or comply with new rules until replaced by a lighter and more powerful triple in 1965. The machine shown here is of the type raced from 1960 to 1961.

"DOLPHIN" FAIRINGS, like the one shown on this machine, were introduced when the FIM banned "Dustbin" fairings in 1957. Although "Dustbin" fairings also covered the front wheel of the motorcycle and they gave better top speed, they were potentially dangerous in windy conditions, especially on the exposed mountain section of the Isle of Man TT course.

•WORLD CHAMPION MV•

In 1956 John Surtees, pictured here at the 1960 Junior TT, became the first rider to win a World Championship on a four-cylinder MV. Over the following years he and other team riders notched up a stunning collection of World Championship victories in the 350cc and 500cc classes.

World Champion John Surtees

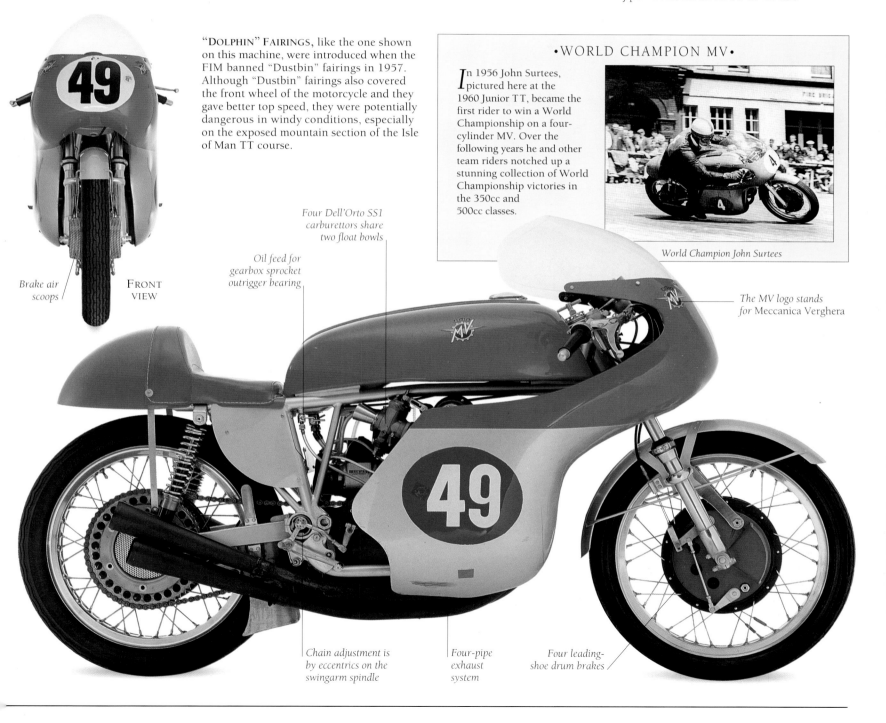

Brake air scoops

FRONT VIEW

Four Dell'Orto SS1 carburettors share two float bowls

Oil feed for gearbox sprocket outrigger bearing

The MV logo stands for Meccanica Verghera

Chain adjustment is by eccentrics on the swingarm spindle

Four-pipe exhaust system

Four leading-shoe drum brakes

MV Agusta 175CS

Capacity 174cc • Power output 11bhp @ 6,700rpm   ITALY
Weight 110kg (242lb) • Top speed 114km/h (71mph)

THE 175CS WAS INTRODUCED for 1954, a year after a more sedate touring version. Both models used an o.h.c. 174cc single-cylinder engine with a four-speed gearbox. The CS was to remain in the range until 1958, and during that time it was one of MV's biggest sellers. The "Disco Volante" nickname is derived from the flying-saucer shape of the lower part of the fuel tank. It was available with telescopic forks or the long leading-link design used on the 1956 model shown here. The model was replaced in the MV range by an o.h.v. machine.

Flying saucer-shaped fuel tank

Long leading-link forks were optional

Unit-construction, o.h.c. engine

MV Agusta
Liberty Sport

Capacity 48cc • Power output not known   ITALY
Weight 58kg (128lb) • Top speed 88km/h (55mph) (estimated)

ITALIAN LAWS ALLOWED MACHINES under 50cc to be used without registration and also by youngsters and in 1962 MV introduced the Liberty to compete in this part of the market. It had a comprehensive specification and was built to the same standards as the rest of the MV range. There was a tiny o.h.v. engine and a three-speed gearbox that was operated by a twistgrip on the left handlebar. Later versions had a four-speed box with footchange. The frame was similar to other MV lightweights with telescopic forks and swingarm rear suspension. The Liberty Sport shown here dates from 1966.

39 x 40-mm engine

MV Agusta 600

Capacity 592cc • Power output 52bhp @ 8,200rpm   ITALY
Weight 221kg (487lb) • Top speed 161km/h (100mph)

DESPITE THE SUCCESS of MV Agusta's four-cylinder racers, a road-going four did not appear until 1966, and when it did appear it was a touring motorcycle rather than the sporting machine that enthusiasts wanted. The luxury specification included cable-operated, twin, front disc brakes and an electric starter-cum-dynamo. Final drive was by shaft. The d.o.h.c. engine layout was based on the racers but the 600 was restricted to two carburettors. The bizarre styling included an oblong headlight from a Fiat car. The 600 continued until 1971, although fewer than 200 were built in that time. The bike pictured here is a 1968 model.

Handlebar-end indicators

Combined dynamo/electric starter mounted underneath the gearbox

---

MV Agusta Minibike

Capacity 48cc • Power output 2bhp   ITALY
Weight not known • Top speed 40km/h (25mph) (estimated)

PHIL READ WON the last two of MV Agusta's 37 World Championships in 1973 and 1974. The first of these minibikes (1972 model shown) was built for Read's son and a limited number was subsequently made for sale to indulgent parents. Behind the authentic-looking red and silver fairing was a humble Franco Morini two-stroke engine. The four exhaust pipes, just like the racers, branched out from a single cylinder.

MV race-style fairing

Four-pipe exhaust system

25-cm (10-in) wheels

MV Agusta America

Capacity 789cc • Power output 75bhp @ 8,500rpm • Weight 240kg (529lb) • Top speed 209 km/h (130mph)

IN **1971 MV PRODUCED** its first sporty four-cylinder road bike. It retained the shaft drive of the touring 600 but capacity and compression ratio were increased. Also supplied with four carburettors, the performance was significantly improved. The new machines also looked better with sporty styling and significant splashes of red. The 1975 model shown here was part of a special batch of machines; intended to impress the American market, they failed to make any impact.

Upmarket specification includes a suede seat

Front brake master cylinder

Silencers for the U.S. market are quiet but ugly

Engine capacity of U.S. models increased to 789cc

Scarab front brake callipers with 28-cm (11-in) discs

MZ RT125

Capacity 123cc • Power output 5hp @ 4,800rpm • Weight 85kg (187lb) • Top speed 75km/h (47mph)

BEFORE **WORLD WAR II** the DKW factory was based at Zschopau. After the war it was situated in the Eastern sector of the divided country. DKW relocated to the West but its old factory continued to produce motorcycles to original DKW designs using, after 1956, the title MZ (Motorrad Zschopau). Originally introduced in 1938, the RT125 re-entered production in 1949, and derivatives of the original design were still produced at Zschopau 40 years later. Simple, reliable, and sturdy, it was ideal for production and use in the Eastern Bloc.

Telescopic front forks and plunger rear suspension were advanced features for a 1938 design

Enclosed chains were used on Zschopau-built bikes after 1954

Two-stroke engine has gear primary drive to a unit-construction three-speed gearbox

MZ RE125

Capacity 124cc • Power output 25bhp • Weight 91kg (200lb) • Top speed 211km/h (131mph)

GERMAN®

PRODUCTION **MZ**S WERE RUGGED, UTILITARIAN MACHINES, yet much of the success of Japanese two-stroke racing machines can be attributed to MZ and its RE125. Chief designer for MZ during the 1960s was Walter Kaaden, a brilliant and much underrated engineer who pioneered many of the advances made in two-stroke technology since World War II. Based at Zschopau in former East Germany, the MZ racing team did not enjoy the resources and funding of their Japanese competitors in the 125cc and 250cc World Championships,

yet they could still produce some remarkable feats of engineering, not least the development of a single-cylinder 125cc engine capable of producing more than 200bhp per litre MZ was dealt a huge blow at the penultimate Grand Prix of the 1961 250cc World Championship when its number one rider, Ernst Degner, left for Suzuki, taking with him the secrets of Kaaden's machines. MZ persevered but was unable to compete with the technical back-up and superior materials available to competitors.

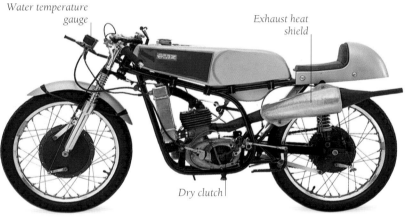

Water temperature gauge

Exhaust heat shield

Dry clutch

DESPITE THE TECHNICAL SUPERIORITY of its 125cc and 250cc two-stroke racers in the late 1950s and early 1960s, MZ never won a World Championship. This can be attributed to the lack of money and resources available to the East German team.

•TWO-STROKE PIONEER•

Much of MZ's designer Walter Kaaden's pioneering work was done in the field of exhaust technology, which was later recognized as central to the efficiency of a two-stroke engine. He realized how the shape of the expansion chamber (exhaust) creates "pressure waves" from exhaust gases and subsequently increases crankcase pressure. In this way, power lost in the combustion process is re-used in a natural "supercharging" effect.

Walter Kaaden in 1993

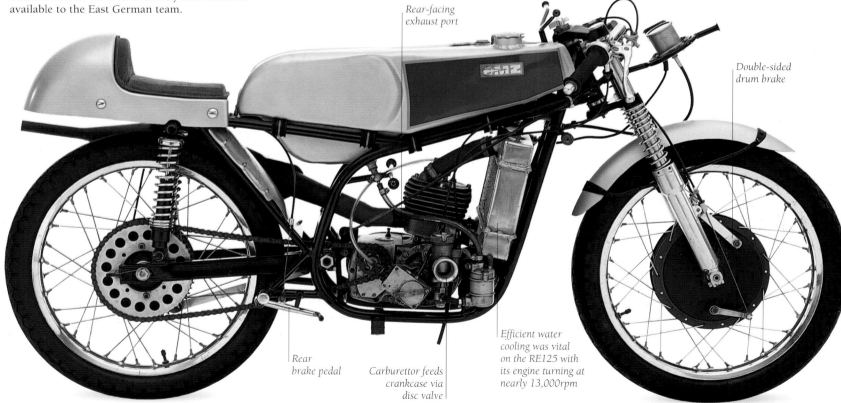

Rear-facing exhaust port

Double-sided drum brake

Rear brake pedal

Carburettor feeds crankcase via disc valve

Efficient water cooling was vital on the RE125 with its engine turning at nearly 13,000rpm

MZ
ES250/2 TROPHY

Capacity 243cc • Power output 17.5bhp
Weight 156kg (344lb) • Top speed 116km/h (72mph)

GERMANY

MZ
ETS250 TROPHY SPORT

Capacity 243cc • Power output 21bhp @ 5200rpm
Weight not known • Top speed 129km/h (80mph)

GERMANY

Ungainly and utilitarian in appearance, the MZ ES250 and its variants became highly valued by riders in the West. They prized reliability, efficiency, economy of purchase, and operation over aesthetic design. For many Eastern Bloc buyers it was the only option. Originally introduced in 1956 the ES250, with its long leading-link front forks and distinctive headlamp cowl, was produced with limited modifications until 1973, the year the machine pictured here was built.

A sporting two-stroke version of the Trophy model was introduced in 1969. The philosophy of simplicity and practicality remained but the appearance and performance of the bike was improved. Power was marginally increased and a 46-cm (18-in) front wheel replaced the 41-cm (16-in) of the original. A massive 22-litre (4.8-gallon) tank was substituted for the unusual fuel tank/headlamp cowl. The distinctive long silencer and the enclosed chain remained. Both ES and ETS models were replaced by a new range in 1973.

Side panels hide air filter and electrics

Earles forks

Integral levers for suspension adjustment

Telescopic units replaced leading-link front forks

Huge 22-litre (4.8-gallon) fuel tank

Drum brakes

Kickstarter on left-hand side

MZ SKORPION

Capacity 660cc • Power output 48bhp @ 6,250rpm • Weight 170kg (375lb) • Top speed 174km/h (108mph)

GERMANY

Introduced in prototype form in 1992, the Skorpion was intended as a machine to take the revamped MZ (now MuZ) company into the next century. Designed by the British Seymour Powell partnership, the production version, like the bike pictured here, appeared in 1994. The five-valve single-cylinder engine was supplied by Yamaha and many of the parts were of Italian origin.

THE TWIN-TUBE STEEL FRAME and single-cylinder engine are common to both the Sport and the Tour versions, although the latter has a more upright riding position and loses the half-fairing. The Skorpion won a British design award.

Headlight from Yamaha

Twin-tube steel frame

Disc brakes front and rear

Cast-alloy wheels

Liquid-cooled, s.o.h.c., five-valve, four-stroke single is mildly tuned for reliability

Adjustable footpegs and handlebars

FRONT VIEW

NER-A-CAR MODEL C

Capacity 348cc • Power output not known • Weight 250lb (113kg) • Top speed 55mph (88km/h)

THE NAME **NER-A-CAR** is a play on words involving the name of the designer, Carl A. Neracher, and the characteristics of the machine. The basis of the machine was a chassis consisting of two pressed-steel side members, between which the engine and gearbox were mounted. At the front a pivoted loop provided limited suspension, the arms of the loop being widely splayed towards the rear to provide steering clearance for the front wheel, which pivoted on an inclined kingpin in the centre of the loop. The handlebars were mounted on a vertical column, the lower end of which carried an arm connected to a steering arm projecting from the front hub by a curved drag link. Comprehensive mudguarding and enclosure made the machine truly "near a car". The first European Ner-a-Car was produced under licence in England – although it was of American origin – by Sheffield Simplex Ltd., and the Model C shown here dates from 1925. *The Motor Cycle* carried out a favourable road test on the machine in September 1924.

THE LOW CENTRE of gravity and its ease of handling made the Ner-a-Car easy to drive. Large mudguards meant it could be ridden in conventional clothing without the rider getting dirty during his or her journey while the open frame enabled riding in a skirt, a kilt, or a cassock. The company advertised extensively in an effort to attract custom from unlikely sources. Vicars were said to bless the Ner-a-Car makers with their custom.

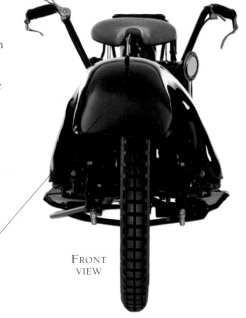

Large front mudguard

FRONT VIEW

•INTERESTING TRANSMISSION•

The original Ner-a-Car had a 211cc single-cylinder, two-stroke engine mounted with its crankshaft running in line with the frame. Capacity of the engine was later increased to 285cc. The interesting part of the design was the transmission, which was by friction from the engine's large flywheel. The driven disc was perpendicular to the flywheel, and its position could be moved by the left-hand twistgrip. Varying the position relative to the circumference of the wheel provided variable gearing.

Ner-a-Car and rider, c.1930

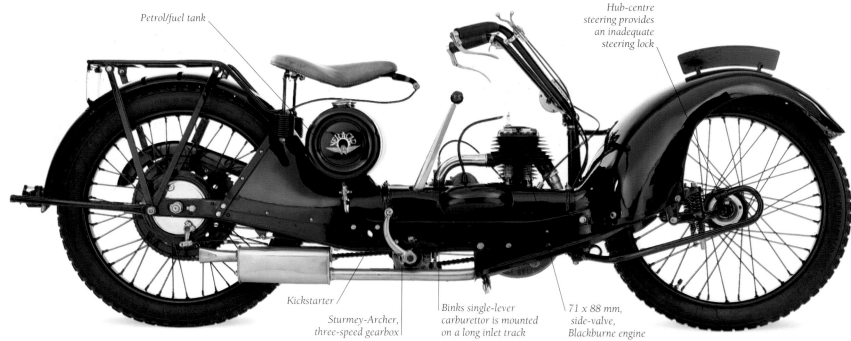

Petrol/fuel tank

Hub-centre steering provides an inadequate steering lock

Kickstarter

Sturmey-Archer, three-speed gearbox

Binks single-lever carburettor is mounted on a long inlet track

71 x 88 mm, side-valve, Blackburne engine

NEW IMPERIAL

Capacity 491cc • Power output 40bhp @ 7,500rpm • Weight not known • Top speed 110mph (177km/h)

ALTHOUGH DESIGNED AS A RACING MACHINE, it was as a record breaker that the 500cc, V-twin New Imperial achieved lasting fame. The engine was virtually two pushrod, o.h.v., 250s on a common crankcase, driven via a four-speed, Sturmey-Archer gearbox. As a racing machine, it was beset with handling problems. Even so, ridden by Ginger Woods, it raised the Brooklands 500cc lap record to 115.82mph (186km/h) in 1935.

IN 1928, *THE MOTOR CYCLE* offered a prize for the first British 500cc multi-cylinder machine to cover 100 miles (161km) in one hour on a British track. Despite the efforts of both Triumph and Ariel with supercharged machines, it was not until the New Imperial twin appeared in 1934 that the prize was won, with 102.27 miles (165km) covered.

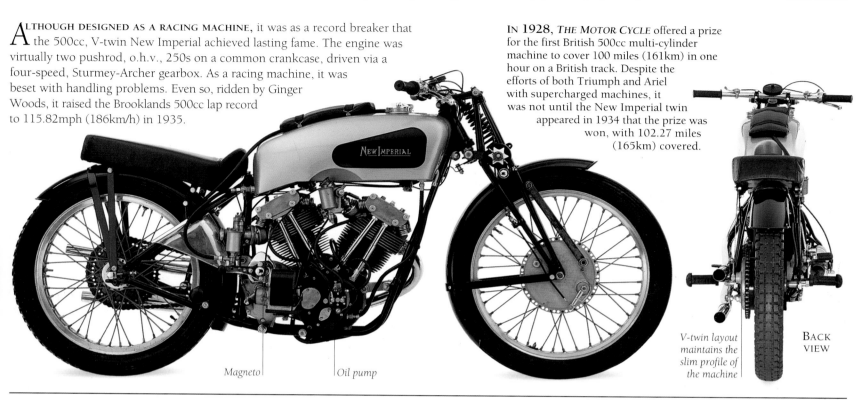

Magneto

Oil pump

V-twin layout maintains the slim profile of the machine

BACK VIEW

NIMBUS MK II

Capacity 746cc • Power output 22bhp @ 4,000rpm • Weight 172kg (380lb) • Top speed 121km/h (75mph)

PRODUCED IN DENMARK, the Nimbus was hardly changed from 1934 to its demise in 1959. Its sophisticated engine was housed in a crude frame made of steel plates and strip. A dash panel incorporating the handlebars carried the instruments and electrical switchgear, while the machine was completed by a fish-tail straight-through exhaust system. The Nimbus was rarely sold outside its country of origin.

THE HEART of this machine was a four-cylinder in-line engine in which the vertical drive shaft to the overhead camshaft doubled as the armature of the dynamo. There was a three-speed gearbox (with footchange after 1935) and shaft drive to the rear wheel.

Pressed-steel handlebars

Metal-plate frame

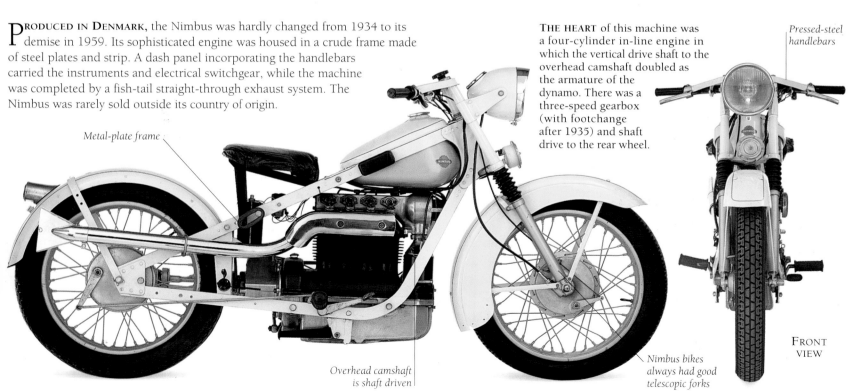

Overhead camshaft is shaft driven

Nimbus bikes always had good telescopic forks

FRONT VIEW

Norton SIDE VALVE

Capacity 490cc • Power output 12bhp @ 3,000rpm
Weight 252lb (114kg) • Top speed 75mph (121km/h)

UNITED KINGDOM

NORTON INTRODUCED ITS OWN PRODUCTION ENGINE in 1908. The company had previously used proprietary power units supplied by Clément, Peugeot, and JAP. This side-valve engine did much to establish Norton's reputation for quality products and sporting success with excellent results at the Brooklands race track. It soon became available in 633cc and 490cc versions. The 490cc engine was used in this 1920 racing model which also had a three-speed gearbox and chain drive. Earlier machines were single-speed, belt-drive devices. Improved versions of this power unit were made until 1954.

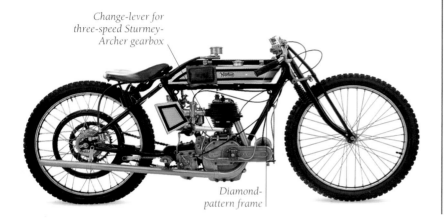

Change-lever for three-speed Sturmey-Archer gearbox

Diamond-pattern frame

Norton MODEL 18

Capacity 490cc • Power output 18bhp
Weight 336lb (152kg) • Top speed 80mph (129km/h)

UNITED KINGDOM

THE MODEL 18 FIRST APPEARED in 1922, along with a number of Norton's new overhead-valve singles. The Model 18 remained available, with some modifications to the suspension and the addition of a four-speed gearbox, until 1954. The bottom half of the engine was virtually identical to that of the Model H side valve, but instead of side valves, the cams operated overhead valves by means of pushrods and rockers. The chain drive to the three-speed Sturmey-Archer gearbox ran in a new pressed-tin "oilbath" case that survived until the 1960s on Norton roadsters. The bike shown here was produced in 1924.

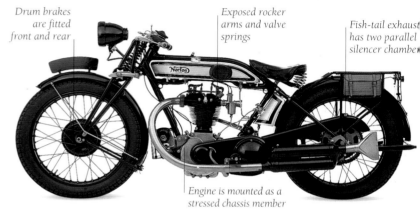

Drum brakes are fitted front and rear

Exposed rocker arms and valve springs

Fish-tail exhaust has two parallel silencer chamber

Engine is mounted as a stressed chassis member

Norton CS1

Capacity 490cc • Power output not known • Weight 330lb (150kg) • Top speed 71mph (114km/h)

UNITED KINGDOM

THE CS1 – MEANING CAMSHAFT ONE – was Norton's first overhead-camshaft machine, and the company stuck with the layout until 1962. It was developed in response to the success of Velocette's overhead-cam racer and unveiled in May 1927. Designed by Walter Moore, who later went to work for NSU, the CS1 had a new cradle frame as well as the new engine and the latest Webb girder forks. The bike shown is from 1928.

THE "CRICKET BAT" CS1, so called because of the shape of its bevel gear housings, gained a more efficient fish-tail silencer in 1928. Production of the CS1 ended in 1929.

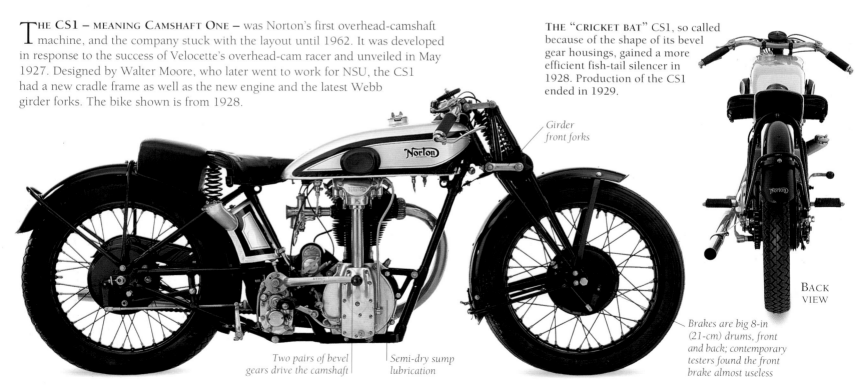

Girder front forks

Two pairs of bevel gears drive the camshaft

Semi-dry sump lubrication

BACK VIEW

Brakes are big 8-in (21-cm) drums, front and back; contemporary testers found the front brake almost useless

NORTON INTERNATIONAL

Capacity 490cc • Power output 29bhp @ 5,000rpm
Weight 355lb (161kg) • Top speed 85mph (137km/h)

UNITED KINGDOM

THE "INTER" WAS INTRODUCED into Norton's range of single-cylinder machines in 1932 and used the improved o.h.c. engine that had been redesigned by Arthur Carroll in 1930. A sports model intended as a fast road bike or a competitive mount for the amateur racer, it was available in 350cc or 500cc models. Lights were not included in the list price, but the otherwise impressive specification included an Amal TT carburettor, Webb competition girder forks, and a four-speed gearbox. The model's popularity waned after World War II, but it survived in various forms until 1958. The machine shown here is a 1936 Model 30.

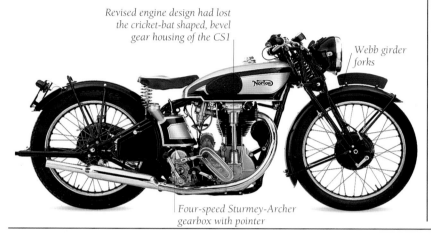

Revised engine design had lost the cricket-bat shaped, bevel gear housing of the CS1

Webb girder forks

Four-speed Sturmey-Archer gearbox with pointer

NORTON 500

Capacity 490cc • Power output 35bhp @ 6,000rpm
Weight 380lb (172kg) • Top speed 110mph (177km/h)

UNITED KINGDOM

NORTON INTRODUCED PLUNGER REAR SUSPENSION on its works racing machines in 1936. Production versions of the chassis, nicknamed the "garden gate", soon followed. This 1938 racing machine is not fitted with the telescopic forks or twin-camshaft engine that appeared on the works bikes that year. Although increasingly uncompetitive against more powerful foreign opposition in international events, the "Manx Specification" o.h.c. Norton with alloy cylinder head was still almost obligatory equipment in the 500 class for amateur racers. The "Manx" name was not adopted until after World War II.

"Garden gate" frame with plunger rear suspension

Alloy cylinder head with exposed hairpin valve springs

Ventilated conical drum brake

Sturmey-Archer-based gearbox

NORTON MODEL 7 DOMINATOR

Capacity 497cc • Power output 29bhp @ 6,000rpm • Weight 420lb (190kg) • Top speed 88mph (142km/h)

UNITED KINGDOM

LIKE OTHER FACTORIES, NORTON was eager to emulate the success of Triumph's Speed Twin (see pp.182–83), but World War II caused a delay until November 1948. The Model 7 Dominator comprised a new 500cc o.h.v. parallel-twin engine with a revised gearbox to fit the shape of the engine in the plunger-framed, rolling chassis from the ES2 single. The new engine had a single camshaft mounted in front of the cylinders, and pushrods passed through a tunnel in the iron barrel. It was designed by Bert Hopwood. Illustrated is a 1949 machine.

Plunger rear suspension

Norton Roadholder front forks

Dynamo is driven by a fibre gear at the end of camshaft

FRONT VIEW

ALTHOUGH THE plunger-framed Model 7 was eclipsed by featherbed-framed versions from 1952 onwards, it was the predecessor to a line of Norton twins that culminated in the Commando (see p.146).

NORTON MANX

Capacity 498cc • Power output 47bhp @ 6,500rpm • Weight 309lb (140kg) • Top speed 140mph (225km/h)

NORTON'S OVERHEAD-CAMSHAFT racing singles had received 35 years of development by the time the final machines emerged from the firm's factory at Bracebridge Street, Birmingham, in 1962. Direct factory involvement was reduced from 1955 but the Manx remained competitive much later. Norton's final TT win was achieved by Mike Hailwood in 1961, and as late as 1969 the bikes achieved top-three finishes in 500cc Grand Prix racing. The most significant post-war improvement to the machine was the use of the famous "featherbed" frame, which endowed the Manx with faultless handling. The engine also received attention. The twin camshaft design, which the factory

bikes used in 1938, was adopted on post-war production models, and a revised short-stroke design was used from 1954. The Manx was available with a 350cc or 500cc engine. The smaller machine used the model number 40M, the 500 30M. The bigger bike was more successful. The model pictured here is a 1962 30M, one of the last of the line of Manx racers. After the final Manx had been built in 1962, Norton's historic home at Bracebridge Street was shut down. Road bike production moved to the AMC factory in south London, ending an era of British motorcycle building.

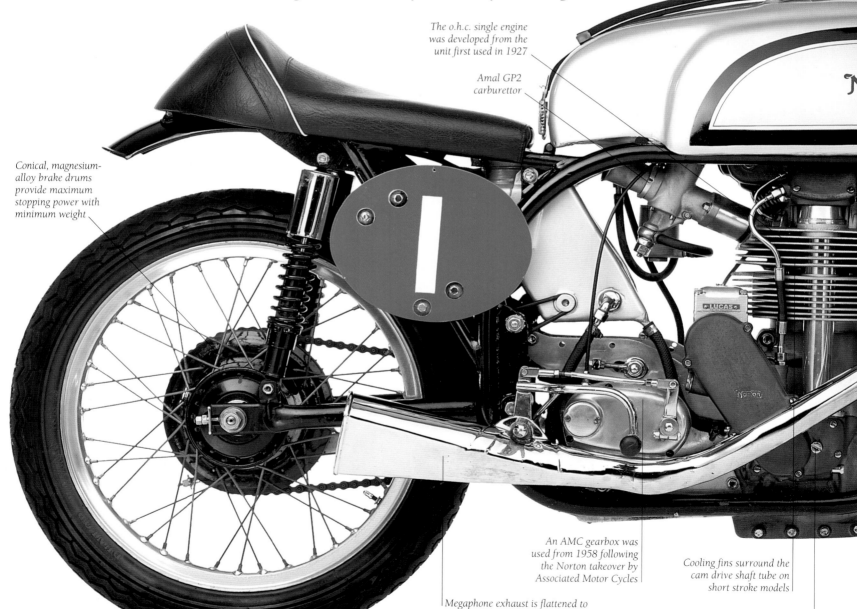

The o.h.c. single engine was developed from the unit first used in 1927

Amal GP2 carburettor

Conical, magnesium-alloy brake drums provide maximum stopping power with minimum weight

An AMC gearbox was used from 1958 following the Norton takeover by Associated Motor Cycles

Cooling fins surround the cam drive shaft tube on short stroke models

Megaphone exhaust is flattened to increase cornering clearance; 350 models use a reverse-cone megaphone

Right-side crank end drives helical gears for the overhead cams, oil pump, and magneto drive

THE "FEATHERBED" FRAME – so-called because works rider Harold Daniell likened its comfort to that of a feather bed – became commercially available after its stunning debut in the 1950 TT when Norton scored a 1-2-3 in both the Senior and Junior races. Developed by Rex McCandless, the double-loop, cradle frame was notable for its stability and steering under racing conditions. It was also cheaper to make and less prone to breakage than the "garden gate" design that it replaced. It was probably the biggest single advance in motorcycle chassis design since the appearance of the "new" Werner layout in 1901.

A "head steady" clamps the engine to the frame, providing extra stiffness for the steering head

Norton's famous Roadholder telescopic forks

•350CC NORTON•

The Manx Norton in action at the 1952 Dutch Grand Prix

From its spectacular debut in 1927 in the Isle of Man Senior TT, to its demise nearly 35 years later, the overhead-camshaft racing Norton was "unapproachable" on the racetrack. The "featherbed"-framed models, introduced in 1950, boasted superb steering and roadholding. Here Geoff Duke takes a corner in his winning ride in the 1952 Dutch Grand Prix. He led the race from start to finish.

BACK
VIEW

Fibreglass numberplate with perspex fly screen was used from 1960

Slim front view gives maximum air penetration; by the late 1950s, most riders fitted fairings

Twin air scoops provide ventilation for the drum brakes

Double-sided drum brake was used on the very last machines

FRONT
VIEW

NORTON
650SS DOMINATOR

Capacity 646cc • Power output 49bhp @ 6,800rpm
Weight 434lb (197kg) • Top speed 115mph (185km/h)

UNITED KINGDOM

MANY CONSIDERED THE 650SS to be the best of the Featherbed Dominators. The engine was enlarged to 646cc and fitted with steeply angled twin Amal carburettors. The lighting system was fed by a 12-volt alternator, but magneto ignition was retained long after other makers had changed to coil. The gearbox was AMC. The revised, "slimline", frame had waisted top rails to accommodate pressed-steel panelling and was fitted to some models from 1960 to 1963. This bike dates from 1962.

Norton's publicity emphasized the featherbed frame's reputation for good handling.

Chromed mudguard

Post-1960 featherbed frames were known as "slimline"

NORTON
FASTBACK COMMANDO

Capacity 745cc • Power output 56bhp @ 6,500rpm
Weight 398lb (180kg) • Top speed 115mph (185km/h)

UNITED KINGDOM

LAUNCHED IN **1967**, the radically styled Commando gained the name Fastback in 1969 (the year of this model), to distinguish it from the more conventional 1968 version. The engine, gearbox, swingarm, exhaust system, and rear wheel were mounted together as a single assembly, held onto the massive tubular spine frame by three "Isolastic" rubber insulators. The Atlas engine was slanted forwards and the four-speed AMC gearbox was driven by an uprated triplex chain. The front wheel gained an efficient twin, leading-shoe brake and the Roadholder forks were retained.

BACK VIEW

Ventilated, twin, leading-shoe drum brakes

Innovative "Isolastic" engine mounts reduce vibration

NORTON COMMANDO INTERSTATE MkIII 850ES

Capacity 829cc • Power output 60bhp @ 6,000rpm • Weight 430lb (195kg) • Top speed 115mph (185km/h)

UNITED KINGDOM

NORTON WAS ON THE VERGE of bankruptcy by 1975 when this bike – the final version of the Commando – was produced. Based on 1973's MkI 850, the MkIII was fitted with an electric starter in addition to the kickstarter. It had tuned silencers, Lockheed disc brakes front and rear, left-hand gearchange, halogen lighting, and a full complement of accessories, such as mirrors and indicators. Production only lasted until 1977.

FOR THE **850ES** to comply with strict environmental legislation in the vital American market, 140 improvements were required. It was sold in Roadster form with black and gold livery, or as the Interstate with Manx-style silver and black as seen here.

Annular discharge silencers were tuned to give a deep engine note

The Commando's pre-unit gearbox was outdated by 1975

Disc brake

FRONT VIEW

NORTON
COMMANDO FORMULA 750

Capacity 750cc • Power output not known
Weight not known • Top speed not known

UNITED KINGDOM

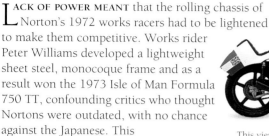

LACK OF POWER MEANT that the rolling chassis of Norton's 1972 works racers had to be lightened to make them competitive. Works rider Peter Williams developed a lightweight sheet steel, monocoque frame and as a result won the 1973 Isle of Man Formula 750 TT, confounding critics who thought Nortons were outdated, with no chance against the Japanese. This bike was produced in 1973.

This view shows the fairing removed, exposing the monocoque frame.

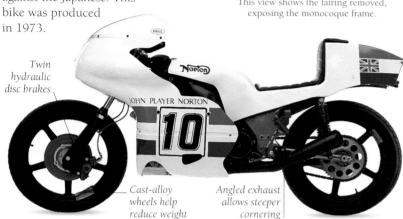

Twin hydraulic disc brakes

Cast-alloy wheels help reduce weight

Angled exhaust allows steeper cornering

NORTON CHALLENGE

Capacity 750cc • Power output 95bhp @ 9,750rpm
Weight not known • Top speed not known

UNITED KINGDOM

BY 1973 THE COMMANDO ENGINE was outdated, so Norton employed Cosworth Engineering to design a 750cc vertical-twin engine for the Formula 750 series. The unit-construction engine was, in effect, two cylinders from Cosworth's water-cooled, 3-litre (13.6-gallon), d.o.h.c., Formula 1 V8 car engine. Lack of funds meant that the Challenge's potential was never realized. Shown here is a 1974 model.

Water and oil radiators

FRONT VIEW

Twin front disc brakes

Engine-mounted alloy swingarm

NORTON NRS588 ROTARY RACER

Capacity 588cc (estimated) • Power output 135bhp (estimated) • Weight not known • Top speed not known

UNITED KINGDOM

TWO DECADES AFTER ITS LAST TT VICTORY, a Norton Wankel ridden by Steve Hislop won 1992's Senior race. The bike was the culmination of 20 years of Wankel development begun by the BSA-Triumph group. The chassis had a twin-spar, alloy frame, with upside-down front forks and monoshock rear suspension. Despite the success of the racers, the Wankel-engined road bikes did not sell well.

Aerodynamic fairing

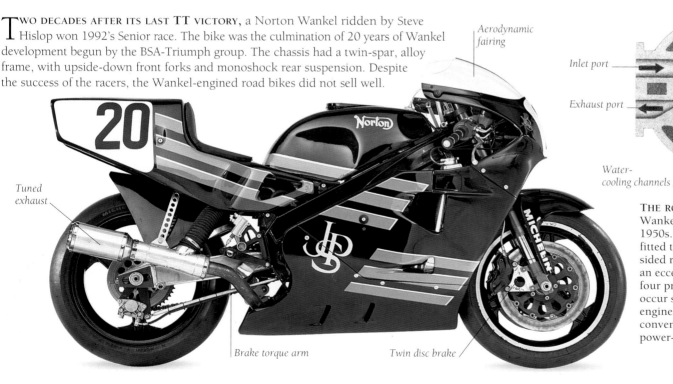

Tuned exhaust

Brake torque arm

Twin disc brake

Three-sided rotor

Inlet port

Exhaust port

Eccentric chamber

Spark plug

Water-cooling channels

Spur gear

THE ROTARY'S INVENTOR, Felix Wankel, developed the engine in the 1950s. It was based on a supercharger fitted to German warplanes. A three-sided rotor spins on a spur gear inside an eccentrically shaped chamber. The four processes of internal combustion occur simultaneously, making the engine more efficient than the conventional four-stroke with its power-sapping inertia stresses.

NSU

Capacity 211cc • Power output 1.25bhp @ 1,500rpm
Weight 40kg (88lb) • Top speed 39km/h (24mph)

GERMANY

LIKE MANY PIONEER motorcycle manufacturers, NSU got into the business via bicycles and, before that, sewing machines. This, the company's first motorcycle, dates from 1901 and was fitted with a Swiss Zedel (Zurcher & Luthi) engine clipped to the front downtube of a strengthened bicycle frame. The rear wheel was driven by a leather belt. There was an automatic inlet valve, manual lubrication, and trembler coil ignition. Although the machine had no suspension, NSU saw the need for a braking system improved from the parent bicycle.

The only suspension is a sprung saddle

External, contracting-band brake

NSU 350TT

Capacity 349cc • Power output 7bhp @ 2,500rpm
Weight not known • Top speed not known

GERMANY

THE ADVANTAGES OF THE TWIN-CYLINDER engine over the single when more power was required were appreciated very early on and, as the V-twin was the easiest form to accommodate in a motorcycle frame, it was that layout which most manufacturers followed. This 349cc NSU from 1912, with its mechanically operated, overhead inlet and side exhaust valves, had an up to date engine but the transmission was crude, with direct belt drive from the engine pulley to the rear wheel. The suspension was non-existent. Even so, the machine achieved fourth and seventh places in the 1913 Isle of Man Junior TT.

Primitive brakes consist of an external contracting band and a V-block in the belt rim

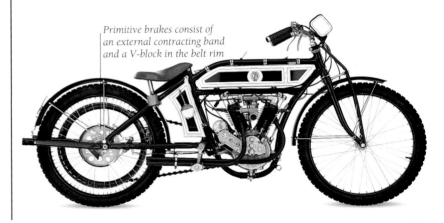

NSU 18PS SPORT

Capacity 1000cc • Power output 15bhp @ 3,800rpm
Weight 160kg (353lb) • Top speed 121km/h (75mph)

GERMANY

BY THE EARLY 1920s the motorcycle was showing little sign of its bicycle parentage. Frames were heavier, longer, and lower; engines were more powerful; the three-speed, countershaft gearbox with clutch and kickstarter was almost universal; and brakes had improved beyond recognition. In the large-capacity class, the V-twin engine reigned supreme, and because the larger engines produced plenty of power, they tended to lag behind the smaller machines in terms of engine development. The i.o.e. engine in this 1924 NSU originated in bikes produced before World War I. Such machines were popular with the fast solo rider as well as for sidecar work.

Final-drive chain

Sprung front forks

NSU 500SS

Capacity 494cc • Power output 22bhp @ 4,400rpm
Weight 165kg (364lb) • Top speed 148km/h (92mph)

GERMANY

SO SIMILAR was the 500cc o.h.c. engine Walter Moore designed for NSU to his Norton design that it was said that NSU stood for "Norton Spares Used". It may be more true to say that, having produced one satisfactory design, he worked along similar lines in designing the NSU. Shown here is a 1931 model.

Walter Moore (left), shortly after joining NSU, with a factory rider

Forged-steel shoe forms lower member of the frame

NSU Kompressor

Capacity 347cc • Power output 46bhp @ 8,000rpm • Weight 200kg (441lb) • Top speed 219km/h (136mph)

ALTHOUGH THE **K**OMPRESSOR **WAS FAMOUS** for its record-breaking activities in post-war years, the supercharged NSU twin was an example of how not to make a racing motorcycle. At a time when the dominant 500cc machine was the 138-kg (304-lb) BMW Kompressor (see p.28), a 200-kg (441-lb) 350 was clearly not the way to proceed, however much power it produced. While it is true that there was much less opposition in the 350cc class, what there was had been developed over a number of years and the main threat to Norton and

Velocette supremacy looked likely to come from DKW. Although it was clear that NSU's frames and suspension designs left much to be desired, the same could not be said of the company's engine which, with double overhead camshafts, unit construction, and supercharging, represented the state of the art at the time. After World War II, the machine reappeared in German national races in both 350cc and 500cc forms, but was never a match for the BMW. The NSU Kompressor illustrated dates from 1939.

THE **NSU K**OMPRESSOR appeared in 1938 at first in rigid-framed form but, by the following year, the engine was mounted in a plunger-sprung frame, still fitted with girder forks. As Moto-Guzzi and Velocette had by then been using pivoted-fork rear suspension for some years and both BMW and Norton were using telescopic front forks, it was clear that NSU was lagging behind the leaders in both frame and suspension design.

FRONT VIEW

Duplex, cradle frame has widely spaced frame tubes

• RECORD BREAKER •

The NSU Kompressor had some racing success – the picture on the right shows Heiner Fleischmann on his way to third place in the 1939 Junior TT – but its greatest triumph was in breaking records. The Kompressor's final achievement came in 1956 when, wrapped in a streamlined shell, it raised the record for the "world's fastest" motorcycle to 340km/h (211mph).

Heiner Fleischmann at the 1939 Junior TT

Plunger rear suspension

Twin overhead camshafts are shaft driven

Hand-formed, alloy fuel tank

53.3-cm (21in) front wheel

Supercharger

NSU Fox

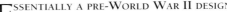

Capacity 98cc • Power output 6bhp @ 6,500rpm
Weight 87kg (192lb) • Top speed 85km/h (53mph)

GERMANY

THE FOX WAS THE FIRST entirely new post-war design from NSU, and broke new ground in being a four-stroke in a class dominated by two-strokes. Presumably in an effort to counter possible sales resistance and to win customers from rival manufacturers, the engine was in the style of a two-stroke. The pressed-steel front fork carried short-leading links, again with the springs enclosed. This bike is a 1949 model.

FRONT VIEW

Frame's centre section houses rear suspension spring

Three-speed gearbox built in-unit with the engine

NSU 251 OSL

Capacity 241cc • Power output 10½bhp @ 5,000rpm
Weight 132kg (291lb) • Top speed 100km/h (62mph)

GERMANY

ESSENTIALLY A PRE-WORLD WAR II DESIGN introduced in 1933, the OSL was put back into production after the war and continued until it was superseded by the Max in 1952. Clever design work gave the engine a similar appearance to the more expensive o.h.c. machines, while at the same time reducing cost and complexity. The performance was very respectable, and the gearbox allowed this to be exploited to the full. The machine had an old-fashioned look; this model dates from 1951.

FRONT VIEW

Fully enclosed final-drive chain

Pushrod o.h.v. engine

Oil compartment at the front of the crankcase

NSU Max

Capacity 247cc • Power output 15bhp @ 5,800rpm • Weight 165kg (364lb) • Top speed 116km/h (72mph)

GERMANY

REVOLUTIONARY is hardly a strong enough word to describe this 1952 Max on its introduction. The cycle parts were basically those of the 200cc Lux introduced the previous year, but the engine was entirely new. Its unique feature was the drive to the overhead camshaft via paired eccentrics and connecting rods.

AS THE ENGINE WARMED UP the tie-rod caused the camshaft housing to rotate slightly around its axis, which also passed through the points of contact between the rockers and the valves, thus maintaining valve clearances as the engine grew taller.

Choke lever mounted on handlebar

Pressed-steel frame ideally suited to mass production

Cover conceals dry clutch

Springing for the rear suspension enclosed in the frame

FRONT VIEW

NSU RENNMAX

Capacity 247cc • Power output 36bhp @ 11,000rpm • Weight 117kg (258lb) • Top speed 210km/h (130mph)

GERMANY

THE RENNMAX WAS INTRODUCED IN **1952** and showed promise from the start, but this 1953 twin-cylinder model was ready to take on the world. Ridden by Werner Haas and backed up by Reg Amstrong, the machine secured the two top placings in the World Championship table from strong Guzzi opposition. Haas repeated his placing the following year on a revised Rennmax. NSU withdrew its factory team at the end of 1954.

THE D.O.H.C. ENGINE had shaft-driven camshafts and a four-speed gearbox. Revised camshaft drive and six-speed box were introduced in 1954. A rudimentary fairing was part of the hand-formed alloy fuel tank. Performance was equal to most machines in the 350cc class.

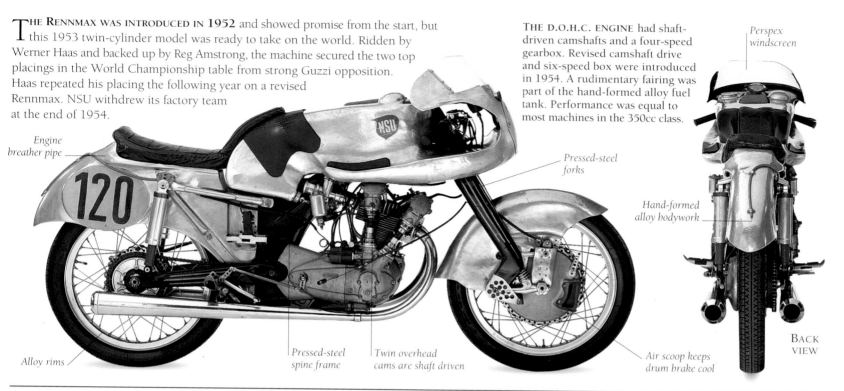

Engine breather pipe

Perspex windscreen

Pressed-steel forks

Hand-formed alloy bodywork

Alloy rims

Pressed-steel spine frame

Twin overhead cams are shaft driven

Air scoop keeps drum brake cool

BACK VIEW

NSU QUICKLY

*Capacity 49cc • Power output 1.5bhp @ 5,000rpm
Weight 33kg (73lb) • Top speed 40km/h (25mph)*

GERMANY

INTRODUCED IN **1953**, the Quickly was the first of a new generation of machines that came to be known as mopeds. It used a 49cc two-stroke engine driven via a twistgrip-operated, two-speed gearbox. The lightweight frame and leading-link forks were made from pressed steel, and as a cheap runabout it was exceptional. More than a million were made before production stopped in 1962. The bike shown here is a 1954 model.

SIDE VIEW

Pressed-steel frame

66-cm (26-in) wheels have small drum brakes

Simple two-stroke engine with two-speed gearbox

NSU SUPERMAX

*Capacity 247cc • Power output 18bhp @ 6,500rpm
Weight 174kg (383lb) • Top speed 126km/h (78mph)*

GERMANY

THE SUPERMAX, introduced in 1956, was the final development of the Max (see p.150). The engine power was increased slightly but so was the weight, so the difference in performance was negligible. By this time, the post-war German "economic miracle" had reached the point where the demand for motorcycles was falling and NSU was gearing up for car production. In fact, the company was taken over by Volkswagen in 1969. This Supermax dates from 1957.

FRONT VIEW

Revised rear suspension with external spring/damper units

Steering damper

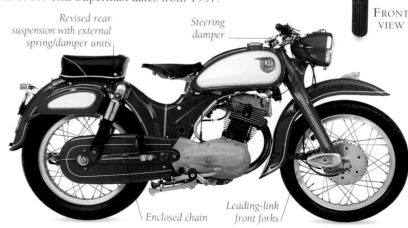

Enclosed chain

Leading-link front forks

OD TS50

Capacity 498cc • Power output 13bhp @ 3,500rpm • Weight 130kg (287lb) • Top speed 115km/h (71mph)

WILLY OSTNER AT DRESDEN (Ostner Dresden – OD) was typical of many small manufacturers in Germany. He built high-quality motorcycles with proprietary components between 1927 and 1935. This 1931 machine is a classic example. It uses an inclined single-cylinder, i.o.e that was made by the Swiss firm MAG, which also supplied larger capacity engines, including V-twins, to OD. Some lightweight models used Bark two-stroke engines.

THIS BIKE has a three-speed Hurth gearbox, Amal carburettor, and Bosch magneto. The silver and blue paintwork was the usual colour scheme for **OD** machines.

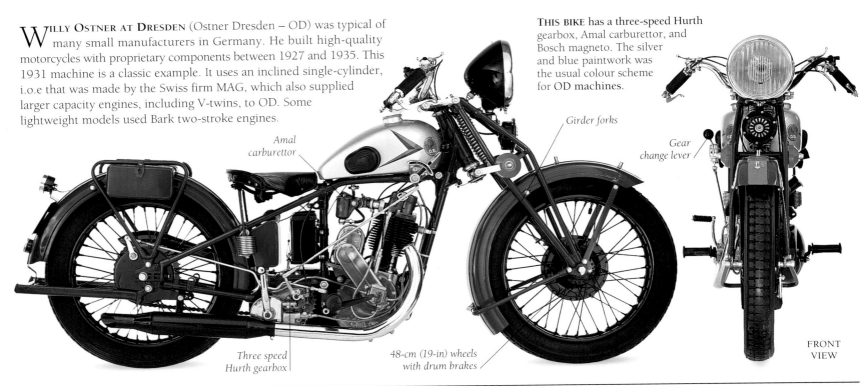

Amal carburettor

Girder forks

Gear change lever

Three speed Hurth gearbox

48-cm (19-in) wheels with drum brakes

FRONT VIEW

OEC COMMANDER

Capacity 498cc • Power output 20bhp (estimated) • Weight 433lb (196kg) • Top speed 75mph (121km/h) (estimated)

THOSE WHO SAID THAT **OEC** stood for Odd Engineering Contraptions were being slightly unkind. However, there can be little doubt that the firm was responsible for some fairly unconventional ideas, showing a progressive outlook even though the execution was unusual. This 1938 Commander model used an AJS/Matchless engine and Burman gearbox, while megaphone exhausts added sporting appeal. Few were sold.

Equipped with a speedometer as standard

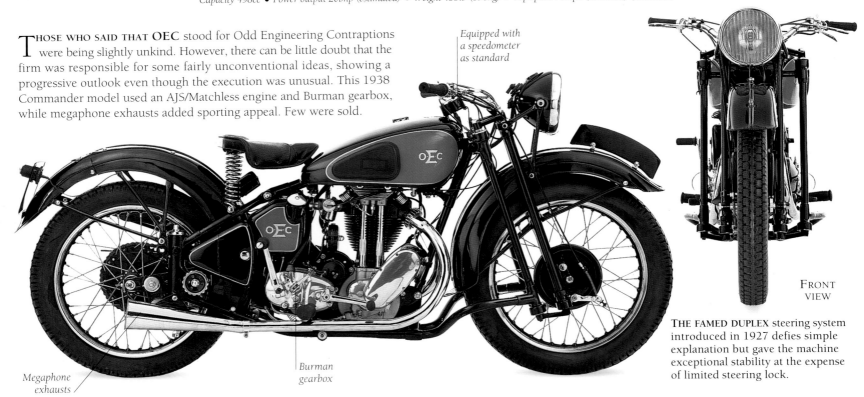

Megaphone exhausts

Burman gearbox

FRONT VIEW

THE FAMED DUPLEX steering system introduced in 1927 defies simple explanation but gave the machine exceptional stability at the expense of limited steering lock.

OK SUPREME

Capacity 248cc • Power output 10bhp (estimated) • Weight 270lb (122kg) (estimated) • Top speed 60mph (97km/h) (estimated)

UNITED KINGDOM

T HE OK SUPREME EARNED THE NICKNAME "Lighthouse" because of the look of its vertical camshaft drive with inspection window at the top. This inspection window provided an instant means of checking the circulation of the oil, which was carried in a compartment integral with the crankcase. The vertical drive shaft carried two cams at its upper end, which operated the valves via tappets and rockers. With a four-speed Burman gearbox and Webb forks, the remainder of the machine was conventional. This model dates from 1932.

Inspection window enables instant checking of oil circulation

Webb forks

FRONT VIEW

Fish-tail exhaust

Four-speed Burman gearbox

THESE DAYS, this bike's nickname is better known than the machine itself. At the time many manufacturers seemed to be jumping on the o.h.c. bandwagon, but none did it quite like this.

OPEL MOTOCLUB

Capacity 496cc • Power output not known • Weight not known • Top speed 109km/h (68mph) (estimated)

GERMANY

T HE OPEL CAR COMPANY built motorcycles intermittently from 1901. The Motoclub was introduced in 1928 and survived until 1930 when Opel stopped motorcycle production entirely. The machine shown here was built in 1929. The advanced pressed-steel frame construction and pivoting forks were originally used on Neander machines. Components are cadmium-plated rather than painted.

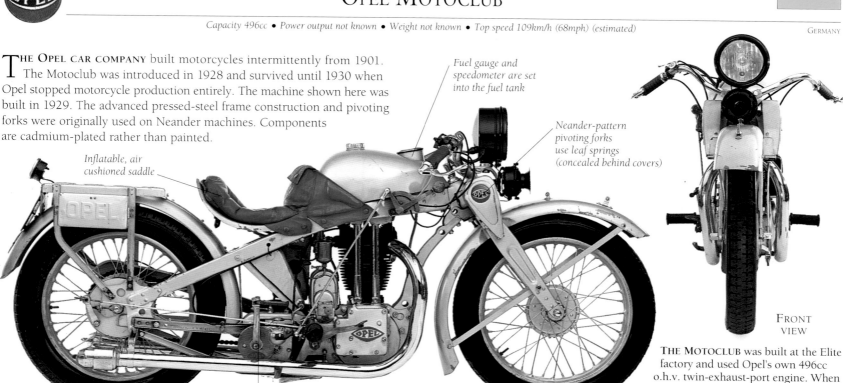

Fuel gauge and speedometer are set into the fuel tank

Neander-pattern pivoting forks use leaf springs (concealed behind covers)

Inflatable, air cushioned saddle

Kickstarter

FRONT VIEW

THE MOTOCLUB was built at the Elite factory and used Opel's own 496cc o.h.v. twin-exhaust-port engine. When Opel production ended, a similar machine was briefly built using o.h.c. single-cylinder Küchen engines.

PANTHER MODEL 100

Capacity 596cc • Power output 26bhp @ 5,000rpm • Weight 353lb (160kg) • Top speed 85mph (137km/h)

JOAH PHELON MADE HIS FIRST MOTORCYCLE in 1900, and two of its features – all-chain drive and a sloping engine taking the place of the front downtube of the frame – were part of the specification of every large-capacity machine that the company produced before its demise in 1966. The Panther name was adopted in 1923 when a revised 500cc overhead-valve engine was introduced. This formed the basis for those that followed. By 1929 the capacity was up to 600cc, rising to 650cc in 1959. This 600 is a 1935 model.

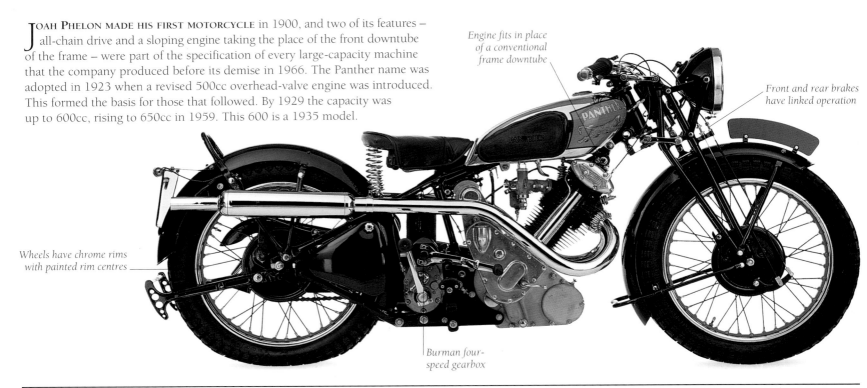

Engine fits in place of a conventional frame downtube

Front and rear brakes have linked operation

Wheels have chrome rims with painted rim centres

Burman four-speed gearbox

PERKS AND BIRCH MOTORWHEEL

Capacity 222cc • Power output 1bhp (estimated) • Weight not known • Top speed 20mph (32km/h) (estimated)

ORIGINALLY, THE MOTORWHEEL was to be used in place of either wheel of a bicycle or the front wheel of a tricycle. This 1900 bike's a.i.v. engine was mounted on a stationary axle. The drive from engine to hub was by gears. The design was sold to Singer, which adopted chain drive and a single-sided wheel.

THE ENTIRE MOTORWHEEL mechanism was housed within a wheel consisting of two dished aluminium castings bolted together at the rims. It was a clever idea, but one that failed to set any new trend in design until resurrected by Cyclemaster 50 years later.

Conventional-style bicycle frame

Wheel consists of two joined castings

Surface carburettor also serves as the fuel tank

BACK VIEW

PEUGEOT

Capacity 248cc • Power output not known • Weight not known • Top speed 88km/h (55mph) (estimated)

NOW FAMOUS FOR ITS CARS, Peugeot was once among France's leading motorcycle manufacturers. It introduced an advanced, new unit-construction 350 in 1926, followed by a range of unit-construction four-strokes. Pictured here is the 250 model from 1932. Designed as a utilitarian machine, the finish was good but not expensive.

IGNITION FOR THE SIDE-VALVE ENGINE was by a camshaft-driven magneto. A hand-operated three-speed gearbox was mounted on the right side of the fuel tank. It also had a Gutner carburettor.

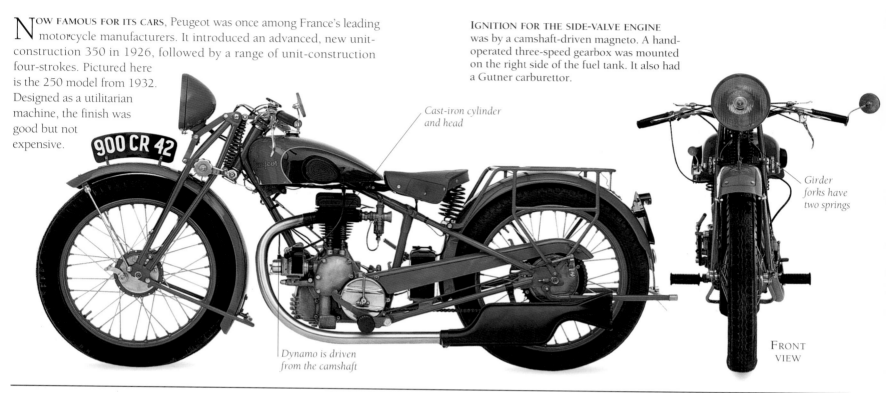

Cast-iron cylinder and head

Dynamo is driven from the camshaft

Girder forks have two springs

FRONT VIEW

PHÄNOMEN

Capacity 98cc • Power output 2.25 bhp • Weight 58kg (128lb) • Top speed 48km/h (30mph) (estimated)

THE FAMOUS PHÄNOMEN MARQUE was among Germany's first motorcycle manufacturers. The company soon concentrated on car construction, but returned to making motorcycles in the mid-1930s (the 1938 model is shown). These lightweight machines were powered by two-stroke Sachs engines. The inadequate power output made pedals necessary for hill climbing as well as starting. Many German manufacturers of this period produced similar cheap utilitarian machines, using engines supplied by Sachs and Ilo.

Pivoting forks have pressed-steel blades

66-cm (26-in) wheels

Chain-driven rear wheel

Two-speed gearbox

POPE

Capacity 997cc • Power output 15bhp @ 3,800rpm • Weight 309lb (140kg) • Top speed 75mph (121km/h)

U.S.A

STEAM, ELECTRICITY, AND PETROL ENGINES had all been used to propel a variety of Pope vehicles in the early years of the century but motorcycles bearing the Pope name did not appear until around 1911. The early machines were simple 26cu. in. (426cc) a.i.v. singles that used loop frames and leaf-sprung front forks, and transmission to the rear wheel was by flat belt. For 1913, Pope introduced an advanced new design. This followed the period's American fashion for V-twin machines, but the new Pope was more sophisticated than most of the opposition. The 45° V-twin engine used pushrod-operated o.h.v.s rather than the i.o.e. and side-valve layouts popular with U.S. manufacturers. A roller-bearing big end was lubricated by mechanical oil pump. Transmission was by chain via a multi-plate clutch and there was an auxiliary hand pump for high speeds. Management problems ended production in 1918.

MOST MACHINES were sold with a three-speed gearbox and kickstarter, although this cost more than a basic single-speed pedal start model.

Clutch

Kickstarter

Gear-change lever

FRONT
VIEW

•A COMFORTABLE RIDE•

The low-revving, large-capacity V-twin engines installed in early American motorcycles were extremely durable. A comfortable ride was ensured by the plunger rear suspension, which complemented the leaf-sprung trailing-link front forks.

A Pope on the open road

Twistgrip controls operate the throttle and valve lifter

Leaf-sprung, trailing-link forks

Plunger rear suspension

There are two rear brakes

Three-speed gearbox has a hand-operated lever

Schebler carburettor

Front wheel has no brakes

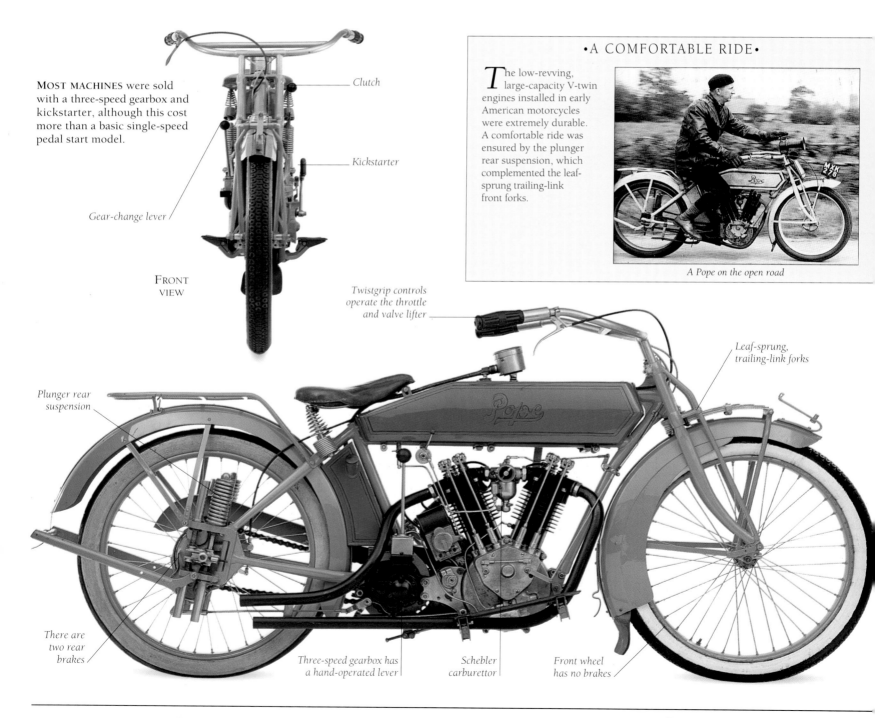

PUCH 220

Capacity 223cc • Power output 4.5bhp • Weight 77kg (170lb) • Top speed 72km/h (45mph)

AUSTRIA

PUCH WAS NEVER AFRAID OF THE UNCONVENTIONAL, as the majority of Puch products through the years demonstrated. The company adopted the "split single" layout – in which the two pistons operate in parallel cylinders and share a common combustion chamber – in 1923 and stuck with it for almost 50 years. Another feature that the firm used for a long time was a clutch built into the rear hub. This is a 1926 model.

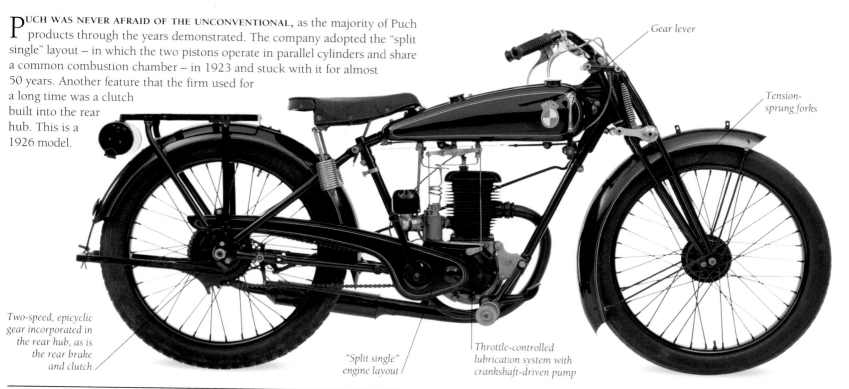

Gear lever

Tension-sprung forks

Two-speed, epicyclic gear incorporated in the rear hub, as is the rear brake and clutch

"Split single" engine layout

Throttle-controlled lubrication system with crankshaft-driven pump

QUASAR

Capacity 848cc • Power output 40bhp @ 5,500rpm • Weight 700lb (318kg) • Top speed 110mph (177km/h) (estimated)

UNITED KINGDOM

DEVELOPED BY MALCOLM NEWALL AND KEN LEAMAN in the mid-1970s, the Quasar was truly revolutionary, perhaps too much so for the buying public. In a reversal of traditional motorcycle ergonomics, the rider sat with his feet to the fore, as in a car. The engine was the same water-cooled, in-line four, 848cc o.h.v. unit as used in the Reliant Robin. A total of 20 machines were sold between 1977 (the year of the pictured Quasar) and 1982.

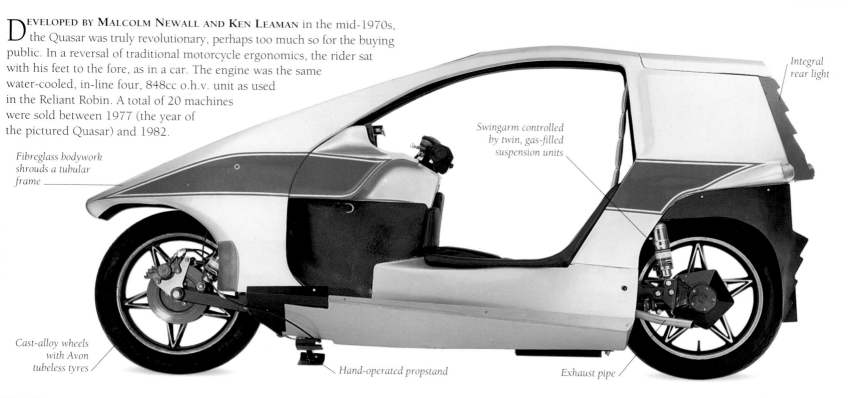

Integral rear light

Swingarm controlled by twin, gas-filled suspension units

Fibreglass bodywork shrouds a tubular frame

Cast-alloy wheels with Avon tubeless tyres

Hand-operated propstand

Exhaust pipe

RALEIGH MODEL 9

Capacity 699cc • Power output not known • Weight 290lb (131kg) • Top speed 55mph (89km/h)

UNITED KINGDOM

Raleigh stopped making motorcycles in 1905 to concentrate on its bicycle business, but a new large-capacity machine was produced in 1921 intended for solo or sidecar use. It was fitted with Raleigh's own side-valve, flat-twin engine and a three-speed gearbox made by Raleigh's Sturmey-Archer subsidiary. Leaf-sprung rear suspension and enclosed primary and final drive were also fitted.

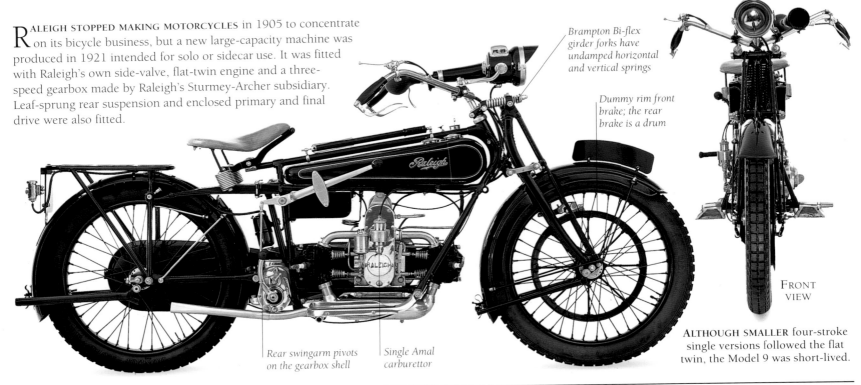

Brampton Bi-flex girder forks have undamped horizontal and vertical springs

Dummy rim front brake; the rear brake is a drum

FRONT VIEW

Rear swingarm pivots on the gearbox shell

Single Amal carburettor

ALTHOUGH SMALLER four-stroke single versions followed the flat twin, the Model 9 was short-lived.

READING STANDARD THOROUGHBRED

Capacity 17.6cu. in. • Power output 2.25hp • Weight 145lb (66kg) • Top speed not known

U.S.A.

The engines for the first Indian motorcycles (see pp.101–110) were built by the Aurora Automatic Machine Company. As part of its arrangement with Indian, Aurora was allowed to sell the engines to other manufacturers using its Thor label. Reading Standard bought Thor engines and produced machines very similar to the Indian.

The A.I.V. engine was incorporated into the seat-post of a bicycle-style frame. Transmission was by chain with a primary reduction. Reading Standard produced its first motorcycles in 1903 and in 1906 became the first U.S. manufacturer to adopt the new side-valve layout. This machine dates from 1905.

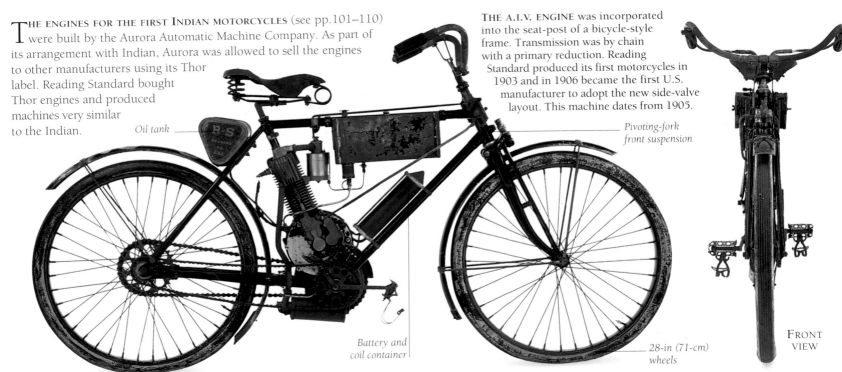

Oil tank

Pivoting-fork front suspension

Battery and coil container

28-in (71-cm) wheels

FRONT VIEW

Rex-Acme

REX-ACME TT SPORTS

Capacity 348cc • Power output not known • Weight 237lb (107kg) • Top speed 85mph (137km/h) (estimated)

REX-ACME FITTED a variety of proprietary engines to its machines after it stopped making its own power units in 1922. Its most famous models of the 1920s were the Blackburne-engined TT Sports machines. The bike shown here was built in 1926, the year after Wal Handley won the Junior TT on a similar machine. The engine is the classic external flywheel single-cylinder, 71 x 88-mm o.h.v. Blackburne.

THE GEARBOX is a three-speed Burman and the carburettor was supplied by Amal. Despite the popularity of these machines among amateur competitors, Rex was in decline by the end of the 1920s.

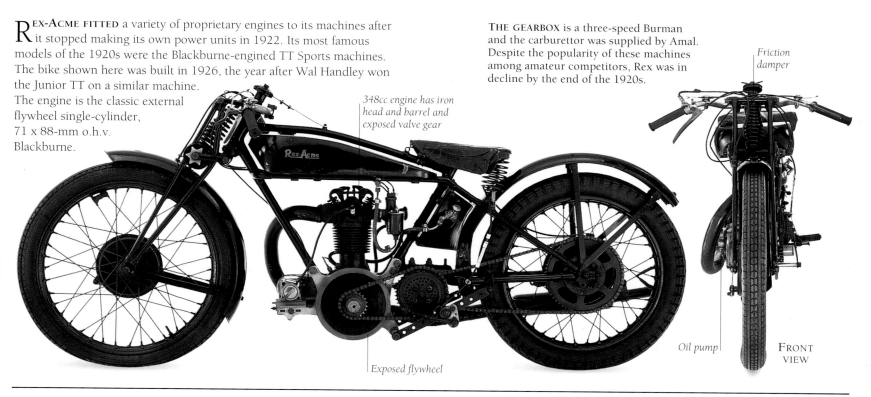

Friction damper

348cc engine has iron head and barrel and exposed valve gear

Exposed flywheel

Oil pump

FRONT VIEW

REYNOLDS RUNABOUT

Capacity 269cc • Power output not known • Weight 210lb (95kg) • Top speed not known

THE REYNOLDS RUNABOUT was one of the better and larger products of the British scooter boom that took place after World War I. The Wall 269cc two-stroke engine was positioned underneath the seat and was concealed behind metal panels. Drive to the rear wheel was via a Moss two-speed gearbox. Chain or belt final drive was optional. Petrol and oil tanks were mounted on the front leg shield and the seat was placed on a sprung platform.

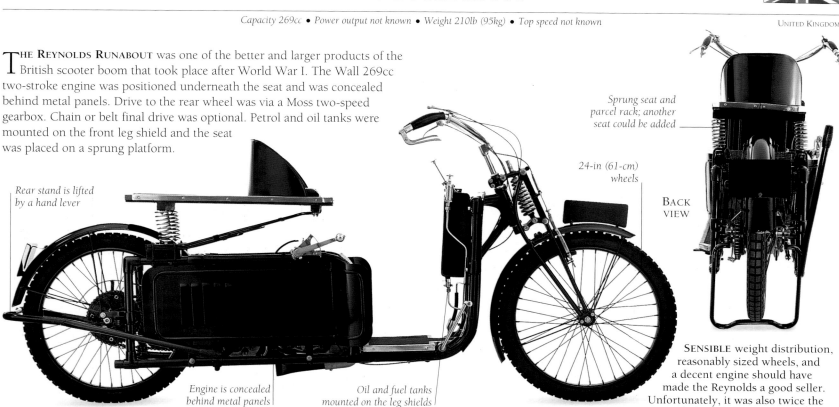

Sprung seat and parcel rack; another seat could be added

24-in (61-cm) wheels

BACK VIEW

Rear stand is lifted by a hand lever

Engine is concealed behind metal panels

Oil and fuel tanks mounted on the leg shields

SENSIBLE weight distribution, reasonably sized wheels, and a decent engine should have made the Reynolds a good seller. Unfortunately, it was also twice the price of a basic lightweight motorcycle.

RICKMAN MÉTISSE MK3 SCRAMBLER

Capacity 649cc • Power output 40bhp @ 6,500rpm • Weight 285lb (129kg) • Top speed 80mph (129km/h)

UNITED KINGDOM

THE RICKMAN BROTHERS began building specials after becoming disillusioned with production scramblers. Their first bikes were an amalgam of Triumph engine in BSA frame. The Métisse name (French for "mongrel") reflects their hybrid form. The Rickmans then began to build their own chassis, available in kit form or complete.

THIS MÉTISSE features a unit-construction Trimph TR6 SS Trophy engine. Fitted with 8.5:1 pistons and T120 camshafts, the engine was in essence a single carburettor version of the Bonneville unit. A single Amal Concentric carburettor was fitted with twin, high-level, open exhaust pipes. It is a replica of a 1965 model.

Wide braced handlebars improve control

Unsilenced exhaust pipes

Duplex cradle frame made of bronze-welded, nickel-plated Reynolds 531 tubing

Mudguards, sidepanels, fuel tank, and seat units are fibreglass

BACK VIEW

RICKMAN ENFIELD MÉTISSE

Capacity 736cc • Power output 52bhp @ 6,000rpm • Weight 353lb (160kg) • Top speed 110mph (177km/h)

UNITED KINGDOM

WHEN THE ROYAL ENFIELD COMPANY ceased production in 1970, the company receiver was left with a batch of about 200 736cc parallel-twin engines intended for Enfield's Mark 2 Interceptors but without frames. A final batch of Enfield-engined machines was assembled using Rickman bike parts. The first of these bikes appeared in 1970, though the model shown here was not registered until four years later.

High-rise handlebars have clip-on mountings

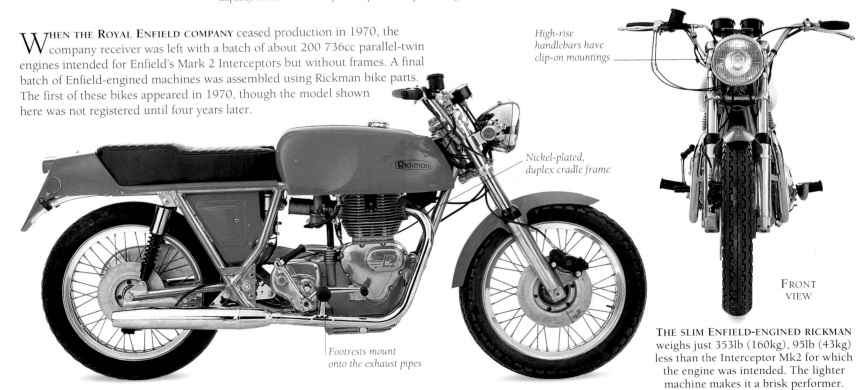

Nickel-plated, duplex cradle frame

Footrests mount onto the exhaust pipes

FRONT VIEW

THE SLIM ENFIELD-ENGINED RICKMAN weighs just 353lb (160kg), 95lb (43kg) less than the Interceptor Mk2 for which the engine was intended. The lighter machine makes it a brisk performer.

ROKON TRAIL-BREAKER

Capacity 146cc • Power output 8bhp @ 7,000rpm • Weight 219lb (99kg) • Top speed 30mph (48km/h) (estimated)

U.S.A.

INTRODUCED IN 1963, the unique Trail-Breaker has been produced intermittently since then without any major modifications. It is the only two-wheel drive motorcycle to have gone into production in a major way. Functional in appearance, it is intended for use by people who need to travel on rugged terrain but who are not experienced motorcyclists. The two-stroke engine is a Chrysler unit originally intended for use as an outboard engine for boats. The machine can also be supplied with several optional extras, including ploughs, trailers, and pumps. The Rokon drive system works by means of a 146cc engine that drives the three-speed gearbox via a belt and a centrifugal clutch; later versions are fitted with a torque converter. The wheels are driven by a series of chains and "T"-gears. A disc brake, mounted on the opposite side of the front "T"-gear, operates on the whole drive train and provides braking on both wheels.

BACK VIEW

A CHAIN from the gearbox drives a "T"-gear mounted above it. This drives a second chain to the rear wheel and also a shaft that runs inside the spine frame. A universal joint at the steering head allows movement. A second "T"-gear mounted over the front wheel turns the drive through 90° once more and a chain drives the front wheel.

Pull-cord starter

Drive-train mounted disc brake

Towbar

Horizontal cylinder, two-stroke engine

Wheels are hollow aluminium tanks capable of holding water or fuel. When empty they can be used as flotation chambers

Universal joint allows front wheel drive to continue to function when steering

Rear luggage frame

Pivoting footrests

Suspension is provided by under-inflated fat tyres

ROYAL ENFIELD

ROYAL ENFIELD V-TWIN

Capacity 425cc • Power output 14bhp • Weight 312lb (141kg) • Top speed 55mph (88km/h)

ROYAL **E**NFIELD STARTED making V-twins in 1910. Initially Enfield fitted MAG or JAP engines, but from 1914 onwards, when this bike was made, Enfield used its own 425cc V-twin engine. Valves were inlet-over-exhaust, and oil was pressure-fed to the big ends. It was fitted with a two-speed, all-chain transmission. Royal Enfield continued to produce V-twins until 1939.

THE V-TWIN had a mechanical oil pump that supplied accurately pressurized oil to the engine. It was a great improvement over other bikes of the period which were fitted with a hand pump that the rider had to remember to prime constantly.

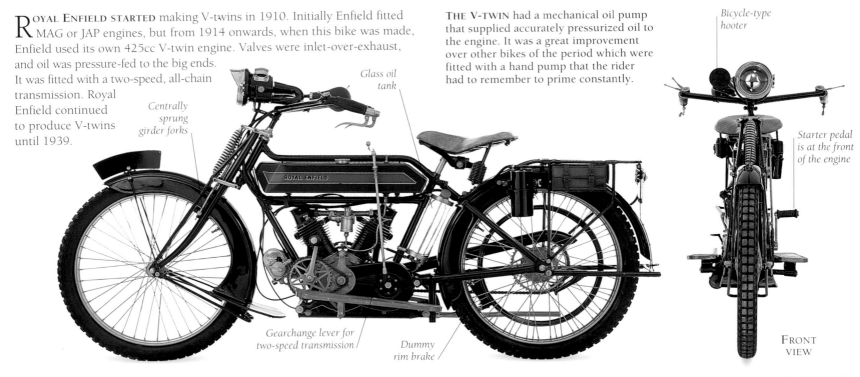

Centrally sprung girder forks

Glass oil tank

Bicycle-type hooter

Starter pedal is at the front of the engine

Gearchange lever for two-speed transmission

Dummy rim brake

FRONT VIEW

ROYAL ENFIELD 225L

Capacity 225cc • Power output 9bhp
Weight 150lb (68kg) • Top speed 44mph (71km/h) (estimated)

FIRST PRODUCED IN **1914**, the 225L was a lightweight 225cc two-stroke. It remained in the range until 1929 in two versions: a normal flat-tank and an open-framed "ladies" model. The three-port engine with deflector piston, outside flywheel, and two-speed gearbox provided modest performance. The open frame was designed to be easily ridden by women wearing long skirts, which were fashionable at the time. The leg shields gave some wet-weather protection. This is a 1924 model.

Barrel fuel tank

Open-frame layout

FRONT VIEW

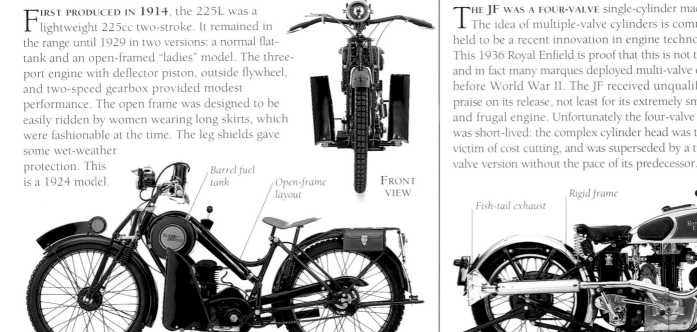

Leg protection

ROYAL ENFIELD JF

Capacity 499cc • Power output 19bhp @ 5,000rpm
Weight 364lb (165kg) • Top speed 80mph (129km/h)

THE **JF** WAS A FOUR-VALVE single-cylinder machine. The idea of multiple-valve cylinders is commonly held to be a recent innovation in engine technology. This 1936 Royal Enfield is proof that this is not the case, and in fact many marques deployed multi-valve engines before World War II. The JF received unqualified praise on its release, not least for its extremely smooth and frugal engine. Unfortunately the four-valve model was short-lived: the complex cylinder head was the victim of cost cutting, and was superseded by a two-valve version without the pace of its predecessor.

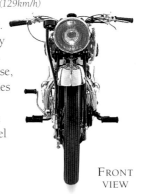

FRONT VIEW

Fish-tail exhaust

Rigid frame

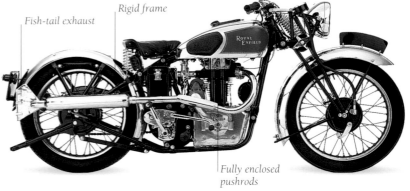

Fully enclosed pushrods

ROYAL ENFIELD TRIALS BULLET

Capacity 346cc • Power output 17bhp @ 5,500rpm • Weight 310lb (141kg) • Top speed 65mph (105km/h)

UNITED KINGDOM

PRODUCTION OF A NEW post-war Bullet started in 1949. UK production ended in 1963, but it is still built in India (see p.57). The 346cc, all-alloy, o.h.v. single-cylinder engine used an integral oil reservoir similar to the pre-war machines, but it was moved behind the engine. A modern frame with swingarm rear suspension was used across the range. The success of the Trials Bullet was convincing publicity for the new suspension system. A less successful 499cc version was built from 1953.

THE BULLET was produced in trials, scrambler, and road versions, with different engine tuning, suspension, mudguards, and other components. The trials machines were especially successful, winning an impressive series of competitions. The bike shown here is a 1950 model.

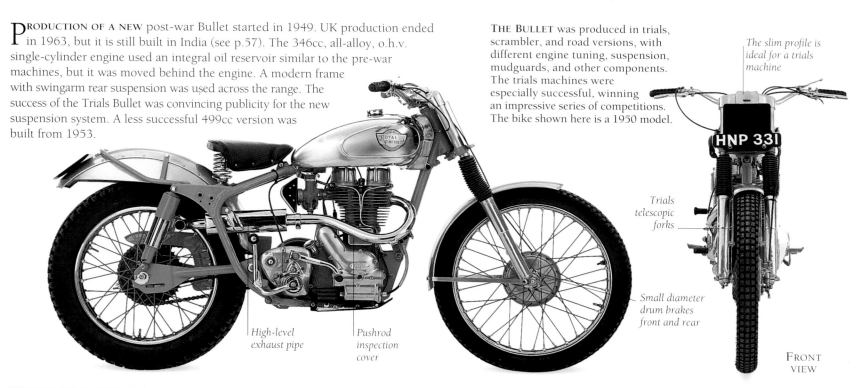

The slim profile is ideal for a trials machine

Trials telescopic forks

High-level exhaust pipe

Pushrod inspection cover

Small diameter drum brakes front and rear

FRONT VIEW

ROYAL ENFIELD 500

Capacity 495cc • Power output 25bhp @ 5,500rpm
Weight 390lb (177kg) • Top speed 78mph (125km/h)

UNITED KINGDOM

FIRST LAUNCHED IN **1948**, this 1951 500 was Royal Enfield's answer to the Triumph Speed Twin (see pp.182–83), and one of many British-made parallel twins exported to America in large numbers. The rear suspension set-up pioneered by the Trials Bullet (see above) was copied on the 500 twin. It remained in production until 1958, although a 750cc version was made until the early 1970s. Enfield twins were also sold in the U.S. under the Indian badge (see p.109).

Front cover of Motor Cycling magazine, September 1952, advertising the 500 twin.

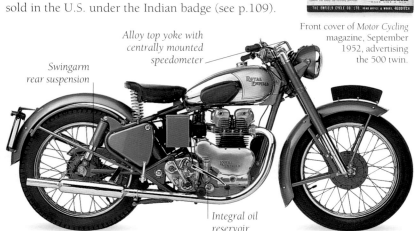

Alloy top yoke with centrally mounted speedometer

Swingarm rear suspension

Integral oil reservoir

ROYAL ENFIELD
CONTINENTAL

Capacity 248cc • Power output 26bhp @ 7,500rpm
Weight 300lb (136kg) • Top speed 86mph (138km/h)

UNITED KINGDOM

THE CONTINENTAL GT gained great popularity in the 1960s for its good looks and "café racer" image. Enfield began producing the practical, unit-construction Crusader 250 in 1956. This evolved into the Crusader Sports, Continental, and finally the Continental GT in 1964. The clip-on handlebars, racing fuel tank, and loud pipe were successful in attracting young buyers. However, the uncomfortable riding position and unreliability of its five-speed gearbox meant that its appeal was short-lived. Production stopped in 1967 when Enfield collapsed and Norton-Villiers took over the company.

"Jelly mould" petrol tank

Large diameter crankcase breather pipe

Front drum brake with cooling discs

A five-speed gearbox is fitted to this 1966 model

RUDGE MULTI-GEAR

Capacity 499cc • Power output 3.5bhp • Weight 241lb (109kg) • Top speed not known

THROUGH AN INGENIOUS SPLIT-BELT PULLEY SYSTEM, the Rudge Multi-gear had infinitely variable gear ratios. First marketed in 1912, it enjoyed considerable success in pre-war racing classes but, after the war, all-chain drives and mechanical gearboxes rendered the Multi-gear system obsolete. By 1924, all Rudge models featured four-speed gearboxes. Shown here is a 1923 Multi.

THE FINAL TT appearance of the Multi in 1922 was a disaster for the Coventry-based Rudge-Whitworth factory. All five machines entered failed to finish.

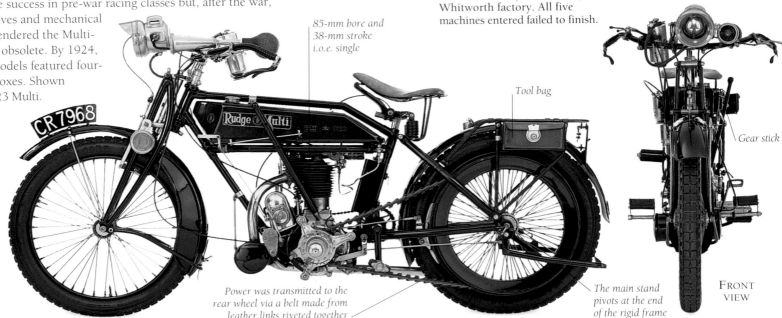

85-mm bore and 38-mm stroke i.o.e. single

Tool bag

Gear stick

Power was transmitted to the rear wheel via a belt made from leather links riveted together

The main stand pivots at the end of the rigid frame

FRONT VIEW

RUDGE TT REPLICA

Capacity 498cc • Power output 32bhp

Weight 290lb (132kg) • Top speed 100mph (161km/h)

AFTER NEARLY 16 YEARS OF SUCCESSFUL RACING, the Rudge-Whitworth factory began production of the TT Replica in 1931. Alongside this 1933 machine, there were 348cc and, later, 248cc engine options, contributing to widespread use by British and Continental racers. A further advantage was the comparatively low cost of these machines for the private buyer. Under the guidance of George Hack, the racing team of Graham Walker, H. G. Tyrell Smith, and Ernie Nott won many Grand Prix, TT, and other races before the factory withdrew from official racing in the early 1930s.

Four valves in the semi-radial head are operated by pushrod

Friction damper

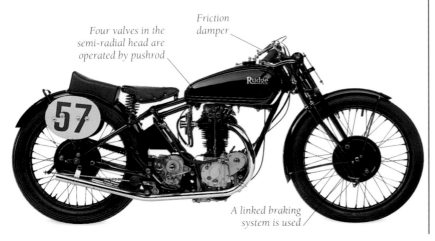

A linked braking system is used

RUDGE ULSTER

Capacity 499cc • Power output 35bhp

Weight 420lb (191kg) • Top speed 95mph (153km/h)

ADVERTISED IN 1937 as "probably the fastest 500cc motorcycle in normal production", the Rudge Ulster offered a degree of comfort and refinement that was unusual for such a high-performance machine. Distinguished from two other 500cc models in the range by its aluminium-bronze-alloy cylinder head, other improvements to the famous Rudge four-valve engine included enclosed valve gear and pumped oil-feed to the top end. Coupled brakes and a hand-operated centre stand added to the luxury specification. This bike is a 1937 model.

Design of the cylinder head is essentially the same as on the 1933 TT Replica

Pillion seat

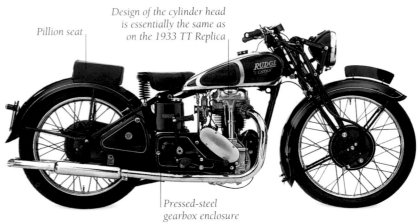

Pressed-steel gearbox enclosure

RUMI

Capacity 125cc • Power output 15bhp • Weight 85kg (187lb) • Top speed 150km/h (93mph)

THE MARKET FOR SMALL-CAPACITY MACHINES has been very important in Italy since World War II. Large and small manufacturers have produced many interesting designs. Moto Rumi of Bergamo introduced its 125cc two-stroke twin in 1949. Production continued until the early 1960s. The machine pictured here is a 1954 model.

THE ENGINE'S twin cylinders are horizontal and the clutch is mounted on the end of the crankshaft. The engine unit is suspended from the machine's tubular-frame structure. The same power unit is also used in Rumi's Formichino scooter.

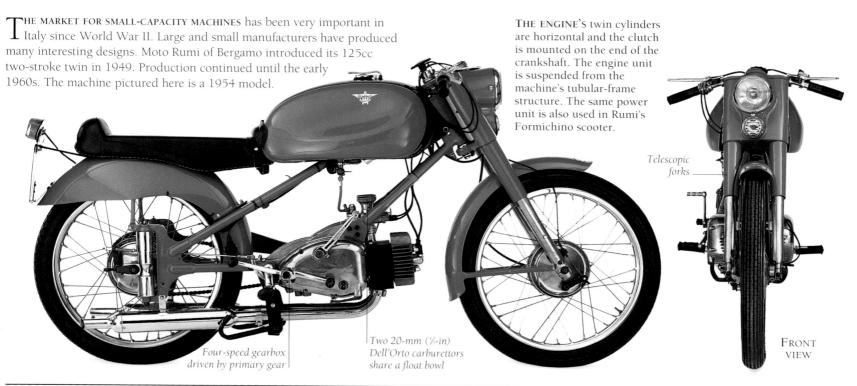

Telescopic forks

Four-speed gearbox driven by primary gear

Two 20-mm (⅞-in) Dell'Orto carburettors share a float bowl

FRONT VIEW

SALSBURY MODEL 85

Capacity not known • Power output 6hp
Weight not known • Top speed 45mph (72km/h) (estimated)

U.S.A.

IN 1935 E. FOSTER SALSBURY began producing scooters in America; his success inspired Cushman and other manufacturers to enter the scooter market. The post-war designs of 1946 were more sophisticated than the pre-war machines but still relied on a simple, single-cylinder, side-valve engine. Torque converter transmission meant controls were simple; the brake and throttle were both foot-operated pedals and there was no gearchange. Front and rear suspension was fitted. The styling was classic late 1940s but production was short lived. The 1949 model shown here was built during the last year of manufacture.

SCHÜTTOFF

Capacity 348cc • Power output 2.5bhp
Weight 105kg (232lb) • Top speed not known

SCHÜTTOFF ENTERED THE MOTORCYCLE MARKET in the mid-1920s with a range of four-stroke singles of 246cc, 348cc, and 496cc with three-speed gearboxes. The model shown here is a 1926 o.h.v. machine with a four-valve cylinder head and a twin-port exhaust layout. The frame is a tubular construction with the chain-stays and seat-post bolted to the back of the gearbox. Schüttoff later made two-stroke machines using engines supplied by DKW, which was also based in Saxony. DKW took complete control in the early 1930s.

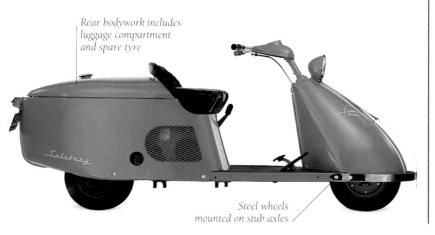

Rear bodywork includes luggage compartment and spare tyre

Steel wheels mounted on stub axles

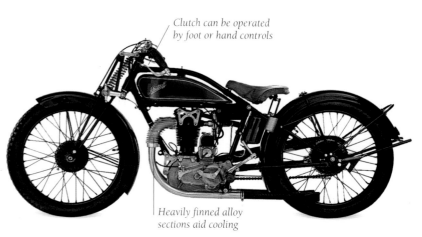

Clutch can be operated by foot or hand controls

Heavily finned alloy sections aid cooling

SCOTT 3¾

Capacity 532cc • Power output 3.75hp • Weight 196lb (89km/h) • Top speed not known

ALFRED ANGUS SCOTT, a true innovator, was responsible for nearly 60 separate motorcycle patents. He had been experimenting with the two-stroke engine for several years when his first production Scott motorcycles appeared in 1908. The very first machines were built by Jowett, but Scott soon established his own production facility at Shipley in Yorkshire. The advanced design included a two-speed gear, all-chain drive, a triangulated frame, telescopic forks, and a kickstarter. The unusual open-frame layout meant that the fuel tank was positioned on the seat-post. The whole machine had an integrated design that was far superior to most of the opposition, which was still little more than powered bicycles. The novel engine was a water-cooled, two-stroke twin with a 180° crankshaft and a capacity of 333cc. Engine size was gradually increased to 532cc by 1912 when this model was produced. The effectiveness of Scott machines was proven in a series of competition successes culminating in Senior TT wins in 1912 and 1913.

•SCOTT PEDALS•

Brake pedal

Gear-change pedal

By providing a kickstarter and an engine of sufficient power to climb severe gradients, Scott was able to dispense with the pedalling gear that was the standard system on most machines of the period. This left the rider's feet free to operate the rear brake and gear-change pedals without taking hands from the handlebars.

THE TRIANGULATED-FRAME design used by Scott offered women motorcyclists other benefits as well as its superior rigidity. This photograph is believed to show Mrs A. B. Wade of Cardiff with her two-speed Scott in 1912. The open-frame layout meant that female riders could keep their skirts in place, while sporting riders of either sex benefitted from the superior handling compared to the more flimsy contemporary opposition.

Mrs A. Wade of Cardiff on a 1912 Scott

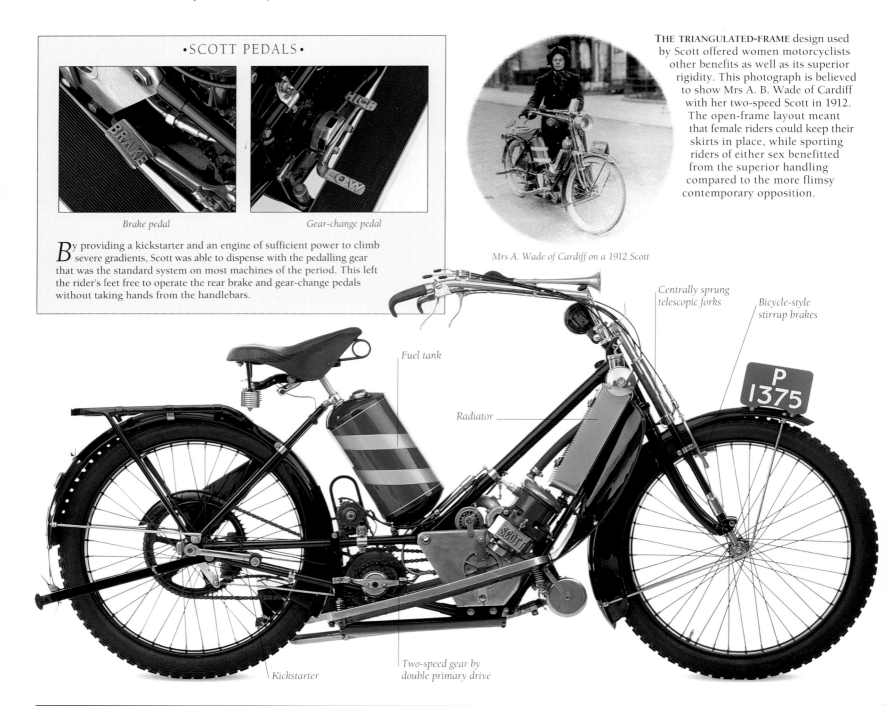

Centrally sprung telescopic forks

Bicycle-style stirrup brakes

Fuel tank

Radiator

Kickstarter

Two-speed gear by double primary drive

SCOTT SUPER SQUIRREL

Capacity 498cc • Power output not known • Weight 235lb (107kg) • Top speed 65mph (105km/h) (estimated)

ALTHOUGH A. A. SCOTT PARTED from the motorcycle company he founded in 1915, subsequent models produced by the Shipley company followed the pattern that he had established. The first Squirrel models appeared in the early 1920s, and were sporting 486cc versions of the existing 532cc machines. The Super Squirrel was introduced in 1924, equipped with a new 498cc or 596cc engine that incorporated water cooling of the cylinder head as well as the barrel. The Super Squirrel remained in production for seven years and was one of the company's most popular models. This is a 1929 model.

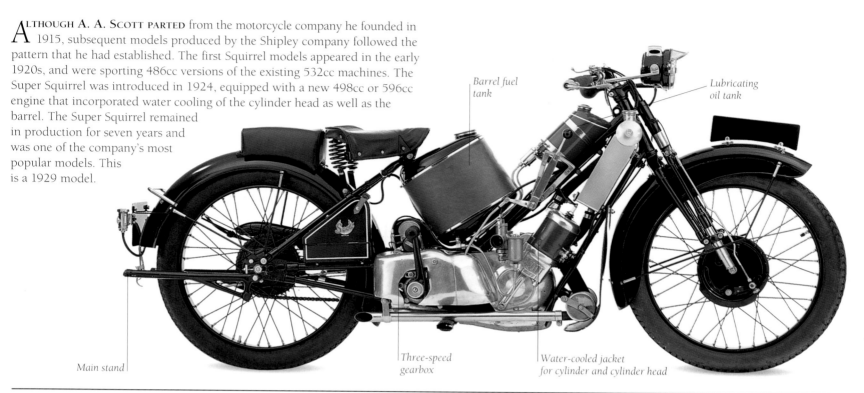

Barrel fuel tank

Lubricating oil tank

Main stand

Three-speed gearbox

Water-cooled jacket for cylinder and cylinder head

SCOTT FLYING SQUIRREL TT REPLICA

Capacity 596cc • Power output not known • Weight 335lb (152kg) • Top speed 80mph (129km/h) (estimated)

IMPROVEMENTS IN FOUR-STROKE OPPOSITION meant that Scott never equalled its pre-World War I successes at the Isle of Man TT, although it did win the manufacturer's prize in 1922. A third place in the 1928 Senior TT was sufficient justification to produce a TT Replica model for 1929 based on the Flying Squirrel. It used the duplex frame that had first appeared in 1927 and incorporated the TT full-frame fuel tank. The company's telescopic forks had additional bracing for extra strength but, sadly, this Scott innovation was replaced from 1931 by proprietary girders.

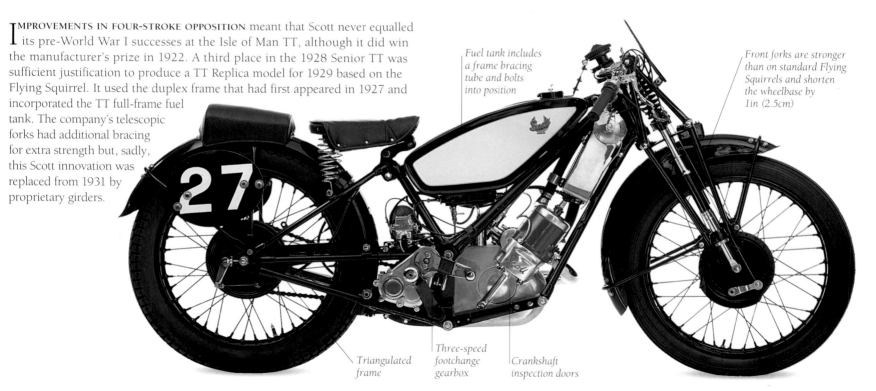

Fuel tank includes a frame bracing tube and bolts into position

Front forks are stronger than on standard Flying Squirrels and shorten the wheelbase by 1in (2.5cm)

Triangulated frame

Three-speed footchange gearbox

Crankshaft inspection doors

SEARS

Capacity 30.5cu. in. (500cc) • Power output 4.5hp • Weight not known • Top speed 45mph (72km/h) (estimated)

U.S.A.

SEARS ROEBUCK, the Chicago-based department store and mail order company, added motorcycles to its catalogue around 1912. Sears motorcycles were probably made by the Excelsior Cycle Co., which also used the DeLuxe brand name. This is a 1914 model. The engine is a single-cylinder, i.o.e. Spacke unit with its distinctive rear-facing exhaust port. Transmission is by two chains with primary and secondary reduction.

MANY OF THESE MACHINES were sold by mail order to remote areas to be ridden and maintained by unskilled novices. They needed to be strong and simple.

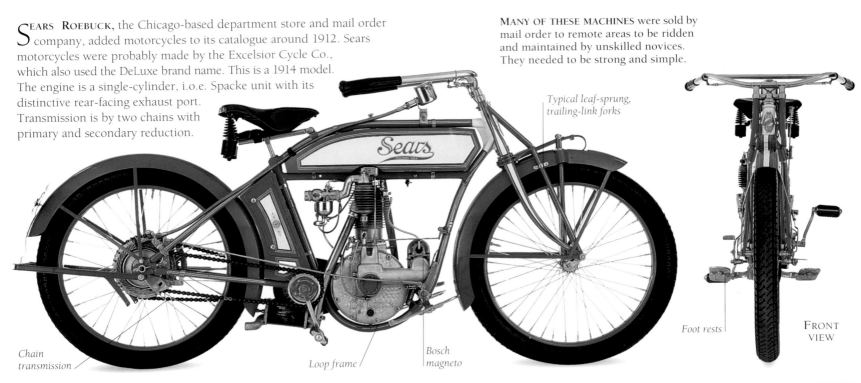

Typical leaf-sprung, trailing-link forks

Chain transmission

Loop frame

Bosch magneto

Foot rests

FRONT VIEW

SEARS 106SS

Capacity 106cc • Power output 9bhp
Weight not known • Top speed 56mph (90km/h)

U.S.A.

SEARS HAD A LONGSTANDING RELATIONSHIP with the Austrian manufacturer Puch and sold large numbers of its machines under the Sears or Allstate badges in the 1950s and 1960s. Sears also imported Italian Gilera motorcycles which were sold under the Sears brand-name in the 1960s. This 1966 106SS is based on the Gilera's 124 (see p.64). It is a typical Italian lightweight of the period with an o.h.v. single-cylinder engine and four-speed gearbox. To keep costs down the Sears-badged machine was built to Gilera's most basic specification.

Engine cases are painted, not polished, to reduce costs

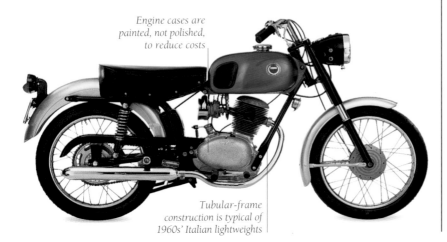

Tubular-frame construction is typical of 1960s' Italian lightweights

---

SEARS

Capacity 49cc • Power output 4.5bhp (estimated)
Weight not known • Top speed 40mph (64km/h) (estimated)

U.S.A.

SEARS BEGAN SELLING Puch-built machines as early as 1954. By the late 1960s this 49cc lightweight machine was typical of its products. It used a fan-cooled, two-stroke engine and had a three-speed gearbox. In the 1950s Sears sold large numbers of scooters and lightweight motorcycles but things got tougher in the next decade. Not only were comparable Japanese motorcycles superior to those sold by Sears but Japanese marketing techniques had vastly improved. Sears dropped out of the motorcycle market soon after this 1968 machine appeared.

Rear view mirror

Pressed-steel frame construction

49cc, fan-cooled two-stroke engine

SERTUM 250

Capacity 250cc • Power output 11bhp (estimated) • Weight 127kg (280lb) (estimated) • Top speed 89km/h (55mph) (estimated)

ITALY

SERTUM BEGAN BUILDING MOTORCYCLES in Milan in 1932 and was among the first to resume production after World War II. The model shown here was built in 1947. The side-valve, single-cylinder machine had unit-construction of the engine and gearbox, with battery and coil ignition charged by dynamo. Despite the obvious quality of construction and advanced features, Sertum production ended in 1951. A 500cc model was also produced at this time.

THE STEEL FRAME uses the engine/gearbox unit as a structural member. Front suspension is by pressed-steel girder forks and the rear has a swingarm with concealed springs.

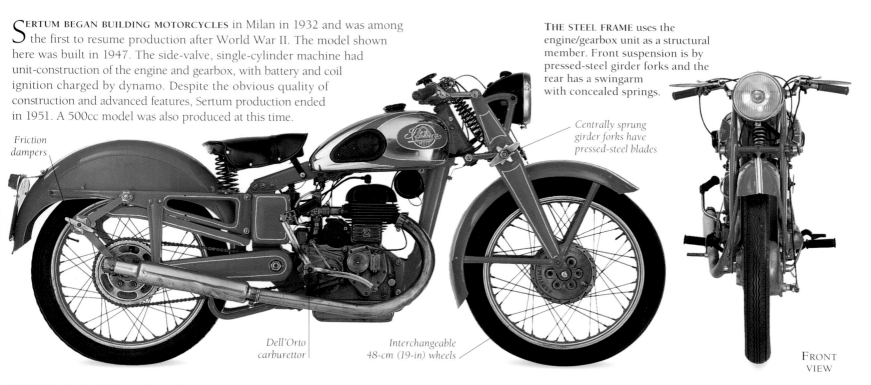

Friction dampers

Centrally sprung girder forks have pressed-steel blades

Dell'Orto carburettor

Interchangeable 48-cm (19-in) wheels

FRONT VIEW

SIMPLEX
SERVI-CYCLE

Capacity 150cc • Power output not known
Weight not known • Top speed 45mph (72km/h)

U.S.A.

FIRST BUILT IN 1935, the Simplex Servi-Cycle was made until 1960. It was the only machine to be built in substantial numbers in America's Southern states. The engine was an air-cooled, rotary valve, two-stroke single with the carburettor mounted behind the crankcase. The Automatic clutch version was introduced in 1953. This is a 1957 model. The Simplex frame was an unusual twin-loop design with each side of the frame made from a single tube. The leading-link fork design was a scaled-down version of the "Springer" design used on early Harleys.

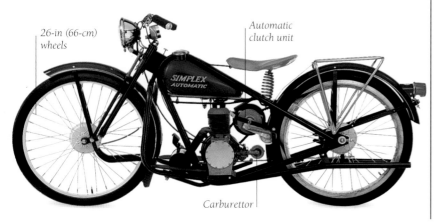

26-in (66-cm) wheels

Automatic clutch unit

Carburettor

SIMPLEX SCOOTER

Capacity 150cc • Power output not known
Weight not known • Top speed 45mph (72km/h)

U.S.A.

THERE WAS A SCOOTER sales boom in America in the 1950s. Simplex tried to cash in with a scooter introduced in 1956 (pictured is the 1958 model). It used the same engine with variable speed gear and belt drive as the Automatic motorcycle (see left). The power unit was fitted into a step-thru frame fitted with 4.00 x 12-in tyres on steel wheels. Not produced in large numbers, the Simplex never challenged the market-leading Cushmans (see p.44). In 1960, Simplex switched to making minibikes and go-karts with proprietary four-stroke engines.

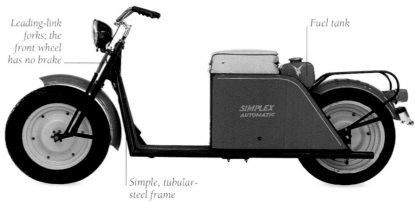

Leading-link forks; the front wheel has no brake

Fuel tank

Simple, tubular-steel frame

SKOOTAMOTA

Capacity 124cc • Power output 1.5bhp • Weight 98lb (44kg) • Top speed 25mph (40km/h)

LIKE THE ABC MOTORCYCLE, the Skootamota was the product of the fertile brain of Granville Bradshaw, although it was actually produced by Gilbert Campling Ltd. There was a minor boom in this type of machine immediately after World War I, and the Skootamota was one of the better examples, being equipped with a seat! In this 1919 model, the engine was mounted horizontally behind the seat and drove the rear wheel via a chain from a sprocket mounted on an extended camshaft.

EARLY EXAMPLES had a side inlet and overhead exhaust valve, but in later models both valves were overhead. The scooter boom was short-lived and production ceased in 1922.

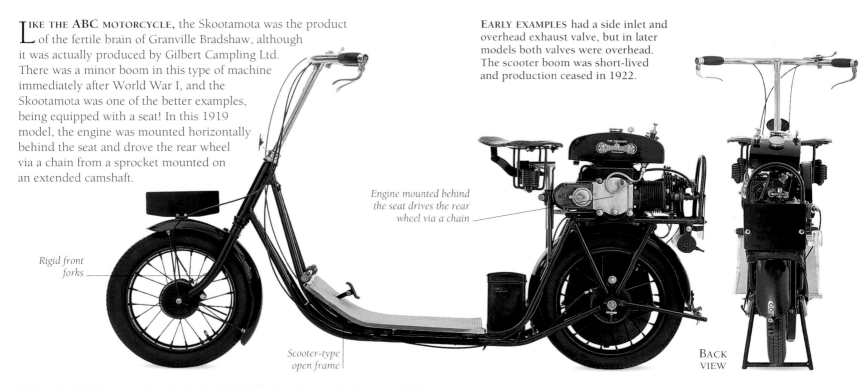

Engine mounted behind the seat drives the rear wheel via a chain

Rigid front forks

Scooter-type open frame

BACK VIEW

SMITH MOTOR WHEEL

Capacity 118cc • Power output not known • Weight not known • Top speed 20mph (32km/h) (estimated)

ORIGINALLY DESIGNED IN BRITAIN by the motorcycling innovator A. W. Wall, this device was first introduced as the Wall Auto Wheel in 1910. Manufacturing rights were subsequently acquired by A. O. Smith & Co. of Milwaukee, Wisconsin, which began producing them in 1914. Smith continued to make the wheel until 1919. This is a 1915 machine.

THE SELF-CONTAINED clip-on engine and wheel unit could be attached to any conventional bicycle. It comprised a 118cc a.i.v. engine that drove the third wheel via a reduction gear. The bicycle could be banked into a turn in the normal way.

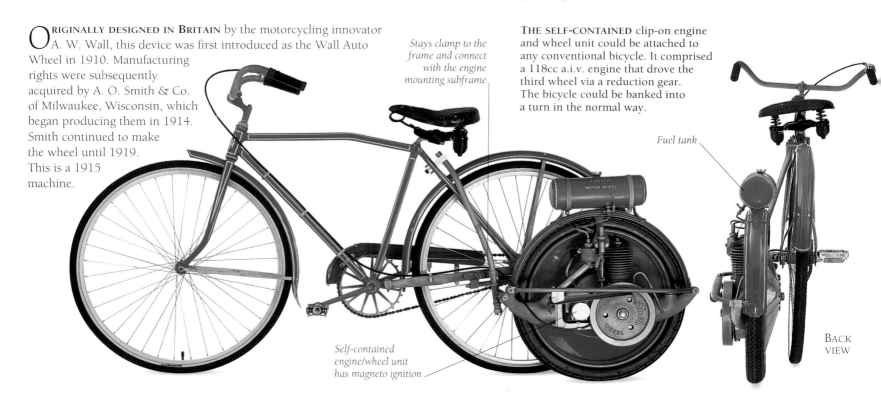

Stays clamp to the frame and connect with the engine mounting subframe

Fuel tank

Self-contained engine/wheel unit has magneto ignition

BACK VIEW

SPIEGLER

THE ADVANCED SPIEGLER FRAME DESIGN comprised a main beam running from the steering head to the rear axle. This was constructed of tubing with a steel skin. The engine and gearbox were supported by a twin-loop tubular cradle bolted to the main beam of the frame. Fuel and oil tanks were within the frame structure. The machine pictured here was built in 1924 and uses Spiegler's own single-cylinder engine. Most machines were built using JAP or Motosacoche engines. The bike has conventional girder forks and dummy rim brakes.

THE ENGINE'S OVERHEAD VALVES can be inspected through a lift-up panel. The lighting kit fitted to this machine was an accessory added after purchase.

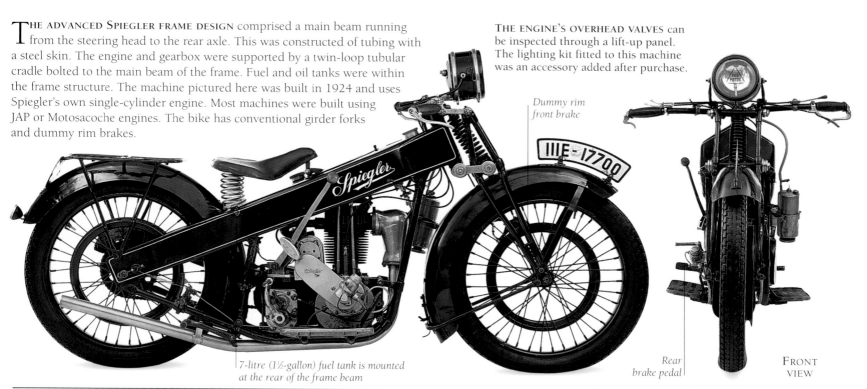

Dummy rim front brake

Rear brake pedal

FRONT VIEW

7-litre (1½-gallon) fuel tank is mounted at the rear of the frame beam

STANDARD REX SPORT

STANDARD HAD USED SINGLE-CYLINDER and V-twin engines supplied by JAP and MAG before the company began making its own engines around 1930. O.h.c. Rex models appeared later. These advanced machines were produced in 348cc and 493cc capacities. The engine had an inclined cylinder, and oil was contained in an integral reservoir. The barrel and head were cast-iron, and there were two exhaust ports. The four-speed Hurth gearbox was bolted to the back of the engine to create a compact power unit.

THE LEADING-LINK forks were made under licence from Brough in England, based on a Harley-Davidson design. The model shown here was built in 1935.

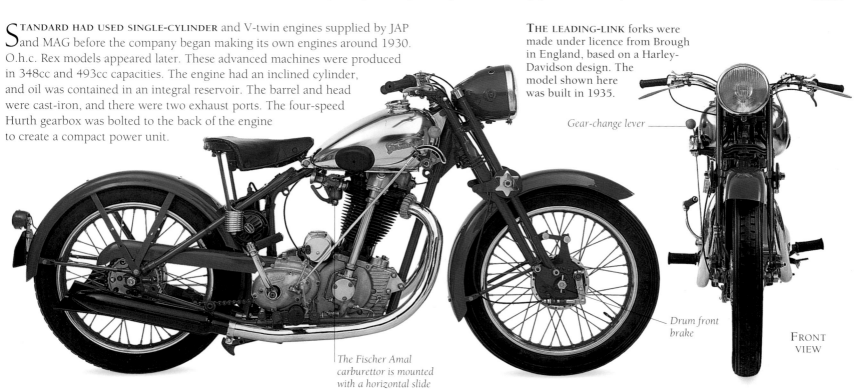

Gear-change lever

Drum front brake

FRONT VIEW

The Fischer Amal carburettor is mounted with a horizontal slide

STEEN

U.S.A.

Capacity 98cc • Power output 10bhp
Weight 140lb (63kg) (estimated) • Top speed 60mph (97km/h)

THE CALIFORNIA COMPANY STEEN entered the booming U.S. minibike market in the early 1960s when the minibike was crude, small-wheeled, often with no suspension, and powered by an industrial engine. Minibike competition (usually among junior riders) forced rapid change, and by the time this Steen/Allsport model was produced in 1973 the demand was for far more sophisticated machines. Essentially it is a scaled-down version of a full-blown motocross bike with 16-in (41-cm) wheels.

Full duplex cradle frame with a 28-in (71-cm) seat height

The engine is a Hodaka two-stroke single

STOCK R119

GERMANY

Capacity 119cc • Power output 1.5bhp @ 3,000rpm
Weight 32kg (70lb) • Top speed 50km/h (31mph)

ALTHOUGH THE U.S. WAS NEVER a lucrative market for the clip-on engine or the lightweight motorcycle, the Cyclemotor Corporation of the U.S.A. introduced a simple 119cc two-stroke clip-on engine for bicycles in 1915. It was followed in 1918 by a complete machine powered by the same engine. This machine, called the Evans, was sold in large numbers in Germany before production ended in 1924. Manufacture was moved to Berlin, where it was built under the Stock name until about 1929.

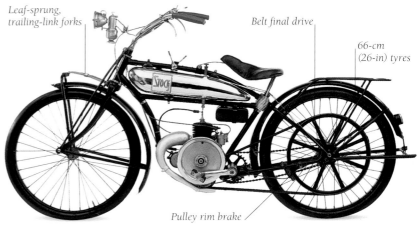

Leaf-sprung, trailing-link forks

Belt final drive

66-cm (26-in) tyres

Pulley rim brake

SUNBEAM
SPORTING MODEL

UNITED KINGDOM

Capacity 499cc • Power output not known
Weight not known • Top speed not known

IN ADDITION TO ROAD-GOING MACHINES (see right), Sunbeam also made competition machines based on the road bikes. Extra power was obtained through careful engine tuning and preparation, and weight was lost by removing auxiliary components. These Sunbeams achieved excellent results and enhanced the firm's reputation. George Dance was almost unbeatable in sprint and hill-climb competitions, while other riders won the 1920 and 1922 Senior TTs, the French Grand Prix, the Italian TT, and the Austrian championship. This machine dates from 1923.

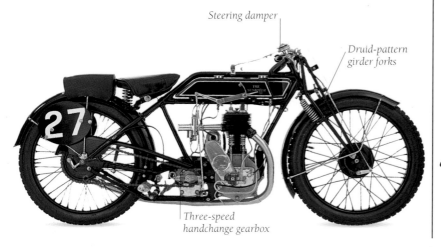

Steering damper

Druid-pattern girder forks

Three-speed handchange gearbox

SUNBEAM MODEL 5

UNITED KINGDOM

Capacity 499cc • Power output 3.5hp
Weight 238lb (108kg) • Top speed 60mph (97km/h) (estimated)

JOHN MARSTON PRODUCED HIS FIRST SUNBEAM MOTORCYCLE – the name was previously used on high-quality bicycles and enamelware – in 1913. The Sunbeam was a side-valve single with enclosed primary - and final-drive chains designed by John Greenwood, previously a designer of Rover motorcycles. Sunbeam established a reputation for high-quality finish and sound engineering and, despite comparatively high prices, the bikes sold well. The machine was improved over the following years but not radically altered. The Model 5 shown here was built in 1925.

High-quality black finish with gold striping

Sunbeam's famous "little oilbath" chaincase

SUNBEAM MODEL 90

Capacity 493cc • Power output not known • Weight 300lb (136kg) • Top speed not known

SUNBEAM INTRODUCED O.H.V. SINGLES during the 1923 racing season, and they appeared in its catalogue alongside the very successful side-valve machines for 1924. The 347cc model 80 and the 493cc Model 90 were originally listed as competition models only and were not equipped with kickstarter or other road-going features. By the time the 1928 model pictured here was built, they were available in road trim with kickstarter, optional lighting kit, and other extras to make life easier for the road rider. The twin-port

cylinder head was an option on the Model 90 during 1926 and became a standard feature the following year. At this time, the twin-port layout was a popular feature on British single-cylinder machines. With two exhaust pipes splayed out into the passing air, it offered improved cooling as well as better gas flow. For 1927–28 a "Bullnose" flat tank was provided, differing from the earlier style with concave corners at the front. The flat tank was dropped for 1929 when more modern-looking saddle tanks were introduced.

THE MODEL 90 was designed by John Greenwood and, in typical Sunbeam fashion, the engine contained no radical features but was of sound design and quality construction, featuring two cams with exposed hollow pushrods and hairpin valve springs. The valves were set at 90° in a heavily finned cast-iron cylinder head.

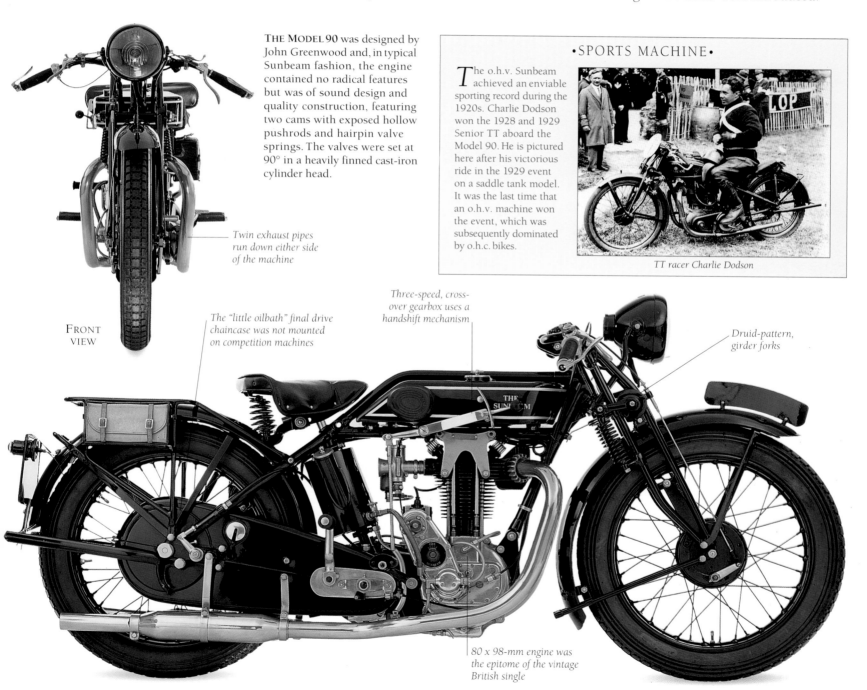

FRONT VIEW

Twin exhaust pipes run down either side of the machine

•SPORTS MACHINE•

The o.h.v. Sunbeam achieved an enviable sporting record during the 1920s. Charlie Dodson won the 1928 and 1929 Senior TT aboard the Model 90. He is pictured here after his victorious ride in the 1929 event on a saddle tank model. It was the last time that an o.h.v. machine won the event, which was subsequently dominated by o.h.c. bikes.

TT racer Charlie Dodson

Three-speed, crossover gearbox uses a handshift mechanism

The "little oilbath" final drive chaincase was not mounted on competition machines

Druid-pattern, girder forks

80 x 98-mm engine was the epitome of the vintage British single

SUNBEAM MODEL S7 DE LUXE

Capacity 487cc • Power output 25bhp • Weight 435lb (197kg) • Top speed 72mph (116km/h)

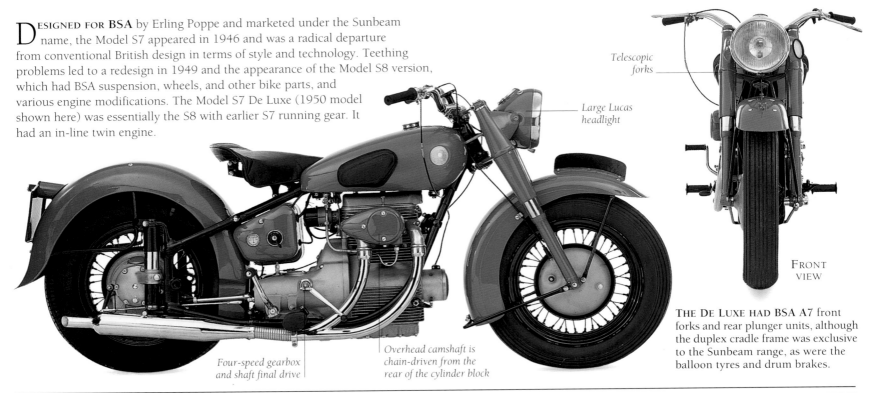

DESIGNED FOR BSA by Erling Poppe and marketed under the Sunbeam name, the Model S7 appeared in 1946 and was a radical departure from conventional British design in terms of style and technology. Teething problems led to a redesign in 1949 and the appearance of the Model S8 version, which had BSA suspension, wheels, and other bike parts, and various engine modifications. The Model S7 De Luxe (1950 model shown here) was essentially the S8 with earlier S7 running gear. It had an in-line twin engine.

Telescopic forks

Large Lucas headlight

FRONT VIEW

Four-speed gearbox and shaft final drive

Overhead camshaft is chain-driven from the rear of the cylinder block

THE DE LUXE HAD BSA A7 front forks and rear plunger units, although the duplex cradle frame was exclusive to the Sunbeam range, as were the balloon tyres and drum brakes.

SUZUKI

SUZUKI RT63

Capacity 124cc • Power output 25.5bhp @ 12,000rpm • Weight 94kg (207lb) • Top speed 183km/h (114mph)

ORIGINALLY A COMPANY that built looms for weaving, Suzuki moved into the world of motor vehicles just after World War II. Its first motorcycle appeared in 1955 and was a 125cc three-geared two-stroke single, after which Suzuki developed rapidly and by 1960 was entering bikes in world-class competition. This RT63 rotary-valve air-cooled twin from 1963 was originally produced with both rear- and forward-facing exhausts (the one shown has rear-facing). The gearbox was eight-speed and of the cassette type, making it easy to remove the gear ratios for alteration.

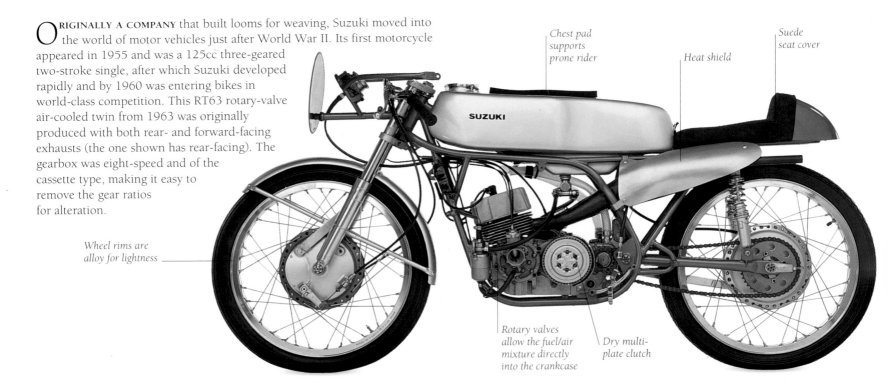

Chest pad supports prone rider

Heat shield

Suede seat cover

Wheel rims are alloy for lightness

Rotary valves allow the fuel/air mixture directly into the crankcase

Dry multi-plate clutch

Suzuki X6 Hustler

Capacity 247cc • Power output 29bhp @ 7,500rpm • Weight 143kg (316lb) • Top speed 145km/h (90mph)

WHEN SUZUKI INTRODUCED the X6 Hustler in 1965 it caused an immediate stir, especially among lovers of high-performance lightweight machines. Despite its small, 247cc air-cooled, two-stroke engine, the X6, as it was known in the U.S. (T20 Super Six in Britain), was capable of 145km/h (90mph) and offered a sophistication rarely seen then on such small motorcycles.

THERE WAS A SIX-SPEED GEARBOX (hence the "Six"), a 20.3-cm (8-in) twin leading-shoe front brake and a separate oil pump instead of the usual pre-mix, petrol/oil system. The X6 Hustler remained in production for three years and, at the height of its popularity, Suzuki produced 5,000 machines per month.

Rear-view mirror

Externally sprung telescopic forks

Twin leading-shoe drum brake

Light alloy barrels have cast-iron liner

Unusually for a Suzuki, the kickstart is on the left

46-cm (18-in) rear wheel

FRONT VIEW

SUZUKI

Suzuki TR500

Capacity 500cc • Power output 64.5bhp @ 8,000rpm • Weight 135kg (298lb) • Top speed 233km/h (145mph)

DEVELOPED FROM THE 500CC parallel-twin Cobra road bike and first seen in 1968, Suzuki's TR500 went on to gain considerable racing success, especially in the U.S. The bike illustrated was ridden by Art Baumann to the company's first U.S. National Championship win at Sears Point on 7 September 1969. In 1970, larger 34-mm (1⅓-in) carburettors were fitted and compression raised to 7.34:1.

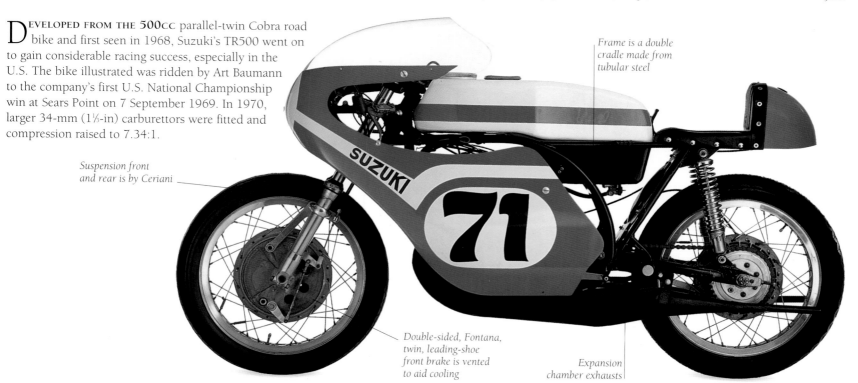

Frame is a double cradle made from tubular steel

Suspension front and rear is by Ceriani

Double-sided, Fontana, twin, leading-shoe front brake is vented to aid cooling

Expansion chamber exhausts

SUZUKI GT750

Capacity 738cc • Power output 67bhp @ 6,500rpm • Weight 238kg (524lb) • Top speed 174km/h (108mph)

LAUNCHED IN 1971, Suzuki's GT750 made an immediate impact thanks to its radical design and rapid acceleration. Building on its success in the 1960s with racing two-strokes, Suzuki decided to create a large-capacity, multi-cylinder sports bike for road riders. Suzuki's first venture into the superbike market was largely successful; the GT stayed in production for five years. The three cylinders were arranged in-line across the frame, which could cause the middle cylinder to overheat, being flanked by a cylinder on either side and shielded from the cooling breeze by the frame downtubes and front forks, hence the use of water cooling. This water jacket not only enabled the engine to perform for lengthy periods at high revs and helped reduce mechanical noise but also earned the GT its nickname "Kettle" in Britain and "Water Buffalo" in the U.S. As with many two-strokes, the price to pay for high performance was poor fuel consumption, which could drop to around 8.86km/l (25mpg) if the bike was ridden hard. The machine pictured is the 1971 model.

RELATIVELY SOPHISTICATED for its time, the cooling system had a four-stage operation in which a thermostat blocked the flow of coolant when the engine was started so that the optimum operating temperature could be reached quickly. As the temperature rose, other ducts opened to allow coolant flow and an electric fan cut in to aid cooling.

• SUZUKI RACERS •

Suzuki won the 50cc and 125cc World Championships in the 1960s but withdrew from the Grand Prix after 1967. It subsequently produced successful race machines based on the 500 road bike and later the 750 triple. Britain's Barry Sheene is shown here on a 500 in 1973.

Barry Sheene competing in the French F750

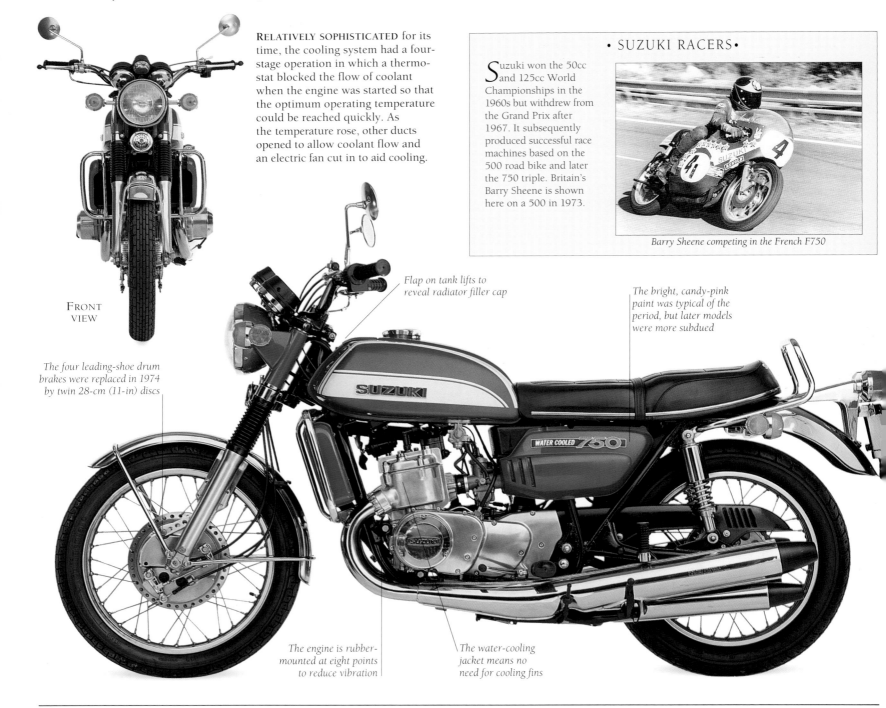

FRONT VIEW

Flap on tank lifts to reveal radiator filler cap

The bright, candy-pink paint was typical of the period, but later models were more subdued

The four leading-shoe drum brakes were replaced in 1974 by twin 28-cm (11-in) discs

WATER COOLED 750

The engine is rubber-mounted at eight points to reduce vibration

The water-cooling jacket means no need for cooling fins

SUZUKI RE5

Capacity 497cc • Power output 62bhp @ 6,500rpm • Weight 230kg (507lb) • Top speed 179km/h (111mph)

THE RE5 MADE ITS DEBUT IN LATE 1974 and was met with suspicion and caution by motorcyclists. The main reason for this was the use of a Wankel-type rotary engine, which was relatively rare for motorcycles. The model shown is the 1975 model. The rotary design is outwardly very different from a conventional piston engine and motorcyclists, notorious for their conservatism, found it hard to accept. Though smooth and fairly powerful for its size, the RE5 also used a lot of fuel, its 20.5-litre (4½-gallon) tank giving a range of about 129km (80 miles), which was insufficient for a touring bike. Production ended in 1977.

Instrument pod roll-top retracts when ignition key is inserted

Large, twin-choke carburettor with accelerator pump

Spherical indicators

Twin disc brakes

Radiators for cooling oil and water are provided for the hot running engine

Wankel engine lacks the visual impact of a piston engine

SUZUKI KATANA

Capacity 997cc • Power output 108bhp @ 8,500rpm • Weight 251kg (554lb) • Top speed 225km/h (140mph)

BY THE EARLY 1980s Suzuki had developed an extremely powerful and attractively compact four-cylinder engine, prefixed by the letters GSX. The company now needed a new design to match the modern performance of this d.o.h.c., 16-valve motor. It turned to former BMW car designer, Jan Fellstrom, and the Katana was the result. Characterized by its integral fuel tank and seat, half-fairing, and two-tone seat, the Katana was an immediate hit with riders wanting reliability and high performance. The 1982 model is shown here.

Recessed fuel cap

Seat material looks good but is a magnet for dirt

Anti-dive mechanism reduces fork movement when braking

48-cm (19-in) front wheel

A 1074cc version of the four-cylinder motor was also produced

TSCC logo advertises Suzuki's twin swirl combustion chamber

SUZUKI GSX-R1100WR

Capacity 1074cc • Power output 130bhp @ 9,700rpm • Weight 230kg (507lb) • Top speed 285km/h (177mph)

SUZUKI'S **GSX-R1100, LAUNCHED IN 1986,** heralded the start of the true racer-replica era. Its four-cylinder, four-stroke, d.o.h.c. engine, race-type features, and outstanding power made it an immediate classic. The GSX-R also became a favourite with racers and there were many track successes. It is still in production and, though tall and heavy by modern standards and no longer the fastest in its field, it is revered by enthusiasts. This bike is a 1994 WR model.

Alloy frame members pass over the top of the engine

Twin-headlamp fairing

Upside-down forks

Three-spoke alloy wheels

Engine covers are magnesium for lightness

"Floating" discs

SWM GUANACO 320TL

Capacity 277cc • Power output 18bhp @ 6,500rpm • Weight 85kg (187lb) • Top speed 113km/h (70mph) (estimated)

IN **1971 SWM STARTED MAKING MOTORCYCLES** specializing in off-road competition machines. Early models used German Sachs two-stroke engines, but by 1978, when the machine pictured here was built, the engines were supplied by the Austrian Rotax company. Based on the successful SWM trials bike, this machine was modified for dual-purpose use. In 1981, French rider Gilles Burgat won the World Trial Championship on an SWM machine.

Lighting kit was a standard fitting

A small speedometer is mounted on the fork leg

Snail-cam chain adjusters

Remote reservoir shock absorbers

Lightweight 125-mm (5-in) conical drum brakes

TERROT 175

Capacity 173cc • Power output 3hp • Weight 110kg (242lb) • Top speed 50km/h (31mph)

FRANCE

Taxation laws in France made lightweight motorcycles of up to 175cc attractive to buyers, and most manufacturers offered machines in this class. Terrot of Dijon, which became one of France's leading motorcycle companies, made neat two-stroke machines with inclined cylinders and loop frames. The model shown here dates from 1924. It used chain primary drive to a two-speed gearbox with belt drive to the rear wheel. The machine followed the style of the 269cc Terrot, which had been introduced in 1922.

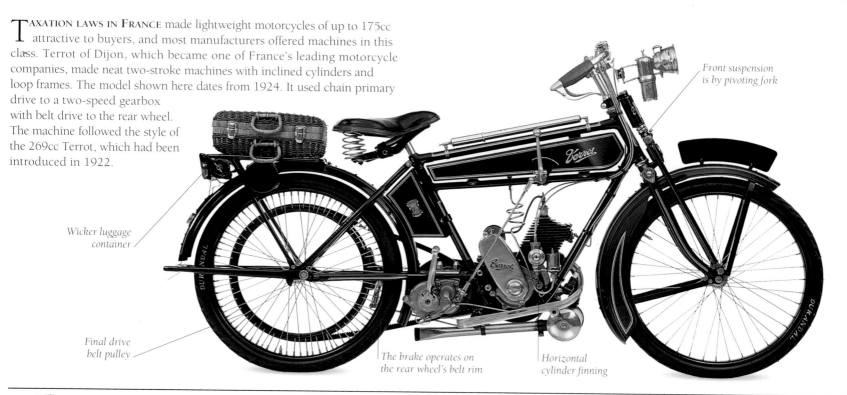

Front suspension is by pivoting fork

Wicker luggage container

Final drive belt pulley

The brake operates on the rear wheel's belt rim

Horizontal cylinder finning

TORNAX SIMPLEX SPORT

Capacity 592cc • Power output 22bhp • Weight 178kg (392lb) • Top speed 120km/h (75mph)

GERMANY

Established in 1925, Tornax soon established a reputation for high-quality sporting machines. It used proprietary engines during its time as a manufacturer. This 1934 Simplex Sport model was typical, using a 592cc twin-port o.h.v. engine supplied by the British firm JAP. The gearbox was a three-speed Hermes unit. The construction is conventional, with a diamond-pattern frame and girder forks. Instruments were recessed into the plated fuel tank. This model was the last of the JAP-engined Tornax machines after government restrictions prohibited the import of foreign components.

Instrument panel illumination light

Plated fuel tank

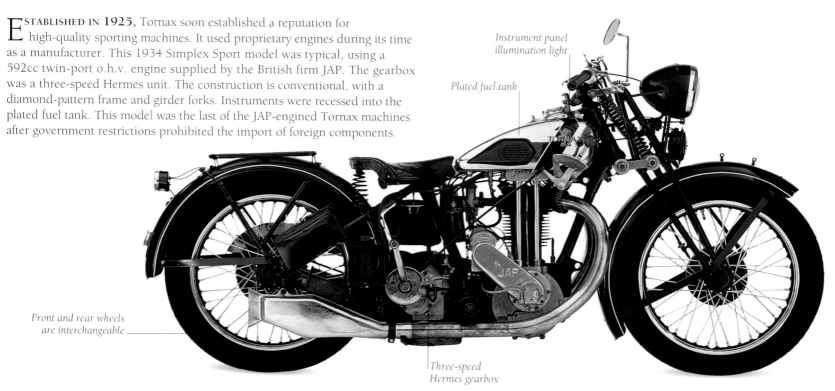

Front and rear wheels are interchangeable

Three-speed Hermes gearbox

TRIUMPH MINERVA

Capacity 239cc • Power output 2.25bhp @ 1,500rpm
Weight not known • Top speed 25mph (40km/h)

UNITED KINGDOM

FOR TRIUMPH, LIKE MANY other bicycle makers, it was relatively simple to produce its first motorcycle. This 1902 machine is little more than a bicycle, lightly modified with an engine, fuel tank, and final drive pulley on the rear wheel. With a mechanical inlet valve and a spray carburettor, the Belgian Minerva engine was more advanced than many of its contemporaries. From 1903 Triumph fitted British-built JAP engines, until introducing its own 363cc s.v. units in 1905.

BACK VIEW

Bicycle-type stirrup brake on front wheel

Longuemare spray carburettor

239cc side-valve engine

TRIUMPH HUB CLUTCH

Capacity 499cc • Power output 3.5hp
Weight not known • Top speed 46mph (74km/h)

UNITED KINGDOM

THIS MODEL APPEARED in 1910, the year that Triumph introduced its new clutch system. Contained in the rear hub and operated by a foot pedal, the clutch further evolved motorcycle practicality as it allowed the machine to be brought to a standstill with the engine still running. This bike was developed from Triumph's 1905 Three Horse model, which was the first to use the company's own side-valve engine and began the move away from bicycle-type frames to a lower diamond frame.

Horizontal-spring forks

FRONT VIEW

Final drive pulley

Clutch-operating pedal

TRIUMPH TYPE R FAST ROADSTER

Capacity 499cc • Power output 20bhp • Weight 240lb (109kg) • Top speed 75mph (121km/h)

UNITED KINGDOM

THE TYPE R WAS BASED ON TRIUMPH'S POPULAR MODEL H. The only major changes were the new cylinder and head designs by engineer Harry Ricardo (see inset). He changed the bike from a 550cc side valve to a 499cc with advanced four-valve cylinder head and centrally positioned spark plug. Performance increased greatly. The Model R, nicknamed "Riccy", made its debut in the 1921 Senior TT and remained in its catalogue until 1927. Triumph concentrated on a two-valve model from 1924; 35 years later Honda realized the potential of four valves. This 1923 bike pre-dates the fitting of drum brakes by one year.

Cycle parts are from Triumph's Model H

Druid-pattern girder forks

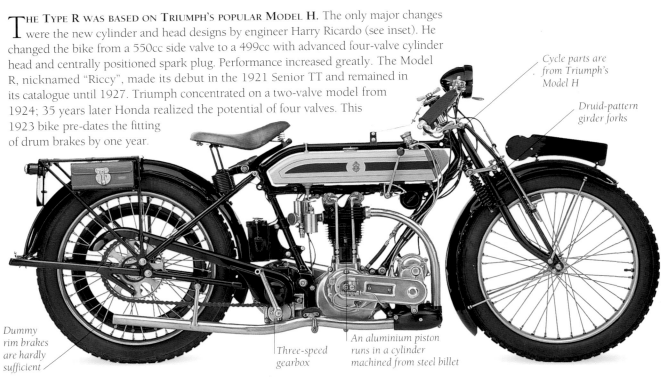

Dummy rim brakes are hardly sufficient

Three-speed gearbox

An aluminium piston runs in a cylinder machined from steel billet

HARRY RICARDO realized that fuel flow improves with more valves due to the greater valve area. Small, lighter valves reduce reciprocating mass allowing higher revs, and a centrally placed spark plug improves cylinder burning because of reduced flame travel. These ideas were neglected until Honda popularized them in the 1960s.

TRIUMPH MODEL SD

UNITED KINGDOM

Capacity 550cc • Power output 5.5hp
Weight 242lb (110kg) • Top speed not known

THE MODEL SD, INTRODUCED IN 1920, was based on the belt-drive three-speed Model H. The new machine had all-chain transmission and was now fitted with a kickstarter rather than pedals. To smooth the drive the gearbox was fitted with a shaft-mounted shock absorber, hence "SD" – Spring Drive. An electric horn and acetylene or dynamo lighting were optional. There were other improvements on this 1923 model, including a front drum brake and Druid-type girder forks.

FRONT
VIEW

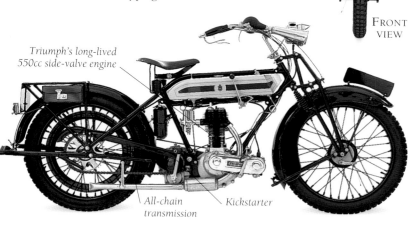

Triumph's long-lived 550cc side-valve engine

All-chain transmission

Kickstarter

TRIUMPH 6/1

UNITED KINGDOM

Capacity 649cc • Power output 25bhp @ 4,500rpm
Weight 435lb (197kg) • Top speed 85mph (137km/h) (estimated)

DESIGNED FOR THE 1934 SEASON by Valentine Page, the Triumph 6/1 introduced many design features later used by major British manufacturers. Although initially fitted with handshift gears, footshift was an option by 1935. The 6/1's chassis comprised a duplex cradle frame with front forks to match. It was aimed principally at the sidecar market. However, despite winning prestigious awards in factory tests, it was quietly dropped after the 1935 season.

FRONT
VIEW

The carburettor is fitted onto a Y-shaped manifold

Timing gear case

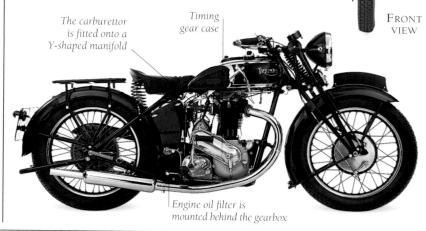

Engine oil filter is mounted behind the gearbox

TRIUMPH TIGER 80

UNITED KINGDOM

Capacity 343cc • Power output 20bhp @ 5,700rpm • Weight 320lb (145kg) • Top speed 75mph (121km/h)

A NEW RANGE OF O.H.V. TRIUMPH SINGLES designed by Val Page appeared in 1933. When the company changed hands in 1936, Edward Turner revised the range with new frames, upswept exhausts, a tank-mounted instrument panel, and more chrome and colour. Called the Tiger 70 (249cc), 80 (343cc), and 90 (493cc), the numbers were an optimistic suggestion of top speed. The new models were better looking, faster, and cheaper. Selling in large numbers, they helped to re-establish the Triumph marque. This 1937 343cc Tiger 80 is a typical example.

Chrome is used extensively on the Tiger range

FRONT
VIEW

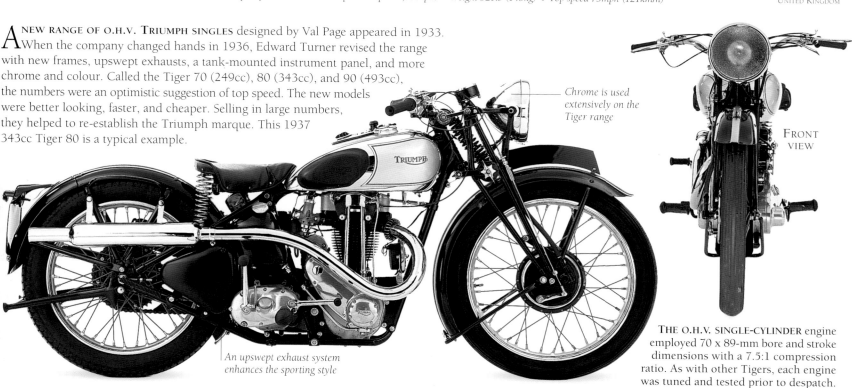

An upswept exhaust system enhances the sporting style

THE O.H.V. SINGLE-CYLINDER engine employed 70 x 89-mm bore and stroke dimensions with a 7.5:1 compression ratio. As with other Tigers, each engine was tuned and tested prior to despatch.

TRIUMPH SPEED TWIN

Capacity 498cc • Power output 27bhp @ 6,300rpm • Weight 378lb (171kg) • Top speed 93mph (150km/h)

TRIUMPH CHIEF DESIGNER Edward Turner launched the 500cc Speed Twin in July 1937, less than two years after the 6/1 had been phased out (see p.181). Turner's talent for marketing style within a tight budget was epitomized by this parallel twin: it was 5lb (2.2kg) lighter than the Tiger 90 sports single but cost only fractionally more. With a 7:1 compression ratio, the understressed 63 x 80-mm engine made the Speed Twin very smooth and powerful compared to its contemporaries, despite its 360° configuration. Running on ballbearings, the crankshaft had a central flywheel and split alloy connecting rods with white-metal lined big-end caps. The engine symmetry was further assisted by twin camshafts positioned fore-and-aft of the cast-iron cylinder block. The pushrods, housed in chromed tubes placed centrally between the cylinders, operated the valve gear, which was enclosed in separate alloy castings bolted onto the cast-iron cylinder head. The double-plunger oil pump and the Lucas Magdyno were driven by the inlet camshaft pinion. A telltale button protruding from the timing cover warned of any drop in oil pressure. The engine was slightly narrower than the Tiger 90 unit, but was fitted into Tiger series running gear with black or maroon livery. Capable of a top speed of more than 90mph (145km/h), the Speed Twin achieved a 74mph (119km/h) quarter mile (400metres) from a standing start. A sporting version appeared for 1939 in the form of the Tiger 100. Turner's Speed Twin not only provided the basis for the Triumph range for the next 50 years, but also instigated the British motorcycle industry's preoccupation with parallel twins throughout the post-war era. This is a 1939 model.

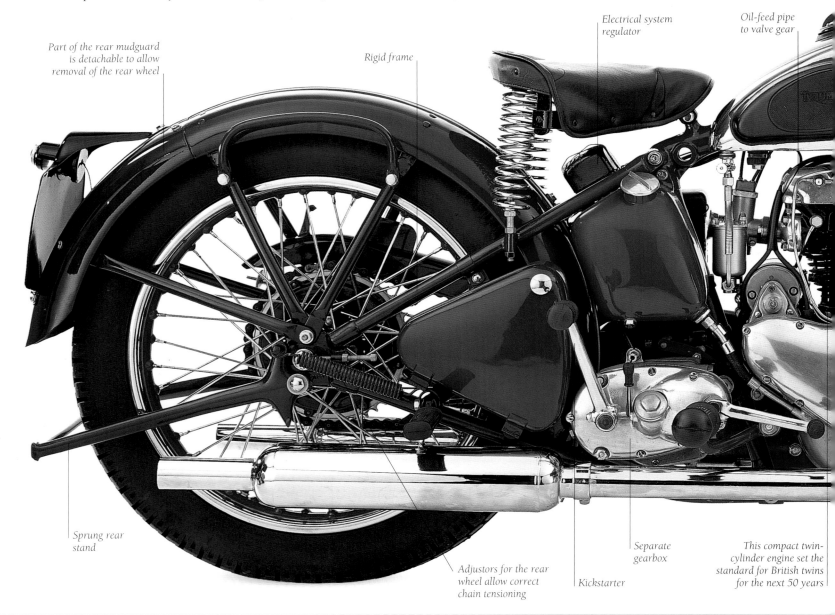

Electrical system regulator

Oil-feed pipe to valve gear

Part of the rear mudguard is detachable to allow removal of the rear wheel

Rigid frame

Sprung rear stand

Adjustors for the rear wheel allow correct chain tensioning

Kickstarter

Separate gearbox

This compact twin-cylinder engine set the standard for British twins for the next 50 years

LIKE MANY OTHER manufactureres of the period, Triumph put an instrument panel on the top of its fuel tanks. Made of an early form of plastic known as bakelite, the panel carried a Lucus three-positioned lighting switch, a large Lucus ammeter, and an oil pressure gauge. A useful device was also fitted to the panel: a detachable inspection lamp for use at night.

•TRIUMPH DESIGNER•

Speed Twin designer Edward Turner was a major figure in British motorcycle design. He started work at Ariel, producing the innovative Square Four (see p.18), and moved to Triumph when Ariel's owners took over that firm in 1936. At Triumph he added chrome and colourful paint to its mundane single-cylinder machines, transforming them into the Tiger range. In post-war years Turner was instrumental in adapting Triumph motorcycles for the American market where they sold in large numbers during the 1950s and 1960s.

Edward Turner at work

Speedometer drive cable

FRONT VIEW

VIEWED FROM ANY ANGLE, Turner's designs are always characterized by graceful lines. Even the 8-in (20-cm) Lucas headlamp does not detract from the Speed Twin's overall slimness. With the twin exhaust pipes well tucked in, its engine was actually narrower than the Tiger's. Turner designed with speed in mind, proven by the need to lean past 45° to ground the footrests or silencers.

TRIUMPH 3TA

Capacity 349cc • Power output 18.5bhp @ 6,500rpm • Weight 349lb (158kg) • Top speed 80mph (129km/h)

ANNOUNCED IN 1957, the 3TA was Triumph's first unit-construction twin. Because of the radical styling of his redesign, Edward Turner may have considered it wise to test the market with the 350cc twin, which was never popular with the buying public. Although the basic layout of the engine remained unaltered, the crankcase was extended to house the gear cluster in a separate compartment. A built-up crank assembly ran in a combination of plain and ball main bearings. Instead of a magneto, the inlet camshaft now drove a distributor that was mounted in the crankcase behind the timing chest through skew gears. The lighting and ignition system were powered by a crankshaft-mounted alternator in the primary drive case. A magnetic speedometer driven off the rear wheel replaced the expensive traditional instrument, and there was a gear indicator on top of the gearbox inner casing. The most radical feature was the rear enclosure – the "bathtub" – but this gave way to a shortened skirting for 1964. The 3TA survived until 1966. This bike is a 1958 model.

THE 3TA had a top gear ratio of 1:5.4 and a 7.5:1 compression ratio. Bore and stroke dimensions of 58.25 x 65.5mm gave the engine its 21cu. in. (349cc) capacity, hence "Twenty-One". The cylinder block was cast-iron with an alloy head and bolt-on manifold carrying an Amal 375 Monobloc carburettor. The gearbox was driven by a duplex chain with no tensioner. The "Twenty-One" was finished in Silver Beige.

FRONT VIEW

•BODY TALK•

The chassis of the 3TA had a simplex cradle frame with swingarm rear and telescopic front suspension. The fuel tank was the first to carry the "mouth organ" badge. The headlamp nacelle was retained and, in Turner's view, complemented by a large front mudguard. The seat was hinged for tool roll and battery access but the air filter and rectifier were almost inaccessible.

Percy Tait testing the prototype in 1957

The unit-construction engine was later enlarged to 490cc to power Triumph's popular 500 twins

The classic Triumph headlamp nacelle is complemented by a large front mudguard

Single Amal Monobloc carburettor

"Mouth organ" tank badge

Radical rear enclosure known as the "bathtub"

The 3TA has a gear indicator situated on top of the gearbox inner casing

The gearbox casing is integral with the crankcase

Camshaft timing-gear case

The rear wheel drives the magnetic speedometer

TRIUMPH
T120 BONNEVILLE

Capacity 650cc • Power output 46bhp @ 6,500rpm
Weight 404lb (183kg) • Top speed 110mph (177km/h)

UNITED KINGDOM

REGARDED AS THE QUINTESSENTIAL British twin, the Bonneville was
introduced in 1959 and continued in various forms until 1989. The
name reflects speed records set by Triumph twins on the Bonneville Salt
Flats, in Utah, USA, during the 1950s. The first Bonnevilles, like the rare
1959 model shown here, had a compression ratio of 8.5:1, and were fitted
with the recently introduced alloy head and a half-race inlet camshaft. Twin
Amal Monobloc carburettors were fed by a remote float chamber. Until
1960 the chassis consisted of the standard simplex frame, with running
gear common to the rest of the 650cc range.

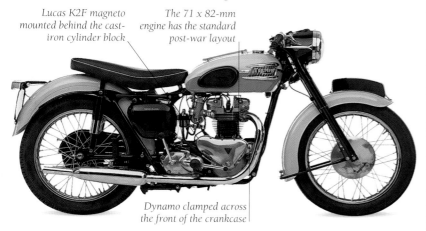

*Lucas K2F magneto
mounted behind the cast-
iron cylinder block*

*The 71 x 82-mm
engine has the standard
post-war layout*

*Dynamo clamped across
the front of the crankcase*

TRIUMPH
T20 TIGER CUB

Capacity 199cc • Power output 10bhp @ 6,000rpm
Weight 240lb (109kg) • Top speed 72mph (116km/h)

UNITED KINGDOM

LAUNCHED IN 1954, the T20 was post-war Britain's only serious attempt
at a four-stroke machine for the lightweight market. Based on the
149cc Triumph Terrier, the Cub was later developed by BSA for the 248cc
C15 (see p.39). Early models had plunger rear suspension, but by the time
this 1959 model appeared they were fitted with a swingarm frame. The
four-speed gearbox was a built-in unit with the engine. The name and
style of the machine suggested a small-scale version of Triumph's popular
twins. The Tiger Cub lasted until 1968.

*Gear indicator
mounted in the
headlamp nacelle*

*63 x 64-mm, o.h.v. all-
alloy, unit-construction
engine with inclined cylinder*

*Duplex chain
drives the gearbox*

TRIUMPH
6T THUNDERBIRD

Capacity 649cc • Power output 34bhp @ 6,300rpm
Weight 385lb (175kg) • Top speed 106mph (171km/h)

UNITED KINGDOM

THE ORIGINAL THUNDERBIRD was introduced in 1949 to satisfy U.S.
market demand for increased capacity. The engine was stretched from
500 to 650cc, establishing a new class for post-war British twins. Marlon
Brando rode a Thunderbird in the 1954 film *The Wild One*. This 1960
model has bathtub styling and a duplex cradle frame, both introduced that
year. In 1961 the engine was fitted with an alloy head, and in 1962 unit
construction was adopted. The Thunderbird name was dropped in 1966,
reappearing briefly in the 1980s on a 650cc twin and again in the 1990s on
a retro-styled version of the 900cc Triumph triple.

*Single Amal Monobloc
carburettor; some earlier models
had a car-type SU instrument*

*Duplex
cradle frame*

*Thunderbird logo – the
name is derived from
American Indian mythology*

TRIUMPH
T120TT BONNEVILLE SPECIAL

Capacity 649cc • Power output 54bhp @ 6,500rpm
Weight 350lb (159kg) • Top speed 120mph (193km/h) (estimated)

UNITED KINGDOM

TRIUMPH AMERICA DEVELOPED the TT Special for the West Coast market
where desert and beach racing were very popular. To save the weight of
a battery, the problematic Energy Transfer ignition was used, while the
duplex frame gave way to a single downtube running into a duplex cradle.
The rear end was stiffened by plates supporting the ends of the swinging
fork pivot. The T120TT was made for only two seasons, and few survived
the rigours of sand racing and the stresses imposed on the bearings. The
advent of genuine scrambles machines made the TT Special obsolete.

*This 1966 model has a
standard U.S. fuel tank
and a hinged dual seat*

*The T120TT came
without lights or
registration plates*

*The specially designed,
straight-through exhaust pipes
sweep in under the engine*

TRIUMPH T150 TRIDENT

Capacity 740cc • Power output 58bhp • Weight 468lb (212kg) • Top speed 125mph (201km/h)

THE T150 TRIDENT APPEARED FOR EXPORT ONLY in 1968; it was not available in Britain until 1969. Its standard Triumph engine layout had camshafts front and rear of the cylinders, with an extra cylinder to increase capacity. A 120° crankshaft made the engine smooth and gave the exhaust a distinctive sound. Despite excellent performance and handling, the Trident was eclipsed by Honda's CB750 (see pp.88–89). The T150V, the 1972 model, had a five-speed gearbox and disc brake. With 1974's major re-styling came an electric starter and left-foot gearchange. A 1972 model is shown here.

From 1971 export models had smaller tanks and higher handlebars

Standard Triumph wheels with a new twin leading-shoe front brake introduced in 1968

The three-into-four-into-two exhaust system ends in a pair of futuristic silencers, popularly known as "ray guns"

The engine has vertical cylinders and is fitted with three concentric carburettors

Simplex cradle frame

TRIUMPH X75 HURRICANE

Capacity 740cc • Power output 58bhp @ 7,250rpm
Weight 444lb (201kg) • Top speed 105mph (169km/h)

UNVEILED IN NOVEMBER 1972, the X75 Hurricane was based on the discontinued BSA Rocket 3 (see p.39), inheriting its duplex frame and inclined cylinders. BSA-Triumph had commissioned U.S. designer Craig Vetter to design a limited edition of chopper-style triples to cash in on the chopper craze caused by the movies *Wild Angels* and *Easy Rider*. By 1972 (the date of the bike shown here), the BSA name had been dropped, and so a Triumph badge was used. The Hurricane was more brash than efficient: the two-gallon (nine-litre) fuel tank restricted distance, the extended forks impaired handling, and the wide handlebars made high speeds difficult.

A small steel fuel tank is hidden inside the fibreglass seat and dummy tank unit

All three exhaust pipes exit on the right-hand side

For style rather than handling, the forks were extended by 1in (2.5cm)

A five-speed Triumph gear cluster is fitted

Ineffective conical-hub twin leading-shoe brake

TRIUMPH T140D BONNEVILLE

Capacity 748cc • Power output 51bhp (claimed)
Weight 410lb (186kg) • Top speed 96mph (154km/h)

THE BONNEVILLE ACQUIRED a new frame with an oil tank in the top tube in 1971, and capacity grew to 748cc in 1973. Launched in 1979 (date of the bike shown here), the T140D Special was substantially modified to meet restrictive U.S. emissions laws. The changes badly affected performance, making the T140D an unworthy successor to the Bonneville name. It was the last Triumph twin exported to North America in significant numbers. Bonneville production continued at Triumph's Meriden factory until the collapse of the workers' cooperative in 1983.

Engine oil is carried in the tubular spine of the duplex frame

A restrictive silencer on the two-into-one exhaust killed the bike's performance

Amal Mk2 carburettors

Seven-spoke Lester cast-alloy wheels

Brake and gearshift operation switched sides to meet U.S. legislation in 1975

TRIUMPH

TRIUMPH SPEED TRIPLE

Capacity 885cc • Power output 99bhp @ 9,000rpm • Weight 461lb (209kg) • Top speed 135mph (217km/h)

UNITED KINGDOM

THE REVIVED TRIUMPH COMPANY introduced its new range of three- and four-cylinder motorcycles in 1991. The design of the d.o.h.c., water-cooled engines was heavily influenced by Kawasaki's GPZ900R (see p.115) and a tubular-steel spine was used across the range. The best machine in the original range was the unfaired, 885cc, three-cylinder Trident. This new, unfaired Triple was produced for 1994. Looks were improved with black paint and it came equipped with uprated brake and suspension components. Its name was inspired by the 1937 Speed Twin.

Removable seat hump conceals passenger seat

Twin front disc brakes with opposed, four-piston callipers

Three-into-two exhaust system with "bean-can"-style silencers

Both wheels are 17in (43cm) equipped with Michelin Hi-Sport tyres

---

TRIUMPH KNIRPS

Capacity 276cc • Power output 3bhp
Weight 130lb (59kg) • Top speed 40mph (64km/h)

GERMANY

TRIUMPH WERKE NÜRNBERG (TWN) was established in 1903 as an offshoot of the Triumph Cycle Co. in Coventry – a logical step because the English company was headed by Siegfried Bettmann from Nuremberg and his compatriot Mauritz Schulte. Following the introduction of the Triumph "Junior" in 1914, the German factory tooled up to make a similar model, the Knirps ("Nipper"), and production started in 1920 (the year of the model shown here). Apart from a slightly larger engine the German machine was almost identical to its English counterpart.

Two-stroke engine driving by chain to a two-speed gearbox and belt to the rear wheel

TRIUMPH BDG 125

Capacity 123cc • Power output 6.5bhp @ 4,800rpm
Weight 176lb (80kg) • Top speed 50mph(80km/h)

GERMANY

AFTER WORLD WAR II, TWN was one of the first German manufacturers to resume production, initially with pre-war designs. In 1949 the company announced new 125cc and 250cc models using the "split single" principle first used in the late 1930s. With this the transfer ports are in one cylinder and the exhaust ports are in another, both having a common combustion chamber. The engine therefore runs as a single, but provides good separation of incoming and exhaust gases. TWN used this layout until it stopped motorcycle production in 1957. This is a 1950 model.

Tubular frame

Telescopic forks

VAN VEEN OCR1000

Capacity 996cc • Power output 100bhp @ 6,000rpm
Weight 295kg (650lb) • Top speed 242km/h (150mph)

AFTER MANY YEARS' INVOLVEMENT with Kreidler 50cc racers, Henk van Veen decided to produce a large-capacity machine under his own name. He used a water-cooled twin-rotor Wankel engine developed in conjunction with Audi/NSU, a four-speed gearbox and shaft drive developed by Porsche, front forks and rear suspension by Koni, and brakes by Brembo. Expensive and produced only to special order, the bike clearly represented a prestigious flagship for the Van Veen organization rather than a serious attempt at becoming a motorcycle manufacturer.

A 4¾-gallon (22-litre) fuel tank is fitted

VELOCETTE D2

Capacity 220cc • Power output 8bhp
Weight 158lb (72kg) • Top speed 40mph (64km/h)

BEST REMEMBERED FOR ITS O.H.V. FOUR-STROKE SINGLES, Velocette also produced some notable two-stroke engines during the "flat tankers" era. Although the D2 looks simplistic to contemporary eyes, it is worth remembering that most early motorcyclists were also their own mechanics, responsible for repairs and servicing on machinery subjected to harsh 1920s road conditions. Brake technology was slow to advance. The D2's stirrup brakes were no worse than its competitors', but then the standard was not very high. This is a 1921 model.

Hand lever operates sliding dog, two-speed gearbox

VELOCETTE MODEL K

Capacity 348cc • Power output not known • Weight 260lb (118kg) • Top speed 65mph (105km/h)

AVAILABLE IN EITHER SPORT OR TOUR FORMATS, the Model K was the first Velocette to feature the Percy Goodman-designed overhead camshaft engine that became synonymous with the Birmingham factory. The new engine was the first four-stroke that Velocette had produced since converting to war production in 1916. It remained essentially unchanged until the early 1930s. The machine shown here is a 1925 Model K.

Druid-type side-sprung forks

BACK VIEW

Oil tank for dry-sump lubrication system

Shaft-driven o.h.c.

MUCH OF Velocette's wartime work involved making parts for Rolls-Royce armoured cars; the association proved to be a positive influence on Velocette's engineering quality.

VELOCETTE MODEL LE

Capacity 149cc • Power output 8bhp @ 6,000rpm • Weight 250lb (113kg) • Top speed 50mph (80km/h)

To a public more familiar with Velocette's sturdy traditional singles, the "Little Engine" came as a shock. Its pressed-steel monocoque frame and shaft-drive, flat-twin, side-valve engine with a reputation for almost silent running failed to overcome the doubts, yet the design had many novel features. The engine, gearbox, radiators, and rear swingarm were mounted on a subframe which unbolted from the main frame for easy maintenance.

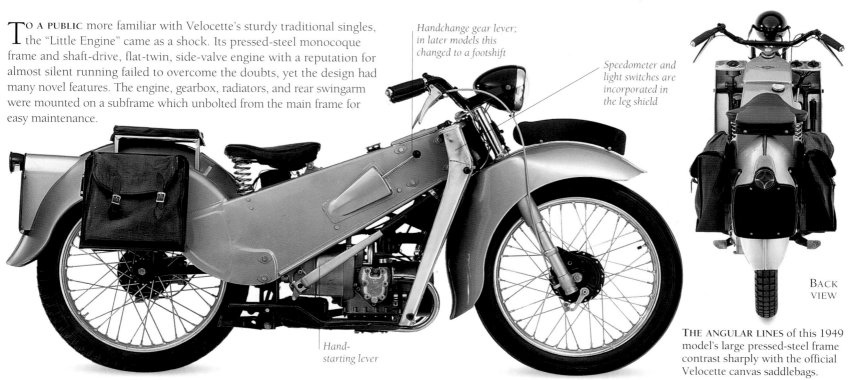

Handchange gear lever; in later models this changed to a footshift

Speedometer and light switches are incorporated in the leg shield

BACK VIEW

Hand-starting lever

THE ANGULAR LINES of this 1949 model's large pressed-steel frame contrast sharply with the official Velocette canvas saddlebags.

VELOCETTE
KTT MK VIII

Capacity 348cc • Power output 34bhp
Weight 320lb (145kg) • Top speed 115mph (185km/h)

Despite a pre-war heritage, variants of the o.h.c. Velocette engine designed by Percy Goodmann were built up until the 1950s, thus signalling the strength of the initial design. The last model to bear the famous moniker, the KTT Mk VIII (1947 model pictured), was introduced a year after the Velocette factory team had cleaned up at the 1938 TT, and soon established a name for reliability that distinguished it among highly temperamental production racers of the era. Modifications after the war were limited, but the winning World Championship machines ridden by Freddie Frith in 1949 and 1950 used double overhead camshafts.

Stainless steel braiding helps to protect the oil lines

VELOCETTE
THRUXTON VENOM

Capacity 499cc • Power output 40bhp @ 6,200rpm
Weight 390lb (177kg) • Top speed 105mph (169km/h)

In essence a tuned version of Velocette's Venom model, the big single engine proved ideally suited to the Thruxton Nine Hour production race, after which later developments of the sports Venom were named. Prior to the introduction of the Thruxton in 1965, the Velocette factory sold a high-performance kit to prospective racers. Ironically, the 1965 500-mile (800-km) race moved to Castle Combe in Wiltshire, but Velocettes still dominated the 500cc class. The Thruxton Venom illustrated here is a 1967 model.

Rear springing is adjusted by moving the upper mounting bolts of the rear damper unit through an arc

The fuel tank is cut away to accommodate the downdraught carburettor

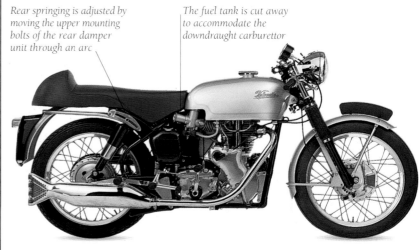

VESPA 150

Capacity 145cc • Power output 7bhp @ 5,000rpm • Weight not known • Top speed 90km/h (56mph)

FIRST INTRODUCED IN **1946**, the Vespa remains in production in the 1990s, updated and improved. It is the longest-lasting production motorcycle ever made. The Vespa was born because of the need for cheap personal transportation in the chaos of post-war Italy and also the need of aircraft makers Piaggio to diversify after the war. It was designed by aircraft designer Corradino d'Ascanio without the preconceived notions that a motorcycle designer would have brought to the task. The frame was a pressed-steel monocoque designed with the intention of providing maximum comfort and convenience to the rider, hence the "step-thru" layout and the integral leg shields. The engine, gearbox, and rear wheel assembly pivoted to provide rear suspension. Wheels were interchangeable and mounted on stub axles like a car. The gearchange was operated by a twistgrip system on the left handlebar. The word *vespa* is Italian for "wasp"; the buzzing of its two-stroke engine and the wasp-like rear section of the machine gave the company its name.

THE ORIGINAL VESPA used a 98cc engine but the capacity increased to 125cc in 1948 and a 150cc model appeared in 1954. Later the capacity of Vespa scooters increased to 198cc. The 150 shown here is a 1965 model. Many owners installed extras on to their scooters, this one has a basket on the inside of the leg shields, a luggage rack with spare wheel, and a pillion seat. This basic model was supplied with just one saddle.

•FASHION ACCESSORY•

Despite being designed as a practical form of transportation, the Vespa was promoted as a stylish fashion accessory for the young. Vespas and Lambrettas became an essential part of British "Mod" culture in the 1960s. Mods would convene in large numbers at British coastal resorts. This picture shows such a gathering in Hastings.

Vespas at Hastings, England

FRONT VIEW

Leg shields help protect clothing

Passenger grab rail

Fuel tank is hidden under the seat

Single-sided front fork uses a trailing-link suspension system

The entire engine gearbox unit pivots to provide rear suspension

20.3-cm (8-in) wheels

VICTORIA KR50S

Capacity 495cc • Power output 18bhp @ 5,000rpm • Weight 150kg (330lb) • Top speed 113km/h (70mph)

VICTORIA INTRODUCED A RANGE of single-cylinder machines in 1928 to supplement the flat-twin models already produced. The new machines were of conventional construction with tubular frames, girder forks, and British-built Sturmey-Archer engines of 198cc to 495cc. The KR50S, a top of the range sports model with three-speed gearbox, was introduced in 1931. Victoria's Sturmey-Archer-engined machines were phased out in the early 1930s: the KR50S was dropped in 1933 while the 198cc side-valve version lasted until 1934. This bike is a 1931 model.

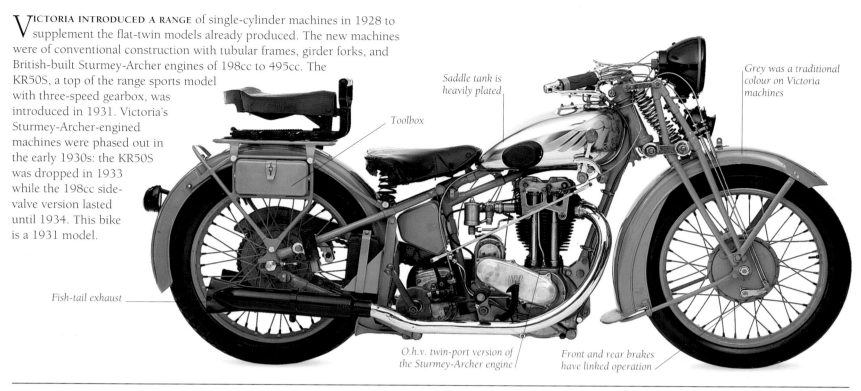

Saddle tank is heavily plated

Toolbox

Grey was a traditional colour on Victoria machines

Fish-tail exhaust

O.h.v. twin-port version of the Sturmey-Archer engine

Front and rear brakes have linked operation

VICTORIA BERGMEISTER

Capacity 347cc • Power output 21bhp @ 6,300rpm • Weight 176kg (389lb) • Top speed 130km/h (81mph)

THE BERGMEISTER was Victoria's first post-war four-stroke. It was introduced in 1951 but production versions were not available until 1953. The bike was designed by Richard Küchen, and the four-speed gearbox used chains rather than pinions. Final drive was by shaft. In 1956, production ended and Victoria returned to the lightweight two-stroke. The Bergmeister's heavy development costs damaged the firm's finances, and it merged with the Zweirad Union in 1958. The Bergmeister shown here dates from 1954.

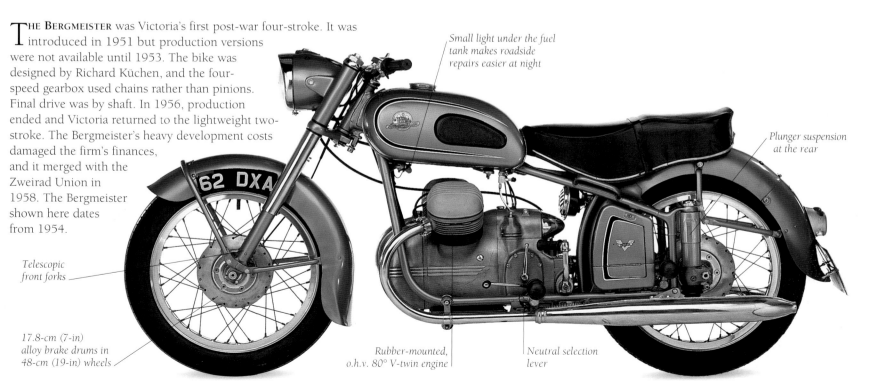

Small light under the fuel tank makes roadside repairs easier at night

Plunger suspension at the rear

Telescopic front forks

17.8-cm (7-in) alloy brake drums in 48-cm (19-in) wheels

Rubber-mounted, o.h.v. 80° V-twin engine

Neutral selection lever

VICTORIA SWING

Capacity 197cc • Power output 11bhp @ 5,300rpm • Weight not known • Top speed 100km/h (62mph)

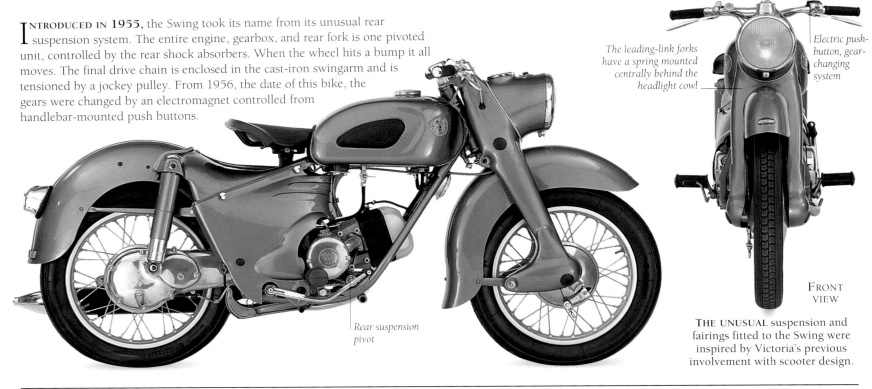

INTRODUCED IN **1955**, the Swing took its name from its unusual rear suspension system. The entire engine, gearbox, and rear fork is one pivoted unit, controlled by the rear shock absorbers. When the wheel hits a bump it all moves. The final drive chain is enclosed in the cast-iron swingarm and is tensioned by a jockey pulley. From 1956, the date of this bike, the gears were changed by an electromagnet controlled from handlebar-mounted push buttons.

The leading-link forks have a spring mounted centrally behind the headlight cowl

Electric push-button, gear-changing system

Rear suspension pivot

FRONT VIEW

THE UNUSUAL suspension and fairings fitted to the Swing were inspired by Victoria's previous involvement with scooter design.

VINCENT-HRD COMET

Capacity 498cc • Power output 25bhp @ 5,300rpm • Weight 385lb (175kg) • Top speed 92mph (148km/h)

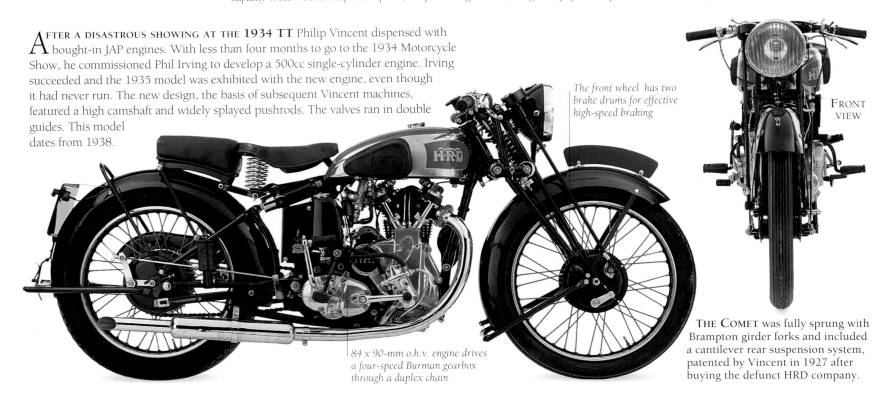

AFTER A DISASTROUS SHOWING AT THE **1934 TT** Philip Vincent dispensed with bought-in JAP engines. With less than four months to go to the 1934 Motorcycle Show, he commissioned Phil Irving to develop a 500cc single-cylinder engine. Irving succeeded and the 1935 model was exhibited with the new engine, even though it had never run. The new design, the basis of subsequent Vincent machines, featured a high camshaft and widely splayed pushrods. The valves ran in double guides. This model dates from 1938.

The front wheel has two brake drums for effective high-speed braking

FRONT VIEW

84 x 90-mm o.h.v. engine drives a four-speed Burman gearbox through a duplex chain

THE COMET was fully sprung with Brampton girder forks and included a cantilever rear suspension system, patented by Vincent in 1927 after buying the defunct HRD company.

VINCENT-HRD SERIES C BLACK SHADOW

Capacity 998cc • Power output 55bhp @ 5,700rpm • Weight 458lb (208kg) • Top speed 125mph (201km/h)

THE BEST-KNOWN OF ALL VINCENT-HRD MODELS, the Black Shadow began as a tuned version of the Series B Rapide, which superseded the pre-war Series A Rapide in 1946. The Series C version appeared in 1949 and was in production until 1954. The 84 x 90-mm, V-twin, unit-construction engine formed an integral part of the rolling chassis, suspended from a spine frame that doubled as an oil tank. The rear subframe pivoted from the rear of the gearbox with twin spring boxes and, from 1949, a damper was mounted between its apex and the rear of the oil tank. Driven through a servo clutch by a triplex chain, the narrow crossover gearbox contained four ratios. At 100mph (161km/h) in top gear the flexible engine was running at just 4,000rpm. When the stands on each side of the bike were used in conjunction with the main stand, it was lifted clear of the ground for maintenance purposes. Another notable feature was a large 150mph (241km/h) speedometer, emphasizing that, at the time, the Vincent was the world's fastest standard motorcycle.

BACK VIEW

THE POST-WAR Black Shadows retained many of the best features of the Series A range: cantilever rear suspension, quickly detachable twin-braked wheels, and, on Series Bs, Brampton girder forks. Series C models were equipped with the firm's own Girdraulic forks, which combined the rigidity of girders with the latest in hydraulic technology.

•THE FIRST BLACK SHADOW•

The 1949 motorcycle shown on the right, with the registration number JRO 102, is the prototype Black Shadow. The production models that followed had a shallower body, and Girdraulic forks replaced the Brampton girder forks. Behind the bike can be seen the former Vincent factory to the right, and Philip Vincent's house on the left.

Prototype Black Shadow in 1949

Stainless steel mudguards

Friction dampers for the rear suspension are fitted at the junction of the seat stays and the swingarm

Side-float Amal 289 carburettor

Two camshafts are driven by an idler gear mounted on the crankshaft

A hydraulic suspension damper is centrally mounted. Springs are contained in the two longer sleeves behind the fork blades

5-in (13-cm) Miller headlamp with switch and ammeter

Eccentric lower link mounts allow steering geometry adjustment for solo or sidecar use

A six-volt 40-watt Miller Dynamo is driven from the clutch

Chain tension adjusters

Oil filter housing

Two 7-in (18-cm) drum brakes are fitted to each wheel

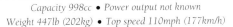

VINCENT
SERIES D RAPIDE

Capacity 998cc • Power output not known
Weight 447lb (202kg) • Top speed 110mph (177km/h)

Vincent intended that all the Series D models should have enclosed bodywork. These streamlined machines were announced in late 1954. A revised frame layout meant that the oil tank moved to a position under the seat. Coil ignition was used and suspension was controlled by Armstrong dampers. But the bodywork, which was made by an outside supplier, could not be delivered in time and so the first 1955 models, like this Rapide, got the improvements without the bodywork. The Series D was the last range produced by Vincent before production ended in 1955.

The dual seat and oil tank are mounted on a tubular subframe

WANDERER

Capacity 308cc • Power output 2.5hp
Weight not known • Top speed 60km/h (37mph) (estimated)

This 1903 machine was one of the earliest produced by the Winkelhofer & Jaenicke company of Saxony. The company built its first motorcycles the previous year. The frame of this simple machine was a loop pattern with a second horizontal bracing tube above the engine. The camshaft on the a.i.v. engine was situated in front of the barrel; a long inlet tract ran from the rear-mounted carburettor situated behind the cylinder. This allowed it to draw warm air from around the barrel. Magneto ignition was supplied. Wanderer was noted for its quality of construction.

Bicycle-style front brake operates on the tyre

Loop frame allows engine to be mounted low

WANDERER K500

Capacity 498cc • Power output 18bhp • Weight 165kg (364lb) • Top speed 120km/h (75mph)

Designed by Alexander Novikoff, this radical machine was introduced in 1928. Intended as a high-quality rival to BMW's shaft-drive twins, the K500's single-cylinder engine was mounted with its crank running longitudinally in the pressed-steel frame. There was a three-speed gearbox and shaft final drive. However, Wanderer staked too much on the new bike and the firm was taken over by NSU in 1930. The takeover ended the bike's production, but its design proved more durable.

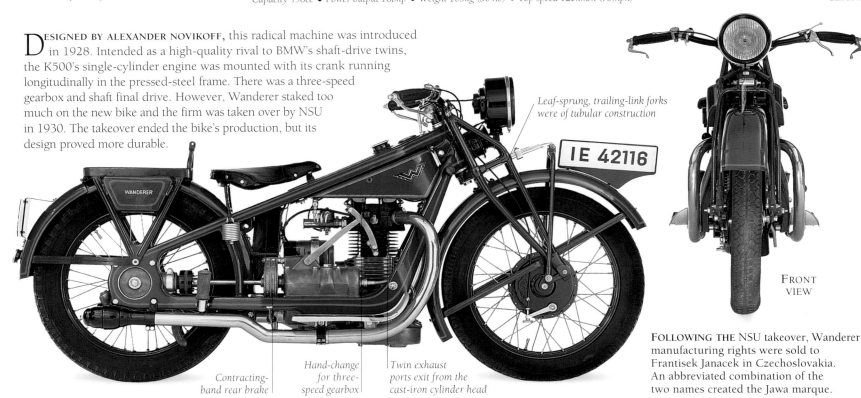

Leaf-sprung, trailing-link forks were of tubular construction

IE 42116

FRONT VIEW

Contracting-band rear brake

Hand-change for three-speed gearbox

Twin exhaust ports exit from the cast-iron cylinder head

FOLLOWING THE NSU takeover, Wanderer manufacturing rights were sold to Frantisek Janacek in Czechoslovakia. An abbreviated combination of the two names created the Jawa marque.

WERNER

Capacity 262cc • Power output 2.5hp • Weight not known • Top speed 32km/h (20mph)

THE WERNER BROTHERS introduced their first motorcycle in 1897 when they fitted a small engine designed by Hippolyte Labitte above the front wheel of a bicycle. It was the first motorcycle built in significant numbers, and it was made under licence in Britain. The engine location of the early Werner, its weight high up on the front fork, made the machine dangerously unstable. But other marques used equally unlikely positions for their power units; within the wheels, under the seat, and even on subframes projecting out behind the rear wheel. The "new" Werner, like the one pictured here, appeared in 1901. This machine moved from the bicycle-and-engine style towards an integrated "motorcycle". Once the problem of ideal engine location was solved, the way was open for further developments in engine and chassis technology. Other significant improvements over the earlier machine included electric ignition, an improved carburettor, and more effective brakes. These helped turn the motorcycle from an eccentric toy into a practical machine.

THE FRAME WAS SPLIT between the bottom bracket and the forked downtube, and the engine was securely bolted into position in the gap. An additional horizontal brace was added above the engine to provide further strengthening of the frame. With the engine now mounted low down and centrally between the wheels, the handling of the machine was much improved.

•IMPRACTICAL MACHINE•

The Werners' first motorcycle was produced in 1897. It featured a small-capacity a.i.v. engine mounted above the front wheel of a bicycle. Viewed a century later, the machine seems hopelessly impractical. It had awful weight distribution, dangerous and temperamental hot-tube ignition, and insufficient power. At the time it was the nearest to a practical motorcycle so far achieved.

Owner with Werner, 1910

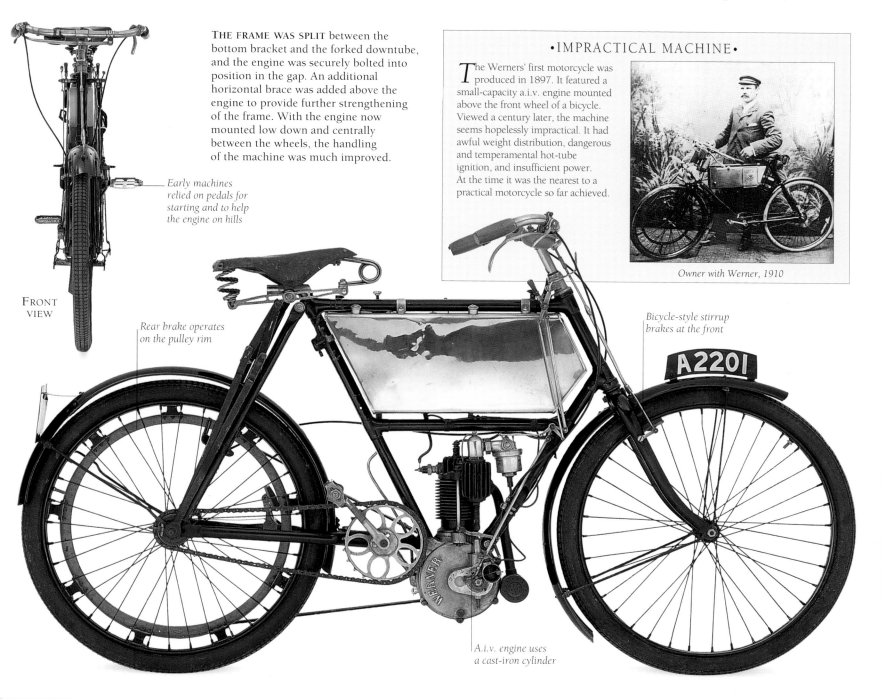

FRONT
VIEW

Early machines relied on pedals for starting and to help the engine on hills

Rear brake operates on the pulley rim

Bicycle-style stirrup brakes at the front

A2201

A.i.v. engine uses a cast-iron cylinder

WESLAKE

Capacity 499cc • Power output 48bhp • Weight 183lb (83kg) • Top speed 60–80mph (97–129km/h)

U.S.A.

THE **SPEEDWAY BIKE** is among the most specialized of motorcycles, and its design has altered little in 60 years. The skeletal lightweight frames and vertically mounted, single-cylinder, four-stroke engines of modern machines differ little from their forebears. Until the four-valve Weslake engine appeared in 1974, two-valve engines made first by JAP and then Jawa had dominated the sport since the 1930s. The new Weslake was more powerful than the two-valve engines and soon became the dominant engine in Speedway. The bike here was used by 1981 World Champion Bruce Penhall.

Pushrod tube for overhead valves

Lightweight telescopic forks

A coloured disc hides a conventional wheel

The front wheel is larger in diameter than the rear but has a narrower tyre

Clutch actuating arm; no gearbox is fitted

WHIZZER MODEL F

Capacity 138cc • Power output 2.5bhp
Weight not known • Top speed 30mph (48km/h) (estimated)

U.S.A.

ORIGINALLY **PRODUCED AS A CLIP-ON ENGINE** to fit any bicycle frame, the Whizzer power unit first appeared in 1939. The simple 138cc side-valve engine could be clamped into any bicycle frame at three mounting points. Drive to the rear tyre was by a belt-driven friction roller mounted under the bottom bracket. In 1943 a revised design was introduced. The Model F, like the machine shown here, had improved engine internals and belt drive to the rear wheel.

Bicycle-style frame

Belt drive

Flexible exhaust pipe allowed easy engine mounting

WHIZZER
PACEMAKER

Capacity 138cc • Power output 3hp
Weight not known • Top speed 35mph (56km/h) (estimated)

U.S.A.

BY **1951, WHEN THIS WHIZZER PACEMAKER** was produced, the American moped had evolved into a complete machine with a Schwinn frame. The bike had a chrome fuel tank, telescopic forks, and two curving frame tubes. Whizzers were economical, and sold in large numbers in the 1940s and 1950s, being especially popular with American teenagers. They were still available in the early 1960s, but were no match for the new lightweight machines arriving from Japan.

Metal cover hides belt-tensioning jockey pulley

Telescopic forks

Curved frame tube

WILKINSON TMC

Capacity 848cc • Power output not known • Weight 320lb (145kg) • Top speed not known

THIS LUXURIOUS AND ADVANCED MACHINE was designed P. G. Tacchi and built by the Wilkinson Sword Company. It was first shown as the TAC (Touring Auto Cycle) in 1909, with shaft drive, leaf-sprung rear suspension, and a three-speed gearbox. Redesigned as the TMC (Touring Motor Cycle) in 1911, the capacity of the four-cylinder side-valve engine was increased to 848cc. The model pictured here is from 1912.

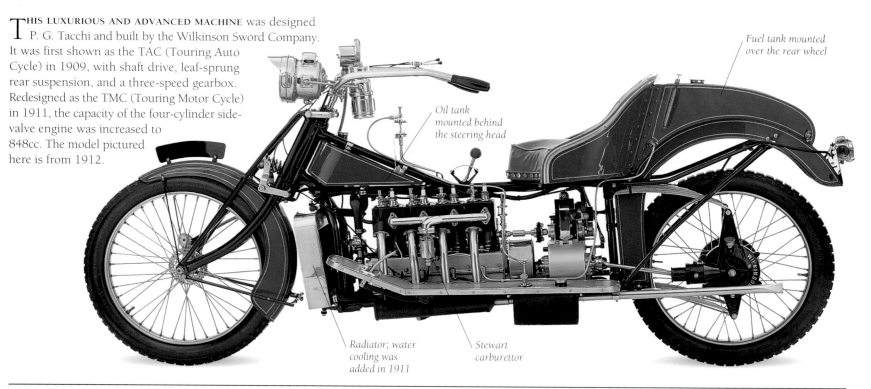

Fuel tank mounted over the rear wheel

Oil tank mounted behind the steering head

Radiator; water cooling was added in 1911

Stewart carburettor

WIMMER GG35

Capacity 344cc • Power output 16bhp • Weight not known • Top speed 113km/h (70mph) (estimated)

THE BAVARIAN FIRM OF B. WIMMER UND SOHN began building motorcycles and clip-on bicycle engines in the early 1920s. The GG35 model shown here dates from 1932 and is typical of its neat design and high-quality construction. The three-speed Hurth gearbox was bolted to the back of the inclined-cylinder 344cc o.h.v. engine to make a rigid semi-unit-construction power unit. The compact frame was a twin-loop cradle structure fitted with conventional girder forks. The engine had a cast-iron cylinder and head with twin exhaust ports.

Bing carburettor

48-cm (19-in) wheels

High-level exhaust pipes

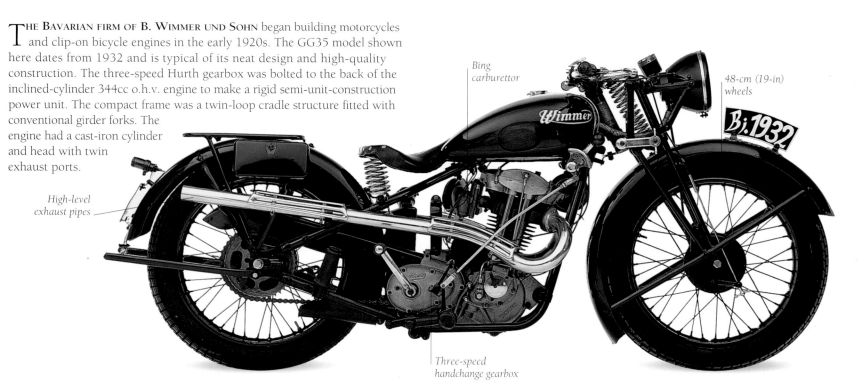

Three-speed handchange gearbox

WINDHOFF

Capacity 748cc • Power output 22bhp @ 4,000rpm • Weight 200kg (441lb) • Top speed 129km/h (80mph)

THE EXTRAORDINARY FOUR-CYLINDER WINDHOFF was shown for the first time at the 1927 Berlin Show. The futuristic design was based around a massive oil-cooled in-line engine unit. There was no frame – the gearbox and rear subframe were bolted to the back of the engine, the steering head assembly bolted to the front. The one-piece engine and cylinder block were made from cast-alloy, and the steel cylinder liners were cooled by oil pumped from the massive sump. Oil capacity was six litres (1.3 gallons). The o.h.c. was gear driven. The model seen here is from 1928.

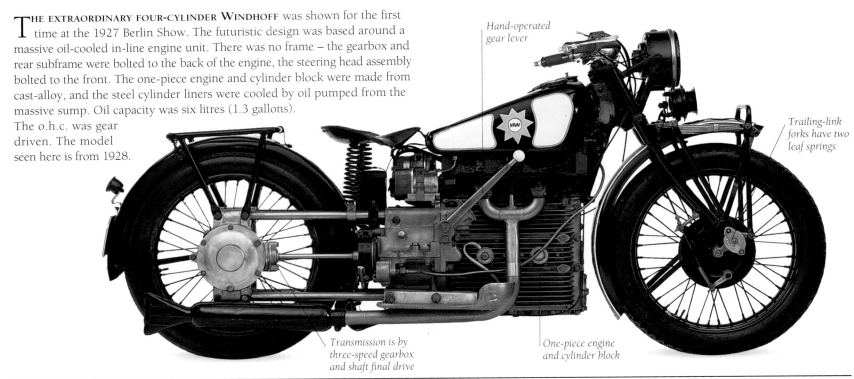

Hand-operated gear lever

Trailing-link forks have two leaf springs

Transmission is by three-speed gearbox and shaft final drive

One-piece engine and cylinder block

WOOLER

Capacity 340cc • Power output 2.75bhp • Weight not known • Top speed not known

JOHN WOOLER PRODUCED A VARIETY of innovative motorcycles over a period from 1913 until the 1950s. Many were produced only in prototype form, but all contained a number of eccentric features. A conventional i.o.e. flat-twin engine was used on production machines between 1919 and 1925.

THE MODEL SHOWN HERE is from 1919. It is equipped with an expanding-pulley variable gear, operated by foot on the right side of the motorcycle.

Acetylene lighting

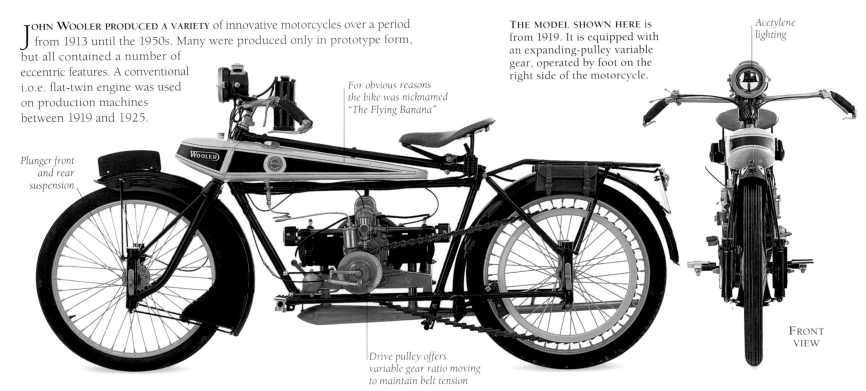

For obvious reasons the bike was nicknamed "The Flying Banana"

Plunger front and rear suspension

Drive pulley offers variable gear ratio moving to maintain belt tension

FRONT VIEW

YALE

Capacity 30.5cu. in. (500cc) • Power output 3.5bhp • Weight 160lb (73kg) • Top speed 45mph (72km/h)

U.S.A.

THE CONSOLIDATED MANUFACTURING COMPANY OF TOLEDO, Ohio, began making motorcycles in 1902 after buying the rights to the California motorcycle. The early machines were called Yale-Calfornias, but the suffix had been dropped by the time this single-cylinder model was built in 1910. The Yale was typical of the rugged machines produced in the U.S. at this time. Throttle and ignition were controlled by twistgrips that operated via complicated linkage arrangements. The engine retained the atmospheric inlet valve, and battery and coil ignition.

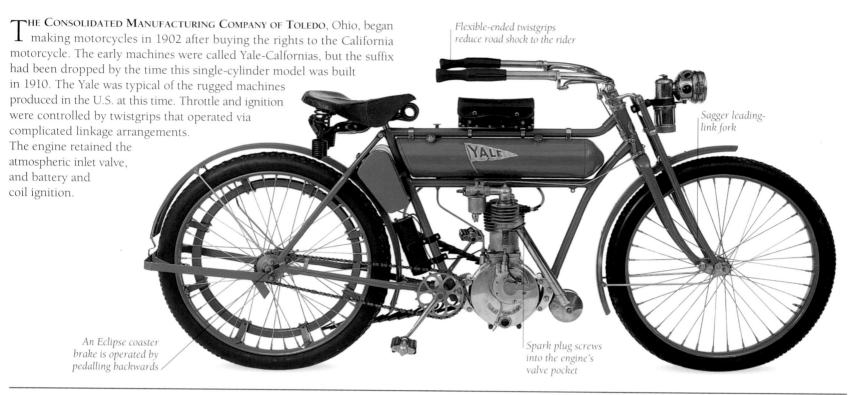

Flexible-ended twistgrips reduce road shock to the rider

Sagger leading-link fork

An Eclipse coaster brake is operated by pedalling backwards

Spark plug screws into the engine's valve pocket

YALE

Capacity 61cu. in. (1000cc) • Power output 6.5bhp • Weight not known • Top speed not known

U.S.A.

YALE FOLLOWED THE TREND SET by other American manufacturers and introduced its own V-twin in 1910. The 61cu. in. (1000cc) engine had its cylinders spaced at 45°, the same angle as Harley-Davidsons. By 1914, when the machine shown here was built, it had been significantly improved from the first Yale twins. Inlet valves were now mechanically operated.

TWO-SPEED PLANETARY GEAR with footchange was standard. A disc clutch operated by lever on the left of the machine was also a standard feature. Primary and final drive were by chain.

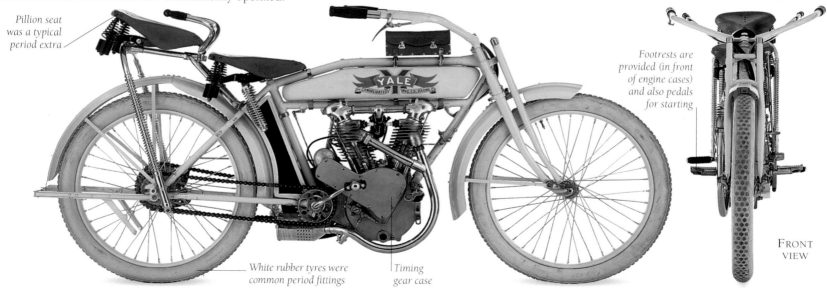

Pillion seat was a typical period extra

Footrests are provided (in front of engine cases) and also pedals for starting

White rubber tyres were common period fittings

Timing gear case

FRONT VIEW

YAMAHA YD2

Capacity 247cc • Power output 14.5bhp @ 6,000rpm • Weight 140kg (309lb) • Top speed 113km/h (70mph) (estimated)

YAMAHA'S FIRST TWO-STROKE TWIN, the YD1, was introduced in 1957. It was heavily inspired by the German Adler M200 (see p.12). In 1959 the YD2 replaced it (the letter D was used on the model name to indicate a 250). The crankcases and cylinders were changed on the new model, and it was the first Yamaha to be exported to the West. The appearance of a more sporty stablemate meant that few were sold. This is a 1959 model.

THE YD2 WAS A PRACTICAL MOTORCYCLE that featured an enclosed chain and deeply valanced mudguards. Styling was typical of Japanese motorcycles of the period.

Single carburettor is concealed behind an alloy cowl

Pressed-steel frame

Combined dynamo/electric starter unit

Clutch mounted on the left end of the crankshaft

Four-ratio gearbox

41-cm (16-in) wheels are fitted

FRONT VIEW

YAMAHA
YDS3C BIG BEAR

Capacity 246cc • Power output 21bhp @ 7,500rpm
Weight 159kg (350lb) • Top speed 135km/h (84mph)

LIKE OTHER JAPANESE MANUFACTURERS, Yamaha produced its first trail bikes by adding high-level pipes to road-going models. The Big Bear, the first Yamaha "street scrambler" (shown below), was introduced for 1965. Based on the YDS3, it was the first of Yamaha's two-strokes to be equipped with an automatic oiling system. The new model's revised frame and suspension improved its handling. Yamaha won its first road racing World Championship in 1964, and the YDS3's sales success was attributable partly to Yamaha's increasing reputation.

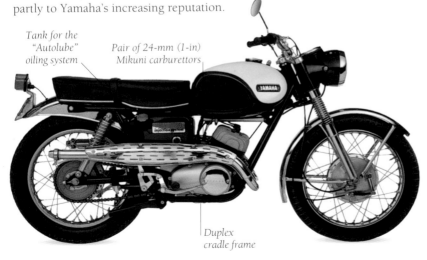

Tank for the "Autolube" oiling system

Pair of 24-mm (1-in) Mikuni carburettors

Duplex cradle frame

YAMAHA
YR2 GP SCRAMBLER

Capacity 348cc • Power output 36bhp @ 7,500rpm
Weight 163kg (360lb) • Top speed 155km/h (96mph)

THE CAPACITY OF YAMAHA'S TWO-STROKE TWINS increased gradually, and the first of the YR models appeared in 1967. This was an entirely new design, and the first Yamaha to have horizontally split engine cases. A restyled version of the conservative YR1, the YR2 was introduced in 1968. The high-level pipes and wide handlebars of this scrambler derivative reduced rider comfort and did not endow the machine with any real off-road ability. The arrival of the DT1 trail bike (see p.202) the same year killed off the Japanese street scrambler.

46-cm (18-in) wheels front and rear

New five-port cylinder barrels

Horizontally split engine cases

YAMAHA LS2

Capacity 97cc • Power output 10.5bhp @ 8,000rpm • Weight 95kg (210lb) • Top speed 109km/h (68mph) (estimated)

JAPAN

Yamaha's commitment to the two-stroke twin meant that it made production versions as small as 90cc. This is a 1971 example of the 97cc LS2 that was produced until 1973. The small-capacity twins were scaled-down versions of Yamaha's bigger two-strokes with, considering their size, excellent performance, handling, and equipment. The LS2 engine thrived on revs, which had to be kept up to achieve maximum performance.

When the RD range was introduced in 1973, the 97cc twins were dropped and a 124cc model became the smallest available.

Equipment included a rev counter

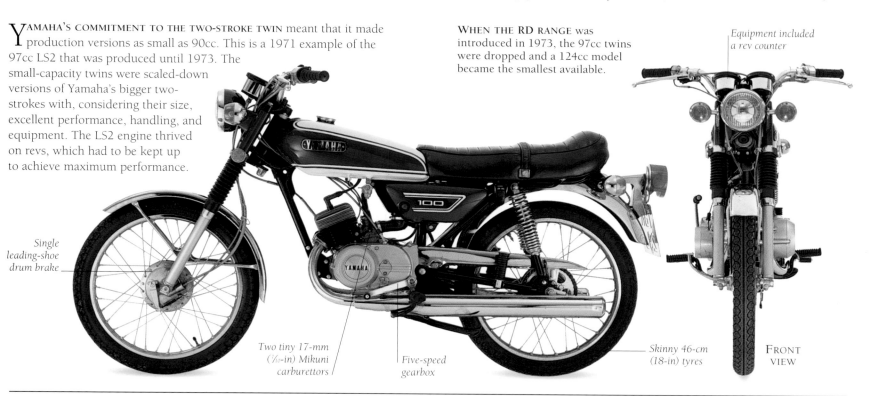

Single leading-shoe drum brake

Two tiny 17-mm (⅔₆-in) Mikuni carburettors

Five-speed gearbox

Skinny 46-cm (18-in) tyres

FRONT VIEW

YAMAHA CS5

JAPAN

Capacity 196cc • Power output 22bhp @ 7,500rpm
Weight 116kg (255lb) • Top speed 137km/h (85mph) (estimated)

Kickstarting a 180cc two-stroke twin is simple, but when Yamaha introduced the YCS1 in 1967 it was equipped with an electric starter. The machine was improved and uprated and evolved into the 196cc CS5, which was available in 1972 and 1973. The 200 had good handling and brisk performance, making it an ideal bike for novices. It was replaced by the RD200, which retained the electric starter. This is the 1972 model.

Matt black cylinder fins with polished edges

Twin leading-shoe drum brake

Open cradle frame

YAMAHA

YAMAHA TR3

JAPAN

Capacity 347cc • Power output 58bhp @ 9,500rpm
Weight 107kg (235lb) • Top speed not known

Yamaha had offered racing versions of its road-going, two-stroke twins since the TD1 of 1961; these had competed successfully at club and national level with riders of varying abilities. The withdrawal, in the late 1960s, of many Japanese factories' teams from international competition meant Yamaha's two-stroke twins came to dominate that field too. The 1972 TR3, shown below, was ridden to victory by Don Emde in the Daytona 322-km (200-mile) race against full-blown 750s.

Box-section swingarm

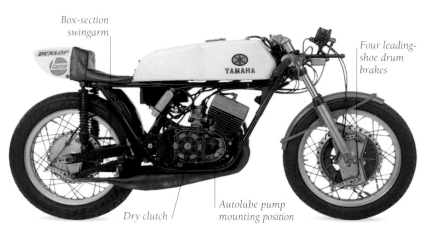

Four leading-shoe drum brakes

Dry clutch

Autolube pump mounting position

YAMAHA DT1

Capacity 246cc • Power output 22bhp @ 6,000rpm • Weight 107kg (235lb) • Top speed 114km/h (71mph)

BEFORE THE ARRIVAL OF THE DT1, Japanese manufacturers had built "street scramblers" by adding high-level exhaust pipes and knobbly tyres to their roadsters (see the Big Bear, p.200). The DT1 was the first purpose-built trail bike, opening up a new market in 1968. Competition riders removed the lights and could increase engine power with a factory-produced tuning kit.

THE DT1 combined light weight with a flexible engine and good suspension to create a usable, off-road motorcycle that looked good, had excellent equipment, and handled well. The trail bike became an essential part of Yamaha's range and the DT prefix was on its two-stroke trail bikes.

48-cm (19-in) front wheel

Folding footrests

FRONT VIEW

Duplex cradle frame with 24-cm (9½-in) ground clearance

Single-cylinder two-stroke engine with five-port barrel

YAMAHA YZ250

Capacity 246cc • Power output 21bhp @ 7,500rpm • Weight 105kg (232lb) • Top speed 142km/h (88mph)

TO WIN MOTOCROSS RACES, a motorcycle must have excellent suspension. Understanding this, in 1974 Yamaha developed the YZ250 with a single long-travel rear suspension unit mounted horizontally underneath the seat and fuel tank. As a result, the YZ250 was probably the best production motocross bike at the time.

DeCarbon Monoshock suspension unit

Telescopic forks have 18cm (7in) of travel

THE FIRST PRODUCTION MODELS appeared in 1974 on the competitive, and lucrative, American market. They were an immediate success, and other manufacturers followed Yamaha's lead. Soon the single shock absorber system was the norm for road bikes as well as off-road competition machines.

Rear suspension allows 16.5cm (6½in) of travel

Lightweight conical brake hubs

Five-speed gearbox

Single-cylinder, air-cooled, two-stroke engine with reed-valve induction

YAMAHA

YAMAHA RD350B

Capacity 347cc • Power output 39bhp @ 7,500rpm • Weight 154kg (340lb) • Top speed 169km/h (105mph)

YAMAHA UPGRADED ITS RANGE of two-stroke twins for 1973, giving the revised line of 124cc to 346cc models the "RD" prefix. The most notable change was the adoption of reed valves throughout the range. Situated between the carburettor and the crankcase, the reed valve operated as a one-way valve. It allowed the motor to run a higher crankcase pressure without risking "blowback" through the carburettor. This increased performance, especially at low and medium revs.

THROUGHOUT THE 1970S, Yamaha twins – such as the 1975 model shown here – were the definitive, sporting two-strokes, with performance capable of outstripping much larger machines. The 350 was replaced by the 398cc RD 400 in 1976.

U.S. models have wide handlebars

Front disc brakes replaced drums in 1974 on the B version of the RD350

Easily tunable twin-cylinder engine made this bike popular with racers

Duplex cradle frame

BACK VIEW

YAMAHA

YAMAHA XS650B

Capacity 653cc • Power output 50bhp @ 7,200rpm • Weight 220kg (485lb) • Top speed 179km/h (111mph)

WHILE OTHER JAPANESE manufacturers introduced flashy, multi-cylinder superbikes, Yamaha's first four-stroke was a conservative 650 twin with styling inspired by traditional British twins. The original version was introduced in 1969 as the XS1. It had drum brakes and no electric starter. By the time the XS650B was introduced in 1975, an electric starter, disc brakes, and an improved frame had been incorporated. The machine shown is a 1975 model.

THE XS650B has a chain-driven overhead camshaft and primary drive to the gearbox is by gear. The engine gained an excellent reputation for reliability and provided the basis for the flat-track racing machines on which Kenny Roberts won the U.S. Championship in both 1973 and 1974. Yamaha also produced more complex 743cc and 498cc parallel twins in the 1970s. Neither was as successful as the well-liked 650.

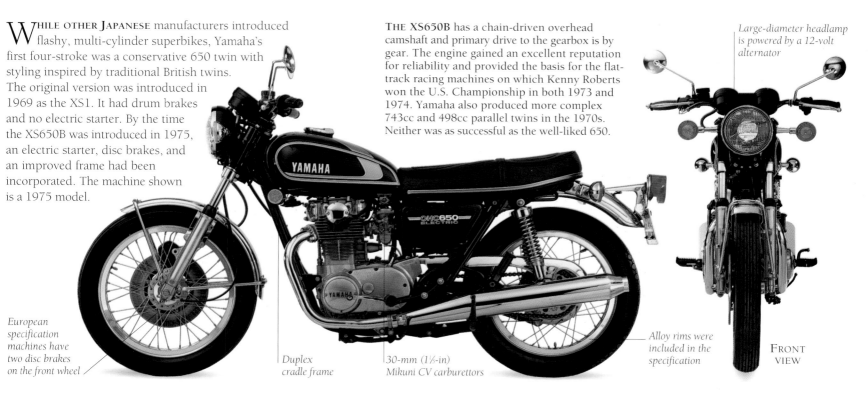

Large-diameter headlamp is powered by a 12-volt alternator

European specification machines have two disc brakes on the front wheel

Duplex cradle frame

30-mm (1⅕-in) Mikuni CV carburettors

Alloy rims were included in the specification

FRONT VIEW

YAMAHA TZ250

Capacity 247cc • Power output 53bhp @ 10,500rpm • Weight 108kg (239lb) • Top speed 225km/h (140mph)

THE WATER-COOLED TZ racers replaced Yamaha's air-cooled TD models when they were introduced for 1973. In the following 15 years a TZ was essential for private racers looking for racing success. The engine layout followed the pattern of Yamaha's road-going two-stroke twins, with parallel cylinders and a 180° crankshaft.

TO MAINTAIN its competitive edge, Yamaha continually improved the TZ. Tuners also worked hard to make them faster and many machines, such as this 1979 model, were heavily modified.

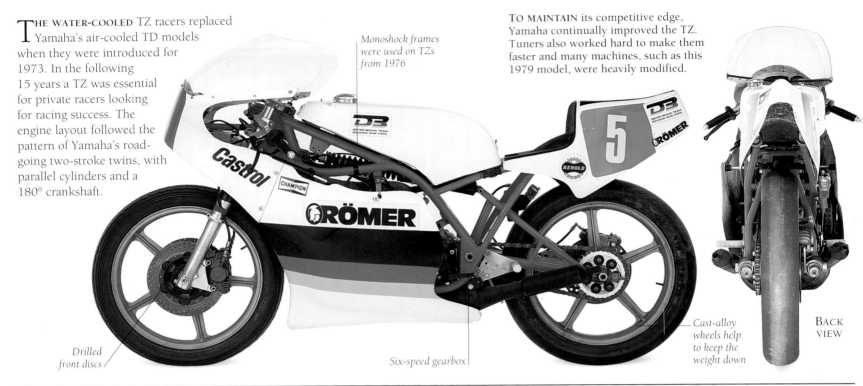

Monoshock frames were used on TZs from 1976

Drilled front discs

Six-speed gearbox

Cast-alloy wheels help to keep the weight down

BACK VIEW

YAMAHA XV920

Capacity 920cc • Power output 65bhp • Weight 224kg (493lb) • Top speed 177km/h (110mph)

IN MOVING AWAY from its reliance on the two-stroke engine, Yamaha tried various configurations. These included the production of the large air-cooled 75° V-twins introduced for 1981. Two models were produced for the American market: the XV750 had custom styling and shaft drive, while this 1981 XV920 had conventional styling and enclosed-chain final drive.

EUROPEAN CUSTOMERS did not receive the XV920. They were offered a similar model but with a capacity of 981cc and the TR1 model number. Neither version was a great success and the custom-style models sold in far greater numbers.

Long tailpiece containing a wallet for a padlock and chain

Box-section frame includes the carburettor airbox

Five-speed gearbox

Fully enclosed final drive chain

FRONT VIEW

YAMAHA RZ500

Capacity 499cc • Power output 87bhp @ 9,500rpm • Weight 180kg (396lb) • Top speed 216km/h (135mph)

JAPAN

AS EMISSION CONTROLS and restrictive legislation closed in on large-capacity two-strokes, Yamaha produced the ultimate version of its race-developed road bikes. Produced from 1984 to 1987, the RZ was a water-cooled twin-crankshaft V4 machine whose engine layout derived from Yamaha's early 1980s' Grand Prix machines. The bike shown is a 1984 model.

LIKE MANY other Japanese machines, the V4 Yamaha was sold in various forms in different world markets. In North America it was the RZ500, in Japan it was the RZV500 with an alloy frame, and in Britain the steel-framed bike was sold as the RD500.

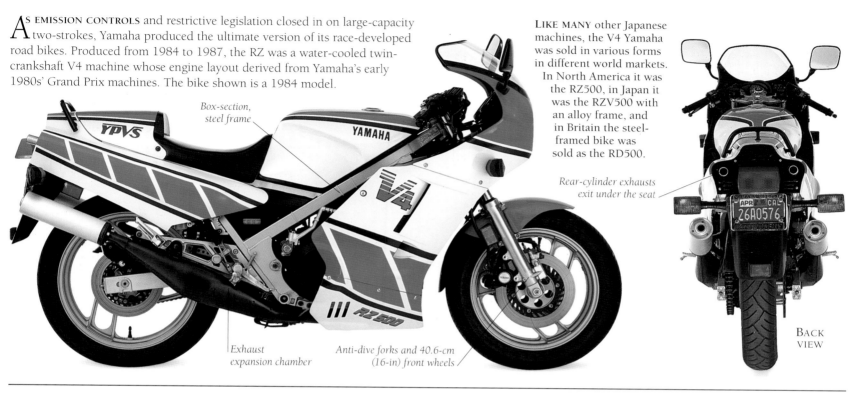

Box-section, steel frame

Rear-cylinder exhausts exit under the seat

BACK VIEW

Exhaust expansion chamber

Anti-dive forks and 40.6-cm (16-in) front wheels

YAMAHA V-MAX

Capacity 1198cc • Power output 145bhp • Weight 270kg (596lb) • Top speed 230km/h (144mph)

JAPAN

ENGLISHMAN JOHN REED was asked to design the V-Max when Yamaha wanted to build the ultimate custom. Since Reed lived in California, the outrageous styling unsurprisingly showed strong American influences. Instead of the usual long low styling of custom bikes, the V-Max had a much denser mechanical look. Its massive water-cooled V4 motor was based on that of the Venture touring bike. This V-Max dates from the first year of production – 1985.

SOME MARKETS, including the U.K., were supplied with a restricted version of the V-Max, with power output cut to 95bhp. In unrestricted form the V-Max is capable of stunning straight-line performance; the handling is less inspiring.

Single speedometer instrument

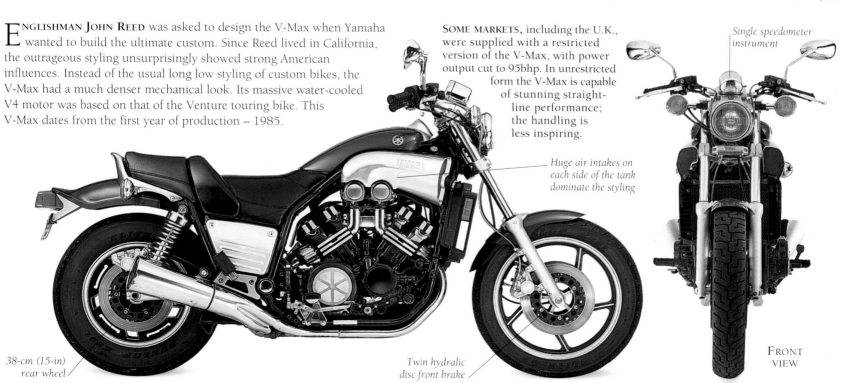

Huge air intakes on each side of the tank dominate the styling

38-cm (15-in) rear wheel

Twin hydralic disc front brake

FRONT VIEW

YAMAHA GTS1000

Capacity 1002cc • Power output 100bhp @ 9,000rpm • Weight 251kg (553lb) • Top speed 213km/h (132mph)

THE **GTS1000** WAS THE FIRST Japanese mass-produced bike to have hub-centre steering in place of the more traditional front fork. Yamaha's "Omega chassis", with single-sided front swingarm and a monoshock rear end, gave it a rock-steady ride and a low centre of gravity. The downside was heavy steering and a poor steering lock. Powered by Yamaha's FZR1000 Exup motor with added fuel injection and catalytic converter, the GTS1000 was aimed at the older, more experienced rider. ABS brakes were an optional extra. The bike shown dates from 1994.

Integral fairing and bodywork

Large, powerful headlamp

Massive, six piston, front brake calliper

Exhaust system features a catalytic converter

Alloy frame

Front suspension swingarm

YAMAHA FZR1000

Capacity 1002cc • Power output 125bhp @ 10,000rpm • Weight 240kg (529lb) • Top speed 269km/h (167mph)

THE **FZR1000** IS YAMAHA'S LARGEST CAPACITY super sports bike. Its history can be traced back to the 1985 FZ750 – the first mass-produced five-valve-per-cylinder bike. The original d.o.h.c. FZR1000 became the FZR1000 Exup in 1989. The Exup's variable exhaust valve offered a wider spread of power while the large frame offered a riding position that suited all. The power output was phenomenal, particularly when de-restricted to 147bhp; this was the standard in some markets. The FZR1000 illustrated dates from 1992.

Massive, alloy, Deltabox chassis

Removable seat hump

Upside-down forks

Three-spoke alloy wheels

Bodywork removed to show internal parts

Twin-disc, four-piston, calliper front brakes

ZÜNDAPP

Capacity 249cc • Power output 4.5bhp @ 3,500rpm • Weight 85kg (187lb) • Top speed 75km/h (47mph)

GERMANY

Iᴺ ᴄᴏᴍᴍᴏɴ ᴡɪᴛʜ ᴍᴀɴʏ ᴏᴛʜᴇʀ ᴍᴀɴᴜꜰᴀᴄᴛᴜʀᴇʀꜱ in the early 1920s, Zündapp broke into the motorcycle business with a 211cc two-stroke that bore more than a passing resemblance to the successful Levis of the same capacity (see p.222). Progressive improvements lead to the introduction of the EM250 model in 1925. This featured a repositioned magneto, allowing the wheelbase to be reduced, the introduction of centre spring forks, and a hub brake for the front wheel in place of the rim type previously used.

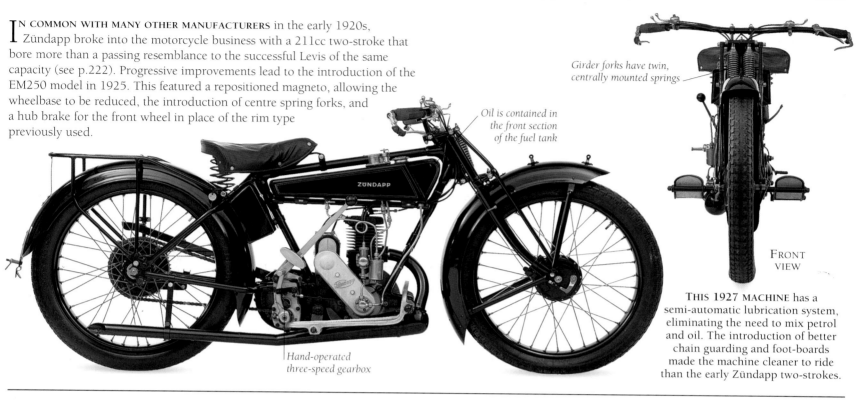

Oil is contained in the front section of the fuel tank

Girder forks have twin, centrally mounted springs

Fʀᴏɴᴛ Vɪᴇᴡ

Hand-operated three-speed gearbox

Tʜɪꜱ 1927 ᴍᴀᴄʜɪɴᴇ has a semi-automatic lubrication system, eliminating the need to mix petrol and oil. The introduction of better chain guarding and foot-boards made the machine cleaner to ride than the early Zündapp two-strokes.

ZÜNDAPP K800

Capacity 800cc • Power output 22bhp @ 4,300rpm • Weight 200kg (440lb) • Top speed 126km/h (78mph)

GERMANY

Iɴᴛʀᴏᴅᴜᴄᴇᴅ ɪɴ 1933 and continued with only minor changes until 1939, the smooth and powerful K800 was the luxury superbike of its era. The horizontally opposed four-cylinder side-valve engine had most of its ancillaries (carburettor, generator, distributor, etc.) enclosed by an aluminium cowling. The output from the engine passed, via a multi-plate clutch in the flywheel, to a four-speed "gearbox" in which four sets of chains and sprockets provided the different ratios. Selection was via a ball change lever, as found in a car. From the gearbox an open shaft was used to drive the rear wheel.

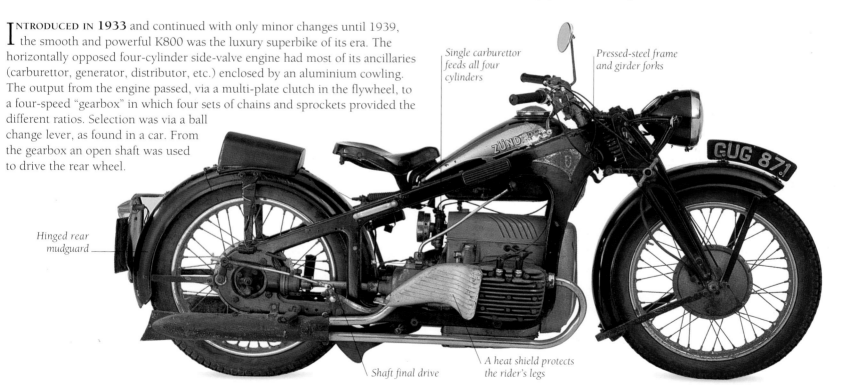

Single carburettor feeds all four cylinders

Pressed-steel frame and girder forks

GUG 871

Hinged rear mudguard

Shaft final drive

A heat shield protects the rider's legs

ZÜNDAPP KS601

Capacity 597cc • Power output 28bhp @ 4,700rpm • Weight 214kg (472lb) • Top speed 140km/h (87mph)

GERMANY

BETTER KNOWN AS THE "GREEN ELEPHANT", the KS601 was Germany's fastest road machine when introduced in 1950. The horizontally opposed, twin-cylinder, o.h.v. engine, and four-speed chain and sprocket "gearbox" were essentially those of pre-war days, but were now mounted in a tubular frame fitted with telescopic forks, plunger rear suspension, and interchangeable wheels. The model shown here dates from 1953.

Tubular frame

Telescopic forks

FRONT VIEW

Shaft drive

O.h.v. flat-twin engine

IN TYPICAL ZÜNDAPP FASHION, the engine was smoothly styled with its ancillaries enclosed as much as possible. It soon became popular with sporting sidecar drivers.

ZÜNDAPP BELLA 201

Capacity 199cc • Power output 10bhp @ 5,200rpm
Weight 139kg (306lb) • Top speed 100km/h (62mph)

GERMANY

AS A RESULT OF THE SUCCESS OF THE SCOOTER in the years following World War II, many established motorcycle manufacturers turned their attention to this type of machine. In their efforts to produce one that handled in an acceptable manner, most adopted the "step-thru" layout and large wheels. The benefits were improved weight distribution resulting from the forward engine location, a stiffer frame due to its greater depth, and better cooling due to the air tunnel through the frame. The Bella was introduced in 1953 and production lasted until 1964. Illustrated is a 1957 Bella 201.

Tubular frame fully enclosed by pressed-steel bodywork

Deep, valanced mudguard

Front swingarm has a single shock absorber on the left side

ZÜNDAPP GS125

Capacity 124cc • Power output 18bhp @ 7,900rpm
Weight 100kg (220lb) (estimated) • Top speed 105km/h (65mph) (estimated)

GERMANY

THE LETTERS GS STAND FOR GELÄNDE SPORT – *Gelände* meaning "terrain". Enduro-type events were very popular in the early 1970s, especially in the U.S. where cheap Japanese trail bikes had given many riders a taste for something more serious. The requirement was for a machine combining good off-road capabilities with a fair turn of speed when necessary, in a form legal on the road. The GS125 fulfilled this, being built on the lines of a motocross machine with lights. The machine shown is a 1972 bike; developed versions of it won the world 125cc Motocross Championship in 1973 and 1974.

High-level exhaust system

Lights fitted to fulfill legal requirements for road use

This Zündapp engine was also supplied to other firms as a proprietary unit

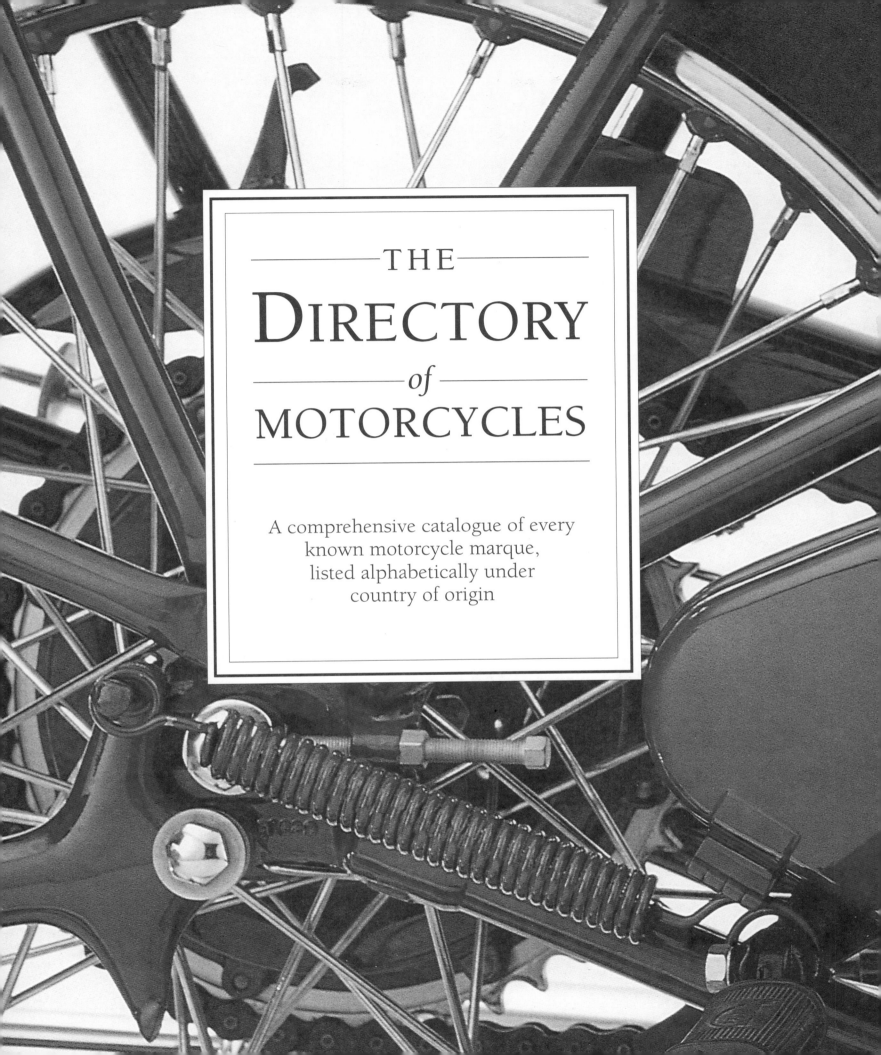

THE
DIRECTORY
of
MOTORCYCLES

A comprehensive catalogue of every
known motorcycle marque,
listed alphabetically under
country of origin

Marques Worldwide

THERE HAS BEEN A STAGGERING NUMBER of motorcycle marques since the first petrol-engined machines were built in 1885 – over 3,000 to date. The marques are listed in the following pages, with details (where available) of the most noteworthy features of the machines each manufacturer made. Some prototypes that did not make it into production have been omitted. The major producers – United Kingdom, Germany, Italy, United States, France, and Japan – are listed first. Countries that have only produced a relatively small number of marques appear in the rest of the world section (see pp.288–308). Where we have been unable to find corroboration of a marque's existence in more than one source, it has been listed as an unconfirmed marque at the end of the entry for the country of manufacture. The use of the  symbol and a cross-reference beside the marque's name indicates the page(s) on which a motorcycle or motorcycles bearing the particular marque appear(s) in the A–Z section of the book. Letters in names are capitalized to show how the marque name evolved. For example, Alba was derived from four letters of its founder's names, shown as ALbert BAruch.

Shaded areas on the map of the world show the countries in which listed motorcycles have been made. The numbers refer to the pages on which each country's marques begin in the directory of motorcycles.

CANADA
p.307

UNITED STATES
OF AMERICA
p.268

MEXICO
p.307

BRAZIL
p.307

ARGENTINA
p.307

NUMBER OF MOTORCYCLE MARQUES PRODUCED IN EACH COUNTRY

COUNTRY OF ORIGIN	NO. OF MARQUES	COUNTRY OF ORIGIN	NO. OF MARQUES
Argentina	4	Japan	68
Australia	30	Mexico	2
Austria	81	The Netherlands	90
Belgium	94	New Zealand	5
Brazil	3	Norway	2
Bulgaria	1	Poland	15
Canada	11	Portugal	8
China	8	Romania	1
Czech Republic and Slovakia	65	Slovenia	2
		South Africa	1
Denmark	4	South Korea	1
France	479	Spain	57
Germany	667	Sweden	20
Hungary	12	Switzerland	91
India	24	Taiwan	3
Ireland	1	United Kingdom	685
Israel	1	United States	340
Italy	567	Former U.S.S.R.	20

The greatest concentration of motorcycle manufacturers has historically been in Europe (see detail, right).

DENMARK
p.305

REPUBLIC OF
IRELAND
p.303

UNITED
KINGDOM
p.212

NETHERLANDS
p.298

POLAND
p.303

GERMANY
p.234

BELGIUM
p.395

CZECH
REPUBLIC
p.301

SLOVAKIA
p.301

FRANCE
p.277

SWITZERLAND
p.292

AUSTRIA
p.290

HUNGARY
p.303

SLOVENIA
p.303

ROMANIA
p.303

BULGARIA
p.303

ITALY
p.252

PORTUGAL
p.289

SPAIN
p.288

NORWAY
p.305

SWEDEN
p.304

FORMER
U.S.S.R.
p.305

EUROPE
SEE DETAIL

ISRAEL
p.308

CHINA
p.308

SOUTH
KOREA
p.308

JAPAN
p.285

INDIA
p.306

TAIWAN
p.308

SOUTH
AFRICA
p.308

AUSTRALIA
p.308

NEW
ZEALAND
p.308

United Kingdom

THE BRITISH MOTORCYCLE INDUSTRY was built on the back of the bicycle trade, which was well established at the end of the 19th century. A parallel industry quickly emerged, supplying large and small makers with engines, gearboxes, and other parts. During the 1920s there were hundreds of manufacturers and British motorcycles had an excellent worldwide reputation. Many small companies collapsed during the Depression in the 1930s, and the marketplace was increasingly dominated by large firms. After 1945 production was concentrated in the hands of a few companies. The BSA (see p.215) and AMC (see p.213) groups were the key players. Sales were good and motorcycles were exported in large numbers, but money was not invested in new products or new production facilities. Short-sighted management in the face of Japanese opposition made the collapse of the industry in the 1970s inevitable. The revival of the Triumph marque (see p.231) in 1992 is symbolic of the re-emergence of prestigious European marques in a new image-conscious market.

ABC p.10
1913 Granville Bradshaw designed 492cc three-speed 3.5hp fore-and-aft flat twins, which were built in limited numbers by the All British (Engine) Co. Inlet-over-exhaust and overhead-valve versions were produced.
1919 A new 398cc ABC, designed by Bradshaw, appeared. It was built by the Sopwith Aircraft Co. in England, and also in France by Gnome & Rhône from 1920. The radical new machine had a transversely mounted overhead-valve flat-twin engine, a four-speed gearbox, front and rear drum brakes, and leaf-sprung front and rear suspension. The design suffered from teething troubles and was expensive to manufacture.
1923 The last ABCs were made in the U.K., but production in France continued until 1925.

ABC
c.1920–24 Another, unrelated, ABC company that made orthodox belt-driven motorcycles with 269cc and 247cc two-stroke Villiers engines.

ABC SKOOTAMOTA p.170
1919–22 A Bradshaw-designed scooter with a 123cc single-cylinder exhaust-over-inlet-valve engine mounted above the rear wheel with the cylinder positioned horizontally. Final drive was by chain. Built by Gilbert Campling Ltd on the Isle of Wight.

ABERDALE
1946–49 Trademark used on 98cc Villiers-engined autocycles built by Bown (see p.215).

ABINGDON
1903 Coxeter & Sons of Abingdon in Berkshire first made 2.5hp Minerva-engined machines with belt drive. The company name soon changed to Abingdon-Ecco Ltd and production switched to Birmingham. It developed its own single-cylinder and V-twin four-stroke engines of 348cc to 794cc and also supplied engines to other makers. An association with the East London Rubber Co., which marketed Kerry motorcycles (see p.222), began with the first Kerry-Abingdon machine in 1907. These were available until 1915. After World War I the range comprised 794cc V-twins and 499cc and 623cc singles, which were produced until 1925.
1926 A new 174cc overhead-valve machine was introduced for 1927, but by this time the bikes were more commonly known by the initials AKD (see right).

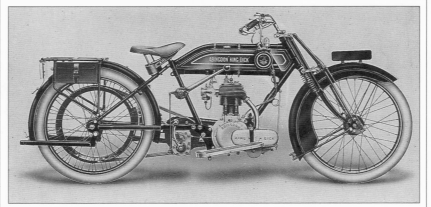

A 1920 Abingdon "King Dick" 499cc side-valve single with belt final drive

ABJ
1949–54 A. B. Jackson made 98cc Villiers-engined lightweights and the 49cc Auto-Minor.

ACKLAND
c.1919–24 William Ackland built a few machines using V-twin JAP engines and Sturmey-Archer gearboxes.

ACME
c.1902 Began making motorcycles and tricars using its own single-cylinder and V-twin engines, as well as power units supplied by Minerva, JAP, and others. After World War I it was taken over by Rex (see p.227).
1922 The Rex-Acme name was adopted.

ADVANCE
1905–07 Built single-cylinder and V-twin motorcycles in Northampton, using its own four-stroke engines.

AEL
1919–24 A. E. Lynes & Co. used 269cc Villiers two-stroke and JAP four-stroke engines in conventional belt-driven bikes with Albion two-speed gearboxes.

AEOLUS
1903–05 Designed by E. R. Owen and built in London, the Aeolus was a 492cc single-cylinder shaft-driven machine.

AEOLUS
1914–16 Built in Birmingham by Bown (see p.215), Aeolus machines used the company's own 205cc or Villiers 269cc two-stroke engines. There was also a model with a single-cylinder side-valve Precision engine. Belt drive was used.

AER
1937–40 A. E. Reynolds built 249cc single- and 344cc twin-cylinder two-stroke machines, which had a four-speed gearbox and flywheel magneto. Reynolds was a successful motorcycle dealer, who had also built the Reynolds Special (see p.228). In the late 1950s AER also produced a prototype Villiers-engined machine with enclosed bodywork.

AIROLITE
c.1921–23 Motorized bicycles equipped with 110cc two-stroke Simplex engines. The makers also offered a sidecar attachment intended for children.

AJAX
1922–25 Cheap Birmingham-built lightweights with 147cc and 269cc two-stroke Villiers engines and belt final drive. There was also a 348cc model with a Blackburne power unit.

AJS pp.13–15
1911 After building engines for other manufacturers, Albert John Stevens and his brothers finally produced a complete machine with the AJS logo. It was a 2.5hp single, but the range soon included V-twins. The marque had a successful competition history and built excellent racing machines, particularly the 350cc overhead-valve and, from 1927, overhead-camshaft singles.
1931 The Stevens brothers overstretched their resources by becoming involved in the manufacturing of radio sets, cars, and commercial vehicles. The slump and subsequent financial difficulties forced them to sell the company to Matchless (see p.223) and production moved from Wolverhampton to southeast London. This merger was to form the basis of the AMC group (see p.213). Increasingly the two marques lost their separate identities and after World War II AJS machines were little more than a Matchless with a different badge. The Stevens brothers resumed motorcycle production using the Stevens name (see p.230) in 1934.
1967 Production of AJS four-stroke machines ended, two-stroke motocross bikes survived. The rights to the name and the manufacturing rights to the motocrossers were bought by Fluff Brown of Andover.

AJR
1925-26 Conventional machines built in Scotland by A. J. Robertson using JAP 246cc to 490cc overhead-valve engines.

AJW
1928–77 Arthur John Wheaton began building quality machines in Exeter using JAP, Anzani, Rudge, and Villiers engines. These included a sensational four-cylinder 1000cc water-cooled bike with link steering. During the war the company moved to Bournemouth, where new owners built a JAP-engined side-valve parallel twin in limited numbers until 1952. It was followed by a 125cc JAP-engined two-stroke, but production was brief. Afterwards the AJW name was used on Italian-built two-strokes, which were distributed by AJW until 1977.

AKD
1926–32 The well-established Abingdon marque also used the name Abingdon

King Dick. From 1926 the name was abbreviated to AKD. In 1927 the old, large-capacity single-cylinder and V-twin machines were replaced by lightweight 174cc overhead-valve four-stroke singles. The AKD range later included models from 146cc to 349cc. AKD also supplied engines to other manufacturers.

AKKENS
1919–22 Basic belt-driven machines with 292cc Union two-stroke engines made in Birmingham by Messrs Thomas and Gilbert.

ALECTO
1919–24 London-built 345cc two-strokes with two-speed gearboxes and belt final drive. The machines were also available with a factory-fitted sidecar.

ALERT
1903–06 Built by Smith & Molesworth in Coventry, the Alert used a single-cylinder 3.25hp engine, which was mounted below the frame downtube. A clutch was mounted on the crankshaft.

ALLDAYS & ONIONS
1903 Alldays & Onions of Birmingham was a motoring pioneer that had built DeDion-powered tricycles as early as 1898. Its first motorcycles used Moto-Rêve and other proprietary engines.
1914 Began production of a 292cc two-stroke using the firm's own engine. This was sold as the Allon (see below), which was then adopted as the marque name.
1926–27 The Alldays & Onions name was reintroduced on a 349cc four-stroke single, which used the oil-cooled Bradshaw engine, and a 680cc JAP V-twin. When motorcycle production ended the firm continued manufacturing equipment for forges.

ALLON
1915–26 Allon was originally used as a model name on a 292cc two-stroke single built by Alldays & Onions. It was an abbreviation of the company's name and also indicated that the model was supplied with all extras fitted – "all on".

ALP
1913–16 Lightweight machines produced by the British branch of the Swiss Moto-Rêve company in Alperton, West London. A 256cc atmospheric-inlet-valve engine was used in a belt-driven loop-framed model. A 3hp two-speed two-stroke was introduced in 1915 but the war restricted production.

ALTA
c.1968–71 Specialized trials machines with 120cc Suzuki engines.

ALWIN
c.1920 A 1.5hp small-wheeled two-stroke scooter. The rider stood on a

A 1954 Ambassador Embassy with a 197cc Villiers engine

platform mounted on a pressed-steel frame. Production numbers not known.

AMBASSADOR
1946–64 Ambassador machines were built in Ascot, Berkshire. A range of motorcycles and scooters was produced using Villiers engines of 147cc to 248cc. The firm also distributed Zündapp machines in the U.K. DMW (see p.218) briefly took over production from 1962.

AMC
1931–66 The basis for Associated Motor Cycles came from the takeover of AJS by Matchless in 1931, although the title was not used until later. Norton, James, and Francis Barnett were later absorbed. AMC was the name of the company and was not attached to the bikes, which retained their established brand-names. AMC collapsed in 1966.

ANGLIAN
1903–12 Built in East Anglia, Anglians had vertically mounted 2.25hp and 2.75hp atmospheric-inlet-valve MMC and DeDion engines and belt final drive. By 1905 JAP engines were also used.

ARIEL 🏍 pp.18–20
1902 Components Ltd made bicycle parts at a factory in Birmingham. It began building motorized tricycles and quadricycles around 1898 using DeDion engines. Its first motorcycles used proprietary engines, although it quickly developed its own power units. These were side-valve singles with a worm-gear-driven camshaft mounted behind the vertical cylinder. The Fleet name was also for some engines and motorcycles.
1910 A new machine with a 498cc White & Poppe side-valve engine was

launched. It was to provide the basis of the Ariel range until 1926, although V-twins with AKD and MAG engines were also produced during this period. In 1924 a smaller model with a 249cc Blackburne engine was introduced.
1926 Ariel entered a new era with the appointment of Val Page as designer. New 557cc side-valve and 496cc overhead-valve singles were produced. Updated versions of these models were still being produced in the 1950s.
1930 The famous Square Four, designed by Edward Turner, was introduced. The design was revised over the years and continued in production until 1959. Ariel owner Jack Sangster took over Triumph in 1936. BSA later bought both companies – Ariel in 1944 and Triumph in 1951. As well as singles and the Square Four, Ariel built 498cc and 646cc parallel twins during the 1950s. The larger twin used a BSA A10 engine.
1958 New two-stroke twins were introduced. They continued until 1965 and were the last true Ariels. The name was finally used on a three-wheeled moped built in 1970.

ARMIS
1920–23 The Birmingham-based Armis Cycle Manufacturing Co. first built a belt-driven bike with a 348cc two-stroke Precision engine. Later it also offered JAP- and MAG-powered four-strokes, including a 654cc side-valve V-twin.

ARMSTRONG
c.1913–14 Armstrong built typical belt-driven 269cc Villiers-engined machines.

ARMSTRONG 🏍 p.21
1980 Motor components manufacturer, Armstrong Equipment moved into

motorcycle production when it took over Cotton (see p.217). The following year CCM (see p.216) were incorporated into the group. Armstrong motorcycles were mainly Rotax-powered road racers, off-road competition machines, and motorcycles for military use.
1987 Armstrong withdrew from the project and CCM reverted to the ownership of Alan Clews. Harley-Davidson acquired a licence to produce the military bike. Production of Rotax powered off-road competition machines was continued by CCM.

ARNO
1906–15 Side-valve singles, equipped with the company's own 493cc engine, produced in Coventry.

ARROW
c.1913–17 Lightweight machines with 211cc two-stroke proprietary engines and Burman two-speed gearboxes built in Birmingham by Kirk & Merifield.

ASCOT
1904–06 Typical pioneer machines built in London using imported engines.

ASCOT-PULLIN 🏍 p.21
1928–30 Built by the Ascot Motor Co. and designed by Cyril Pullin, who also produced the Pullin-Groom (see p.227), Ascot-Pullin machines were advanced. A 498cc overhead-valve single-cylinder engine was mounted horizontally in a pressed-steel frame and the wheels had hydraulic brakes.

ASHFORD
1904 Motorcycles and tricars assembled in Ashford, Middlesex using Minerva and Antoine engines.

ASL
c.1907–15 Air Springs Ltd produced motorcycles with front and rear air-sprung suspension. It used Fafnir, White & Poppe, and single-cylinder and V-twin JAP engines with belt final drive.

ATLAS
c.1913–14 Sporting single-cylinder machines built in Coventry using JAP and Blumfield 500cc engines.

ATLAS
1921–25 Made by the Aston Motor & Engineering Co. in Aston, Birmingham, Atlas machines were 142cc belt-driven three-port two-strokes. They may also have been sold under the Aston name.

AURORA
1901–07 W. H. Halliwell of Coventry built belt-driven loop-framed machines using his own and proprietary engines.

AURORA
c.1919–21 Aurora motorcycles were made on the Isle of Man with 318cc Dalm two-stroke engines and belt drive.

AUSTEN
c.1903–06 Installed vertically mounted Kelecom engines in loop frames.

AUTOGLIDER
1919–22 Built a small-wheeled scooter with a 292cc Union two-stroke engine.

AUTOSCO
c.1920–21 A tubular-framed scooter with an 117cc atmospheric-inlet-valve engine mounted next to the gear-driven rear wheel. The power unit was probably a Wall Auto-Wheel.

AYRES-LEYLAND
1920 Also known as Ayres-Hayman, this machine used a 688cc Coventry-Victor flat-twin engine in a duplex tubular frame of the company's own design.

BAC
1950–53 After selling the rights to the stressed-skin aluminium-framed Bond motorcycle, the Bond Aircraft and Engineering Co. built conventional tubular-framed lightweight machines. It produced two models using 98cc Villiers or 123cc JAP two-stroke engines. There was a small-scale motorcycle called the Lilliput and the Gazelle scooter.

BAKER
1926–30 Frank Baker founded the Precision company (see p.226), which merged with Beardmore to create Beardmore Precision in 1919. After that venture folded in 1924, Baker developed a range of 147cc to 247cc Villiers-engined machines, which were sold under his name. A 249cc side-valve model with an inclined cylinder and an Albion three-speed gearbox appeared in 1930, shortly before the company was taken over by James (see p.221).

BANSHEE
1921–24 The Banshee motorcycle was built at Bromsgrove using 269cc to 497cc engines supplied by Villiers, Blackburne, Bradshaw, and Barr & Stroud. They were made by George Bell, who later worked for Triumph.

BARNES
1904 G. A. Barnes built tricars and forecars, as well as motorcycles using MMC and Minerva engines.

BARON
c.1920–21 Baron built orthodox belt-driven bikes with two-stroke Villiers and 348cc side-valve Blackburne engines.

BARRON
1977 Assembled in the U.K., the Barron was an unlikely union of Polish cycle components and an Italian 123cc Minarelli engine.

BARTER
1902–05 Before developing the Fée flat-twin motorcycle (see p.219), J. Barter designed a single-cylinder machine in which the drive pulley was driven from the camshaft. A complete machine with a vertically mounted engine was exhibited at the Crystal Palace Show in 1903.

BAT  p.22
1902 Company founded by S. R. Batson in south London.
1904 Taken over by the Tessier family who used the slogan "Best after Test". Reliability, comfort, and sporting success were Bat sales points. Most machines used JAP single-cylinder and V-twin engines of 346cc to 976cc.
1923 It took over Martinsyde (see p.223).
1926 Production stopped.

BAUGHAN
1930–36 Harry Baughan produced specialized trials bikes in Stroud, Gloucestershire. They had 250cc to 500cc side-valve and overhead-valve JAP and Blackburne engines. A sidecar outfit with a driven third wheel was also built.

BEARDMORE PRECISION
1919 F. E. Baker's Precision company (see p.226) had become involved with the giant Beardmore industrial group around 1915, but the first Beardmore Precision motorcycles did not appear until 1919. The first models were unit-construction two-speed 348cc two-stroke singles with leaf-sprung front and rear suspension and an innovative frame design in which the pressed-steel fuel tank was a structural member. Side-valve singles of 348cc to 596cc were soon added to the range. Barr & Stroud sleeve-valve and Blackburne 350cc side-valve engines were also used.
1925 Beardmore's interest was expensive and short-lived. Sales were dropping and after poor results in the 1924 TT, the company closed in 1925. Beardmore continued a tenuous connection with motorcycle production through its interest in Dunford & Elliot, maker of the Dunelt motorcycle (see p.218). Baker established a new firm under his own name (see left).

BEAUFORT
c.1923–26 The Argson Engineering Co. of Beaufort Works, Twickenham, built the Argson invalid carriage. It also made 170cc two-stroke scooters and a 175cc overhead-valve flat twin.

BEAU IDEAL
1904–07 The Richards Beau Ideal Cycle Co. of Wolverhampton produced conventional belt-driven motorcycles using engines supplied by Minerva, Peugeot, and others. It also sold the Dutch Eysink motorcycle (see p.298).

BEAUMONT
1921–22 Orthodox machines built in Leeds with 269cc Wall two-stroke engines and 348cc Blackburne side-valve engines. Occasionally the Leeds-built 309cc side-valve three-cylinder Redrup radial engine was used.

BEESTON
1898–1905 Humber was originally based in Beeston near Nottingham. It used the Beeston name on superior versions of its machines, even when they were made at its Coventry factory.

BERWICK
1929 Named after the designer's native town, where the prototype machine was built, the Berwick used 246cc to 346cc Villiers engines. It was exhibited at the Olympia Motorcycle Show in 1929 but probably never went into production.

BINKS
1903–06 Charles Binks of Nottingham was among the first to produce a four-cylinder motorcycle with the cylinders set in-line. His 411cc and 803cc atmospheric-inlet-valve machines had chain drive, a kickstarter, and either an in-line or transverse engine. Production machines were sold and possibly built by

A 1923 Beardmore Precision with unit-construction 596cc side-valve engine and frame with integral fuel tank

Evart-Hall (see p.219). Binks also made an improved spray carburettor and built New Leader cars from 1905 to 1909.

BIRCH

1902–05 John North Birch was one of the British motorcycle pioneers. With his partner Edwin Perks, he produced the Perks & Birch Motorwheel (see p.226). After the production rights for the Motorwheel were sold to Singer in 1900, Birch developed new designs in which the engine cases formed the bottom bracket of a triangular tubular frame to which they were brazed. This design was licenced to Bradbury. Birch also built his own machines to the same pattern under the name George Elliot. He apparently knew the author Mary Ann Evans, who used this pseudonym.

BLACKBURNE

1913 Aircraft pioneer Geoffrey DeHaviland began to develop motorcycle engines around 1904. In 1909 he sold the manufacturing rights to Cecil and Alick Burney who intended to build complete motorcycles. Major Blackburne joined the brothers as a partner. A 499cc side-valve motorcycle with Blackburne's distinctive outside flywheel engine was announced in 1913. These machines may have used frames made by OEC. During the war the Burney brothers enlisted. They later produced bikes under their own name (see p.216).
1919 Production of Blackburne motorcycles was resumed after World War I. The demand for engines led to the transfer of motorcycle manufacturing to OEC (see p.225). Machines were sold under the Blackburne name until 1922, when the OEC name took precedence.

BLACK-PRINCE

c.1919–20 The Black-Prince was an unusual machine that may not have progressed beyond prototype stage. It had a 500cc flat-twin two-stroke engine, which was mounted in a pressed-steel frame. Another machine with a pressed-steel frame and a 292cc Union two-stroke engine was also produced, as was a wooden-framed two-stroke engined car. E. W. Cameron produced the machines, first in Doncaster and then in Barnard Castle, County Durham.

BLUMFIELD

c.1908–14 Primarily an engine maker, Blumfield also built some complete machines, including competition models.

BOND

1949–53 Lawrence Bond was involved in a variety of two-, three-, and four-wheeled projects, which were built by several companies from the late 1940s to the 1960s. The first motorcycle was an advanced lightweight with a stressed-skin aluminium frame. It used a 98cc Villiers or 123cc JAP two-stroke engine. From 1950 to 1953 new machines were produced under the BAC name (see p.214) and Bond was also involved in the prototype Oscar scooter, which was exhibited in 1953.
1958–62 Bond built new scooters with fibreglass bodywork and 147cc to 197cc Villiers engines before quitting scooters to concentrate on cars.

BOOTH

1901–03 The Booth Motor Syndicate of Putney, southwest London, produced conventional belt-driven machines with Minerva engines. From 1903 they were also sold under the Hulbert-Bramley name (see p.221).

BORD

c.1902–06 An early clip-on bicycle engine with belt drive, which fitted vertically in the triangle of the frame.

BOWDEN

1902–05 Frank Bowden invented the Bowden cable and founded the Raleigh company (see p.227). He also briefly built machines under his own name, using single-cylinder engines supplied by FN and Simms, among others.

BOWN

1919–24 Before World War I Bown built Aeolus machines (see p.212). After the war it assembled simple belt-driven machines mainly using 269cc and 247cc Villiers two-stroke engines, although 350cc four-strokes with Blackburne and JAP engines were also offered. When motorcycle production stopped the company relocated to North London and continued to make bicycles.
1946–49 Built 98cc Villiers-engined autocycles under the Aberdale trademark (see p.212).
1950–58 Bown relocated to Tonypandy in Wales and the Bown name was reintroduced on 98cc and 122cc Villiers-engined lightweights. From 1955 it built 47cc Sachs-engined mopeds.

BRADBURY

1901–25 Bradbury machines were built in Oldham, Lancashire by a company that also made bicycles, baby carriages, and sewing machines. The Peerless name was used on its first motorcycles. They were single-cylinder atmospheric-inlet-valve models made under a J. N. Birch patent (see Birch, left).
1914 New 499cc side-valve horizontally opposed twins and 749cc side-valve V-twins were introduced. Capacity of the V-twins later increased to 871cc. The company concentrated on quality rather than design innovation.

BRITAX

1954–56 Motor accessory company that made scooters and a 50cc racer using Ducati Cucciolo engines. It bought the Excelsior company (see p.219) in 1964.

BRITISH-RADIAL

1921–23 British-Radial produced an unusual machine using a 309cc Redrup 120° three-cylinder radial engine in a Chater-Lea frame. A two-speed Sturmey-Archer gearbox with belt final drive was fitted. In 1923 the company may have built a 123cc four-stroke single.

BRITISH SALMSON See Cyclaid (p.217).

BRITISH-STANDARD

c.1919–23 Built orthodox belt-driven machines in Birmingham using Arden and Villiers two-stroke and Blackburne four-stroke engines.

BROCKHOUSE

1946–55 Brockhouse was the company that produced the Corgi minibike (see p.217). It became a key shareholder in the Indian marque (see p.271) in the early 1950s and it was Brockhouse that ordered the end of Indian production in the U.S. In the U.K. it produced a basic 250cc side-valve machine, which was sold as the Indian Brave. Most of the production was sold in the U.S.

BROUGH

1908–25 William Brough built motorcycles in Nottingham, but it was his son George (see Brough Superior, below) who made the family name famous. William Brough made single-cylinder and V-twin engines before adopting the flat-twin as his favoured engine layout. Motorcycles with fore-and-aft flat-twin engines of up to 692cc were built. Production was limited.

BROUGH SUPERIOR 🏍 pp.34–35

1920 George Brough's first machines were shown at Olympia in 1920. They used 986cc V-twin JAP engines, available in side- and overhead-valve form. Later versions also used Matchless and MAG engines. The *Motor Cycle* magazine once described them as "The Rolls Royce of motorcycles"; George Brough made sure that the tag was remembered. They were expensive, high-quality, high-speed bikes. They also achieved considerable sporting success. Over the years various prototypes and limited runs were built, including a machine powered by an Austin 7 car engine and the Golden Dream shaft-driven four. The company gained a reputation for large-capacity V-twins of up to 1150cc, although smaller versions were also produced.
1940 Motorcycle manufacturing ceased when the firm switched to war work.

BROWN

1901–15 Accessory supplier Brown Brothers also sold complete motorcycles.

Its first models had BSA bicycle frames with a 1.5hp engine. In 1902 it adopted the "new" Werner engine position using 2hp Minerva engines. Later models were typical machines equipped with 292cc to 499cc single-cylinder four-stroke engines. Brown also sold machines with the Vindec trademark until 1928.

BROWN BICAR See Midget Bicar (p.224).

BSA 🏍 pp.36–39

1910 The Birmingham Small Arms company diversified into the production of bicycle parts in the late 19th century. Motorcycle components followed but it did not build complete motorcycles until 1910. BSA built solid, simple, and cheap motorcycles. Early models were 499cc side-valve singles. Soon there were also 557cc singles, and in 1919 770cc V-twins. By 1939, when the firm switched to war production, V-twins of 500cc to 1000cc were available. In the 1920s and 1930s the range included a 175cc two-stroke, as well as side- and overhead-valve singles, including the Sloper and the first of the Star singles, the 1933 Blue Star. It was followed by the Empire Star and finally Gold Star models.
1943 BSA bought the Sunbeam name from AMC (see p.213). After World War II it was attached to an upmarket shaft-driven machine and subsequently an unsuccessful scooter.
1944 Acquired the Ariel marque.
1946 New 498cc BSA overhead-valve parallel twins were introduced in response to Triumph's Speed Twin, followed by 646cc versions.
1948 Began production of the 123cc two-stroke Bantam. BSA acquired the design from DKW as part of the war reparations programme. Built until 1971, it was BSA's best-selling model.
1951 BSA took over Triumph, although both firms maintained separate identities for many years. The arrival of small-capacity Japanese machines in the 1950s saw British makers retreat into building large-capacity motorcycles like the 740cc three-cylinder Rocket 3, introduced in 1968. The collapse of the market for large machines left them in big trouble.
1973 The company collapsed. Norton Villiers took control and dropped the BSA name. It was revived later in the decade and attached to Yamaha-engined trail bikes, primarily intended for export.

BULLDOG

1920 Built in Birmingham by H. H. Timbrell, the Bulldog had a horizontally opposed Coventry-Victor engine mounted in a duplex cradle frame.

BURFORD

c.1914–15 Conventional machines with either a 500cc side-valve single-cylinder or 269cc Villiers two-stroke engine.

BURNEY
1923–27 Burney machines were built by Alick and Cecil Burney, after they split from Blackburne. They first built a 495cc side-valve chain-driven single. A V-twin with a 680cc side-valve JAP engine appeared in 1927.

CAIRNS MOCYC
1949–51 A 49cc two-stroke clip-on bicycle engine that mounted on a subframe above the front wheel, which was driven by friction roller. It was also known as the GYS Motamite.

CALCOTT
1910–15 A Coventry-based company that built cars from 1904. Its first motorcycles used 3.5hp White & Poppe engines. Later it also produced its own 292cc side-valve engines.

CALTHORPE
1909 First exhibited at the Stanley Cycle Show, Calthorpe machines were built in Birmingham by George Hands. Early models, using 3.5hp White & Poppe engines, were followed by 211cc two-strokes and proprietary-engined four-strokes. After World War I Villiers, JAP, Blackburne, Peco, and Precision all supplied engines to Calthorpe before it began to make its own 350cc overhead-valve and 500cc overhead-camshaft engines in 1925. It soon dropped the overhead-camshaft engine in favour of the overhead-valve unit, which was supplied in 247cc to 493cc capacities.
1928 Introduced the Ivory model with sloping engine and ivory paintwork. It remained in the range until 1935.
1938 New owners moved the firm to Bristol, where they intended to build Matchless-engined machines.
1939 The new factory was requisitioned for the war effort before production could begin.

CALVERT
c.1900–04 Built in Stoke Newington, North London, Calvert machines were equipped with the firm's own single-cylinder and V-twin engines with external flywheels.

CAMPION
c.1901–25 The Campion Cycle Co. of Nottingham also built motorcycles. They were orthodox machines equipped with JAP, Precision, and Villiers engines, ranging from 269cc two-strokes to 1000cc V-twins. It also built motorcycles for the Scottish company New Gerrard (see p.224) for a period from 1924.

CARFIELD
1919–27 Built at Smethwick, Birmingham, the first Carfield machines used the 269cc Villiers two-stroke engine, an Albion two-speed gearbox, and belt final drive. The company was soon producing a range of machines with engines supplied by Villiers, JAP, and Coventry-Victor. For 1927 a new chain-driven lightweight, with a 175cc Aza two-stroke engine, was introduced. The company folded soon afterwards.

CARLTON
1936–39 Orthodox 122cc Villiers-engined motorcycles built by a bicycle company. They were also sold as the Grose-Spur by a London motorcycle dealer. Carlton is now part of the Raleigh bicycle group.

CASTELL
1903 Short-lived London manufacturer that used vertical atmospheric-inlet-valve engines in its machines.

CASSWELL
1904–05 Casswell assembled machines using a Chater-Lea frame with a water-cooled Fafnir 3.5hp engine.

CAYENNE
1912–13 Produced by the Hayes-Pankhurst Manufacturing Co. in Sussex, the Cayenne was a 499cc overhead-valve single with water cooling.

CC
c.1921–24 Charles Chamberlain built a limited number of machines using Villiers two-stroke and single-cylinder and V-twin four-stroke engines.

CCM
1971 Clews Competition Motorcycles began making high-quality motocross bikes based on the single-cylinder overhead-valve BSA B50 engine. These machines were very successful during the mid-1970s despite the theoretical advantages of the two-stroke opposition.
1981 CCM became part of the Armstrong group, and for the following six years motorcycle production continued under that name.
1987 CCM bought the company back from Armstrong and continued making small numbers of specialized off-road machines using Rotax engines.

CEDOS
1919–29 Built in Northampton by CEDric and OScar Hanwell using their own 198cc to 246cc two-stroke engines. Later they also installed Villiers and Peco two-stroke engines, as well as four-stroke units from Blackburne, Bradshaw, and JAP, including 976cc V-twins.

CENTAUR
1901–15 The first Centaur motorcycles followed the Minerva pattern. In 1904 Centaur introduced a new frame that incorporated the silencer into the front downtube. It used single-cylinder and V-twin engines. A prototype inlet-over-exhaust parallel twin with a central flywheel was shown in 1910.

CENTURY
c.1899–1905 Limited production of motorcycles, tandems, and forecars with Aster and other proprietary engines.

CHASE
1902–06 The Chase brothers were enthusiastic competition motorcyclists. They built loop-framed, belt-driven machines, with 2.5hp to 4hp MMC and Ariel engines, similar to those they rode.

CHATER-LEA
1900 Chater-Lea was a well-established cycle components company, which supplied fittings to other companies before building its own machines. Early models had single-cylinder and V-twin engines supplied by Minerva, Peugeot, JAP, Sarolea, and others. Although it soon developed its own V-twin and single-cylinder engines, it continued to offer customers the option of using proprietary power units. In 1908 it introduced the Model 7, which was equipped with a 350cc engine with all chain transmission.
1919 Resumed motorcycle production after World War I with a range of 350cc to 550cc side-valve and overhead-valve singles using Blackburne, JAP, and its own engines. From 1922 machines with Blackburne 350cc overhead-valve and its own 545cc side-valve engines were popular. The latter sold well to the Automobile Association for sidecar use until 1936. Chater-Lea's own 350cc engines, including its famous face-cam single, were developed for sporting use.
1936 Motorcycle production ceased but the company continued to trade.

CHELL
1938–39 Limited production of 98cc and 122cc Villiers-engined lightweights.

CHENEY
1962– Cheney offers specialized off-road competition machines, which have used various power units, including Triumph, BSA, and Sachs.

CLARENDON
1901–11 Built machines using its own and proprietary units. By 1903 it was using loop frames and possibly water cooling. Mechanical inlet valves appeared on some models in 1904.

CLÉMENT-GARRARD
1902–11 Charles Garrard imported French Clément engines, which were mounted in frames from James Norton. Norton also produced similar machines under the name Energette (see p.219).

CLEVELAND
c.1911–14 Built in Middlesborough by Egerton Price using Precision engines. Freddie Dixon made his TT debut in 1912 aboard a Cleveland machine.

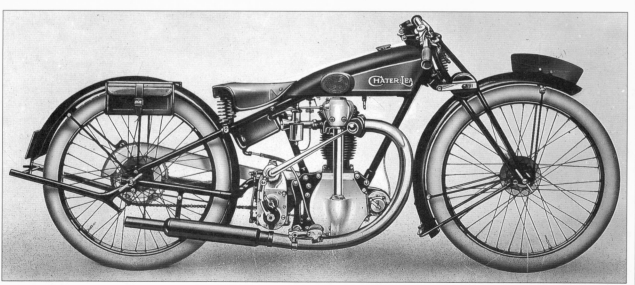

A 1926 face-cam-engined Chater-Lea Super Sport

CLYDE

1899–1926 Built in Leicester by G. H. Wait, Clyde was among the first to use loop frames, magneto ignition, and spray carburettors. It used Simms power units on early machines, before switching to single-cylinder and V-twin JAP engines. It also produced cars.

CLYNO

1909 Clyno machines were built in Thrapston, Northamptonshire. Early models used Clyno's own variable ratio gear and proprietary parts, including Stevens 386cc single and 744cc V-twin engines, both with overhead valves. In 1910 the single was dropped and Clyno concentrated on the twin. It acquired the manufacturing rights to the Stevens V-twin engine and moved to a factory in Wolverhampton, which was formerly occupied by Stevens. In 1913 a belt-driven two-speed 269cc two-stroke with an inclined cylinder was introduced.
1914 Clyno benefited from the war when the army selected the V-twin combination for use as a machine gun mount. Post-war production was based on the two-stroke and the V-twin.
1923 Demand for Clyno's light car stopped motorcycle production.

CMM

c.1919–21 CMM machines were built by Coventry Motor Mart, using 292cc Union two-stroke engines.

COMERY

1919–22 Nottingham-based firm that built belt-driven 247cc Villiers-engined machines. A sidecar was also offered.

COMET

c.1902–07 Belt-driven Minerva-engined machines built in southeast London.

COMMANDER

1952–53 A futuristic-looking prototype lightweight shown in 1952. It had a 98cc or a 122cc Villiers engine.

CONNAUGHT

1910–27 Birmingham-built 293cc and 348cc two-stroke singles with petroil lubrication and belt drive. In 1924 the company took over JES (see p.222) and added four-stroke machines to its range. These included its own 348cc and 490cc side-valve singles and other models with Bradshaw, Blackburne, and JAP engines.

CONSUL

1916–23 Norwich-based company that built conventional 269cc and 246cc Villiers-engined belt-driven two-strokes.

CORAH

c.1905–11 R. N. Corah of King's Norton built machines using proprietary engines mainly supplied by JAP. A prototype rotary-valve machine was also built.

CORGI

1946–55 A small-wheeled two-stroke scooter built by Brockhouse, the Corgi had a 98cc Excelsior Spryt engine with a horizontally mounted cylinder. The design was based on wartime Excelsior Welbike paratroopers motorcycles. It sold in the U.S. as an Indian Papoose.

CORONA-JUNIOR

1919–23 Built in North London by the Meteor Manufacturing Co., a 447cc side-valve single with a vertical cylinder and external flywheel. The basic model was a single-speed belt-driven machine.

CORYDON

1904–08 Single-cylinder and V-twin loop-framed machines built in Croydon.

COTTON p.43

1919 Frank Willoughby Cotton began making machines using his patented triangulated frame design. Early machines had 269cc Villiers and 350cc side-valve Blackburne engines. Later 150cc to 600cc proprietary engines were used. The excellent handling of the straight-tube frame made the Cotton a successful racer. World War II interrupted manufacturing.
1953 Production resumed with Villiers- and Anzani-engined machines of up to 250cc with conventional frames. Cotton racers and Minarelli-engined trials bikes were successful in the 1960s. In 1976 new Rotax-engined racers appeared.
1980 Cotton was taken over by Armstrong and the name vanished.

COULSON-B

1919–23 The Coulson-B was originally built in London. It had leaf-sprung rear suspension, a 348cc side-valve Blackburne engine – hence the B suffix – and a two-speed gearbox with belt final drive. A 499cc model appeared in 1920.

A. W. Wall (see Wall p.232) took over production in 1921 and in 1923, under the ownership of H. R. Backhouse & Co., the marque became New Coulson.

COVENTRY B&D

1923–26 Machines made by Barbary & Downes, which also built bikes under the Wee McGregor (see p.232) and Three Spires (see p.231) names. It used single-cylinder and V-twin JAP engines of 346cc to 976cc and 348cc Barr & Stroud power units. The company was also known as Coventry Bicycles Ltd.

COVENTRY-CHALLENGE

1903–11 Built orthodox belt-driven motorcycles with Minerva engines.

COVENTRY-EAGLE

1901 Bicycle factory that installed MMC, DeDion, and Buchet engines in bicycle frames to make its first machines. From 1904 production was limited.
1921 Production resumed with 500cc single-cylinder and 680cc V-twin JAP-engined machines. Later models varied from 147cc Villiers-powered two-strokes to the 996cc JAP V-twin, the Flying Eight. The 250cc Villiers-engined Pullman was introduced in 1933.
1939 The war stopped production.

COVENTRY-MASCOT

1922–24 Built side-valve, overhead-valve, and sleeve-valve 350cc machines using Blackburne, Bradshaw, and Barr & Stroud engines.

COVENTRY-PREMIER See Premier
(p.227).

COVENTRY-VICTOR

1919–35 Built flat-twins using its own 499cc, 688cc, and 907cc engines. It also made a three-wheeled light car. Engine manufacturing continued after 1935.

CRESCENT

1915 Name used on a utilitarian model built by Rudge-Whitworth using 269cc Villiers engines.

CROFT CAMERON

1923–26 The Croft Cameron Super-Eight was built in limited numbers using V-twin Anzani engines.

CROWNFIELD

1903–04 Name used on a 2.25hp Kerry-engined ladies' model with an open tubular frame.

CRYPTO

1901–08 Built by W. G. James in London, Crypto machines were equipped with a variety of proprietary engines, including MMC and Peugeot.

CURRY

1913 The Curry was a diamond framed JAP-engined side-valve single.

CYC-AUTO p.45

1934–55 The Cyc-Auto was a 98cc autocycle with a modified bicycle-style frame. The engine had a vertical cylinder and longitudinal crankshaft. A worm gear turned the drive through 90° and allowed the use of chain drive to the rear wheel. The company used its own power units before briefly switching to Villiers and Scott engines. A 98cc motorcycle based on the Cyc-Auto engine, but with shaft drive and plunger rear suspension, was offered in 1955.

CYCLAID

c.1950–56 British Salmson built 31cc clip-on two-stroke engines, which mounted on the rear carrier.

CYCLEMASTER/CYCLEMATE

1951–60 A powered wheel with a 26cc and later 33cc two-stroke engine, the

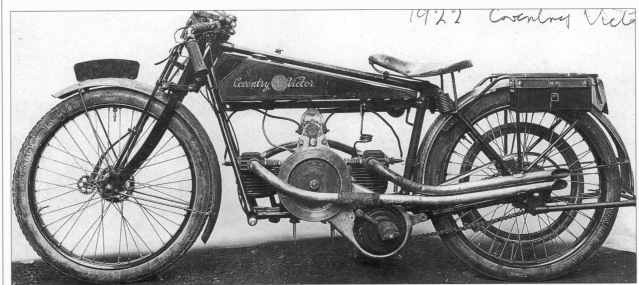

A 1922 Coventry-Victor 688cc sports model with the gearbox mounted under the rear cylinder

Cyclemaster could be fitted in place of the rear wheel on a conventional bicycle. From 1955 the firm also offered a complete machine called the Cyclemate.

CYKELAID
c.1920–26 Cykelaid produced 133cc two-stroke clip-on bicycle engines.

CYMOTA
c.1950–52 A 45cc two-stroke clip-on engine that mounted above the friction-driven front wheel.

DALESMAN
1969–74 Off-road competition machine that used a 124cc Puch two-stroke engine in a British-made frame.

DALTON
1920–22 Limited production of motorcycles with proprietary engines.

DART
1923–24 Built a few advanced 350cc overhead-camshaft singles.

DAVIS
1910 A JAP-engined sidecar outfit in which the driver sat in the sidecar and steered with a tiller.

DAVISON
1902–08 Davison used Simms and Minerva engines in bicycle-style frames.

DAW
1902–05 Engine makers Dalton And Wade also built a few complete machines.

DAWN See Pearson & Cox (p.226).

DAY-LEEDS See Eclipse (p.219).

DAYTON
1913–15 Bicycle maker Charles Day offered a 162cc belt-driven two-stroke. The engines may have been made by Stuart Turner and were also available as a clip-on attachment for bicycles.
1921–22 Built motorcycles using 269cc Villiers engines.
1938–39 Resumed production with a 98cc Villiers-engined autocycle.
1954–60 Produced 174cc to 249cc Villiers-engined scooters.

DEFY-ALL
1921–22 Built Villiers- and Blackburne-engined motorcycles with leaf-sprung rear suspension.

DE LUXE
1914–24 The De Luxe used either TDC and Villiers two-stroke engines or Barr & Stroud sleeve-valve motors.

DENE
1903–c.1923 Produced in Newcastle-upon-Tyne using proprietary engines, including Minerva, Precision, and JAP.

DENNELL
c.1903–08 Used proprietary engines, including Minerva and unusual 660cc three-cylinder JAP power units.

DERBY
1901–02 Built bicycle-style machines with 1hp atmospheric-inlet-valve engines. It also supplied engines to other makers.

DESPATCH-RIDER
1915–17 Lightweight machines with proprietary 211cc two-stroke engines.

DIAMOND
1908–31 This Wolverhampton-based company built its first motorcycles using single-cylinder and V-twin FN engines. An advanced unit-construction two-speed machine appeared in 1912 but production ended in World War I. After the war it built orthodox machines with Villiers, JAP, and Bradshaw engines. The company pursued an active competition programme. Serious production ended in 1931 after an ambitious but unsuccessful TT effort. The company continued to offer machines to order.

DKR
1957–66 Built Villiers-powered scooters of 147cc to 249cc. The fuel tank was mounted in the bulbous front fairing.

DMB
c.1927 Diamond-framed belt-driven lightweights with 247cc and 342cc Villiers engines, built by the Derby Cycle Manufacturing Co. of Birmingham.

DMW
1945–71 Dawson's Motor Works made Metal Profiles forks and wheel hubs as well as Villiers-engined motorcycles, including off-road competition machines and utility lightweights. It bought Villiers stock when that company closed and it still supplies Villiers spares.

DORMAN See Whirlwind (p.232).

DOT p.50
1902–32 Harry Reed began making motorcycles using Fafnir, Peugeot, and JAP engines. Before and after World War I Dot built successful racing machines. In the 1920s JAP, Blackburne, and the oil-cooled Bradshaw 350cc engine were used. In 1928 it launched a range of Villiers-engined machines of 98cc to 346cc. The Depression ended production in 1932.
1949–73 Dot resumed production of Villiers-engined machines, especially off-road competition bikes. In the 1950s it imported German Victoria mopeds and in the 1960s the Italian Guazzoni motorcycle. When Villiers quit engine making Dot used Minarelli two-stroke engines, but production soon stopped.

DOUGLAS p.51
1907 The Douglas Brothers foundry produced castings for J. Barter's Light Motors Ltd, maker of the Fée motorcycle (see p.219). When Light Motors failed, Barter went to work for Douglas taking his designs with him. Douglas produced flat twins for the next 50 years. Its first machine was a belt-driven 350cc model. It was soon established as one of the major British manufacturers and enjoyed competition success. Machines were supplied to the military during World War I. By 1922 it was producing a range of flat twins of 348cc to 735cc. During the 1930s it built lightweights using its own and Villiers engines. The 1935 500cc shaft-driven Endeavor was the first Douglas to use a transverse engine. In the 1930s the firm had a number of owners and went into decline.
1946 Introduced new 348cc flat twins with transversely-mounted engines.
1951 Douglas began making the Italian Vespa scooter under licence.
1957 Motorcycle manufacturing ended. Production of Vespa scooters continued until about 1964 and Douglas continued to import Vespa scooters into the 1980s.

DREADNOUGHT
1915–23 Belt-driven 269cc Villiers-engined machines built by W. A. Lloyd & Co. in Birmingham. Some bikes may also have been sold under the Walco brand-name. Lloyd also made the Lloyd motorcycle (see p.223).

DUNELT p.56
1919–35 Sheffield steel maker Dunford & Elliot offered a very novel stepped-piston two-stroke single. A 499cc model was produced from 1919 to 1927 and a 249cc from 1926 to 1935. From 1929 Sturmey-Archer and Villiers engines were also used. Very late machines were offered with Python and JAP engines.
1957 A 49cc moped was made using a German Rex two-stroke engine.

DUNKLEY
c.1913 Birmingham-built machines with proprietary engines, including 170cc side-valve Pecision and 349cc Peco two-strokes. The machines used conventional diamond frames and larger capacity JAP and Precision engines could be specified.

DUNKLEY
c.1957–59 Pram maker that built light scooters and mopeds using its own overhead-valve 65cc engines.

A 1923 499cc stepped-piston Dunelt two-stroke with a Sturmey-Archer three-speed gearbox

DUZMO
1919–24 Sporting 496cc singles and 992cc 50° V-twins designed by John Wallace and built in Enfield.

ECLIPSE
1903–05 Eclipse produced motorcycles with a wide-angle V-twin engine with atmospheric-inlet-valve and belt drive.

ECLIPSE
1912–14 Engineering company Job Day & Sons Ltd of Leeds produced single-cylinder and V-twin engines, cycle cars, and motorcycles with its own 499cc inlet-over-exhaust single-cylinder engine. Motorcycles were also sold under the Day-Leeds trademark.

ECONOMIC
1921–23 Early machines had a 165cc two-stroke flat-twin engine positioned in-line, but later models had a transverse engine layout in a duplex cradle frame.

EDMONTON
c.1903–05 Built in Edmonton using vertical atmospheric-inlet-valve engines mounted in front of the bottom bracket.

EDMUND
c.1907–26 Charles Edmund built motorcycles using engines supplied by JAP and Blackburne, among others.

ELF
c.1913 Built by the Nestor Motor Co. of Blackpool, a loop-framed 149cc machine with an inlet-over-exhaust engine.

ELF-KING
c.1907–09 Shown at the 1907 Stanley Show, the Elf-King was a typical early belt-driven 443cc motorcycle.

ELFSON
1923–25 Wilson & Elford built a limited number of lightweights using its own 292cc two-stroke engines and the overhead-valve 170cc Norman engine.

ELI
1911–12 Assembled Precision-engined motorcycles and sidecars in Bristol.

ELLISON
c.1911 Sprung-frame machines available with Peugeot or JAP engines.

ELMDON
1915–21 Typical lightweights with 269cc Villiers engines and belt drive.

ELSWICK
1903–21 Bicycle maker that used single-cylinder side-valve Precision engines in its first motorcycles. It was taken over by Hopper and moved from Elswick to Barton-on-Humber. Hopper also produced an almost identical machine under the Torpedo badge (see p.231).

EMC
1947 Dr Josef Ehrlich's Motorcycle Company first made a 348cc split-single two-stroke, but it was not popular and production soon ended. A 125cc Puch-engined racer was built from 1952.
1960 Ehrlich produced a few racing two-strokes with mixed success.
1981 EMC became associated with the Waddon Engineering Co. in the development of Rotax-engined race bikes.
1982 Ehrlich split from Waddon to produce his own machines. The high point of the venture was Eddie Laycock's win in the 1987 Junior TT.

EMERALD
c.1903 Built 1.75hp and 2.75hp bikes with loop frames and two-speed gear.

ENDRICK
c.1911–15 Built in Birmingham using proprietary engines, including Fafnir.

ENDURANCE
c.1909–24 C. B. Harrison built two-stroke machines using the company's own and Villiers engines.

ENERGETTE
1902–07 Name used on some early Norton motorcycles (see p.225).

EVART-HALL
1903–05 Built a single-cylinder machine before taking a licence to produce the four-cylinder Binks (see p.214).

EXCELSIOR p.60
1896–1964 Bayliss, Thomas & Co. fitted a 1.25hp Minerva engine onto an Excelsior bicycle to make its first motorcycle. It was one of the first motorcycles available to the British buyer. MMC and JAP engines were also used in the early days.
1919 R. Walker & Son – maker of the Monarch motorcycle – took over the company. Villiers, JAP, and Blackburne engines were used. Its most famous machines were the single-cylinder four-valve Mechanical Marvels and overhead-camshaft Manxman models of the 1930s. It also made more mundane two-strokes. During World War II it built the 98cc Welbike for parachute landing. After the war it built a range of 98cc to 197cc machines using Villiers and its own two-stroke power units.
1949 Introduced the 249cc Talisman two-stroke twin. Capacity grew to 328cc before production stopped in 1962. An unsuccessful scooter was launched at the end of the 1950s, but the company was in decline. In 1964 it was bought by Britax (see p.215) and production ended.

FAIRFIELD
c.1914–15 Conventional 269cc two-strokes built by Alfred Forster & Co.

FAIRY See Fée (see right).

FB
1913–22 Fowler & Bingham built 269cc two-stroke engines, which were supplied to other manufacturers. It also built some complete machines. Later versions were known as FB Wizard.

FEDERAL/FEDERATION
1919–37 Built in Birmingham by the Co-Operative Society and available through Co-Op shops, these were orthodox machines with 122cc to 344cc Villiers and 248cc to 680cc JAP engines.

FÉE
1905–07 J. Barter (see p.214) had built a single-cylinder engine before making a 200cc flat-twin power unit, probably the first engine of this type to be used in a motorcycle. Barter formed Light Motors Ltd to produce the machines under the Fée name – soon anglicized to Fairy. A larger capacity machine was also built. Following financial troubles Barter took the design to Douglas (p.218), who used the flat-twin layout for the next 50 years.

FEW-PARAMOUNT
1920–27 Unusual two-wheeled car built in limited numbers by F. E. Waller. The rider and passenger sat in bucket seats. JAP and Blackburne single-cylinder and V-twin engines were used. Machines made from 1926 to 1927 used the Paramount-Duo trademark.

FLEET See Ariel (p.213).

FLM
c.1951–53 Built in Leeds by Frank Leach, former designer for Panther, FLM machines were Villiers- and JAP-powered two-stroke lightweights with rear springing. The FLM venture was unsuccessful and Frank Leach returned to Panther.

FORWARD
1909–15 Forward produced its own 339cc and 479cc side-valve V-twin engines, which were mounted on conventional belt-driven machines. It competed in the early TT races.

Mr P. W. Owen riding a 339cc V-twin Forward in the 1912 Junior TT

FRANCIS-BARNETT  p.63

1919 Production of Gordon Francis' innovative motorcycle with bolted-up straight tubular frames and a JAP engine began in 1920. Villiers-powered two-stroke machines soon followed.

1933 Introduction of the 249cc Villiers-engined Cruiser with semi-enclosed bodywork and a frame that combined I-section forgings with pressed-steel sections.

1947 The company became part of the AMC group. Post-war products were conventional machines using Villiers and AMC's own two-stroke engines of up to 250cc. Later models were identical to James machines; they were both part of the AMC group and were eventually built at the same factory.

1966 Production ended.

GABY

1914–20 Gaby built belt-driven two-strokes using 269cc Metro engines. After the war they were sold with Arden engines of the same type and capacity.

GAMAGE

1900–24 Gamages department store sold motorcycles built by other makers with its own badge. Early models included Fafnir-powered models, later it offered typical Villiers 269cc two-strokes and larger capacity side-valve singles.

GARRARD See Clément-Garrard (p.216).

GB

1905–08 GB produced long, low machines with single-cylinder and V-twin engines. The 1908 military model had a fan-cooled 5.5hp V-twin engine and a two-speed hub gear.

GEORGE ELLIOT See Birch (p.215).

GERRARD

1913–15 These belt-driven lightweights were made in Birmingham and had 269cc Villiers engines.

GLENCAIRN

1902 An assembled machine intended for export. Production was minimal.

GLENDALE

c.1920–21 Small numbers of bikes with 550cc side-valve Blackburne engines were built in Wooler, Northumberland.

GLOBE

c.1901–05 Built in Coventry by Clarke, Cluley & Co., which originally made textile-making machines. Its motorcycles used vertical engines in loop frames.

GLORIA

1924–25 Almost a typical British lightweight of the 1920s, the Gloria used Druid forks and a two-speed Albion

Captain Peatty astride a Blackburne-engined Hawker racer, c.1926

gearbox with belt final drive. An unusual feature was the French Train 123cc two-stroke engine.

GLORIA

1931–33 A cheap stopgap model using a 98cc Villiers engine built by Triumph to take advantage of new tax classes.

GOUGH

c.1920–23 Gough built motorcycles using JAP and Blackburne side-valve single-cylinder engines.

GOVERNMENT

1914 A 292cc JAP-engined four-stroke, which incorporated a variable ratio belt pulley on the engine shaft.

GRANDEX

1910–16 Orthodox belt-driven bikes using single-cylinder and V-twin JAP and Precision engines. In 1916 Grandex produced a two-stroke model with a 232cc Precision engine. The primary drive chain also drove the magneto.

GRAVES

1914–15 Mail order company Graves offered the inappropriately named Speed King motorcycle in its pre-war catalogue. The diamond-framed belt-driven machine with 292cc side-valve JAP engine was built by New Imperial (see p.224).

GREEN

1903–04 Built by a Cheltenham gunmaker using Simms engines and magnetos. The machine had rear suspension, and the fuel and oil tanks were incorporated into the large-diameter frame tubes.

GREEN

1910–23 Charles Green's machines used Precision-based engines with water cooling. These engines were also used by the pre-war Regal marque.

GREEVES  p.66

1953–72 Greeves built invalid cars and produced a prototype motorcycle in 1951 to test a rubber suspension system. Most early machines had 197cc Villiers engines, although later 250cc Villiers and Anzani engines were used. From the late 1950s Greeves was very successful in trials and scrambling. Large numbers of off-road machines were exported. From the early 1960s, 250cc road racers were also built. Availability of Spanish and Japanese off-road machines from the late 1960s and the end of Villiers engine production helped to kill the company.

1975 After a failed attempt to revive the marque, it finally closed around 1977.

GRI

1921–22 Designed by G. R. Inshaw and built in Glasgow, the GRI combined a single-overhead poppet valve with a rotary valve to control gases. Only a few 349cc, 420cc, and 499cc versions were produced.

GRIGG

1920–25 Grigg built a 161cc two-stroke scooter, then small-capacity motorcycles using its own engines. Larger models used engines by Villiers, Blackburne, and the rare B&H 990cc V-twin.

GRINDLAY-PEERLESS

1923–34 An established sidecar maker, its first motorcycle used a 1000cc Barr &

Stroud sleeve-valve V-twin engine. This was followed by models using engines from 172cc supplied by Villiers, JAP, Python, and Barr & Stroud.

GROSE-SPUR

1916 Dalm-engined belt-driven two-strokes probably built by another manufacturer but sold by London motorcycle dealer James Grose Ltd.

1938–40 Villiers-engined lightweight built by Carlton but again sold under the Grose badge. It had a 122cc engine with three-speed gearbox.

GSD

1922–23 The GSD (Grant Shaft Drive) had a transverse-mounted, White & Poppe 345cc single-cylinder two-stroke engine, a four-speed gearbox, shaft drive, and a duplex tubular cradle frame. Production numbers were minimal.

G&W

1902–06 Guy & Wheeler of Liverpool built motorcycles using Aster and other proprietary engines. The 1903 machine had the engine mounted vertically behind the downtube of a long-wheelbase frame.

GYS MOTAMITE See Cairns Mocyc (p.216).

HACK

1920–23 Scooter with a 110cc Simplex two-stroke engine mounted in front of the chain-driven rear wheel.

HADEN

1912 A. H. Haden's 4.5hp model with a three-speed gearbox was exhibited under his own name. He also produced the New Comet marque (see p.224).

1920–24 Haden again attached his own name to his product. This model used a 347cc Precision two-stroke engine.

HAGG-TANDEM

1920–23 The Hagg-Tandem was designed by Arthur Hagg and made in limited numbers by Taylor & Haytor. It had extensive bodywork, leaf-sprung rear suspension, and a removable pillion seat. The engine was a 349cc sleeve-valve Barr & Stroud single. In 1923 the name was shortened to HT and a more conventional machine, also with a Barr & Stroud engine, was produced.

HAMILTON

1901–07 Made single-cylinder and V-twin engines and complete machines.

HAMPTON

c.1912–14 These 492cc side-valve machines used TDC engines.

HARPER

1954–55 Built in Exeter, the Harper Scootamobile used a Villiers two-stroke engine and fibreglass bodywork.

HAWKER
1920–24 Harry Hawker had been the chief test pilot at the Sopwith Aircraft Co. After World War I, Sopwith diversified into motorcycles through the ill-fated ABC venture (see p.212). A new company was then established with Hawker as the front man. Its first model was a 292cc two-stroke with its own gearbox and belt final drive. It remained in production until 1924. Other bikes, introduced from 1922, used 248cc to 550cc side-valve and overhead-valve Blackburne engines.

HAZEL
c.1906–11 London-built machines using first Peugeot then JAP engines.

HAZLEWOOD
1905–25 Built in Coventry, the final models were 676cc and 976cc JAP-engined V-twins that used Hazlewood's own three-speed gearboxes.

HB
1919–23 Orthodox 348cc to 550cc side-valve and overhead-valve Blackburne-engined machines built by Hill Brothers of Wolverhampton.

HEC
1922–23 Built in Taunton by the Hewin Engineering Co., the HEC was a belt-driven lightweight with a 247cc Villiers engine and a Sturmey-Archer gearbox.

HEC
1938–40 The Hepburn Engineering Co. of Kings Cross, London, built an 80cc two-stroke autocycle with a Levis engine.

HENLEY
1920–26 A variety of machines built by the Clarke brothers, using vertically mounted single-cylinder four-stroke engines of up to 545cc, supplied by Blackburne, Bradshaw, and JAP. The name became New Henley in 1926.

HERCULES
1912–14 Hercules was a Birmingham bicycle manufacturer that dabbled in the motorcycle market. Its first machines used Precision and Sarolea single-cylinder side-valve engines. In 1914 it offered a 211cc belt-driven two-stroke.
1955–61 Mopeds were produced to capitalize on the British moped boom. First shown in 1955 with 49cc two-stroke JAP engines, later models used French Lavalette power units.

HESKETH p.81
1981– Ambitious but ill-fated plan to produce a new British superbike. A 992cc eight-valve double overhead-camshaft engine was developed by Weslake and prototype machines were running by 1980. Early models were beset with problems. Improved

machines were produced until 1988 and are still available to special order.

HJ
1920–21 Howard & Johnson of Birmingham used 269cc two-stroke engines supplied by Liberty and Villiers.

HJH
1954–56 H. J. Hulsman built Villiers-engined machines in Wales. It used frames made from square-section tubing.

HOBART
1901–24 Built in Coventry by bicycle makers Hobart, Bird & Co., these orthodox machines had a vertical engine and belt drive. Later there were V-twins. Precision engines were used from 1911 and the firm also offered ladies' models. Post-war production initially focused on lightweights with 269cc Villiers two-stroke engines. JAP and Blackburne four-stroke engines were added later.

HOCKLEY
1914–16 Built in Birmingham, these 269cc proprietary-engined two-strokes with belt drive were intended for export.

HOLDEN
1897–1902 The first four-cylinder motorcycle was developed by Colonel H. C. L. Holden. The Holden was a brave and innovative design, but it was soon outdated by other developments. It was produced commercially by the Motor Traction Company of London from 1899 to 1902. Holden later designed the famous Brooklands race track.

HOLROYD
1922 Orthodox sporting machines built in limited numbers by motorcycle racer J. S. Holroyd using single-cylinder JAP engines with Burman gearboxes and belt final drive.

HOSKISON
1919–22 Hoskison was a maker of typical period machines with proprietary parts. The engines were 292cc Union two-strokes, and Blackburne 349cc and 499cc side-valve singles.

HOWARD
1904–7 Built in Coalville, Leicester, by Howard & Co., this machine featured a horizontal engine with the crankcases attached to the seat-post of a bicycle-style frame. The carburettor was replaced by a simple petrol vaporizer.

H&R
1922–25 Coventry-built belt-driven lightweight with a 147cc Villiers engine. (Initials sometimes reversed – R&H.)

HRD p.97
1924–28 Howard R. Davies had been an apprentice at AJS and raced Sunbeam

motorcycles before World War I. He later won the 1921 Senior TT on a 350cc AJS before starting his own marque. HRD machines were designed by E. J. Massey and used JAP single-cylinder 344cc and 490cc engines; a 597cc model was also available for 1927. HRD closed down in 1927. The rights were bought by the maker of OK Supreme motorcycles (see p.225), which then sold them to Phillip Vincent, creator of Vincent-HRD (see p.231).

HT See Hagg-Tandem (p.220).

HULBERT-BRAMLEY
1903–06 Successors to the Booth Motor Company, Hulbert-Bramley made single-cylinder machines with Minerva engines. The company also built forecars and ladies' motorcycles.

HUMBER p.97
1898 Thomas Humber began building bicycles at Beeston near Nottingham around 1870. The first motorized machines were the result of the involvement of Harry J. Lawson and his Motor Manufacturing Co. based in Coventry. Humber used these MMC engines, as well as Minerva power units, in motorized bicycles, tricycles, and quadricycles produced around 1900.
1902 Humber began building a 344cc single designed by Joah Phelon, who soon began production of a very similar machine under the P&M name. It had the inclined engine positioned as the downtube of the frame and used chain drive. Between 1906 and 1908 the demand for Humber cars interrupted production. In 1909 it returned with an almost orthodox 500cc belt-driven machine that used its front downtube as a silencer. There was also a 198cc side-valve lightweight and in 1911 a 340cc two-speed side-valve V-twin that won that year's Junior TT. Other designs included a water-cooled 500cc single and a 750cc flat twin.
1919 The post-war range included 500cc and 600cc flat twins; by the mid-1920s Humber specialized in overhead-valve and side-valve 350cc singles.
1930 Humber quit motorcycle production to concentrate on cars.

HUNTER
1904 These were built in London using vertical atmospheric-inlet-valve engines and a chain drive system incorporating a transmission shock absorber.

IMPERIAL
1901–04 The Imperial Cycle & Motor Co. of Birmingham mounted atmospheric-inlet-valve Coronet engines onto loop frames of various styles.

INDIAN PRINCE See Silver Prince (p.229).

INVICTA
1913–23 Built in Coventry by Arthur Barnett, who became a partner in Francis-Barnett from 1919. Invicta used Villiers, Abingdon, and JAP engines of 147cc to 654cc.

IRELAND
c.1912 Diamond-framed machines built in Wolverhampton using Blumfield single-cylinder and V-twin engines.

IVEL
1901–05 Built in Biggleswade, Bedfordshire, by an agricultural engineer turned bicycle and car maker. The Ivel motorcycle used DeDion and MMC engines in bicycle frames.

IVY
c.1908–32 Ivy motorcycles were built by bicycle maker S. A. Newman Ltd in Birmingham. The early motorcycles had JAP and Precision engines. After World War I Ivy produced its own single-cylinder two-stroke engines of 225cc to 348cc. Later it reverted to proprietary power units.

IXION
c.1910–23 Built in Birmingham, Ixion bikes had proprietary engines including JAP, Villiers, Precision, and Peco.

IXION
1929–30 New Hudson briefly revived the Ixion name and attached it to an existing 249cc side-valve machine.

JAMES p.111
1902 Birmingham bicycle maker that used Minerva and FN engines to make its first motorcycles. A radical new machine appeared in 1908, which used drum brakes and had hub-centre steering and a one-sided chassis. It used James' own 523cc engine. Conventional machines followed; these used James' own lightweight two-stroke, 500cc side-valve V-twin, and 600cc side-valve single-cylinder engines.
1922 Full-scale production resumed during the 1920s. James built a range of single-cylinder and V-twin machines from 250cc to 750cc with side-valve and overhead-valve engines. Villiers two-stroke lightweights were also added after the Baker marque was taken over in 1930. By the mid-1930s only Villiers-engined two-strokes were made. After World War II James focused on the production of utility machines and off-road motorcycles using Villiers engines.
1951 The company was taken over by AMC, which also owned the Francis-Barnett marque. The products of the two brands became increasingly similar.
1966 Lack of identity and problems with the AMC two-stroke engine caused the company problems, but it was finally finished by the collapse of AMC.

JAP
1903–08 J. A. Prestwich produced complete motorcycles for a short time before concentrating on making engines. **1932–39** JAP introduced its own frames for its successful speedway engines.

JD
c.1920–26 Built by the Bowden Wire Co., this was a 116cc clip-on engine also available attached to a reinforced bicycle chassis (ladies' or gents' model).

JEHU
1901–c.1910 The 1903 London-built Jehu motorcycle was equipped with chain drive and its own clutch. It used Minerva and MMC engines.

JES
1913–24 J. E. Smith and Co. of Gloucester made a 116cc atmospheric-inlet-valve clip-on engine that mounted vertically in the bicycle frame. The rear wheel was driven by belt. Complete motorcycles with 169cc two-stroke engines were introduced from 1922. A JES four-speed gearbox and chain drive were optional. In 1924 production was taken over by Connaught and moved to Birmingham. A conventional machine with a 348cc Blackburne engine was sold with the JES badge.

JESMOND
1902–03 Jesmond produced typical pioneer machines that used Fafnir engines. They were made in Newcastle and preceded the Dene marque (see p.218). (Jesmond Dene is a park in the Newcastle suburbs.)

JH
c.1913–15 James Howarth of Oldham built a range of machines powered by Villiers, JAP, and MAG engines.

JNU
1920–22 The JNU was a Dalm-engined 318cc two-stroke with an open frame.

JOYBIKE
1958–60 Built by H. V. Powell (Cycles) in Birmingham, Joybikes were offered as mopeds or "scooterettes" with 49cc Trojan or 79cc JAP two-stroke engines.

JP IMPREGNABLE
c.1912–14 London motorcycle accessory supplier John Piggot Ltd also sold these 300cc TDC-engined machines, which were made elsewhere.

JUCKES
1902–25 T. C. Juckes and his company, The Efficient Engineering and Motor Co., built motorcycles intermittently from 1902. From the early 1920s a 274cc two-stroke was offered. In 1924 a 347cc overhead-valve machine with a four-speed gearbox and diagonally braced frame was introduced.

JUNO
1904 Built by the London Machinists Co. using a vertically mounted 353cc atmospheric-inlet-valve Fafnir engine and belt final drive. **1914–16** The marque was reintroduced by the same company with a typical belt-driven Villiers-engined lightweight; a V-twin JAP-engined machine was offered in 1916.

JUPP
1921–24 A scooter-type machine that used a 269cc Villiers two-stroke engine. It had large mudguards and bucket seats. A later model used a 147cc Villiers engine in a more conventional frame.

KEMPTON
1921–22 Lightweight motorcycles and scooters built by William Hooper using the 124cc ABC Skootamota engine. Hooper was also responsible for the prototype Superb Four.

KENILWORTH
1919–24 This scooter-type machine was developed by a Captain G. Smith-Clarke. Production models used a 142cc overhead-valve Norman engine mounted at the front of the tubular frame.

KERRY
1902–14 Marque name for machines sold by the East London Rubber Company. The first Kerry bikes had loop frames with an inclined single-cylinder engine and belt drive. Kelecom and FN engines were used and it is probable that the complete machines were built in Belgium. The introduction of a 308cc chain-driven machine in 1907 began an association with Abingdon that resulted in Kerry-Abingdon machines being produced. **1960–66** After nearly 50 years, Kerry re-entered the motorcycle market with a range of Italian-built mopeds.

KESTREL
c.1903 Early make that used Minerva and possibly other proprietary engines.

KIEFT
1955–57 German Hercules scooters sold under the name of its importer in the U.K., where the Hercules trademark was owned by Raleigh bicycles. At other times the Prior name was used.

KING
1901–07 King built tricycles and belt-driven machines with DeDion, Minerva, MMC, and DAW engines.

KINGSBURY
1919–23 During the first British scooter boom the Kingsbury Aviation Co. built a small-wheeled stand-up scooter with a 2.25hp two-stroke engine. It also produced orthodox motorcycles with 349cc and 254cc two-stroke engines.

KINGSWAY
1921–23 Built in Coventry with a 269cc Arden two-stroke engine and belt drive.

KUMFURT
1914–16 Conventional machines offered with Villiers, Vitesse, Precision, or JAP engines. They had extensive mudguards and luggage racks, patent hammock footboards, and a detachable feather pad on the seat – hence the name.

KYNOCH
1903–04 A Birmingham armaments company that built chain-driven singles with the inclined cylinder mounted in place of the frame downtube. **1911–13** The company returned with conventional side-valve JAP-engined single-cylinder and V-twin machines.

LAGONDA
1902–05 More famous as a manufacturer of quality cars, Lagonda built a few motorcycles with its own engines. A 2.75hp model of 1903 had the inclined engine mounted underneath the downtube of a bicycle-style frame.

LAKE & ELLIOT
c.1904–05 Built a motorcycle using its own 3hp engine with mechanical valves.

LEA FRANCIS
1912–24 Bicycle and car maker that also built high-quality V-twin motorcycles with MAG and JAP engines.

LEONARD
1903–06 Limited production using Minerva, MCC, and Fafnir engines in bicycle-style and loop frames.

LETHBRIDGE
c.1923 Offered a 293cc two-stroke and a Blackburne-engined 350cc four-stroke.

LEVIS
1911 The first Levis machines produced by Bob Newey and the Butterfield brothers were 211cc two-strokes. Levis

Mr Frears of Leicester on his single-speed 211cc Levis two-stroke, c.1914

continued to develop the two-stroke engine, increasing its capacity to 247cc. The "Six-port" model of 1929/30 was the first to use transfer ports in the piston skirt to cool the underside of the piston. Levis also achieved competition success in racing and trials with the small-capacity machines.

1927 Levis introduced its first four-stroke, an overhead-valve 346cc single. Later four-stroke machines included the overhead-camshaft 247cc single of 1933, and larger capacity 498cc and 592cc overhead-valve singles. It continued with good-quality, utilitarian two-strokes.
1939 With the onset of war, Levis switched to making compressors.

LGC
1926–31 The Leonard Gundle Motor Co. built small numbers of Villiers- and JAP-engined motorcycles as well as commercial three-wheelers.

LINCOLN-ELK
c.1902–15 These bikes were built in Lincoln by James Kirby, originally with proprietary engines but soon with Kirby's own power units. A 770cc V-twin was introduced around 1913.
1919–26 Production resumed after the war with a range of conventional bikes using the company's own side-valve 349cc and 597cc single-cylinder, and 770cc 50° V-twin engines. Final drive was by belt.

LITTLE GIANT
1913–15 Built in Uxbridge, these lightweights used Precision 225cc two-stroke and 199cc side-valve engines.

LLOYD
1902–03 Built by W. A. Lloyd's Cycle Fittings Ltd in Birmingham using the company's own 2hp engine. W. A. Lloyd had been involved with W. J. Lloyd at the Quadrant bicycle company. The Villiers-engined Dreadnought was made by W. A. Lloyd from 1915 to 1923.

LLOYD THOMAS
c.1905–10 A Welsh marque that used proprietary engines including Minerva and Antoine power units.

LMC
1907–23 Lloyd Motor Engineering Co. was formed by W. J. Lloyd after he split from Quadrant in 1907. Prior to World War I it produced 499cc and 596cc side-valve singles with belt drive. In 1909 it also produced a parallel twin. Post-war LMC built side-valve V-twins of 832cc to 960cc equipped with three-speed Sturmey-Archer gearboxes.

LONDON
c.1904 These were built by Rex Patents, using its own vertically mounted 3.5hp side-valve engine.

Michael McEvoy and designer George Patchett with a JAP-engined V-twin, 1926

LUGTON
c.1912–14 Limited production of single-cylinder proprietary-engined four-strokes.

MABON
c.1904–05 Built in London, Mabon bikes used proprietary engines mounted vertically in bicycle-type frames.

MACKLUM
1920–22 Early small-wheeled scooters designed by F. MacCallum and built by Alfred Wiseman, maker of the Verus (see p.231). The Macklum used a 292cc Union two-stroke engine mounted above the chain-driven front wheel.

MAJESTIC
1933 A de luxe model produced by OK Supreme using 250cc, 350cc, and 500cc Ajax single-cylinder overhead-valve engines. The engines were constructed by the Stevens brothers after they had sold their AJS company to the Matchless marque (see right).

MARLOE
1920–22 Marloe used Precision two-stroke or Blackburne single-cylinder four-stroke engines. A ladies' model was offered alongside the conventional diamond-framed machine.

MARS
1921–25 Coventry-based Mars used Villiers, JAP, Bradshaw, and Barr & Stroud engines. It was one of the first British firms to use saddle tanks.

MARSEEL
1920–21 An early, short-lived scooter that had a single-cylinder 232cc two-stroke engine with a horizontal cylinder mounted underneath the footboards.

MARTIN
1911–22 Built by H. Martin & Co. of Croydon using Precision and JAP engines of 198cc to 498cc, including V-twins in conventional diamond-pattern frames. Racing machines were also produced and used at Brooklands and the TT by Harry Martin and other riders.

MARTIN-COMERFORD
c.1933–57 Specialized speedway machines originally designed by George Wallis. Subsequently Thames-Ditton dealer Comerfords took up the design. The machines also appeared as Martin-Rudge and Martin-JAP.

MARTINSHAW
1923–26 Built in Twickenham in limited numbers using side-valve and overhead-valve Blackburne engines of 348cc to 998cc.

MARTINSYDE
1919 Helmuth MARTIN and George HandaSYDE's aircraft company, like many others, diversified after World War I. The new motorcycle used its own 678cc exhaust-over-inlet 50° V-twin. This was followed by a 738cc version in 1922. A 346cc single was added but could not save the company.
1923–25 Bat (see p.214) bought the name and briefly continued production.

MASON & BROWN
1904–c.1908 This was a bicycle-style machine with a 2hp or 3hp engine mounted horizontally above the pedals. Final drive was by belt. Conventional cooling fins were replaced by a cylindrical metal jacket with holes in the front end. It used a primitive fuel-injection system.

MASSEY-ARRAN
1920–24 Built in small numbers by E. J. Massey using proprietary engines of 172cc to 490cc made by Villiers, JAP, Blackburne, and Bradshaw. Competition machines were also produced.

MATADOR
1922–27 Built by Bert Houlding in Preston, Lancashire, Matador machines had a diamond frame with Blackburne 350cc side-valve and overhead-valve engines. The oil-cooled 349cc Bradshaw engine was also used. Matador also produced Toreador machines.

MATCHLESS 🏍 pp.123–25
1899 H. Collier & Sons built its first motorcycles using MMC 2.75hp engines in bicycle-style frames. It soon adopted V-twin JAP engines for road bikes and successful racers.
1912 Matchless began to make its own 488cc single-cylinder engines. It adopted the inlet-over-exhaust 1000cc MAG V-twin for use in a sidecar machine. Matchless' own V-twin and single-cylinder side-valve and overhead-valve engines were soon available in sizes from 250cc to 990cc. There was also a 350cc overhead-camshaft model.
1930 A novel but unsuccessful 400cc V-twin was introduced, followed by a 593cc overhead-camshaft V4.
1931 The Wolverhampton AJS company was bought and production transferred to London. This association formed the basis of Associated Motor Cycles (see AMC, p.213); which later incorporated Norton, James, and Francis-Barnett.
1948 A new 500cc parallel twin was built with swingarm rear suspension. Capacity was later enlarged to 650cc. Single-cylinder machines based on the earlier 350cc and 500cc models were also produced and new 250cc and 350cc singles appeared in 1958.
1966 AMC collapsed; it was resurrected as Norton Villiers Ltd. The Norton name took precedence in the new company. By 1969 the Matchless had disappeared.
1987 The name was revived briefly on a single-cylinder machine that used a Rotax 500cc overhead-camshaft engine.

MCEVOY
1925–29 A range of machines was built in Derby by Michael McEvoy, financed by Cecil Birkin, and designed by George Patchett. They had proprietary engines from 172cc Villiers two-strokes to 998cc Anzani V-twins. There were also JAP and Blackburne four-stroke singles and V-twins including competition machines.

MCKECHNIE
1921–22 Built in small numbers by a Colonel McKechnie, the McKechnie used a 688cc Coventry-Victor flat-twin engine in a weird sprung frame.

MCKENZIE
1921–25 Lightweight machines that used proprietary two-stroke engines of 147cc and 169cc with belt final drive, available in ladies' and gents' frames.

MEAD
1911–16 Built in Liverpool, the 1914 lightweight model used a 170cc Precision four-stroke engine with two-speed gear and belt final drive in a diamond frame.

MERCURY
c.1937–39 Just five of these unusual Scott-engined Duralumin-framed touring machines were built.

MERCURY
1956–59 Bicycle company that produced lightweight motorcycles and scooters using 98cc Villiers engines. It also built the 49cc Mercury Mercette.

METRO
1912–18 These belt-driven lightweights used Metro's own 269cc two-stroke engines. The company merged with Tyler in 1919 to make Metro-Tyler motorcycles (see below).

METRO-TYLER
1919–23 The Tyler Apparatus Co. (see p.231) took over Metro (see above) in 1919 and the two names were merged. Production of belt-driven 269cc two-strokes continued. In 1922/23 a 696cc V-twin was also listed.

MIDGET BICAR
c.1904–12 Designed and built by J. T. Brown, the machine used pressed-steel frame construction and belt drive with a variable pulley gear. It used proprietary engines including 500cc and 600cc Precisions. The Midget Bicar was also built under licence in the U.S.

MILLIONMOBILE
c.1902–03 Early models were powered bicycles with a 1.5hp engine over the front wheel or behind the steering head. In 1903 a loop-framed motorcycle with a 3.25hp Aster engine was produced.

MOHAWK
c.1903 A bicycle manufacturer that built motorcycles using 2.25hp and 3hp engines mounted vertically in new Werner-style frames.
1920–25 Mohawk made diamond-framed bikes using 269cc Villiers two-stroke, 499cc AKD side-valve single-cylinder, and 293cc and 346cc JAP engines. It also offered the American Economic 154cc two-stroke flat-twin clip-on engine on one of its bicycles.

MONARCH
c.1919–21 R. Walker & Son used the Monarch name on 269cc Villiers-engined and 292cc JAP-engined bikes. Walker took over the Bayliss Thomas Excelsior marque (see p.219) in 1919 and the Monarch name was soon dropped.

MONOPOLE
1902 Monopole exhibited a motorized bicycle, equipped with an inclined engine that mounted below the downtube, at the Stanley Show.
1911–27 Monopole re-entered the market with Precision-engined machines. It later produced a range of models using proprietary engines supplied by Villiers and JAP from 147cc two-strokes to a 676cc V-twin.

MONTGOMERY
c.1902 William Montgomery began building limited numbers of motorcycles using Fafnir and FN engines.
1911–39 After a move to Coventry, motorcycle and sidecar production resumed. Before World War I it built a 688cc side-valve flat twin. Post-war production resumed in 1922, using proprietary engines supplied by JAP, Anzani, Bradshaw, and Villiers. P&P motorcycles were also built at the Montgomery works. A fire interrupted production in 1925. New machines were introduced for 1926 with Villiers and JAP engines, and saddle tanks.

MOONBEAM
1920 The Moonbeam was a belt-driven lightweight with a Villiers 269cc engine.

MORRIS
c.1902–05 William Morris was later famous as a car manufacturer. His early motorcycles had DeDion and MMC engines.

MORRIS-WARNE
1921–22 These 247cc two-stroke singles were made in London. Two models were offered.

MORTON-ADAM
1923–26 The first machine sold under the Morton-Adam marque was a 246cc two-stroke single with the company's own engine. In 1924 a 246cc overhead-camshaft machine was introduced.

MOTORPED
c.1920–22 A complete machine incorporating a Simplex 105cc two-stroke engine on a bicycle frame.

MOUNTAINEER
1920–24 Yorkshire-built lightweight machines with 269cc two-stroke engines with belt drive and diamond frames.

MPH
1920–24 The MPH was a diamond-framed belt-driven lightweight powered by a Wall 269cc two-stroke engine.

NER-A-CAR   p.140
1921–26 Developed in the U.S. by Carl A. Neracher, the Ner-a-Car was also built in England by the Sheffield Simplex company. The first British-made Ner-a-Cars used the same 211cc two-stroke engine and variable-ratio friction drive as the U.S. version. Capacity of the engine was increased to 285cc and for 1925 a 348cc Blackburne side-valve single-cylinder engine and three-speed Sturmey-Archer gearbox were offered in an attempt to improve performance.

NEW BOWDON
1902–03 Built by H. Cragg & Sons, this machine had a 2hp Simms engine mounted in front of the rear wheel.

NEW COMET
c.1905–28 The New Comet was built by bicycle fittings manufacturer A. H. Haden, who also used his own name on some early machines. By 1910 a range of 2.5hp, 3hp, and 3.5hp machines was made. Precision and water-cooled Green-Precision engines were used in some machines before World War I. After, production focused on two-stroke machines with 147cc, 269cc, and 292cc engines supplied by Peco, Villiers, and Climax.

NEW COULSON
1923–24 Formerly the Coulson-B (see p.217), the name changed after the make was taken over by H. R. Backhouse & Co. It used proprietary engines of 269cc to 498cc supplied by Liberty, Blackburne, and Bradshaw. The unique leaf-sprung frame was still optional.

NEW COURIER
1919–23 These were cheap versions of Olympic machines (see p.226).

NEW ERA
c.1920–22 Built in Liverpool using 318cc single-cylinder two-stroke engines supplied by Dalm and 499cc Blackburne four-stroke singles.

NEW GERRARD
1922–40 Built in Edinburgh and designed by Jock Porter, who won TT races in 1923 and 1924 for the marque. During the sales boom that followed, production was sub-contracted to the Campion firm until 1927. Blackburne engines were used in most early machines though some had JAP and the Scottish-built Barr & Stroud sleeve-valve single-cylinder power unit. From 1933 a single model using an 346cc overhead-valve JAP engine was listed.

NEW HENLEY
1926–30 New name for the Henley marque (see p.221) after it was taken over by J. Crump. A 348cc overhead-valve MAG-engined model appeared in 1926. Other models continued to use JAP and Blackburne single-cylinder and V-twin engines of up to 748cc. In the final year 172cc and 247cc Villiers-engined two-strokes were also offered.

NEW HUDSON
c.1903 New Hudson was an established bicycle company whose first motorcycles were Minerva-engined bicycles.
1910 Proper production began using JAP engines. The following year it started to use its own 499cc side-valve single-cylinder engine. A 350cc single and a 700cc side-valve V-twin followed. In 1914 a 211cc two-stroke based on the Levis design was added. Overhead-valve models were made from the mid-1920s.
1931 New 350cc and 500cc overhead-valve and side-valve sloping singles were introduced.
1933 Motorcycle manufacturing ended and production switched to suspension and brake components for Girling.
1939 A lightweight autocycle with a 98cc Villiers engine was introduced. It offered economic and popular wartime transport. The manufacturing rights were sold to BSA, which built an updated model until 1958.

NEW IMPERIAL   p.141
1901 The first New Imperial motorcycle had an 500cc engine mounted above the front wheel. It failed to sell.
1910 Production restarted. The first machine used a 292cc JAP side-valve engine. The company continued to use single-cylinder and V-twin engines supplied by JAP into the late 1920s. Successful racing machines were also developed.
1925 It began to build its own engines, which were mainly 250cc to 500cc four-stroke singles.
1931 A 146cc overhead-valve unit-construction lightweight was introduced, followed by advanced unit-construction overhead-valve singles. Cantilever rear suspension was offered. A 500cc 60° V-twin racer set records in 1934.
1938 The company was sold to Jack Sangster, owner of Ariel and Triumph, but with the onset of war in 1939 production stopped.

NEW KNIGHT
c.1923–27 Conventional machines built in small quantities in Bedford by Messrs Holloway and Knight. They used 147cc and 247cc Villiers two-stroke and JAP 292cc and 343cc engines.

NEWMOUNT
1929–33 These were German Zündapp machines assembled in Coventry with a different tank badge. Some models used Python 348cc and 498cc four-valve single-cylinder engines, but the 198cc, 248cc, and 298cc models used Zündapp two-stroke engines.

Mrs O. Miller on a 1930s Ariel single (see p.213)

NEW PARAGON

c.1922–23 Formerly known as the Paragon, the bikes used the company's own two-stroke engines. The one model listed for 1922/23 was a 358cc single.

NEW RYDER

1914–22 These Birmingham-made bikes used 269cc Villiers and Peco two-stroke engines. A 293cc JAP-engined four-stroke was offered for 1916.

NEW SCALE

1919–25 Known from 1913 to 1919 as the Scale, these machines reappeared in 1920 as the New Scale. They used Precision 348cc two-stroke and 499cc side-valve Blackburne engines; 350cc four-strokes using JAP, Bradshaw, and Blackburne engines were also built. The company was absorbed by Dot (p.218).

NEWTON

1920–22 Inexpensive belt-driven machines with 269cc Villiers engines.

NICKSON

1920–26 J. Nickson of Preston built machines using Blackburne 348cc to 546cc four-stroke singles, and the Bradshaw 346cc oil-cooled overhead-valve single. The company also produced the open-framed, 318cc Dalm-engined JNU two-stroke.

NLG

1905–12 North London Garages built orthodox motorcycles using JAP 499cc single and 770cc V-twin engines. Track racing versions were very successful.

NOBLE

c.1901–06 Noble used its own engines with mechanical inlet valves, although early machines may have used DeDion, MMC, Minerva, and Coronet engines. From 1904 it had a Chater-Lea frame that followed the "new" Werner layout.

NOBLE-PRECISION

1912 Built by Alfred Noble & Co., this diamond-framed belt-driven machine used a 499cc side-valve Precision engine.

NORBRECK

1921–24 Made by D. H. Valentine, using Villiers and Arden two-stroke engines, although some may have had Blackburne four-stroke engines.

NORMAN

c.1937 Kent bicycle maker that first built a 98cc Villiers-engined autocycle called the Mobyk.
1948 Models included the autocycle and motorcycles of 98cc to 249cc. These included off-road competition models. All used Villiers engines except for the short-lived 1956 Uni-twin, which used a 242cc British Anzani engine.
1958 Norman bought the rights to make a Sachs-engined 49cc moped from the defunct German marque Achilles, which was sold as the Norman Lido.
1963 Production stopped, the company having been sold to Raleigh in 1961.

NORTON   pp.142–47

1902 James Lansdowne Norton supplied cycle components, including frames for Clément-Garrard motorbicycles. A Clément-engined Norton machine soon followed. Other machines with Moto-Rêve and Peugeot engines followed. Rem Fowler won the 1907 TT on a Peugeot V-twin engined model. It was the first of many major racing successes for Norton.
1908 Norton began to make its own 490cc side-valve singles, which remained in production for over 40 years. From 1922 overhead-valve singles were built.
1927 Overhead-camshaft racing machines were introduced. These were very successful and gradually evolved into the famous Manx.
1948 A new 497cc overhead-valve parallel twin was built to challenge the Triumph Speed Twin. This engine was gradually enlarged to 828cc.
1950 The "featherbed" frame was introduced on racing machines, then on the road-going singles and twins.
1952 Norton was absorbed by AMC (see p.213). Production moved to the Matchless factory. When AMC collapsed in 1966 the group amalgamated with the Villiers engine company, reappearing as Norton Villiers.
1967 The Commando was launched. It used a 745cc (later 828cc) version of Norton's ageing twin-cylinder engine mounted in a new frame that isolated the engine and vastly reduced vibration.
1973 Norton Villiers took over the ailing BSA-Triumph group and became Norton Villiers Triumph (NVT). The new company suffered serious financial and labour problems. An Italian-engined step-thru moped appeared in 1976.
1977 NVT collapsed.
1983 The Norton name re-emerged on a Wankel-engined machine that was sold to the British Police. From 1988 the Wankel was available to the public. Racing versions were very successful. The company has changed hands several times since 1992; motorcycle sales were never sufficient to make it viable.

NUT

1912 The initials NuT referred to the home of the marque in Newcastle-upon-Tyne. Some early machines used Moto-Rêve engines but most were equipped with JAP V-twin engines of 350cc to 1000cc. Founder Hugh Mason rode a JAP-engined 350 to victory in the 1913 Junior TT. Production restarted after World War I, concentrating on V-twins of up to 750cc with JAP and its own engines. There was also a utility model with a 172cc Villiers engine.
1933 Financial problems had often interrupted production in the 1920s and the firm had a succession of owners. The slump finally killed it.

NVT See Norton (left).

NYE

1910 Conventional machines with JAP and Precision engines sold by a London motorcycle dealer of the same name.

OEC   p.152

c.1901 The Osborn Engineering Co. made its first machines using Minerva engines around 1901, but few were built.
1922 OEC motorcycles appeared. They were identical to the Blackburne bikes that disappeared at the same time. OEC had been making the Blackburne motorcycles since at least 1920. Now the bikes were OECs, but they still had Blackburne engines, although other power units were also used. A racing model used the overhead-camshaft 350cc Blackburne engine and some road bikes had the oil-cooled Bradshaw 350cc power unit. Frames were also built for speed record attempts.
1927 The first of the novel duplex-steered machines appeared. Wags dubbed the company "Odd Engineering Contraptions". A range of both bizarre and conventional machines using JAP, Villiers, Blackburne, Matchless, and Python engines of 147cc to 998cc followed. OEC would build almost anything that a client specified. Production was halted by the war.
1949 Production resumed with conventional 122cc and 197cc Villiers-engined lightweights. One model used the 250cc side-valve Brockhouse engine.
1954 Production finally ended.

OGSTON

1914–16 Ogston took over production of the four-cylinder Wilkinson-TMC at the outbreak of World War I.

OK (OK SUPREME)   p.153

1899 Bicycle maker Humphries & Dawes began making powered two-wheelers with DeDion, Minerva, JAP, and Precision engines. The most successful pre-war model used a 200cc inlet-over-exhaust engine supplied by NSU. Post-war, OK made lightweight machines powered by Villiers and Union two-stroke engines of 246cc, 269cc, and 292cc. These were sold under the OK Junior name. JAP-, Blackburne-, and Bradshaw-powered four-strokes were added to the range from 1923.
1926 Dawes left the company while Humphries tried to take OK upmarket. He changed the name to OK Supreme.
1927 Humphries hired former HRD designer E. J. Massey. He also bought the

Hugh Mason with his JAP-engined NuT motorcycle after winning the 1913 Junior TT

remains of the bankrupt HRD marque (see p.221) before selling it to Phillip Vincent. New models with OK's 250cc overhead-camshaft engines were devised but the JAP-engined bikes were more popular.
1939 Production ended but a few JAP-engined grass trackers arrived in 1946.

OLIVOS
1920–21 Spring frame machines with side-valve Blackburne 496cc engines.

OLYMPIC
1902–23 Built by F. H. Parkyn, originally with MMC and Minerva engines. Proper production started in 1919 with Verus 269cc two-stroke engines in straight-tube frames; Orbit 261cc engines were used in 1920. Soon available with Villiers, JAP, and Blackburne engines. Cheaper models were sold under the New Courier name.

OMC
1930 The OMC was a 172cc Villiers-engined machine with a bolt-up frame.

OMEGA
1909 Lightweights with 1.75hp engines in bicycle-style frames.

OMEGA
1913–16 Built by W. J. Green, the first Omegas had 345cc two-stroke Omega engines. A side-valve 292cc JAP-engined bike was introduced for 1916, but war-time restrictions soon ended production.
1919–27 Post-war production began with the 292cc JAP and the 345 two-stroke. A 170cc two-stroke with two-speed gear and belt final drive followed. Various proprietary engines were used.

ONAWAY
c.1905–08 Onaway used Kelecom V-twin or Bercley parallel-twin engines.

ORBIT
1913–24 Proper production began in 1919 with a two-stroke Orbit-engined bike. Later models also had JAP, Levis, Bradshaw, and MAG engines.

ORMONDE
c.1900–05 Built a 3hp atmospheric-inlet-valve belt-driven machine with a Kelecom engine. The frame was supplied by Taylor-Gue, who in 1905 bought the Kelecom and Ormonde interests and produced machines as Veloce. This evolved into the Velocette (see p.231).

ORTONA
1904–06 Built a 3.5hp atmospheric-inlet-valve single with a long wheelbase and a vertically mounted engine.

OSBORNE
1910–11 Osborne used single-cylinder and V-twin engines. Novelties included a four-speed belt pulley and a facility to tension the drive belt while in motion.

OSMOND
1902 Osmond exhibited motorcycles at the Stanley Show, but soon reverted to bicycle production. The company was taken over by James (see p.221) in 1911.
1920 The motorcycles reappeared. An open-framed 103cc two-stroke was built. In 1923 an orthodox motorcycle with a 239cc two-stroke engine was introduced.
1926 The marque name was dropped.

OVERSEAS
1913–23 Rugged export machines built by W. J. Lloyd, who also made LMC bikes (see p.223). They used the same 499cc side-valve singles and 832cc and 960cc side-valve 50° V-twins as LMC.

PACER
1914–15 Lightweights built in Guernsey with JES 116cc inlet-over-exhaust engines.

PACKMAN & POPPE See P&P (right).

PANTHER (P&M)   p.154
1900 Joah Phelon built his first prototype motorbike. The engine's inclined cylinder was used in place of a front downtube, becoming one of the longest-lasting motorcycle designs. Chain drive was used. The design was licenced to Humber (see p.221), which produced it under its own name from 1902 to 1905. Phelon entered a partnership with Richard Moore in 1904, for proper production to start. The P&M kept improving until the 1960s. The engine grew to 555cc; later there were 598cc and 645cc models. A 770cc 90° V-twin was developed before the war but never went into production.
1923 The Panther name was adopted from 1923, when Granville Bradshaw redesigned the bike using overhead valves.
1927 Bradshaw designed a new 250cc transverse unit-construction V-twin – the Panthette. It did not sell. Villiers-engined 147cc to 247cc lightweights followed.
1932 Overhead-valve 250cc and 350cc singles appeared. These economy bikes, called Red Panthers, were sold cheaply by a London dealer. Big-single production continued with detail changes. After the war, 197cc to 249cc Villiers-engined bikes reappeared alongside redesigned 250cc and 350cc singles. The big single, popular with sidecar drivers, grew to 645cc. Production ended in 1967.

PARAGON
1914–23 Two-stroke singles, with belt final drive and conventional diamond frames, built by Portaway-Cooper. Later known as New Paragon (see p.225).

PARAMOUNT-DUO See FEW-Paramount (p.219).

PARKYN
1902–04 Parkyn used Minerva engines with mechanical valves in a strong frame. Later became Olympic (see left).

PAX
1920–23 Blackburne 348cc and 499cc side-valve engines in diamond frames.

PEARSON
c.1903–04 Built in Southsea, Hampshire, with French-made 3hp Aster engines.

PEARSON & COX
1912–14 A steam-powered machine with a kerosene-fired boiler. The "engine" was mounted under the seat, driving the rear wheel by belt. The boiler was under the front downtube and the kerosene tank fitted into the triangle of the frame. Some machines used the Dawn name.

PEBOK
c.1903–09 Motorcycles with Pebok's own 2.25hp to 3.5hp atmospheric-inlet-valve engines, loop frame, and belt drive.

PECO
c.1913–15 PEarson & COle built 346cc single-cylinder two-stroke engines as well as a limited number of complete bikes.

PEERLESS See Bradbury (p.215).

PENNINGTON
1897 American E. J. Pennington's design had twin cylinders behind the rear wheel; connecting rods operated directly onto the rear axle. He sold the rights to H. J. Lawson who built two prototypes at his Humber (see p.221) works, proving the design's inadequacy.

PERKS & BIRCH   p.154
1899–1900 The original motorwheel was built by Edwin Perks and John North Birch (see Birch p.215). It was a 222cc atmospheric-inlet-valve engine with magneto and fuel tank mounted in a gear-driven wheel. The self-contained unit could be attached to any suitable bicycle in place of either wheel. In 1900, the rights were sold to Singer (see p.229).

PETERS
1921–25 Unusual machine with front and rear suspension that used the fuel tank as a stressed frame member. It used Peters' own 347cc two-stroke engines, and later proprietary power units.

PHILLIPS
1953–65 Mopeds sold by the Raleigh group; mainly re-badged imports.

PHOENIX
1900–08 Pioneering machines by J. V. Hooydonk. Advanced features included two-speed gearboxes, clutches, and spray carburettors.

PHOENIX
1956–64 These 147cc to 322cc Villiers-engined scooters were built in London by Ernie Barrett. He also produced and rode Phoenix-JAP racing machines.

PIATTI
1954–58 Scooter designed by Vincenzo Piatti and built by Britax. The engine and wheels were hidden beneath a stressed skin structure. Also built in Belgium, it looked like a ride-on vacuum cleaner.

PILOT
1910–16 Accessory and frame maker that built complete machines. Early models used JAP and Sarolea engines but later also Precision and Dalm. It also produced a sprung telescopic fork.

PMC
c.1909–15 Premier Motor Co. built the three-wheeled Premier Motorette before starting motorbike production. Unable to use the Premier name, its bikes had PMC, Premo, Rex-JAP, and Warwick badges.

PORTLAND
1910–11 Made for and sold exclusively by Maudes Motor Mart, London, these bikes used JAP and Peugeot engines.
1920 A 2.75hp two-stroke Arden-engined belt-driven machine was offered.

POUNCY
1930–36 Built in Dorchester, Dorset, with 147cc to 346cc Villiers engines.

POWELL
1921–26 Powell used 546cc side-valve Blackburne engines before switching to its own 169cc to 245cc two-strokes.

POWERFUL
c.1903–06 Coventry-built machines with Buchet and other proprietary engines in bicycle-style frames.

P&P
1922 Erling Poppe and Gilmour Packman built their first prototype machine with a White & Poppe (Erling's father) two-stroke engine. Production machines used JAP and Barr & Stroud engines. Frames had straight tubes from the headstock to the live rear axle. By the mid-1920s manufacturing was sub-contracted to Montgomery (see p.224).
1925 Gilmour Packman was killed in a brawl with an employee, and a fire at the Montgomery factory ended production. Poppe sold to John Wooler in 1926, and limited production continued in London.
1930 Production ceased. Poppe later designed the Sunbeam S7 for the BSA group (see p.215).

PRECISION
1912–19 Frank Baker's firm made its first bike engine in 1910, a 499cc side-valve single. By 1912 it was supplying single-cylinders and V-twins of 293cc to 760cc to much of the British industry. From 1912 it built complete motorbikes. It became involved with giant industrial group Beardmore in 1915, and in 1919 Beardmore-Precision machines appeared.

PREMIER
1908 The Premier Cycle Co. of Coventry joined the motorcycle market with a White & Poppe-engined single-cylinder 427cc side-valve machine.
1910 It began to use its own 499cc side-valve engines. A German subsidiary was established and moved to Czechoslovakia three years later. Czech production lasted until 1933 (see p.302).
1911 A 246cc model was introduced. The next year a 548cc 90° V-twin was added to the range. A 322cc two-stroke twin and a 998cc four-stroke V-twin were launched in 1914 but few were built before World War I. Around this time the name changed to Coventry-Premier.
c.1916 During the war some 499cc machines were sold to the military but production did not resume after the war.

PREMO
1909 Two-stroke 345cc single built by PREmier MOtor Co. (PMC) of Coventry.

PRIDE & CLARKE
1939 This big London dealer briefly sold 98cc and 122cc Villiers-engined lightweights under its own name.

PRINCEPS
1902–07 Built by J. E. Hutton, early machines were powered bicycles with Princeps' own 1.75hp engines above the downtube in an inclined position. Later, more powerful engines included single-cylinder and V-twin designs.

PRIOR
c.1936 German Hercules machines (see p.240) were sold as Priors in the U.K. The Sachs-, Villiers-, and JAP-engined bikes were exhibited at the 1936 Olympia Show. From 1955 to 1957 Hercules bikes were sold in Britain under the Kieft name.
1957–60 The Prior name was reintroduced after a change of importer.

PRIORY
1919–26 Two-stroke 147cc to 292cc bikes with engines by Union, Arden, and Villiers. Also a JAP 292cc four-stroke.

PROGRESS
1901–08 An early user of the loop frame layout. It had Forman, Simms, and other proprietary engines.

P&S
1919–21 A utilitarian 292cc side-valve belt-driven JAP-engined diamond-framed bike built by Pearson & Sopwith.

PULLIN-GROOM
1920–25 Designed by Cyril Pullin and, like his later Ascot-Pullin machine (see p.213), well ahead of its time, the Pullin-Groom had a pressed-steel step-thru frame and swingarm rear suspension. The 216cc (later 350cc) horizontally mounted two-stroke engine was hidden within the frame. A two-speed gearbox was attached and final drive was by enclosed chain.

PV
1910–25 Produced proprietary-engined bikes – from 996cc JAP V-twins to 246cc Villiers two-strokes – with its own frames.

QUADRANT
1901 The first Quadrant motorcycle – the Autocyclette – had a 211cc Minerva engine in a bicycle frame. Began making 250cc atmospheric-inlet-valve engines in 1903; later, 450cc and 500cc singles.
1907 W. J. Lloyd left Quadrant to create LMC (see p.223). His partner, Thomas Silver, also left to form Silver (see p.229), rejoining soon after. He left and returned yet again two years later. Before the war, V-twins of up to 1129cc appeared.
1918–28 Post-war production consisted of 490cc to 780cc singles. Quadrant went into decline, finally disappearing in 1928.

QUASAR 🏍 p.157
1977–85 The Quasar was a weird bike with a roof. The engine came from a 750 Reliant car and the rider sat low with his feet forward. The Phasar, a later version, had a six-cylinder Kawasaki engine.

RADCO
1913 E. A. RADnall & CO. began making 211cc, later 247cc, two-strokes using its own engines.
1926–30 Made JAP 246cc, 293cc, and 490cc four-strokes. After 1930 Radnall reverted to two-strokes, making 147cc and 196cc Villiers-engined bikes alongside its own 247cc two-strokes.
1954–56 Radnall made a conventional 98cc Villiers-engined lightweight.
1966 A 75cc minibike with a Villiers lawnmower engine was produced.

RAGLAN
1903 Bicycle maker Raglan first exhibited forecars and 2.75hp motorcycles.
c.1909–13 New machines used 292cc to 496cc Precision engines.

RALEIGH 🏍 p.158
1899 This bicycle maker's first motorbike had a Schwann atmospheric-inlet-valve engine above the front wheel.
1903 Began making good 2hp and 3hp bikes with all-chain transmission, a clutch, and a twistgrip throttle.
1905 Motorcycle production stopped.
1919–33 A 698cc side-valve flat twin appeared. Single-cylinder (174cc to 496cc) and V-twin (598cc and 998cc) side- and overhead-valve bikes followed. Its gearboxes and engines were sold to other companies such as Sturmey-Archer. Lack of demand ended production.
1958 It began making mopeds. Raleigh designs were soon replaced by licence-built Mobylettes. A 78cc Bianchi scooter was built under licence as Raleigh Roma.
1967 Motorcycle production ended.

RAMBLER
c.1951–61 Villiers-engined 98cc, 122cc, and 197cc machines built by Norman (see p.225) for export.

RAY
1919–20 These 331cc and 269cc two-stroke singles were built in London.

RAY
1922–25 A 198cc bike with two-speed unit-construction gearbox. Another had a 172cc Villiers-Jardine engine/gearbox.

RAYNAL
c.1914–22 Bicycle maker built Villiers-engined 269cc two-stroke lightweights.
1937–50 Raynal produced a 98cc autocycle, again using Villiers engines.

READY
1920–22 Built by D. Read using JAP 293cc and 346cc side-valve engines.

REBRO
c.1922–25 REad BROs. of Tunbridge Wells built 147cc and 247cc Villiers-engined, belt-driven lightweights.

REGAL
c.1909–15 Used 349cc Peco two-stroke and 196cc to 602cc Precision engines. Racing and sports machines came with Blumfield or water-cooled Green-Precision engines. Bought by New Comet (see p.224) in 1913.

REGENT
1920 Regent Motor Cycles of London sold this 688cc machine with a Coventry-Victor side-valve flat-twin engine, a Sturmey-Archer three-speed gearbox, and a conventional tubular frame. Probably built in small numbers.

REGINA
1902–05 Belt-driven machines with vertically mounted proprietary engines probably by MMC, Fafnir, and Minerva.

REGINA
1914–15 S. Barnett built 292cc two-strokes using its own engine with a vertical cylinder in a diamond frame. A two-speed gearbox was optional.

REMUS
1914–22 Birmingham-built belt-driven two-stroke with a 211cc Radco engine.

REVERE
1915–22 Villiers-engined 269cc bike built by W. H. Whitehouse & Co.

REVOLUTION
1904–06 Used 2.75hp and 3.5hp engines mounted in an inclined position under the downtube of a bicycle-style frame. Made its own engines with the NRCC logo.

REX (REX-ACME) 🏍 p.159
1899 Marque founded by Billy and Harold Williamson.
1900 First Rex motorcycle had a 398cc atmospheric-inlet-valve single-cylinder engine. By 1905 it also produced a 465cc side-valve single and 726cc inlet-over-exhaust V-twins.
1911 The Williamsons quit the firm; Billy founded Williamson (see p.233), while Harold went to Singer (see p.229).
1919 Rex took over the Coventry Acme Motor Co. and built the first Rex-Acme in 1921: a 348cc Blackburne-engined bike.

S. F. Garrett astride a water-cooled Regal Precision on the Isle of Man, 1912

From 1922 only proprietary engines were used. Two- and four-stroke engines of 170cc to 550cc were supplied by many companies, but Rex-Acme was in decline. **1930–33** The factory closed and the name was bought by sidecar maker Mills-Fulford to use on overhead-valve 175cc to 250cc singles with AKD engines.

REX-JAP
1908–15 Apparently unconnected with Rex-Acme, the Rex-JAP was built by the Premier Motor Co., also known as PMC (see p.226) and Premo (see p.227).

REYNOLDS RUNABOUT p.159
1919–23 Scooter-style machines that used 269cc Liberty two-stroke engines and two-speed Moss gearboxes.

REYNOLDS SPECIAL
1931–35 Built by Scott and sold solely by A. E. Reynolds Ltd, the Reynolds Special was based on 498cc and 596cc Scott TT replica engines. It had premium-quality components and accessories. Early versions were called Aero Specials. Reynolds later built the AER (see p.212).

REYRE-NEWSON
1921 Sports 248cc single with a vertically mounted face-cam engine and Sturmey-Archer gearbox, with belt final drive.

R&H See H&R (p.221).

RICHARDS See Beau Ideal (p.214).

RICKMAN p.160
1962–86 Successful scramblers the Rickman brothers began making Métisse frames for competition bikes with Triumph and other British engines. Later there were road and racing machines, and also lightweight off-road bikes with Zündapp and other two-stroke engines. In the 1970s, 736cc twin-cylinder Royal Enfield-engined machines were followed by large road bikes using Kawasaki and Honda four-cylinder engines. Pat French took over Métisse frame production in 1982, but Rickman still made a few kits for Japanese engines until 1986.

RILEY
1901–08 Previously made powered tricycles and forecars. Its first motorbike had Minerva and MMC engines, soon replaced with Riley's own singles and V-twins. The Riley was the first British engine with a mechanical inlet valve and the company also pioneered valve timing overlap. Riley's car successes led to the cessation of its motorcycle production.

ROC
1903–15 Apparently funded by the author Sir Arthur Conan Doyle, the Roc was designed and built by A. W. Wall, later responsible for the Wall Auto Wheel (see p.232) and the Liberty two-stroke

A 499cc side-valve Rover demonstrates its passenger-carrying capabilities

engine. The Roc ditched the high bicycle-style frame and pedals for a longer, lower frame and footrests. It had hub clutch and gear assemblies with up to four ratios. It used both its own and Precision engines.

ROCKSON
1920–23 Villiers- and Blackburne-engined bikes by J. E. ROCK & SONs.

ROLFE
1911–14 Machines that used 498cc JAP singles and 770cc Precision V-twins.

ROMPER
1920 Belt-driven diamond-framed machines that used 292cc Union engines.

ROVER
1903–05 This bicycle firm's first motorbike had a 300cc side-valve engine. **1910–22** A 3.5hp 499cc side-valve machine, designed by John Greenwood, formed the basis of the range until the 1920s. An Ariel three-speed gearbox was added from 1915. JAP-engined V-twins were also built from World War I. **1923–25** Unit-construction 250cc and 350cc machines appeared. Increasing car production ended motorcycle building.

ROYAL-AJAX
c.1904 Bicycle-style machines with belt drive and vertical single-cylinder engines.

ROYAL ENFIELD pp.162–63
c.1898 The Enfield Cycle Co. began to develop tricycles and quadricycles with DeDion, Minerva, and MMC engines. Motorcycles followed in 1900. One model had the engine in front of the steering head. Motorcycle production stopped in 1905. **1910** Motorcycle production resumed with a 2.25hp MAG-engined V-twin. Larger versions followed with 770cc JAP engines. It soon built its own 425cc

inlet-over-exhaust V-twin, and before the war a 225cc two-stroke. After the war the company concentrated on the large-capacity twin, which used a 976cc Royal Enfield engine and production of the 225cc two-stroke continued. **1924** A four-stroke 350 was introduced; its JAP engine was soon replaced by Enfield's own 350cc side-valve and overhead-valve engines. Capacity grew to 488cc in 1927, when a four-speed gearbox was offered. A new 225cc side-valve bike was built from 1928. In 1931 a four-valve single and the 146cc two-stroke Cycar arrived. The V-twin grew to 1140cc by the end of the 1930s. **1948** Post-war production was based on pre-war machines until the arrival of the new 500cc parallel twin, followed in 1949 by the 350cc Bullet overhead-valve single. Both were housed in new frames with swingarm rear suspension. By 1952 the machines ranged from a 125cc two-stroke to the 692cc Meteor twin. New 250cc overhead-valve singles appeared in 1954, and were succeeded by the unit-construction Crusader series in 1957. **1962** The company was sold. A new two-stroke 250 racer was not a success. Capacity of the big twin grew to 736cc. **1967** The factory closed. The tooling to make the 350cc and 500cc Bullet went to India, where production continues. Assembly of 736cc Interceptor twins continued in Bradford-on-Avon using parts supplied by sub-contractors. **1970** The company went into liquidation. The remaining Interceptor engines were fitted into Rickman chassis (see left).

ROYAL GEORGE
c.1903 Bicycle-style machine with a 2hp Minerva engine below the downtube.

ROYAL MAIL
c.1902 Equipped with Clément and Kelecom engines and chain drive.

ROYAL ROEBUCK
c.1902 Loop-framed machines built by J. F. James with 1.75hp to 2.25hp engines and belt final drive. Kelecom and other proprietary engines were used.

ROYAL-RUBY
c.1909–22 Used its own 275cc and 350cc side-valve engines. Also used Villiers two-strokes and JAP V-twins of up to 1000cc. The company closed in 1922 and the name changed hands. **1927–32** Production restarted with mainly Villiers-engined machines, although some had JAP power units.

ROYAL SCOT
1922–24 This bike was one of the first machines to use the 348cc sleeve-valve Barr & Stroud engine. It had a diamond-pattern frame, a three-speed Burman gearbox, and saddle tank.

ROYAL SOVEREIGN
c.1902–03 This bike had a centrally mounted Minerva 211cc engine.

R&P
1902–06 Robinson & Price produced a motorbike in which the crankcases were cast as one piece with lugs for mounting the frame tubes. The 346cc atmospheric-inlet-valve engine's cylinder was mounted vertically. Belt drive was used.

RUDGE p.164
1911 Coventry's Rudge-Whitworth bicycle factory began making 499cc inlet-over-exhaust motorcycles. **1912** The Rudge-Multi variable gearing system was introduced, lasting until 1923. Larger single-cylinder (750cc) and V-twin (998cc) engines were added to the range in 1913 and 1915. **1924** Rudge's first four-valve single was built. It developed over the years in 250cc to 500cc capacities. The first 250s had two-valve JAP engines. The four-valve Rudge engines and its gearboxes were also sold to other manufacturers under the Python name. **1933** Rudge went into liquidation but production and development continued. In 1935 a two-valve 250 was introduced and the company was taken over by EMI, relocating to Middlesex in 1938. The factory switched to radar production at the start of the war. A 98cc Villiers-powered Rudge autocycle was built by Norman (see p.225) until 1941.

RUDGE-WEDGE
1903–04 Run by the son of the founder of Rudge (see above), Rudge-Wedge made a limited number of bikes before being absorbed by the larger Rudge company.

RUSSELL
1913 Inlet-over-exhaust 172cc machine with a diamond frame and belt drive. Pedals were fitted for starting and hills.

RW SCOUT

1919–21 Built by R. Weatherell & Co. using 318cc Dalm two-stroke engines in diamond frames with belt drive. From 1922 it was known as the Weatherell, and the range expanded to include Blackburne-engined four-strokes.

SALTLEY

1919–25 Used mainly Villiers two-stroke engines of 147cc, 247cc, and 269cc. Also built some bikes with 499cc side-valve Blackburne and Vulcanus (possibly Anzani under another name) engines. Orthodox machines with belt final drive.

SARACEN

1967–73 Specialized off-road 123cc to 188cc two-stroke Sachs-engined bikes.

SARCO-RELIANCE

1921–25 Built diamond-framed 269cc and 292cc two-strokes with two-speed Albion gearboxes and belt final drive.

SAXESSORIES

1923 Villiers-engined 247cc bikes with belt final drive sold by accessory maker Saxelby's of Coventry.

SCALE

1913–19 Diamond-framed two-strokes built in Manchester. Early models had 318cc Dalm engines. The war halted production. New Precision-engined 348cc bikes appeared in 1919. Originally built by Harry Scale, post-war bikes were made by Roberts & Hibbs – from 1920 they were sold as New Scale (see p.225).

SCARLET

1915 Orthodox two-stroke lightweight with a 269cc Metro two-stroke engine.

SCORPION

1963–65 Built in trials, scrambler, and road racing form, Scorpions had monocoque frames and Villiers engines. Also available as a frame kit.

SCOTT  pp.166–67

1908 Alfred Angas Scott produced one of the first viable two-strokes. The first production machine was a 333cc parallel twin with a water-cooled cylinder head, all-chain drive, a kickstarter, a two-speed gear, triangulated frame, and telescopic forks. The first bikes were built for Scott by car maker Jowett, although production soon transferred to Scott's own premises. Capacity gradually increased to 532cc by 1912 and water cooling was extended to the cylinder block. Scott machines were very succesful in competition.
1911 A rotary valve was added to the competition machines. Scotts won the TT in 1912 and 1913. During World War I, A. A. Scott left to develop a three-wheeled vehicle. The company went into decline, and its finances were precarious during the 1920s and 1930s. Production during the inter-war years was mainly of Scott's traditional two-stroke twins in 500cc and 600cc capacities. A 298cc single was built between 1929 and 1930, but was unsuccessful.
1934 A large-capacity (747cc then 986cc) water-cooled in-line triple was introduced. Only nine were produced.
1938 Took over Cyc-Auto (see p.217) and produced its own 98cc engine. After World War II motorcycle production resumed but Scott was in trouble.
1954–65 Under new ownership a redesigned machine was introduced. Using Scott's old engine and gearbox in a more modern frame, they were made in limited numbers in Birmingham. The marque faded out without officially ending production.

SEAL

1912–23 "Sociable, Economical, And Light", the Seal looked like a normal motorcycle and sidecar but was driven from the sidecar. There was no seat or handlebars on the "motorcycle". It had a 980cc JAP V-twin engine. The "sidecar" on some models could seat four.

SEELEY

1966–72 Sidecar racer and motorcycle dealer Colin Seeley took over the manufacturing rights to Matchless G50 and AJS 7R overhead-camshaft racers four years after AMC (see p.213) stopped production. New frame designs were produced and these exceptionally successful racing machines remained in production until 1972. A road bike was also developed, but few were made. Special frames were produced for other power units, including Suzukis and Hondas. Ducati commissioned Seeley to produce frames for its first V-twins.

SERVICE

c.1911–15 The Service Co. of London sold a variety of motorcycles, some with its own badge.

SHARRATT

c.1920–30 West Bromwich-based family bicycle company, Sharratt built orthodox machines using JAP engines in. Production was limited. In 1923 it introduced a 147cc two-stroke, which was among the first machines to use the JAP-built Aza engine.

SHAW

c.1901–08 Pioneer maker from Crawley in Sussex that built 2.25hp or 2.75hp machines. The vertical single-cylinder engine was mounted behind the seat-post and drove the rear wheel by belt or chain.

SHEFFIELD-HENDERSON

1919–23 Originally a sidecar maker, the company's first bike had a 3hp two-stroke engine with an inclined cylinder. It was soon superseded by Blackburne-engined 348cc and 498cc machines.

SILK

1975–79 Having earlier produced a machine based on an uprated Scott engine, George Silk built a few complete bikes with a Scott-inspired, but totally redesigned, 653cc water-cooled two-stroke engine/gearbox unit.

SILVA

1919–20 Early scooter with front-wheel drive provided by a 118cc atmospheric-inlet-valve Wall Auto Wheel.

SILVER

1907 Thomas Silver left Quadrant (see p.227) and built identical machines, advertised as "An old friend under a new name". In under a year they were reunited. The story was repeated in 1909.

SILVER PRINCE

1920–24 Built in Birmingham by the Tyrus Cycle Co., these conventional machines used 269cc Villiers and 292cc JAP engines. The same machines were sometimes sold as the Indian Prince. A bicycle-style machine with a 187cc two-stroke engine was also produced.

SIMMS

c.1902 A maker of engines, magnetos, and some complete motorcycles.

SINGER

1900 This bicycle and sewing machine company bought the manufacturing rights to the Perks & Birch Motorwheel (see p.226). The Motorwheel was superseded by a more orthodox motorcycle, but Singer stopped manufacturing motorcycles by 1906.
1908 Singer resumed motorcycle production with bicycle-style machines using Motosacoche engine units.
1911 Singer began making its own complete machines with 299cc side-valve engines. A 499cc model was also built. Subsequently a unit-construction 535cc side-valve single with two-speed gearbox and multi-plate clutch appeared. The same layout was soon adopted on the 300. A 350cc two-stroke was unveiled in 1914, but few were made.
1915 World War I stopped production.

Harold Petty leaving Ramsey, the Isle of Man, on a 3.5hp Singer in the 1912 Senior TT

SIRRAH
1921–26 Built in Birmingham by Alfred Wiseman Ltd, the maker of the Verus motorcycle (see p.231), Sirrahs were designed by a Mr Harris whose name reversed gave the marque its name. A 292cc Union-engined single was made and the Sirrah name was later used on cheap versions of the Verus range.

SKOOTAMOTA
See ABC Skootamota (p.212).

SLANEY
1921–22 Slaney used a 688cc Coventry-Victor flat-twin engine.

SMS
1913–14 S. M. Swingler built these 211cc two-stroke motorcycles. The unusual engine design included an extra air port and a simple non-return valve, which was situated between the carburettor and the crankcase.

SOS
1927–40 The Super Onslow-Special was built by Len Vale-Onslow using 172cc and 250cc water-cooled Villiers engines. Other models had JAP and Blackburne single-cylinder four-stroke engines and were among the first to use all-welded tubular frames.

SOUTHEY
c.1921–22 Orthodox machines that came with belt final drive and other proprietary components. Engines used included 346cc two-stroke singles.

SPARK
1903–04 This machine was built in London with Spark's own vertically mounted 2hp engine.

SPARK
1921–23 Sparkbrook (see below) built a 247cc Villiers-engined lightweight.

SPARKBROOK
1912–24 Before the war Sparkbrook used single-cylinder and V-twin JAP engines on its machines. A 269cc Villiers-engined lightweight appeared in 1914. From 1922 it built 350cc four-strokes using JAP and sleeve-valve Barr & Stroud engines.

SPARTAN
1920–22 Built in Nottingham, this 349cc diamond-framed two-stroke with belt drive and Broler engine was previously known as the Welland B and the Broler.

SPARTON
c.1976–78 This racer combined a Suzuki-inspired square-four two-stroke Barton engine with a Spondon chassis.

SPEED KING
See Graves (p.220).

SPRITE
1964–74 Sprite built specialized trials and motocross machines, often supplied in kit form. It used Husqvarna, Maico, Villiers, and later its own 360cc to 405cc power units.

SPUR
See Grose-Spur (p.220).

STAFFORD PUP
1920 This 142cc overhead-valve scooter was made by T. G. John, who later produced the Alvis car.

STAG
1912–14 Orthodox machines that were powered by Precision engines.

STANGER
1921–23 Unusual 538cc two-stroke V-twin in which the cylinders were set at 45°, but a 135° crankshaft kept the firing intervals equal.

STAR
1903–1915 This Wolverhampton-based car and tricycle maker offered the 2hp Star Griffon motorcycle, which was most probably imported from France. From 1903 to 1905 Star built Griffin-inspired motorcycles. In 1913 it made bikes with single-cylinder and V-twin JAP engines.

STARLEY
1902–04 The Starley motorcycle was developed by William Starley and built by Swift (see p.231). The engine, placed in front of the bottom bracket of a braced bicycle-style frame, had a longitudinal crankshaft. A worm gear turned the drive through 90° and it was transmitted to the rear wheel by chain.

STELLAR
1912–14 Stuart Turner built a 784cc two-stroke in-line twin with water cooling. It was also sold as a Stuart.

STEVENS
1934–38 Built by the Stevens brothers after the sale of AJS (see p.212) to Matchless (see p.223), Stevens machines were orthodox 249cc, 348cc, and 495cc overhead-valve singles with duplex cradle frames. The engines were sold to other marques.

STUART
See Stellar (above).

SUN
1911 A bicycle maker that began making 270cc to 590cc motorcycles with Precision engines. In 1913 Sun was one of few to use a 346cc inlet-over-exhaust Villiers engine, which was soon replaced by the 269cc Villiers two-stroke. Sun also used the 269cc two-stroke Vitesse (VTS – Valveless Two-Stroke) engine with disc valves in TT events of the early 1920s. Road machines used Villiers, Vitesse, Blackburne, and JAP engines of 98cc to 650cc.
1932 Motorcycle production stopped.
1948 A 98cc Villiers-powered autocycle, motorcycles, and scooters of up to 250cc were built, as were off-road machines.
1961 Sun was sold to Raleigh, but no more motorcycles were made.

SUNBEAM pp.172–74
1912 John Marston built quality bicycles with the Sunbeam trademark at the Sunbeamland works in Wolverhampton. The first Sunbeam motorcycle was a 347cc side-valve single with two-speed gearbox. Primary and final drive chains were enclosed in Sunbeam's famous "little oil bath" chaincases. A 499cc model soon followed. From 1913 to 1923 V-twin models that used JAP, MAG, and AKD engines were offered.
1918 Sunbeam was sold to a chemical company. Senior TT wins in 1920 and 1922, coupled with the undeniable quality of the machines, gave Sunbeam an excellent reputation.
1924 Overhead-valve singles appeared with TT victories in 1928 and 1929. A less successful overhead-camshaft racer was built in 1925. By the late 1920s its road bikes were lagging behind the opposition and the pressure to compete saw the quality drop. New 250cc, 500cc, and updated saddle-tank models arrived in the early 1930s.
1936 The company was sold to AMC (see p.213) and relocated to London. In 1939 250cc to 500cc high-camshaft overhead-valve singles appeared, but the outbreak of war ended production.
1947–56 Having bought Sunbeam in 1943, the BSA group used the name on its 487cc shaft-driven in-line twins.
1959–64 The final insult was the use of the name on 173cc two-stroke and 249cc overhead-valve twin BSA scooters. In 1964 the last BSA scooters were sold and the Sunbeam name disappeared.

SUPERB FOUR
1920 William Hooper of the Kempton marque (see p.222) built a prototype 998cc overhead-camshaft in-line four.

SUPREMOCO
c.1921–23 Built in Manchester with two- and four-stroke proprietary engines and belt final drive. Few were made.

SWALLOW
1946–51 Sidecar maker Swallow built the Gadabout, a tubular-framed small-wheeled scooter with 122cc or 197cc

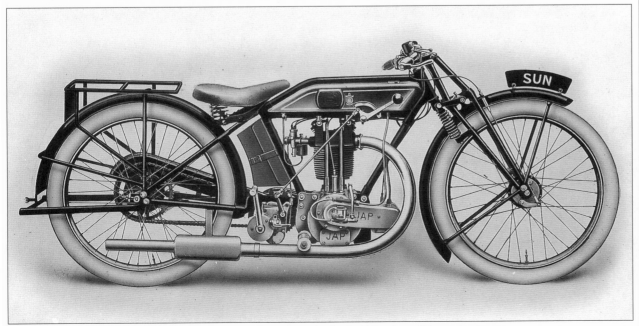

A 1926 Sun motorcycle with a 500cc overhead-valve JAP engine and Burman gearbox

Villiers engines. Swallow helped lay the foundation for the Jaguar car company.

SWAN
1911–13 H. F. Thornton built advanced Precision- and JAP-engined machines with sheet-metal open frames.

SWIFT
1898–1915 Swift, a bicycle maker, was involved in the construction of Starley machines around the turn of the century, but left the motorcycle scene around 1905. Involved with the Ariel marque (see p.213), the Swift machines that reappeared in 1910 were similar to Ariel motorcycles of the period, using the same White & Poppe 492cc side-valve power units. Swift later used a 670cc Abingdon V-twin engine.

TANDON
1948–57 Tandon used 122cc to 322cc Villiers and British Anzani two-stroke engines. Its first models had bolt-up frames with straight tubes, but later used a more conventional construction.

THOMAS SILVER See Silver (p.229).

THREE SPIRES
1931–32 A 147cc Villiers-engined two-stroke made by Coventry Bicycles. It previously built the Wee McGregor and Coventry B&D machines (see p.232).

TICKLE
1967–73 Tickle acquired the rights and tooling for Manx Norton machines after the AMC race shop closed. Limited numbers were built in 350cc, 500cc, and 600cc versions.

TOOLEY'S BI-CAR See Zenith (p.233).

TOREADOR
1924–28 Bert Houlding built Toreadors and Matadors (see p.223) in Preston. The first motorcycle had a 496cc overhead-valve MAG V-twin engine, which was mounted in a diamond frame. In 1925 he built 344cc to 492cc single-cylinder machines with JAP and oil-cooled Bradshaw engines.

TORPEDO
1910–20 Built in Barton-on-Humber by the Hopper bicycle company, which also produced the Elswick (see p.219). Both machines were identical except for colour. They used 294cc to 499cc two- and four-stroke Precision engines.

TREBLOC
1922–25 Built 63cc clip-on engines.

TRIPLE-H
1921–23 The two Hobbis brothers and Horrell built a 246cc Morris-engined two-stroke. The Hobbis brothers later produced the Triplette (see right).

TRIPLETTE
1923–25 The Hobbis brothers built this 147cc Villiers-engined machine.

TRIUMPH pp.180–87
1902 Germans Siegfied Bettman and Maurice Schulte began making Triumph bicycles in Coventry in 1887. Their first motorcycles were built in 1902 using 2.25hp Minerva engines fitted to bicycle-style frames. JAP and Fafnir engines were also used, and in 1904 Triumph adopted the "new" Werner engine position.
1905 Began to make its own 363cc side-valve engines. By 1910 capacity had grown to 499cc. An experimental 600cc side-valve vertical twin was also built.
1913 The 225cc two-stroke Junior model appeared, staying in production until 1925. The side-valve single was further improved and capacity increased to 550cc. A three-speed gearbox was fitted in 1915 to create the Model H, which was supplied in large numbers to the military during World War I.
1920 The 550cc all-chain drive SD single appeared. In 1921 a new cylinder head with four overhead valves was added to a sporting version of the bike.
1924 Triumph introduced the Model P, a cheap 494cc side-valve single that sold in vast numbers.
1932 A range of 250cc to 500cc overhead-valve singles appeared, followed by 550cc side-valve singles, 650cc parallel twins, and 147cc overhead-valve lightweights. Focusing on car production during the depression in 1936, Triumph sold the bike company to Jack Sangster, owner of the Ariel marque (see p.213).
1937 The 498cc Edward Turner-designed Speed Twin arrived. It was the basis of the Triumph range for the next 50 years. The company moved to a new factory in Meriden during World War II.
1951 Triumph was sold to the BSA group. It maintained a separate identity until the late 1960s. The Triumph range was dominated by parallel twins of up to 650cc, which were exported to the U.S. in large numbers. A 150cc single-cylinder unit-construction lightweight was introduced in 1954.
1957 A 350cc unit-construction twin was built. The 650cc Bonneville model was launched in 1959. There was also an unsuccessful attempt to make scooters.
1968 The three-cylinder 740cc Trident (also produced as the BSA Rocket 3) was launched. The 500cc and 650cc twins continued in production and a 250cc BSA single was sold as a Triumph.
1973 The BSA/Triumph Group folded. The remnants joined with the Norton-Villiers company to create Norton Villiers Triumph (NVT).
1975 After a long dispute a workers co-operative was established at Meriden to make the 750cc twins. Production of Tridents continued at NVT's Small Heath factory until 1977 when NVT crashed.

1983 The co-operative collapsed. The Triumph name and rights were bought by businessman John Bloor.
1985–88 Limited production of 750cc twins was resumed by spare parts manufacturer Les Harris, while Bloor's team developed all-new machines.
1990 Bloor's all-new Hinkley-built machines arrived with 750cc to 1200cc water-cooled double overhead-camshaft engines with three or four cylinders in a steel spine frame. By now, the Triumph name was its only link with the past.

TROBIKE
c.1960–61 Built a 98cc minibike.

TRUMP
c.1910–23 Built in Byfleet, Trump achieved considerable sporting success at the nearby Brooklands race track. Production machines used JAP and Anzani single-cylinder and V-twin engines. A 269cc Peco-engined two-stroke was built prior to World War I.

TURNER "BY-VAN"
1946–50 A two-wheeled goods transporter that had a 148cc two-stroke engine mounted on the front forks. Its pressed-steel body could carry up to 76kg (1.5cwt).

TUSROKE
c.1919 Built a 350cc belt-driven two-stroke using the company's own engine.

TYLER
1913–18 Built in London by the Tyler Apparatus Co. using a 198cc side-valve four-stroke Precision engine or a 269cc two-stroke engine. Tyler became associated with the Metro marque from 1918 and subsequently produced the Metro-Tyler motorcycle (see p.224).

UNIBUS
1920–22 A 269cc two-stroke scooter built by the Gloucestershire Aircraft Company. Its advanced specification led to a high price and poor sales.

VAL
1913–14 The orthodox Val had a 488cc side-valve JAP engine. The Val Motor Co. of Birmingham also made sidecars.

VASCO
1921–23 Vasco built a lightweight two-stroke with 261cc Orbit engines. It later used 349cc Broler power units.

VAUXHALL
c.1923–24 Car maker that developed a 931cc shaft-driven overhead-valve four-cylinder machine. It never reached full production.

VELOCETTE pp.188–89
1905 Cycle maker Taylor-Gue supplied frames for the Kelecom-engined

Ormonde motorcycle (see p.226). When Ormonde folded, Taylor-Gue took over production under the Veloce name.
1910 An advanced 276cc four-stroke with wet-sump lubrication and a unit-construction two-speed gearbox was built. It was replaced by an orthodox 500cc side-valve single sold under the VMC (Veloce Motor Co.) banner.
1913 The 206cc Velocette two-stroke was introduced, and the name was used on all subsequent machines. The little two-stroke formed the basis of the post-war range and capacity grew to 249cc.
1925 The overhead-camshaft Model K appeared. Overhead-camshaft racing versions of 350cc and 500cc included the KTT, which won the 350 World Championship in 1949 and 1950.
1933 New 249cc, 346cc, and 495cc overhead-valve singles were introduced.
1948 The LE model appeared. This innovative 149cc, later 192cc, water-cooled flat twin was expensive compared to other similar models. Derivatives, including an air-cooled overhead-valve sports bike, were made in the following years, as was a short-lived 247cc flat-twin two-stroke scooter. The rest of the range was made up of the old-fashioned 349cc and 499cc overhead-valve singles.
1971 The company closed.

VENUS
1920–22 Venus built 318cc machines using Dalm two-stroke engines.

VERUS
1919–25 Built by Alfred Wiseman Ltd, which also made Sirrah (see p.230) and Weaver machines (see p.232). First available with 211cc and 269cc two-stroke engines, by 1923 the range was exclusively four-strokes, which were equipped with Blackburne and JAP single-cylinder and V-twin power units.

VICTORIA
c.1902–28 The Victoria, made in Glasgow using proprietary components, was one of the few motorbikes built in Scotland. Early machines used single-cylinder Precision engines. Later 147cc to 688cc Coventry-Victor, JAP, and Villiers engines were used.

VINCENT (VINCENT-HRD) pp.192–94
1928 Philip C. Vincent bought the well-regarded HRD trademark for his new machines. Early models used overhead-valve single-cylinder JAP and Python (Rudge) engines of 350cc and 500cc in tubular frames with cantilever rear suspension. Vincent machines were well engineered and high quality.
1934 Began to make its own 498cc overhead-valve single-cylinder engines.
1936 The single was doubled up to produce a 998cc V-twin. Both machines were redesigned after World War II. The

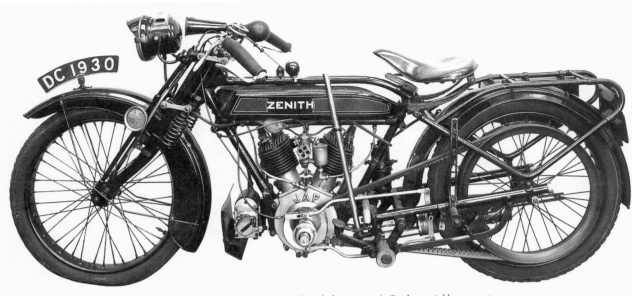

A 1920 JAP-engined 5hp Zenith motorcycle with the company's Gradua variable gear system

twin was justifiably billed as the world's fastest production motorcycle, but was expensive to make and to buy. Vincent was never in a financially strong position and attempted to diversify with a 48cc cyclemotor engine and by distributing NSU machines in the United Kingdom. **1955** Vincent production stopped.

VINCO
1903–05 Minerva-engined motorcycles produced by W. H. Heighton Ltd of Peterborough, which also made forecars.

VINDEC
1914–28 Brown Brothers sold a 226cc two-stroke under this name. It also sold four-stroke models of larger capacity under the Brown badge (see p.215). After World War I all its motorcycles used the Vindec badge. These included single-cylinder and V-twin JAP-engined four-strokes and 147cc Aza-engined two-stroke lightweights from the mid-1920s.

VINDEC-SPECIAL (VS)
1903–14 This name was used on the German-built Allright motorcycles for the British market.

VIPER
1919–22 Vipers were orthodox bikes with 292cc side-valve JAP engines.

VULCAN
1922–23 The Vulcan used 250cc two-stroke and 292cc side-valve JAP engines.

WADDON-EHRLICH
1981–82 A 250cc Rotax-engined racer project in which Joe Ehrlich developed the engine and Waddon Engineering was responsible for the rest of the machine. The project soon foundered, but led to the revival of Ehrlich's EMC marque (see p.219).

WAG
c.1925 An unusual 496cc two-stroke V-twin built by Wright and Gasking.

WALL
1909–16 The Wall Auto Wheel was a powered wheel with a 118cc atmospheric-inlet-valve engine, which mounted next to the rear wheel of a conventional bicycle. The design was by A. W. Wall, who was also the producer of the Roc motorcycle (see p.228). From 1914 a revised version was produced in the United States as the Smith Motor Wheel (see p.275).

WALLIS
1925–26 These unorthodox motorcycles had hub-centre steering and leaf-sprung front suspension. The 346cc and 490cc JAP and 348cc Blackburne engines were mounted in an inclined position.

WARD
1915–16 Orthodox 298cc two-strokes built in Yorkshire.

WARDILL
c.1926 An unusual 346cc two-stroke that had a separate charging cylinder wrapped around the conventional cylinder so that the crankcase was not part of the combustion process.

WARLAND
1923 The Warland used a 348cc Blackburne side-valve engine. Drive was by chain. Warland was taken over by Connaught (see p.217).

WARWICK See PMC (p.226).

WASP
1963– An off-road competition sidecar outfit specialist, Wasp also constructed some solos and an eight-valve parallel-twin engine in limited numbers.

WASSELL
1970–75 Specialized motocross and trials bikes built by motorcycle accessory supplier W. E. Wassell. Sachs, Bantam, BSA, and Puch engines were used.

WAVERLEY
1921–23 Built in Birmingham, Waverley motorcycles were equipped with 269cc Peco two-stroke and 348cc to 499cc Blackburne side-valve engines.

WD
1912–13 A 499cc inlet-over-exhaust single built by Wartnaby & Draper. Oil was contained in an engine sump and pressure-fed to the crankshaft.

WEARWELL
1901–03 An established bicycle firm, Wearwell made motorcycles using 2.5hp atmospheric-inlet-valve engines built by the Stevens brothers, who became AJS (see p.212). The engine was mounted above the frame downtube and drove the rear wheel by belt. When the machine was improved around 1903 the Wolf name (see p.233) was adopted.

WEATHERELL
1922–23 R. Weatherell & Co previously used the RW Scout name (see p.229) on orthodox singles and V-twins, which had Blackburne engines of 249cc to 696cc.

WEAVER
1922–25 The maker of Verus bikes (see p.231) built a lightweight using 142cc overhead-valve Wiseman engines and 147cc two-stroke Villiers or Aza engines.

WEE MCGREGOR
1922–25 A 170cc belt-driven Hobart-engined two-stroke built by the maker of the Coventry B&D machines.

WELLAND B See Spartan (p.230).

WELLER
1902–05 Weller made cars and motorcycles using its own engines.

WESTFIELD
c.1902–04 Made motorcycles using MMC and other proprietary engines.

WESTOVIAN
1914–16 R. V. Heath of South Shields offered a range of models with engines supplied by Villiers, JAP, and others.

W&G
1927–28 This 490cc two-stroke twin was mounted in a diamond frame.

WHIPPET
c.1903 Built motorcycles and forecars using Aster and FN engines in London.

WHIPPET
1920–21 A small-wheeled scooter built by G. C. Hayward & Co. with a 150cc overhead-valve engine placed vertically in front of the chain-driven rear wheel.

WHIRLWIND
1900–03 Brand-name used by Dorman & Co. on its motorcycles. It produced its own engines of 1.75hp to 3hp. Early models had bicycle frames, but later used loop frames and water cooling.

WHITE & POPPE
c.1902 White & Poppe may have built some complete machines before establishing itself as an engine supplier.

WHITLEY
c.1902–04 The company offered 2.75hp and 3.5hp engines, some with water cooling, and complete motorcycles.

WHITWOOD
1934–36 Few were sold of this two-wheeled car built by OEC. It had fully enclosed bodywork and stabilizer wheels with a range of engines from 250cc Villiers to 1000cc JAP power units.

WIGAN-BARLOW
1921–22 Machines made in Coventry with 292cc side-valve JAP and 346cc Barr & Stroud sleeve-valve engines.

WILKIN
c.1920 A diamond-framed bike, built in Sheffield, which used 348cc and 499cc Blackburne side-valve engines with an enclosed chain drive.

WILKINSON 🏍 p.197
c.1903–05 The Wilkinson Sword company's first motorcycle was a loop-framed machine with an Antoine engine and belt final drive.
1908–14 The company developed a radical new bike designed by P. G. Tacchi. The TAC (Touring Auto Cycle), was shown at the 1909 Stanley

Show. It had a 676cc air-cooled in-line four-cylinder engine with atmospheric inlet valve. The rider sat in a bucket seat.
1911 An improved 848cc TMC (Touring Motor Cycle) model was water cooled with side valves. The capacity soon increased again to 996cc.
1912 Wilkinson was involved in a project to make the unconventional two-stroke Wooler motorcycle (see below).
1914 Concentrated on armaments manufacturing. Production of the TMC was transferred to the Ogston Motor Co. (see p.225), which continued to build the machines for two more years.

WILLIAMSON
1912–20 Billy Williamson built his own luxury motorcycles after leaving the Rex company (see p.227). A 964cc flat-twin engine with air- or water-cooling was built by Douglas especially for the Williamson. After World War I it used 770cc side-valve JAP V-twin engines.

WILLOW
1920 A very basic scooter powered by a 118cc Wall Auto Wheel.

WIN
1910–14 The Win was an orthodox motorbike that used 499cc and 599cc side-valve Precision engines.

WITALL
1919–23 Limited production of simple belt-driven lightweights using 269cc TDC and Arden two-stroke engines.

WIZARD See FB (p.219).

WIZARD
1920–22 Built in Wales using 269cc Liberty engines in a bolt-up frame.

WOLF
1903–39 The Wolf name was adopted for Wearwell machines (see p.232). It used Stevens engines until 1909. Moto-Rêve engines may also have been used.
1912 The Wulfruna name was used on a new line of single-cylinder and V-twin JAP-engined machines with diamond frames. It was among the first to use the Villiers two-stroke engine. After World War I Blackburne engines were also used and the Wulfruna name was dropped. Production stopped around 1928.
1931–40 It returned with a range of conventional 98cc to 197cc Villiers-powered lightweights, which remained in production until World War II.

WOOLER 🏍 p.198
c.1909 John Wooler's first machine was an unusual two-stroke single with a double-ended piston and connecting rods. A variable ratio belt-drive system was fitted and the machine had front and rear plunger suspension. A 344cc model was briefly built by the Wilkinson-TMC

company from 1912 to 1914.
1911 Wooler built a fore-and-aft flat twin with a 348cc inlet-over-exhaust engine mounted in line with the frame.
1923 An updated engine appeared. Its worm-gear-driven camshaft operated overhead valves that were located at 90° to the cylinder.
1926 Wooler acquired P&P (see p.226) and restarted production in limited numbers. He also built a prototype 511cc single with a vertical camshaft.
1930 Wooler closed P&P.
1948 Reappeared with a new bike that had an unorthodox flat four-cylinder beam engine in which the pistons worked in coupled pairs.
1956 Wooler's death signalled the end of the company.

WULFRUNA See Wolf (left).

WYNNE
c.1919 Built by J. W. Oates, the Wynne was a 2.75hp scooter with front and rear suspension.

XL
1921–23 Built in Worthing by the Norfolk Engineering Company, these solid machines had horizontal chain-stay tubes extended to the front downtube. The XL used 490cc to 550cc single-cylinder JAP and Blackburne engines.

YOUNG
1919–23 The Mohawk bicycle company offered an improbably large 269cc clip-on two-stroke engine. Subsequently there was a more plausible 130cc model. Both mounted behind the rider's seat.

ZENITH
1905 Zenith produced Tooley's patent Bicar, a strange two-wheeler with a low tubular frame with hub-centre steering. Various proprietary engines, including Sarolea V-twins, were used.
1907 The sprung-frame Zenette motorcycle appeared with a 482cc side-valve Fafnir engine. From 1908 it was available with the Zenith Gradua gear, which was a feature in its machines until 1923. It used an opening engine pulley to offer a variable gear ratio. The pulley control also moved the rear wheel so that belt tension was maintained. The device offered huge hillclimbing advantages. From 1914 mainly V-twin JAP engines were used, but the Bradshaw oil-cooled flat twin was also offered from 1920.
1922 The first all-chain drive Zeniths appeared. These used JAP, Bradshaw, and Blackburne engines of up to 998cc. Machines of larger capacity were raced successfully. There was also a 172cc Villiers-engined lightweight. Declining sales stopped production in 1930.
1931 After the company changed hands, limited production of conventional JAP-engined machines restarted. World

War II interrupted production, which stopped for good in 1949.

ZEPHYR
1918–20 Zephyr built a 131cc clip-on two-stroke engine for bicycles, as well as a complete machine.

Unconfirmed Marques

Abbotsford *1919–20*
AGA *1921 350*
Arab *1923–26*
Arden Coventry *1912–20*
Argyle
Armstrong London *1902–05*
Aston Birmingham *1923–24*
Avon *1919–20*
Avondale
AWJ
Bamber
Bentinck
Blackford *c.1902–04*
Borham *1902–05*
Bounds–JAP *1909–12*
Caesar *1922–23*
Camber *1920–21*
Carlton *1922*
Charlton *1904–08*
Colonial *1911–13*
Condor *1907–14*
Coventry-Star *1919–21*
Crest *1923*
Dane *1919–20*
Dart *1901–06*
Downer Groves
Dux *1904–06*
Dyson-Motorette *1920–22*
Eagle-Tandem *1903–05*
Eagre
EBO Leicester *1910–c.1914*
Ever-Upright
Farnell
Force
Frays
Frogmore
Fuller
Givaudan *1908–14*
Graphic *1903–06*
Greyhound Hampstead *1905-07*
Hansan *1920–22*
Harewood *1920*
Haxel-JAP *1911–13*
Hercules Derby *1902*
Invicta *1902–06*
Ixion *1901–03.*
JD *c.1902*
Lancer *c.1904*
Large *1903*
L&C *c.1904*
Lily *1906–14*
Marlow *1920–22*
Mars *1905–08*
Marvel-JAP *1909–12*
Maxim *1919–21*
May Bros *1903–06*
MCC London *1903–1910*
Mead *1922–24*
M&M *1914*
Morris *1913–22.*
Mountaineer *c.1902*

Moveo *c.1907*
ND *1928*
Neal-Dalm *1919*
Neall *1910–14*
Nestor *1913–14*
New Crescent *1912*
Nicholas London
Overdale *1921–22*
Pallion *1905–14*
PDC London *1903–06*
Peerless *1913–14*
Pick *c.1908*
Planet *1919–20*
Precision Northampton *1902–06*
Prim *1906–07*
Radmill *1912–14*
Reliance Southampton *c.1902*
RIP London *1905–08*
Romp *1913–14*
Roulette *1918–19*
Royal-Eagle *1901–10*
Royal Wellington *c.1901*
Saturn *1925–26*
Scout *1912–13*
SL *1924–25*
Slade-JAP Manchester *1920–23*
SPA-JAP Scarborough *1921–23*
Stafford *c.1898*
Stan *c.1919*
Stanley *c.1902*
Star *1919–21*
Sudbrook *1919–20*
Symplex *1913–22*
Tee-Bee Glasgow *1908–11*
Thomas *1904*
Thorough *1903*
Tilston *1917–19*
Townend Coventry *1901–04*
Trafalgar *1902–05*
Trafford *1919–22*
Trent *1902–c.1906*
Victa *1912–13*
Waddington *1902–06*
Wakefield *c.1902.*
Warrior *1921–23*
Watney *1922–23*
Wheatcroft *1924*
Wilbee *1902–c.1906*
Winco *1920–22*
Wirral *1902–c.1906*

Germany

Both the internal combustion engine and the motorcycle were first built in Germany. Hildebrand & Wolfmüller (see p.241) built the first "production" motorcycles in Munich in 1894. Adler (see p.234), NSU (see p.245), and others began making motorized bicycles at the turn of the century. The industry took off after World War I, when hundreds of small companies emerged to supply the demand for motorized transport. Few lasted beyond the crash of the German economy in the mid-1920s. Survivors were able to expand during the 1930s, when DKW (see p.236) was the biggest manufacturer in the world. After World War II the renewed demand for economical personal transportation was satisfied by makers of low-cost, utilitarian machines. Increasing affluence and the advent of the cheap car meant that this boom was short-lived and the industry was in decline after the mid-1950s. By the mid-1980s BMW (see p.235) was the only significant company still in business.

ABAKO
1923–25 Nuremberg-based company that built 129cc three-port two-strokes with chain drive.

ABC
1922–24 A small company that made 149cc two-strokes in Berlin.

ABENDSONNE
1933–34 Abendsonne built a limited number of machines using two 98cc Villiers engines coupled together to create a two-stroke parallel twin.

ACHILLES
1953–57 Made 48cc to 123cc Sachs-engined mopeds and scooters. When Achilles stopped production, the Norman company in England acquired the tooling and rights, which were used to produce the Norman Lido moped.

ADLER p.12
1900–07 Adler started out as a bicycle, typewriter, and car maker in Frankfurt. It built its first motorcycles using DeDion engines, but soon developed its own single-cylinder and V-twin engines. Demand for cars ended motorcycle production.
1949–58 New machines with single- and twin-cylinder, two-stroke engines of 98cc to 247cc were introduced. The 200cc to 250cc twins were widely copied by other manufacturers. Production ceased during the sales slump of the late 1950s. The company, now owned by Grundig, has survived as a leading manufacturer of office equipment.

ADRIA
1921–28 Adria built four-stroke engines, and complete belt-driven motorcycles of 276cc to 346cc. Its engines were also supplied to other motorcycle manufacturers.

AGON
c.1924–28 Built a variety of conventional machines using proprietary engines, among which was the oil-cooled, 346cc overhead-valve Bradshaw.

ALBA
1919–24 Loop-framed, 198cc to 249cc side-valve and overhead-valve singles built at Stettin by ALbert BAruch. The engines were also sold to other manufacturers. Some machines had two-speed, in-unit gearboxes with belt drive.

ALBERT
1922–24 Open-framed 183cc two-strokes built in Saxony. Few machines were built.

ALBERTUS
1922–24 Albertus produced standard lightweights. It used 118cc to 146cc two-stroke Löwy engines with belt drive mounted in simple loop frames.

ALGE
1923–31 ALfred GEissler of Leipzig built machines from 173cc to 498cc using two- and four-stroke British engines.

ALLRIGHT p.15
1901 Allright machines were built by Köln-Lindenthaler Metallwerke AG.

Single-cylinder and V-twin Kelecom, Minerva, FN, and Fafnir engines were used in its early motorcycles. Later it used engines supplied by JAP, MAG, and others in orthodox machines. The same models were sold in some markets under the Vindec-Special (see p.249), Tiger (see p.248), and Roland (see p.247) brand-names.
1923 Allright acquired the Cito marque, which at that time made the 497cc shaft-driven, KG motorcycle.
1927 Motorcycle production stopped.

ALMORA
c.1924–25 Almora briefly produced a machine that used the 113cc to 176cc Löwy-designed two-stroke engine, which ran (badly) on crude oil.

AMAG
1924–25 Berlin-based company that built Bekamo-engined, 149cc two-strokes.

AMI
1921–25 The Ami was a 94cc four-stroke overhead-valve clip-on engine for bicycles that mounted below the pedal bracket. It was built by Auto Motoren Ind in Berlin.

AMMON
1923–25 An unusual lightweight built in Berlin, the Ammon used small-capacity proprietary engines, including the 200cc side-valve Paqué and various two-stroke power units, in a pressed-steel and tubular frame.

AMO
c.1921–24 Amo produced a typical belt-driven 146cc two-stroke lightweight.

AMO
1953–55 Small company located in Berlin that built 48cc mopeds.

ANDREES
c.1923–29 Andrees machines were built in Düsseldorf by H. W. Andrees using proprietary engines of 346cc to 598cc supplied by Bradshaw, MAG, and Blackburne. The machines were conventional, but they were built to a high standard. In later models Andrees used its own 198cc two-stroke engine.

ANKER
1949–53 An established bicycle manufacturer that produced a range of motorcycles and mopeds using 48cc to 244cc Sachs and Ilo engines. After 1952 production moved to a different factory, where identical machines were produced and were briefly sold with the Pamag badge (see p.245).

ARCO
c.1922–31 Arco built a range of water-cooled, four-stroke singles of 248cc,

346cc, and 498cc. The 498cc version was equipped with overhead camshaft, and smaller models were of overhead-valve design. All had a forward-facing carburettor and rear-facing exhaust port with vertical cylinders.

ARDIE p.17
1919 Arno Dietrich began building 305cc and 348cc two-stroke machines.
1922 Dietrich was killed in an accident, but production continued, soon switching to a range of machines with JAP, Rudge, Küchen, and Bark engines of 246cc to 996cc. After World War II the firm was owned by Dürkopp (see p.237) and built 122cc to 346cc two-strokes.
1958 Production stopped.

ARGEO
1924–27 Berlin-based firm that built 198cc and 246cc two-stroke singles.

ARISTOS
1922–24 Built in Berlin, this unconventional machine used a water-cooled, flat-twin, side-valve, 614cc engine in a pressed-steel, box-section frame. The machines were also sold under the Menos (see p.244) and Sterna (see p.248) names.

ARMINIA
1925–31 Utilitarian machines built in limited numbers by the maker of EPA motorcycles (see p.237) using proprietary engines.

ASTORIA
1923–25 The Astoria was a 289cc two-stroke built at Nuremberg. After financial trouble the company was taken over by Nestoria (see p.245).

ASTRA
c.1921–25 Built in Munich using 339cc horizontally opposed flat-twin Bosch-Douglas engines. Other models used single-cylinder JAP and Blackburne engines of 293cc to 496cc.

ATLANTIC
1921–22 Small Berlin company that built motorcycles using Hansa 193cc side-valve engines.

ATLANTIK
1925–26 Small Bamberg-based company that made primitive 173cc two-strokes in limited numbers.

ATLAS
1924–29 Leipzig-built machines equipped with Atlas's own 248cc and 348cc two-stroke engines.

AUTINAG
c.1924–25 Autinag motorcycles were built by Düsseldorfer Motorenfabrik. The range comprised 127cc and 198cc belt-driven two-strokes with the firm's own

engines, and a 496cc machine with a MAG four-stroke engine. A sporting version of the 198cc model was called the Dümo.

AUTOFIX
1950–53 Autofix produced a weird scooter with a 120cc two-stroke engine and a three-speed gearbox mounted above the front wheel. The engine and fork assembly was covered by a cowl.

AUTOFLUG
1921–23 Built lightweight, belt-driven motorcycles and scooters in Berlin using two-stroke Bekamo engines.

AVIS-CELER
c.1925–31 Built orthodox 172cc to 498cc machines with Villiers, JAP, and MAG engines.

AWD
1921–59 Augustus Wurring of Düsseldorf founded his motorcycle company when he was just 21 years old. Pre-war machines used DKW, Villiers, and Blackburne engines. After the war the company built utilitarian machines with Ilo and Sachs two-stroke engines. Production stopped in 1959, but AWD machines were available by special order until the 1980s. The Wurring name (see p.250) was also used.

AWO
1950–61 The AWO was a shaft-driven 250cc overhead-valve single-cylinder BMW clone built in East Germany. The name was subsequently changed to Simson and production switched to lightweight two-strokes.

BAIER
1924–29 Initially Baier built 173cc to 248cc two-stroke singles and later 500cc two-stroke split-singles with twin exhaust ports.

BALALUWA
c.1924–25 A short-lived firm that built a 346cc overhead-valve single. The firm was located in Munich.

BAM
c.1933–37 Berlin Aachener Motorradwerke assembled Belgian FN machines in Germany to circumvent import restrictions.

BAMO
1923–25 A small firm, located in Saxony, that built 148cc and 172cc machines with DKW engines.

BASTERT
1949–55 Bastert built a variety of motorcycles and scooters using Ilo and Sachs engines of 98cc to 197cc, including the Einspurauto luxury scooter.

BAUER
1936–53 Built 74cc and 98cc Sachs-engined mopeds before World War II. After the war it produced models with 97cc to 174cc Sachs and Ilo two-stroke engines. In 1952 a new machine with the company's own 248cc overhead-valve, single-cylinder engine was introduced. It had a rear-facing exhaust port and carburettor. Development costs drained resources and the company had to close.

BAYERN
c.1923–26 Early models were equipped with 293cc flat-twin Bosch-Douglas engines. Later Bayern extended the range to include 498cc to 998cc MAG-engined V-twins.

BE-BE
1924–27 Small firm that made 117cc two-strokes.

BECKER
1903–06 Built in Dresden by Karl Becker using his own and Fafnir single-cylinder and V-twin engines.

BEKAMO
1922–25 Bekamo machines were advanced, 129cc two-strokes built in Berlin and designed by Hugo Ruppe, who had previously worked for DKW (see p.236). The Bekamo had a pumping piston at the bottom of the crankcases and wooden frames were used. The company suffered in the German economic crisis and was bankrupt in 1924. Production of tubular-framed Bekamo machines continued in Czechoslovakia until 1930.

BERGFEX
1904–09 Berlin-based firm that built motorcycles using its own and Fafnir single-cylinder and V-twin engines.

BERLIN
c.1958–65 East European scooter with a 148cc MZ engine (see Pitty p.246).

BEUKER
c.1921–29 Beuker built 211cc side-valve four-strokes with its own engines

incorporating two-speed gearboxes. Final drive was by belt. They were made in Nordrhein Westfalen.

BIMOFA
c.1922–25 Bimofa made loop-framed, belt-driven lightweights with Hansa side-valve engines.

BINZ
1954–58 Binz built a strange, large-wheeled moped-cum-scooter. It had 49cc Sachs and Ilo engines.

BISCHOFF & PEDALL
1926–31 Took over production of the Astoria/Nestoria (see p.234) two-stroke. The firm also built machines with Küchen, Motosacoche, and Sturmey-Archer four-stroke engines. Some sporting success was achieved. Built at Nuremberg.

BISMARCK
1904–08 A major bicycle maker, whose first motorcycles were typical pioneer machines with proprietary engines.
1931 Introduced utilitarian mopeds with 74cc and 98cc two-stroke engines.
1950–57 Made a range of 98cc to 174cc motorcycles with Sachs and Ilo engines. The company collapsed following a dramatic sales drop in 1956.

BLEHA
1923–26 Bleha made a limited number of motorcycles using DKW and its own 174cc to 247cc two-stroke engines.

BMW 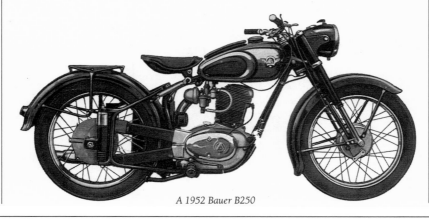 pp.26–33
1923 Post-World War I restrictions on the manufacturing of aircraft forced aero engine maker BMW (Bavarian Motor Works) to diversify. It supplied side-valve flat-twin cylinder engines to other manufacturers and was also involved in production of the lightweight Flink (see p.238) and the Helios (see p.240) motorcycles before it started making machines using its own badge. The first BMW-badged machine, the R32, had a flat-twin cylinder engine mounted across the frame and used shaft drive to the rear wheel. This engine and transmission layout is still used by BMW. The design

was uprated in the following years with the introduction of overhead valves and other detail improvements. Single-cylinder models were also produced. These had vertical cylinders and retained shaft drive. Their quality build and high specification made them too expensive for the utilitarian market.
1935 The 745cc side-valve R12 was introduced. This was the first production motorcycle equipped with hydraulically damped telescopic forks. It also had a four-speed gearbox. In the 1930s supercharged competition machines, which established new speed records, were also built. Sidecar outfits, including machines with driven sidecar wheels, were supplied to the German military during World War II. Production of shaft-driven singles and twins resumed after the war. Revised overhead-camshaft racing machines were produced. They failed to achieve major success in the solo classes, but dominated world championship sidecar racing for 20 years from 1954. The road bike range comprised 245cc singles to 594cc twins that, from 1954, were fitted with Earles forks and swingarm rear suspension. Quality of construction continued to make BMWs expensive machines. The singles were dropped in 1967.
1969 An all-new range of machines was introduced. The 498cc, 599cc, and 746cc models now had telescopic forks and a far more modern look than their predecessors. Capacity of the air-cooled twins later grew to 898cc, then 980cc. The range was enlarged to include sports and touring models with fairings.
1978 Lightweight 473cc and 649cc twins were introduced to extend the appeal of the BMW range.
1983 Breaking with 60 years of tradition, a new range of in-line, water-cooled, fuel-injected 740cc to 987cc three- and four-cylinder models was introduced. Shaft drive was retained. Touring, sports, and unfaired models were produced. The new bikes were intended to match the performance of multi-cylinder Japanese machines and also to meet the increasingly strict noise and emissions legislation. Four-valve cylinder heads and a 1081cc version were produced later.
1993 BMW reverted to the flat-twin layout on new machines intended to take the company into the 21st century. The 1085cc and 850cc engines had four valves per cylinder with a high camshaft layout. Electronic injection and oil cooling were used. The engine was an integral member of the frame, which had a wishbone front suspension system. An even more radical departure was the introduction of a 652cc single-cylinder motorcycle with chain drive. This machine was built in Italy, to BMW specifications, by Aprilia using Austrian Rotax engines.

A 1952 Bauer B250

BOGE
c.1923–27 Made conventional machines using the company's own 295cc side-valve engine and belt drive. Burman or Sturmey-Archer three-speed gearboxes were used. The company still exists and makes compressors.

BÖHME
1925–30 Built advanced 130cc water-cooled two-strokes with stepped pistons and horizontal cylinders.

BRAND
1925–30 Berlin-built lightweight with a horizontal-cylinder two-stroke engine supplied by Bekamo. The machine had belt drive, unit construction, a girder fork, and a two-speed gearbox. It was built by Brand & Sohne and sometimes sold under the B&S name (see below).

BRENNABOR
1902–12 Brennabor was one of the first German motorcycle manufacturers. Its early machines had a single-cylinder, atmospheric-inlet-valve engine mounted in a diamond frame in the "new" Werner position. Zedel, Fafnir, and the firm's own single-cylinder and V-twin engines were used. Motorcycle production was stopped to concentrate on producing cars and bicycles.
1933–40 Motorcycle production was resumed. Mopeds and lightweight machines with proprietary two-stroke engines were made.

B&S
1925–30 B&S is an abbreviation of Brand & Sohne. It built Bekamo-engined two-strokes (see also Brand).

BÜCKER
1922–58 Franz Bücker built machines using a variety of proprietary engines of up to 1000cc before World War II. From 1948 he built Ilo-engined lightweights of 125cc to 200cc.

BUSSE
c.1922–26 The Busse was a single-cylinder, 141cc belt-driven two-stroke built at Magdeburg.

CAMBRA
1921–26 Berlin-based firm that built two-speed, loop-framed, side-valve lightweights with belt drive.

CHARLETT
1921–24 The Charlett was a lightweight machine with a 195cc side-valve engine.

CITO
1905–27 Bicycle maker that used single-cylinder and V-twin Fafnir engines in its early machines. After World War I it built 346cc machines equipped with the firm's own single-cylinder two-stroke engine.

1922 Cito took over production of the KG, shaft-driven, triangular-framed, 497cc overhead-valve motorcycle.
1923 The firm was acquired by Allright.
1927 Production stopped.

CITYFIX
1949–53 Cityfix built a spine-framed, 98cc Sachs-engined lightweight and also some crude scooters.

CL
1951 Short-lived company that built a few 48cc two-stroke scooters.

CM
c.1921–23 Basic belt-driven, open-framed lightweights built at Munich. DKW engines were used.

COCKERELL
1919–24 Built at Munich by Fritz Cockerell, who also designed the Megola (see p.244). These were 110cc to 169cc two-strokes with a horizontal cylinder. They were superior to most of the small-capacity bikes on the German market at this time. Sporting versions achieved competition success. Engines were also sold to other manufacturers. A prototype two-stroke four-cylinder machine was designed. The owners of the Abako marque (see p.234) bought the firm.

COLUMBUS
1922–24 Columbus was the maker of the Gnom 63cc clip-on bicycle engine. It produced the overhead-valve, 250cc engines used in the first Horex motorcycles (see p.241) and subsequently concentrated on engine production. The company was absorbed by Horex in 1926, but continued to supply engines to other manufacturers.

CONDOR
1953–54 Built 48cc scooters.

CORONA
1902–07 Built loop-framed, belt-driven motorcycles and tandems with vertically mounted, atmospheric-inlet-valve Zedel and Fafnir engines.
c.1922–24 Production was resumed, again using proprietary engines, including BMW flat twins.

CUDELL
c.1898–1905 Built pioneer machines with DeDion engines.

CURWY (CURSY)
c.1911–31 Curwy built orthodox machines using its own 350cc and 500cc side-valve and overhead-valve single-cylinder engines. The name was changed to Cursy in 1927.

CYKLON p.45
1901–05 Cyklon was located in Berlin. Its first machines used the early Werner

layout with the engine mounted above the front wheel, but it soon adopted a more conventional layout. DeDion, Werner, and Zedel engines were used.

DAIMLER p.46
c.1885 The Daimler was the world's first motorcycle with an internal combustion engine. The wooden-framed machine was built to test Gottlieb Wilhelm Daimler's engine. He was later involved in the Daimler-Benz concern, which now makes Mercedes-Benz cars and trucks.

DAK
1923–25 The Deutsche Automobil-Konzern built 117cc and 147cc machines, using Ilo two-stroke engines.

DAW
c.1924–25 Diana-Werke GmbH built a 407cc single-cylinder two-stroke. This unusual machine, designed by Ernst Köhler, had pressed-steel bodywork and disc wheels (see Köhler p.242).

DEFA
1921–24 Deutsche Fahrradbau of Berlin built loop-framed, belt-driven machines with 198cc four-stroke engines.

DELTA
c.1924 Delta built a strange-looking machine with angular, enclosed bodywork concealing a 499cc single-cylinder two-stroke engine. The machine had a pillion seat and rear suspension. Very few were built.

DERAD
1923–26 Deutsche Industriewerke built a 393cc fore-and-aft flat-twin. Later the the name changed to D-Rad (see p.237).

DGW
1927–28 The DGW name was sometimes used on DKW machines (see below), particularly in export markets.

DIAG
1921–28 Diag first built small-capacity, clip-on engines. It later produced a range of complete machines, including four-stroke singles of up to 346cc.

DIAMANT p.47
1903–07 Built typical machines using Fafnir V-twin engines and later, its own engines.
1926 Diamant resumed motorcycle production using mainly Kühne engines in diamond framed machines. It merged with Elite (see p.237) in the late 1920s and from 1928 to 1931 it produced the Opel (see p.245) and EO (see p.237) motorcycles with Duralumin frames and Opel and Küchen engines.
1937–40 It made lightweight machines with 74cc to 124cc Sachs two-stroke engines. The company still exists as a bicycle manufacturer.

DIETERLE-DESSAU
c.1921–25 Wilhelm Dieterle built simple belt-driven machines at Dessau. Alba supplied 198cc and 247cc side-valve engines that were installed in bicycle frames. The same machine may also have been sold under the Dreipunkt or FEM-Alba brand-names.

DIHL
1923–24 Belt-driven, 269cc two-strokes that were never built in quantity. Made in Berlin.

DKF
1923–24 Lightweight machines with side-valve engines produced in Berlin by Deutsche Kleinmotoren & Fahrzeugwerke.

DKW pp.48–50
1919 DKW, founded by an expatriate Dane, Jörgen Skafte Rasmussen, began production with a 118cc two-stroke clip-on engine for bicycles. It was nicknamed *das kleine Wunder*, meaning "the little miracle". Over the following years different slogans were used to fit the DKW initials. The company produced a succession of advanced and well-engineered, two-stroke machines. Engines were also supplied to other manufacturers.
1921 The first complete machines were 122cc Golem scooters. The 142cc Lomos scooter appeared the following year, but neither model was very successful. However DKW's lightweight motorcycles, which appeared from 1922, sold in large numbers. DKW adopted pressed-steel frame construction and offered fan- and water-cooled machines in the 1920s.
1930s By the 1930s DKW was the largest motorcycle manufacturer in the world. In 1932 it merged with Audi, Wanderer, and Horch to create the Auto Union and began making two-stroke cars in addition to motorcycles. Racers with supercharged split-single cylinder engines were developed in the 1930s, Ewald Kluge won the 1938 Lightweight TT and the 1938 and 1939 European Championships aboard DKW machines.
1945 After World War II DKW moved from Zschopau in East Germany and relocated to the West. The post-war two-stroke range included singles and twins of up to 350cc. Small-capacity machines were based on the much copied pre-war RT125 model. MZ motorcycles (see p.244) were made at the old premises in Zschopau. DKW racers appeared in the mid-1950s but did not repeat the success of the pre-war machines.
1958 With the German motorcycle industry in severe depression, DKW merged with Victoria (see p.249) and Express (see p.238) to form the Zweirad Union (see p.251).
1966 The engine makers Fichtel & Sachs, owners of the Hercules marque

(see p.240), took over the Zweirad Union. The DKW name was briefly used on Sachs-engined lightweights. It lasted longer in some export markets, where Hercules machines, including its Wankel-engined motorcycle, carried a DKW badge until the late 1970s.

DOBRO-MOTORIST
1923–25 A small Berlin-based company that assembled machines using DKW and JAP engines in Cotton-style triangulated frames.

DOLF
c.1922–25 Dolf built unusual machines that used the firm's own 198cc two-stroke engines.

D-RAD
1926–33 Deutsche Industriewerke built motorcycles from 1923, after buying the Star marque (see p.248) and its 393cc side-valve flat-twin machine. The early machines were named Derad (see p.236) but the D-Rad logo was introduced in 1926. The following year a 498cc side-valve single, with an inclined cylinder, and unit-construction, three-speed gearbox, replaced the flat twin. An overhead-valve version was produced later. Smaller capacity machines with Bark two-stroke engines were also offered. NSU bought and closed the company in 1933.

DÜRKOPP
1899–1907 A bicycle and sewing machine company that built a range of motorcycles before World War I. It subsequently quit motorcycle production to make cars. In the 1930s it made motorized bicycles.
1949–60 Resumed motorcycle manufacturing with a range 100cc to 200cc two-stroke machines. Initially Ilo and Sachs engines were used, but the company quickly developed its own 147cc to 194cc two-stroke power units. It also made the successful Diana scooter. In 1955 Dürkopp merged with Ardie (see p.234), but production stopped five years later. Dürkopp still manufactures industrial sewing machines.

DWB
1924–26 Dorko Werke Bamberg took over production of the two-stroke Juhö machine (see p.241) when that firm closed. It built 198cc and 269cc versions of the motorcycle, but only in small numbers.

EBER
1924–28 A small manufacturer that used Blackburne, Kühne, and Küchen engines of 347cc to 498cc.

EBS
1927–30 Ernst Bauermeister & Son built an extensive range of machines at its Berlin premises. It used its own four-stroke engines of 198cc to 796cc. Some models were equipped with Villiers two-stroke engines.

ECA
c.1923–24 Eca manufactured a standard two-stroke lightweight with a loop frame and belt drive. The company was based in Hamburg.

ECEKA
1924–25 A short-lived company that produced small-capacity machines, using an assortment of proprietary engines.

EGA
1922–26 EGA built single-cylinder two-strokes fitted with its own 246cc and 346cc single-cylinder engines.

EICHELSDÖRFER
1929–31 Eichelsdörfer assembled utilitarian machines, using 198cc and 298cc JAP engines.

EICHLER
1920–25 Eichler was more prolific than the average small German manufacturer of the period. It built lightweight, two-stroke machines using engines supplied by Bekamo and DKW. The DKW Lomos and Golem scooters were also made under licence. The company was based in Berlin.

EISENHAMMER
1923–26 Built loop-framed belt-driven machines, using DKW two-stroke engines of 206cc to 225cc.

EKA
1924–25 EKA built a limited number of motorcycles equipped with DKW two-stroke engines.

ELFA
c.1926–40 Elfa used an assortment of proprietary engines in sizes of up to 500cc. During the 1930s the company mainly produced motorized bicycles.

ELFE
1923–25 Small Leipzig-based company that built two-stroke machines, using its own 196cc two-stroke engines.

ELITE
c.1924–40 Formerly a car maker, Elite merged with Diamant around 1924 and began producing motorcycles. It used Kühne 350cc to 500cc four-stroke engines. From 1932 it built the Elite-Opel – the EO – (see below) using the unusual Opel pressed-steel frame and an overhead-camshaft Küchen engine. Elite also used JAP engines and produced Sachs-engined two-strokes.

ELRING
1924–25 The Elring name was sometimes used on 196cc ELFE two-strokes (see above).

ELSTER
c.1924–26 Built a few unremarkable, small-capacity side-valve machines.

EMA
c.1922–26 Built by Eduard Molitor in Aalen, EMA motorcycles were simple, belt-driven lightweights that used 145cc DKW engines. Molitor also produced larger machines under his own name (see p.244).

EMW
c.1945–56 EMW was located in East Germany. It produced a 340cc shaft-driven single, with a pressed-steel frame and plunger rear suspension, based on the pre-World War II BMW design.

ENAG
1924–25 ENAG motorcycles were designed by Theo Steininger and built by Erie & Nestler at Nuremberg. They were unorthodox 250cc and 350cc two-strokes with water cooling.

ENLAG
1925–27 Enlag was the new name given to Eschag machines from 1925.

EO
1930–31 The Elite-Opel was built by the Elite-Diamant works. It combined the licence-built Neander frame of the Opel Motoclub with 347cc and 498cc overhead-camshaft Küchen engines.

EPA
1924–33 EPA machines were designed by Peter Pazicky. The company built a limited number of motorcycles using JAP engines. Lightweight utilitarian models were also produced under the Arminia brand-name (see p.234).

ERKA
1923–24 A short-lived company that built utilitarian, 269cc two-strokes in small quantities.

A 1958 Dürkopp Fratz moped with typical period pressed-steel construction

ERKÖ

1922–24 Erko was one of the many small German makes that appeared briefly in the early 1920s. It used 145cc DKW engines.

ERMAG

1923–30 Early models produced by Ermag were radical, 246cc stepped-piston two-strokes with disc valves. From 1926 it made 500cc four-strokes and during the last year of production it used MAG engines.

ERNST

c.1924–30 Built a range of conventional machines fitted with MAG engines. These included 348cc singles, and 498cc to 996cc V-twins.

ESCHAG

1923–25 Built small-capacity, belt-driven two-strokes. The name was changed to Enlag from 1925.

ESCH-REKORD

c.1927–30 Based in Cologne, Esch-Rekord built sporting machines equipped with a variety of British engines.

EUROPA

c.1931–33 Europa made motorcycles with two-stroke Villiers and Schliha engines. The factory was in Munich.

EVEREST

1925–26 Everest briefly produced an overhead-valve 500cc single.

EWABRA

c.1921–24 Ewabra made conventional 600cc side-valve singles with belt drive and three-speed gearbox.

EXCELSIOR

c.1901–39 A bicycle manufacturer that, over a long period, built unremarkable motorcycles with proprietary engines. The factory was located in Brandenburg. The marque vanished at the beginning of World War II.

EXPRESS

c.1903–08 Express was an established bicycle firm that fitted Fafnir engines into bicycle-style frames to make its first motorcycles. It produced a V-twin machine as early as 1904, but soon gave up motorcycle manufacturing.
1933–39 Resumed production with simple mopeds and lightweights with Sachs engines.
1949–58 Built mopeds and motorcycles up to 250cc using its own, Ilo, and Sachs engines. By 1958 production had dwindled to two models, and the company joined DKW (see p.236) and Victoria (see p.249) in the Zweirad Union (see p.251). The Express brand-name was soon dropped.

FA

1952 FA produced 175cc Sachs-engined cabin scooters.

FABULA

c.1922–24 Bielefeld-based firm, Fabula built an advanced, 246cc shaft-driven two-stroke with a triangulated, tubular frame. The design was influenced by the KG motorcycle. Few were built.

FADAG

c.1921–25 Initially Fadag built 118cc clip-on bicycle engines. It later added a 497cc single-cylinder four-stroke machine to its range.

FAFNIR

c.1900–14 Famous as a maker and supplier of engines for other manufacturers, Fafnir also made complete motorcycles for a short period.

FAKA

1952–57 Beneath jet-age styling were conventional 147cc to 197cc Ilo-engined scooters, produced by Fahrzeugwerke Kannenberg.

FALKE

c.1923–25 Falke produced lightweight two-strokes with proprietary engines.

FALTER

1952–63 Small manufacturer that concentrated exclusively on the production of mopeds.

FAMO

c.1923–26 Famo built simple belt-driven 127cc two-strokes.

FAVORIT

1933–38 Favorit built sidecars as well as motorcycles. Early machines were fitted with large-capacity V-twin JAP engines. Later the company produced two-strokes with Sachs engines.

FERBEDO

1953–54 Short-lived, 48cc Zündapp-engined scooter built by a toy manufacturer.

FEX

1923–24 A Berlin manufacturer that appeared briefly in the early 1920s. Its motorcycles used DKW and Bekamo two-stroke engines.

FIFI

1923–24 The Fifi was a 2hp clip-on two-stroke engine produced by Eichler. It mounted inside the wheel.

FIX

1922–26 The Lloyd car company built 144cc two-strokes in Bremen. It also sold them under its own name (see Lloyd p.243). Fix also supplied engines to other manufacturers.

A 1956 advertisement for a 49cc Express moped

FKS

1921–25 Frank Krause built 149cc lightweights and an unusual 298cc flat-twin two-stroke with belt drive. His premises were in Berlin.

FLINK

1920–22 Apparently the Flink was the first motorcycle built by BMW (see p.235). It was an ordinary belt-driven lightweight with a 148cc Kurier two-stroke engine.

FLOTTWEG

c.1921–37 Flottweg was one of many manufacturers to begin production with clip-on bicycle engines. The engines were 119cc four-strokes. Later the company offered complete motorcycles with 183cc and 243cc overhead-valve engines. JAP power units were used in some machines. The last models produced by Flottweg were equipped with the firm's own 198cc overhead-valve engines.

FKS

1923–24 Small Berlin-based company that made machines using proprietary two-stroke engines.

FORELLE

1955–58 Bicycle maker that briefly built 49cc Ilo- and Sachs-engined mopeds.

FORTUNA

1921–28 Fortuna built well-made but unremarkable two-strokes with 247cc and 297cc engines. It was located in Nuremberg.

FRANKONIA

1923 Frankonia assembled machines using horizontally mounted 145cc DKW engines.

FRANZANI

1923–31 Franzani produced a limited number of machines using its own two-stroke engines. It later switched to JAP and Küchen four-stroke power units.

FRANZENBURG
c.1925 Klaus Franzenburg from Nuremberg built a range of 350cc and 500cc single-cylinder machines with twin downtube frames. Production numbers are unknown.

FREITAL
1925–26 The Freital name was briefly used by DKW on 173cc two-stroke motorcycles.

FREUDENIA
1925 Freudenia was another small marque that used DKW engines.

FRIMA
c.1923–24 The Frima motorcycle, built by FRIedrich MArquardt, used a two-stroke engine.

FRIMO
c.1923–25 The Frimo motorcycle was a 246cc two-stroke built by the makers of VIS machines (see p.249).

FRISCHAUF
1928–40 Frischauf built conventional motorcycles in limited quantities. It used JAP, Blackburne, Küchen, and Villiers engines until 1933, and subsequently it made Sachs-engined lightweights.

GEHA
1920–24 During its limited period of manufacture, Geha made bicycle-style machines with small two-stroke engines.

GEIER
1934–54 During the 1930s Geier used Ilo engines to power its machines. Production was interrupted by the war and was not resumed until 1950. Its new range included Ilo- and Sachs-engined machines of up to 175cc, and a tricycle.

GEKA
c.1924–25 Geka produced typical DKW-engined lightweights, using a 173cc fan-cooled engine with two-speed gearbox and belt drive.

GE-MA-HI
c.1924–27 Built a wide range of lightweight two-strokes using a variety of proprietary engines. Some models had unusual, steel box-frames.

GERMANIA
1901–08 The Germania tradename was used on Laurin & Klement (see p.300), single-cylinder and V-twin machines that were built under licence, in Dresden, by Siedel & Naumann (see S&N p.248).

GLAS-GOGGO
1951–56 Glas-Goggo made Ilo-engined scooters with 123cc, 148cc, and 197cc engines. In 1955 production switched to light cars, which it continued to make

until the mid-1960s. Soviet copies of the Goggo-designed scooter later appeared under the Tula name (see p.305).

GNÄDIG
1925 Franz Gnädig was involved in the production of the KG – Krieger Gnädig – (see p.242) motorcycle, but when KG was taken over by Allright, Gnädig left to develop his own overhead-valve 350cc motorcycle. The complete machine was only built for a short time, and subsequently Kühne took over production of the engine. Gnädig later worked for Diamant (see p.236) and Opel (see p.245).

GNOM
c.1921–23 An overhead-valve clip-on bicycle engine made by Columbus (see p.236) in Oberursel. Gnom later became part of the Horex marque (see p.241).

GOEBEL
1951–79 Small company that produced only mopeds.

GOETZ
1925–35 Built a limited number of machines to special order using proprietary engines.

GOGGO
1951–56 Goggo made Ilo-engined scooters of 123cc to 197cc (see also Glas-Goggo).

GÖRICKE
1903–12 Bielefeld-based bicycle factory that produced motorcycles intermittently. The first motorcycles were typical belt-driven single-cylinder and V-twin machines.
1928–33 Introduced a new range of machines using MAG, Blackburne, and Villiers engines.
1949–c.1959 Made Sachs- and Ilo-engined machines of 48cc to 247cc. Göricke still manufactures bicycles.

GOUVERNEUR
c.1902–07 Pioneer company that installed 3.5hp engines on its machines.

GRADE
c.1903–25 Two-stroke specialist that also made aeroplanes and cars. The motorcycles used mainly 118cc and 132cc engines.

GRITZNER p.66
1903–08 Sewing machine manufacturer that built single-cylinder and V-twin Fafnir-engined motorcycles in the early days of the industry.
1953–62 Resumed production with a range of Sachs-engined lightweights. In 1958 Gritzner took over production of the Monza model from the defunct Mars factory (see p.243). It also built a KTM scooter under licence.

GROTE
1924–25 Built a 305cc two-stroke single in Berlin. Adding extra engines created a 610cc twin or a 915cc triple.

GRÜCO
c.1924–25 A short-lived company that built motorcycles using 346cc Kühne engines.

GRUHN
1921–32 Richard Gruhn may have built motorcycles as early as 1906, but serious production did not begin until after World War I. Gruhn motorcycles were 196cc side-valve four-strokes with loop frames and belt drive. Some overhead-valve machines were also made and one model had shaft drive. They were made in Berlin.

GRUTZENA
c.1925–26 Grutzena used 348cc overhead-valve Kühne engines mounted in orthodox frames with leaf-sprung, trailing-link front fork.

GS
c.1920–24 Gustav Schultz made clip-on, 129cc two-stroke bicycle engines and complete lightweight machines with loop frames and belt drive.

GS
1923–25 Built by George Schroff in Berlin, GS motorcycles were known also as Schroff-Record (see p.247). The machines were equipped with 145cc Gruhn engines.

GSM
1926 GSM machines, made in Saxony by G. Schultz, were equipped with 206cc DKW engines.

GÜLDNER
c.1925 Güldner briefly ventured into the motorcycle industry with its British-style, flat-tank 497cc overhead-valve single. The vertical engine was mounted on frame rails that passed along the top of the crankcases. The company was based at Aschaffenburg.

GUSTLOFF
c.1934–40 Gustloff made 74cc to 123cc lightweight machines. They were equipped with Sachs-engines.

HABROS
1927–30 Habros built a moped-like scooter with an engine that clipped onto the left side of the rear wheel. The company's factory was based in Nuremberg.

A Göricke Gorette step-thru photographed in 1955

HAGEL
1925 As a brief and unsuccessful foray into motorcycle production, Hagel offered a 247cc two-stroke equipped with its own engine. Based at Nuremberg.

HAKO
c.1924–25 HAns KOrn built JAP-engined machines inspired by the British HRD (see p.221). It was later known as HKR (see p.241).

HANFLAND
1920–25 Berlin-based company that built belt-driven 147cc two-strokes, using its own engines. The motorcycles were sometimes sold under the Kurier name (see p.243).

HANSA
c.1922–26 Built 148cc, 198cc, and 248cc two- and four-stroke machines.

HAPAMEE
c.1925–26 Built belt-driven machines equipped with the firm's own 198cc and 246cc two-stroke engines.

HARRAS
1922–25 Harras was one of the many short-lived Berlin companies that sprang up in the 1920s. It used 139cc and 145cc two-stroke Bekamo engines.

HASCHÜT
1929–31 HAns SCHÜTze of Dresden built 172cc Villiers-engined machines.

HAWEKA
c.1923–26 Haweka built four-strokes, using JAP and MAG single-cylinder engines.

HECKER
1922 Hans Hecker founded this company. Early production included 245cc two-strokes and 346cc overhead-valve machines with engines of his own design. From 1926 Hecker motorcycles were powered by JAP units of 198cc to 546cc, and other proprietary engines, including MAG.
1931 Production shifted to lightweight machines furnished with Sachs 73cc and 98cc two-stroke engines. The war interrupted production and when manufacture was resumed in 1948 it built lightweight machines with Ilo and Villiers two-stroke engines.
1957 Production ceased.

HEIDEMANN
1949–52 An established bicycle firm that briefly built a Sachs-engined 125cc lightweight motorcycle.

HEILO
1924–25 250cc and 350cc two-stroke single-cylinder machines built at Nuremberg by Heilbron & Co.

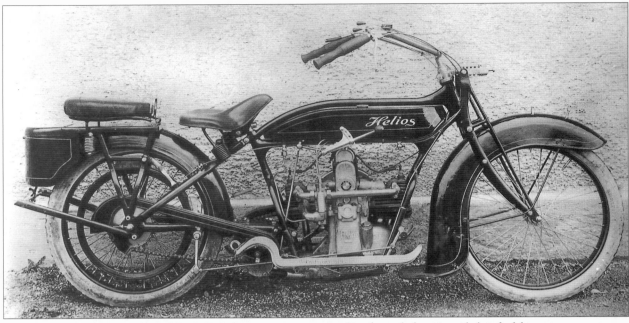

A 1922 Helios built by BMW; the flat-twin engine was mounted in a fore-and-aft position with chain final drive

HEINKEL p.77
1953–65 Post-war limitations on aircraft manufacturing made Heinkel switch to production of mopeds and scooters. The 150cc overhead-valve Tourist scooter appeared in 1953 and the Perle moped in 1954. The scooter was immensely successful.

HELI
1923–25 Berlin-built motorcycle with a 246cc water-cooled two-stroke engine, leaf-sprung fork, and belt drive.

HELIOS
1921–22 The Helios was a horizonally opposed twin built by BMW (though this was not BMW's first entry into the motorcycle market – see also Flink p.238) before it adopted the tranverse layout. The Helios machine followed the Douglas layout with fore-and-aft cylinders and chain drive. The engine, a 486cc side-valve unit, was also sold to other manufacturers, including Victoria. Legend says that problems with this machine encouraged BMW to design a new motorcycle with shaft drive and a transverse engine.

HELLA
c.1921–24 Hella built 147cc and 183cc two-stroke singles with belt drive. The engine was mounted horizontally in bicycle-style frames.

HELLER
1923–26 Heller built a machine using a 493cc BMW flat-twin engine. It offered a water-cooled version of this bike and also a limited number of two-strokes.

HELO
1923–25 Short-lived manufacturer of 149cc two-strokes with Bekamo engines.

HENKEL
1927–32 Paul Henkel took over the rights and tooling to make the single-cylinder shaft-driven KG motorcycle from Allright (see p.234) when it stopped making motorcycles. From 1929 he also built a smaller machine with a 198cc Blackburne engine.

HERCULES p.81
1904 The first motorcycle built by this Nuremberg-based bicycle company was a typical atmospheric-inlet-valve single-cylinder machine with belt drive. Production was halted by World War I.
1924–26 Limited motorcycle production was resumed, using proprietary engines of 75cc to 500cc. These were supplied by JAP, Sachs, Küchen, and Bark, among others.
1950 After World War II production began again with a range of machines using Sachs and Ilo two-stroke engines of 100cc to 250cc in orthodox chassis. Hercules soon grew to become one of the largest German manufacturers of the 1950s. It was subsequently bought by Fichtel & Sachs.
1966 Merged with the Zweirad Union, an amalgamation of the DKW (see p.236), Express (see p.238), and Victoria (see p.249) marques.
1974 The W2000, the first Wankel-engined motorcycle in production, was launched. The rest of the model range was made up of two-strokes. The number of models available decreased throughout the 1970s and since the 1980s Hercules has primarily produced mopeds.

HERKO
c.1922–25 Herko built a variety of complete machines, including 122cc and 158cc belt-driven two-strokes with an inclined cylinder, and a 198cc model with side-valve engine.

HERMA
c.1921–24 Manufactured 148cc clip-on engines for bicycles.

HERMES
c.1918–25 Stettin-based company that produced advanced, 150cc horizontal-cylinder two-strokes with all-chain transmission.

HERMES
1924–25 Hermes was another of the small companies to tackle motorcycle production in the 1920s. It made a very limited number of open-framed machines that were equipped with JAP engines.

HEROS
1921–29 A Saxony-based firm that was originally called H&R (see p.241), Heros produced a variety of two- and four-stroke motorcycles of 155cc to 247cc.

HEROS
1923–24 This Heros was made in Berlin, using 142cc DKW engines.

HERTHA
1925 The short-lived Hertha company built machines using 142cc DKW engines.

HESS
1925 Hess offered a 748cc air-cooled in-line four-cylinder machine. Few were actually built.

HEXE
1924–25 Hexe made clip-on bicycle engines and complete lightweight motorcycles in Bamberg.

HIEKEL
1925–32 Leipzig-built, triangular-framed machine with a 348cc single-cylinder two-stroke engine.

HILDEBRAND & WOLFMÜLLER pp.82–83
1894–97 Hildebrand & Wolfmüller built a steam-powered bicycle before developing petrol engines. After two years of experiments it began building the first commercially built motorcycle. It was not a practical machine and did not survive once the novelty vanished.

HIRSCH
1923–25 The company made small-capacity two-strokes, using its own and DKW engines. The machines were built in Berlin.

HIRTH
1923–26 Hirth made a limited number of 144cc and 244cc water-cooled racing two-strokes, which were raced with great success in the 1920s.

HKR
1925–26 HKR was the new name for The Hako motorcycle (see p.240). It still looked like the British HRD machine and it still used a JAP engine. The initials stood for Hans Korn of Rothenburg.

HOCHLAND
c.1926–27 The Hochland motorcycle was a 496cc overhead-valve flat twin. The engine was mounted with fore-and-aft cylinders in a typical, tubular frame.

HOCO
1924–28 Hoco followed Bekamo's example and used a wooden frame construction. Steel fittings were bolted to the ash sections for the steering head and engine mountings. Villiers and DKW two-strokes, as well as JAP four-stroke engines were used.

HOFFMANN p.84
1949 Jakob Oswald Hoffmann started building Ilo-engined motorcycles, and also acquired the licence to build Vespa scooters in Germany.
1951 Introduced a BMW-style, 250cc flat twin, but expensive development costs strained company finances.
1954 The Vespa licence expired, and without it Hoffmann could not survive.

HOREX p.96
1923 The Horex motorcycle was the unlikely product of diversification by the HOmburg-based REX Glassware Co. The first machines used 250cc to 600cc four-stroke engines supplied by the Oberursel engine company, which also made the Gnom clip-on engine (see p.239).
1926 Oberursel was taken over.
1930 Lack of success with Oberursel engines encouraged Horex to begin building 350cc to 500cc Sturmey-Archer engines under licence. These and other engine designs were made under the Columbus name (see p.236). They were also sold to other manufacturers. There followed an assortment of models using single-cylinder and parallel-twin, four-stroke engines with side-valve, overhead-valve, and overhead-camshaft operation.
1948 Post-war production restarted with the pre-war, overhead-valve 350cc single. Some 250cc singles and a 500cc parallel twin were added to the range in the 1950s, but production stopped in 1960.
1980 A range of Sachs-engined mopeds appeared with the Horex name but soon vanished. The name is still used on Honda-engined machines produced in limited numbers in Japan for the Japanese market.

H&R
1921–25 Hartmann & Richter was the predecessor of the Heros marque (see p.240). It built a range of two- and four-stroke machines.

HUC
1924–25 Huc made lightweights using 145cc and 172cc DKW engines.

HUCKE-RINNE
c.1924–26 Built by Max Hucke using Rinne two-stroke engines of 124cc, 174cc, and 247cc.

HULLA
c.1925–32 Hulla installed DKW and JAP engines on orthodox frames of its own design.

HUMMEL
1951–54 Made motorcycles, scooters, and mopeds from 49cc to 247cc, using Ilo engines. The scooters were largely sold under the Sitta label (see p.248).

HUY
1922–26 Huy used its own and MAG engines of 198cc to 346cc. It made lightweight machines with an inclined-cylinder engine mounted in a loop frame with belt drive. Built in Dresden.

IDEAL
1922–25 Dresden-built, loop-framed lightweights with belt drive and Triumph-type pivoting forks. Ideal originally used a 1.5hp four-stroke engine but later versions may have had a 173cc two-stroke power unit.

IFA p.100
1947 After World War II, the former DKW (see p.236) factory was within the boundaries of communist East Germany. DKW relocated to West Germany, and the machines built at the old factory were named IFA. Most models were two-stroke 98cc to 298cc singles based on previous DKW designs, but there was also a 350cc two-stroke flat twin.
1960 The machines were renamed MZ (see p.244), an abbreviation for Motorradwerke Zschopau.

ILO
c.1923–25 Ilo, a well-known manufacturer of two-stroke engines, briefly built complete machines. They were typical belt-driven lightweights.

IMME p.100
1948–51 The Imme was a novel and advanced, 99cc two-stroke machine designed by Norbert Riedel. The wheels were mounted on stub axles, allowing single-sided swingarm and front forks. The engine pivoted with the swingarm, which doubled as the exhaust pipe, and rubber-sprung suspension was used. A 148cc twin-cylinder version was also built in limited numbers.

IMPERIA
1923–25 Imperia built a limited number of motorcycles furnished with 350cc to 500cc JAP engines.

IMPERIA
1924 Began making machines with MAG, JAP, Bradshaw, and Blackburne engines of 350cc to 1000cc. It enjoyed considerable competition success with the racing versions of these machines.
1926 The company changed owners and production moved from Cologne to Bad Godesberg. Manufacturing of motorcycles continued, using a variety of proprietary engines. In the 1930s attempts were made to develop unconventional, supercharged two-stroke engines and hydraulic transmissions.
1935 These experiments drained the company coffers and production stopped.

INDUS
1924–25 Built a few machines in Berlin. JAP, Kühne, and Küchen engines were used in frames with front and rear leaf-sprung suspension.

JAVON
1929–32 J. A. Volger acquired the remains of the Abako marque (see p.234) with manufacturing rights for the Cockerell two-stroke engine. Small-capacity two-strokes and JAP-engined four-strokes were made in limited numbers in Nuremberg.

JCZ
c.1925 Josef Cemanek at Zittau assembled machines, in limited numbers, using proprietary components.

JHC
1921 Nuremberg-based firm that made a handful of 183cc two-strokes.

JOOS
c.1900–07 Pioneer company that originally produced horizontal twins with its own engines. Later models were equipped with Fafnir single-cylinder and V-twin engines.

JUHÖ
1922–24 JUlius HÖflich used his own 195cc two-stroke and Alba's 148cc side-valve engines in conventional, belt-driven machines. Production rights passed to DWB (see p.237), which continued production until 1927.

JURISCH
1926–30 Two-stroke specialist Carl Jurisch made this competition machine in Leipzig. It was a supercharged 250cc twin-cyclinder bike with water cooling.

KARÜ
c.1922–24 The Karü motorcycle was built by KArl RÜhmer at the Stockdorfer Motoren Werk where the similar SMW (see p.248) machine was also built. The bikes were fitted with Bosch-Douglas and BMW flat-twin engines.

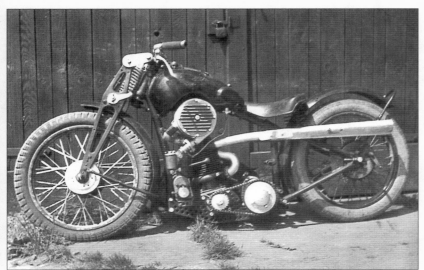

A 1935 Imperia 348cc two-stroke with supercharger mounted on top of the cylinder

The 1982 Krauser MKM 1000 with a multi-tubular frame and BMW flat-twin engine

K-C
c.1920–24 Kircheim & Co. of Magdeburg built a 105cc two-stroke bicycle engine with rotary valve, which mounted above the rear wheel. It also offered an unusual 257cc motorcycle with a rotary-valve, two-stroke flat-twin engine and belt drive.

KENI
1921–25 Berlin-based firm that built typical belt-driven lightweights. The company used its own 145cc and 158cc two-stroke engines which were mounted in loop frames.

KG
1919 The KG was an advanced machine produced by Franz Gnädig and the Krieger brothers. It had a single-cylinder 497cc overhead-valve engine with an in-unit three-speed gearbox and shaft drive to the rear wheel. The frame was a triangulated tubular structure and it was fitted with girder forks.
1922 Due to economic circumstances, Cito (see p.236) took over production of the KG motorcycle. The following year Cito was absorbed by Allright (see p.234), which continued making the KG under the Allright-KG name. The Krieger brothers established a rival operation making a similar machine, which they called the Original-Krieger (see p.245).
1927 Allright stopped making motorcycles and production of the KG was taken over by Paul Henkel.
1932 After a varied history spanning 13 years, the KG went out of production.

KILLINGER & FREUND
1938 Produced a prototype machine with a three-cylinder two-stroke radial engine, which mounted in the front wheel like a Megola (see p.244). It also featured streamlined bodywork.

KLEINSCHNITTGEN
c.1954 A small firm that produced a few 49cc Ilo-engined scooters. It also built small cars.

KLOTZ
c.1923–26 Stuttgart-based firm that built two-strokes, using its own 246cc engines.

KMB
1923–26 Köln Motorradwerk Becker made single-cylinder four-stroke bikes.

KÖBO
c.1923–26 Köbo built a belt-driven, 276cc two-stroke single with three gears.

KOFA
1923–25 Kofa produced a few 276cc two-strokes.

KÖHLER
1922–25 Designed by Ernst Köhler and built in Munich by Diana-Werke GmbH, it was also known by the initials DAW (see p.236). The machine had a 407cc single-cylinder two-stroke engine hidden behind strange pressed-steel bodywork, which extended forward to provide a cowl for the headlamp. The wheels were steel discs and it was fitted with a trailing-link front fork.

KOMET
1902–05 Komet built 1hp to 4hp two-stroke engines under licence from Ixion (see p.280) in France. These were fitted to its own bicycle-style frames.

KONDOR
1924–25 Kondor built conventional machines in Berlin using proprietary two- and four-stroke engines.

KÖNIG
1969–76 A manufacturer of outboard engines for boats, König also developed a 500cc racing motorcycle with a horizontally opposed, flat-four-cylinder two-stroke engine. The engine was also built in 680cc form. Kim Newcombe won the Yugoslav Grand Prix in 1973 and the firm enjoyed many other competition successes in both solo and sidecar races. Newcombe's death and the appearance of more developed engines from other manufacturers, signalled the end of König's brief but memorable career.

KOSTER
c.1923–25 Koster developed an unusual-looking machine with a pressed-steel and tubular frame, probably inspired by the Mars design. The motorcycles had small-capacity two-stroke Bekamo or Cockerell engines. The drive chain was enclosed and disc wheels were used.

KRAMER
1977–85 Kramer built motocross and enduro machines that housed Rotax engines of 124cc to 280cc. It was linked with the Italian Kram-It firm (see p.259).

KRAUSER
1976– BMW dealer and motorcycle luggage manufacturer Mike Krauser developed a special eight-valve version of the BMW Rennsport engine in 1976 in an effort to keep it competitive in sidecar racing against the two-stroke opposition. He subsequently supported, and then took over first the Kreidler, then the Zündapp race teams when those companies closed. The 50cc World Championship in 1983 and the 80cc title in 1985 were both won on Krauser-backed machines. After the failure of the BMW-derived engine in sidecar racing, four-cylinder two-stroke engines for racing sidecars were also produced. Between 1982–83 he built 200 special, multi-tubular frames to take BMW flat-twin engines. These were sold in kit form or as a complete motorcycle, with a BMW warranty. In the late 1980s Krauser produced the Domani, a sidecar outfit based on the K-series BMW engine and transmission.

KREIDLER p.118
1951–82 Kreidler machines were built in Stuttgart by a metals company. It specialized in 50cc motorcycles and mopeds throughout its history. From the mid-1950s it dominated sales in the 50cc category and at one time it was the largest motorcycle manufacturer in Germany. Kreidler products used a horizontal-cylinder two-stroke engine. The Florett models, which were first introduced in 1956, were especially popular. The first Kreidler racing machines were introduced in 1959 and were modelled on the company's own road bikes. The design was developed in the early 1960s and Kreidler quickly achieved World Championship success. It won six 50cc World Championships and set speed records in the 50cc category. Sales fell in the early 1980s and the firm went into liquidation.

KRIEGER
c.1925–26 Soon after the KG marque (see above) was taken over by Allright (see p.234), the Krieger brothers established a new company. They built machines with single-cylinder Blackburne engines, which had triangulated frames and were similar to the KG. They also used the name Original-Krieger (see p.245).

KRUPP
c.1919–22 For a brief period of time, Krupp built the U.S.-designed Autoped scooter (see p.268) under licence. The fuel tank and the small atmospheric-inlet-valve engine were mounted on the front fork. Pushing the handlebars forward engaged drive, pulling them back disengaged the drive and applied the brake. The handlebars could be folded down for covenient storage.

KSB
1924–29 Small Saxony-based company that used 142cc to 498cc two- and four-stroke engines supplied by Blackburne, DKW, JAP, and Kühne. The initials KSB stood for Kurt Schiebach of Bautzen.

KURIER
1921–24 Kurier built a lightweight, loop-framed, belt-driven two-stroke, which from around 1922 was offered with a simple rear suspension system. Transmission was by belt and the inclined-cylinder engine had a capacity of 154cc.

KZ
1924–25 KZ motorcycles were built in very limited numbers by Kolb & Ziegler using Alba 198cc side-valve and Kühne 348cc overhead-valve engines.

LEBELT
1924–25 Paul Lebelt built a limited number of machines with his own two- and four-stroke engines.

LEOPARD
c.1921–26 Magdeburg-based firm that built orthodox machines with its own 249cc and 350cc overhead-valve two-stroke engines.

LEOPARD
c.1958–66 The German Panther marque used this name in some export markets for its lightweight, Sachs-engined two-stroke motorcycles to avoid confusion with the British-built Panther (see p.226).

LEVANTE
1954 Levante used a 34cc Rex engine that mounted above the belt-driven front wheel.

LFG
1921–25 Luftfahrzeug GmbH of Berlin was in the airship business before it diversified into clip-on bicycle engines. It also produced a fully enclosed motorcycle with authentic Zeppelin styling. It had a 305cc two-stroke engine.

LINSER
c.1922–24 Built flat-twin machines with Bosch-Douglas and BMW engines.

LLOYD
c.1922–26 A standard two-stroke built by the Lloyd car company, using a 144cc engine. The Lloyd was also sold under the Fix name (see p.238).

LLOYD
1923–29 Lloyd was the brand-name used for larger capacity machines built along with the more utilitarian Ocra marque (see p.245). They were fitted with proprietary four-stroke engines.

LMS
c.1922 LMS was another company that attempted to switch to motorcycle production from airships. The result was a weird machine with enclosed bodywork that concealed 350cc and 500cc four-stroke twin-cylinder engines. A 142cc DKW-powered version was also offered. Unsurprisingly, not many were built.

LORENZ
c.1921–22 Lorenz built a limited number of 211cc two-stroke scooters. It was located in Stetten.

LORENZ
1921–24 Berlin-based firm that built a 126cc flat-twin two-stroke engine, which was available either as a bicycle attachment or in a complete machine.

LUPUS
1923–26 Small company that built two-strokes using its own 148cc engine.

LUTRAU
c.1924–33 Built a range of 200cc to 350cc two-stroke singles and a 500cc side-valve single.

LUTZ
1949–54 Lutz made unremarkable 58cc and 174cc scooters.

LUWE
1924–28 LUdwig WEber built a range of bikes using proprietary engines, supplied by Paqué, Kühne, Blackburne, MAG, and JAP.

MABECO
1922–27 The Mabeco motorcycle was built in Berlin by MAx BErnhardt & CO. A copy of the Indian Scout, it was available in 596cc and 749cc versions. Some models were developed with overhead-valve rather than side-valve operation. A few motorcycles were also built using a licence-built, split-single Garelli two-stroke engine.

MAFA
1923–27 Mafa offered a range of machines equipped with small-capacity, DKW two-stroke engines and Kühne four-stroke singles of 119cc to 496cc.

MAGNET
1901–14 A pioneer company that built machines using its own single-cylinder and V-twin engines.

MAICO p.122
1935 MAIsch & CO began building lightweight motorcycles and mopeds using Ilo and Sachs two-stroke engines. The war stopped production.
1948 After the war Maico launched a new 123cc machine that used its own single-cylinder two-stroke engine. By 1953 it was offering a range of bikes of up to 400cc, as well as the fully faired Maico-Mobil. From 1955 a proper scooter, the Maicoletta, was built and the company took an increasing interest in off-road competition. A large number of motocross and enduro machines were built and exported from the 1960s.
1983 Production of road and off-road machines stopped when the company went bankrupt. Subsequently intermittent and limited production of enduro and motocross machines has been continued by another company, which has retained the Maico badge.

MAMMUT
1924–33 Formerly a machine tool manufacturer, this Nuremberg-based firm began building motorcycles in 1924. It used its own 197cc and 246cc two-stroke engines, as well as MAG, JAP, and Blackburne four-strokes. From 1929 it used Coventry-Eagle pressed-steel frames, which it built under licence.

MAMMUT
1953–56 An established bicycle manufacturer that also made motorcycles in the 1950s, Mammut produced a range of mopeds and lightweight motorcycles of up to 197cc. It used Ilo, Zündapp, and Sachs two-stroke engines to power its machines, which were also sold under the Meister (see p.244) and Phänomen (see p.246) names.

MAMMUT (MAMMOTH)
1966– Mammut – "Mammoth" – was the name for the first model built by Friedl Münch (see p.244). It was a monster bike with a NSU car engine. From 1966 to 1977, when Münch lost the rights to his own name, the same bike was known as the Münch. In 1977 Münch revived the Mammut name on a limited number of machines.

MARS (MA) p.123
1903–14 Mars began construction of motorcycles at its factory in Nuremberg. Early machines were equipped with Zedel and Fafnir engines.
1920 Introduced the "Weiss Mars", which used a 948cc side-valve horizontally opposed engine built by Maybach. This was mounted longitudinally in a box-section frame. Bankruptcy and the German economic crisis stopped production between 1925–27. When production resumed the firm was prevented from using the Mars trademark and the machines were known by the initials MA. It launched a range of new models using MAG, Sturmey-Archer, and Villiers engines. Throughout the 1930s the company concentrated on making Sachs-engined lightweights. This trend continued after World War II, when 98cc to 174cc Sachs-engined machines were produced.
1958 Mars folded and production of its 49cc Monza model was taken over by Gritzner (see p.239).

MAURER
1922–26 Two-stroke specialist that built rotary-valve clip-on engines and a few complete motorcycles. A 294cc flat twin and a 247cc single were produced. Both used water cooling. The twin engine was also used to power a car.

A 1919 example of the Krupp folding scooter

MAUSER
1924–27 The Mauser was a weird cross between car and motorcycle. The chassis used two pressed-steel members with a 510cc water-cooled side-valve engine mounted horizontally at the rear, underneath the passenger seat. Girder forks and leaf-sprung rear swingarm were used. The machine boasted narrow, car-style bodywork and outrigger wheels, which were retractable when the machine was moving. It was also built under licence in France by Monotrace (see p.281).
1927–32 Production was continued by Gustav Winkler.

MAX
1924–25 Berlin-built machines that used the company's own 180cc two-stroke and 446cc side-valve engines.

MEGOLA p.126
1921–25 The Megola was designed by Fritz Cockerell, who also produced lightweight two-stroke machines under his own name (see p.236). The 640cc five-cylinder radial engine was inspired by radial aircraft engines. It mounted in the front wheel and rotated around a stationary crankshaft. There was no clutch or gearbox. The frame was a pressed-steel, box-section girder and leaf-sprung rear suspension was used. Racing versions were also produced.

MEISTER
1951–56 An established bicycle company that produced a range of motorcycles using a variety of proprietary engines. Zündapp-powered mopeds were built as well as Sachs- and Ilo-engined lightweight motorcycles and scooters of up to 197cc. Some models were also sold under the Mammut (see p.243) and Phänomen (see p.246) brand-names.

MENOS
1922–23 Menos machines were also sold under the Aristos (see p.234) and Sterna (see p.248) names. All the machines were built at the Berlin factory, and used the same 614cc water-cooled flat-twin engine and pressed-steel frame. The Menos was distinguishable by its striking, striped design.

MERCO
1922–24 Merco built lightweights using its own 148cc two-stroke engines.

MESSERSCHMITT-VESPA
1954–64 An aircraft manufacturer that took over the licence to build Vespas in Germany from Hoffman. It also made bubble cars.

MF
1922–25 A dairy engineer, Max Fischer, began building motorcycles in 1922. MF machines were fitted with 492cc side-valve flat-twin BMW engines; 347cc and 497cc side-valve single-cylinder Blackburne engines; and some two-stroke DKW engines.

MFZ
1921–28 Berlin-based company that built simple and strong machines. It used its own 198cc, 247cc, and 347cc overhead-valve engines.

MGF
1923–26 Berlin-based firm that built orthodox two-strokes of 122cc to 198cc.

MIELE
1933–62 Formerly a bicycle manufacturer, Miele began installing 73cc and 98cc Sachs engines in its own bicycle frames in 1933. After World War II the company continued building Sachs-powered lightweight motorcycles of up to 190cc. From 1955 to its demise in 1962 it concentrated on moped production.

MJ
c.1924–25 MJ produced a 339cc air-cooled horizontally opposed twin with a three-speed, unit-construction gearbox and chain final drive. The machine had a duplex cradle frame and trailing-link forks. A water-cooled version and a 249cc two-stroke may also have been produced.

MJS
1924–25 Short-lived firm that made a few simple 245cc two-strokes.

MÖFA
1926 Albert Möser built a limited number of machines, using four-stroke single-cyclinder Blackburne engines.

MOLITOR
c.1926 A British-style machine built by Eduard Molitor, who also produced the EMA lightweights (see p.237). Molitor machines were 500cc and 600cc four-stroke singles that used proprietary engines and other components.

MOTAG
1923–24 Built by Becker & Co. of Leipzig in very limited numbers, the Motag had an unusual cast-alloy frame. It was available with 514cc to 804cc vertical-twin engines with air or water cooling.

MOTA-WIESEL
1948–52 The Mota-Wiesel was a small-wheeled moped equipped with a 74cc or 98cc two-stroke engine.

MÜCO
1921–24 Müco briefly offered a 98cc two-stroke clip-on bicycle engine, which mounted at the rear wheel.

MÜNCH p.133
1966 Constructor Friedl Münch made several road and racing machines, but the Mammut – "Mammoth" – (see p.243) is his monument. It was built using the engine from an NSU car. Capacity was originally 996cc, but it later grew to 1177cc and beyond.
1974 The company was taken over by Heinz W. Henke, who retained the Münch name.
1977 Friedl Münch split with Henke. Henke kept the Münch brand-name and continued to produce machines until the early 1980s. Friedl Münch revived the Mammut name, which he had used on his original model in 1966. He was also involved in an attempt to re-launch the Horex marque (see p.241) in the 1980s.

MUZ
1991– MuZ was the renamed descendant of the MZ marque (see right). It launched a range of four-strokes with Yamaha and Rotax engines.

MW
c.1923–26 MW machines had an unusual frame made of cast-alloy and pressed-steel sections. All models had rear suspension and used either a 249cc overhead-valve single-cylinder engine or a 144cc in-line twin.

MZ pp.137–139
1960 The products of Motorradwerke Zschopau previously used the IFA badge (see p.241). The factory at Zchopau was the pre-war home of DKW (see p.236). MZ machines were based on earlier DKW designs, and MZ continued the tradition of two-stroke development from its predecessors. Its 125/150cc models were based on the pre-war DKW RT125 and were a mainstay of production for 40 years. There was also an unusual 350cc horizontally opposed, shaft-driven two-stroke twin. It was replaced by 250cc single-cylinder road bikes, which were also developed into successful enduro machines. In road racing, MZ engineer Walter Kaaden was responsible for developing 125cc and 250cc machines, which led the world in two-stroke technology during the 1960s.
1991 With the reunification of Germany MZ was denationalized and renamed MuZ. New four-stroke models with

A Mauser Einspuranto with stabilizer wheels retracted

Rotax and Yamaha engines were produced. Two-strokes were pushed into the background.

NAMAPO
c.1921–24 Built 147cc and 197cc side-valve single-cylinder machines.

NEANDER
c.1924–32 Ernst Neander designed and built motorcycles using engines of up to 1000cc, supplied by Villiers, Küchen, MAG, and JAP. The advanced frame design was made from Duralumin section and featured pivoting forks. The design was also made under licence by Opel (see below) and EO (see p.237).

NEMALETTE
1924–25 Nemalette produced a bizarre machine with enclosed bodywork and twin rear wheels. It was powered by a 173cc DKW two-stroke engine. Unsurprisingly, very few were built.

NERA
1948–50 The Nera was an early post-war scooter, which used 120cc Ilo and 149cc Sachs, two-stroke engines.

NESTORIA
1925–31 Nestoria took over production of the Astoria marque (see p.234) in 1925. Its machines, produced at the Nuremberg factory, used the firm's own 289cc and 346cc two-stroke engines. In 1926 it was taken over by Bischoff & Pedall (see p.235) and began using proprietary four-stroke engines. These included the overhead-camshaft, three-valve Küchen; 496cc and 596cc inlet-over-exhaust MAG singles; and Sturmey-Archer four-stroke singles.

NKF
1924–25 Norddeutsche Kühlerfabrik built 132cc machines in Berlin. It used the Bekamo two-stroke engine.

NSH
c.1923–28 Built orthodox machines using Villiers and JAP engines of up to 490cc.

NSU  p.148–151
1900 Around 1890 Neckarsulm Strickmaschinen – "knitting machine" – Union began making bicycles. At the turn of the century it installed a 1.5hp Swiss Zedel engine into a bicycle-style frame to create its first motorcycle. By 1903 the company had begun making its own 329cc 2.5hp engines. The next year it started building an 804cc V-twin. In the years preceeding World War I NSU built a variety of single-cylinder and V-twin machines, including racers. It also exported in quantity. After the war the firm continued making both singles and V-twins.
1929 British designer Walter Moore joined NSU from Norton (see p.142). He created new, 348cc to 596cc overhead-camshaft racing singles. More mundane two- and four-stroke machines, for mass production, were also developed. These included the OSL range of 250cc to 600cc overhead-valve singles and 98cc and 200cc two-stroke singles.
1949 Post-war production started slowly, but in 1949 the new 98cc overhead-valve Fox was introduced. The Fox had a pressed-steel frame with leading-link forks and cantilever rear suspension. The following year NSU began making the Lambretta scooter under licence. The OSL range continued in production until 1952 when the Max appeared. In 1953 NSU began to produce the highly successful Quickly moped. Over a million were made in the next decade. The Prima scooter replaced the Lambretta design in 1956.
1963 Increased commitment to car manufacturing ended motorcycle production, but mopeds continued to be built until 1965.

NUX
1924–25 Short-lived company that made 170cc two-strokes in Berlin.

OCRA
1923–25 Ottamar CRAmer built a 137cc two-stroke engine that attached to a bicycle. He also made larger capacity Lloyd motorcycles (see p.243).

OD 🏍 p.152
1927–35 Willy Ostner of Dresden made quality machines with proprietary engines. Most models were equipped with MAG single-cylinder and V-twin engines of 347cc to 996cc. Some small motorcycles were also made using Bark 198cc and 246cc two-stroke engines.

ODIN
1923–24 K. L. Konrad built a limited number of 124cc two-strokes.

OGE
1921–24 OGE produced a 118cc lightweight two-stroke.

OHB
1928 Otto Hoffmann built a limited number of machines using 490cc overhead-valve single-cylinder JAP engines.

OKUR
c.1922 See Oruk (right).

OMNIA
1931–33 Imperia (see p.241) used the Omnia name for a range of cheap two-strokes, which used 98cc and 147cc Villiers and 198cc Bark engines.

OPEL 🏍 p.153
1901–30 The famous car maker Opel also built motorcycles. Until 1907 it made conventional single-cylinder machines of 1.75hp to 2.75hp. Production resumed after World War I, making 140cc side-valve clip-on bicycle engines and later, complete machines with 148cc inlet-over-exhaust engines. From 1926 it made 498cc side-valve singles and in 1928 it launched the Motoclub motorcycle, which was based on the Neander design. Motoclub machines had the company's own 499cc side-valve and overhead-valve engines. These machines were actually built at the Diamant-Elite factory.

ORIAL
c.1929–31 Orial was the name used in export markets on German-built Triumph machines after the company split from the British Triumph firm. From 1931 the initials TWN – "Triumph Werke Nürnberg" – were used instead.

ORIGINAL-KRIEGER
1925–26 The Krieger brothers and Franz Gnädig began building an advanced, 497cc shaft-driven single under the name KG (see p.242) in 1919. A subsequent merger with Cito (see p.236), followed by a takeover by Allright (see p.234) in 1923, saw them part company with their creation. They subsequently built the very similar Blackburne-engined Original-Krieger machine, but legal action by Allright halted production.

ORIONETTE
1921–25 Orionette built conventional 129cc to 346cc two-strokes in Berlin. It also produced a prototype with an exhaust valve in the cylinder head.

ORTLOFF
1924–25 A short-lived company that built lightweights with 185cc and 198cc side-valve engines from Gruhn.

ORUK
1922–24 Oruk built an open-framed lightweight with a 189cc side-valve engine, which was mounted beside the rear wheel. During the first year of production the name Okur (see left) was sometimes used. Twenty-five years later Vespa used a similar idea. Its design was far more successful than the Oruk.

OSCHA
1924–25 Otto SCHAaf built 496cc water-cooled horizontally opposed twins in limited numbers at Leipzig.

PAFFRATH
c.1923–26 The MW machine (see p.244) designed by Paul Paffrath was also sold under his name. It used an unorthodox, cast-alloy and pressed-steel frame.

PAMAG
1952–53 PAderborner Maschinenbau AG took over production of Anker motorcycles (see p.234). It briefly produced Sachs- and Ilo-powered machines.

PAN
1924–25 Berlin-based company that built machines using 346cc overhead-valve, single-cylinder Kühne engines. The frame was a triangulated tubular structure fitted with a leaf-sprung, trailing-link front fork.

PANTHER
1933–59 A bicycle firm that began motorcycle production with Sachs- and Ilo-engined 73cc and 98cc two-stroke lightweights. After World War II the range expanded to include machines of 49cc to 173cc using Sachs engines. These were sold in some export markets under the Leopard name (see p.243) to avoid confusion with the British Panther marque (see p.226). Production of mopeds continued until the mid-1970s.

KS 175 S

The "Swinging Frame" Model with Remarkable Roadability Handsomer and Quieter

The Panther KS 175S with a 173cc Sachs engine as shown in the 1956 catalogue

A 1955 version of Rabeneick's Universal-engined shaft-drive 250 model

PAQUÉ
c.1921–25 Based at Augsburg, Bavaria, Paqué began production in 1921 with 137cc clip-on bicycle engines. It later made complete motorcycles with 147cc and 197cc overhead-valve engines and a few overhead-camshaft 198cc and 497cc side-valve machines. It supplied engines to other manufacturers.

PATRIA
1925–27 Built overhead-camshaft 250cc and 350cc four-stroke singles.
1949–52 Briefly resumed production with Ilo-engined two-strokes.

PAWA
1922 The Pawa was a strange and unsurprisingly short-lived machine. It had a long wheelbase, front and rear suspension, a large fairing, and bucket seats. A 226cc two-stroke single or a horizontally opposed, 340cc four-stroke twin-cylinder engine was used.

PAWI
1922–24 Pawi built a limited number of BMW-engined machines. It was located in Berlin.

PER
1925–26 PER used a 308cc two-stroke engine in a strange, pressed-steel frame. Bucket seats were used and the engine was hidden behind enclosed bodywork. It was the work of Kurt Passow, who earlier had built the even weirder Pawa.

PERLE
c.1920 Competition machines built in limited numbers by racer Hans Perle.

PETERS
1924 Small Berlin factory that produced motorcycles using 143cc DKW engines.

PHÄNOMEN p.155
1903–40 Phänomen originally built motorcycles with Fafnir 487cc single-cylinder and 507cc V-twin engines. Production stopped before World War I. From 1930, Sachs-engined 73cc to 123cc two-strokes were built.

PHÄNOMEN
1951–56 The Phänomen name was used on the range of lightweight machines built by Meister (see p.244).

PHANTOM
1921–28 Berlin-based company that built conventional four-stroke machines. Phantom used its own 148cc to 265cc single-cylinder four-stroke engines. Later models were available with JAP engines.

PHOENIX
c.1933–39 The Phoenix brand-name was used by RMW (see p.247) on orthodox machines.

PIMPH
c.1924–26 Pimph produced machines fitted with single-cylinder and V-twin engines supplied by JAP and MAG.

PIROL
1949–54 Pirol took over production of Schweppe scooters (see p.247). The scooters were available with 143cc to 198cc two-stroke engines supplied by Ilo, Sachs, and Küchen.

PITTY
1954–64 Eastern bloc scooter that used a 149cc MZ engine.

POSTLER
1920–24 Walter Postler built a scooter with a 252cc inlet-over-exhaust engine and a 246cc overhead-valve motorcycle.

PREMIER
1910–13 This was a branch of the British Premier company (see p.227), which built 346cc side-valve and 270cc two-stroke machines. When production stopped in Nuremberg the factory was re-established at Eger in Czechoslovakia, where production continued until 1933.

PRESTO
1901–40 Originally Presto used Fafnir, Minerva, and Zedel engines. Production was intermittent. After World War I it made lightweights with 197cc side-valve Alba engines. Machines produced in the final years used 74cc and 98cc Sachs engines. Presto also made cars.

PRIOR
c.1935 The Prior trademark was adopted for German-built Hercules machines when sold in the United Kingdom. The British Hercules marque was owned by Raleigh.

PROGRESS
1901–14 An early manufacturer, based in Berlin, that initially used Zedel and Fafnir single-cylinder and V-twin engines to power its machines. Later Progress produced its own engines.

PROGRESS
c.1953–60 Progress produced Sachs-engined scooters of 147cc to 191cc, which were also known by the Strolch name (see p.248).

RABENEICK
1933–63 Cycle components and bicycle maker August Rabeneick built some 74cc Sachs-engined mopeds before World War II. In 1947 it reintroduced powered bicycles and from 1950 it built proper motorcycles with Sachs and Ilo engines of up to 247cc. From 1953 it also made a few overhead-valve shaft-driven singles with Universal engines. After 1958 Rabeneick ceased making larger machines to concentrate on mopeds and 98cc lightweights. In 1963 the company was taken over by Fichtel & Sachs, the owners of the Hercules marque (see p.240). Two-wheeler production ceased soon after in favour of vehicle clutches.

RECORD
1922–24 Record offered orthodox machines, which used its own 98cc two-stroke engines.

REH
1948–53 REH motorcycles were built by Richard Engelbrecht of Hamburg. 173cc to 248cc Ilo engines were used.

RENNER-ORIGINAL
1924–32 Dresden-based firm that built mainly JAP-engined machines, using single-cylinder and V-twin engines of 198cc to 996cc. It also offered some small two-strokes with Villiers engines.

RENNSTEIG
c.1925–30 Rennsteig played a part in the convoluted history of Krieger bikes. It took over production of the Original-Krieger (see p.245) in 1925 and used 198cc to 497cc Blackburne engines.

REX
1923–25 A short-lived company that made orthodox two-strokes fitted with 283cc engines.

REX
1948–64 Rex began production with clip-on bicycle engines. It later built complete mopeds and lightweight motorbikes using its own engines, and a 123cc Villiers-engined motorcycle.

R&F

c.1924–26 R&F produced a 348cc motorcycle fitted with its own overhead-valve engine.

RIBI

1923–25 Berlin-based company that built motorcycles using its own 196cc to 248cc overhead-valve engines.

RIEDEL

1948–51 See Imme (p.241).

RINNE

1925–30 Small company, located in Berlin, that made a limited number of 124cc to 248cc two-strokes.

RIXE

1934–59 The first machines that Rixe made were mopeds with 73cc to 98cc Sachs engines. After the war it increased production to include Sachs-engined models of 49cc to 248cc. It continued building mopeds until the 1970s.

RMW

1925–55 RMW commenced production with 132cc to 198cc two-strokes equipped with its own engines. It later added a range of four-stroke models, which had MAG, Möser, Küchen, and other engines of up to 498cc. RMW also produced identical machines under the Phoenix brand-name (see p.246). After World War II it built very few machines.

ROBAKO

1924–26 The Robako was built in Berlin using 129cc and 132cc Bekamo and MGF engines.

ROCO

1922–25 The Roco was one of the many Berlin-built, lightweight two-strokes. 110cc and 147cc models were offered.

ROCONOVA

1924–26 Roconova built a very limited number of 248cc and 348cc overhead-camshaft singles with its own engines.

RÖHR

1952–57 Röhr briefly entered the two-wheeler market with a scooter powered by a 197cc Ilo engine.

ROLAND

1904–07 Roland was one of the several names used on products produced by the Köln-Lindenthaler Metallwerke AG (see Allright p.234).

ROLAND

1923–24 Built small two-strokes in Berlin using 132cc Bekamo and 145cc DKW engines.

ROTER TEUFEL

1923–25 Berlin-built 170cc side-valve machines.

ROYAL

1902–12 Royal built typical early machines using engines supplied by FN, Minerva, and others.

RS

1924–25 Rogge & Stiller of Berlin built an unconventional, 380cc two-stroke twin with a rotary valve.

RUD

1927–30 Richard Uhlmann of Dresden built machines using Kühne, MAG, and JAP engines of 348cc to 748cc.

RUNGE

1923–24 Hermann Runge built a Paqué-engined four-stroke lightweight in Nuremberg.

RUNGE

1923–26 Harold Runge built small-capacity four-strokes in Hannover.

RUPPE

1927–30 After the demise of his Bekamo marque (see p.235), Hugo Ruppe re-established a business making 98cc clip-on bicycle engines.

RUT

1923–24 RUT experimented with simple 124cc two-strokes before switching to manufacturing components.

RUWISCH

1948–49 The Ruwisch was a scooter powered by a 38cc Victoria engine. Few were built.

SACHS

1980– Fichtel & Sachs began making two-stroke engines in the 1930s. The company took over Hercules (see p.240), Rabeneick (see p.246), and the Zweirad Union (see p.251) during the 1930s. The Sachs name did not appear on a complete motorcycle until 1980. The same models were often available as a Hercules or DKW (see p.236).

SAR

1923–30 Berlin-based company that built motorcycles equipped with its own 122cc to 198cc two-stroke engines.

SATURN

1921–27 Saturn built two- and four-stroke machines using its own 149cc to 497cc engines, including side-valve V-twins. It also made a clip-on engine.

SBD

c.1923–24 SBD offered a single model, which used the 293cc Bosch-Douglas flat-twin engine.

SCHLIHA

1924–30 The Schliha was an unusual two-stroke machine with an inlet valve in the cylinder head. Engine capacity ranged from 129cc to 596cc. The Schliha factory was in Berlin.

SCHMIDT

1921–24 Robert Schmidt built clip-on engines for bicycles and complete motorcycles with 196cc four-stroke engines.

SCHNEIDER

1924–26 Schneider assembled machines using 142cc to 206cc DKW engines.

SCHNELL-HOREX

1952–54 Robert Schnell built racing motorcycles at the Horex factory. These were 248cc, 348cc, and 498cc single-cylinder racing machines that were equipped with gear-driven double overhead camshafts.

SCHROFF-RECORD

1923–25 Schroff-Record was another name used on Berlin-built GS machines (see p.239). They were simple 148cc belt-driven two-strokes.

SCHÜRHOFF

1949–53 Schürhoff built mopeds and Ilo-engined motorcycles of 125cc to 175cc. They continued to produce mopeds until the late 1950s.

SCHÜTT

c.1933–34 Paul Schütt built two-strokes fitted with his own 196cc two-cylinder engines in alloy frames.

SCHÜTTOFF p.165

1924–33 Built motorcycles in Chemnitz in Saxony using its own 246cc to 496cc side-valve or overhead-valve single-cylinder engines. DKW (see p.236) bought a stake in the company in 1928. It subsequently built 198cc to 298cc models with DKW engines and a DKW-badged 500cc four-stroke single. In 1932 it was absorbed by DKW and production stopped.

SCHWALBE

c.1922–24 The Schwalbe motorcycle was built by the Spiegler brothers, who later built motorcycles under their own name (see p.248). This was a 124cc to 198cc flat-twin which was available either as a clip-on engine or as a complete machine.

SCHWEPPE

1949–50 Built 143cc to 198cc scooters equipped with Ilo, Sachs, and Küchen engines. These were later sold under the Pirol name (see p.246).

SEEGARD

1924–25 Berlin-based firm that built a few lightweights with its own 146cc and 197cc side-valve engines.

SEITH

1949–50 Seith built children's motorcycles powered by 38cc Victoria moped engines.

SERVOS

1953 Servos briefly produced a scooter using a 38cc Victoria engine, which was mounted above the front wheel.

S&G

1924–32 Scharrer & Gross built and sold engines to other manufacturers from 1922 before producing complete machines. It made four-stroke singles of 346cc to 596cc and also Villiers-engined two-strokes.

SIEG

c.1922–30 Sieg assembled machines fitted with a wide variety of proprietary engines from 110cc to 598cc.

SIMSON

1950– Simson produced 250cc overhead-valve shaft-driven singles derived from the pre-war BMW-design, which were originally known by the AWO name (see p.235). Production of

The Sachs GS125 enduro was sold alongside the Hercules range in 1979

49cc and 74cc two-stroke mopeds and lightweight motorcycles began in the late 1950s, and the shaft-driven 250cc was dropped soon after. Simson also produced successful small-capacity off-road competition models.

SITTA
1950–55 Hummel built mopeds, scooters, and motorcycles at its Bremen premises, using 49cc to 247cc Ilo, two-stroke engines. The scooters were sold under the Sitta label.

SMW
c.1923–33 Karl Rühmer built machines at the Stockdorfer Motoren Werk under the Karü name (see p.241), before adopting the SWM trademark.

S&N
1901–08 Seidel & Naumann built Laurin & Klement machines (see p.301) under licence using the Slavia and Germania names.

SNOB
c.1921–25 Built 154cc to 184cc four-strokes in Düsseldorf. Most models were equipped with inlet-over-exhaust engines with an inclined cylinder and belt drive. They were more successful than most of the small machines offered in Germany at the time.

SOLO
1949–82 Solo produced mopeds and lightweight motorcycles using its own 49cc two-stroke engines.

SPIEGLER p.171
c.1923–32 The Spiegler brothers installed JAP and MAG engines of 198cc to 598cc into unorthodox, pressed-steel beam frames that ran from the steering head to the rear axle.

SPIESS
1902–07 Built in Berlin by Otto Spiess, these machines used Minerva, Zedel, and Fafnir engines.

STANDARD p.171
1925–39 Wilhelm Gutbrod began assembling MAG- and JAP-engined motorcycles in Stuttgart. He established a Swiss branch (see Standard p.294) in 1931. During the 1930s the firm made its own two- and four-stroke engines. Production ended in Stuttgart in 1939, continuing in Switzerland until 1952.

STAR
1920–23 Designed by H. F. Günther of Berlin, the Star was a 393cc side-valve horizontally opposed twin. The design was bought by the munitions company Deutsche Industriewerke, forming the basis of its subsequent Derad/D-Rad machines (see pp.236-237).

STEIDINGER
c.1925–27 Built 199cc two-strokes with triangulated frames.

STEINBACH
1981–85 Steinbach made a limited number of Rotax-engined four-stroke single-cylinder machines.

STERNA
1922–24 The Sterna motorcycle, a 614cc flat-twin machine, was also sold under the Aristos (see p.234) and Menos (see p.244) names.

STOCK p.172
1924–33 The 119cc U.S.-built Evans lightweight was popular in Germany. When the Cyclemotor Corporation of New York stopped manufacturing it, it was produced in Berlin, under licence by Stock. Starting in 1929 new models with 173cc to 298cc two-stroke engines and shaft drive were built.

STROLCH
c.1953–60 Strolch built 98cc to 191cc Sachs-engined scooters, which were also known by the Progress name (see p.246).

STUDEMANN
1953 Studemann briefly entered the two-wheeler market with a 38cc Victoria-powered moped.

SUDBRACK
1950–51 A bicycle company that built Ilo-powered 98cc and 123cc machines.

SUT
1921–27 Built by Scholz Und Tegener of Berlin, the SUT was a lightweight machine with a 196cc four-stroke engine and belt drive. The engine was suspended from a low, tubular frame with leaf-sprung, trailing-link suspension.

TAS
c.1924–31 TAS equipped its machines with 173cc to 499cc two- and four-stroke Gnome & Rhône engines. It later switched to 350cc to 500cc MAG single-cylinder engines.

TAUTZ
1921–23 Frank Tautz built tubular-framed scooter-style machines powered by 119cc DKW engines. The company was located in Leipzig.

TECO
c.1920–26 Stettin-based company that used 198cc four-stroke Alba engines, which were built in the same city. Later models had 350cc Kühne engines.

TERRA
c.1922–24 Terra built standard two-strokes of 125cc to 175cc.

TETGE
1923–26 Tetge built a limited number of machines using its own 150cc and 175cc side-valve engines and 597cc MAG V-twins.

TIGER
c.1901–07 Tiger was one of the names used on machines made by the Köln-Lindenthaler Metallwerke AG (see Allright p.234).

TORNAX p.179
1926–55 Tornax made quality motorcycles at Wuppertal using JAP and Columbus engines of 350cc to 1000cc in its own frames. It also produced some successful competition machines. In the 1930s it added a lightweight Ilo-engined two-stroke. After the war Tornax resumed production of 125cc to 250cc Ilo-engined two-strokes and also offered a 250cc overhead-valve twin. In 1953 it introduced an innovative, 250cc four-stroke twin. Unfortunately, although the bike enjoyed some commercial success, the company was unable to recover its development costs and ceased production in 1955.

TORNAX
1982–84 The name Tornax was briefly revived for a range of 50cc to 80cc Minarelli-engined lightweights.

TORPEDO
1928 A bicycle firm that built 198cc single-cylinder machines until 1934.
1950 Resumed production with two-stroke lightweights, using Ilo and Sachs engines of 49cc to 174cc.
1953 Ceased production of motorcycles, but continued to manufacture bicycles and mopeds.

TREMO
1925–27 Berlin-based company that built a small number of motorcycles

A 1967 Simson ISDT machine; it was produced in 49cc and 73cc versions

equipped with its own 308cc side-valve and overhead-valve engines.

TRIANON
c.1922–26 Trianon used its own 232cc two-stroke engine in a lightweight belt-driven machine.

TRIUMPH  p.187
1903 This company was a subsidiary of the British Triumph company, which had been established by a German. It began making motorcycles using Minerva and Fafnir engines. When the British parent company began to make its own engines, these were used, but falling demand stopped motorcycle production in Nuremberg in 1908.
1920 Production restarted with the introduction of the 276cc two-stroke, Knirps model. It was based on the British Baby Triumph. From 1924 it also imported British-built four-stroke models.
1930 After splitting from Triumph in England, 350cc to 750cc single-cylinder and V-twin engines were supplied by MAG. From 1934 the company also offered Sachs-engined lightweights. The initials TWN – "Triumph Werke Nürnberg" – and the Orial name (see p.245) were adopted in export markets to differentiate the machines from the British product. New two-strokes of 170cc to 350cc were also developed, including a rotary-valve 250cc split-single that appeared in 1939.
1948 Triumph resumed production after the war. By 1953 it built a range of solid, rather than sporting, two-stroke split-singles of 125cc to 350cc. The 200cc Contessa scooter was included in this range.
1957 Unable to survive the decline in the motorcycle market, the company was taken over by Grundig and motorcycle production stopped.

TX
1924–27 The TX was built in Berlin, using Bekamo 132cc and 174cc engines. The TX frame had a wide diameter top tube that also acted as the fuel tank.

UDE
c.1924–25 UDE produced a limited number of 249cc two-strokes.

UNIVERSELLE (UNIVERSAL)
1925–29 Dresden-based company, Müller & Co. built motorcycles using its own four-stroke engines of 183cc to 247cc. The unit-construction gearbox was mounted in front of the engine. Final drive was by belt.

UNO
1980– UNO offers specialized racing machines and café-racer style road bikes, which use various single-cylinder four-stroke engines in single-shock frames.

A 1986 Uno café racer with a 450cc Ducati single-cylinder engine

URANIA
c.1934–39 Urania built lightweight machines using Sachs and Ilo engines.

URS
1966–70 The URS was a specialized racing machine that had a 500cc double overhead-camshaft four-cylinder racing engine built by Helmut Fath. It took its name from the village of URSenbach, where it was made. Fath won the sidecar World Championship in 1968 with a URS outfit. A solo racer was developed with less success. In 1970 the team was sold to the U.S.-financed Münch set-up. Fath later developed a 500cc two-stroke flat four under his name.

UT
1925–59 UT used its own 246cc horizontal-cylinder two-stroke engine before switching to Blackburne, JAP, and Küchen engines of 125cc to 500cc. After the war it made Ilo-engined two-strokes of 125cc to 250cc.

VAN VEEN  p.188
1978–1981 Van Veen distributed Kreidler mopeds (see p.242) in Holland. It built lightweight machines, including racers, with Kreidler engines at its German factory. There was also a large-capacity Wankel-engined machine, which was built in limited numbers.

VAREL
1951–53 Varel built two-stroke mopeds and scooters using its own 43cc engine

and 99cc Mota power units. Some models had the engine mounted above the front wheel.

VATERLAND
c.1933–39 Built 98cc and 123cc Sachs-engined lightweights.

VENUS
1953–55 Venus produced a range of Sachs-engined scooters. The larger models were available with optional electric starters.

VICTORIA  pp.191–192
1899 Nuremberg bicycle maker that made its first motorcycle in the usual manner by bolting a proprietary engine to a bicycle frame. Production did not begin until around 1905 when belt-driven machines were produced using Zedel and Fafnir single-cylinder engines. After World War I they built fore-and-aft flat twins. The first versions used BMW engines, but from 1923 Victoria built its own engines. In the late 1920s it began to build single-cylinder machines using proprietary engines. It also offered small-capacity two-strokes and a 498cc parallel twin with inclined cylinders and a four-speed in-unit gearbox.
1945 After the war Victoria concentrated on 38cc to 247cc two-stroke machines.
1951 Launched the V35 Bergmeister. The shaft-driven 347cc V-twin was produced until 1958, when the declining German market forced the company to

concentrate on lightweight machines. There were some new two-stroke designs and from 1956 Italian Parilla engines were used in some machines.
1958 Victoria joined DKW (see p.236) and Express (see p.238) in the Zweirad Union (see p.251). The Victoria brand-name was used on a variety of mopeds and scooters.
1966 The name was finally dropped.

VINDEC-SPECIAL
c.1903–14 Vindec-Special was one of the several names used on machines made by the Köln-Lindenthaler Motorenwerke (see Allright p.234).

VIS
c.1922–25 VIS offered single- and twin-cylinder two-strokes of 250cc and 500cc.

VOMO
1922–31 DKW dealer Eugen Seeler also built two-stroke mopeds. VOMO is an abbreviation of VOlksMOtorrad.

VORAN
1921–24 Berlin-based firm that built 150cc two-strokes.

VS
c.1922–24 Veit Schuh built a very limited number of machines.

WACKER
1922–23 Julius Wacker made motorcycles in very limited numbers in Nuremberg.

WALBA
1949–52 Walba built 98cc to 173cc Ilo-engined scooters.

WALTER
c.1903–42 Walter used Fafnir engines in its early machines. In the 1920s and 1930s it produced a range of two-strokes with engines supplied by Villiers, Sachs, and Ilo.

WANDERER 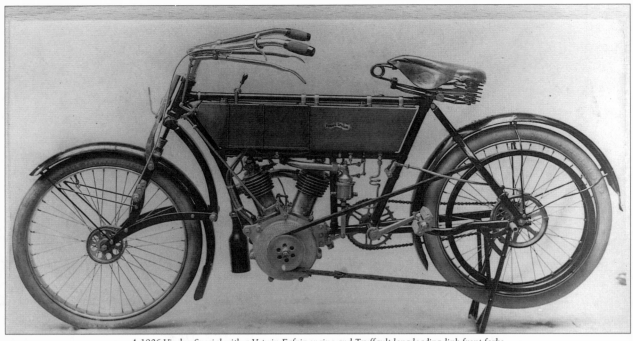 p.194
1902 Wanderer followed the normal pattern of installing an engine in a bicycle frame to create its first machine. It subsequently produced a range of motorcycles that included a side-valve 250cc single and a 500cc side-valve V-twin. Capacity of the post-World War I twin grew to 616cc and then 750cc, and chain drive was fitted. The last of the V-twins had four exhaust ports. Smaller capacity machines were also produced.
1928 A brand-new machine replaced existing models. This unconventional design used a 498cc overhead-valve single-cylinder engine, three-speed in-unit gearbox, shaft drive, and a pressed-steel frame. Investment in this machine probably led to the company's demise.
1929 The firm collapsed, but the design of the shaft-driven single was sold to F. Janacek and production moved to Prague. The name of the JAnacek-WAnderer was subsequently abbreviated to Jawa (see p.301). A Sachs-engined lightweight with a Wanderer badge was produced sometime in the 1930s.

WEGRO
1922–23 The Wegro was a strange, long-wheelbase machine fitted with a 452cc two-stroke twin engine. It was built in Berlin by VIS-Ges.

WELS
1925–26 Wels assembled motorcycles using 348cc Kühne and 490cc JAP engines.

WERNO
1925–33 Werno motorcycles were orthodox lightweights fitted with 154cc four-stroke and 143cc two-stroke engines. They were built in Berlin by WERner NOel.

WIMMER 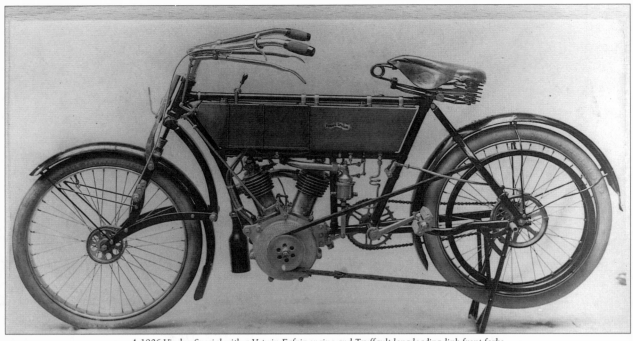 p.197
1921–39 Quality machines built in Bavaria using Wimmer's own overhead-valve engines from 137cc to 497cc. Some models used Bark two-stroke engines.

WINDHOFF 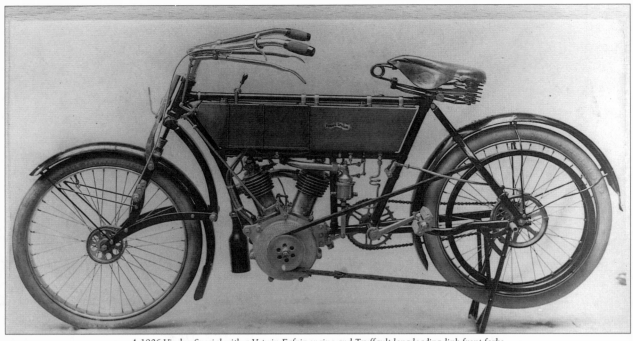 p.198
1925 The first machines were 122cc and 173cc two-strokes with engines, built under licence, from Bekamo. Some models were water-cooled and all used a secondary pumping piston.

A 1906 Vindec-Special with a V-twin Fafnir engine and Truffault long leading-link front forks

1927 A very advanced 746cc oil-cooled overhead-camshaft in-line shaft-driven four was introduced. This used the engine as the chassis, to which the steering head and rear frame members were bolted. Two years later it was replaced by a 996cc shaft-driven flat twin. Neither model sold well.
1932 Demand for expensive large-capacity machines was minimal. Windhoff's last machines used licence-built, Villiers two-stroke engines.
1933 Motorcycle production stopped.

WITTEKIND
1952–54 Built 40cc mopeds.

WITTLER
1924–53 Wittler began motorcycle production with a 250cc two-stroke. After World War II it made mopeds and lightweight motorcycles with Sachs and Zündapp engines.

WK
1920–22 The WK was a 249cc motorwheel that attached to a bicycle.

WOLF-SUPERIOR
c.1927 A small number of 500cc singles built by racer Hans Wolf at Nuremberg.

WOTAN
1923–25 Leipzig-based firm that built 170cc two-strokes.

WSE
1924–25 Built by W. Elsel and fitted with its own 249cc side-valve engine.

WURRING
1921–59 August Wurring of Düsseldorf also sold his motorcycles under the AWD initials (see p.235). Pre-war machines housed a variety of British and German proprietary engines. Post-war models used two-stroke engines from 100cc to 250cc.

WURTTEMBERGIA
1925–33 Berlin company that used Blackburne engines of 198cc to 596cc in conventional frames.

ZEGEMO
1924–25 Short-lived company that built 248cc machines in Dresden.

ZETGE/ZETTGE
1922–25 Zetge built low-framed lightweights with horizontal-cylinder DKW engines of 142cc to 173cc.

ZEUGNER
1902 A pioneer company that assembled machines using proprietary engines. It was based in Berlin.

ZEUS
1925–27 Asseembled in Leipzig by Klotz & Becker using 348cc and 498cc overhead-camshaft Küchen engines.

ZIEJANÜ
1923–27 Albert ZIEgelgängsberger and Hans JAkob of NÜrnberg used their own 211cc and 246cc two-stroke engines and also fitted 348cc and 498cc JAP engines. They later abbreviated the name to ZJN.

ZIRO
1920–25 Ziro produced rotary-valve 148cc and 346cc horizontal-cylinder two-strokes with three-speed belt-driven transmission. BMW-style tubular frames were used. The bike was designed by Albert Roder, who soon left to join Ermag (see p.238).

ZITTAVIA
1924–25 Zittavia built motorcycles to order using Alba, JAP, and Blackburne engines.

ZÜNDAPP 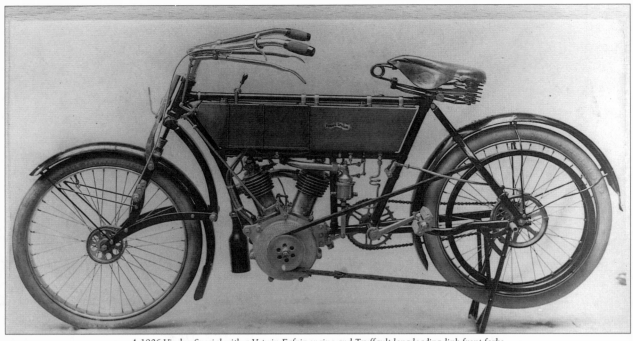 pp.207–208
1921 Nuremberg armaments company, ZUNDer und APParatebau copied the design of its first machines from the British Levis. These were simple, belt-driven 211cc two-strokes. Capacity was later increased to 249cc, gearboxes were added from 1924, and by 1930 there was a range of lightweight two-strokes from 200cc to 300cc. Zündapp was soon among Germany's largest manufacturers. Some four-stroke singles were also produced using British Rudge-Python engines. Zündapp machines were also assembled in Britain under the Newmount name (see p.224).
1933 The first Zündapp four-stroke engines appeared. These were shaft-driven 398cc and 498cc flat twins and 598cc and 797cc flat fours. During World War II KS750 flat twins, as well as other machines, were supplied to the German army. After the war the 597cc flat twin and 198cc two-strokes were reintroduced.
1953 The 147cc Bella scooter and a 48cc clip-on engine for bicycles were introduced. The range of lightweight machines was soon expanded to include two-strokes of 48cc to 249cc. The four-stroke flat twins were dropped in 1957. Road and off-road two-strokes were developed throughout the 1960s and 1970s. These included off-road competition models, mopeds, scooters, and water-cooled machines of up to 250cc. An 80cc Zündapp racer won the 1984 World Championship, but it did not save the company.

1984 Zündapp finally collapsed and the remains of the company were sold to China.

ZWEIRAD UNION
1958–74 Victoria (see p.249), Express (see p.238), and DKW (see p.236) merged in response to the decline of the German motorcycle market. They continued to use the individual marque names. Hercules joined the group in 1966 and is the only survivor, following a takeover by the Fichtel & Sachs industrial group in 1969.

ZWERG
1923–25 Zwerg, a manufacturer of pumps and stationary engines, briefly built lightweight two-strokes of 147cc and 187cc.

Unconfirmed Marques

ADMA *1924–26*
Aeroplan *1922–25*
AFW *1923–25*
Alfa *1925–28*
Ambag *1923*
Apex *1925–26*
Argul *1923–26*
Ari *1924–25*
Atlantis *1926–32*
Auto-Ell *1924–26*
Bamar *1923–25*
Bayerland *1924–30*
BB *1923–25*
Beco *1923–25*
Befag *1922–24*
Behag *1924–26*
Beresa *1923–25*
Bergo *1924*
Bero *1924–25*
Bismarck *1921–23*
BNF *1903–07*
Bodo *1924–25*
Braak *1923–25*
Bravis *1924–26*
Bubi *1921–24*
Bullo *1924–26*
Bulow *1923–25*
Burkhardita *1904–08*
Centaur *1924–25*
Charlkron *1925*
Claed *1904–08*
CR *1926–30*
Cyclop *1922–25*
Danibus *1923–24*
Deloma *1924*
DFB *1922–25*
Difra *1923–25*
DMG *1921–24*
DSW Berlin *1922–23*
Dringos Berlin *1924–25*
Dümo *1924–25*
EBW *1923–24*
ECKL *1923–26*
ED *1923–25*
EMH *1927–29*
EMWE *1924–25*
Engee *1925*

Ernst-Eichler *1924–25*
Evans-Pondorf *1924–25*
Evo *1923–25*
Excelsior *1923–24*
Fagard *1923–25*
Fama *1923–25*
FB *1923–25*
Fechtel *1924–26*
FG *1923–25*
FHG *1927–29*
Fiamc *1951–53*
Fiame *1951–53*
Fortonia *1924–25*
Freco *1923–25*
FSW Berlin *1923–26*
Fubo *1923–25*
Furch *1924–25*
Gaggenau *1925–27*
GAR *1924–26*
Geppert *1925–26*
Gervo *1924–25*
Gloria-Rekord *1924–1925*
Golbi
Gold-Rad *1952–81*
Haja *1924–25*
Hako *1924–25*
Halumo *1923–26*
Harsho *1925–26*
Hascho *1923–26*
Hauser *1981–*
Herbi *1928–32*
Herkra *1922–23*
Hesco
Hessrad *1923–25*
HMW *1923–28*
Hoock *1926–28*
Hüffer *1923–25*
Husar *1923–25*
JAK *1922–25*
Jale *1923–25*
Jeanette Berlin *1949–50*
JSL *1923–25*
Kadi *1924–30*
Karrenberg
Katho *1923–25*
King-Jap *1928–31*
K&K *1924–25*
KM *1924–26*
KMS *1922–24*
Kolibri *1923–30*
KR *1924–25*
KR *1930–33*
Kroboth *1951–54*
KRS *1921–26*
Kuli Berlin *1922–24*
Kurras *1925–27*
KV *1924–27*
LDR *1922–25*
Leifa *1924–25*
Leto *1926–28*
Liliput *1923–26*
Lord *1929–31*
Lucas *1923–24*
Ludolph *1924–26*
LWD *1923–26*
Mabret *1927–28*
Maco *1921–26*
Mamof *1922–24*
MAS *1923–24*
Mascotten
Matador *1925–26*

Mawi *1923–30*
Mederer *c.1920*
Meteor *1924–26*
Meybrein *1922–26*
Meybra *1923–25*
MFB *1923–24*
MFB *1925–26*
Mimoa *1924*
MMM *1925–27*
Möfa *1923–27*
Möwe *1903–08*
MUFI (Imperator) *1925–26*
Nassovia *1925*
Neve-Ilo *1924–26*
NIS *1925–26*
Nordstern *1922–24*
Norved *1924–25*
Oberle *1927–29*
Oda *1925–26*
Ofran *1923–25*
OM *1923–25*
Ori *1923–25*
Otto *1921–37*
Pe *1923–24*
Perkeo Berlin *1924–26*
Perlex *1924–26*
Permo *1952–54*
Phönix *1933–39*
Ponny *1924–26*
Pony *1924–26*
Potthoff *1924–26*
PSW *1924–29*
Radex *1951–late 1950s*
Rapid Berlin *1924*
Ratingia *1923–25*
Real *1981–*
Riwina *1924–25*
Rotter *1924–25*
Rueder *late 1910s–early 1920s*
Sarolette Berlin *1949–52*
Sartorius *1924–26*
Schlimme *1924–25*
Schunk *1924–26*
SCK *1924–25*
Sewut *1924–26*
SFW *1924–26*
SH *1925–28*
Siegfried *1925*
SMW *1923–33*
Spindler *1922–25*
Standard *1922–24*
Star *1895–c.1900*
Sticherling *1923–26*
Stoewer *1904–05*
Stolco *1922–24*
Struco *1922–25*
Sturm *1923–25*
Tempo *1924–27*
Thumann *1925–26*
Tika *1921–24*
Torpedo *1901–07*
Tropfen *1923–24*
TUK *1921–22*
Vesuv *1924–26*
Vollblut *1925–27*
Wackwitz *1920–22*
Walmet *1924–26*
Weber-Mag *1926–27*
Wecoob *1925–30*
Weiss *1925–28*
Wela *1925–28*

Welt-Rad *1901–07*
Westfalia *1901–06*
Wiga *1928–32*
Wikro *1924–26*
WMB *1924–26*
WSM *1919–23*
Wuco *1925*
Zehner *1924–26*
Zurtz-Rekord *1922–26*

Italy

THROUGHOUT THE 20TH century, Italy has been the only country to have consistently produced motorcycles. Initially less prolific than other countries, the industry blossomed after World War I with family companies such as Benelli (see p.253) and Gilera (see p.257) building high-quality machines with impressive sporting pedigrees. After World War II the need for low-cost personal transport brought about a scooter boom, led by the Lambretta (see p.259) and the Vespa (see p.267). As it did elsewhere, the arrival of cheap cars in the 1950s and 1960s caused a depression in the industry and destroyed many of the smaller marques. While the British companies were crushed by Japanese opposition, large import tariffs protected the Italian concerns. Famous marques such as Ducati (see p.255) and Laverda (see p.257) sold machines at home while finding export markets for their prestigious sports models. In the 1990s the industry continues to produce machines of all sizes with unrivalled style and sporting heritage.

ABIGNENTE
1926–29 Built a limited number of 345cc two-stroke motorcycles.

ABRA
1923–27 Small manufacturer that used DKW and its own engines.

ACCOSATO
1976–90 Lightweights that used engines by Minarelli and Hiro.

AERMACCHI ⊞ p.74
1945 Famous aircraft manufacturer from Varese that started making the Macchitre commercial tricycle. It was driven by a flat-twin engine.
1951 Built the 125cc two-stroke Macchi scooter. It was a motorcycle-cum-scooter with large wheels.
1956 The futuristic Chimera was introduced. Its 175cc horizontal overhead-valve engine formed the basis for the Aermacchi range of 175cc to 350cc machines for many years.
1960 Harley-Davidson bought 50 per cent of Aermacchi and sold the machines under its label in the United States. A 125cc two-stroke single was introduced in 1967 and other two-strokes followed. Twin-cylinder two-stroke racers won the 250 and 350 World Championships. Harley-Davidson took complete control of Aermacchi in 1974.
1978 Harley-Davidson sold Aermacchi to Cagiva (see p.254). The Cagiva name was used on subsequent machines.

AERO-CAPRONI
1947 The Caproni aircraft company moved into motorcycle production after

World War II and built a 48cc four-stroke motorcycle and the CCC moped.
1951 The 75cc Capriolo motorcycle was introduced. It had an advanced face-cam-overhead-valve engine, a four-speed gearbox, and a pressed-steel frame. Some 100cc and 125cc versions of the face-cam single were later produced.
1954 The Cento 50, a 150cc transverse flat twin, was introduced. Face-cam operated valves, a pressed-steel frame, and chain final drive were installed.
1958 The company changed its name to Aeromere, but its range of 75cc, 100cc, and 125cc face-cam machines were still known by the Capriolo name.
1964 Motorcycle production stopped.

AESTER
1932–35 Turin-based manufacturer that constructed machines using 150cc and 500cc four-stroke engines.

AETOS
1912–14 A 492cc V-twin with magneto ignition and belt drive that was made in Turin in limited numbers.

AGOSTINI
1991– Makes 50cc two-stroke mopeds with Franco Morini engines. No relation to the ex-world champion.

AGRATI
1958–65 This long-established maker of bicycle components introduced 70cc, 80cc, and 125cc two-stroke Capri scooters in 1958. The 48cc Como scooter was also built. In 1960 it took over Garelli (see p.257) and the Garelli name was used exclusively from 1965.

AIM
1974–78 Built off-road lightweights with two-stroke proprietary engines.

ALATO
1923–25 Made in Turin with its own 131cc two-stroke engines.

ALCYON ITALIANA
1926–28 Built 98cc and 173cc French Alcyon machines under licence.

ALDBERT
1953–59 Aldbert constructed motorbikes in Milan with its own 49cc to 173cc two-stroke and 174cc to 246cc overhead-valve engines.

ALFA
1923–26 Alfa used JAP, 170cc Norman, and 348cc Blackburne overhead-valve engines in its machines. Production was on a limited scale.

ALGAT
1992 Algat built a 22cc folding moped, which it named the Plico.

ALIPRANDI
1925–30 The Aliprandi brothers built 173cc to 498cc machines using Moser, JAP, and Sturmey-Archer engines. Production was limited.

ALKRO
1992– Makes 48cc folding mopeds.

ALMIA
1924–26 A small marque that built two-stroke lightweight motorcycles.

ALPINA
1923–26 A small marque that produced two-stroke lightweight motorcycles.

ALPINO
1945–63 A 48cc clip-on bicycle engine was later followed by 48cc, 125cc, and 175cc two- and four-stroke scooters, mopeds, and three-wheelers. Alpino also constructed racers and successful record-breaking machines.

ALTEA
1939–41 Alberico Seiling, who had earlier made MAS (see p.260) and Seiling (see p.265) motorcycles, constructed this 196cc overhead-valve motorbike. It was equipped with cantilever rear suspension.

AMISA
1946–50 Amisa was a producer of small commercial tricycles, which were later followed by a lightweight motorcycle with a 125cc Rumi engine.

AMR
1979–1985 Built 125cc to 400cc Sachs-engined off-road competition machines.

ANCILOTTI
1967–85 This small marque specialized in mopeds and lightweight sporting and off-road motorcycles powered by 50cc, 125cc, and 250cc Franco Morini, Hiro, and Sachs engines.

ANCORA
1926–39 Constructed in Milan with 147cc to 347cc Villiers two-stroke engines. From 1936 the new owner Umberto Dei (see p.255) made 60cc to 98cc models. After 1939 the Dei name was used exclusively.

ANZANI
1922–25 In 1907 Italian pioneer Alessandro Anzani began making engines for aircraft and motorcycles in France. He established a branch factory in his native Milan and built a 500cc overhead-valve V-twin motorcycle in 1922. Some 750cc and 1000cc side-valve versions were also made.

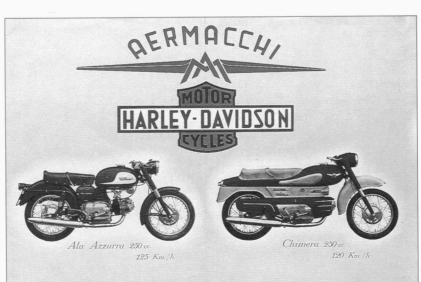

Aermacchi's distinctive Chimera featured pressed-steel bodywork

APE
1923–25 Lightweight motorcycles using Train engines that were made in Pesaro.

APRILIA  pp.16–17
1960 Bicycle company Aprilia built its first mopeds in Noale, near Vicenza.
1975 Developed off-road motorcycles using Rotax, Sachs, and Hiro engines. It included the Scarabeo model.
1982 Introduced road models and began to develop road-racing machines, initially using two-stroke Rotax engines. It won the 125 World Championship in 1992 and both 125 and 250 classes in 1994. The company also built Rotax-engined four-stroke singles. From 1995 its range will include a large-capacity V-twin with Aprilia's own engine.

AQUILA
1927–35 First produced DKW-engined bicycles in Bologna. Motorcycles with 247cc and 498cc Küchen, Python, and OMB engines were made later. Angelo Blatto designed the last machines.

AQUILA
1953–58 A later Aquila marque built 48cc to 174cc machines including an overhead-camshaft 175. Few were made.

ARDEA
1931–34 Built on a small scale in Gallarate, its range included a 250cc overhead-valve horizontal-cylinder single with a three-speed gearbox.

ARDITO
1951–56 Made a 48cc clip-on engine and a moped, followed by a range of two- and four-stroke lightweights, some including overhead camshafts.

ARES
1932–35 A 175cc overhead-valve machine made in Turin.

ARIZ
1952–54 Armido RIZzetto of Milan built 48cc friction-drive clip-on engines and some complete machines.

ARZANI
1904–06 Francesco Arzani built this belt-driven vertical single-cylinder racer.

ASPES
1967–82 A manufacturer of mopeds and lightweight sports machines with Franco Morini and Minarelli engines. Its own 124cc two-stroke engine was used in road, racing, and motocross machines.

ASPI
1946–51 Built clip-on engines and later 125cc shaft-driven two-stroke flat twins.

ASSO
1927–31 A 175cc overhead-valve sloping-cylinder single built in Turin.

ASSO
1947–52 Built a clip-on 48cc engine.

ASTORIA
1934–36 Astoria first used 250cc and 500cc British Ajax engines. In 1935 it built its own engines, but the marque folded the following year.
1947–57 Reappeared with a machine using a 498cc overhead-valve engine. Lightweight models used Villiers and its own two-stroke engines.

ASTRA
1931–51 Astra, founded by Max Türkheimer (see p.267), built motorcycles in Milan using Ariel and its own engines of 175cc to 500cc.

ASTRO
1950–53 Built 47cc clip-on engines.

ATALA
1923– Bicycle maker Atala built JAP- and Blackburne-engined motorcycles before World War II. After the war it produced mopeds with various engines. It was taken over by Rizzato (p.265) in 1977. Moped production with the Atala name continues. Its motorcycle production was very intermittent.

ATTOLINI
1920–23 Produced 269cc Villiers-engined machines in limited numbers.

AUGUSTA
1924–31 Built 125cc, 175cc, and 350cc overhead-camshaft singles, designed by Angelo Blatto, in limited numbers.

AZZARITI
1933–34 In 1931 Vincenzo Azzariti built a 175cc desmodromic overhead-valve engine. He later produced a 344cc overhead-camshaft twin-cylinder engine.

BANTAM
1947–49 Bantam produced a 123cc two-stroke scooter.

BARONI
1957–59 Built mopeds and 175cc motorcycles in limited numbers.

BARTALI
1953–61 Made 48cc and 175cc two- and four-stroke mopeds and motorcycles including the Gabbiano (see p.257).

BAUDO
1920–31 Founded by Antonio Baudo, it first built 474cc to 1000cc V-twins. In 1927 machines using 250cc Train and 350cc Bradshaw engines were made. He joined with Augusto Monaco to make the 500cc side-valve Monaco-Baudo (see p.261). In 1928 Baudo left to form BM (see p.254). The new management introduced Mauser and Chaise engines and Durandal pressed-steel frames.

A 1960 version of Agrati's 80cc Capri scooter

BAZZONI
1951 Built a small number of 135cc four-stroke scooters.

BB
1927–30 Built machines in Parma using its own 123cc two-stroke engine.

BECCACCINO-BETTOCCHI
1951–56 Built Demm-engined mopeds.

BECCARIA
1924–28 Built by Beccaria and Revelli with 350cc Blackburne four-stroke and Villiers two-stroke engines.

BENELLI  p.23
1921 Founded in 1911 by the Benelli brothers, the company built its first motorcycle, a 98cc two-stroke, in 1921. Engine capacity later grew to 125cc, 150cc, and 175cc.
1927 A 175cc overhead-camshaft four-stroke single was built. It became one of the largest Italian marques in the 1930s.
1950 Giuseppe Benelli left to form MotoBi (see p.262). Dario Ambrosini won the 250 World Championship for Benelli. In the 1950s and 1960s a range of two- and four-strokes under 250cc was built. Four-cylinder racers arrived in 1960 and Kel Carruthers won the 1969 250 World Championship on a Benelli. A 643cc overhead-valve twin-cylinder road bike appeared in 1970.
1972 The ailing marque was bought by Alessandro de Tomaso. He invested in a Japanese-inspired range of modern two- and four-stroke machines including the 748cc six-cylinder Sei.
1992 Benelli again changed owners. Moped production continues.

BENOTTO
1947–58 Bicycle company that built some proprietary-engined lightweights.

BERNARDI
1894 This machine, hailed as the first Italian motorbike, was built in Padua by Professor Enrico Bernardi. It had a four-stroke engine mounted in a trailer, which was attached to a normal bicycle.

BERNEG
1955–61 Built in Bologna and designed by Alfonso Drusiani. The engines were 160cc and 175cc vertical twins with a chain-driven overhead camshaft.

BERTONI
1953–55 Produced 160cc two-stroke machines in limited numbers.

BETA
1948– At first Giuseppe Bianchi built 153cc to 199cc overhead-valve singles in Florence. He later used his own two-stroke engine. Since the 1970s Beta has been making off-road models, including successful trials bikes.

BIANCHI  p.23
1897 Already an established bicycle maker, Edoardo Bianchi built an atmospheric-inlet-valve clip-on engine, later followed by cars and tricycles. By World War I Bianchi was a leading Italian marque with both single-cylinder and V-twin ranges of machines.
1925 New 348cc overhead-camshaft single-cylinder racers appeared along with 171cc to 498cc single-cylinder and side-valve V-twin road bikes. After World War II it built 125cc to 250cc

two- and four-strokes. Some 248cc to 482cc overhead-camshaft twin-cylinder racing models arrived in 1960, while Bianchi's range of road-going machines included scooters and mopeds.
1967 Motorcycle production ended.

BIKRON
1924–36 Built lightweight motorbikes.

BIMM (MOTOBIMM)
1965–80 Built 50cc to 125cc off-road and sporting mopeds and motorbikes using proprietary engines.

BIMOTA 🏍 pp.24–25
1972 Founded by BIanchi MOrri and TAmburini, it built improved frames for racing and sports machines. While its first chassis used a 750cc Honda engine, it later used engines from all the major Japanese firms and from Ducati. Bimota built a reputation for innovative design, quality engineering, and high prices. Production numbers were restricted.
1984 Built the Tesi prototype with hub-centre steering, but the bike did not begin production until 1991. In the early 1990s it developed its own two-stroke racer engine.

BIMOTOR
1984– Builds mopeds with proprietary engines, including off-road models.

BLATTO
1924–27 Built an overhead-camshaft lightweight motorbike. Designer Angelo Blatto was later a partner in the Ladetto & Blatto company (see p.259).

BM
1928–31 Antonio Baudo (see p.253) and sidecar maker Meldi (see p.261) built a small number of 498cc overhead-valve motorcycles using JAP engines.

BMA
1972– Constructs mopeds in limited numbers.

BM BONVICINI
1950–72 Mario Bonvicini built lightweights using Ilo, NSU, and his own engines. Remarkable 50cc and 175cc overhead-camshaft racers were made. He later concentrated on building mopeds.

BMP
1920–25 The Malasagna brothers, based near Turin, built a 240cc two-stroke with four-speed gearbox and belt drive.

BORGHI See Olympia (p.263).

BORGO (MOTOBORGO)
1906–1926 Founded in Turin by the Borgo brothers, it soon emerged as a major producer of advanced machines. Its first bikes were 498cc, 693cc, and 827cc inlet-over-exhaust-valve singles.

It introduced aluminium pistons in 1911 and a variable ratio belt drive in 1914. In 1920 it built 477cc unit-construction V-twins with oil contained in the tubes of the frame. Motorcycle production ended in 1926 when Borgo began specializing in piston manufacturing. This business continues today.

B&P
1926–29 Built lightweights with 125cc twin-cylinder Della Ferrera and 175cc Brouiller engines.

BREDA
1946–49 A 65cc two-stroke motorized bicycle constructed by a large engineering company.

BRM
1954–58 The Bellentani brothers made mopeds using their own engines.

BROUILLER
1926–29 Assembled with 125cc and 175cc French Brouiller engines in Turin.

BS VILLA
1992–94 Produced small scooters using 49cc two-stroke Yamaha engines.

BUCHER (BUCHER AND ZEDA)
1911–20 Famous marque that began by making 342cc to 568cc single-cylinder four-strokes. After World War I it resumed production with a 500cc single-cylinder machine.

BUSI-NETTUNIA
1950–54 Athos Busi built 98cc, 125cc, and 160cc Parilla-engined two-strokes.

CABRERA
1979–83 Produced 125cc to 175cc off-road two-strokes in limited numbers.

CAGIVA 🏍 p.42
1978 The Castiglioni brothers bought the Aermacchi marque (see p.252) when Harley-Davidson sold off its Italian interests. The first Cagivas were 123cc two-strokes based on the earlier Harley-Davidson models. Motocross and 350cc four-stroke trail motorcycles were also constructed. In 1983 a deal with Ducati enabled them to build bigger machines. During the next decade, Cagiva was to expand rapidly. It took over Ducati (see p.255) in 1985, Husqvarna (see p.304) in 1986, Morini (see p.261) in 1987, and CZ (p.301) in 1993. Despite these incorporations, the Cagiva name is mainly used on small-capacity and trail motorbikes.

CALCATERRA
1926–29 Built a 175cc two-stroke.

CALVI
1923–24 Produced a 280cc single-cylinder four-stroke machine.

CAMPANELLA
1927–28 Built lightweight motorcycles.

CAPELLO
1911–15 Made 3.5hp singles and 5.5hp V-twins in Turin. A clutch and gearbox were optional extras.

CAPPA
1905–10 Giulio Cappa, who later designed engines, built this shaft-driven single-cylinder bike with water cooling.

CAPPONI
1924–26 Produced a limited number of 175cc two-stroke motorcycles.

CAPRI See Agrati (p.252).

CAPRIOLO See Aero-Caproni (p.252).

CAPRONI-VIZZOLA
1953–59 Another Aero-Caproni subsidiary (see p.252) that produced motorcycles with NSU engines of 98cc to 247cc in pressed-steel spine frames.

CARCANO
1899–1902 Pioneer that placed a four-stroke engine into a bicycle-style frame.

CARDA
1946–54 Built a 43cc clip-on engine.

CARDANI
1967–69 CARlo Savaré and DANIele Fontana (a brake manufacturer) built a 498cc three-cylinder racer with twin overhead camshafts and four valves per cylinder. It was never fully developed.

CARNIELLI
1931–39 Teodoro Carnielli, a bicycle maker, built 98cc to 500cc bikes with Sachs, JAP, and Rudge Python engines.
1950–60 Carnielli returned with lightweights using Sachs, Ilo, and other proprietary engines. It also made three-wheelers with the Vittorio label.
1968–80 Began producing the Graziella folding moped with a 48cc Sachs engine.

CARNITI
1953–54 Boat engine maker that made the unsuccessful Automoto scooter. The unusual design had a three-cylinder two-stroke engine of 186cc and variable ratio friction drive in a pressed-steel frame.

CARRÙ
1927–60 First built a 175cc two-stroke. Overhead-camshaft racers of 250cc to 500cc were made in the 1940s.

CASALINI
1958– Makes 50cc and 125cc two- and three-wheelers for carrying goods.

CASOLINI
1928–33 Built two-strokes with Villiers and its own engines on a small scale.

CAVICCHIOLI
1923–24 Built 349cc two-strokes with a double-diameter piston.

CBR
1912–15 Cigala, Barberis, and Ruda built 255cc and 346cc sloping-cylinder four-strokes and a 3hp two-stroke.

CECCATO
1950–63 Built a variety of two- and four-strokes including 75cc to 98cc gear-driven overhead-camshaft sports models.

CENTAURUS
1946–50 The Bergami brothers took over the MG company (see p.261), which had made MG and Taurus (see p.266) bikes before World War II. Centaurus built 250cc and 500cc four-strokes based on the earlier machines.

CF
1927–36 Catelli and Fiorani founded this marque in Piacenza and made a 175cc overhead-valve model. In 1934 250cc face-cam bikes were introduced followed by a 500cc side-valve twin. CF collapsed in 1936 and its patents were acquired by Fusi (see p.257).

CFG
1926–29 Built by Columbo, Folli, and Genesini using overhead-camshaft four-stroke engines of 175cc and 250cc.

CHIANALE
1927–30 Built in Cunea using 350cc Chaise engines.

CHIORDA
1952–57 Bicycle maker that built two- and four-stroke proprietary-engined lightweights. A 100cc vertical twin with overhead valves was exhibited in 1954.

CICALA
1952–53 A small scooter with a 49cc two-stroke engine and large wheels.

CIGNO
1953–54 Produced a small 48cc scooter.

CIMA
1927–29 Cima constructed a machine that was powered by a single-cylinder four-stroke Blackburne engine.

CIMATTI
1949–84 Bicycle company that made 50cc mopeds from the post-war boom until its closure in 1984. It also built 100cc to 175cc models in the late 1950s and throughout the 1970s.

CISLAGHI
1922–27 A motor-uno rather than a motorbike. It had one large wheel, and the power unit and rider sat within it. Apparently capable of 100km/h (62mph), the buying public was not convinced.

CM
1930–57 Mario Cavedagni and Oreste Drusiani of Bologna made a 175cc overhead-valve model, followed by 250cc and 500cc overhead-valve and overhead-camshaft machines in the 1930s and 1940s. In 1950 CM introduced 125cc single-cylinder and 250cc twin-cylinder two-stroke models.

CMK
1967–75 Off-road competition bikes, which first used 50cc Zündapp engines. These were followed by the company's own machines with 50cc to 173cc two-stroke engines. Production of these motorcycles was minimal.

CMP
1953–56 Lightweights built on a small scale with 50cc, 75cc, 100cc, and 125cc Ceccato and Sachs engines.

COLELLA
1988–93 Built a folding moped.

COLOMBO
1923–25 Made lightweight motorcycles.

COMET
1953–57 Designer Alfonso Drusiani constructed these advanced machines. The first model had a 175cc twin-cylinder engine with twin overhead camshafts and overhung cranks. A complex 250cc sleeve-valve single-cylinder machine was also made.

COMFORT
1923–26 Constructed in Milan using 350cc Bradshaw, Barr & Stroud, and Blackburne engines.

CONTI
1935–39 Conti produced a 175cc overhead-valve motorcycle with three-speed gearbox.

COPPI
1958–60 Built 48cc two-stroke mopeds.

COZZO
1954–55 Cozzi built a 175cc overhead-camshaft single with a horizontal cylinder and shaft drive in a beam frame.

CRT
1925–29 Built a few machines using 175cc to 350cc Blackburne engines.

DALL'OGLIO
1926–30 Guido Dall'Oglio left GD (see p.257) to build his own 123cc two-stroke motorcycle.

DARDO
1926–29 Built by Fara in Turin, Dardo machines used 124cc and 132cc horizontal-cylinder two-stroke engines, two gears, and a cone clutch in the rear hub. In 1928 it built a 175cc overhead-valve horizontal-cylinder four-stroke in a tubular frame.

DE AGOSTINI
1925–27 Few of these bikes were made. They used 125cc twin-cylinder two-stroke Della Ferrera engines.

DECA
1955–58 A small company that made a 48cc four-stroke moped and a 100cc overhead-valve vertical twin with four-speed gearbox. A 125cc version of the twin was also made from 1957.

DEI
1906–14 Umberto Dei of Turin was a bicycle maker. Before World War I he made conventional single-cylinder four-stroke motorcycles.
1934–66 Production was resumed with 74cc and 98cc lightweights with Sachs engines. These were followed by motorcycles with Villiers and JAP engines of 250cc and 500cc. In 1940 Dei built the 98cc Sachs-engined Dei and a 60cc motorized bicycle. After World War II the company produced Garelli Mosquito-engined mopeds and 150cc Sachs-engined motorcycles.

DELLA FERRERA
1909–38 Founded in Turin by the Della Ferrera brothers, it soon emerged as one of the leading Italian marques. Its first high-quality, hand-built machines were 330cc and 500cc overhead-valve singles. In 1914 a 500cc V-twin and a single with four valves and variable ratio belt-drive system were introduced. In 1921 a 1048cc unit-construction V-twin with four-speed gearbox appeared. In 1925 it built a luxurious 1394cc sports model and a 125cc two-stroke twin. After 1930 Della Ferrera concentrated on 175cc and 350cc four-stroke motorcycles.

DEMM
1953–82 The Demm brothers of Milan built a range of lightweights from 50cc two-stroke mopeds to 175cc shaft-driven overhead-camshaft motorcycles. Demm engines were also supplied to other companies.

DE TOGIN
1932–33 Bolognese oddity that was installed with a 175cc two-stroke DKW engine and side-by-side seating for two.

DEVIL
1953–57 See OCMA (p.263).

DI BLASI
1988–92 Assembled a folding moped.

DIK DIK
1950–52 Made a 43cc clip-on engine.

DIONISI
1924–27 Alberto Dionisi constructed 123cc two-stroke motorcycles.

DI PIETRO
1921–24 Di Pietro produced a clip-on bicycle engine.

DOGLIOLI
1929–35 A small marque that built machines on a small scale using 173cc to 500cc British proprietary engines.

DOMINISSINI
1924–28 Constructed lightweight motorcycles with DKW engines.

DONISELLI
1951–61 Having built commercial three-wheelers for transporting goods before World War II, Doniselli later produced the 49cc Demm-engined Vedetta scooter and traditional mopeds.

DOTTA
1924–35 Dotta built 125cc two-stroke lightweight motorcycles with Piazza engines and commercial three-wheelers. After 1930, it concentrated on the latter.

DP
1923–26 DP was a small manufacturer of lightweight two-strokes.

DUCATI 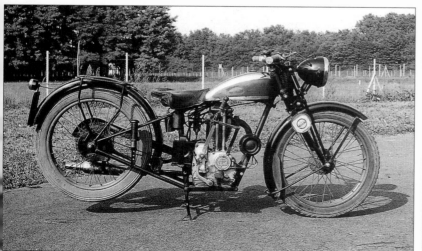 pp.52–55
1946 Production began with the 48cc overhead-valve clip-on Cucciolo engine (see Siata, p.266). From 1950 it built motorcycles and scooters using Cucciolo power units.
1952 The advanced 175cc overhead-valve Cruiser scooter with automatic transmission and electric starting was introduced, but it failed to sell well. Lightweight overhead-valve motorcycles followed.
1954 Engineer Fabio Taglioni joined Ducati and influenced the design of its machines for the next 30 years. His first bike, a 98cc overhead-camshaft single, appeared in 1955. Later 98cc to 436cc singles were based on this design.
1956 Desmodromic valve gear was used for the first time on Ducati racers. It is now a Ducati trademark feature. The 1950s and 1960s saw development of single-cylinder bikes continue. Twin-cylinder racers and a prototype 1257cc V4 were also made.
1970 Based on its single-cylinder technology, a 748cc V-twin was built using shaft- and bevel-driven overhead camshafts. Capacity grew to 864cc and 973cc and successful racing models were also developed. It was built until 1986.
1977 Ducati created a 500cc overhead-camshaft V-twin with belt drive and began its production in 1979. By 1994 the capacity of the air-cooled two-valve engine had reached 904cc. Again the road bikes were developed into successful racing machines.
1985 Cagiva took over Ducati.
1988 A new 851cc four-valve V-twin with fuel injection and water cooling was built. Capacity grew to 916cc and its racers dominated World Superbike racing. Production continues today.

EASY BIKE
1992–94 Built an electric moped.

ELECT
1920–23 Built a fore-and-aft flat twin in Turin. Twin camshafts operated four valves per cylinder. The transmission had three gears and belt final drive.

ELSA
1920–25 Elettromeccanica Lucini Società Anonima was the maker of a 75cc clip-on engine.

EOLO
1947–48 Built a 46cc clip-on engine.

ERCOLI-CAVALLONE
1922–23 Built a small number of 500cc unit-construction two-stroke V-twins.

ERFIM See Moretti (p.261).

EST
1932–34 Built by Claudio Petinnetto using 500cc four-stroke FN engines.

A 1930s Della Ferrera with a unit-construction overhead-valve engine

EUROCROSS
1969–70 Made 125cc motocross bikes with two-stroke Aermacchi engines.

EXCELSIORETTE
1924–26 Produced motorized bicycles.

FAGGI
1950–53 Built conventional lightweight bikes powered by Villiers engines.

FAINI
1923–27 Built two-stroke lightweights of 108cc and 198cc. The designer was Pietro Vassena, who later created the Rumi engine (p.265).

FALCO
1950–53 Constructed Sachs-powered lightweights.

FANTIC  p.61
1968– Fantic builds mopeds and minibikes with two-stroke Minarelli and Franco Morini engines. It developed off-road competition machines including world championship-winning trials bikes with its own engines.

FB
1970–72 Built off-road machines with 125cc two-stroke Aermacchi engines.

FB MINARELLI
1957– The new name for FBM (see below) after Franco Morini left. Chiefly an engine supplier, it intermittently builds racing and record-breaking bikes.

FB MONDIAL p.61
1933–79 Before World War II the Boselli brothers (Fratelli Boselli) built commercial three-wheelers. After the war Giuseppe Boselli created the Mondial marque – the FB initials paid tribute to the earlier enterprise. Racing success was crucial to Mondial and in 1949 its first machine, a 125cc twin overhead-camshaft racer, won the 125 World Championship. Production began in 1950 with overhead-valve 125s. Two- and four-stroke scooters and motorbikes soon followed. The marque declined in the 1960s, and by the mid-1970s it was producing mopeds and Sachs-engined machines before shutting down in 1979.
1987 The marque was relaunched. Building its bikes at the Villa company's factory, it did not survive long.
1989 Mondial reappeared yet again with a small production of 125cc two-strokes and 600cc four-stroke machines.

FBM
1951–57 Franco Morini and Vittorio Minarelli built the 125cc single-cylinder two-stroke Gabbiano and the 200cc four-stroke Vampire. In 1956 FBM became a supplier of 48cc and 175cc two- and four-stroke engines to other marques. Morini left to form his own

company (see p.261) in 1957 and the FB Minarelli name was adopted (see left). Production of the Gabbiano was continued by Bartali (see p.253).

FERRARI
1952–60 Unrelated to Ferrari cars, these were high-quality 125cc to 160cc two-strokes. A 175cc double overhead-camshaft twin was introduced in 1954. Limited numbers were made.

FERRARIS
1903 Ferraris installed Peugeot engines into strengthened bicycle frames.

FERT
1926–29 Ferruccio Calamida built a machine with a 175cc shaft-driven overhead-camshaft engine in Milan.

FIAM
1923–25 Built lightweight motorcycles.

FIAMC
1952–55 A 125cc two-stroke was made in Parma on a small scale.

FIAMMA
1935–38 Built in Turin with an all-alloy overhead-camshaft engine, a sloping cylinder, and three-speed gearbox.

FIAT
1938 A 98cc Sachs-engined scooter built by the car firm in prototype form only.

FIGINI
1898–1910 Luigi Figinio built his first motorcycle with a single-cylinder engine mounted in the seat-post (Indian style) of a bicycle-type frame. It was briefly associated with Lazzati (see p.259).

FINZI
1922–25 An advanced 650cc side-valve tranverse V-twin designed by Gino Finzi. Its inlet-over-exhaust engine had a single disc clutch and an enclosed chain drive. It never reached large-scale production.

FIORELLI
1951–68 Made Ilo-engined lightweights before switching to moped production.

FIT
1950–52 Built a 50cc clip-on engine.

FLY
1946–49 Built a 50cc clip-on engine that mounted above the rear wheel.

FM MOLTENI
1925–27 The Molteni Brothers of Milan built MAG- and Bradshaw-engined motorcycles equipped with cast-alloy frame, forks, and mudguards.
1950–56 Returned to production with a cast-alloy beam-framed scooter with a 125cc two-stroke engine. It introduced a conventional 125cc motorcycle in 1952.

A 500cc Frera with atmospheric-inlet-valve engine, c.1907

FMT
1928–30 Mattarello of Treviso made a few 132cc open-framed two-strokes for clergymen. Unrelated to the other FMT.

FMT
1922–30 Fratelli Mattarollo of Turin built 124cc two-strokes.

FOCESI
1948–56 Bicycle maker Alberto Focesi also used the Gloria name on his motorcycles. Early 48cc two-strokes had pivoted-engine swingarm assembly. A 100cc overhead-valve single with a pressed-steel frame was introduced in 1953. A 160cc two-stroke with Earles forks followed.

FOCHJ
1954–57 Built lightweight motorcycles with 98cc four-stroke NSU engines.

FONGRI
1910–30 Founded in Turin by FONtan and GRIgnani, the company used its own 500cc and 580cc fore-and-aft flat-twin engines. A three-speed gearbox with enclosed chain final drive was used. In the 1920s it made 500cc water-cooled twin-cylinder engines and a 125cc model, but financial troubles ended production in 1930.

FORONI
1984–87 Produced folding mopeds and motocross bikes in limited numbers.

FPM PUCH See Frigerio (right).

FRANCHI
1950–58 A bicycle accessories company that also built lightweight motorcycles and mopeds with 50cc, 98cc, and 125cc Sachs engines.

FRECCIA AZZURA
1951–53 Built a limited number of scooters and lightweight motorbikes using 125cc Puch split-single two-stroke engines and 147cc Sachs engines.

FREJUS
1956–68 Built mopeds and lightweights generally with FB Minarelli engines.

FRERA
1906–36 Corrado Frera of Milan established what was to be the largest marque in Italy until 1930. Before World War I it built 300cc to 1140cc single-cylinder and V-twin machines with belt drive. Large numbers were supplied to the army during the war. In the 1920s production of 250cc to 500cc singles and large-capacity V-twins continued. A 500cc racer was built using a four-valve engine. After 1930 the marque went into decline in the face of market domination by Moto Guzzi.

FRERA LEONARDO See Leonardo Frera (p.259).

FRIGERIO
1969–88 The Frigerio brothers of Treviglio built 175cc to 350cc off-road competition bikes based on four-stroke Gilera Regolaritas. It later used 125cc to 250cc Puch engines on its machines that were sold under the FPM name. It also made mopeds.

FRISONI
1951–57 Built a 123cc Villiers-engined motorbike and a 160cc scooter.

FUCHS (TAPPELLA-FUCHS)
1953–57 Built clip-on engines and complete bikes with 124cc two-stroke and 159cc overhead-valve engines.

FULGOR
1922–26 Made 143cc clip-on engines.

FURETTO
1948–49 Built a 65cc two-stroke scooter with 30.5-cm (12-in) wheels, a tubular frame, and pressed-steel bodywork. It became the basis for the Iso (see p.258).

FUSI
1936–58 Founded in Milan by Achille Fusi, who had previously produced JAP-engined Ras motorcycles (see p.264). He took over the CF marque in 1936 (see p.254) and started producing the 250cc face-cam CF machine under his own name. Production of this model resumed after World War II alongside Garelli Mosquito-engined mopeds.

FVL
1925–36 Ex-racer Francesco Vincenzo Lanfranchi built his first machines using 124cc and 174cc Moser engines. From 1931 onwards, FVL built its own 174cc and 248cc overhead-camshaft and overhead-valve engines.

GA
1925–27 GA used a 700cc Blackburne V-twin engine in a pressed-steel frame.

GABBIANO
1951–61 A horizontal two-stroke single of 123cc was constructed in very limited numbers. See FB Minarelli (p.256) and Bartali (p.253).

GABBIANO
1985–88 Produced lightweight machines with 50cc Minarelli and Franco Morini engines.

GAIA
1922–32 First made powered bicycles with Rubinelli engines, followed by lightweight motorcycles using Moser and Ladetto & Blatto engines.

GAIO
1947–48 Constructed a 48cc side-valve clip-on engine with friction drive.

GALATOR
1933–35 Built a limited number of 74cc and 98cc Sachs-engined lightweights.

GALBAI
1921–25 Built a small number of two-stroke motorcycles of 276 to 492cc.

GALBUSERA
1934–56 Galbusera first built machines with 175cc to 500cc Rudge Python engines. Radical new designs were presented at the 1938 Milan Salon. However the supercharged 250cc two-stroke V4 and 500cc two-stroke V8 never made it into production. After the war Galbusera constructed conventional motorcycles and three-wheelers of 175cc

to 500cc with Sachs, Villiers, and its own power units.

GALIMBERTI
1933–35 Cesare Galimberti produced uprated versions of Maffeis machines (see p.259).

GALL-MOTOR
1956–57 Produced a 42cc two-stroke clip-on engine, that could run on petrol or diesel.

GALLONI
1920–31 Built 500cc and 750cc side-valve V-twins followed by 250cc to 500cc four-stroke singles. Despite the popularity of its machine, the marque closed due to financial problems. Its last bikes had 175cc Blackburne engines.

GANNA
1923–67 These pre-war machines used 175cc to 500cc four-stroke British proprietary engines. After World War II, it installed Minarelli, Puch, and Sachs two-stroke engines.

GARABELLO
1903–29 Francesco Garabello built his first belt-driven motorbike with a 240cc single-cylinder engine. Its capacity soon increased to 480cc. In 1922 a 984cc shaft-driven in-line four with water cooling was produced, but proved too costly to sell in large quantities. A 175cc water-cooled rotary-valve model with shaft drive was also produced before the company shut down in 1929.

GARAFFA
1923–26 Produced clip-on engines.

GARANZINI
1921–30 Oreste Garanzini imported the English Verus machine and sold modified versions under the Veros name (see p.267). From 1922 Garanzini produced machines under his own name with JAP, Blackburne, and Villiers engines. Overhead-camshaft engines were also used on later motorcycles.

GARAVAGLIA
1904 Probably the world's first Dynasphere, it had a single, large-diameter wheel with the engine and the rider positioned inside.

GARELLI
1919–35 This company was founded by Adalberto Garelli, who had begun to develop two-stroke split singles in 1912. The 350cc Garelli achieved considerable sporting success. By the late 1920s the company had moved into the production of military equipment. Garelli ended motorcycle production in 1935.
1945 To satisfy the demand for cheap transport, the company returned to motorcycle production and built the

38cc two-stroke Mosquito engine for bicycles. It mounted underneath the bottom bracket and drove the rear wheel by friction roller. Over two-million Mosquito engines were produced. It also produced complete motorcycles.
1961 Garelli merged with Agrati (see p.252) and produced an extensive range of mopeds and lightweight motorcycles of up to 125cc. In the 1980s it returned to racing, winning several 125 World Championships between 1982 and 1987. Moped production continues.

GARLASCHELLI
1922–27 Constructed small-capacity two-stroke and 173cc overhead-valve motorcycles.

GATTI
1904–06 Early Italian marque that placed DeDion power units in bicycle-style frames.

GAZZELLA
1946–51 Built clip-on engines.

GAZZI
1929–32 Built motorcycles in limited numbers using its own 173cc overhead-valve engines.

GC
1932–35 Built 70cc clip-on engines.

GD
1923–47 A famous producer of lightweight machines, its first motorcycle was a 123cc two-stroke with two-speed gearbox. In 1929 it introduced a 175cc overhead-camshaft model. Production ended in 1933, but in 1939 it began construction of commercial tricycles.

GEMS
1921–23 Produced machines on a limited scale with a 269cc two-stroke engine, two-speed gearbox, and chain transmission.

GERBI
1952–54 Giovanni Gerbi built limited numbers of lightweights with 48cc to 173cc two-stroke Sachs engines.

GEROSA
1953–75 First used its own 125cc and 175cc overhead-valve engines. It later installed Minarelli two-stroke engines.

GG
1928–34 Founded by Ugo Gasparetti and Albano Ghisellini of Padua, it built 75cc clip-on engines for bicycles and 100cc and 125cc two-stroke engines for lightweight motorcycles.

GHIRRONI
1968–93 Built utilitarian and sports mopeds powered by two-stroke Franco Morini engines.

GIACOMASSO
1926–35 Founded by Felice Giacomasso, it used 175cc Moser and 125cc Della Ferrera engines. The company later constructed its own 175cc four-stroke model, as well as 489cc and 595cc overhead-valve engines.

GIANOGLIO
1930–35 Quality 175cc and 250cc motorbikes made in limited numbers.

GILERA pp.64–65
1909 This famous company was founded in Milan by Giuseppe Gilera. The first machine used a vertically mounted 317cc overhead-valve engine with belt drive in a diamond-pattern frame. Subsequent machines used side-valve engines until 1926, when overhead-valve designs reappeared.
1935 Gilera acquired rights for the Rondine four-cylinder machine (see p.265). It formed the basis of Gilera's Grand Prix racers until the early 1960s. From the mid-1930s, a range of four-stroke road bikes of up to 500cc was introduced. The famous 500cc overhead-valve Saturno appeared in 1939. The post-war range was based on four-stroke singles and parallel twins of 100cc to 500cc.
1969 The company was acquired by the Piaggio group, makers of the Vespa scooter (see p.267). It introduced new two-stroke bikes of 49cc to 125cc and continued to develop earlier four-stroke machines. From 1985 a new 350cc four-stroke single appeared. Its capacity later increased to 558cc and was used to power trail bikes and the café racer-style Nuovo Saturno. There was also a return to Grand Prix racing in the 250cc class.
1993 Piaggio unexpectedly closed the Gilera factory at Arcore to end 84 years of motorcycle manufacturing.

GIORDANI See Ome (p.263).

GIRARDENGO
1951–54 Built mopeds and lightweight motorbikes with proprietary engines.

GITAN
1950–85 GIno TANsini built lightweight motorbikes with its own 125cc two-stroke and 160cc overhead-valve engines. A 175cc four-stroke was made in 1955. Gitan later concentrated on the production of utilitarian and sports mopeds.

GIULIETTA
1957–80 Peripoli (see p.264) built these 49cc Minarelli-engined mopeds and motorcycles.

GKD
1978–85 GKD constructed mopeds, minibikes, and off-road machines in limited numbers.

The 1977 Gori Valli Replica named after the Italian hillclimb champion

GLORIA See Focesi (p.256).

GM
1946–48 Built a clip-on engine.

GN
1920–25 Built by Giuseppe Navone in Turin with British components.

GORI
1969–71 The Gori brothers produced uprated versions of 50cc and 60cc Bimm motocross bikes (see p.254) with Minarelli engines at their workshop in Florence under the Gori-Bimm label.
1971–83 Built 50cc to 245cc sporting and off-road machines using Sachs, Franco Morini, and Rotax two-stroke engines. Taken over by SWM in 1980 (see p.266), it had disappeared before SWM collapsed in 1985.

GR
1924–25 Lightweight racing machines built by Count Gino Revelli using 489cc JAP engines and an Antonio Baudo-designed frame with leading-link forks. It won the Grand Prix of the Nations at Monza in 1925. From 1926 the bike was sold as a Revelli.

GRASSETTI
1962–65 Grassetti produced 123cc and 148cc two-stroke motorcycles in a limited production.

GRAZIELLA See Carnielli (p.254).

GRG
1926–27 A 125cc twin-cylinder Della Ferrera-engined two-stroke with rear suspension built in limited numbers.

GRIM
1945–50 Built clip-on bicycle engines.

GS-GIOIELLO
1950–54 Made a 48cc clip-on engine.

GUALANDI
1911–14 Built 2hp single-cylinder motorcycles in small quantities.

GUARALDI
1905–16 Built machines with Fafnir and Sarolea engines in Lodi. A 1905 sidecar outfit had a hand crank to assist the passenger during hillclimbs.

GUARASCHI
1951–56 Roberto Guaraschi produced 123cc two-strokes with orthodox frames and trailing-link forks. Few were made.

GUAZZONI
1935–79 Before World War II, the Guazzoni brothers built machines with Calthorpe engines. In 1950 two- and four-strokes of 125cc to 250cc were made. Guazzoni built successful 50cc to 125cc rotary-valve two-stroke racing and off-road bikes. During the 1970s it concentrated on mopeds and 50cc motorcycles.

GUIA
1950–54 A 125cc two-stroke Sachs-engined lightweight with a pressed-steel frame was made in limited numbers.

GUIZZARDI
1926–32 A limited production of 125cc and 175cc four-strokes that had the magneto driven from the camshaft.

GUIZZO
1955–62 Guizzo built mopeds and an unsuccessful 149cc scooter.

HIRUNDO
1951 Limited production of a 123cc twin-cylinder scooter built in Turin.

HM
1994– This new marque builds sports mopeds with 49cc two-stroke Morini and Minarelli engines on a small scale.

HRD
1980– Builds mopeds and lightweight motorcycles with Tau engines. Taken over by Kram-It in 1987 (see p.259).

IBIS
1925–28 The Ibis had a 173cc overhead-valve Piazza engine mounted in an open frame. It was built in Turin.

IBIS
1947–51 Ibis made 49cc to 98cc two-strokes in Bologna. These included split-single and twin-cylinder models.

ICEMI
1927–30 Built bikes with Blackburne, JAP, and its own engines of 175cc to 500cc in limited numbers.

IDRA
1923–25 Built 125cc overhead-valve lightweights in a limited production.

IDROFLEX
1949–54 Idroflex built 105cc and 125cc horizontal-cylinder two-strokes in Milan. The engine pivoted with the rear suspension.

IMN
1950–58 Industria Meccanica Napoletana diversified from weapons to motorcycles after World War II. IMN made the Garelli Mosquito engine under licence and built 49cc and 98cc four-stroke and 49cc to 248cc two-stroke motorcycles. An innovative 199cc shaft-driven overhead-valve flat twin was built in 1956. However, its machines were often overpriced and underdeveloped.

INNOCENTI See Lambretta (p.259).

INTRAMOTOR
1971–81 Built Minarelli-engined mopeds and 125cc off-road competition machines.

INVICTA
1950–52 Built a limited number of 73cc and 123cc two-stroke machines.

IPREM
1977–81 Grand Prix racer based on the 50cc two-stroke Kreidler. Eugenio Lazzarini won the 50cc world title on an Iprem in 1980. A less successful 125cc twin was also built.

IRIS
1952–53 Used 123cc Ilo engines.

ISO
1949–63 Established maker of fridges and railway equipment, Iso Thermos bought the rights for the Furetto scooter (see p.256). It introduced a revised 123cc split-single two-stroke in 1950. A 236cc version was later offered with separate lubrication and shaft drive.

The engine was also used in the Isetta bubble-car, later built under licence by BMW. A range of 125cc and 175cc motorcycles appeared in 1961. In 1963 Iso switched to making luxury cars, though some motorcycles were still made under licence in Spain.

ITALA
1933–39 Giuseppe Navone of Turin (see also GN, left) built 100cc to 586cc motorcycles with Train, Chaise, and four-valve Rudge Python engines. In 1933 he also made the 750cc Chaise V4-engined Super Itala. The racing models had pressed-steel frames and were built under licence from Durandal. In 1936 it produced the Piccola Italiana – "little Italian bike" – with a 98cc Train engine.

ITALEMMEZETA
1958–66 These MZ-engined bikes were built by Leopoldo Tartarini, who later formed Italjet (see below).

ITALJET 🏍 p.110
1966– Leopoldo Tartarini used CZ and Triumph engines in his early machines. The Velocette Indian was built for Floyd Clymer in the late 1950s. From the 1970s it concentrated on children's minibikes. It was also responsible for the styling of the Ducati Darmah. In the 1980s Italjet built 350cc road, custom, and trial two- and four-strokes.

ITALMOTO
1952–54 Italmoto made orthodox 125cc two-stroke and 160cc overhead-valve lightweight motorcycles in Bologna.

ITOM
1945–68 Itom first produced a 48cc clip-on engine with friction drive and complete, three-geared mopeds. A 65cc motorcycle was introduced later. From 1960 it specialized in mopeds and 50cc and 60cc lightweight sports machines, which were successful in the early years of 50cc racing.

JANGA
1922–25 Built two-stroke lightweight machines in limited numbers. Engines were also sold separately.

JENIS
1922–24 Produced two-stroke motorized bicycles in limited numbers. The engine was sold separately.

JUNIOR
1924–36 Based in Livorno, its first bikes had 350cc two-stroke engines with two gears and belt final drive. All bolts were the same size so that the bike could be taken apart with one spanner. In 1927 it used 175cc, 250cc, and 350cc JAP and Blackburne four-stroke engines. The company closed in 1936 when the founder died during the war in Ethiopia.

K2
1954–56 Built a 175cc shaft-driven two-stroke with swingarm rear suspension.

KOSMOS
1978–84 Built off-road machines that used 125cc to 480cc two-stroke engines.

KRAMER See Kram-It (below).

KRAM-IT
1981– Originally constructed under the Kramer name using engines supplied by the German Kramer company. When the German marque closed in 1985, the name was changed to Kram-It. Minarelli and Rotax engines were used. It absorbed the HRD marque (see p.258) in 1987.

KYMCO
1994– Builds utilitarian mopeds.

KZ
1954–56 Pietro Vassena built a 175cc two-stroke with shaft drive in Lecco.

LADETTO (LADETTO & BLATTO)
c.1923–27 The Ladetto brothers made engines and lightweight motorcycles as well as designing machines for several other manufacturers.
1927–32 Giovanni Ladetto went into partnership with fellow designer Angelo Blatto (see p.254). Ladetto & Blatto built two- and four-stroke engines and motorcycles of 132cc to 247cc. Blatto left in 1930 and production continued under the Ladetto name. Rear suspension was available in 1932, but production ended later that year.

L'ALBA
1924–26 Lightweight motorcycles made in small numbers by Giorgio Valeri using 198cc side-valve German Alba engines.

LAMBRETTA 🏍 p.119
1947 Post-war diversification by the Innocenti metal company resulted in the very successful Lambretta scooter. The first model was a 125cc shaft-driven two-stroke in a pressed-steel and tubular frame. Bodywork became an option in 1950 when a 250cc V-twin racing bike was built. In 1951 a new large-diameter tubular spine frame was introduced. A moped was produced from 1954 and 150cc scooters were also offered.
1957 A new design appeared with chain drive and four-speed gearbox. It was also restyled with the front mudguard now attached to the bodywork instead of the forks. Engine capacity grew to 173cc and later to 198cc.
1972 Lambretta production ended in Italy, but continued under licence in India and Spain.

LAMPO
1925–30 Produced a small number of lightweights with 125cc two-stroke and 175cc and 250cc four-stroke engines. Production was interrupted between 1928 and 1929, when a 175cc overhead-valve model was produced.

LANDI
1923–26 Lamberto Landi made 125cc and 175cc two-strokes in Turin.

LARDORI
1924–27 Built in limited numbers near Siena using 350cc Train engines and other proprietary components.

LAVERDA 🏍 pp.120–122
1949 Laverda was a farm machinery manufacturer that initially built a 74cc overhead-valve motorcycle with a pressed-steel frame. It was the first in a series of small-capacity models.
1968 A new 653cc overhead-camshaft machine, based on the Honda CB77 design, was constructed. Capacity grew to 748cc and it was soon exported.
1973 Laverda introduced 980cc double overhead-camshaft triples. A 1115cc version followed. Excellent performance ensured a legendary reputation despite its flaws, as later versions became more refined but less desirable. A 500cc twin and a prototype V6 racer were also built, as were smaller capacity two-stroke machines using Zündapp and its own water-cooled engines. By the mid-1980s Laverda was in trouble and production eventually stopped in 1988.
1994 After several false starts, the production of a 650cc twin began at a new factory.

LAZZATI
1899–1904 Placed DeDion engines in bicycle frames. See also Figini (p.256).

LECCE
1930–32 Engineer Otello Albanese from Lecce built a very limited number of motorcycles with modified 175cc Moser engines. They had a three-valve cylinder head with two exhaust valves.

LEGNANO
1932–68 A bicycle company that had earlier produced motorcycles under the Wolsit label (see p.267). After World War II it built mopeds with Garelli Mosquito and Sachs engines.

LEM
1974 Built mopeds and children's minibikes with Minarelli and Franco Morini engines in Bologna.

LEONARDO FRERA
1931–34 A marque established by Leonardo Frera following the takeover of his father's marque (see Frera p.257) by Emilio Fossio. Motorcycles with four-stroke JAP engines of 175cc and 350cc were produced.
1949–60 The marque returned with a limited production of mopeds and motorcycles with Sterzi and its own 50cc to 150cc engines.

LEONE
1946–48 Produced a 49cc clip-on two-stroke engine that was mounted in front of the pedals.

LEPROTTO
1951–57 Made a small number of motorcycles in Turin using its own 160cc and 200cc twin-cylinder two-stroke engines. By 1957 it was constructing mopeds that were powered by 49cc Demm engines.

LILLIPUT See Rosselli (p.265).

LINTO
1947–48 The first bikes made by LINo TOnti with the Linto name were 75cc racers with twin overhead camshafts.
1967–71 Tonti built a new racer by combining two 250cc Aermacchi Ala d'Oro engines to create a 497cc overhead-valve twin with horizontal cylinders and six-speed gearbox. For a short period the Linto was used by several private riders, but was soon eclipsed by Japanese two-stroke racers.

LINX
1929–41 Sports machines built with Rudge Python, JAP, Blackburne, and later Piazza engines. Few were made.

LIVIA
1932–35 Built lightweights with 98cc and 125cc two-stroke Sachs engines.

LUCINI
1921–25 Built clip-on engines.

LUSARDI
1984–85 Kreidler-inspired 50cc and 80cc racers built in small numbers.

LUZI
1970–72 Cesare Luzi built a 50cc racer using a modified FB Minarelli engine.

MAFALDA
1923–26 Small marque that built 123cc and 173cc two-stroke lightweights.

MAFFEIS
1903–35 Bernardo Maffeis may have built a motorcycle as early as 1895. In 1903 a motorbike with a 2hp Sarolea

The 1957 50cc Itom Super Sport with three-speed gearbox

engine was produced. The Maffeis brothers subsequently built V-twin machines. They made bikes with 250cc to 500cc side-valve and overhead-valve Blackburne engines in the 1920s.

MAGNI
1928–30 An interesting 350cc twin with horizontal cylinders and shaft-driven overhead camshaft built by Luigi Magni of Milan. It never reached series production. A conventional 500cc vertical single was also made in 1930.

MAGNI
1977– Formerly with MV Agusta, Arturo Magni set up his own business when MV closed. He builds a limited number of motorcycles with his own frames. Most machines use Moto Guzzi engines, but BMW, MV, and Honda power units have also been installed.

MAININI
1966–70 The Mainini brothers built racers with modified 125cc two-stroke Aermacchi engines in very low chassis.

MAINO
1902–10 Pioneer motorcycle manufacturer that used Souverain engines in its early machines.
1953–60 After World War II Maino built Garelli Mosquito-powered mopeds. Small motorcycles with 98cc NSU and 147cc Sachs and Ilo engines followed.

MAJOR
c.1947–48 Built in Turin by Salvatore Majorca in limited numbers. It was a 350cc shaft-driven overhead-valve machine with enclosed bodywork.

MALAGUTI
1945– Bicycle maker Antonio Malaguti made his first mopeds using 38cc Garelli Mosquito engines. Subsequently Sachs and Franco Morini two-stroke engines were used on a range of mopeds and motorcycles of up to 125cc. Production now concentrates on mopeds.

MALANCA
1956–86 Built 124cc and 149cc twin-cylinder two-stroke motorcycles, as well as some mopeds. Racing machines were also produced.

MALFARDA
1923–28 Small marque that built 123cc and 173cc two-stroke lightweights.

MANTOVANI
1902–10 Belt-driven bikes that used 1.5hp, 2.75hp, and 4hp single-cylinder engines with air or water cooling.

MARCHAND
1899–1910 Paolo and Leone Marchand from Piacenza were among the most important Italian motorcycle producers

in the early 1900s. Attilio Orio was a partner and the bikes sometimes carried a Marchand-Orio badge. Single-cylinder inlet-over-exhaust engines of 1.75hp to 3.5hp were used. A two ratio belt-drive system and rear suspension were also developed. They also made successful racing machines. The company soon turned to car production.

MARCHITELLI
1947–48 A powered wheel with a 38cc two-stroke engine that replaced the bicycle's rear wheel.

MARIANI
1930–34 Built by Enrico Mariani of Monza. It was a 500cc side-valve single available in either petrol- or diesel-fuelled models. The diesel version had two exhaust valves and had to be started on petrol. Few were built.

MARINI
1924–28 A 124cc two-stroke produced in limited quantities.

MARTINA
1924–32 First built motorcycles with a 175cc JAP engine. Later models were built with the client's choice of engines.

MAS
1920 Made in Milan by Alberico Seiling. The first machines were installed with 123cc overhead-valve engines in bicycle-style frames. They were soon followed by a range of side-valve and overhead-valve four-stroke singles of 123cc to 568cc. By the late 1930s, rear suspension was available on MAS machines.
1937 Seiling left the MAS marque to establish his own marque (see p.265). MAS supplied the Italian army with motorcycles during the war. After World

War II it never achieved its pre-war success; the 122cc overhead-valve Stella Alpina model with forced air cooling and a 500cc overhead-camshaft vertical twin were both unsuccessful. A 500cc Grand Prix twin with double overhead camshafts was developed in 1953, but never left the prototype stage. Soon MAS was reduced to building 125cc bikes and mopeds with two-stroke Sachs engines.
1956 The company closed.

MASERATI
1953–61 The Maserati family parted with its sports car company in the late 1940s, but retained the rights to use the name and logo. From 1953 to 1961 it made spark plugs and a small number of high-quality motorbikes including 125cc two-stroke, 160cc and 250cc overhead-valve and 175cc overhead-camshaft models, as well as various mopeds.

MASSARINI
1926–30 Built on a limited scale in Piacenza using its own 118cc, 125cc, and 148cc two-stroke engines.

MAV
1954–56 Built clip-on engines.

MAV
1973–82 Small factory that made off-road competition machines with 50cc, 125cc, and 175cc two-stroke engines by Minarelli, Hiro, and Sachs.

MAXIMA
1920–25 Built 690cc and 750cc fore-and-aft flat twins with three gears and chain drive in orthodox frames.

MAZZILLI
1970–78 Giorgi Mazzilli built a few off-road competition bikes with modified

125cc to 250cc two-stroke Sachs engines in conventional frames.

MAZZUCCHELI
1925–28 Built lightweights in small quantities with 198cc German Alba engines in orthodox frames.

MBA
1977–85 Small factory linked to the Benelli family's arms company and also to the makers of Morbidelli racers (see p.261). It built mopeds with Sachs and other proprietary engines. MBA was also involved in making successful production versions of the 125cc twin-cylinder Morbidelli racing machines with monocoque frames and water cooling.

MBM
1974–81 MBM constructed Minarelli-engined mopeds.

MBR
1924–26 Produced 124cc two-strokes.

MDS
1955–60 The Scoccimarro brothers, Moto Di Scoccimarro, made a 65cc overhead-valve lightweight with an open frame with 41-cm (16-in) wheels. It was followed by more orthodox motorcycles using 70cc to 80cc engines.

ME
1953–55 Moto Emilia of Bologna built 175cc motorcycles in limited numbers. It installed overhead valves on the touring bike, overhead camshaft on the sports bike, and twin overhead camshafts on the Supersport.

MEDUSA
1957–58 Sports motorbikes designed by Luciano Pasini and built by Vasco Loro,

A MAS overhead-valve single, c.1930

the famous racer. It was a 175cc double overhead-camshaft parallel twin with an orthodox frame.

MELDI
1927–37 Meldi built limited numbers of competition machines using overhead-valve single-cylinder JAP and Rudge Python engines of 250cc to 500cc. He was also involved with Antonio Baudo and the BM marque (see p.254).

MEMINI
1946–47 A carburettor factory that built the Electa, a lightweight 173cc two-stroke with telescopic forks and rear suspension. Despite excellent features, it never reached series production.

MENGOLI
1952–54 A 175cc four-stroke machine with overhead camshafts and telescopic forks produced in small numbers.

MENON
1930–32 Used 173cc and 198cc side-valve engines in a limited production.

MERLONGHI
1927–30 Based in Tolentino, it built a motorized bicycle with a 132cc two-stroke engine and two-speed gearbox.

METEORA
1953–66 Angelo Zanasi built the first Meteora using a 175cc overhead-camshaft OMS engine. From 1955 the lightweight machines used FB, NSU, and Franco Morini engines of 50cc to 100cc.

MFB
1957–64 MFB built 50cc to 175cc two-stroke and 174cc overhead-valve bikes.

MFG
1921–27 Francesco Garinzini, brother of Oreste (see Garinzini, p.257), built lightweights with his own 142cc two-stroke engines. He also used larger capacity overhead-valve single-cylinder Blackburne engines in his own frames.

MG
1926–50 The marque was founded in Modena by Vittorio Guerzoni. The first machine was a Train-engined model. In 1932 the Guarinoni-Marninoni company took over production to build 250cc and 500cc overhead-valve and overhead-camshaft machines. From 1933 almost identical models were produced under the Taurus name (see p.266). After World War II MG was taken over by the Bergamini brothers, who continued to build the 250cc and 500cc bikes under the Centaurus brand-name (see p.254).

MIGNON
1922–32 Vittorio Guerzoni (see MG, above) also used the Mignon label. He

first produced a 125cc four-stroke lightweight and made a 250cc twin in 1926 by doubling up the 125cc engine. A sporting version was capable of 120km/h (74.5mph). A 500cc racer with single or double overhead camshafts was also produced.

MILANI
1970–81 Minarelli-engined mopeds and off-road bikes built in small numbers.

MILLER-BALSAMO
1921–59 The Balsamo brothers sold the American Excelsior machines in Milan before making their own motorcycles with 175cc Moser engines. In 1928 they built their own 175cc overhead-valve engine, which established an excellent sporting reputation. In the 1930s Miller built motorbikes with 250cc to 500cc four-valve Rudge Python engines and with its own 98cc and 250cc engines. In 1939 a fully faired machine with a 200cc overhead-valve engine was made and was revived after the war as the Jupiter. A 175cc overhead-camshaft model and conventional 250cc and 500cc machines were also produced. It built economy mopeds in its final years of production.

MINARELLI See FB Minarelli (p.256).

MINERVA
1929–31 A 175cc four-stroke built in limited numbers in Turin. It was unconnected with the Belgian Minerva.

MINETTI
1924–27 The Minetti brothers built 124cc two-strokes in Turin.

MINIMOTOR
1945–56 Clip-on engines of 49cc and, later, 87cc were designed by Vincenzo Piatti, who subsequently created the Piatti scooter, which was built in Belgium and Britain. The Motorminima was a complete machine with a folding frame.

MINIZETA
1989 Built 38cc clip-on engines, complete mopeds, and minibikes.

MI-VAL
1950–67 Its first motorcycles were 125cc two-strokes, which achieved great sporting success. Some 125cc to 250cc overhead-valve models were made from 1954 and a double overhead-camshaft racer was also produced. It also built the three-wheeled Messerschmitt bubble-car under licence. Its final machines were mopeds and four-stroke motocross 250s.

MM
1924–64 Founded in Bologna by Angelo Mattei, Mario Mazzetti, Alfonso Morini, and Giuseppe Massi. In 1927 Mattei and Massi left, and Dr Antonio Salva joined. The company's first machine was a

125cc two-stroke racer with two-speed gearbox. It won the 125cc class at the 1927 Grand Prix of the Nations. In the 1930s MM began building overhead-valve and side-valve machines of up to 496cc. Some 123cc and 173cc overhead-camshaft racers were also built. Alfonso Morini left the company in 1937 to establish his own marque (see Morini, right). After World War II MM built 350cc and 500cc machines based on the pre-war designs, and an exceptional 250cc model with chain-driven overhead camshaft and telescopic suspension. Sadly the company could not reproduce its pre-war success. The last machines that MM built were 125cc utilitarian two-strokes.

MOLARONI
1921–27 The Molaroni brothers built two-stroke machines in Pesaro, including 296cc and 344cc singles and a 596cc flat twin. Single-cylinder four-stroke Blackburne engines were also used.

MOLTENI See FM Molteni (p.256).

MONACO
1950–55 Vittorio Monaco built a 125cc two-stroke motorcycle with enclosed bodywork and a bucket seat for the rider. It failed to sell well. A second version used the Montanto name.

MONACO-BAUDO
1927–28 Augusto Monaco and Antonio Baudo (see p.253) joined together to produce a 500cc side-valve single with a three-speed gearbox and a conventional frame. Monaco had earlier built a 250cc four-stroke twin in association with Della Ferrera.

MONDIAL See FB Mondial (p.256).

MONTANTO See Monaco (above).

MONTEROSA
1954–58 Small company that made utilitarian mopeds with proprietary power units.

MONTÙ
1903–10 Alessandrian manufacturer that built motorcycles with Carcano power units and, later, DeDion engines.

MONVISO
1951–56 A small marque that made mopeds and lightweight motorcycles with 50cc to 175cc Sachs engines.

MORBIDELLI 🏍 p.127
1969–82 It began as a hobby for motorcycle-mad industrialist Giancarlo Morbidelli. His advanced two-stroke racers of 50cc to 250cc won six world championships in the mid-1970s, but his 350cc and 500cc four-cylinder racing models were not as successful. MBA, a

co-operative venture between Morbidelli and Benelli Armi, built customer versions of a 125cc disc-valve twin-cylinder machine with water cooling.
1994 Morbidelli introduced a new touring motorcycle with an 850cc V8 engine and shaft drive. A high price tag and styling by Pininfarina ensured low consumer demand. The public reaction to the new model resulted in a redesign by Bimota.

MORETTI
1934–52 Giovanni Moretti began making motorcycles in Turin using Ladetto, DKW, and JAP engines. In 1946 Moretti produced a 125cc double overhead-camshaft machine with oval frame tubes designed by Angelo Blattò. A 250cc version followed. A 250cc flat twin with overhead valves and shaft drive was introduced in 1947 and was sold under the Erfim name.

MORINI 🏍 pp.128–29
1937 Alfonso Morini left MM (see left) and established his own company, which began making commercial tricycles.
1946 Morini began production of a 123cc two-stroke inspired by the DKW RT 125. A 246cc two-stroke single appeared in 1949.
1950 A new 123cc overhead-camshaft racer appeared. Development of Morini's overhead-camshaft single-cylinder racers continued into the 1960s. The 174cc Rebello, an overhead-camshaft racing machine of 1955, provided the basis of the 247cc twin which came close to beating Honda to the 250 World Championship in 1963.
1952 The first 175cc overhead-valve single-cylinder road bikes were introduced. From these came the successful Settebello sports bikes. The capacities of the overhead-valve singles later ranged from 50cc to 250cc.
1973 New 72° overhead-valve V-twins began production. The very advanced design used Heron cylinder heads and electronic ignition. The first models were 344cc, but 239cc and 479cc versions were built later. The modular design allowed the production of 125cc and 250cc singles using many components from the V-twin engine. This power unit was still in production 20 years later. A turbocharged prototype based on the 500cc V-twin was displayed in 1981, but never reached full production.
1987 Morini was sold to Cagiva. Custom and trail-style bikes using the long-lasting V-twin engine continue in production, mainly for sale in the domestic market.

MOTOBI
1950 After he split from the family business, Giuseppe Benelli (see p.253) built 98cc two-strokes with horizontal cylinders and an egg-shaped engine, which became a MotoBi trademark.

Two-stroke singles and twins of 98cc to 248cc were also built.
1956 Introduced 123cc and 172cc overhead-valve four-stroke singles using the same engine style. The engine capacity was later increased to 245cc.
1962 Giuseppe died and MotoBi was absorbed back into the Benelli fold. For a while it retained a separate identity, but eventually the machines became Benellis with a different badge.
1976–80 The last identifiably different MotoBi was a café racer-style bike based on Benelli's 250cc two-stroke twin.

MOTOBIMM See Bimm (p.254).

MOTO BM
1982–88 Built a small number of mopeds and 50cc motorcycles with two-stroke Minarelli engines.

MOTO-BORGO See Borgo (p.254).

MOTOCLIPPER
1948–49 Built a lightweight motorbike with a 60cc four-stroke Ducati engine.

MOTODELTA
1970–73 Made off-road competition bikes with 125cc Sachs engines.

MOTO FUTURO
1948–49 Made an open-framed 98cc to 250cc machine with a bucket seat.

MOTO GUZZI 🏍 pp.130–132
1921 Founded in Mandello del Lario by Carlo Guzzi and Giorgio Parodi. Its first production machine was a 498cc

horizontal single with an exhaust-over-inlet-valve layout. The horizontal four-stroke single was the basis of the Guzzi range until the mid-1960s and its 500cc singles retained the 88 x 82-mm dimensions of the original bike until 1976. In 1924 the 500cc overhead-camshaft four-valve appeared and won the first European Championship. From 1926 it built 250cc and special racing models. Guzzi stuck to the single for road bikes but developed a series of unusual racers including a 120° V-twin, supercharged singles, triples, and fours, in-line overhead-camshaft fours, and the incredible 500cc V8 in 1955. After World War II, Moto Guzzi built small-capacity motorcycles, such as the successful two-stroke Motoleggera 65, the 98cc and 110cc Zigolo, the 160cc, 175cc, and the 192cc large-wheeled four-stroke Galletto scooter. The 250cc and 500cc external fly-wheel horizontal models continued in production.
1967 A 703cc shaft-driven V-twin was introduced; its overhead-valve engine had originally been intended for use in a military three-wheeler. The V7 model became the basis for Guzzi machines, which are still made today. Touring and sports versions were also built. Engine capacity had grown to 1100cc by 1994.
1971 Alessandro de Tomaso, owner of Benelli (see p.253), bought the troubled company. A V-twin range was developed as was a range of two- and four-cylinder four-strokes identical to Benelli models. A smaller, shaft-driven V-twin appeared in 1977. Some 350cc, 500cc, and 650cc models were eventually made.

1993 A revised Guzzi V-twin appeared. The 992cc Daytona has four-valve heads, overhead-camshaft, and fuel injection.

MOTOM
1947–71 First built clip-on four-stroke engines and complete mopeds. Its first motorcycle was the unusual 147cc overhead-valve Delfino built in 1950. It had a fan-cooled engine mounted under the rider's seat. The radical 1953 98TS model had a 98cc horizontal overhead-valve engine mounted in a pressed-steel frame and featured rubber-sprung suspension. Conventional four-stroke lightweights were built during the 1950s. In the 1960s Motom declined, though 49cc two-strokes using Peugeot and Zündapp engines were produced.

MOTOMEC
1985–89 This multi-functional moped could be used as a mobile pump, a compressor, or a battery charger.

MOTO PIANA
1926–31 Gualtiero Piana (see Piana p.264) built Villiers- and JAP-engined motorcycles until 1927 when he made his own 250cc side-valve engine.

MOTO-RÊVE ITALIANA
1912–15 Built 300cc to 497cc V-twin and single-cylinder machines under licence from Moto-Rêve of Switzerland.

MOTO V
1927–30 A 355cc inlet-over-exhaust-valve single with a pressed-steel frame made in Turin.

MOTRON
1977– This marque builds Minarelli-engined mopeds.

MP
1934–35 Few were made of this 500cc bike with an overhead-valve Sturmey-Archer engine in a pressed-steel frame.

MR
1924–26 Built Train-engined machines in limited numbers.

MT 34
1943–49 A 34cc clip-on engine designed by Giuseppe Remondini.

MT See Muratore (below).

MÜLLER
1950–79 Bruno Müller's first machine was a short-lived 98cc lightweight with a NSU engine. Production resumed in 1968 with off-road bikes using Zündapp, Hiro, Sachs, and Franco Morini engines.

MURATORE
1948–53 Teresio Muratore built a 250cc machine with an inclined twin-cylinder overhead-camshaft engine in an orthodox frame. Made in small numbers, it was also known by the MT name.

MUSA
1947–49 Built a 70cc two-stroke with cantilever rear suspension. Musa also built Ducati Cucciolo-engined mopeds.

MV AGUSTA 🏍 pp.134–137
1945 Aircraft company Agusta needed to diversify after World War II. The first MVs (Meccanica Verghera) were 98cc and 125cc lightweight two-strokes.
1947 A 250cc four-stroke single was built. MV increasingly used four-stroke engines on its road bikes. By the mid-1950s there was a range of lightweights and scooters of 50cc to 175cc. From 1967 250cc and 350cc twins were built. Unlike the racers the road bikes, except for the later fours, were uninspiring.
1950 The first four-cylinder MV racer was built after key personnel had moved from Gilera. The overhead-camshaft 500 had torsion-bar suspension and shaft drive. A 125cc single was also built. Both machines became successful racers and 250cc and 350cc competition bikes were also built. Although 125cc and 250cc production racers were built, the fours were only produced for the factory's own team. MV won 37 World Championships before it withdrew from racing in 1976.
1966 The first four-cylinder road bike appeared, a 600cc shaft-driven tourer. It was built until 1971 when a 750cc sports bike appeared. Double overhead-camshaft road-going fours were also made in small numbers.
1977 Increasingly subsidized by its parent aircraft company, the motorcycle

A 1976 MotoBi based on a 250cc Benelli two-stroke twin

division soon ended production and the name was later sold to Cagiva (see p.254). Its revival is often rumoured.

MVB
1954–56 Built mopeds and lightweights with proprietary two-stroke engines.

NAGAS & RAY
1925–28 Alessandro Nagas and Tullio Ray distributed Indian and Zündapp machines in Italy. Designed by Giuseppe Remondini, their bikes were 348cc side- and overhead-valve singles with three-speed gearbox and external fly-wheel.

NASSETTI
1951–60 Nassetti, a maker of magnetos and aircraft parts, built 49cc two-stroke clip-on engines called the Pellegrino. From 1956 it built complete machines with conventional and spine frames.

NAVONE
1928–29 Giuseppe Navone produced the GN (see p.258) and Itala (see p.258) marques, as well lightweights with 175cc side-valve French PM engines.

NAZZARO
1926–28 Eugenio Nazzaro constructed lightweight motorcycles in Turin with 175cc overhead-valve engines.

NECCHI
1948–54 Few were made of these lightweights, which used up to 123cc Ducati Cucciolo, Garelli Mosquito, Villiers, and Sachs engines.

NEGRINI
1956–86 Built mopeds, minibikes, and lightweight machines of up to 125cc.

NENCIONI
1926–28 Nencioni built twin-cylinder two-stroke lightweights with Della Ferrera engines.

NEPTUNIA See Busi-Nettunia (p.254).

NEPTUNNS
1924–26 Made two-stroke lightweights in limited numbers.

NETTUNIA See Busi-Nettunia (p.254).

NIBBIO
1946–52 The first Italian scooter, it had a 98cc two-stroke engine and a tubular frame. Initially built by Gianca of Monza, San Cristoforo (see p.265) of Milan took over in 1949 and constructed a new 125cc disc-valve two-stroke. In 1952 it was modified further and sold as the Simonetta (see p.266).

NOVARA
1930–35 Angelo Novara of Legnano built a limited number of bikes with 175cc JAP, Chaise, and FN engines.

An overhead-valve Oliverio, c.1930

NVB
1956–57 Mopeds and lightweights with 50cc and 150cc two-stroke and 125cc four-stroke engines. Few were built.

OASA
1930–32 A successor to the Aliprandi marque (see p.252), OASA machines used 173cc four-stroke Ladetto and 246cc and 346cc JAP engines.

OCMA (DEVIL)
1953–58 The Officine Costruzioni Martinelli of Bergamo, a maker of car spares, built its first 125cc and 160cc two-stroke motorcycles and mopeds under the Devil name in 1953. A 175cc four-stroke and a double overhead-camshaft sports model were also made, as were commercial tricycles.

OLIVERIO
1929–32 Built 346cc and 496cc bikes with overhead-valve Sturmey-Archer engines on a small scale in Turin.

OLIVIA
1920–25 The Olivia Brothers built motorized bicycles and, later, a 175cc Train-engined two-stroke lightweight.

OLLEARO
1921–53 Neftali Ollearo of Turin first made a 125cc two-stroke with a cradle frame. Overhead-valve singles of 175cc to 500cc were built later. These had a unit-construction engine and gearbox, and shaft drive. In 1937 it was the first Italian marque to use telescopic forks as standard. In 1945 it resumed production of the pre-war designs and built 45cc two-stroke clip-on engines.

OLMO
1951–61 Built mopeds and lightweights with 49cc proprietary engines.

OLYMPIA
1951–54 Borghi's bicycle company built two-stroke mopeds and lightweights of 50cc and 125cc in small numbers.

OMA
1952–55 Few were built of these 173cc four-stroke singles with either overhead camshafts or overhead valves.

OMAN
1927–28 Diesel-engined machines made in small numbers.

OMB
1933–34 Founded by Angelo Blatto after splitting with Ladetto (see p.259). The machines ranged from a 175cc bike to a 500cc overhead-camshaft racer.

OMC
1933–35 Orthodox 175cc overhead-valve machine that was designed by Giovanni Ladetto and built by the Officine Meccaniche Calabresi.

OMC
1985– OMC produce on- and off-road sports mopeds with Minarelli and Franco Morini engines. It has also been building Testi machines (see p.266) since 1987.

OME
1920–21 An electric motorbike built by Ernest Giordani. The 6/12V and 250W engine gave the machine a top speed of 25km/h (15mph).

OMEA
1950–53 Designed by Carlo Bottari and built in Milan, the Omea was a 124cc two-stroke with three-speed gearbox. It had a cast-alloy frame with swingarm rear suspension. Its centrally sprung leading-link forks were hydraulically damped. Limited numbers were built.

OMER
1968–81 Built Minarelli- and Morini-engined mopeds in small numbers.

OMN
1924–25 Built 147cc and 172cc bikes with Villiers engines in small numbers.

OMT See Muratore (p.262).

OPRA
1927–29 An advanced 490cc four-cylinder racer designed by Pietro Remor and Carlo Gianni and made by Officine di Precisione Romane Automobilistiche. The transverse engine had gear-driven overhead camshafts. Despite its success, high costs ended the project, though it became the basis of Rondine (see p.265) and Gilera (see p.257) racers.

OR
1928–31 Built clip-on engines and also motorcycles with 175cc overhead- or side-valve engines in limited numbers.

ORIONE
1923–28 Guido Carpi constructed 87cc and 125cc two-strokes and a 124cc overhead-valve model in Milan. Engines were also sold separately.

ORIX-PRINA
1949–54 Bicycle maker that built 125cc and 175cc two-stroke scooters and motorcycles in limited numbers.

OSCAR
1965–82 Built utilitarian and sports mopeds with Franco Morini or Minarelli engines. A 60cc racer was made in 1966.

OTTOLENGHI
1928–32 Made in small numbers with 173cc to 346cc Piazza, Ladetto & Blatto, JAP, Ladetto, and its own engines.

OTTINO

1926–35 Built motorized bicycles and lightweight motorcycles with 125cc two-stroke Della Ferrera and 175cc four-stroke JAP, Della Ferrera, and CF engines.

PAGLIANTI

1948–66 Built small scooters and mopeds using Ducati Cucciolo, Garelli Mosquito, and, later, Minarelli and Franco Morini engines.

PANDA

1980–85 Lightweight off-road bikes with 79cc Sachs engines.

PARILLA

1946 Giovanni Parrilla first built 247cc overhead-camshaft racers. Production bikes were available in 1947. By 1950 the range included 98cc, 123cc, and 249cc single-cylinder two-stroke road bikes.
1952 Launched a 174cc single and a 348cc overhead-camshaft parallel twin. Mopeds and scooters were also built.
1956 The 98cc and 123cc Slughi with semi-enclosed bodywork appeared. It was available with a horizontal single-cylinder two- or four-stroke engine. Singles of 175cc and 250cc were exported in road, racing, and scrambler variants.
1967 Production stopped when the industrial group, which had earlier bought Parilla, collapsed.

PARVUS

1921–26 Built 104cc clip-on two-stroke engines and a 123cc two-stroke model.

PASSONI

1902–04 Milanese pioneer who placed 2hp engines into bicycle-style frames.

PATON

1958–85 Giuseppe PAttoni, formerly with Mondial, built competitive racers on a shoestring budget. Lino TONti helped modify his first 125cc and 175cc bikes. In 1964 Paton created a 250cc twin with double overhead camshafts. Four-stroke twins of 350cc and 500cc were developed later. In 1976 a 500cc two-stroke four was produced. Two-stroke development continued into the mid-1980s, but lack of funds hampered and eventually ended the project.

PATRIARCA

1907–10 Gustavo Patriarca built a two-stroke clip-on engine before switching his interest to aircraft.
1925–33 Patriarca made 125cc and 175cc overhead-valve bikes with unit-construction engine and gearbox.
1951–53 Built the Mottina using a 248cc overhead-valve engine.

PEGASO

1955–64 Former Motom employees made high-quality four-stroke mopeds

A 1958 Turismo version of Parilla's 350cc overhead-camshaft twin

and 60cc motorcycles in limited numbers. They used overhead-valve engines, which pivoted with the rear suspension, in pressed-steel frames.

PERIPOLI

1957– Builds 49cc two-stroke mopeds and motorcycles under the Giulietta name (see p 237). Production continues.

PERUGINA

1953–62 Made in Perugia by Giuseppe Menicucci in small numbers, these were 173cc and 248cc overhead-camshaft singles and 158cc two-strokes.

PFG See Piola (right).

PG-PARASACCO

1929 Parasacco and Guarino from Turin built lightweight 175cc overhead-valve machines in a very limited production.

PG-PARENA

1927–31 Built clip-on engines and 125cc and 175cc side-valve lightweights.

PGO

1992– Produces 49cc two-stroke utilitarian mopeds and small scooters.

PIAGGIO

1946– Founded in 1884 by Rinaldo Piaggio in Genoa to build ship fittings, it began to build aeroplanes in 1915. In 1946 it diversified to include scooters and began to build the famous Vespa (see p.267). It absorbed Gilera (see p.257) in 1969. A new range of plastic-bodied scooters appeared in 1990. Piaggio is now the third largest maker of motorized two-wheelers in the world.

PIANA

1923–26 Piana built machines with two-stroke Villiers and four-stroke JAP engines of up to 490cc in Florence. The name changed to Moto Piana (see p.262).

PIAZZA

1924–35 Antonio Piazza of Turin built a 124cc clip-on engine and complete 173cc overhead-valve motorcycles. The engines were also sold to other marques. A 1934 model had a 500cc JAP engine.

PICOT

1946–48 Picot made a 148cc Condor-engined scooter in limited numbers.

PIOLA

1919–21 G. Piola & Sons built a limited number of 620cc chain-driven side-valve flat twins. Also known as the PFG.

PIOVATICCA

1973–75 Built 50cc and 125cc disc-valve two-stroke racers with water cooling. Financial problems forced its sale to Bultaco, who went on to win four world titles with Piovaticca designs.

PIROTTA

1949–58 Small Milanese company that built 40cc clip-on engines, mopeds, and lightweights of 75cc, 125cc, and 160cc.

PIUMA

1989–92 Enduro machines with Husqvarna-derived four-stroke engines.

PIVA

1922–24 Piva built 135cc two-stroke lightweights.

PIVIERE

1953–56 Built a two-stroke moped with friction drive in a pressed-steel frame.

PIZETA

1993– Mopeds with electric power and two-strokes built in limited numbers.

PO

1921–23 A 350cc two-stroke with automatic lubrication built by Pagni & Occhialini of Florence.

POLENGHI

1945–58 Its 58cc clip-on engine, which had opposing pistons and friction drive, was later replaced by orthodox mopeds.

POLET

1923–24 Famous Milanese racer Achille Polet built a few motorcycles with a 481cc inlet-over-exhaust-valve engine.

PONY

1946–49 Built a 44cc clip-on engine.

POSDAM

1926–29 The da Milano brothers made 125cc lightweights with inlet-over-exhaust-valve engines in Turin.

PR

1935–36 Pietro Rosati built a 500cc overhead-camshaft single on a small scale in Turin.

PREMOLI

1935–37 Hand-built by Guido Premoli in Varese using 175cc OMB-Blatto and 500cc Rudge Python engines.

PRINA See Orix-Prina (p.263).

PRINETTI & STUCCHI

1898–1926 A bicycle company that built a DeDion-style tricycle in 1898 and its own 2hp four-stroke engine in 1901. A year later the Stucchi name took precedence. By 1905 Carlo Liedi had designed 3hp and 4hp belt-driven side-valve models. Some 500cc, 750cc, and 1000cc V-twins were built in 1919. Production had slowed by 1924, though 350cc and 500cc singles were made until 1926. Ettore Bugatti, later famous as a car maker, and Alberto Garelli (see p.257) were both former employees.

QUAGLIOTTI

1902–07 Carlo Quagliotti of Turin was one of the most important Italian constructors in the early 1900s. He built single-cylinder Peugeot-engined bikes and 5hp V-twins with chain transmission and primary reduction gear.

RANZANI

1923–31 Lightweight machines that used 175cc Heros and 170cc Norman overhead-valve engines.

RAPID

1953–55 Built 48cc clip-on engines.

RAS

1932–36 Built in Milan by Achille Fusi (see p.257) with 175cc to 490cc JAP engines in orthodox frames. He began using the Fusi name when the rights to the CF marque were acquired.

REGGIOLI

1969–70 Built 60cc Minarelli-engined motocross bikes in limited numbers.

REITER
1927–29 Built in Turin with Blackburne and four-stroke Bradshaw engines.

REVELLI See GR (p.258).

RIGAT
1912–14 Made motorcycles with 487cc Fafnir engines and belt final drive.

RINGHINI
1973–75 Built a 50cc two-stroke racing machine.

RIVA
1928 A supercharged 500cc four with double overhead camshafts and water cooling built by RIdde VAlerio. It made a brief appearance at the 1928 Monza Grand Prix, blowing up on the first lap.

RIVARA
1984 Built off-road Franco Morini- and Minarelli-engined minibikes and mopeds.

RIZZATO
1979– Builds lightweights using Franco Morini and Minarelli engines of up to 123cc. It bought Atala (see p.253) and production continues under both names.

ROMANO
1904–06 The Romano brothers of Turin built a single-cylinder four-stroke motorized bicycle with front suspension.

ROMEO
1969–75 Constructed Minarelli-engined mopeds and minibikes.

ROMERO
1934–36 Built bikes on a small scale in Turin using 500cc horizontal-cylinder engines with side valves and four gears.

RONDINE
1923–28 Produced motorized bicycles with 98cc two-stroke Train engines.

RONDINE
1934–35 A four-cylinder racer built by the Compagnia Nazionale di Aeronautica. It was developed from the earlier OPRA (see p.263). The 499cc transverse engine had gear-driven double overhead camshafts and was supercharged. The inclined cylinders were water cooled. The machine was very successful and when CNA closed, Gilera (see p.257) bought Rondine, which provided the basis for Gilera's four-cylinder racers.

RONDINE
1952–57 This Rondine was a 123cc two-stroke lightweight with a cast-alloy section frame built on a small scale.

RONDINE-COPETA
1967–72 Built 48cc Franco Morini- and Minarelli-engined mopeds and off-road bikes. Not linked to the other Rondines.

ROSSELLI
1899–1910 Based in Turin and originally known as Rosselli & Castellazzi, it built a 1hp four-stroke motorized bicycle called the Lilliput. Engines were also sold separately. Later 258cc belt-driven models were made.

ROSETTA
1950–52 Villiers-engined machines produced in limited numbers.

ROSSI
1929 A 350cc 90° side-valve V-twin in an aluminium frame that used Fiat car parts. Few were made.

ROSSI
1950–55 Built orthodox 123cc Sachs-engined lightweights on a small scale.

ROTA
1950–54 A 500cc overhead-valve single made by Felice Rota in small numbers.

ROVETTA
1900–06 Giovanni Rovetta built clip-on engines, including a 2.25hp water-cooled model and a version that fitted on the front fork and drove the wheel by belt.

ROYAL
1923–28 The Santagostino brothers built 123cc two-strokes. Some four-strokes were made with JAP engines.

RUBINELLI
1921–27 Built 122cc and 172cc two-strokes in Milan. The engines were also used on the Gaia motorized bicycles.

RUMI p.165
1949 Fonderia of Bergamo built one of the most popular Italian sports bikes in the 1950s. It had a 125cc horizontal twin-cylinder two-stroke engine in a tubular frame. A 200cc model was made later alongside the Formichino ("little ant") and Scoiattolo ("squirrel") scooters.
1955 A 175cc overhead-valve single was introduced but it was soon discontinued.
1960 New 98cc, 125cc, and 174cc 90° overhead-valve V-twins were introduced but they never reached full production.
1962 The company closed.
1991 The name reappeared on racers, including a 650cc alloy-framed four-stroke single with a Honda engine.

RUSPA
1925–29 Made a 124cc two-stroke and a 175cc overhead-valve machine. Also built 350cc overhead-camshaft singles under the Ruspa and Gaeta name.

S4
1939–50 Sergio Secondo built 350cc and 500cc overhead-camshaft transverse four-cylinder racers. Updated post-war models achieved modest racing success.

SACOM
1985– Constructs mopeds with proprietary engines in Palermo.

SALETTA
1912–15 Saletta of Turin sold the British Premier and Sunbeam bikes. It also built machines with its own badge using a number of British components.

SALVE
1925–26 Salve constructed a 496cc side-valve single with a tubular cradle frame in Milan.

SAMA
1923–26 Built 350cc overhead-valve singles on a limited scale.

SANCINETO
1933–35 Produced lightweights and three-wheelers with 175cc JAP engines.

SAN CRISTOFORO See Nibbio (p.263) and Simonetta (p.266).

SANTAMARIA
1951–63 Built proprietary-engined mopeds and lightweight motorcycles.

SANVENERO
1980–83 Made 125cc, 250cc, and 500cc two-stroke Grand Prix racers in very small numbers with some success.

SAR
1920–26 Built 500cc overhead- and side-valve flat twins. Also used 350cc and 500cc oil-cooled Bradshaw engines.

SCARAB
1967–85 This name was sometimes used on Ancilotti machines (see p.252).

SEGALE
1985–94 Sports bikes constructed with four-cylinder Japanese engines mounted in lightweight frames.

SEGONI
1967–74 Segoni built sports and racing machines with alloy monocoque frames and 750cc Laverda engines.

SEILING (SEI)
1937–38 Alberico Seiling founded the Seiling marque after he left MAS (see p.260). He produced a 305cc side-valve single equipped with a built-in three-speed gearbox, an external fly-wheel, and rear suspension. In 1939 the name changed to Altea (see p.252).

SENIOR
1913–14 Built by Bonzi & Marchi of Milan using single-cylinder and V-twin Moser engines with belt or chain drive.

SERTUM p.169
1932–51 Sertum – Latin for "crown" – was a major Italian marque in the 1930s. Its first model was a 175cc side-valve bike with unitary construction of the engine and gearbox and a tubular frame. It later developed similar models of 200cc, 250cc, and 500cc. A 500cc side-valve parallel twin, a 120cc two-stroke with a pressed-steel frame, and a 250cc overhead-valve machine were also built. During World War II, many machines were supplied to the Italian military. After the war Sertum reintroduced 250cc and 500cc four-stroke singles and 500cc parallel twins with side or overhead valves. Post-war models had pressed-steel frames with rear suspension and girder forks. Financial difficulties forced Sertum to close.

SESSA
1950–56 Sessa built 150cc two-stroke lightweights with the engine suspended below a single-tube spine frame. From 1953 leading-link forks and torsion-bar rear suspension were used.

SHIFTY
1975–78 Ugo Grandis of Padua built a huge chain-driven machine with a 907cc water-cooled four-cylinder engine from a Fiat 127 car. It was not very successful.

The Fiat-engined Shifty, c.1976

SIAMT
1907–14 These machines were built by La Società Italiana Automobili Motocicli Torino and designed by Luigi Semeria. The bikes, 262cc and 344cc singles and 494cc and 731cc V-twins with a chain and belt transmission system, were also successful in competition.

SIAT
1924–26 SIAT built clip-on bicycle engines and complete motorcycles of 98cc to 198cc.

SIATA
1945–55 La Società Italiana Applicazioni Tecniche Automobilistiche di Torino constructed a 48cc clip-on overhead-valve engine, which was called the Cucciolo – Italian for "puppy". It achieved great success and was also made by Ducati (see p.255) from 1947. From 1952 SIATA built a complete moped using the Cucciolo engine and a 160cc two-stroke called the Dinghi.

SIGNORELLI
1928–30 Built 173cc two-strokes in a very limited production.

SIM
c.1951–56 La Società Italiana Motoscooters built the Ariete scooter with its own 150cc two-stroke power unit, shaft drive, and rubber-sprung suspension. The later Moretti model had a 125cc Puch split-single engine, but neither sold in large numbers.

SIMONCELLI
1927–35 Built lightweight machines with 175cc overhead-valve JAP engines and cantilever rear suspension.

SIMONETTA
1952–54 Upgraded version of the 125cc Nibbio scooter (see p.263) built by San Cristoforo. It was also made under licence in France by Ravat.

SIMONINI
1970–83 Simonini built specialized motocross and enduro machines using 49cc to 247cc two-stroke Sachs engines. It also made utilitarian mopeds.

SIMPLEX
1921–50 Turin-based company Simplex first made clip-on engines, which were soon followed by complete machines with 123cc two-stroke engines. In 1927 150cc and 175cc four-strokes were built. In 1930 the 175cc overhead-valve Ala d'Oro – Italian for "Golden Wing" – was introduced with a 500cc version following in 1934. After World War II the 250cc and 500cc machines were reintroduced with little success.

SIRIO
1945–48 Built 58cc clip-on engines.

A 1980 Trans-Ama enduro machine with a 244cc Hiro engine

SIRTORI
1900–02 Produced a small number of motorcycles with 1.5hp engines.

STELLA
1927–29 Built a lightweight motorcycle with a 175cc overhead-valve Blackburne engine in a conventional frame.

STERZI
1939–62 Sterzi made 98cc and 123cc Sachs-engined machines before World War II. Production resumed in 1948 with its own 125cc two-stroke. In 1954 a 160cc two-stroke and a 175cc four-stroke were built. A 49cc four-stroke moped, a 160cc two-stroke scooter, and a 65cc four-stroke bike soon followed.

STILMA
1948–49 A 500cc single-cylinder four-stroke made in Turin with a tubular and pressed-steel frame. It was equipped with telescopic forks and a parallelogram rear suspension, but few were made.

STORERO
1899–1904 Storero of Turin built a DeDion-engined tricycle and, in 1903, a motorbike with the engine placed in the triangle of a bicycle-style frame. The engine drove the rear wheel using the same chain as the pedals.

STUCCHI See Prinetti & Stucchi (p.264).

SUPERBA
1928–35 Built 175cc Piazza- and JAP-engined lightweights in limited numbers.

SUPERIOR
1934–36 Built by Giuseppe Milanaccio with a 220cc overhead-camshaft engine.

SUPERMOTO
1925–26 An advanced machine built in Milan by Luigi Angelino. It had an open frame using a 350cc horizontal-cylinder side-valve engine with fan cooling.

SVM
1985–87 An unsuccessful attempt to revive the SWM marque (see below).

SWM p.178
1971–85 Successful off-road competition machines equipped with Sachs and Rotax two-stroke engines of 50cc to 320cc. SWM took over Gori (see p.258) in 1979, but over-extended itself in doing so. There was a short-lived revival under the SVM name.

TAPPELLA-FUCHS See Fuchs-Tappella (p.256).

TARBO
1967–69 Two-stroke motorcycles of 49cc to 350cc that were powered by Jawa engines. They were produced by Italemmezeta (see p.258) in a very limited production.

TAUMA
1949–53 Built a 49cc clip-on engine.

TAURA
1927–39 Motorcycles built in Turin by Giulio Doglioli using 175cc to 500cc single-cylinder and V-twin JAP engines.

TAURUS
1933–66 Taurus was an established bicycle company that became a part-owner of the MG marque (see p.261) in 1932. Subsequently almost identical machines were available with the Taurus badge. Models with 175cc to 500cc single-cylinder overhead-valve and overhead-camshaft power units were listed. Some of these were equipped with torsion-bar rear suspension. A double overhead-camshaft racing motorcycle was built in 1938, but was never fully developed. After World War II Taurus built mopeds and motorcycles, including a 175cc overhead-camshaft model, a 160cc two-stroke, and a 250cc overhead-valve machine.

TECHNOMOTO
1968–79 Originally a producer of off-road competition machines with Zündapp and Franco Morini engines, it later made motorcycles for children.

TESTI
1951–83 Lightweights built in Bologna using two-stroke proprietary engines. It specialized in 50cc sports machines. Some models were sold abroad with Horex or Gitane badges. Production resumed on a limited scale in 1987 alongside OMC machines (see p.263).

TGM
1974–85 Maker of successful motocross and enduro bikes that used 50cc to 250cc Hiro and Villa two-stroke engines.

TGR
1979–87 Electric mopeds that were produced in limited numbers.

TIGLI
1950–52 The Tigli was a 75cc two-stroke motorcycle built by Amedeo Tigli and Franco Morini.

TM
1968–92 TM was a maker of mopeds, lightweight motorcycles, and off-road competition machines using 48cc to 125cc Franco Morini and Zündapp two-stroke engines. It later constructed its own engines, which were also sold to other marques.

TOMASELLI
1931–39 Built a limited number of bikes using 173cc to 490cc JAP engines.

TOMMASI
1926–27 This small Genoese factory used 123cc twin-cylinder two-stroke Della Ferrera engines. A 246cc model was made by doubling up the 123cc engine.

TORPADO
1950–62 A bicycle company that made utilitarian mopeds in small numbers. Garelli Mosquito engines were first used, later replaced by Minarelli power units.

TRAIN ITALIANA
1932–35 Lightweight motorbikes that used 100cc Train engines. They were built by Giuseppe Navone (see p.263).

TRANS-AMA
1978–85 Marque that was based in Pesaro. It built a limited number of specialized off-road competition machines that used 48cc to 320cc two-stroke engines.

TRESPIDI
1925–30 Paolo Trespidi of Stradella built 175cc and 250cc two-stroke motorcycles with his own engines. After World War II he created the Alpino marque (see p.252).

TREVISAN
1900–02 Antonio Trevisan of Padua built a twin-cylinder motorcycle with direct drive to the rear wheel. An ignition cut-out killed the engine when the rider took his foot off the footrest.

TÜRKHEIMER
1902–05 Italian motorcycle pioneer Max Türkheimer had been an importer of German Hildebrand & Wolfmüller machines from 1894 before producing his own machines. He used vertical and horizontal single-cylinder engines. In 1931 he created the Astra motorcycle marque (see p.253).

TWM
1979–86 Built 125cc to 250cc off-road competition machines on a small scale.

UFO
1976–83 Mopeds, minibikes, and off-road bikes using Minarelli engines.

UNIMOTO
1985–88 Minarelli-engined mopeds and sports motorcycles using 125cc two-stroke Tau engines with water cooling.

VAGA
1925–34 Mario Vaga built lightweight machines using 175cc Blackburne, JAP, Sturmey-Archer, and CF engines. They were extensively chrome plated.

VALENTI
1979–84 Off-road competition machines that were powered by 125cc to 250cc two-stroke engines.

VANONI
1926–27 A 500cc overhead-camshaft single built by Nino Vanoni in Gallarate.

VASCHETTO
1936–38 Built in Turin by Giuseppe Vaschetto using 250cc and 500cc engines.

VASSENA
1926–29 Engine designer Pietro Vassena built a complete lightweight machine with a 125cc horizontal-cylinder two-stroke engine. After World War II he designed engines for Rumi (see p.265).

VECCHIETTI
1954–57 Built 49cc mopeds using Victoria engines in limited numbers.

VEGA
1947–49 Built a 38cc clip-on engine to mount under the bottom bracket.

VÉLOSOLEX
1948–56 The French VéloSolex moped was built under licence by Sifacin.

VELOX TECNICA
1951–53 A friction-driven moped with the engine above the rear wheel.

VELTA
1939–40 Engineer Vittorio Belmondo built this scooter using a 98cc Sachs engine. Although production was limited, it was to influence subsequent Italian scooter design.

VELTRO
1954–55 A moped made in Bologna.

VERGA
1951–54 Verga made utilitarian mopeds and a lightweight motorcycle with a 75cc two-stroke engine in a pressed-steel frame with swingarm rear suspension.

VEROS
1922–24 Oreste Garanzini (see p.257) built a modified version of the British Verus motorcycle (see p.231).

VESPA p.190
1946 Developed by aircraft maker Piaggio (see p.264) after World War II, the Vespa was designed by Corradino d'Ascanio as cheap utilitarian transport. It has become one of the most successful vehicles ever produced and continues in production over 50 years later. The name Vespa – Italian for "wasp" – derives from its buzzing exhaust note. The first version in 1946 had a 98cc horizontal two-stroke engine with fan cooling and a twistgrip-operated three-speed gearbox. It had a pressed-steel monocoque frame and bodywork with detachable pressed-steel wheels and 8-in tyres. Capacity gradually increased with 125cc, 150cc, 160cc, 180cc, and 200cc models being made. An extra gear was added and the wheels were increased in size to 25cm (10in), but the basic structure remained unchanged. A 50cc version was built from 1963. The Vespa was, and still is, built under licence in many other countries. Piaggio introduced a new range of plastic-bodied scooters in 1990, but the traditional Vespa model continues in production.

VG
1931–35 Vittorio Grilli built machines with JAP engines in limited numbers.

VICENTINI
1925–26 A 250cc two-stroke machine, the design had an additional pumping cylinder and ran on diesel.

VICINI
1984–88 Vicini mopeds had Franco Morini engines and were produced in limited numbers.

VICTRIX
1924–27 Lightweight two-strokes that were built in very limited numbers.

VILLA
1968–88 Francesco and Walter Villa were both successful road racers. However most of their motorcycles were 50cc to 350cc off-road competition bikes using their own or Franco Morini two-stroke engines. Some road racers were also made, including the 250cc two-stroke V4 of 1969.

VILLANI
1925–37 Andrea Villani of Bologna built 175cc single-cylinder two-stroke motorcycles. A 350cc parallel twin was built by doubling up the single.

VI-VI
1955–57 Mopeds made in Milan by VIberti using two-stroke VIctoria power units. Various versions were built.

Production was taken over by SAS when Viberti closed.

VOLTA
1902–07 The French Dalifol steam engine was built under licence in Italy by Volta. It was equipped with a central boiler, coal firebox, and a single-cylinder engine with direct transmission. See also Dalifol (p.278).

VOLUGRAFO
1939–42 Volugrafo built two scooter models; a civilian model had a 98cc Sachs engine, while military versions designed for parachute drops had a 125cc engine and folding handlebars.

VVV-GARLASCHELLI
1926–28 Angelo Garlaschelli made a small number of 125cc two-strokes.

WILIER TRIESTINA
1960–70 Giovanni Parrilla (see p.264) built a limited number of mopeds.

WOLSIT
1910–14 Bicycle maker Legnano used the Wolsit marque name on its early 3.5hp three-speed motorcycles.
c.1932 The Wolsit name reappeared on a motorized bicycle with a NSU Motosulm engine mounted above the front wheel. Legnano later made mopeds under its own name (see p.259).

ZANNETTI
1967–75 Zannetti built a moped with the engine mounted above the front wheel. Engines were also sold separately.

ZENIT ITALIANA
1953–56 Built 160cc and 175cc machines with French AMC engines.

ZETA
1947–52 A small scooter that was equipped with a Ducati Cucciolo engine, 46-cm (18-in) wheels and a partial fairing. It was constructed in Genoa.

A 1975 247cc Villa motocross machine

United States

THE U.S. MOTORCYCLE industry prospered between 1905 and 1915 when many companies produced rugged and simple machines, and Indian (see p.271) was the largest motorcycle manufacturer in the world. But the arrival of low-cost, mass-produced cars diminished the popularity of the motorcycle as an economical means of transportation so that only three major manufacturers survived the 1920s. The closure of Excelsior-Henderson (see p.270) in 1931 left just Indian and Harley-Davidson (see p.271). The effects of poor management in the 1930s and 1940s led to the end of the American Indian in 1953. A post-war scooter boom created several specialized firms, led by Cushman (see p.269). The craze for minibikes in the 1960s was satisfied by small domestic producers, until the Japanese manufacturers entered that marketplace. In the 1980s and 1990s a new, image-led demand for retro-style machines has revived the fortunes of the Harley-Davidson marque.

ACE p.11
1919 Bill and Tom Henderson had created the Henderson marque (see p.271) in 1912. The company was sold to Ignatz Schwinn, the owner of Excelsior, in 1917 and production moved to Schwinn's Chicago factory. Bill Henderson split from his new employer two years later to create the Ace. This was a large-capacity, high-performance four-cylinder machine in the style of the original Henderson. The new company was based in Philadelphia, Pennsylvania. **1922** Bill Henderson died in a motorcycle accident, but production of the Ace continued. Arthur O. Lemon was appointed the new chief designer. **1924** Financial problems broke the company. During the following two years a few Ace machines were built by the Michigan Motors Corporation. **1927** Indian acquired the manufacturing rights to the Ace. The Ace design formed the basis of the four-cylinder Indians made from 1927 to 1942.

ADB
1993 The American Dirt Bike company was established by a group of people who were formerly involved with the ATK concern. It produces off-road competition machines using 350cc to 620cc single overhead-camshaft Rotax engines mounted in unusual frames with a low centre of gravity and enclosed bodywork.

ALLSTATE p.16
1951–65 In 1951 the Sears chain of stores began selling Cushman scooters under its Allstate badge. In 1954 it added Austrian Puch motorcycles to its catalogue, and later also imported the Italian Vespa scooter between 1951 and 1963. It continued to sell Puch and Gilera machines with Sears badges (see p.274) until the late 1960s.

AMC
1912–15 The Allied Motors Corporation took over the Armac factory in Chicago when that firm folded in 1912. AMC built 30.5cu. in. (500cc) singles and 61cu. in. (1000cc) V-twins with inlet-over-exhaust engines and conventional loop frames.

AMERICA
1904–c.1906 The America was an Indian-style single-cylinder machine with the engine incorporated into the seat-post. A novelty was provided by fitting a steering wheel instead of handlebars. It was made by the Great Western Manufacturing Co. of La Porte, Indiana, which later built Crown motorcycles (see p.269).

AMERICAN
1911–14 The American Motorcycle Co. of Chicago built 30.5cu. in. (500cc) and 31cu. in. (508cc) singles and 62.2cu. in. (1016cc) V-twins. All models had atmospheric inlet valves.

AMERICAN EAGLE
1967–69 Laverda 750cc twins were marketed in America under this name. The AE company also unsuccessfully attempted to sell British-made off-road machines and Kawasaki-engined 350cc motorcycles under the same banner.

AMERICAN-ROCKET
1952 The American-Rocket was a prototype machine built by Indian specialist Sam Pierce. It was based on a modified and rubber-mounted 60.8cu. in. (996cc) Chief engine.

AMERICAN-X
c.1910–31 To avoid confusion with the British-built Excelsior marque, American Excelsior machines were renamed American-X in some export markets.

ANTHONY
1900–01 American pioneer E. J. Anthony, of Colorado Springs, Colorado, fitted an internal combustion engine behind the rear wheel of a bicycle. It was mounted on a simple sub-frame and drove the wheel via a belt.

APACHE
1907–11 The Apache was built in Denver by Brown & Beck. It was equipped with a single-cylinder 3hp Thor engine with forward-facing carburettor and rear-exit exhaust.

ARGYLE
1957–61 The Argyle was a tiny fold-away scooter that used a 2.5hp two-stroke Clinton engine. It was built in Memphis by C&E Manufacturing.

ARMAC
1905–13 Armac produced an unusual machine that incorporated fuel and oil tanks in large-diameter frame tubes. The firm also made its own engines. Early machines were 25cu. in. (410cc) atmospheric-inlet-valve singles. Later capacity was increased to 30cu. in. (492cc), and there were also 60cu. in. (983cc) V-twins. In 1906 production moved from St Paul, Minnesota, to Chicago, Illinois. When the company closed, AMC took over the factory.

ARROW
1909–14 Chicago-based firm that produced an orthodox machine equipped with the company's own 5hp single-cylinder 28.5cu. in. (467cc) atmospheric-inlet-valve engine. A leaf-sprung fork and belt drive were used.

ATK
1983– ATK builds off-road machines, which incorporate a system for maintaining constant chain tension and eliminating transmission snatch despite the long-travel rear suspension. The rear brake is a disc mounted on the gearbox output-shaft. Two- and four-stroke Rotax engines are used. The machines are made in southern California.

AUSTIN
1868 W. W. Austin of Winthrop, Massachusetts, built a steam-powered two-wheeler with a coal-burning engine.

AUTO-BI
1900–09 E. R. Thomas was among the first to make motorcycles in America. He mounted an engine near the headstock of a bicycle frame. A belt connected the crankshaft to a pulley under the seat, which drove the rear wheel by friction on the tyre. Later models used a 3hp engine with an inclined cylinder and belt drive direct to the rear wheel. They were made in Buffalo, New York, and were also known as the Thomas Auto-Bi (see p.275). From 1909 the Greyhound name (see p.271) was used.

AUTO-GLIDE
1936–46 The Auto-Glide name was used on machines built by Cushman (see p.269) until World War II.

AUTOPED p.22
1915–21 An early folding scooter which used a 9.5cu. in. (155cc) atmospheric-inlet-valve engine that was mounted beside the front wheel. The Autoped was also constructed under licence in Britain and Germany.

BADGER
1919–21 The Badger was built in Milwaukee, Wisconsin. It was equipped with a 10cu. in. (161cc) engine within the back wheel.

BAILEY FLYER
1913–17 The Bailey Flyer was an unusual 62cu. in. (1016cc) fore-and-aft flat twin with shaft drive, a two-speed gearbox, and a rear hub clutch.

BANGOR
c.1938–40 Bangor, inspired by the Cushman scooter, produced the Clinton-engined Scootmaster.

BEAM See Doodlebug (p.270).

BI-AUTO-GO
c.1913 The Bi-Auto-Go was a bizarre two-wheeled car with a 335cu. in. (5494cc) V8 engine, four-speed gearbox, stabilizer wheels, and automobile-style bodywork. It was a product of the fertile mind of Detroit's James Scripps-Booth, who later manufactured a cyclecar. Only one Bi-Auto-Go was ever built.

BI-CAR
1911 The Bi-Car was a strange cross between a car and a motorcycle. It used a four-cylinder engine in a steel section frame. It also featured shaft drive and a two-speed gearbox.

BLACK DIAMOND
1903–c.1905 Reeser & MacKenzie of Philadelphia, Pennsylvania produced a loop-framed motorcycle equipped with a 18.25cu. in. (299cc) 2.5hp engine. Transmission was by chain with a countershaft-mounted reduction gear.

BLACK HAWK

1912–14 The Black Hawk was a conventional, 30.5cu. in. (500cc) inlet-over-exhaust single with a keystone frame built in Rock Island, Illinois. A 61cu. in. (1000cc) overhead-valve V-twin was listed for 1914, but production numbers were minimal.

BONANZA

1967–69 California-based firm that built two-stroke minibikes.

BOSS HOSS

1990– The Boss Hoss uses a 5735cc V8 Chevrolet engine in a custom-style rolling chassis on a massive scale. The engine's torque is sufficient to obviate the need for a gearbox. The Boss Hoss has just one gear that is capable of taking the machine from zero to a claimed 160mph (257km/h). Production numbers exceed 150.

BRADLEY

c.1910–14 Small Philadelphia company that built 3.5hp belt-driven singles.

BRIGGS & STRATTON

1919 Briggs & Stratton took over production of the Smith Motor Wheel (see p.275) and briefly made it under the firm's own name. It is now famous as an industrial engine company.

BUELL 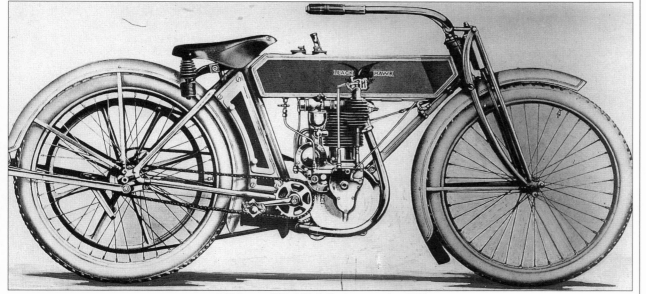 p.40

1985 The company was founded by former Harley-Davidson employee Eric Buell. It built expensive, high-quality sports bikes using Harley-Davidson engines on multi-tubular frames. Early models were encased in strange, bulbous bodywork. In 1993 Harley-Davidson bought a significant share in the company and a new model was introduced. Harley-Davidson was interested in producing sports machines without alienating its traditional buyers. The Thunderbolt was intended for higher volume production at a lower cost than previous Buell machines. It was sold through Harley-Davidson dealers with a factory warranty.

CALIFORNIA

1901–04 California machines, built in San Francisco, California, were probably based on the earlier Marks machine (see p.272). A DeDion-type engine was used in a bicycle-style frame with belt drive. In 1903 a motorcycle of this type became the first motor vehicle to cross America. Manufacturing rights to the design were bought by the Consolidated Manufacturing Co. of Toledo, Ohio, makers of Yale bicycles. It used the design to construct its first motorcycles, called Yale-Californias (see p.275).

CAULFIELD

1953–58 A clip-on engine kit for bicycles made by Lowell Caulfield of Temperance, Michigan.

CHAMPION

1914 Champion built the bizarre 77cu. in. (1261cc) four-cylinder Militaire motorcycle-cum-car under licence in St Louis, Missouri.

CLEMENS

c.1902 Chester Clemens of Springfield, Massachusetts, built a machine that was similar in appearance to the early Indian motorcycles, built in the same city.

CLEVELAND 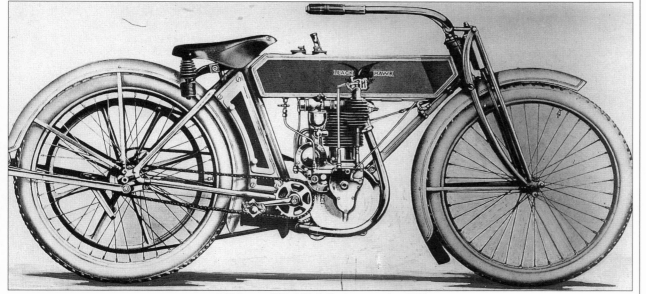 pp.42–43

1915 The Cleveland Motorcycle Manufacturing Co. began production of 13.5cu. in. (222cc) two-stroke singles with in-line crankshafts and chain final drive. Later capacity was increased to 16.5cu. in. (269cc). These machines were very successful and sold well.
1922 Cleveland bought the Reading-Standard Company.
1924 A 21.5cu. in. (350cc) side-valve single was introduced. Its layout and frame design were very similar to the two-stroke, but it was not as successful.
1925 A 36.5cu. in. (598cc) four-cylinder machine, based on the Fowler-Four design, was introduced. It failed to compete with larger capacity Henderson and Ace fours.
1926 A redesigned 45cu. in. (737cc) four appeared. Subsequently a 61cu. in. (1000cc) version was also built.
1929 Despite the quality of its product Cleveland was forced out of business following the Wall Street Crash.

COLUMBIA

c.1900–05 Columbia was a trademark owned by ABC – American Bicycle Company – which was controlled by Colonel Albert Pope from 1903. Pope (see p.274) manufactured motorcycles under its own name from 1911.

COOPER

1972–73 Built in Mexico by Islo (see p.307), but sold in America under the importer's name, the Cooper was an off-road competition machine with a single-cylinder two-stroke engine.

COPELAND

c.1884–c.1892 Copeland built steam-powered tricycles after producing a steam-engined two-wheeler.

CRAWFORD

1913–15 Michigan bicycle maker R. S. Crawford built conventional loop-framed V-twins using a Spacke engine and chain drive. The Crawford was almost identical to the De Luxe (see p.270), and it is possible that it was produced by the same manufacturer and sold with a different badge.

CROCKER

1933 The first motorcycles made by Los Angeles Indian dealer Al Crocker were intended for the booming Speedway scene. Sadly the Crocker could not compete against the successful British-built JAP, and not many were made.
1935 Development work began on a new, overhead-valve 45° V-twin intended for sporting use. Very limited production of the new motorcycle began the following year. Capacity ranged from 61cu. in. (1000cc) to 90cu. in. (1475cc) and the Crocker had performance that was well ahead of comparable, but much cheaper, Harley-Davidsons.
1941 The war stopped large-scale production, although about 100 machines were built and a stylish scooter was also made in small numbers.

CROUCH

1904–09 Small manufacturer of conventional 3hp single-cylinder machines with belt drive. They were made in Stoneham, Massachusetts.

CROWN

1910 The Crown was a belt-driven 29cu. in. (475cc) single built in La Porte, Indiana, by The Great Western Manufacturing Co., which had earlier made the America (see p.268).

CURTISS

1902–10 Aviation pioneer Glenn Curtiss also built motorcycles in Hammondsport, New York. The most famous motorcycle was the V8-engined machine, which achieved a record-breaking speed of more than 136mph (219km/h) in 1907. Production machines used single-cylinder and 50° V-twin engines. In 1909 the firm also offered an unusual three-cylinder model with an extra cylinder placed between the V of a V-twin (W-triple). The makers claimed that this was the world's fastest production motorcycle. Aeronautical interests took over from 1910, although Curtiss continued to produce the Marvel motorcycle (see p.272) until 1914.

CUSHMAN 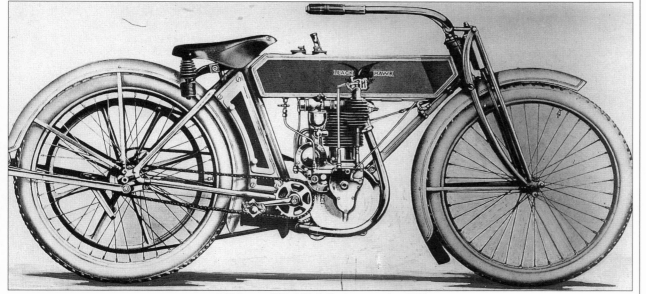 p.44

1936–65 Cushman made the side-valve, industrial Husky engine and developed scooters using these engines as a sideline. The Auto-Glide name (see p.268) was used until after World War II. During the war machines were supplied to the military for parachute landing. Cushman enjoyed the post-war scooter boom in America, building a range of models. Demand declined in the 1960s, partly due to the success of the Honda Cub, and Cushman switched to making golf buggies.

A 30.5cu. in. (500cc) Black Hawk motorcycle, c.1912

CVS

1911–12 C. V. Stahl made 27cu. in. (442cc) singles and 57cu. in. (934cc) V-twins in Philadelphia, Pennsylvania. Both had atmospheric inlet valve, belt drive, and loop frames.

CYCLEMOTOR

1915–24 A clip-on 5.5cu. in. (90cc) two-stroke engine for bicycles, which mounted vertically in a conventional bicycle frame and drove the rear wheel by belt. From 1918 it was available as a complete machine under the Evans brand-name (see below).

CYCLE-SCOOT

1953–55 Cycle-Scoots were industrial-engined scooters.

CYCLONE

c.1912–16 Cyclone motorcycles were built in St Paul, Minnesota, by Joerns Motors, which had previously made the Thiem (see p.275). Cyclone was famous for its advanced and powerful 61cu. in. (1000cc) V-twins, which used shaft- and bevel-gear-driven overhead camshaft. Factory rider J. A. McNeil hit 111mph (179km/h) aboard a Cyclone in 1915.

DAYTON

1911–17 Built in Dayton, Ohio, using Spacke V-twin engines. Two models were made, a 61cu. in. (1000cc) and a 71cu. in. (1163cc). Loop frames and leaf-sprung trailing-link forks were used. In 1915 a lightweight was introduced. It had a 1.5hp engine mounted beside the front wheel in a bicycle-style frame.

DE LONG

c.1902 Built by the Industrial Machine Co. of Phoenix, New York, the layout of the De Long was similar to the Indian, with the engine forming the seat-post of the frame. The De Long used the frame tubes to provide fuel and oil tanks, and containers for the battery and coil.

DE LONG

c.1936 The De Long was a strange belt-driven 13.5cu. in. (220cc) two-stroke with a pressed-steel frame. Production numbers are not known.

DE LUXE

1912–15 The De Luxe was built by the Excelsior Cycle Co. in Chicago (not to be confused with the Chicago-based Excelsior Supply Co., which built similar-looking machines). The De Luxe used inlet-over-exhaust, V-twin Spacke engines and chain drive.

DETROIT

1910–11 The Detroit was a 4hp belt-driven single that used a Pierce-style frame with fuel and oil tanks incorporated in large-diameter frame tubes.

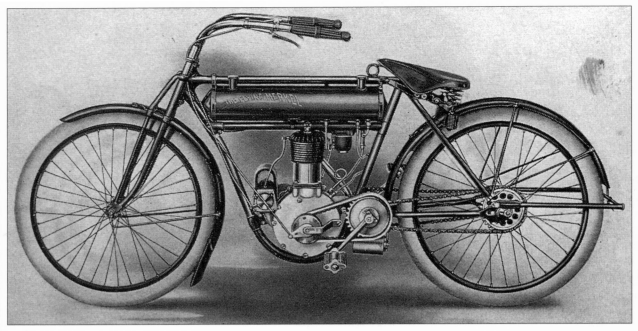

A 1913 Flying Merkel with a loop frame and all-chain transmission

DOODLEBUG

1954–58 A scooter powered by either a Briggs & Stratton or a Clinton 1.5hp industrial engine. It was built by the Beam Manufacturing Co. and sold by the Gambles store chain in competition with Sears' Allstate-badged Cushmans.

DRIVER

c.1902 Large-capacity 7hp atmospheric-inlet-valve single with belt drive built in Pennsylvania by William Driver.

DUCK

c.1902–c.1904 The Duck was possibly related to the early San Francisco-built Marks (see p.272) and California (see p.269) machines.

DYNACYCLE

1949–53 A clip-on bicycle engine built in St Louis, Missouri.

EAGLE

1909–15 Single-cylinder and V-twin machines with inlet-over-exhaust Spacke engines of 30.5cu. in. (500cc) to 61cu. in. (1000cc). Early models used keystone frames and belt drive, but loop frames and chain drive were adopted later. From about 1912 they were built by the American Motors Co., makers of the MM (see p.273).

ELECTRA

c.1911 The Electra was an early attempt at an electric motorcycle. "Alterations are still necessary to perfect the machine", said *Motor Cycling* magazine in 1911. It was not heard of again.

EMBLEM 🏍 p.56

1907–25 Built in Angola, New York, the first Emblems used Thor engines mounted in the seat-post of a bicycle-style frame. From 1909 the company built its own engines, which were fitted into loop frames and used belt drive. V-twins were built from 1910, including a 76.6cu. in. (1254cc) version, which appeared in 1913. Few Emblems were sold in America after 1918, but a 32.4cu. in. (531cc) V-twin was exported to Europe until about 1925.

ERIE

1905–09 The Erie was originally built in Buffalo, on Lake Erie, but production shifted to Hammondsport, New York, when Glenn Curtiss (see p.269) became involved with the marque. Early models used bicycle-style frames, but from 1908 a loop frame was used. The firm used its own and proprietary engines.

EVANS

1918–24 A lightweight 7cu. in. (119cc) two-stroke machine built by the Cyclemotor Corporation of Buffalo, New York. Many were exported to Europe, and after production stopped in America they were built in Germany under the Stock name (see p.248).

EXCELSIOR 🏍 pp.58–59

1907 The Excelsior Supply Co. of Chicago began making 29cu. in. (475cc) single-cylinder motorcycles with its own engines. V-twins followed in 1910.

1911 The company was bought by bicycle maker Ignatz Schwinn, who continued production of inlet-over-exhaust singles and V-twins of up to 61cu. in. (1000cc). Excelsior quickly established itself as the smallest of the "Big Three" motorcycle makers, after Indian and Harley-Davidson.

1917 Schwinn bought the Henderson marque (see p.271).

1925 The Super-X model was launched. It was the first American 45cu. in. (737cc) V-twin. Harley-Davidson and Indian soon followed with their own forty-fives.

1931 With the onset of the Depression Schwinn quit the motorcycle business.

1990s The rights to the Excelsior and Henderson names have been acquired by the Hanlon Manufacturing Co. of Minnesota, which has announced its intention to manufacture a new range of Excelsior/Henderson machines.

FEILBACH

1912–15 Feilbach built 34.5cu. in. (565cc) singles and 79cu. in. (1301cc) V-twins in Milwaukee. Engines were inlet over exhaust and a loop frame was used. From 1914 the Limited name (see p.272) was used.

FLANDERS

1911–14 Built by the makers of the Flanders car, the original motorcycle was a 4hp single with loop frame and belt drive. A side-valve V-twin with enclosed all-chain drive appeared in 1914 but production stopped the same year.

FLESCHER FLYER

1913 The Flescher Flyer was possibly only built in prototype form. It was powered by a 9hp De Luxe engine and equipped with dual-rate springing forks.

FLYING MERKEL

1913–15 The "Flying Merkel" slogan was first used in about 1910 for Merkel machines (see p.272). It was adopted as the official name from 1913 after production shifted to the Miami factory in Middletown, Ohio.

FOWLER-FOUR
1924 Detroit engineer L. E. Fowler built a 36.5cu. in. (600cc) four-cylinder machine with a T-head and shaft drive. Cleveland (see p.269) bought the design and used it as the basis of its first, unsuccessful, four-cylinder machines.

FREYER & MILLER
c.1902 Single-cylinder machines built in Columbus, Ohio.

GEER
1905–09 Built in St Louis, Missouri, by Harry R. Geer & Co., the Geer was available with the firm's own 2.5hp single or 4hp V-twin engines. Both models had belt drive and loop frames.

GERHART
1913–14 Gerhart produced a limited number of four-cylinder machines, inspired by the Belgian FN. The in-line engine used overhead valve and final drive was by chain.

GIBSON
c.1902 Cecil Gibson of Indianapolis, Indiana, built Merkel-engined, belt-driven tandems and possibly some solos.

GLOBESTAR
c.1948–50 Globestar scooters had an 8cu. in. (130cc) four-stroke engine, centrifugal clutch, variable belt-driven transmission, and a cast-alloy frame.

GO-KART CO.
c.1960–72 The Go-Kart Co. was one of the more successful of the many minibike manufacturers of the 1960s.

GREYHOUND
c.1907–14 Greyhound motorcycles were made in Aurora, Illinois, using 4.5hp single-cylinder Thor engines.

GREYHOUND
1909–14 A reorganization of the Thomas Auto-Bi company resulted in a new machine and a new name. The Greyhound had a 30cu. in. (494cc) engine mounted vertically in a keystone frame. Later capacity was increased to 32cu. in. (524cc).

HARLEY-DAVIDSON pp.67–77
1903 William S. Harley and Arthur Davidson built their first motorcycle, a 25cu. in. (410cc) atmospheric-inlet-valve single.
1904 Production began in a shed behind the Davidson family home. The machine was a 30cu. in. (494cc) single, which was later dubbed the Silent Gray Fellow. The Davidson brothers, William and Walter, later joined the firm too.
1907 Harley-Davidson built a prototype V-twin. Production models were listed in 1909 but were not fully developed until 1911. Production of 45° V-twins has been continuous since then, although flat-twin and single-cylinder machines were also produced. Harley-Davidson quickly established itself as the second largest American manufacturer behind Indian. Machine development was evolutionary rather than radical, with side-valve machines replacing inlet-over-exhaust designs in the late 1920s.
1936 The overhead-valve "Knucklehead" model was introduced. This machine was the basis for all subsequent "Big Twins". The demise of Indian in the 1950s left Harley-Davidson as the only large-scale American motorcycle manufacturer. The firm's post-war range included two-strokes and even a scooter.
1960 Harley-Davidson bought the Italian Aermacchi company. Italian-built lightweights were sold in America under the Harley-Davidson name until 1978, when the Italian operation was sold.

HAUSMANN
1918 Hausmann offered a lightweight motorcycle powered by a Smith Motor Wheel (see p.275).

HAVERFORD
1909–14 Haverford built simple machines with the firm's own 30.5cu. in. (500cc) atmospheric-inlet-valve engines.

HENDERSON pp.78–80
1912 Bill and Tom Henderson began building 56cu. in. (920cc) in-line four-cylinder machines with chain drive in Detroit, Michigan. The early machines had inlet-over-exhaust engines and used long-wheelbase frames. In the following years the machines evolved, but Henderson only ever made in-line fours.
1917 The company was bought by bicycle maker Ignatz Schwinn, who also owned the Excelsior marque (see p.270). Production moved to Chicago, Illinois.
1919 The Henderson brothers quit the firm. Bill Henderson established the Ace marque (see p.268). The Henderson company continued to build luxury four-cylinder models under Schwinn.
1931 Schwinn closed his motorcycle division at the onset of the Depression, and Henderson production ended.

HILAMAN
c.1906–13 A. J. Hilaman of New Jersey built chain-driven 3.5hp 29cu. in. (475cc) singles and 7hp 58cu. in. (950cc) V-twins in limited numbers.

1969 American Metal Foundaries – AMF – took over Harley-Davidson.
1981 Harley-Davidson bought the company back from AMF and developed new models and a new image for the company. Quality and reliability were improved and the style and heritage of the machines were emphasized.

INDIAN pp.101–110
1901 George Hendee and Oscar Hedstrom began production of Indian machines in Springfield, Massachusetts. They built high-quality, single-cylinder machines with all-chain transmission and twistgrip controls. These were followed by V-twins in 1907. Indian quickly established itself as the largest motorcycle company in the world.
1914 Indian produced the first motorcycle with an electric starter.
1916 Side-valve singles and V-twins designed by Charles Gustafson replaced the previous inlet-over-exhaust designs. Side-valve engines were to feature on Indian machines until 1953. In 1917 a lightweight flat twin was introduced, but it was short-lived.
1920 Introduction of the Scout, which was followed in 1922 by the Chief. These two models formed the bulk of Indian production until World War II, but lack of development put Indian at a disadvantage to Harley-Davidson in later years. The side-valve and overhead-valve single-cylinder Prince model was produced from 1925 to 1928.
1927 Indian bought the rights to the Ace four-cylinder machine and built in-line fours until 1942.
1945 Ralph B. Rogers took control of Indian. New vertical-single and parallel-twin machines, designed by Torque, were built, but they were never successful.
1953 The last Indian Chiefs were built. Afterwards the name was attached to a variety of unworthy imports as ownership of the name changed several times. The first imported Indians were mundane side-valve 250cc singles built by the British firm Brockhouse. Later in the 1950s there were Indian-badged Royal Enfields. In 1970 a batch of Italian-framed Velocette hybrids were produced followed by assorted small-capacity two-strokes.
1990s Rumours suggest a revival of the marque.

IVER-JOHNSON
1911–20 An established guns and bicycles company that began building single-cylinder motorcycles using its own "truss" frame, which featured a curved bracing strut between the headstock and the seat-post. Early machines were side-valve 31cu. in. (508cc) singles with belt drive. Leaf-sprung rear suspension was available from 1913. In 1914 the firm introduced a 62cu. in. (1016cc) side-valve V-twin, which had a two-throw crankshaft and 60° cylinder angle. A two-speed gear hub was optional.

JEEPETTE
1943 The Jeepette was a miniature motorcycle in the style of the Powell A-V-8 and the Cushman Eagle.

A 1920 Iver-Johnson side-valve V-twin with a "truss" frame

The "underslung" Militaire had wooden spoked wheels

JEFFERSON
1912–15 The Jefferson was built by the Waverley Manufacturing Co. of Jefferson, Wisconsin. The firm had made engines and complete machines under the Waverley name (see p.275) from 1905 to 1912 and had also briefly used the PEM badge (see p.273). The machines had overhead-valve single-cylinder and V-twin engines of 30.5cu. in. (500cc) and 61cu. in. (1000cc).

JOERNS-THIEM
1908–16 Makers of the famous overhead-camshaft Cyclone V-twin (see p.270), Joerns-Thiem had previously built 31cu. in. (508cc) side-valve singles and 66cu. in. (1082cc) side-valve V-twins. The Thiem name (see p.275) was more commonly used before 1910.

JOHNSON
1918–19 Johnson offered a 9.5cu. in. (155cc) horizontally opposed, twin-cylinder, two-stroke clip-on engine for bicycles, which mounted above the chain-driven rear wheel.

KEATING
c.1902 The Keating, built by the Eisenhuth Horseless Vehicle Co., featured a single-cylinder engine that mounted behind the seat-post of a bicycle-style frame. Novelties included a float-feed carburettor, a clutch, chain drive, and a hollow rear mudguard that served as the exhaust silencer.

KEEN
1936–c.1944 Basic Cushman-style scooter with a small-capacity side-valve Lauson industrial engine.

KENZLER
c.1910–11 Kenzler built motorcycles at Cambridge, Wisconsin, before merging with Waverley (see p.275) and shifting production to the Waverley factory in

Jefferson, Wisconsin, where the amalgamated company produced Jefferson machines (see left).

KOKOMO
1910–11 A neat 21cu. in. (346cc) side-valve single with belt drive made at Kokomo, Indiana. A loop frame with leaf-sprung leading-link fork was used.

LA RAY
1946–48 Milwaukee-based firm that made lightweights with Clinton industrial engines.

LE JAY
c.1939 Le Jay produced the world's first electric scooter.

LIBERTY
1918 The Liberty was a 60.34cu. in. (989cc) inlet-over-exhaust V-twin machine developed for the U.S. military by the Government Quartermasters Dept. Representatives from Harley-Davidson, Indian, and Excelsior were involved in the design.

LIGHT THOR-BRED
1901–09 The Light Manufacturing and Foundry Co. of Pottstown, Pennsylvania, built motorcycles using Thor engines. In 1909 it amalgamated with Merkel (see right). The 1910 models were billed as Merkel-Light before the Light name was dropped.

LIMITED
1914–15 The Limited name was used on the tank of Feilbach (see p.270) machines during their final years.

MANSON
c.1901–08 The first Mansons, built in New York State, had an open frame with a vertically mounted DeDion-type engine. Moving production to the Fowler Manson Sherman Co. of Chicago,

Illinois, single-cylinder Thor-engined motorcycles and delivery tricycles were built. A V-twin was listed for 1908.

MARKS
c.1898–c.1904 West Coast pioneer Roy C. Marks had a number of motorcycle patents to his name. His simple bicycle-style machine was probably the basis of the California (see p.269) and, later, Yale-California (see p.275) motorcycles.

MARSH
c.1900–06 Marsh motorcycles were built in Brockton, Massachusetts, by the American Motor Co. The crankcases of the engines were used as an integral part of the frame, and the cylinder was incorporated into the seat-post in the style of the Indian. The company amalgamated with Metz (see right) in 1905, and the first MM machines (see p.273) appeared the following year.

MARVEL
1910–13 From 1910 Curtiss (see p.269) concentrated on the aircraft business, but continued to produce the Marvel motorcycle. Most were overhead-valve 30cu. in. (492cc) singles.

MAYO
c.1903–08 Mayo machines were made by the Mayo Damper Co. of Pottstown, Pennsylvania. Early models had an inclined single-cylinder engine in a bicycle-style frame. Later versions used a loop frame with 24.5cu. in. (401cc) single-cylinder and 49cu. in. (803cc) V-twin engines with belt drive.

MCM
1994– Builds 1000cc V-twin off-road machines with Folan engines.

MERKEL
1902 Joe Merkel began building motorcycles in Milwaukee, Wisconsin.

He used his own single-cylinder atmospheric-inlet-valve engines and later also built V-twins. He was the first American manufacturer to equip his machines with a spring frame.
1909 Amalgamated with the Light Manufacturing and Foundry Co. of Pottstown, Pennsylvania (see left). In 1910 the Light name was dropped in favour of the Flying Merkel slogan.
1911 The Miami Cycle Co., makers of the Moto-Racycle (see Racycle p.274), bought out Merkel-Light and production moved to its base in Middletown, Ohio. Joe Merkel subsequently left the company in 1913. For 1914 a spring starter was available on the V-twins, but it was not a success.
1917 Production ended.

MERKEL MOTOR WHEEL
1917–22 Designed by Joe Merkel, the Motor Wheel was a clip-on bicycle engine that mounted beside the rear wheel. The last batch was produced at the Indian factory.

METZ
1902–06 Charles Metz was involved in the production of the Orient machine (see p.273) before making motorcycles under his own name. His machines had an inclined cylinder, and the crankcases were an integral part of the frame. Chain drive was used and a two-speed gear appeared in 1903. In 1905 Metz merged with the American Motor Co., makers of the Marsh motorcycle (see left). The Marsh-Metz name was adopted in 1906. V-twin engines were available during the final year of Metz production.

MEYERS
c.1969 Beach buggy manufacturer Bruce Meyers built minibikes equipped with Briggs & Stratton engines.

MIAMI
1914–16 The Miami Cycle Co. built the Moto-Racycle (see Racycle p.274) and then Merkel motorcycles (see above). The firm also used its name on a cheap, lightweight side-valve machine that was sold alongside the larger Merkels.

MICHAELSON
1913–15 J. M. Michaelson, who was formerly involved with the Minneapolis concern (see p.273), built 36cu. in. (590cc) singles and 72cu. in. (1180cc) V-twins using Spacke inlet-over-exhaust engines. Loop frames with leaf-sprung trailing-link forks were fitted.

MIDGET-BICAR
1908–09 The Walton Motor Co. of New York built the British-designed Midget Bicar (see p.224) under licence. Machines were equipped with Peugeot and Sarolea V-twin or single-cylinder Fafnir engines.

MILITAIRE

1911–19 A bizarre motorcycle-cum-car that was intended for military use. Early versions used a 29cu. in. (480cc) single-cylinder side-valve engine in a strange car-style chassis, which used side beams, hub-centre steering, and reverse gear. Later an 80cu. in. (1306cc) four-cylinder engine was added. It was not successful. The Militor name was also used for the same machines, and the licence-built Champion (see p.269) was almost identical.

MINNEAPOLIS

1908–15 Early Minneapolis machines used 19.3cu. in. (316cc) Thiem engines and featured chain drive and two-speed gears. Thor and Spacke V-twins and the firm's own single-cylinder side-valve engines with unit-construction gearboxes were used on later models. From 1912 the V-twins were available with sprung frames.

MITCHELL

1901–06 A pioneer machine built by the Wisconsin Wheel Works. It used a 1.5hp engine mounted near the steering head of a bicycle-style frame. A twisted rawhide belt drove the rear wheel.

MM

1906–13 Charles Metz created the first Orient motorcycle (see right) and also produced machines under his own name (see Metz p.272). William Marsh was another pioneer. They teamed up in 1905 under the banner of the American Motor Co. and produced the first Marsh-Metz machines the following year. As well as conventional 30.5cu. in. (500cc) single-cylinder machines, they also built a unique 61cu. in. (1000cc) 90° V-twin. The engine was used as an integral part of the frame.

MONARCH

1912–14 Monarch succeeded the Reliance marque (see p.274). They were 33.5cu. in. (549cc) inlet-over-exhaust singles and 67cu. in. (1098cc) inlet-over-exhaust V-twins built in Oswego, New York, by the Ives Motorcycle Co.

MON-AUTO

1916–17 The Mon-Auto was a bizarre minibike with a 16cu. in. (264cc) engine mounted beside the rear wheel. The frame was a single large-diameter tube and the rider's footrests were on the front axle. It was also referred to as the Gibson Mon-Auto.

MONTGOMERY WARD

c.1911–12 American department store and mail-order chain that sold motorcycles under its own brand-name. The actual manufacturer is not known.
c.1959–69 The company resumed motorcycle retail. This time it sold Japanese Mitsubishi scooters and Italian-built Benelli motorcycles under the Ward Riverside label.

MORGAN

c.1902 A bicycle-style machine, built in Brooklyn, New York, the Morgan had an inclined engine mounted near the steering head.

MORSE-BEAUREGARD

1912–17 The Morse-Beauregard was an advanced, 40cu. in. (655cc) and later 50cu. in. (819cc) in-line twin with shaft drive. It had a T-head side-valve engine and horizontally split crankcases. The engine was used as a stressed member of the frame.

MOTORMASTER

1939 A bicycle equipped with a two-stroke Evinrude engine. It was made by the Cleveland Welding Co. in Ohio.

MOTO-SCOOT

1936–48 Simple industrial-engined scooters built in Chicago, Illinois.

MUSTANG 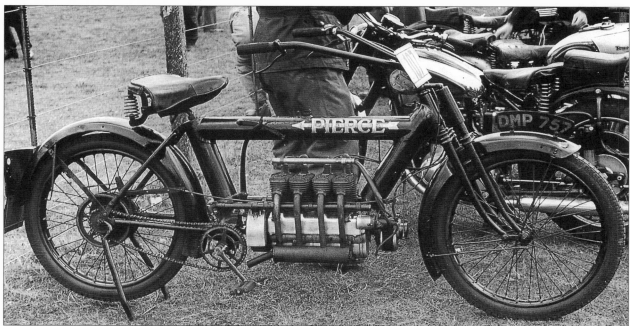 p.134

1946–65 The Mustang was a strange and simple, small-wheeled motorcycle built in Glendale, California. The first versions were equipped with Villiers engines, but later models had 19.5cu. in. (320cc) side-valve industrial motors. Mustangs were popular transportation for college students in the 1950s.

NER-A-CAR p.140

1922 An innovative machine, with a low chassis and hub-centre steering, designed by Carl A. Neracher. Production had begun a year earlier in Britain, where it was made by the Sheffield-Simplex Co. All American models used a 13cu. in. (211cc) two-stroke engine, but the capacity of British models increased to 285cc in 1922 and a 348cc four-stroke Blackburne engine was offered from 1924.
1926 Production stopped on both sides of the Atlantic. In the U.K. the parent company collapsed, in the U.S. the Ner-a-Car did not sell as hoped.

NEW ERA

1908–13 An unusual machine designed by E. L. LeFevre. A 30.5cu. in. (500cc) engine was mounted underneath a bucket seat and a footchange two-speed gearbox was used. The company went bankrupt in 1912 but briefly re-appeared the following year with a 61cu. in. (1000cc) vertical-twin as well as the single-cylinder model.

ORIENT

1899–c.1904 Charles H. Metz was the designer for the bicycle manufacturer, Orient. The company's first motorized two-wheelers were pace-setters for racing bicycles made in about 1898. From there it was a short step to making simple belt-driven motorcycles. The first machines used French Aster engines, but by 1903 the firm produced its own line of 21cu. in. (344cc) to 30cu. in. (492cc) atmospheric-inlet-valve engines. From 1902 Metz produced motorcycles under his own name (see p.272). Orient turned its attention to making cars.

PARAMOUNT

1917 A lightweight 19.4cu. in. (318cc) fore-and-aft flat twin built in Columbus, Ohio. The camshaft was positioned at 90° to the crankshaft and drive was from the camshaft to a multi-plate clutch.

PEERLESS

1911 The Peerless name was briefly used on SD machines (see p.274).

PEERLESS

1912–15 Boston-based firm that made 33cu. in. (541cc) inlet-over-exhaust singles. The engine cases were an integral part of the frame and belt-driven transmission was used.

PEM

1912 The initials of designer Perry E. Mack were briefly used on the 30.5cu. in. (500cc) overhead-valve singles built by Waverley (see p.275). In less than a year the name was changed to Jefferson (see p.272).

PIERCE

1909–13 Pierce made cars and bicycles before building motorcycles. The first motorcycle was inspired by the Belgian FN four. It had a 36.5cu. in. (598cc) side-valve in-line four-cylinder engine mounted in a frame of 3½ in (8.9cm) diameter tubing, which incorporated the fuel and oil tanks. Final drive was by shaft. A two-speed gearbox and a clutch were added in 1910 and a simpler, belt-driven single was also produced.

PILOT

1912 A single-cylinder machine built by the Oberwegner Motor Co. using a 30cu. in. (492cc) Thor engine in a loop frame.

PIRATE

1913–15 Made in Milwaukee, Wisconsin, the Pirate range included inlet-over-exhaust 35cu. in. (574cc) singles and 69cu. in. (1130cc) V-twins. They used countershaft clutch and all-chain drive in a loop frame.

An early Pierce Arrow machine, c.1909, showing the in-line four-cylinder engine

POPE  p.156

1911–18 Colonel Albert A. Pope was an early motor industry magnate whose companies built cars, bicycles, and motorcycles around the turn of the century. These included the Columbia (see p.269) and Rambler (see right) motorcycle marques. The first motorcycle made under the Pope name used the firm's own 26cu. in. (426cc) single-cylinder atmospheric-inlet-valve engines. In 1913 an advanced 61cu. in. (1000cc) overhead-valve V-twin with plunger rear suspension was introduced.

POWELL

1939–51 In 1939 the Powell brothers, from Los Angeles, California, began building typical American industrial-engined scooters. The following year they introduced the A-V-8 (Aviate), which used the company's own 21cu. in. (344cc) engine in a scaled-down motorcycle-style frame. The design of the A-V-8 set a trend for post-war motorcycle-style minibikes.
1967–72 The Powell name reappeared on industrial-engined minibikes.

PUDDLEJUMPER

c.1938 A stylish scooter built in Nebraska by the Midget Motors Corporation. It was apparently available with a side-valve industrial engine or a rechargable electrical power-unit.

RACYCLE (MOTO-RACYCLE)

1905–12 The Racycle was built by the Miami Cycle Co. of Middletown, Ohio. It was similar in style to the early Indian, using a 2.25hp Thor engine mounted as the seat-post of a bicycle-style frame. Later models had a 30cu. in. (492cc) Thor engine mounted in a keystone frame. The Racycle name was dropped when Miami bought Merkel (see p.272).

RAMBLER

1902–14 Rambler motorcycles were typical, Indian-style machines that incorporated the engine's cylinder into the seat-post and drove the rear wheel by chain. Rambler was part of the American Bicycle Co./Pope group of companies.

READING STANDARD  p.158

1903 The first motorcycles, built in Reading, Pennsylvania, were Thor-engined copies of the Indian design.
1907 Reading Standard became the first American manufacturer to build side-valve engines. These were designed by Charles Gustafson, who later worked for Indian. Single-cylinder and V-twin engines of up to 61cu. in. (1000cc) soon followed.
1922 Reading Standard folded and the firm was bought by Cleveland (see p.269).
1923 After selling the remaining stock, Cleveland let the name die.

RELIANCE

1904–12 New York based company that built 21cu. in. (344cc) atmospheric-inlet-valve machines using its own engines and loop frames. When the firm closed, Monarch (see p.273) took over.

RIVERSIDE

c.1959–69 The Montgomery Ward chain of stores used the Riverside brand-name on Mitsubishi Silver Pigeon scooters and Benelli motorcycles, which could be bought by mail order.

ROCK-OLA

1938–40 Rock-Ola, the famous juke-box maker, built scooters too. They were typical small-wheeled machines with side-valve industrial engines. A three-wheeled delivery model was also built.

ROKON  p.161

1959– The original Rokon was a two-wheel drive motorcycle designed for popular non-competitive off-road use by hunters and forestry workers. It had a 134cc Chrysler two-stroke engine intended for marine use. There was no suspension, but it was equipped with fat, low-pressure tyres. Production of machines based on the original design has continued at various locations and with occasional interruptions since 1959. New off-road competition machines entered production in 1973 with 340cc Sachs two-stroke engines and automatic transmission. The machines were innovative and well-made, and they proved successful in competition. The arrival of cheap, Japanese competition machines in the mid-1970s ended Rokon's aspirations as a manufacturer of competition bikes. After an interruption from 1979–81, production of the two-wheel-drive Rokon continued, and the machine remains in production in Portsmouth, New Hampshire.

ROLLAWAY

1919–21 Rollaway built a two-stroke engine for bicycles that mounted on the front fork like the later French VéloSolex.

ROYAL

1901–10 Emil Hafelfinger built his first 1.25hp motorcycle in 1901. It did not reach production until 1907, by which time power output was up to 2.75hp and capacity was 19.3cu. in. (316cc). The layout was similar to the early Indian but the engine, mounted on the seat-post, was surrounded by a four-tube cage. The name was enlarged to Royal-Pioneer in 1909 when an overhead-valve engine, with valves positioned at 90° to the bore, appeared.

RUGOMOBILE

c.1903 The Rugomobile was a strange, open-framed machine, which used a crank-started 3hp engine. It is possible that it was also known as the Ruggles.

SAFTICYCLE

1946–50 Built in La Crosse, Wisconsin, the Safticycle was a odd amalgam of scooter and bicycle.

SALSBURY  p.165

1935–42 The Salsbury was the inspiration for the classic American scooters of the 1940s and 1950s. E. Foster Salsbury's first machines used Evinrude two-stroke engines and friction drive on the rear tyre. Soon four-stroke engines and chain drive were used. The design of the Salsbury influenced and encouraged succeeding American scooter manufacturers.
1946–49 A new company owned by Northrop Aviation produced the post-war Salsburys. Production lasted only a few years.

SCHICKEL

1912–19 Schickel built unusual, 30cu. in. (492cc) and 42cu. in. (688cc) two-stroke singles at Stamford, Connecticut. The company pioneered the use of pre-mixed oil in petrol for two-stroke lubrication. From 1915 a lightweight model with flywheel magneto was produced. Some models used the SMC label (see p.275).

SCOUT

1911–13 A 30.5cu. in. (500cc) belt-driven single made by the Michigan Motorcycle Co. of Detroit.

SD

1909–11 The SD initials stand for both the makers Spangler & Dewald of Brooklyn, New York, and for shaft drive. The motorcycle was a 27cu. in (442cc) single. The Peerless name (see p.273) was briefly used in 1911.

SEARS  p.168

1912–16 Sears stores sold machines built by other manufacturers with their own label. From 1913 to 1914 these were built by Thor. Later machines used Spacke engines and were probably built by the Excelsior Cycle Co. (see De Luxe p.270).
c.1964–69 Sears resumed the sale of imported machines. This time Gilera and Puch machines were sold under the Sears label. The company's Allstate badge (see p.268) was also used on Puch and Cushman machines from 1951.

SHAW

1912–20 Shaw built a 3.5hp single equipped with the firm's own side-valve engine. It was possibly based on the earlier Kokomo machine (see p.272).

The c.1912 two-stroke Schickel's fuel tank was a structural part of the frame

A 2.5hp engine was also available as a bicycle attachment. The company was based in Galesburg, Illinois.

SIMPLEX
1906–09 The Prospect Motor Manufacturing Co. of Brooklyn, New York, sold Peugeot-engined V-twins under the Simplex brand-name. It's unclear if these were made in America or imported.

SIMPLEX 🏍 p.169
1935–75 Simplex made the Servi-Cycle, a successful and long-lived lightweight machine. The 7.5cu. in. (125cc) two-stroke engine used an overhung crankshaft and rotary valve. Final drive was by belt and it had an automatic transmission from the early 1940s. A scooter version was built from the late 1950s. From 1960 Simplex made minibikes with industrial engines.

SMC
1916–18 SMC was the name used on some Schickel two-strokes (see p.274).

SMITH MOTOR WHEEL 🏍 p.170
1914–19 The Motor Wheel was a third-wheel attachment for bicycles that incorporated an 8.9cu. in. (146cc) one-cylinder four-stroke engine. It was built under licence from British designer A. W. Wall, although the American product was slightly different. It was made by Briggs & Stratton (see p.269) from 1919.

STAHL
c.1902–12 C. V. Stahl's original machine used a vertical engine in a modified bicycle-style frame, which incorporated a loop in the downtube to hold the crankcases. Later machines were 27cu. in. (442cc) singles and 57cu. in. (934cc) V-twins with loop frames. They were also known by the initials CVS (see p.270).

STEEN 🏍 p.172
c.1962–75 Californian minibike manufacturers that began production with typical small-wheeled machines. Later the company built more sophisticated competition models with Hodaka engines.

STEFFEY
c.1902–05 Probably the first water-cooled bike produced in the U.S., the Steffey also featured external flywheels. The 1.5hp engine was mounted in a bicycle-style frame with chain drive.

STRATTON
c.1901 Made in New York, the Stratton was a bicycle-style machine with an atmospheric-inlet-valve engine mounted on the lower downtube, which drove the rear wheel by belt.

THIEM
1908–14 Thiem supplied engines to other makers before building complete motorcycles. The firm made typical belt-driven atmospheric-inlet-valve singles of 17.8cu. in. (292cc) to 29cu. in. (475cc) before making side-valve V-twins. Thiem amalgamated with Joerns (see p.272) and later built the famous overhead-camshaft Cyclone V-twin (see p.270).

THOMAS
1900–09 E. R. Thomas was a pioneer manufacturer responsible for the Auto-Bi machine (see p.268), which was also called the Thomas. They were built in Buffalo, New York, and were succeeded by the Greyhound marque (see p.271).

THOR
1907–19 The Aurora Automatic Machine Co. built engines, to the design of Oscar Hedstrom, for the first Indian machines. It also supplied these engines to other manufacturers using the Thor brand-name. Reading-Standard, Racycle, Emblem, and others used Thor engines in their early machines. The first complete Thor motorcycles appeared in 1907. They were 2.25hp and 3hp atmospheric-inlet-valve, loop-framed singles with girder forks. In 1908 there were 5hp 50° V-twins. Power output increased and mechanical inlet valves were introduced in the following years.

THOROUGHBRED
c.1904 The Thoroughbred name was used on early Reading-Standard machines (see p.274).

TIGER
1915–16 The Tiger was a lightweight, 15.25cu. in. (250cc) belt-driven two-stroke motorcycle built in New York by Frederickson & Stenger.

TORPEDO
1907–09 Torpedo used Antoine and Thor single-cylinder and V-twin engines with direct chain drive.

TORQUE
c.1945 A New Jersey engineering company that developed a range of motorcycles. The designer was Briggs Weaver, who had formerly worked with Indian. The "modular" design allowed a 22cu. in. (360cc) single, a 44cu. in. (721cc) twin, and an 88cu. in. (1442cc) four to be built using common components. In 1945 Ralph B. Rogers bought the Torque company, and then acquired Indian (see p.271). Torque designs formed the basis of the post-war Indian range, although the four was only built as a prototype.

TOURIST
c.1904–10 Tourist motorcycles were built in Newark, New Jersey. The

atmospheric-inlet-valve engine was fitted in an inclined position in a loop frame with belt drive. The final versions had 4hp inlet-over-exhaust engines and optional two-speed hub gear.

TRAUB
c.1916 A typical American side-valve V-twin built in Chicago, the Traub was only ever made in prototype form.

TRIUMPH
1907–09 The Triumph name was used on a 17.5cu. in. (287cc) Thor-engined machine built by the makers of the Excelsior motorcycle (see p.270).

VALIANT
c.1964–65 The Valiant was a 197cc Villiers-engined version of the Simplex minibike (see left).

VARD
c.1944 The Vard, made in Pasadena, California, was probably only made as a prototype. It was a 21.5cu. in. (350cc) side-valve single with an inclined cylinder in a swing-arm frame.

WAGNER
1901–14 Single-cylinder machines built in St Paul, Minnesota, using Wagner's own or Thor engines. Loop frames with a diagonal bracing strut were used. The company also made tandems.

WAVERLEY
1905–12 The Waverley motorcycle was built by the Waverley Manufacturing Co. For a short time in 1912 it took the initials of the designer, Perry E. Mack (see PEM p.273), and from 1912 to 1915 it was marketed as the Jefferson (see p.272).

WHIPPLE
1903–05 Built in Chicago, Illinois, using a bicycle-style frame with the single-cylinder engine mounted parallel to the seat-post. Final drive was by belt and a two-speed gear with clutch was used.

WHIZZER 🏍 p.196
1939–62 Whizzer produced a 8.4cu. in. (138cc) side-valve clip-on bicycle engine. After World War II a complete belt-driven machine with a Schwinn frame was available.

WILLIAMS
1915 An unusual machine with a three-cylinder radial engine mounted in the back wheel. Built in New York.

WYSECYCLE
1946–50 The Wysecycle, built in Dayton, Ohio, was a small-wheeled novelty for college students. It was equipped with a 19.6cu. in. (322cc) engine and semi-enclosed bodywork.

YALE 🏍 p.199
1903–15 The Yale name was used on machines built by the Consolidated Manufacturing Co. of Toledo, Ohio. The first machines were based on the California design (see p.269) and used the Yale-California name. The company subsequently built a range of single-cylinder and V-twin machines from 17.8cu. in. (292cc) to 61cu. in. (1000cc).

YANKEE
1920–23 The Illinois Motor Co. of Chicago built lightweight 15.25cu. in. (250cc) two-strokes.

YANKEE
1972–75 A 488cc two-stroke twin-cylinder dirt bike built by Ossa of Spain for its American importers, the Yankee Motors Corporation, which sold it under the Yankee name.

Unconfirmed marques

Airman Chicago, IL *c.1948*
American Hartford, CT *c.1903*
American Rahway, NJ *c.1903*
American Denver, CO *c.1909*
American Louisville, KY *c.1921*
Atco Pittsburgh, PA *c.1912*
Autobike Chicago, IL *c.1915*
Auto Car Pittsburgh, PA *c.1900*
Auto Four Chicago, IL *c.1971*
Auto Scoot *c.1938*
Barber Brooklyn, NY *c.1900*
Barr Middletown, OH *c.1940*
Baysdorfer-Dumbleton
    Omaha, NE *c.1903*
Bean Boston, MA *c.1903*
Bearcat Rochester, NY *c.1950*
Beard & Abel Boston, MA *c.1903*
Boland Rahway, NJ *c.1903*
Bowman New York, NY *c.1905*
Bradford Bradford, PA *c.1907*
Breed Bay City, MI *c.1912*
Buckeye Columbus, OH *c.1905*
Buffalo Buffalo, NY *c.1984*
Caille Detroit, MI *c.1935*
Camden Camden, NJ *c.1906*
Centaur New York, NY *c.1961*
Century Chicago, IL *c.1917*
Chicago 400 Chicago, IL *c.1905*
Clark Torrington, CT *c.1903*
Clarke St Louis, MO
Clemcut Hartford, CT *c.1908*
Clement Hartford, CT *c.1906*
Cleveland Hartford, CT *c.1903*
Clinton-Tower Cleveland, OH *c.1895*
Comet Elwood, IL *c.1911*
Commando Minneapolis, MN *c.1950*
Crescent Hartford, CT *c.1905*
Crosley Cincinnati, OH *c.1943*
Culp Columbus, OH *c.1903*
Cyclone South Gate, CA *c.1948*
Day Lake View, NY *c.1903*
Delaware Delaware, OH *c.1908*
Duesenberg Rockford, IA *c.1903*
Dukelow Chicago, IL *c.1913*
Dyke St Louis, MO *c.1905*
Eagle Brockton, MA *c.1908*
Eagle St Louis, MO *c.1911*
Economy Detroit, MI *c.1908*
Elk Elkhart, IN *c.1911*
Eshelman Baltimore, MD *c.1954*
Fairchild Pasadena, CA
Fleming White Plains, NY *c.1901*
F&M Columbus, OH *c.1905*
Francke-Johannsmeyer Milwaukee, WI
    c.1905
Franklin Mount Vernon, WA *c.1900*
Grady *c.1909*
Greyhound Reading, PA *c.1924*
Hampden Springfield, MA *c.1903*
Harper New York, NY *c.1908*
Hartford Hartford, CT *c.1907*
Hawthorne Chicago, IL *c.1912*
Heald Benton Harbour, MI *c.1976*
Hemingway Glenwood, IL *c.1905*
Hercules Hammondsport, NY *c.1904*
Herring St Joseph, MO *c.1899*
H&H San Diego, CA *c.1903*
Holley Bradford, PA *c.1906*
Holmes *c.1900*

Hudson Middletown, OH *c.1910*
Imperial *c.1903*
Industrial Syracuse, NY *c.1903*
Kaestner Chicago, IL *c.1903*
Kaye-Pennington Racine, WI *c.1895*
Kelsey *c.1911*
Kenzler-Waverley Cambridge, WI
    c.1912
Kiefler Buffalo, NY *c.1910*
Kirkham Bath, NY *c.1903*
Kulture Rochester, NY *c.1909*
Landgraf Chicago, IL *c.1906*
Langford Denver, CO *c.1920*
Leader Milwaukee, WI *c.1906*
Leo Oakland, CA *c.1905*
Lewis Brooklyn, NY *c.1901*
Lightning Joliet, IL *c.1948*
Lunford Marble, NC *c.1916*
Lyons *c.1909*
Magnacycle
Majestic *c.1912*
Maltby Brooklyn, NY *c.1903*
Mansen-Marsh Brockton, MA *c.1906*
Marathon Hartford, CT *c.1910*
Marman Inglewood, CA *c.1948*
Maxim Hartford, CT *c.1893*
McDonald Chicago, IL *c.1905*
Meadowbrook Hempstead, NY *c.1905*
Mears Brooklyn, NY *c.1903*
Mecky Philadelphia, PA *c.1903*
Menns-VanHorn Boston, MA *c.1903*
MOHS *c.1960s*
Monarch Hartford, CT *c.1903*
Monark Chicago, IL *c.1952*
Monnot Canton, OH *c.1903*
Moore Indianpolis, IN *c.1917*
Morris-Corkhill Rochester, NY *c.1903*
Moto-Glide Los Angeles, CA *c.1930s*
Motopede Rutherford, NY *c.1921*
Nelk Palo Alto, CA *c.1909*
Nioga Whitney Point, NY *c.1903*
Nyberg Chicago, IL *c.1913*
Oakes Johnstown, PA *c.1916*
OK Brooklyn, NY *c.1916*
Pansy *c.1905*
Parkin-Leflem Philadelphia, PA *c.1903*
Patee Indianapolis, IN *c.1901*

Phoenix Milwaukee, WI *c.1906*
Pioneer Jersey City, NJ *c.1903*
Pioneer Worcester, MA *c.1909*
Playboy Oakland, CA *c.1956*
Pony Clarkston, MI *c.1955*
Pratt Four Elkhart, IN *c.1912*
P-T New York, NY *c.1900*
Ranger Chicago, IL *c.1938*
Razoux Boston, MA *c.1903*
Redman *c.1907*
Regas Rochester, NY *c.1901*
R & H Brockton, MA *c.1905*
Riotte New York, NY *c.1895*
Rocket Columbus, NE *c.1962*
Roper Roxbury, MA *c.1869*
Ruggles Brooklyn, NY *c.1903*
Rupp Mansfield, OH *c.1960s*
Salisbury Chicago, IL *c.1895*
Skootmobile Chicago, IL *c.1938*
Slattery Brooklyn, NY *c.1903*
Snell Toledo, OH *c.1905*
Spiral New York, NY *c.1896*
Starlin Tonawanda, NY *c.1903*
Starlite Crystal Lake, IL *c.1960s*
Stormer Hartford, CT *c.1907*
Suddard Providence, RI *c.1905*
Thompson Beverly Farms, MA *c.1909*
Tinkham New Haven, CT *c.1899*
Tribune Hartford, CT *c.1908*
Trimoto Hartford, CT *c.1900*
Twombly Portland, ME *c.1895*
Victor Cleveland, OH *c.1911*
Victory
Warwick Springfield, MA *c.1903*
Wasson Haverhill, MA *c.1903*
Westfield Westfield, MA *c.1917*
Westover Denver, CO *c.1913*
Widmayer New York, NY *c.1907*
Williamson Philadelphia, PA *c.1903*
Willis New York, NY *c.1903*
Wilson Wichita, KS *c.1910*
Wizzard *c.1950s*
Woods Denver, CO *c.1914*
Woods-Meagher Richmond, VA *c.1896*
Yardman Jackson, MI *c.1959*

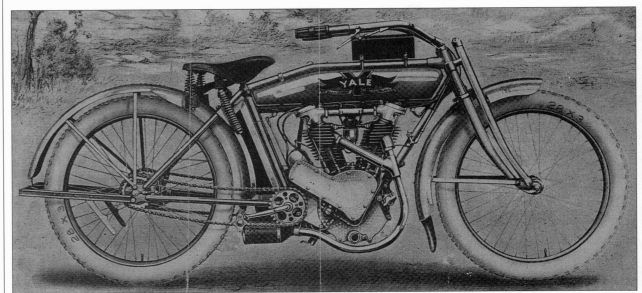

A chain-driven Yale Model 37, c.1913

France

ALBERT DEDION and Georges Bouton's development of an improved internal combustion engine gave motor vehicles better performance and reliability. This was advertised through high-profile motor races. As a result, many small companies sprang up to satisfy the growing demand for motorcycles and tricycles and, by the end of the 19th century, France could boast that it was home to the world's motor industry. But the French lead was short lived: from the end of World War I Britain and Germany were the most important motorcycle manufacturing countries. The French industry survived to satisfy domestic demand but its machines were never exported in large numbers. Between the wars production was gradually concentrated into the hands of a few large companies like Peugeot (see p.282), Alcyon (see below), and Motobécane (see p.281). The arrival of the cheap car after World War II destroyed the domestic motorcycle industry though Peugeot and Motobécane (now owned by Yamaha) continued to make powered two-wheelers.

ABC
c.1920–24 The aircraft engine maker Gnome & Rhône (see p.279) began production with an improved version of the British ABC flat-twin design.

ACMA
1952–62 ACMA built the Vespa scooter in large numbers under licence.

ADER
1903–06 Clément Ader made a limited number of shaft-driven V-twins in Paris.

ADONIS
1950–52 Made mopeds and 48cc to 75cc VAP-engined lightweight machines.

AGF
1947–56 Built a scooter and a 123cc to 173cc Jonghi-engined two-stroke bike. Joined with Guiller (see p.280) in 1954.

AIGLON
1900–54 Pioneer maker that built cars and bicycles, as well as orthodox bikes with Mirus and other proprietary engines. It was bought by Peugeot in 1922, and subsequent machines were just Peugeots with a different badge.

ALCYON
c.1904–57 Edmond Gentil named the marque after a mythological bird. Early models used Zédel, Zürcher, and other engines. After World War I, the Alcyon group acquired Armor, La Français (see p.279), Labor (see p.280), Olympique (see p.282), and Thomann (see p.283), and built 98cc to 498cc two- and four-stroke machines. After World War II it

made mopeds and AMC-, Zürcher-, and VAP-engined motorcycles of up to 248cc.

ALLELUIA
1922–56 Built mopeds and lightweight motorcycles using proprietary engines.

ALMA
1949–59 Built 50cc to 175cc Ydral- and Poulain-engined lightweights.

ALPHA
1983–91 Specialized in trials machines using Honda power units. It later used its own 239cc two-stroke engine.

ALPHONSE THOMANN
1908–23 Made 98cc to 173cc two-strokes, including competition models.

ALTER
1955–56 Built lightweight machines.

ANZANI
1900–c.1939 Famous engine maker that built some complete motorcycles, including large-capacity machines for pacing bicycle races.

ARBINET
1924–34 Dijon-based firm that built a range of 98cc to 497cc two-strokes.

ARDENT
1950–54 Built a 49cc to 85cc VAP-, Le Poulain-, and Lavalette-engined scooter.

ARGENTRE
1930–33 Made 247cc to 498cc side-valve and overhead-valve singles using proprietary engines by JAP and LPL.

ARLIGUE
1950–54 Produced mopeds.

ARMOR See Alcyon (left).

ASTER
1898–1910 Engine supplier that also built some complete machines.

ATLANTIC
1929–32 The company produced 250cc to 500cc bikes with Blackburne, Chaise, and other engines.

AUSTRAL
c.1904–30 Austral built Aster-powered motorcycles. Poinsard, JAP, and Zürcher engines were used after 1918.

AUTO-FAUTEUIL
1902–06 Unusual machines built with the Aster engine placed under the rider's bucket seat, hence the name *Fauteuil* – French for "armchair".

AUTOMOTIONETTE
1934–39 Powered bicycles with 100cc Sachs and Aubier-Dunne engines.

AUTOMOTO
1901 Chavanet, Gros, Pichard & Cie., once a car firm, used up to 500cc JAP, Blackburne, Aubier-Dunne, Peugeot, and its own engines on the first Automotos.
1931 Peugeot took over the marque and built machines up to 250cc with proprietary engines. After World War II it made motorcycles with Villiers and AMC engines, and mopeds with VAP, Motobloc, and Marquet engines.
1962 Production stopped.

BABY MOTO
c.1950–52 This was a tubular-framed scooter built with 49cc Gucciolo or 70cc Lavalette engines.

BAILLEUL
1903–10 Bailleul made Peugeot- and Buchet-engined belt-driven machines.

BARIGO 🏍 p.22
1982– Barigo builds specialized machines with single-cylinder four-stroke Rotax engines. Successful in desert raid, enduro, and super motard races, it is one of few French marques that is still producing motorcycles in the 1990s.

BARRE
c.1925 Made two-stroke motorcycles.

BCR
1923–30 Built its own 125cc and 350cc two-stroke engines and fitted proprietary four-strokes, some with rear suspension.

BENOIT-GONIN
1908–28 Made by a former jeweller who used Zédel, Anzani, and other engines.

BERNARDET
1947–57 The Bernardet brothers built scooters with 49cc to 246cc Ydral, Violet, and its own two-stroke engines.

BERNASSE
1907–c.1920 Max Bernasse hand-built these single-cylinder and V-twin bikes.

BFG
1978–83 Boccardo, Favrio, and Grange did not build a large number of this all-French motorcycle. It used a 1299cc flat-four Citroën car engine with a five-speed gearbox. Boccardo also created the MF motorcycle (see p.281).

BICHRONE
1902–07 Produced an unusual two-stroke V-twin which had one pumping and one combustion cylinder.

BLAUSERETTE
c.1924 Paul Blauseur built these 125cc to 175cc belt-driven two-strokes in Paris.

BLÉRIOT
1919–23 Aircraft maker that built a 497cc parallel twin after World War I.

The stylish 1957 Alcyon Paris-Nice scooter had a 125cc two-stroke engine

Specifications included a three-speed gearbox with chain drive.

BLOTTO
1929–55 Built machines using 123cc to 348cc two-stroke proprietary engines.

BOIVIN
1896–1904 Boivin produced motorcycles and powered wheels.

BOLIDE
1902–10 Made motorcycles in Pantin.

BOUGERY
1896–1902 Built single-cylinder bikes.

BPS
1973–78 Boudet, Portal (see p.282), and Seurat built 49cc to 124cc two-strokes with proprietary engines.

BREUIL
1902–08 Breuil used Peugeot, Aster, and Zürcher engines in its own frames.

BRILLANT
c.1900–04 Built a Zédel-engined model.

BRUNEAU
c.1900–10 Put Zédel engines in bicycle frames, later moved to the "new" Werner position. It added shaft drive in 1904 and vertical-twin engines in 1905.

BRUTUS
1900 Brutus produced engines and complete belt-driven machines.

BUCHET
1900–11 Engine and car maker Buchet also built some motorcycles, including a 4500cc machine for pacing bicycle races.

BUT
1978 Racing machines built by Eric Offenstadt. These innovative 350cc and 500cc water-cooled two-stroke twins were named after their sponsor.

CAMILE-FOUCAUX
1952–54 Made scooters and mopeds.

CARPIO
1930–35 This marque built Aubier-Dunne-engined lightweights.

CARREAU
1902–03 Marque that built machines powered by DeDion and Aster engines.

CAZANAVE
1950–58 Made mopeds, AMC-engined scooters, and lightweight motorcycles.

CEM
c.1920 Built side-valve models in Lyon.

CEMEC
1948–55 CEMEC took over production of the BMW-style flat twins at CMR (see

The 497cc Blériot parallel twin with disc wheels

below) before changing its name to Ratier (see p.282).

CFC
c.1902–06 Compagnie Française des Cycles built motorcycles with single- and twin-cylinder Onfray engines.

CHAPELLE
c.1901–02 This marque was soon absorbed by Rochet (see p.283).

CHOUBERSKY
1899 Tricycle and tandem made under licence from DeDion in Paris.

CHRISTOPHE
c.1925 Made 100cc and 175cc belt-driven two-stroke motorcycles.

CL DELAGE
1924–30 These 175cc to 250cc two-strokes used mainly LPL engines.

CLÉMENT
1896–35 Adolphe Clément's bicycle company merged with Gladiator (see p.279) to create Clément-Gladiator. It sold the 142cc inlet-over-exhaust Autocyclette to other firms. By 1913 Clément were buying MAG and JAP engines, used in the later machines, but also made a 43cc clip-on engine. Later bikes had triangulated frames and cantilever rear suspension.

CMR
1945–48 See CEMEC (above).

COCYMO
1956–59 Assembled mopeds and motorcycles using proprietary parts. Engines used included Lavalette, VAP, Mistral, Sachs, and Ydral. They were then sold under names such as Drévon, Métropole, Racer, Sterling, and VBF.

COINTOT
c.1950s Built unusual lightweights with front and rear suspension.

COLOMB
1950–54 An established bicycle company that briefly built mopeds.

CONTAL
1906–13 Built tricycles and tandems under licence from DeDion in Paris.

COTTEREAU
c.1903–09 Dijon car maker built a bike that used its own or proprietary engines.

CP-ROLÉO
1927–39 Built in Paris using LMP, Harissard, and Staub engines. The frame, with the fuel tank incorporated, was a pressed-steel box section linking the steering head to the rear axle.

LA CYCLETTE
1922–30 Built a 91cc two-stroke-engined bicycle in styles for both sexes.

CYCLEX
c.1950 Cyclex produced clip-on two-stroke engines.

CYCLOTRACTEUR
1914–22 Built a 108cc four-stroke clip-on engine to mount on the front fork.

DALIFOL
c.1895–1900 Made a steam-engined motorcycle with a centrally mounted boiler and direct drive to the rear wheel.

DAX
1932–39 Built quality 98cc, 348cc, and 498cc overhead-valve singles.

DEAUVILLE & CIE
c.1907–09 Built by Alcyon (see p.277).

DE-DE
1923–39 This marque built a range of 98cc to 498cc machines in Courbevoie.

DEDION BOUTON  p.47
1895–1910 Pioneer company that built tricycles and, later, motorcycles. It also sold its engines to other marques. Its motorcycle had its engine vertically placed behind the seat-post and the rear wheel was driven by belt. DeDion soon turned to car production.

DELAPLACE
c.1952 Made simple lightweights.

DEPREZ
c.1920 Proprietary-engined lightweights.

DERNY
1949–58 Built 100cc Zürcher-engined mopeds and tandems. The Roger Tallon-designed 125cc AMC-powered Taon appeared in 1957.

DERONZIÈRE p.47
1906–14 Francisque Croizier de Ronzière made his first machine in Lyon. He used proprietary and his own 288cc engines with atmospheric inlet valves. Bikes were also sold by Manufrance under the RPF, Superior, Hirondelle, and Rupta badges.

DFR
1921–33 Built 175cc two-strokes. It also used proprietary engines including the 350cc oil-cooled Bradshaw single. DFR was sold to Dresch (see p.279) in 1926.

DIAMON
c.1930 Diamon built 100cc to 350cc Chaise-powered models in Toulouse.

DILCETA
1929–39 Dilceta produced 98cc Zürcher-engined lightweights.

DOLLAR
1922–39 The company made 125cc to 350cc overhead-valve machines. A Chaise-engined 750cc V4 was made in very limited numbers.

DORION
1932–36 Built 98cc and 123cc Aubier-Dunne-powered two-stroke lightweights.

DRESCH 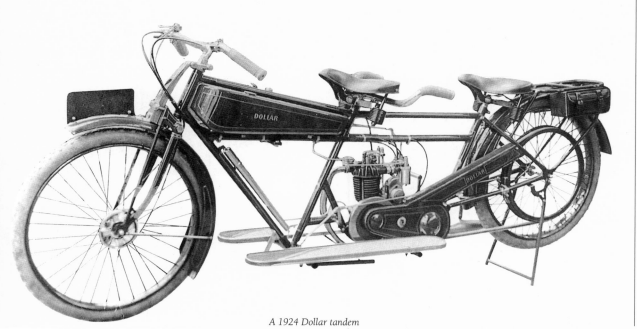 p.52·
1923–39 Henri Dresch, after acquiring the DFR (see p.278) and Le Grimpeur (see p.280) marques, built competitively priced, quality machines using 250cc and 350cc MAG engines. It later built its own engines. A 500cc in-line twin motorcycle was launched in 1930. World War II ended production.

DS-MALTERRE
1922–58 Before World War II the company built a 500cc single. JAP, Ydral, and AMC side-valve engines were used in its machines after the war.

DUCOMMUN
1900 Built an early 1.5hp machine.

DUNCAN-SUPERBIE
c.1894 Built the German Hildebrand & Wolfmüller motorcycle under licence.

DURANDAL
1926–33 Produced motorcycles using proprietary engines, including Zürcher and Sturmey-Archer. Durandal also built the 350cc and 500cc four-valve Rudge Python. Some of these machines had pressed-steel frames.

DUTEMPLE
c.1903–06 Minor marque that made shaft-driven and belt-driven machines.

ELF
1978–88 Innovative hub-centre-steered endurance and Grand Prix racers, financed by the Elf oil company. Real success eluded the company, though its machines were advanced for their time.

EMERAUDE
1902–10 Built single-cylinder machines.

EOLE
c.1930 Favor (see below) used this name for 98cc lightweights.

ESPER
1928–30 Used 175cc to 500cc engines by Moser, Zürcher, Chaise, and JAP.

ETOILE
1933–39 Made 98cc to 198cc Aubier-Dunne- and Sachs-engined two-strokes.

FASTEX
1952 Made 120cc Ilo-engined scooters.

FAVOR
1919–59 The Guillaume brothers used both their own engine and a JAP power unit in early machines. After World War II they built 48cc to 174cc Alter- and AMC-engined mopeds and bikes.

FELIX MILLET
1887–1900 Felix Millet built a machine using a five-cylinder rotary engine.

FEMINIA
1933–36 Feminia built Aubier-Dunne- and Stainless-engined two-strokes.

FIOR
c.1978 Christian Fior constructed an innovative 500cc four-cylinder two-stroke road-racing motorcycle.

FLINOIS
c.1900–02 Built a clip-on engine.

FOLLIS
1951–60 Bicycle manufacturer that built mopeds and motorcycles of up to 250cc with Sachs, Ydral, and AMC engines.

LA FRANÇAISE DIAMANT
1902–54 This bicycle maker was also known by the names La Français and Diamant. Early machines were powered by a 1.25hp proprietary engine mounted on the downtube of a bicycle-style frame. In 1913 it built a 289cc motorcycle with its own engine. After World War I it still continued to manufacture but it was absorbed by Alcyon (see p.277) in 1926.

LA FRANCE
c.1922 Built a two-stroke lightweight.

GARIN
1950–53 Made mopeds and small bikes.

GARREAU
c.1896–1903 Built a motorized bicycle.

GAUTHIER
1973–82 Small marque that built 123cc to 247cc Sachs-engined sport machines.

GÉCO-HERSTAL
1927–28 Having previously made the Harlette lightweight (see p.280), Gerkinet & Co. merged with the Belgian Gillet-Herstal marque and built its machines in France.

GENIAL-LUCIFER
1928–56 Built in Paris, this mail order motorcycle was sold by Mestre et Blatgé. It used MAG, Chaise, and other two- and four-stroke proprietary engines.

GEORGES RICHARD
1903–1909 Pioneer that made bicycles, cars, and motorcycles with proprietary engines, including Zédel. Later it was known by the Trèfle-à-quatre name.

GEORGIA KNAP
1901–05 First mounted next to the rear wheel, the 250cc atmospheric-inlet-valve engine of these machines was later moved to a more conventional position. The company soon turned to making cars.

GERALD
1927–32 Charles Gerald built this bike in Paris using Aubier-Dunne, JAP, and Chaise engines from 98cc to 498cc.

GIMA
1947–56 Owned by Favor (see left), this marque used two- and four-stroke AMC and Ydral engines of up to 250cc.

GITANE
c.1947–80 Until the 1960s this bicycle manufacturer built mopeds and motorcycles using 100cc to 175cc VAP, Ydral, and Sachs engines. In the 1970s it sold a 49cc Italian Testi with a Gitane badge, but this ended when Renault took over the company in 1980.

GL
1919–21 Orial (see p.282) built these 1000cc JAP- and MAG-engined V-twins.

GLADIATOR
c.1902–12 Founded by Darracq, Gladiator was sold to Clément (see p.278) around 1897. Clément used the Gladiator name on some machines.

GLORIOL
c.1924–28 Made proprietary-engined machines including 125cc two-strokes.

GNOME & RHÔNE p.65
1919 An aircraft engine maker that began production with the licence-built Bradshaw-designed ABC (see p.277).
1923 Started building its own excellent 300cc, 350cc, and 500cc singles.
1931 Began producing innovative, BMW-style shaft-driven flat twins and a 250cc single. After the 724cc Type X appeared in 1935, an 800cc side-valve twin was built prior to the outbreak of the war for military use.
1945–59 Post-war production was concentrated on well-designed and constructed 125cc to 200cc two-strokes.

GOBRON-MINERVA
1903–04 Produced motorcycles powered by Minerva engines.

GOLIATH
c.1920–22 Built a 124cc clip-on engine.

GRATIEUX
1919–21 Built a 250cc two-stroke.

A 1924 Dollar tandem

GRIFFON
1902–55 This famous marque built single-cylinder and V-twin machines before World War I. After the war it made Zédel- and Anzani-engined singles and V-twins, and some 175cc to 350cc utilitarian two-strokes. Peugeot took over production in 1927 and Griffon became merely another rebadged Peugeot after World War II.

LE GRIMPEUR
1900 Its first machines used an assortment of engines supplied by Stainless, JAP, Aubier-Dunne, and others. In the early 1920s it built successful two-stroke lightweights.
1926 Dresch (p.278) bought the company. Subsequent models used licence-built MAG single-cylinder engines from 250cc to 500cc.
1932 Dresch dropped the name in favour of the Dresch badge.

GUERRY
c.1904 Engine manufacturer that also built complete 250cc to 350cc machines.

GUIGNARD
1933–38 Jean Guignard built 98cc and 123cc two-stroke motorcycles.

GUILLER
1949–56 The Guiller brothers used AMC, Aubier-Dunne, Ydral, and VAP engines to produce mopeds to 250cc singles. It built Italian SIM scooters under licence, merging with AGF (see p.277) in 1954.

GURTNER
c.1922 Built Train-engined two-strokes.

HARLETTE
1923–28 First built by Goode and Co., Harley-Davidson's French importer, the Harlette lightweight used 125cc to 175cc LPL two-stroke engines. Production moved to Gerkinet & Co. around 1925. The revised Harlette-Géco was also built with 175cc to 250cc Gillet-Herstal four-stroke engines.

HASTY
1930–34 Built powered bicycles with 98cc two-stroke engines.

HELYETT
1926–55 Small firm that used 98cc to 996cc mainly JAP and Chaise engines. A few 750cc JAP-engined transverse V-twins with shaft drive were made around 1928. After World War II its machines were mainly small-capacity two-strokes.

HEMY
c.1950 Built a clip-on bicycle engine.

HERDTLÉ-BRUNEAU
1903–14 Made 150cc inlet-over-exhaust clip-on bicycle engines in Paris.

Expensive but high-quality, it was available with water cooling.

HIRONDELLE
1921–54 Sold by mail order, its first machines were rebadged Deronzières (see p.278). Utilitarian models were produced until the 1950s.

HUNTER
1922–26 Made a belt-driven two-stroke.

HURTU
c.1900–58 Engine maker that produced motorcycles intermittently. Made a belt-driven side-valve motorcycle as early as 1906. Produced 49cc two-stroke mopeds after World War II.

IMPETUS
c.1901 Racing cyclist Baron Impetus (Max Hertel) built this 1.5hp machine.

ISOFLEX
1950 Built an unusual 98cc Villiers-engined step-thru with pivoting frame suspension.

IXION
c.1901–05 Two-stoke pioneer who developed and patented a rotary-valve engine, making a 275cc model in 1905.

JACK SPORT
1927–31 A subsidiary of Utilia (see p.283) that built 350cc and 500cc JAP-engined single-cylinder machines.

JANOIR
1919–24 Innovative 964cc flat twins built by aircraft maker Louis Janoir. Later models had pressed-steel frames.

JAPAUTO
1969–75 Parisienne Honda dealer that built endurance racing machines with 750cc four-cylinder Honda engines.

J-B LOUVET
c.1913–30 Produced motorcycles using JAP and Aubier-Dunne engines.

JCM
1983– Joël Carrow built this specialized trials machine driven by a Tau engine. It later used Spanish Gas Gas power units.

JEAN THOMANN
1920–50 Built mainly small utilitarian two-strokes with proprietary engines.

JOCHUM
c.1901–02 Made 1.75hp machine with a seat-post-mounted engine.

JONGHI
1930–56 Expatriate Italians, Tito Jonghi and Giuseppe Remondi, built excellent 173cc to 348cc singles in the 1930s. They also made small two-strokes with proprietary engines. In 1936 Jonghi

merged with Prester (see p.282). After World War II it produced a superb 125cc racer and 98cc to 248cc two-strokes.

JOUCLARD
1903–07 Built in Dijon, it competed in the 1904 Paris-Bordeaux-Paris race.

JUNCKER
1935–37 Built lightweight motorcycles with 98cc, 123cc, and 147cc Stainless and Aubier-Dunne engines.

KD
1906–10 This marque built clip-on engines and complete motorcycles.

KOEHLER ESCOFFIER
c.1912 Based in Lyon its first machine, a 491cc V-twin, had an excellent sporting reputation. The 1926 499cc single doubled up to create a 980cc overhead-camshaft V-twin – one of the most famous French machines ever built. The company also made road bikes with MAG and Chaise engines.
1929 Monet Goyon (see p.281) took over and used the company's technology to create an MG-badged, all-French racer. The products of the two marques became increasingly similar especially after World War II, when Koehler Escoffier machines were two-strokes of up to 250cc using Villiers engines.
1957 The marque ended production.

LABOR
1908–60 Its earlier models used Zürcher engines. Alycon (see p.277) took over the marque in 1924.

LAMAUDIÈRE
c.1900–07 Early manufacturer of racing models, including a 942cc single. The machines were also known by the names LaMaudière-Labre and Lamaudière et Mauger.

LAMBORGHINI
1985 Using the name of the famous Italian sports car, Yves Kerlo and the Boxer company built this machine with restyled bodywork. It was based on a Kawasaki GPZ1000.

LANDRU
1899-1900 Henri-Désiré Landru was more famous as a serial killer than for his chain-driven four-stroke motorcycles.

LELOIR
1922–24 Paris-built 125cc to 175cc Train-engined two-strokes. It also produced twin-cylinder motorcycles powered by Anzani engines.

LIBERATOR
c.1900–27 Built motorcycles and tricycles using proprietary engines, including Sarolea single-cylinder and V-twin power units.

LIBERIA
1951–56 Built two-strokes up to 250cc using a variety of proprietary engines before concentrating on moped production. Made in Grenoble.

LORIOT
1927–30 Built utilitarian 250cc to 350cc two- and four-stroke motorcycles. In 1928 it built shaft-driven JAP-engined machines equipped with Bredier et Charon bolt-on gearboxes.

LA LORRAINE
1922–25 Built in an area more famous for quiche, La Lorraine used 98cc to 248cc two-stroke engines made to its own recipe.

LOUIS CLÉMENT
1920–32 Another aircraft maker who diversified after World War I with an innovative 540cc overhead-camshaft V-twin. The one-piece cylinder head covered both cylinders and a single camshaft operated the enclosed valve gear. The pressed-steel frame had a tubular rear sub-frame and front downtube. It also had pivoting leaf-sprung forks, alloy disc wheels, and an enclosed chain drive. The quality of design and construction made it an expensive machine. A 996cc version was also built, but it was making two-stroke lightweights by the 1930s.

LOUISSON
1931–33 Lightweights built in St Étienne with proprietary 74cc to 98cc two-stroke engines.

LUCER
1953–58 Used 173cc AMC four-stroke engines. Also built Aubier-Dunne- and VAP-engined two-strokes.

LUCIFER See Genial-Lucifer (p.279).

LUMEN
c.1919–25 Mounted next to the rear wheel, this 150cc overhead-valve clip-on engine was first attached to scooter-style machines.

LURQUIN-COUDERT
1899–1914 A seller of single-cylinder and V-twin engines, some water cooled, it also built complete machines.

LUTÉCE
1921–26 Built a 1000cc in-line shaft-driven twin-cylinder machine. Its sturdy duplex frame had rear suspension.

LUTETIA
c.1922–23 Built a 98cc clip-on engine to mount above the rear wheel.

MACQUET
1951–54 Produced 123cc and 174cc two-strokes.

The 1956 125cc Magnat Debon M4DL was based on a Terrot model

MAGNAT DEBON
1906 Founded by Joseph Magnat and Louis Debon in 1893, it built its first machines in 1906 with single-cylinder and V-twin proprietary engines by Moser and Moto-Rêve. It later built its own.
1924 Taken over by Terrot (see p.283), the marques' machines became identical.
1958 The last Magnat Debon was built.

MAJESTIC
1928–34 M. Roy, maker of the New Motorcycle (see right), built this odd bike with hub-centre steering and extensive bodywork. Proprietary engines, including four-cylinder power units, were used.

MANON
1902–c.1906 Made a motorized bicycle with Kratos and its own 1.5hp engines.

MANUFRANCE
1951–55 Built 125cc and 175cc two-stroke lightweights. Also built machines for the Serge (see p.283) and Hirondelle (see p.280) marques.

MANURHIN
1956–62 Built the 74cc two-stroke DKW Hobby scooter under licence.

MARC
1926–51 Built machines using LMP and JAP single-cylinder four-stroke engines.

MAROT-GARDON
1897–1901 DeDion-engined tricycles.

LA MASCOTTE
c.1924 Named after the black cat on the fuel tank, it built 125cc two-strokes.

MAZOYER
1950–54 René Mazoyer built a 500cc motocross machine.

MAZUÉ
1911–14 Mazué used its own 346cc and 496cc single-cylinder engines.

MBK
1984– A new name for Motobécane (see right). It was soon taken over by Yamaha. Still builds mopeds in France.

MERCIER
1950–62 This bicycle maker built mopeds and, later, motorcycles with Lavalette, Ydral, and other engines.

METROPOLE
c.1902–03 Built by M. Chapelle using a vertically mounted 1.5hp engine. He may have built DeDion-engined tricycles under the Acatène name.

MF
1981–82 Moto Français married a 652cc Citroën car engine to a Guzzi gearbox for this touring machine. Few were built.

MGC
1927–36 Built 250cc to 600cc Chaise- and JAP-engined machines.

MICROMOTEUR
c.1922 Built a clip-on engine.

MILLET
1887–1900 Produced tricycles and motorcycles with a five-cylinder engine.

MINISCOOT
c.1960–62 Built a 74cc folding scooter.

MOBYLETTE
1949–84 Motobécane (see right) used this name on its very successful mopeds.

MOCHET
1950–55 Built lightweight machines with 149cc Ydral two-stroke engines.

MONET GOYON
1917 Began by selling the British Wall Auto Wheel under its own name. In 1922 it probably used a Wall engine to built its own 119cc machine.
1923 Launched a 147cc Villiers-engined

machine. From 1926 it used 350cc and 500cc MAG overhead-valve engines and its own 250cc to 350cc engines.
1929 Took over Koehler Escoffier (see p.280) and used its engines to build an all-French racer. It also led to the creation of a mundane side-valve single.
1934 Began production of 98cc to 342cc Villiers engines under licence. Four-strokes were also made in the 1930s.
1945–58 Production concentrated on utilitarian Villiers-engined machines.

MONOTRACE
1926–29 Strange single-track car with retractable stabilizer wheels and 500cc water-cooled engine built under licence from the German Mauser company.

MORS (SPEED)
1951–56 Built innovative 60cc, 115cc, and 124cc Ydral-engined two-stroke scooters. Taken over by Alcyon in 1955.

MOTEURCYCLE
1921–24 Built a 206cc friction-drive clip-on two-stroke engine.

MOTO-BÉCANE
c.1906 Motorized bicycles and motorcycles built in Paris, also known by the Etoile and Amstoutz names.

MOTOBÉCANE 🏍 p.129
1923 Charles Benoit and Abel Bardin started making a cheap 172cc belt-driven two-stroke lightweight. They called it the Motobécane – "motorbike".
1925 A 308cc model was built under the Motoconfort name (see right).
1927 Made a Blackburne-engined four-stroke machine. In 1929 a 500cc side-valve in-line four was built, but, like its 750cc overhead-camshaft four successor, had little impact and few were made.
1930 Produced 175cc to 500cc unit-construction four-stroke single. V-twins, parallel twins and in-line fours of 100cc to 750cc followed. The 100cc to 175cc overhead-valve model was the most popular and was built until 1960.
1949 The 49cc two-stroke Mobylette moped appeared and sold in millions.
1964 Motorcycle production stopped.
1969 Motorcycle production restarted with 125cc two-stroke twins. Built until 1978, successful racing versions were also made. A 350cc triple was built from 1972 to 1978.
1984 Name changed to MBK (see left).

MOTOBLOC
1948–54 Built lightweights with Villiers and Aubier-Dunne engines. It also used 123cc and 248cc AMC engines. Built the Sulky scooter (see p.283).

MOTO CARDAN
1903–08 Built DeDion-engined bikes and helped pioneer shaft drive, which is sometimes called cardan drive.

MOTOCONFORT
1925–63 Motobécane (see left) used this name for its 308cc two-stroke single. Later models were sold with both badges.

MOTO MONTE
1927–38 Utilitarian two-strokes of 175cc to 250cc built in St Étienne.

MOTOPEDALE
c.1931–39 This marque used 98cc to 123cc Aubier-Dunne two-stroke engines. Also produced larger motorcycles with JAP and Python single-cylinder four-stroke engines.

MOTO PORTEUR
c.1919–23 Powered sidecar that could be attached to any bicycle.

MOTO RECORD
c.1930 Made machines with two- and four-stroke proprietary engines.

MOTOR FLY
c.1921 This two-stroke powered wheel was sometimes called the Fly-Voisin.

MOTOSOLO
1919–23 Assembled a 248cc motorcycle with a two-stroke Sicam engine.

MOTO TRACTEUR
c.1914 Made a clip-on bicycle engine.

MR
c.1934–55 Mandille et Roux produced lightweights using Sachs, Ydral, and other engines.

NARCISSE
1950–53 Made bikes to 98cc with Sachs and Aubier-Dunne two-stroke engines.

NERVOR
1947–58 Built by Radior (see p.282) using its own and AMC engines.

NEW IMPERIA
1947–58 Built 125cc to 175cc AMC-engined lightweights. One motorcycle used a frame with a forged spine and alloy side plates.

NEW MAP
1920–58 Founded in Lyon by Paul Martin, New Map used Chaise, MAG, JAP, and other engines. Its models ranged from 98cc two-strokes to 998cc V-twins. After World War II it built mopeds, scooters, and motorcycles of up to 248cc with Ydral, AMC, and Sachs two- and four-stroke engines.

NEW MOTORCYCLE
c.1925–30 Employed a 246cc Train two-stroke engine and 350cc to 500cc overhead-camshaft Chaise engines within a pressed-steel frame. Designer M. Roy also built the radical Majestic motorcycle (see left).

NINON
1928–39 Built a limited number of orthodox 100cc to 500cc motorcycles and commercial tricycles.

NOUGIER
1937–72 The Nougier brothers were Magnat Debon dealers in Avignon. They made successful hand-built racers, from 250cc singles to 500cc fours.

OLYMPIQUE
1922–54 Orthodox two-stroke bikes that used proprietary engines. The post-war models had AMC engines of 123cc to 248cc. Scooters were also made. It was part of the Alcyon group (see p.277).

OMEGA
1899 Produced a motorized bicycle.

OREOL
c.1903–14 Used its own single-cylinder as well as V-twin engines supplied by Zédel and Moto-Rêve.

ORIAL
1920–27 Built in Lyon using 750cc MAG single-cylinder engines. Orial also produced a V-twin model under the GL name (see p.279).

ORIGAN
1929–50 These orthodox 174cc to 350cc machines were built by the Guiller brothers before using their own name (see p.280).

OSA-LIBERTY
1926–35 Omer SAmin built 173cc to 246cc two-strokes and also used 350cc and 500cc single-cylinder JAP engines.

PALOMA
1954–64 Michel Humblot, the importer of the Austrian Puch, built lightweights with Gillet and Lavalette engines.

PASQUET
1932–c.1939 Made lightweights with 98cc to 123cc Aubier-Dunne engines.

PÉCOURT
1900–05 Built pioneer machines with Zédel 0.5hp and 2.5hp engines.

PERNOD
1981–83 A two-stroke 247cc Grand Prix racer paid for by the Pernod aperitif company. Jacques Bolle won the British Grand Prix on a Pernod bike in 1983.

PERNOT
1899 Used a 1.25hp engine, which was placed on a frame behind the rear wheel.

PERREAUX
1871 Louis-Guillaume Perreaux built probably the first powered two-wheeler by attaching a small steam engine to a Michaux bone-shaker bicycle.

PÉTROCYCLETTE
c.1901–07 Macquart & Cie. offered a 2hp powered bicycle.

PEUGEOT 🏍 p.155
1899 The Peugeot brothers attached a proprietary engine to one of their bicycle frames. Peugeot soon became a leading marque, making its own atmospheric-inlet-valve engine in 1903.
1906 Made 726cc V-twins, which were also sold to other makers. Later 345cc to 994cc V-twins were produced, and from 1907 it began car production.
1913 Its advanced and successful 500cc parallel-twin racers with overhead camshafts and four valves per cylinder first appeared. Post-war, an improved V-twin and a new two-stroke arrived.
1926 Made unit-construction 350cc side-valve singles. Some 175cc to 500cc singles followed. Lightweight two-strokes continued but the 500cc twin-cylinder racer was abandoned after 1927.
1949 Post-war production resumed with a range of two-strokes from mopeds and scooters to 350cc twins. The 125cc Peugeot was a big seller.
1959 Lack of profit ended motorcycle, though not moped, production.
1980 Began building 80cc motorcycles alongside the mopeds and developed a 124cc motorcycle with the Italian Gilera company. Neither project was very successful. An 80cc Honda-engined scooter sold well, and Peugeot moped and scooter production continues.

PIERTON
1922–25 Built bikes with 98cc to 498cc proprietary two- and four-stroke engines.

LA PIZE
1930–37 Built machines using engines from Aubier-Dunne, JAP, and LMP.

POPP
c.1904–06 Henri Popp & Cie. of Paris sold clip-on engines and motorcycles.

PORTAL
1977–c.1982 Built Sachs- and Rotax-engined off-road competition bikes. Portal was earlier involved in BPS (see p.278).

PP ROUSSEY
1931–56 Initially Pierre and Paul Roussey built motorcycles with 98cc to 498cc Chaise, Aubier-Dunne, and Staub engines. After World War II it made a high-tech scooter with a 170cc water-cooled two-stroke engine.

PRESTER
1930–55 Built machines from 98cc to 496cc using Chaise, Aubier-Dunne, and other engines. Merging with Jonghi (see p.280) in 1936, both marques built similar products. After World War II it built 98cc to 248cc two- and four-stroke motorcycles and a 123cc scooter.

PRESTO
1931–33 This marque produced 74cc and 98cc Sachs-engined lightweights.

QUENTIN
1904–07 An engine supplier that also built its own machines, including racers.

RADIOR
1904–55 First used Peugeot and Antoine engines. After World War I it built 98cc to 247cc two-stroke engines and fitted JAP and Chaise four-strokes of up to 500cc. From 1945 it built NSU-engined mopeds and motorcycles to 250cc with Nervor and AMC engines.

RASSER
1922–23 Made 98cc and 350cc two-strokes, some with pressed-steel frames.

RATIER
1959–62 Ratier took over CEMEC (see p.278). It made 494cc and 594cc BMW-inspired all-French flat twins, which were sold mainly to the police and army.

RAVAT
1922–54 Bicycle firm that first built a 98cc proprietary-engined lightweight. It soon made its own 175cc to 350cc two-strokes. It also fitted Chaise, Blackburne, and Zürcher engines. Later, it built VAP-, Villiers-, and Ydral-engined lightweights.

REGINA
1905–10 Built a Rochet-engined bike.

RENÉ-GILLET
1898–1957 Its first machine had its engine mounted on the front fork. The

The 125cc Portal Ranger of 1981 with a Rotax two-stroke engine

first of its famous 500cc V-twins arrived in 1904. Capacity later grew to 750cc and 1000cc. After World War II it built its own 98cc to 250cc two-strokes.

RHONSON
1952–58 Produced mopeds and 123cc lightweight motorcycles.

RHONY-X
1924–32 Built 98cc to 498cc bikes in Lyon with two- and four-stroke JAP, Chaise, LMP, and Stainless engines. It made a 490cc overhead-camshaft unit-construction Chaise-engined model.

RIVA-SPORT
c.1950s Produced 98cc AMC-engined lightweights. Built Motobloc (see p.281) and Sporting machines.

RIVIERRE
c.1898–c.1904 Gaston Rivierre made DeDion-engined bicycles, and developed radial engines and an epicyclic gearbox.

RM
1920–23 Unusual 344cc single-cylinder two-stroke that had a pressed-steel frame. Its friction-drive system had several ratios.

ROCHESTER
1923–29 Built lightweights up to 174cc.

ROCHET
1900–10 Bicycle firm that built DeDion-engined machines. It later made its own 219cc single and 654cc vertical twin.

ROLAND
c.1906 Used Rochet engines. In 1906 it offered an in-line twin with chain drive.

ROSENGART
1922–23 Made two-stroke lightweights.

ROTO SIM
1922 Built a power-wheel for bicycles.

ROVIN
1920–34 Built two-strokes of 100cc to 175cc, and a limited number of 500cc JAP-powered single-cylinder racers.

ROYAL-MOTO
1923–33 This engine supplier produced 244cc two-strokes and limited numbers of 246cc to 498cc four-strokes.

RUPTA See Deronzière (p.279).

SADEM
1951–54 Produced mopeds and lightweight motorcycles of up to 98cc.

SANCHOC
1922–24 Produced 100cc to 250cc two-strokes and 350cc side-valve machines.

SANCIOME
c.1899 Built a single-cylinder machine.

SAN-SOU-PAP
1923–36 Its 175cc to 250cc two-strokes gave San-Sou-Pap – "without valves" – its name. From 1929 it also used 250cc to 500cc JAP, MAG, Velocette, and its own four-stroke engines.

SAVARD/SAVAGE
1987–91 This successful 500cc Honda-engined bike with two-wheel drive raced in Super Motard and hillclimbing events.

SCA
c.1895–98 Société Continental d'Automobile made a motorized bicycle and a tranverse flat-twin tricycle.

SCOOTAVIA
c.1951–54 Morin built luxurious Ydral-engined two-stroke scooters that later had 175cc overhead-camshaft AMC units.

SCOTO
1949–50 Made a simple 38cc Garelli Mosquito-engined scooter.

SCYLLA
1928–37 Machines built with 98cc and 123cc Aubier-Dunne two-stroke and larger capacity Train four-stroke engines.

SEVITAME
1937–39 The Simca car company built few of these twin-cylinder two-stroke motorcycles, intended for military use.

SIC
1921–25 Made 98cc to 346cc machines powered by DKW and other engines.

SICAM
1921–22 Built a 98cc clip-on engine.

SICRAF
1947–53 Built Ydral- and AMC-engined mopeds and motorcycles of up to 246cc.

SIMARD
1951–54 This 174cc Ydral-engined scooter was built by a sidecar maker.

SMART
1922–27 Built two-stroke lightweights.

SOLEX
1946–91 Paul Mennesson designed the original, successful VéloSolex moped with its front fork-mounted engine. Taken over by Motobécane in 1974, it is still built in Hungary in huge numbers.

SOYER
1920–35 Aircraft part maker that built small-capacity two-strokes until 1928. It later built four-stroke singles with JAP, Chaise, and other engines, including its own face-cam engine.

SPADA
c.1922 Built a 190cc twin-cylinder two-stroke, scooter-style machine.

The BMW-inspired 600cc Ratier of 1962

STANDARD
c.1900 Belt-driven motorcycles built in Paris by bicycle maker A. Rogalle.

STERVA (STERLING)
c.1951–56 Built 123cc Ydral-engined scooters. It also made mopeds.

STIMULA
c.1902–14 Attached Minerva, Buchet, Peugeot, and its own engines to tricycles and motorcycles.

STYL'SON
1919–34 Machines built in St Étienne with Moser, Blackburne, and other proprietary engines and components.

SULKY
1954–57 Motobloc (see p.281) built 98cc to 124cc scooters powered by AMC engines.

SYPHAX
1952–53 Built 98cc to 174cc two- and four-stroke lightweights in Nantes.

TALBOT
1953–57 Mopeds and two-strokes of up to 125cc built by the famous car maker.

TAVERNIER
1921–23 Built 175cc to 500cc machines that used Zürcher, JAP, and other proprietary engines.

TENDIL
c.1950 Bicycle company that built 100cc to 170cc lightweights.

TERROT 🏍 .p.179
1901 Charles Terrot made bicycles and motorized quadricycles before building motorcycles with Bruneau, MAG, Zédel, and Dufaux engines. After the war Terrot also used 250cc to 500cc JAP engines and its own 173cc to 250cc two-strokes.

1927 Took over Magnat Debon and made its own four-stroke engines. **1930** A 680cc JAP-engined V-twin was followed by its own 750cc V-twin in 1934. Terrot was soon France's leading marque with a range of lightweights and excellent 175cc to 500cc racing machines. After the war it revised its 498cc overhead-valve single, which was made until 1958. It also built small two-strokes, including a 125cc scooter. The very popular 125cc and 175cc singles were built until 1962.
1954–61 Peugeot took over and moved production to its Automoto factory.

THOMANN
1914–54 Built 98cc to 248cc two-strokes. Absorbed by Alcyon (see p.277).

TITANIA
1901–03 Built a 2.5hp motorcycle.

TOTEY
1901–04 Produced a motorized bicycle.

TRACTOCYCLETTE
1906 Made a Garreau-engined bicycle.

TRAIN
1913–39 Engine supplier that built 98cc to 995cc two- and four-stroke machines.

TRÈFLE-À-QUATRE See Georges Richard (p.279).

ULTIMA
1908–58 Lyon engine maker that made a 98cc two-stroke and a 500cc V-twin.

UTILIA
1929–36 Built 100cc to 500cc two- and four-strokes with JAP and other engines.

VALLÉE
1949–54 Paul Vallée built 125cc and 175cc Ydral two-stroke scooters.

VAP

1951–early 1970s Built 48cc moped engines before making complete lightweights, some using Sachs engines.

VÉLOSTYLE

c.1952 Made scooter/moped devices with 49cc VAP and Mochet engines.

VÉLOSOLEX See Solex (p.283).

VÉLOTOURIST

1922 Built 113cc clip-on two-strokes.

VERLOR

1930–38 Radior (see p.282) built these 100cc to 125cc lightweights. Verlor used its own and Sachs engines.

VICTOIRE

c.1900 Built bikes with Zédel engines.

VILLEMAIN

c.1904–05 Built a single-cylinder bike.

VIRATELLE

1906–24 Advanced 180cc and 350cc water-cooled single-cylinder and 700cc twin-cylinder machines built in Lyon.

WERNER  p.195

1897 Michel and Eugène Werner developed a motorcycle with a 1.5hp belt-driven engine above the front wheel.
1901 A new 1.75hp engine was bolted in front of the pedals, the first to use this layout. Power grew to 2hp and 2.5hp.
1905 A 3.25 and 4hp parallel-twin engine was built.
1908 Michel died and production ended.

WILLIAM

c.1950 Built 100cc proprietary-engined bicycles and tandems in Orleans.

YVEL

1919–24 Made Villiers-engined two-strokes and JAP-engined four-strokes.

ZÉDEL

1902–15 Built single-cylinder and V-twin machines in France using the engines of its Swiss parent company.

Unconfirmed marques

Albatros *1904*
Albert-Jean *1901*
Amstoutz *1900*
Andre *c.1930*
Andru *1903*
Annino *c.1950*
Aquillon *c.1909*
Astral *1919-23*
Audax *1904*
Autocyclette *c.1899*
Automotion *c.1929*
Aviator *1906*
Axa *c.1927*
Bagys *1903*
Benjamin *c.1925*

Bertin *1955–58*
Birma *1949–late 1950s*
BJS *1930–35*
Blanche Hermine *c.1922*
Boccardo *c.1989–92*
Bon Avion *c.1927*
Bonin *c.1905*
Bonin *c.1930*
Boudier *1957*
Bouilly *1899*
Bozier *1903*
Breton *1951–54*
Brooklyn *c.1932*
Brouiller *c.1926*
Cazalex *1951–55*
Cecile *c.1899*
Centaure *c.1900–05*
Chansid *c.1913*
Charles Gerald *c.1927*
Chartier *1902*
Codridex *1952–56*
Columbia *1922–26*
Constantin *c.1900*
Corre *1901–10*
Creanche *c.1900*
Cyclocette *c.1950*
Cyclorex *c.1950*
Deckert *1903*
De Dion Bouton *1926–30*
Degre *c.1903*
Diem. *c.1950*
Doué *c.1903*
Dupuy *c.1925*
Durand *1920–23*
Duten *c.1931*
Eler *c.1950*
Elie Huin *c.1950s–c.1960s*
Elvish *c.1950*
Eriac *c.1950*
Eriol *1932–39*
Eyrant *1904*
Everest *1926*
Excelsior *1905–12*
Exshaw *1922–23*
Famocyclette *1922*
FOR *1924*

FR *1954*
France *1931–35*
Gallia-Sport *c.1930*
Gauthier-Wehrlé *1897*
GD *c.1928*
Genest *1926*
Gimbretiere *c.1951*
Givaudan *c.1902–03*
Grandiere *c.1953*
Hallot *1904*
Harding-JAP *1912–14*
Horsy *1952–53*
Jacquelin *1902*
Jog *c.1906*
Jubocette *c.1922*
Keops *c.1926*
Kervran *c.1927*
Lacombe *1948*
Laforge-Palmanthier *c.1902*
Lafour & Nougier *1927–36*
Lamblin *1910*
Latscha *1948–53*
Liaudois *1923–27*
Libertas *1902*
Lobin *1902*
Magali *1904*
Magaty *1931–37*
Magda *1933–36*
Magnier *1901*
Marant *1922*
Marmonnier *1947–51*
Max *1927–30*
Mercier *1939*
Metropole *c.1955*
MGD *1943*
Mistral *1902*
MOM *1905*
Monarque *1904*
Monoto *1929–54*
Moto-Bijou *1921–22*
Motocette *1922*
Moto Maitre *c.1926*
Motorette *1900*
Motte *c.1910*
M&P *late 1920s–late 1930s*
Myriam *c.1930*

Neva *1926–27*
Omega *c.1910*
Onoto *1922–54*
Otobirou *1921*
Pal *1905*
Pannetonc *1906*
La Pantherre *1928–32*
La Parisienne *1927*
Patimo *1947*
Pauvert *1933–c.1939*
Peregrine *c.1933*
Perraud (PAP) *c.1926*
Petit *1903*
Petit Breton *c.1926*
Phebus *c.1904*
Pierme *1926*
Pipres *c.1903*
Plasson *1921–24*
Poinard *1951–56*
La Préférée *1913*
Progrés *1901*
Propul *1923–26*
Presto *1904*
The Pretty *c.1905*
Quidet *c.1922*
Racer *1953–56*
Racing *1906*
Radiola *1933–39*
RD *c.1950*
Renouard *1904*
Rex *1900*
Ridel *c.1899*
Rivolier *1905–10*
Roés *1932–34*
Roll *1923–24*
Rovlante *1929–35*
Royal Sport *c.1929*
Ruche *1952–54*
Salvatator *c.1901*
Sauvage *c.1950*
Schneider *1902*
Scoot-Air *1953*
Scot *1953*
Sept *c.1937*
Serrus *c.1929*
Sia *1905–12*
Siccardi *1981*
Siphax *1951–56*
Socomia *1951*
Sommaire *c.1908*
Special-Monneret *1952–58*
Sphinx *1899*
Sphynx *1923*
Starnord *c.1953*
Stella *1922–53*
Strock *c.1903*
Sublime *c.1947*
Succès *1904*
Supplexa *1922–32*
Suzy *1932–33*
Svelte *1935*
Teddy *1922–24*
Tortue *1900*
Trilby *1904*
Tungnaud-Cavellier *1902*
Turgan-Foy *1900*
L'Universel *1901*
Vallièrre *1903*
Velox *1904*
Vierge *1900*
D'Yrsan *1925*

The 49cc two-stroke S3300 VéloSolex, sold as "The bicycle which runs by itself"

Japan

Before World War II Japan had no significant motorcycle industry, but in the chaos that followed, there was a huge demand for inexpensive personal transportation. Small workshops began producing low-cost, but crude motorized bicycles using simple engines. Soon, a few efficient companies such as Honda (see below), and Suzuki (see p.287) emerged as producers of proper motorcycles. Other companies diversified into motorcycle production, and some, including musical instrument makers Yamaha (see p.287), and the aircraft- and boat-building Kawasaki group (see pp.285–86), prospered. Competition on the domestic market was fierce, which resulted in a superb product. The industry grew at a phenomenal rate and accelerated when exports began in the late 1950s. Japanese motorcycles became established as reliable, clean, and fun to ride. By the 1960s Honda was the biggest manufacturer in the world. It still is. Since 1974 Japanese producers have dominated the world market.

ABE-STAR
1949–55 Abe-Star produced high-quality, costly machines, which never achieved mass production. The main product was a 142cc four-stroke single followed in 1954 by a 338cc overhead-valve V-twin with strange, four-leg telescopic forks.

AUTO-BIT
1952–62 Built 125cc and 250cc four-stroke machines. The 249cc overhead-valve single-cylinder SS model, which appeared in 1959, featured electric starting and adjustable rear suspension.

BRIDGESTONE p.34
1953–67 Bridgestone built bicycles with cast-alloy frames and from 1953 also supplied clip-on two-stroke bicycle engines. Its first complete mopeds were produced in 1958, and lightweight motorcycles followed in the early 1960s. Bridgestone exploited the benefits of the rotary disc valve to produce a range of high-quality two-strokes from 88cc singles to 348cc twins. Bridgestone achieved a reputation for excellent performance and high build quality. Its motorcycles were exported, but never in the same quantities as bikes produced by the big four Japanese manufacturers. Production stopped in 1967 and Bridgestone concentrated on making motorcycle tyres, which it supplied to other Japanese motorcycle makers.

CABTON
1935–60 Cabton motorcycles were built in Osaka by Koushiro Nakagawa and his son. The company's name is derived from the catchy slogan "Come And Buy To Osaka Nakagawa". The first machines were 346cc overhead-valve singles copied from the British Ariel. In 1946 Cabton produced a clip-on two-stroke bicycle engine and by the mid-1950s it built a range of 250cc to 600cc overhead-valve singles and twins. These machines had tubular frames with plunger rear suspension and telescopic forks. The engine design was heavily influenced by Indian's unsuccessful range of vertical-singles and twins. Small-capacity machines were marketed under the Mizuho name (see p.286). During the mid-1950s Cabton was the fourth largest motorcycle producer in Japan, but it was bankrupt by 1960.

DNB
1957–c.1962 DNB machines, simple, single-cylinder two-strokes of 125cc and 250cc, were built by Fuji Motor and also sold under that name (see right).

DSK
1954–62 The Daito Seiki company made machines for making socks. It also produced a 247cc shaft-driven single-cylinder BMW R25 clone.

ECHO
1958–60 50cc two-stroke built by Tosyo, a joint venture by Showa (see p.287) and Tohatsu (see p.287). They also produced the Pandra (see p.286).

EMURO
1957–58 Short-lived company that produced two-stroke machines. Models ranged from 90cc singles to a 494cc twin, which was made by doubling up the firm's 248cc single.

FUJI KOGYO
1946–68 Fuji Kogyo was the maker of Rabbit scooters (see p.286) and Hurricane motorcycles (see right). It was an aircraft company that diversified into motorcycle manufacturing after World War II. It subsequently changed its name to Fuji Heavy Industries – not to be confused with Fuji Motors Corporation, makers of the DNB motorcycle (see left).

FUJI MOTOR See DNB (left).

HIRANO
1952–61 Hirano built a range of 60cc to 165cc two-stroke scooters under the Pop name (see p.286). It also produced a 121cc motorcycle and built the French-designed 49cc Valmobile folding scooter under licence.

HODAKA p.84
1964–78 Hodaka supplied engines to the Yamaguchi (see p.287) marque and built complete motorcycles after Yamaguchi collapsed in 1963. These were developed and sold in the U.S.A. by the Pacific Basin Trading Co. (PABATCO). Hodakas were not sold on the Japanese market. The motorcycles were excellent 100cc and 125cc two-stroke singles that were mainly for off-road use. A 250cc model was available from 1975, but the company did not last much longer.

HONDA pp.85–95
1948 Soichiro Honda started making motorcycles by bolting army surplus engines into bicycle frames. By 1960 Honda was the largest motorcycle-manufacturing company in the world. The first machines were followed by 50cc bicycle-style machines with Honda-designed two-stroke engines. In 1949 a proper motorcycle with a 98cc two-stroke engine and pressed-steel frame was produced. It was called the Dream.
1953 Honda built its first four-stroke. The model range expanded to include motorcycles of up to 250cc, as well as scooters and mopeds.
1958 It introduced the Super Cub. Over 20 million have been built since and its derivatives are still in production.
1959 Honda began to export motorcycles to the West and its international racing career started. By the end of 1967 Honda had won 17 World Championships, and it quit racing. Honda promoted a clean, fun image of motorcycling and offered reliable bikes with electric starters and other novel features. Car production began in 1963.
1969 Introduction of the Honda CB750, the first mass-produced four-cylinder motorcycle. It was also the first to have disc brakes and one of few large-capacity machines with an electric starter. It was an enormous success and was followed by smaller versions. Honda continued to dominate the market for utilitarian machines. Since 1969 there have been numerous new models and innumerable competition wins in all classes.
1974 The 1000cc flat-four water-cooled Gold Wing was introduced. In 1981 production of the Gold Wing was moved to Honda's factory in the U.S. The capacity of the machine was later increased to 1500cc with the addition of another pair of cylinders.
1983 While other manufacturers accepted the across-the-frame four as the standard superbike layout, Honda introduced new V4 designs. These were never as successful as the in-line four, although 750cc versions are still in production and are the basis of Honda's superbike racing machines. In the 1990s Honda is still the largest and most successful manufacturer in the world. Soichiro Honda died in 1992.

HOSK
1953–57 A range of motorcycles produced by the aptly named Nippon Kousoku Kikan – "Japanese Highspeed Organization". The first machines, 196cc and 235cc four-stroke singles, were followed by 123cc and 143cc split-single two-strokes. There were also 350cc and 500cc four-stroke singles and twins. The bikes were given grandiose names such as Hosk Road King and Road Queen. Production did not last long.

HURRICANE
1953–68 The Hurricane was a British-style machine made by Fuji Heavy Industries – formerly Fuji Kogyo (see left). The engine was a 346cc overhead-valve single.

KATAKURA
1958–c.1962 Katakura built 120cc to 200cc two-stroke singles and twins.

KAWASAKI pp.111–117
1960 Kawasaki supplied engines to Meihatsu (see p.286) before starting production of its own machines. It is a huge company that builds aircraft, ships, industrial robots, and more; but it is the smallest of the "Big Four" Japanese motorcycle manufacturers. The first Kawasaki-badged machines were 50cc two-strokes followed by 125cc two-stroke singles and twins.
1964 Kawasaki acquired the Meguro marque (see p.286) and its British-inspired 650cc twins became the first large-capacity Kawasaki machines.
1965 Kawasaki began exporting machines to the U.S.
1969 The introduction of new three-cylinder two-strokes established Kawasaki's sporting reputation. By the mid-1970s the triples were available in

250cc to 750cc versions, but restrictive U.S. emissions legislation killed off the performance two-stroke road bike and alternative machines had to be developed.

1972 Introduced the 903cc four-cylinder Kawasaki Z1. It replaced the Honda 750 as top superbike. The eight-valve air-cooled four-cylinder engine was eventually produced in various sizes from 400cc to 1100cc. Some models used shaft drive. Derivatives of the Z1 are still in production.

1984 Kawasaki introduced the GPZ900R. The sixteen-valve water-cooled machine represented the next stage in superbike development and re-affirmed Kawasaki as the choice of enthusiasts. Unlike other Japanese manufacturers, Kawasaki never took much interest in the market for utility motorcycles.

LILAC

1949–67 Shaft-driven motorcycles built by the Marusho Co. (see below) using the Lilac brand-name. Early models were 148cc four-stroke single-cylinder machines with two-speed gearbox and pressed-steel frames. Later models had tubular frames and Earles forks, and some had automatic transmission. The baby Lilac, a 90cc overhead-valve machine with shaft drive, was launched in 1953. It was a huge commercial success. The firm's first horizontally opposed twin was a 339cc machine made in 1954. A 247cc V-twin with a duplex cradle frame was launched in 1959, followed by 288cc versions. In 1964 a new 493cc horizontally opposed BMW-style twin was produced. It was sold in the U.S. under the Marusho name but was not a success.

LINER

1955–56 The Liner was built by Kitagawa, who also produced the Portly-Robbin motorcycle (see right). A 247cc in-line four-stroke twin with shaft drive, the design was a scaled-down copy of the British Sunbeam S7 (see p.174).

MARTIN

1953–c.1961 Martin built 125cc to 199cc two-stroke singles. It was the first Japanese manufacturer to use swingarm rear suspension.

MARUSHO

1964–67 Masashi Ito's Marusho company built shaft-driven motorcycles under the Lilac brand-name (see above) from 1949 to 1967. The Lilac R92 was exported to the U.S. as the Marusho Magnum. It was a 493cc horizontally opposed BMW-style twin-cylinder motorcycle. The model was dogged by awful build quality and poor design detail. Fewer than 1,000 machines were built.

MEGURO

1937–64 Meguro was founded in 1924 to make components for motorcycles and cars. Its first complete motorcycle was the 500cc four-stroke single-cylinder Z-97 model of 1937. After the war it built a range of British-style, overhead-valve single-cylinder and parallel-twin machines of 248cc to 651cc. From 1957 Meguro also produced a 125cc lightweight. The four-stroke twins were based on the BSA A10 design. Meguro was taken over by Kawasaki (see p.285) in 1961, and 248cc and 651cc models were briefly sold under the Kawasaki label.

MEIHATSU

1953–61 Meihatsu made 58cc to 247cc two-stroke singles and twins equipped with Kawasaki engines. Production stopped when Kawasaki started to produce machines under its own brand-name.

MIYATA

1913–63 Still a famous bicycle manufacturer, Miyata started as a gun maker and built its first bicycles around 1892. Its first prototype motorcycle was a 175cc two-stroke based on the design of the Baby Triumph. Full production did not begin until 1933 when the 250cc four-stroke Asahi – "Sun Rise" – model was introduced. This was followed by a 171cc two-stroke model in 1935. The 350cc single-cylinder overhead-valve JA-350 model appeared in 1956 and was heavily based on the German Horex Regina design. Mopeds, scooters, and a 125cc twin-cylinder two-stroke motorcycle were launched in the late 1950s and early 1960s. The company decided to quit motorcycle production in 1963 to concentrate once again on the manufacture of bicycles.

MIZUHO

c.1934–56 The maker of the larger capacity Cabton (see p.285) motorcycle also produced 125cc to 250cc machines under the Mizuho trademark.

MONARCH

1952–57 Small company founded by Fusao Nomura and Fujio Murata. It produced sporting machines that were successful in early Japanese motorcycle races. The first machines used the 142cc Meguro engine and were sold as Pony-Monarch (see right). In 1954 it introduced a 230cc overhead-valve single based on the design of the high-camshaft overhead-valve Velocette single. The capacity of the machines was later increased to 246cc.

NISSAN

1954 Nissan, an internationally renowned car manufacturer, briefly built 60cc overhead-valve lightweights.

OLYMPUS-KING

1956–62 Olympus-King built a range of machines that had an obvious German influence. Early machines were 250cc to 350cc four-stroke singles, some with Earles forks. Later models were 123cc two-stroke single-cylinder and 246cc two-stroke twin-cylinder motorcycles, with horizontal cylinders, pressed-steel frames, and telescopic forks.

PANDRA

1958–60 The Pandra was a 123cc two-stroke scooter with Cadillac styling. It was built by Tosyo, who also produced the Echo (see p.285).

POINTER

1947–63 The Shin-Meiwa company first made 56cc two-stroke clip-on bicycle engines. In 1949 it produced a 146cc

four-stroke engine that was mounted on a frame supplied by Osaka-Sankyo and was sold under the Pointer name. In 1953 the firm produced a complete machine with a 248cc four-stroke engine. It was the first of a range of machines of up to 250cc, which were produced until 1963 when motorcycle production ended. In the 1960s, 90cc and 155cc two-strokes with pressed-steel frames and leading-link forks were produced. Some of these machines were exported to the U.S.

PONY-MONARCH

1951–55 Pony-Monarch was the name used on the 142cc overhead-valve Meguro-engined machines built by Monarch (see left).

POP/POPMANLEE

1953–61 Built by Hirano (see p.285), the Pop models were 60cc to 161cc two-stroke scooters.

PORTLY-ROBBIN

1950–56 The Portly-Robbin was built by frame maker Kitagawa, using a 140cc engine supplied by Fuji Kogyo. The machine sold sufficiently well to finance the development of the Liner motorcycle (see left) by the same company.

RABBIT

1946–68 Rabbit scooters were built by Fuji Heavy Industries (see Fuji Kogyo p.285) when it diversified from aircraft production after World War II. The early Rabbit, the first Japanese scooter, was a crude device similar in appearance to pre-war American scooters. It was powered by a 135cc four-stroke engine. Styling and finish improved and engine power increased over the following years. By 1957 its top model was the 250cc Superflow with electric starter, automatic transmission, and a raft of other gizmos. Styling was typical period pastiche. There were also lightweight machines from 50cc. Large-wheel step-thrus were built in the 1960s to compete with Honda's Cub.

RIKUO

1935–62 The Sankyo pharmaceutical company began importing Harley-Davidson motorcycles to Japan in 1920 and subsequently obtained a licence to produce them in Japan. The first Rikuo – "King of the Land" – was built in 1935. The company continued to built Harley-Davidson-inspired side-valve and overhead-valve V-twins of 750cc to 1200cc until production ended in 1962. During World War II machines were supplied to the Japanese military, including outfits with a driven sidecar wheel. Inspired by BMW machines, the company also produced 248cc and 348cc overhead-valve shaft-driven single-cylinder models from 1953.

MF-39 **Type 300c.c.** (Sport Type)

The MF-39 Lilac with a 288cc V-twin engine and shaft drive

SANYO

1953–c.1960 Small manufacturer that produced a 150cc four-stroke single. A 248cc overhead-valve machine was produced from 1957.

SHOWA

1948–60 Bicycle and office equipment company that may have produced a moped with a German Sachs engine during the 1930s. In 1948 it began making clip-on two-stroke engines. The following year it produced a complete 100cc two-stroke machine. Later, 150cc to 250cc four-strokes were also introduced. In 1959 arrived a new 246cc two-stroke single with pressed-steel frame, Earles forks, and typically bizarre Japanese styling. The following year it launched a new 125cc two-stroke machine, but the company was taken over by Yamaha (see right). The name is still used by a supplier of motorcycle suspension components.

SILVER PIGEON

1946–64 Aircraft makers Mitsubishi made the typical move into scooter production after the war. Its Silver Pigeon range was the main Japanese opposition to Fuji's Rabbit scooters. A variety of two- and four-stroke machines of 115cc to 210cc were produced. Early models were inspired by the pre-war Salsbury from the United States while later versions took their styling inspiration from Lambretta. They were imported in the U.S. by Rockford and also sold by Montgomery Ward under its Riverside badge (see p.274).

SUMITA

1953–55 90cc to 250cc four-strokes built in Simta, Tokyo.

SUZUKI 🏍 pp.174–178

1952 An established manufacturer of weaving machinery, Suzuki's first motorcycle was a bicycle with a 36cc two-stroke engine. The rear wheel was driven by belt. Adequate performance and reliability combined with the demand for cheap transportation in post-war Japan made it a success. Capacity was later increased to 58cc.

1955 Suzuki produced its first real motorcycle, a 100cc two-speed machine with telescopic forks. Plunger rear suspension was an optional extra. In 1956 an improved 125cc model appeared, followed by a 250cc two-stroke single in 1957. In 1958 Suzuki began mass production and in 1959 a 125cc twin-cylinder two-stroke and a new moped were launched.

1960 The first Suzukis appeared in the West at the Isle of Man TT races. Records did not fall. Exports to Europe began in 1961, and the United States got 50cc to 250cc machines in 1962. Racing success was achieved by luring East German rider Ernst Degner to defect to the West in 1961. He brought MZ's two-stroke tuning secrets with him. By the end of 1968 Suzuki had won seven 50cc and 125cc World Championships.

1965 The X-6 Hustler was launched. It was a 250cc two-stroke parallel twin and had a six-speed gearbox and automatic lubrication system. It was the first Suzuki designed primarily for Western market and its performance made it a hit. A range of twin-cylinder, two-stroke road bikes of 125cc to 500cc followed. In 1967 Suzuki was the first Japanese marque to build serious motocross machines. Three years later it won its first motocross World Championship.

1971 The GT750 was Suzuki's answer to Honda's 750 four and an attempt to break into the big bike market. It also built 380cc and 550cc triples but only the biggest version had water cooling. Successful racing versions of the 750cc triple were also produced. U.S. pollution restrictions meant that the days of large-capacity two-stroke road bikes were numbered. Suzuki also developed a Wankel rotary-engined machine, but it did not sell well. The company returned to Grand Prix racing with the twin-crankshaft square-four RG500 in 1974. Subsequently it won the 500cc World Championship in 1976, 1977, 1980, and 1981.

1976 Suzuki unveiled its first four-stroke. The GS 750 was a double overhead-camshaft four-cylinder Kawasaki-inspired machine. A 398cc twin and a 997cc four followed. In 1979 Suzuki adopted a four-valves-per-cylinder layout on its four-stroke range.

1985 The oil-cooled and alloy-framed GSX-R750 was introduced. It was the first of a new breed of race replica road bikes, which eventually became available in sizes from 250cc to 1100cc. Water cooling was added in 1991. Like the remaining Japanese manufacturers, Suzuki now produces a range of machines from mopeds to megabikes.

TOHATSU

1950–66 The first motorcyles offered by TOkyo HATSUdoki – "Tokyo Engine Factory" – were bicycles equipped with 48cc two-stroke engines and belt final drive. A range of two-stroke motorcycles and mopeds followed. This included a 123cc single based on the much-copied DKW RT125. Small-capacity racers were also made, including 50cc and 125cc twins. Tohatsu still exists as a maker of marine two-stroke pumps.

TOYO MOTOR

1949–59 Toyo Motor was the third best-selling motorcycle in Japan in 1952. The machine was a motorized bicycle. Proper motorcycles with front and rear suspension and an 88cc engine were produced from 1955. The following year 124cc single-cylinder two-stroke models appeared. Later there was a 200cc version with enclosed chain and pressed-steel leading-link forks.

TSUBASA

1955–60 Tsubasa, the makers of Daihatsu cars, built 246cc to 345cc overhead-valve singles and after 1958, a 125cc two-stroke single.

YAMAGUCHI

1955–63 A bicycle manufacturer that built 50cc to 125cc two-stroke mopeds and lightweight motorcycles. The 1960 125cc Super Twin was inspired by the Ariel leader. Hodaka engines were used from 1962, and when Yamaguchi shut down, Hodaka (see p.285) began production of complete machines.

YAMAHA 🏍 pp.200–206

1954– Musical instrument maker that diversified into motorcycle production. Its first machines were copies of the DKW RT125. In 1957 a 250cc twin was introduced. This design was based on the Adler MB250. It was the first in a series of excellent, two-stroke twins of up to 398cc, which are still being made.

1960 Yamaha began exporting machines to the U.S. Specialized racing models were also developed, and Yamaha competed in its first TT in 1961. By the end of the decade it had won five World Championships. During the 1970s and 1980s it was even more successful. Yamaha production racing machines amassed numerous wins.

1969 Yamaha's first four-stroke was introduced. The XS1 was a conservative 654cc overhead-camshaft parallel twin. A variety of 250cc to 750cc twins followed as Yamaha moved away from its reliance on the two-stroke. Increased involvement in off-road competition led to the development of single-shock rear suspension systems and a range of two- and four-stroke trail bikes.

1977 The XS750, a three-cylinder shaft-driven double overhead-camshaft bike, was the first of a new generation of four-strokes. Four-cylinder machines of 550cc to 1100cc followed, emphasizing a further shift from the two-stroke. Four-stroke V-twins first appeared in 1982.

1984 Based on its Grand Prix technology, Yamaha produced the ultimate road-going two-stroke. It was a 500cc twin-crank V-four. Restrictive legislation and advancing four-stroke technology killed it. Now most Yamaha road bikes are four-strokes.

1985 Another new range of four-strokes was launched with the water-cooled four-cylinder twenty-valve FZ750. Yamaha now produces a huge variety of machines at factories in Japan and the rest of the world.

Unconfirmed Marques

Asahi *c.1953–65*
BIM *c.1956–61*
Center *c.1950–62*
Cruiser
Gasden
Happy
Hope Star
IMC
Jet
Kanto *c.1957–60*
Lancer *1957–early 1960s*
Marine
Mikasa (Baby Twin)
Mishima
NMC *1950s–1960s*
Omega *1960s*
Pearl
Popet *1957–early 1960s*
Queen Bee
Rotary *early 1950s–1961*
Shin Meiwa *1950s–1960s*
Silver Star *1953–58*
SJK *1956–early 1960s*
Taiyo

1962 Tohatsu brochure shows 125cc Sport model

Rest of the World

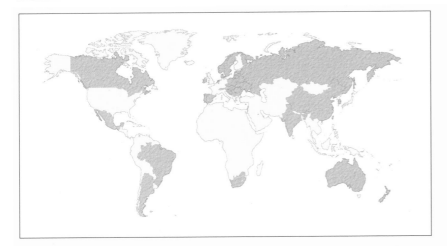

EARLY MANUFACTURERS THAT WERE NOT in large markets found it hard to get established and were often reliant on components from stronger motorcycle-producing countries. Fluctuating markets have made small companies vulnerable and led to the demise of many established firms and the emergence of new makers. While few manufacturers survive in Spain, Austria, and Scandinavia, the rapidly expanding industries in Asia, India, and South America have created a vast number of machines to satisfy the demand. Many of the new manufacturers build machines under licence from European and Japanese companies, while others make bikes to their own designs.

Spain

ALEU
1953–56 Barcelona company that made 198cc and 247cc two-stroke singles.

ALFER
1980– This company produces mainly off-road competition machines using Rotax power units.

AMS
1954–65 Built in Malaga using 124cc to 248cc Hispano-Villiers engines.

ARC
1954–56 Few were made of this 123cc Hispano-Villiers-engined bike.

AVELLO
1960– Avello originally built small-capacity MV Agusta machines (see p.262) under licence from MV, and its own 49cc two-stroke, switching to Puch-based machines in 1970. In 1987 Avello linked up with Suzuki to produce small-capacity Suzuki bikes. It also distributes the larger Suzuki models in Spain.

BJR
1953–61 Made 123cc and 174cc unit-construction two-stroke singles. A 175cc overhead-valve single was also built.

BULTACO p.41
1958 Founded by Francisco Bulto after he left Montesa (see right), Bultaco produced 124cc single-cylinder two-stroke road and racing bikes.
1964 The Sherpa trials bike, developed by Sammy Miller, achieved worldwide success ending with five straight wins in the World Trials Championship between 1975 and 1979. Motocross and enduro machines of 125cc and 370cc were exported, while road bikes sold in Spain.
1976 Bultaco returned to Grand Prix racing with 50cc and 125cc bikes based on Piovaticci designs. It won the 50cc world title in 1976, 1978, and 1981.
1979 Production ended due to market decline and industrial unrest. Re-opened in 1980 but had shut for good by 1983.

CLUA
1952–64 Built Italian Alpinos (see p.252), 74cc and 123cc two-strokes, and an overhead-valve single in Barcelona.

COBAS
1982– Antonio Cobas, a specialist constructor, led race bike chassis design in the 1980s with his alloy twin-spar frame. A Rotax-powered Cobas won the 125cc World Championship in 1989.

CORONAT
c.1952 Advanced, 200cc overhead-valve single-cylinder machine. Few were made.

DERBI p.47
1949– Derbi (DERivados de BIcicletus), an established bicycle company, began building 48cc two-stroke mopeds. In 1950 it made a 250cc two-stroke single. A range of mopeds and motorcycles of up to 350cc was built during the 1950s. It now concentrates on mopeds, but some road and off-road motorcycles were built in the late 1970s and early 1980s. Its racers have won several World Championships.

DUCATI
1957–82 Mototrans (see p.289) built 125cc to 350cc overhead-camshaft single-cylinder Ducatis under licence from the Italian parent company. It also made small-capacity two-strokes.

DUCSON
c.1950–80 Ducson was a successful maker of mopeds, 49cc and 65cc motorcycles, and also 50cc racers in Barcelona.

EDETA
1951–60 Edeta built a limited number of 147cc and 173cc two-strokes.

ELIG
1956–59 Made a limited number of machines using Hispano-Villiers engines.

EVYSCA
1956 Evysca built a few 173cc unit-construction overhead-valve machines.

GAS GAS
1986– Rising from the ashes of the Merlin marque (see right), Gas Gas specializes in competitive off-road bikes for trials and enduro use with its own, TM, and Cagiva power units.

GIMSON
c.1956–64 Bicycle manufacturer that also built mopeds and 65cc motorcycles.
1977–86 Again produced mopeds and 50cc bikes but its revival was short-lived.

IRUNA
c.1953–59 Iruna built two-stroke scooters, using its own 123cc engine.

KOBAS See Cobas (see left).

LUBE
1949–65 Based in Bilbao, Lube used two- and four-stroke German NSU engines of 49cc to 247cc in its pressed-steel frames. On NSU's demise in 1963 it briefly built its own two-stroke engines.

LUTETIA
c.1927 Lutetia built a limited number of 172cc diamond-framed Villiers-engined lightweights.

MAVISA
1957–60 Built a 248cc two-stroke twin.

MECATECNO
c.1982– Builds trials machines and children's minibikes.

MERLIN
1982–86 Specialized in trial machines using 347cc Cagiva two-stroke engines. Partly founded by Ignacio Bulto, son of Francisco Bulto, the founder of Bultaco.

MONFORT
1957–59 Limited run of 123cc to 197cc machines using Hispano-Villiers engines.

MONTESA p.127
1945 Founded in Barcelona by Francisco Bulto and Pedro Permanyer, Montesa's first motorcycle was a 98cc two-stroke. A 125cc model followed in 1946. By the end of the 1940s, Montesa was competing internationally.

A 1955 Derbi 350cc two-stroke twin

1958 Bulto left to set up the Bultaco marque. Production of lightweight two-stroke machines continued.
1962 The 175cc Impala, one of the most successful and enduring Spanish bikes, was introduced. With its all-new engine, a racing and a 250cc version were built. Trials and motocross machines were also developed. Montesa exported competition machines of 123cc to 349cc in the 1970s. The company also produced road bikes of 49cc to 349cc, until the industry collapsed at the end of the decade.
1981 The Impala was successfully reintroduced, yet Montesa was still taken over by Honda. It now assembles Honda mopeds but still makes the famous Cota trials machine.

MOTOBIC
1949–65 Motobic built mopeds and 122cc Hispano-Villiers-powered two-stroke lightweights. From 1963 it built 98cc Italian Agrati Capri scooters under licence and a 98cc motorcycle.

MOTO HISPANIA
1951– Once built small-capacity Moto Guzzis, it now makes its own mopeds.

MOTOTRANS
1978–82 Built Ducati machines (see p.288) under licence from 1957. In 1978 it introduced its own 410cc overhead-camshaft single-cylinder trail bike, which it sold under its MTV badge. Later it also sold Zündapp-powered two-strokes under the MTV badge.

MYMSA
c.1955–62 Built 75cc to 175cc two-stroke machines in Barcelona.

NARCLA
1955–67 Gerona-built 123cc two-stroke single sold in Touring and Sport models.

OSSA
1949 Motorcycle enthusiast Manuel Giro owned a company that made film projectors (Orpheo Sincronia SA). The Ossa logo shows a version of the Geneva Escarpment mechanism used in moving film cameras and projectors. Its first bike was a 124cc two-stroke single. Mopeds were built from 1951. It made its only four-stroke, a 172cc overhead-valve machine, from 1958 to 1963.
1962 A 159cc machine, designed by Manuel's son Eduardo, was introduced. As capacity grew to 175cc and 230cc, it powered most Ossas for 20 years. Ossa developed and heavily exported off-road competition bikes from the late 1960s.
1967 A 249cc disc-valve two-stroke racer was developed. The U.S. importer of Ossa bikes requested a 461cc twin model which was created by doubling up a 230cc single. Not on sale until 1972 the twin failed to sell well, although it was made until 1982. A 976cc four-cylinder prototype was also built but proved too powerful for the early-1970s frame and tyre technology. Ossa continued successfully in motocross and trials, but life became difficult in post-Franco Spain. Despite new street and off-road models using 244cc to 302cc engines, Ossa did not survive the era.
1984 Ossa, replaced by a workers' co-operative, lasted for only one more year.

PONY
1952–54 Pony machines were powered by a 123cc Hispano-Villiers engine.

REDDIS
1957–60 Built in Reus, south of Barcelona, it used Hispano-Villiers engines in its limited production.

RIEJU
1952– Its models included 124cc and 174cc overhead-valve AMC-powered machines. It now concentrates on 49cc to 74cc mopeds and lightweights.

ROA
1952–63 Built in Madrid using 197cc to 325cc Hispano-Villiers engines.

ROVENA
1963–68 Sold under the Rovena name, this range of two-strokes was built by Sanglas (see below) using twin-cylinder 249cc and 323cc Hispano-Villiers engines with conventional cycle parts.

RUTER
1957–60 Built at Figueras using 98cc and 124cc Hispano-Villiers engines.

SADRIAN
1956–63 Sadrian produced 123cc and 197cc machines powered by Hispano-Villiers engines.

SANGLAS
1942 Built heavyweight 295cc to 497cc unit-construction overhead-valve four-stroke singles, mostly for the Spanish police.
1962 Began building lightweight two-strokes with Zündapp and Hispano-Villiers engines of 49cc to 325cc under the Rovena name (see above). When two-stroke production stopped in 1968, it gradually developed a single. Limited numbers were exported in the 1970s.
1978 Produced a parallel-twin cylinder bike with a 392cc Yamaha engine.
1981 Yamaha took over completely, and the Sanglas name was dropped.

SERVETA
1973– Builds Lambretta scooters under licence in Bilbao. It had previously made 49cc mopeds and motorcycles.

SETTER
1954–56 Setter built 60cc lightweights.

TORROT
1960–85 Once a subsidiary of the French Terrot company (see p.283), it later concentrated on mopeds.

VILLOF
1951–61 Villof built 75cc to 125cc lightweight two-strokes using Hispano-Villiers and its own engines.

Unconfirmed marques

BH *1956–60*
Cofersa *c.1953–60*
Darlan
Gorrion *1952–55*
Huracan *1957–59*
Iresa *1956–59*
Movesa *1952–62*

Portugal

CASAL
1964– Built industrial engines before making mopeds, scooters, and Zündapp-derived two-stroke lightweights of up to 125cc. A 250cc bike was also made.

EFS
c.1967–79 Casal- and Sachs-powered lightweights. A 125cc Puch-engined machine was made in the late 1970s.

FAMEL
c.1960– It builds specialized small-capacity bikes. A 49cc DKW engine was used in a pressed-steel and tubular frame in early models. It now builds Zündapp-derived two-strokes and mopeds.

FORVEL
c.1977–82 Used 125cc Hodaka engines before switching to small-capacity Casal-powered road and off-road machines.

SIS
c.1950– Bicycle maker that makes mopeds and 49cc to 98cc Sachs-powered two-stroke lightweights, sold briefly in Germany under the Horex label.

Unconfirmed marques

Macal Husquevarna
Motali
Pachancho

A 1976 Ossa Pioneer enduro bike with a 310cc engine

Austria

ALFA-GNOM
1926–28 Franz and Anton Rumpler built a limited number of 594cc overhead-camshaft singles. They also produced JAP-engined FAR motorcycles.

ALKO
1927–30 ALois KOuril built motorcycles in Vienna. He used single-cylinder and V-twin JAP and MAG engines, but most other components were made in-house.

AUSTRIA
c.1903–07 Austria made a two-stroke clip-on bicycle engine, which mounted above the belt-driven front wheel. Later the engine moved behind the steering head and the drive was taken by belt to the rear wheel.

AUSTRIA
1930–33 The Austria firm was founded by H. Hauler – formerly the H of DSH (see right) – and K. Lamberts. Early models were based on the German Ardie design and used alloy frames and 246cc to 347cc engines from JAP, Villiers, Blackburne, and Sturmey-Archer.

AUSTRIA-ALPHA
1935–52 Before World War II Josef Illichmann built a limited number of innovative racing motorcycles. A 250cc

to 350cc V-twin engine with a single shaft-driven overhead camshaft was used. In 1950 he produced a new range using Puch and Ilo two-stroke engines. They were good machines that were too expensive to sell in large numbers.

AUSTRO-ILO
1938 Austro-Ilo briefly produced lightweight machines with Ilo two-stroke engines.

AUSTRO-MOTORETTE
c.1922–27 This bicycle maker from Graz offered a 72cc and 82cc clip-on two-stroke engine. It mounted beside the front wheel on a braced front fork. This engine was doubled up to produce a lightweight motorcycle with a 144cc parallel-twin engine, which was first produced in 1925. Production was short-lived, but led to the development of the Titan motorcycle (see p.292).

AUSTRO-OMEGA
1931–38 The Austro-Omega was created by Josef Pruckner from the remains of the York marque (see p.292). He also made sidecars. The motorcycles were made from British components, including 348cc to 1150cc JAP and Sturmey Archer engines, mounted on Pruckner's own frames. Production of sidecars continued after World War II.

BARTISCH
1926–28 Franz Bartisch developed advanced 348cc and 498cc overhead-

camshaft single-cylinder engines. A very limited number of complete machines were produced.

BISON
1924–26 Bison built Douglas-style, fore-and-aft flat-twins using engines of 298cc to 688cc, supplied by Bosch-Douglas, BMW, and Coventry-Victor. Chain or belt final drive was used with a British-made three-speed gearbox.

BOCK & HOLLÄNDER
1904–11 Built cars before making belt-driven single-cylinder motorcycles. It adopted the "new" Werner layout with the engine bolted into position between the bottom bracket and the front downtube. In 1905 a four-cylinder two-speed machine with shaft drive was produced.

BOP
c.1923–24 Hans Bostik built a small number of machines using a 196cc overhead-valve Paqué engine with unit-construction two-speed gearbox. A duplex cradle frame was used.

BRÉE
c.1902–04 Theodore Brée fitted lightweight 1.5hp two-stroke engines into bicycle-style frames.

CLESS & PLESSING
c.1903–06 Graz-based firm that built motorcycles using its own 2.25hp to 3hp single-cylinder and V-twin, automatic-

inlet-valve engines with belt drive. They were sometimes known by the Noricum brand-name (see p.291).

COLIBRI
1952–54 Colibri built a few scooters with DKW engines.

DEGEN
1924–38 Franz Degen built a limited number of motorcycles, using Villiers and JAP engines, before switching to bicycle manufacturing.

DELTA-GNOM
1923–28 Began production of a 123cc clip-on bicycle engine. It was enlarged to 170cc the following year to power a lightweight, belt-driven motorcycle with a loop frame. A 248cc two-stroke was launched in 1925, which used front and rear drum brakes. Its first four-strokes were built in 1926 using JAP engines. The next year it began to make its own 498cc overhead-valve single. Production was stopped in 1928 because of the country's economic collapse.
1932–38 Resumed production with updated versions of the earlier machines. In 1935 it stopped producing its own engines and relied on JAP power units of up to 600cc.
1953–c.1963 After World War II it made mopeds and lightweight motorcycles of 98cc to 175cc using Rotax and Ilo engines.

DSH
1924–32 Döller, Seidl, and Hauler imported Humber motorcycles into Austria, as well as making its own quality machines using Villiers, JAP, and MAG engines of 117cc to 748cc. Production stopped in 1928. In 1929 after reorganization, it moved to Vienna. Subsequently, only JAP single-cylinder and V-twin engines were used.

EM
1928–29 Orthodox motorcycles assembled by Ernst Minkus in Vienna. They used proprietary components, including MAG engines.

ERR-ZETT
1938 Err-Zett built lightweight two-strokes that used 98cc Sachs engines.

FAR
1924–28 Franz and Anton Rumpler built 350cc and 500cc single-cylinder machines with JAP and Blackburne engines. The Rumpler brothers also produced the Alfa-Gnom motorcycle which used their own 594cc overhead-camshaft engine.

FORCE
c.1925–26 A short-lived company that built 350cc two-stroke singles with an inclined cylinder and belt final drive.

A 1957 HMW Super Sports moped

FREYLER

1927–28 The Freyler was an under-developed rotary-valve 350cc four-stroke single. The project collapsed due to fundamental design problems.

GAZDA

1924–26 Limited production of 246cc twin-port two-strokes with a second supercharging cylinder in the bottom of the crankcases.

GIGANT

1936–38 Sturdy motorcycles built in Vienna by Johann Teichert. Single-cylinder and V-twin JAP engines and other proprietary components were used in most machines. A few were made with an overhead-valve Husqvarna engine.

GOLO

1923–25 Golo made conventional machines with JAP and Blackburne engines and other proprietary components.

HAI

1938–39 Bargmann & Co. designed a neat machine using its own 108cc two-stroke engine. This was mounted in an advanced cast-alloy frame, which included an integral fuel tank. A few were made after World War II.

HMK

1937–38 HMK used JAP single-cylinder engines in orthodox machines. Production stopped during the war.
c.1948 For a short time, after World War II, it produced a model with an overhead-valve 250cc Bark engine.

HMW

1949–57 HMW made 49cc to 74cc two-stroke mopeds, scooters, and lightweight motorcycles using its own engines.

KAUBA

1953–55 Kauba made 98cc two-stroke Rotax-engined scooters.

KOHOUT

1904–06 Kohout built cars and motorcycles. It used Minerva and Fafnir engines for its motorcycles.

KRAMMER

1923–29 Krammer assembled a limited number of machines using proprietary components. Villiers, Persch, Anzani, and MAG engines were all used in conventional machines.

KTM 🏍 p.118

1955– The KTM initials originally stood for Kraftfahrzeuge Trunkenpolz, Mattighofen. Its first motorbike, built in 1953, was a 98cc Rotax-engined Moser machine. The KTM brand-name was adopted after Ernst Kronreif became

Hans Trunkenpolz's partner in 1955. KTM made advanced and high-quality lightweight motorcycles and mopeds using two-stroke engines supplied by Sachs, Rotax, and Puch, although an early double overhead-camshaft 125cc racer was based on an MV Augusta four-stroke. In 1956 it began to build scooters and the following year it produced the stylish-looking Tarzan 125. From 1960 to 1965 it concentrated solely on moped production and from 1967 it began to develop motocross machines, which used its own two-stroke engines. These machines went on to win countless M-X championships. Four-stroke singles appeared in the 1980s.

LAG

1921–29 Liesinger AG of Vienna was an armaments company that diversified into building 118cc clip-on bicycle engines. Subsequently it made high-quality motorcycles with its own 147cc to 346cc two-stroke engines and JAP four-stroke singles of up to 496cc.

LANCO

1924–26 Lanco was the new name for the JW machine. The new name came from the backers LANgsteiner and COeln. As well as the overhead-valve 496cc JW, it also produced a side-valve model. Its attempt to produce its own engines was short-lived and it soon switched to MAG power units.

LOHNER

1950–c.1958 Lohner built scooters in Vienna using Ilo and Rotax two-stroke engines of 47cc to 199cc. The production of the Sissy moped continued into the 1960s.

M See EM (p.290).

MESSNER

c.1928–33 Messner produced a few 250cc competition machines with overhead-valve JAP engines or its own overhead-camshaft power-unit.

MEZO

1923–24 MEdinger and ZOgelmann built triangulated tubular frames and used DKW, Villiers, Blackburn, and JAP engines. Very few were actually built.

MONTLHÉRY

1926–28 Montlhéry motorcycles, built in Vienna, were named after the famous French racing circuit. The machines were equipped with Blackburne and JAP power units and other proprietary parts. Small numbers were built.

MOSER

1953–54 A 98cc Rotax-engined lightweight built at Mattighofen by the forerunner of the KTM company.

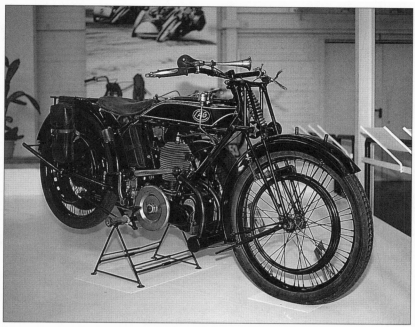

A 1925 LAG 250cc two-stroke

MT

1925–35 Austrian Villiers importer M. Thun sold Villiers- and JAP-engined motorcycles under his MT badge. Some of these machines were British-made Sun motorcycles to which the MT badge was attached. Belgian La Mondiale machines, using an improved two-cylinder Villiers engine, were also sold under the MT label. Racing versions were produced.

NIESNER

1905–14 Josef Niesner of Vienna built a limited number of high-quality machines using single-cylinder and V-twin Fafnir engines of 3hp to 5hp.

NORICUM

c.1903–06 The Noricum name was sometimes used on Cless & Plessing (see p.290) machines sold in parts of the Austro-Hungarian Empire.

O&B

1903–07 The first machine built by Opel & Beyschlag in Vienna was a copy of the German Opel. The following year it began to produce its own designs in co-operation with the German parent company. These were shaft-driven 2.25hp singles and a 3.5hp V-twin.

PERPEDES

1923–27 Albert Stouratz produced a 148cc two-stroke clip-on engine for bicycles. It was mounted above the rear wheel, which was driven by belt. It was apparently unconnected with the other Perpedes (see below).

PERPEDES

1924–25 Karl Heinisch built a limited number of machines using either a 122cc LAG engine or a Persch two-stroke engine with a two-speed gearbox.

PERSCH

1923–25 Persch produced a 118cc two-stroke engine with an external flywheel, which was sold as a clip-on bicycle engine. It also built some complete machines.

PUCH 🏍 p.157

1903 Johann Puch produced his first 244cc motorcycle in 1903. He also built tricycles and cars. Motorcycles used single-cylinder and then V-twin engines. It soon became the leading Austrian motorcycle manufacturer. Successful competition machines were also built.
1923 The first of Puch's two-stroke split-singles designed by Giovanni Marcelino appeared. This design was the basis for most Puch motorcycles over the next 50 years. The first versions were 122cc but capacity soon grew to 250cc. Successful racing versions were also built. In 1931 a 500cc model was produced by doubling up the 250cc to create a four-piston split-twin.
1934 Steyer-Daimler-Puch was created by the amalgamation of three firms. New models followed, including the 1936 800cc side-valve horizontally opposed four, of which many were supplied to the state authorities. Anschluss stopped production but manufacturing of lightweight machines continued. A lightweight powered bicycle appeared in 1937 similar to Scott's Cyc-auto. There was also a 125cc single in 1940. This formed the basis of post-war machines.
1946 Post-war production of 125cc singles and 175cc to 250cc split-singles resumed. Many were exported. In the U.S. Sears, Roebuck stores sold them under the Sears (see p.274) and Allstate (see p.268) badges. Pressed-steel frames were introduced in 1951. Mopeds and scooters with conventional fan-cooled

two-stroke engines of 49cc to 125cc were built from 1952. Off-road competition machines were successful in enduro and motocross. Harry Everts won the 1975 250cc World Motocross Championship. The 49cc Maxi moped was introduced in 1968, which sold in large numbers. Puch concentrated on 50cc machines from the mid-1970s. In 1987 Piaggio took over the marque and production in Austria ended.

REFORM
1903–c.1905 Vienna-based firm that produced a limited number of single-cylinder machines using Monarch engines.

REPUBLIK
1899–1908 Name used on some Laurin & Klement machines built in Bohemia, now part of the Czech Republic.

RWC
1954–60 Bicycle manufacturer RWC built 98cc lightweights using Rotax engines.

SCHEIBERT
c.1907–13 Originally Scheibert put its 1.75hp four-stroke engine in an inclined position on the downtube of a bicycle frame. Transmission to the rear wheel was by twisted rawhide belt with a tensioning pulley. Later the engine was mounted above the front wheel, which was driven by friction roller.

SMART
1924–32 Smart made orthodox bikes with 172cc to 600cc engines supplied by Villiers, Blackburne, and JAP.

STYRIA
1904–08 The firm was founded in 1891 by Johann Puch to make bicycles. He sold out in 1897 and went on to start a new company under his own name (see p.291). The first Styria motorcycle had a single-cylinder 1.75hp engine that was used as a stressed member in a diamond frame. The advanced engine had mechanical side-valve operation and magneto ignition. Final drive was by belt. It later built loop-framed V-twins as well, and some machines were exported.

TITAN
1927–32 Titan was the successor to Austro-Motorette (see p.290). It produced a 346cc two-stroke single designed by Karl Schüber, which used an early type of reed valve to control induction. A few 500cc JAP- and Blackburne-engined four-stroke machines were also made.

WERNER
1928–29 Werner built machines using mainly single-cylinder and V-twin MAG engines of up to 996cc, although it also made a few machines with JAP engines. All models had sturdy frames with twin downtubes and optional rear suspension.

WERTAL
1953 Wertal built sporting machines using split-single Puch engines. The chassis design was inspired by the Featherbed Norton and the forks by Greeves. They were sold as a kit to which the Puch components were added. It could also use other motors. Very few machines were produced.

WESPE
1937–38 The Wespe was a 122cc Villiers-engined lightweight sold by Thomas Harbourn, the importer of British Triumph motorcycles.

YORK
1927–29 York assembled motorcycles with British components including JAP engines of 350cc to 750cc. In 1929 production moved from Vienna to Halle in Germany. The marque disappeared the following year.

Unconfirmed marques

Amak Vienna *1922–23*
Assman Leibnitz *1938–39*
Conieri *1954–56*
Danneck Vienna *c.1907*
Fulgur *c.1935–39*
Glockner
JLS Stockerau *1926–30*
Junior *1933–39*
JW *1923*
Kosty *1952*
LS *1923–24*
Lux *1953–55*
Muller *1924–26*
Rotor *1924–38*
RZ
Seklehner-Roscer *1937*
Venus Vienna *c.1923*
Vylea *1926–27*
Wega Vienna *1923–24*
We-Ka-Be *1922–23*
WKB *1923–24*
W&W *1925–27*

Switzerland

ALESIA
1966–70 Alesia, based in Martigny, was a constructor of snow-scooters. These were powered by 49cc Sachs two-stroke engines which drove a caterpillar track on the rear. A ski was attached to the front forks to steer the machine. Around 200 were built.

ALLEGRO
1923–50 Cycles Allegro in Neuchâtel began building motorcycles in 1923. A range of 147cc to 347cc machines with Villiers engines were constructed, as well as some successful racing derivatives. MAG, Sturmey-Archer, and Gillet-Herstal engines were used later. Motorcycle production ended in 1950, but the Allegro marque continues to manufacture bicycles and mopeds.

AMI
1950–56 A cross between a motorcycle and a scooter, the Ami combined a motorcycle layout with small wheels and extensive bodywork. It was powered by Sachs engines of 98cc to 174cc.

AMSLER
1948–50 Amsler & Co. built a number of lightweight motorcycles, which used 98cc single-cylinder Sachs engines.

ARNI
1950–54 This company first produced a Sachs-engined minibike. Later, in association with Achilles Wilhelmshaven, it made scooters with 150cc, 175cc, and 200cc engines.

AUXI
1921 Auxi produced 134cc motorcycles with belt drive to the rear wheel.

BIANCHETTI
1913–26 Bianchetti bikes were equipped with 125cc twin-cylinder two-stroke Della Ferrera engines.

BPR
1929–32 Buratti, Ponti, and Roch of Acacias, former employees of Moto-Rêve and Motosacoche, were based near Geneva. BPR motorcycles were equipped with 350cc to 500cc overhead-valve and side-valve MAG engines. Production was halted by a lack of funds.

BÜTIKOFER
1894 Swiss pioneer Eduard Bütikofer built a Hildebrand & Wolfmüller-style single-cylinder motorcycle.

CASEY
1925–55 Marcel Casey of Geneva began production with motorcycles powered by 500cc Blackburne engines. After 1945 he built a range of machines equipped with 122cc Villiers, 49cc four-stroke Cucciolo, and Sachs engines.

LA CHAINE
1905 Walter Schmied of Geneva built a motorcycle with two-speed friction-drive transmission and rear suspension.

CILO
c.1961 Cilo was a bicycle manufacturer that also produced mopeds with 50cc two-stroke engines.

COLOMBE
1905–06 Louis Ischy built twin-cylinder machines of 2.75hp to 3.5hp.

CONDOR
1901 Condor was already an established bicycle manufacturer, located in Courfaivre, when it diversified into motorcycle manufacturing. It became the second-largest motorcycle maker in Switzerland after Motosacoche. Its first motorcycle was a 1.5hp lightweight. Early machines used proprietary engines mainly supplied by Zédel but later the company used single-cylinder and V-twin MAG four-stroke and Villiers two-stroke engines in its machines.
1947 Built the Condor EC580, the first motorcycle to use Condor's own engine. It was a 597cc side-valve flat-twin engine with shaft drive. Capacity was later increased and versions for military use were also produced. In 1950 Condor introduced a 350cc two-stroke twin, and in 1956, a prototype 250cc model with an overhead-camshaft single-cylinder Maserati engine. The A250, an overhead-camshaft single with shaft drive appeared in 1959. It was Condor's last production machine. Condor continued its involvement with motorcycles as an importer of Italian bikes.

COSMOS
1902–10 Cosmos fitted 3hp and 4hp proprietary engines by Fafnir and Zédel into its own bicycle-style frames.

DARLING
1924–29 Friedrich Lochner built motorcycles using his own 250cc two-stroke engine, which was positioned in an open frame.

DUFAUX
See HADC (p.293) and Motosacoche (p.293).

EFF-EFF
1904 Furrer & Fröhlicker made 3hp water-cooled machines.

EGLI
1968– Fritz Egli began by building special frames for Vincent V-twins. Later these chassis housed a variety of Italian and Japanese engines. Egli designs usually have a large-diameter top tube.

FAMO
c.1921 Built in Hinwil near Zurich, the Famo was a lightweight motorcycle with an auxiliary engine that mounted in a bicycle-style frame.

FIDUCIA
1902–06 J. Weber & Co. of Uster produced a 450cc motorcycle using its own engine.

FORSTER
1921–32 The Forster motorcycle was designed by K. Kirshbaum and constructed by the Forster brothers. It was equipped with the company's own two-stroke engines of 140cc, 200cc, and 247cc. The Forster was built in Hinwil near Zurich.

FREI
1925–32 Jacob Frei of Geneva built several motorcycles based on the design of British James machines.

GIROUD
1926–27 Louis Giroud produced a limited number of motorcycles based on the British James machines.

HADC
1901–05 The Dufaux brothers, later to become famous as the creators of the Motosacoche marque (see right), originally used the HADC name on their machines. HADC is an abbreviation of H. & A. Dufaux & Cie.

HELVETIA
1905 G. A. Saurer, a manufacturer that was later known for its vans, offered single-cylinder and twin-cylinder motorcycles. These were powered by proprietary engines supplied by Zédel. The company was located in Arbon.

HELVETIA
1927–30 Unconnected to the other company of the same name (above), Helvetia was the marque name used by Universal (see p.294) on a 190cc PA-engined two-stroke motorcycle.

HIRONDELLE See Schwalbe (p.294).

HISPANO-SUIZA
1947–49 Hispano-Suiza made the famous VéloSolex moped in Switzerland. It was constructed under licence from the French Solex marque.

IDEAL
1903–04 Built in Geneva by Van Leisen, Ideal motorcycles were equipped with a number of proprietary engines including Souvairan, Zédel, Taddeoli, Favre, and Clement power units.

IMHOLZ
1924–27 Imholz built a limited number of motorcycles with its own 125cc and 175cc two-stroke engines. Some 173cc overhead-camshaft proprietary engines by Moser were also used.

JENNY
1932 Period advertising claimed that the Jenny was the "fastest, simplest, and most modern small motorcycle". The 125cc single-cylinder two-stroke engine had an inclined cylinder. Transmission was by a three-speed Albion gearbox and chain drive. The Jenny also had front and rear suspension.

KELLER
1929–32 The Keller was an unusual motorcycle constructed by Charles Keller. It had a 397cc side-valve single-cylinder engine with three-speed gearbox built in-unit. The design was clean and functional and the quality of construction was excellent, but it never sold in significant numbers.

LCR
1976– Louis Christen Racing (LCR) have, to date, built approximately 150 sidecar racing units using Yamaha, Krauser, ADM, and Swiss Auto V4 engines. The marque has won world championships an astounding 12 times – several times with Rolf Biland. In addition, LCR has built approximately 100 road-going sidecar outfits as well as monocoque motorcycle chassis for Krauser, MBA, and Rotax.

LA LEOPARDE
1904–10 Rudolphe Born was the constructor of La Leoparde motorcycles, which were powered by 2.75hp twin-cylinder Moser proprietary engines.

MALLAVALLON
c.1903 Founded in Geneva by Pierre Dunant, Mallavallon built motorcycles with 3hp air- or water-cooled four-stroke engines.

MOSER
1902–35 Fritz Moser made complete motorcycles as well as supplying engines to other manufacturers. He built single-cylinder and V-twin engines of up to 598cc. In the 1920s Moser offered 123cc and 173cc overhead-camshaft singles,

which were very successful. In 1932 the company was taken over by Allegro and its name soon disappeared.

MOTOCLETTE
1906–16 Michaud & Cie. made motorcycles in Geneva using Moser and Zédel engines.

MOTO FAURE
1901–05 Charles Faure of Geneva built several motorcycles with 2.5hp to 3hp engines.

MOTO GENEVE
1908–12 The Moto Geneve was a single-cylinder motorcycle powered by a Zédel engine.

MOTORBLOC
1921 Philip Zucker of Bâle produced a clip-on engine that mounted on the rear luggage rack.

MOTO-RÊVE
1904–25 As well as supplying engines to other companies, Moto-Rêve also built complete machines. The company's earlier models were single cylinder but V-twins were also made, and in 1909 this marque was among the first to build parallel-twin motorcycles. Moto-Rêve also had a factory in England (see Alp p.213). The 1911 Senior TT was won aboard a Moto-Rêve. The marque continued to build machines until 1925.

MOTOSACOCHE (MAG)
pp.132–33
1898–1905 Motosacoche is the most famous and was the most successful Swiss marque. Henri and Armand Dufaux & Cie. (see HADC, left) began by experimenting with internal combustion engines and produced some machines under theDufaux and HADC brand-names. These included a 216cc seven-cylinder radial engine, which mounted on the rear wheel of a bicycle.
1905 The Dufaux brothers produced a 215cc atmospheric-inlet-valve clip-on engine unit for bicycles, which the company named La Motosacoche, "the motor in a bag". The engine and fuel tank were mounted on a tubular subframe that could be placed within the triangle of a bicycle frame. The power unit could also be enclosed behind a fairing. Complete machines soon followed. The Dufaux brothers were also aviation pioneers and made the first Swiss motorized flight in December 1906. In August 1910 they flew the first Swiss biplane – of their own design – over Lake Leman.
1908 A 438cc side-valve V-twin motorcycle was introduced. The capacity of the clip-on engine soon grew to 250cc, and a 750cc inlet-over-exhaust V-twin appeared later. Motosacoche used this valve arrangement on some

A 1911 Moto-Rêve twin with chain final drive

machines until the 1930s.

1911 A separate entity was established to sell proprietary engines to other manufacturers. MAG (Motosacoche Acacias Geneva) soon established itself as a major supplier of engines throughout Europe. MAG produced a range of engines including 350cc to 1000cc V-twins and 350cc to 500cc singles. The company also produced some overhead-camshaft racing singles.
1917 The Motasacoche brand-name was finally adopted.
1923 The French company New-MAP began to build MAG engines under licence and was constructing complete machines by 1930.
1945 After World War II Motosacoche built a 250cc shaft-driven overhead-camshaft single and acquired the rights to the 250cc overhead-camshaft twin-cylinder Opti motorcycle, which was made from 1955.
1956 Over half a century since its first engine was constructed, Motosacoche finally withdrew from the motorcycle market.

MOTO WALTHER
1972–75 Ernest Walther produced 250cc, 500cc, and 750cc motorcycles powered by Honda, Kawasaki and Aermacchi engines, which were fitted into his own frames. Few were built.

NOVA
c.1907 Hurlimann & Cie. built these 1.75hp motorcycles.

ORIS
c.1903 An early company based in Liestal that produced machines of 2hp, 2.5hp, and 3hp, which were powered by Zédel engines.

PERAVES
1988– Peraves manufactures the fully-enclosed Ecomobile, designed by Swissair pilot Arnold Wagner. The Ecomobile uses a BMW K-series engine and transmission. The driver and the passenger sit in a cockpit similar to that of an aircraft. The machine also has retractable stabilizer wheels. Production is on a limited scale and the machine is extremely expensive.

PERFECTA
1946–50 Perfecta built motorcycles equipped with 123cc to 173cc overhead-valve French AMC engines.

PERILLARD
1906–09 Jule Emile Perillard of Geneva built four-stroke motorcycles using a 1.25hp engine, which was mounted on the rear wheel.

PICCOLO
1948–49 These 48cc scooters were produced in Bâle.

QUICK
1918–30 Paul Speidel first built motorcycles using Müller and Vogel engines. From 1924 a British-style machine with a Bradshaw engine was also available.

RB
1923–24 A 497cc four-valve single-cylinder motorcycle was produced by Roger Barbier. It had a forward-facing carburettor and a pair of rear-facing exhaust ports.

ROLO
c.1923 A 2hp four-stroke motorcycle produced by the partnership between engineer ROth and financier LOcher.

LA ROUTIÉRE
1903–05 La Routiére constructed an early 2.75hp motorcycle. Production was limited.

ROYAL
1900–08 Pioneer manufacturer, Philipp Zucker of Bâle, constructed a range of machines from 1.5hp to 3.5hp using mainly single-cylinder and V-twin Zédel power units.

ROYAL STANDARD
1928–32 Produced by the Ateliers des Charmilles, Geneva, the Royal Standard was an interesting 400cc unit-construction in-line twin with shaft-driven overhead-camshaft and chain final drive. It had a tubular cradle frame.

SCHÄFERSOHN
1927 A motorcycle built by Schäfer and Sohn in Bâle using a 350cc side-valve JAP engine.

SCHWALBE (HIRONDELLE)
1901–05 The established bicycle manufacturer Ruegg & Co. briefly produced single-cylinder motorcycles using Zédel 2.75hp engines mounted in bicycle-style frames.

SEYMAZ
1975–88 These racing sidecar units, powered by Yamaha, Krauser, and Fath proprietary engines, were built in Jussy. Seymaz racing bikes won the World Championships in 1977 and 1983.

SOUVAIRAN
1902–03 Very limited production of motorcycles in Geneva.

STANDARD
1931–52 The Standard marque was established in Germany in 1925. Following the take over of the Swiss company Zehnder, Standard began parallel production of motorcycles at the Zehnder premises in Gränichen. Pre-war bikes were identical to those produced in Germany and used MAG, Ilo, and Standard's own 350cc and 500cc Rex overhead-camshaft engines in frames that had Brough-style leading-link forks. Ironically the Swiss company outlived the German Standard marque, which did not resume manufacturing after World War II.

SWISS-BOY
1951 Shown at the Geneva car show in 1951, the Swiss Boy was a 125cc Ilo-engined scooter.

TICINO
1958 Built a 49cc lightweight powered by a Demm engine.

TOURISTE
c.1903 Motorcycles ranging from 2hp to 3hp were constructed by F. Despland & Co. in Lausanne.

UNIVERSAL
1928–64 Universal first produced two-stroke lightweight motorcycles under the Helvetia name (see p.293). It subsequently used single-cylinder two- and four-stroke and V-twin proprietary engines supplied by JAP, Ilo, Anzani, and Python in a variety of orthodox machines. From the mid-1930s Universal also introduced its own 676cc and 990cc side-valve V-twins. It continued to build motorcycles after World War II producing 580cc flat-twins and 248cc overhead-valve singles. Both of these models had shaft drive and were powered by Universal's own engines. A 250cc two-stroke twin using an Ilo engine was also produced.

VICTOIRE
1899–1902 Victoire was a brand-name used on complete machines produced by Zürcher et Luthi (see Zédel, below), which was more famous for its engines.

ZÉDEL
c.1897 Primarily a producer of engines which were supplied to other makers, Zédel – also known as ZL or Zürcher et Luthi – may have made a limited number of complete machines (see also Victoire, above).

ZEHNDER
1923–30 J. Zehnder & Sons of Gränichen began production of engines in 1896. Starting in 1923 it offered a complete 110cc two-stroke lightweight motorcycle with a horizontal cylinder and belt final drive. It had an open frame and pivoting forks. A 248cc two-stroke with a vertical cylinder, rear-facing exhaust port, and chain drive was introduced in 1928. Zehnder was bought by the Swiss Standard company in 1930.

Unconfirmed marques

Corbeau
Doraule *Geneva 1906*
Famocyclette *Geneva 1921–23*
Geneva *c.1902*
Gex *Geneva*
Haller
HMO (Hegi Moto Ottenbach)
Imme
La Saint Aubin
MACO
Molino
Motosport *1923*
Motox *1951*
Müller-Vogel *1905–16*
Rapid
Rebo (Rébo) *1955–78*
Sim-Roto
SNA *1903*
Taddeoli *1901–03*
Thury *1877*
Trezza *1920s*
Vanleisen *1875*

Belgium

ADS
1949–c.1957 Sachs- and Ilo-engined lightweights and mopeds built in Aalst by A. De Smaele.

ALDIMI
1953 Initiated by coachbuilder Albert d'Ieteren and racing champion René Milhoux, this firm made a Sarolea-engined scooter named Prince de Liège. Only ten machines were built.

ALERION
1919 Made engines in Brussels prior to World War I. In 1919 it produced a 500cc motorcycle for sidecar use. Few were built.

ANTOINE
1903–c.1910 Founded in Liège in 1899, Antoine initially made light cars. From 1903 it made motorcycles using its own single-cylinder and V-twin atmospheric-inlet-valve and side-valve engines as well as Kelecom-designed power units. From 1905 it also offered some four-cylinder motorcycles.

L'ARDENTE
c.1951–52 Mopeds built by H. Vassen in Liège, with 98cc Sachs engines.

AUTOMOTEURS
1902 Motorcycles made in Leuven, in the Delin works, by Eugène Mathieu.

L'AVENIR
c.1955 Made mopeds with Sachs and HWM engines in Lier.

BARBE
1926–c.1933 Principally JAP- and Blackburne-engined motorcycles, ranging from 125cc to 350cc, made in Herstal. Barbe achieved some sporting success.

BASSE-WEZ
1903–04 Made some single-cylinder motorcycles.

BELGIAN CUSHMAN
1950–c.1955 The American Cushman scooter (see p.269) was built under licence at the Ateliers de Fontaine l'Evêque in Anderlues. It had a 295cc engine, automatic clutch, and optional gearbox. In 1952 designer René Milhoux made some improvements. The scooter had some success in Belgium.

BERCLEY
1904–c.1908 Founded by N. C. Nielsen, this Brussels-based firm originally made bicycles. In 1904 it began production of single-cylinder machines. The following year it introduced a model with a parallel-twin 616cc engine, designed by the engineer Kindermans. It used a 360° three-bearing crankshaft and mechanical valve-operation (side-valve) engine mounted tranversely in the frame.

BOVY
c.1914–32 Founded in Liège in 1888, Bovy made arms, and later bicycles. It built a few motorcycles prior to 1914. After World War I motorcycles using Anzani, Villiers, JAP and Blackburne engines of 100cc to 600cc were made. Racing machines were also produced. A lightweight machine with a 98cc Villiers engine and pressed-steel forks was produced in 1932.

BRONDOIT
1919–30 Nicolas Brondoit of Herstal began production with 97cc two-stroke auxiliary engines for bicycles. In 1920 he built mopeds under the name of Ideal-Brondoit and later Brondoit. In 1922 the firm built a simple, 250cc two-stroke belt-driven motorcycle. Brondoit won the French Bol d'Or in the 250 class in 1925. Conventional machines with 500cc MAG engines were also produced before manufacturing ceased in 1930. Some models were later assembled using spare parts.

BURY
1932–33 An established cycle maker in Brussels, Bury built a 100cc Sachs-engined moped and in 1933 a light motorcycle with a 125cc Gillet engine.

BUYDENS
1950–56 Charles Buydens built quality motorcycles with French Ydral engines of 100cc, 125cc, and 175cc. Some had Earles front forks. About 100 machines were built.

CASTADOT
1900–01 Belgian pioneer machines with Zédel engines.

C. DEVOS
1930s Brussels' Camille Devos equipped bicycles and tandems with a Sachs wheel. In 1950 he built Sachs-engined mopeds.

CIE
1900–c.1905 The initials CIE stand for Compagnie Internationale d'Electricité. It built Kelecom-designed belt-driven motorcycles of 3hp and 4hp in Liège.

CITA
1922–c.1925 CITA – Comptoir Industriel Technique Automobile – machines were made by engineer Henri Gonthier in Liège. From 1919 he built auxiliary engines for bicycles. In 1922 he offered a range of motorcycles powered by his own side-valve and overhead-valve engines of 175cc to 500cc. Gonthier died in 1925 and production stopped soon after.

CMB
1923 A single-cylinder belt-driven motorcycle shown in Brussels in 1923.

COLIBRI
c.1951–52 Sachs-engined mopeds and light motorcycles made by Valère Ransy of Charleroi.

COMET
c.1950 Built bicycles and tandems using a 63cc two-stroke engine, which was mounted in the centre of the rear wheel. Engines were supplied by the Belgian company Hanrez.

CYCLON
1952–55 Designed by René and André Milhoux and made by Moorkens of Antwerp, Cyclon machines used 125cc BSA and DKW engines.

DAVENTRY
1949–56 Jules Delmotte of Brussels had been an established bicycle accessories trader since 1920 and in 1949 he began building light motorcycles with Sachs engines. By 1953 the range included 250cc Ilo-engined mopeds and Sachs- and Ilo-engined motorcycles of 98cc to 250cc. In 1955 Daventry produced 50cc and 175cc Sachs-engined scooters with rubber suspension.

DELIN
1900–02 Joseph Delin founded a bicycle factory under the Derby name in Leuven in 1890. Delin made motorcycles from 1900, some under the Derby name, and in 1902 the company name changed to Automoteurs (see left).

DIAMOND
1931–32 Mopeds with Sachs engines made by bicycle builder Brasseur of Liège.

DOBBELEEN
c.1930 Made in Denderwindeke near Ninove, Dobbeleen motorcycles were equipped with 350cc and 500cc JAP side-valve engines. Very few of these primitive machines were built.

DUVAL
1950–c.1955 Duval built a limited number of machines using 125cc Royal Enfield engines in Antwerp.

DYMAX
1951–54 Built the French Poulain engine under licence, and from 1954 also offered Husqvarna-engined mopeds.

ELITE
1931 Mopeds with Sachs and Gillet engines made in Liège by Counotte, a bicycle manufacturer.

ELVE
c.1958–63 Sachs-engined mopeds made by Vanderhulst.

EMVA
1949–c.1956 An established bicycle maker in Ans near Liège, this company began building mopeds and motorized tandems in 1949 with 98cc Sachs engines. From 1951 it also produced 150cc and 175cc Sachs-engined light motorcycles with telescopic forks front and rear. By 1955 some had Ilo engines. Annually the firm produced around 2,000 mopeds and almost 1,000 motorcycles. Some motorcycles were built under the Ensia name.

EOLE
c.1900–07 A. Wafflard of Liège made belt-driven machines using Fafnir and Kelecom engines.

ESCOL
1923–39 Founded by Jules Escol in 1914 in Châtelet near Charleroi to make winches for coal mines. Escol's sons, Felix and Maurice, made a prototype motorcycle in 1923 called Super Moto. It was equipped with a 1000cc Anzani engine, a pressed-steel frame, and front and rear suspension and weighed 330kg (728lb). It never went into production. However in 1932, Escol made some 500cc and 600c JAP-engined machines also with pressed-steel frames. Later lighter models were added to the range with Villiers 200cc and 250cc two-stroke engines and Villiers and JAP 350cc engines. World War II stopped production in 1939.

FLANDRIA
1951–81 Bicycle maker in Zedelgem since 1896, Flandria began producing successful mopeds in 1951, making 25,000 in the first year. During the 1950s it also made light motorcycles and Ilo-engined scooters. From 1957 Flandria concentrated on moped production. It then made its own engines, exporting them all over the world during the 1960s and 1970s before going bankrupt in 1981.

FLY
c.1949 Made by Ateliers Louis Vits of Brussels, the Fly was a type of large-wheeled scooter with a 99cc Villiers engine positioned horizontally. It had no gearbox and some of the models had rear suspension.

FN p.62
1901 Fabrique Nationale was an armaments firm that diversified into bicycle – then motorcycle – production. The first machines used a 133cc single fitted into a bicycle frame.
1904 Designer Paul Kelecom produced a 360cc four-cylinder machine with shaft drive. Taking motorcycle design beyond the bicycle and an engine, it was the first production multi-cylinder motorcycle. Capacity of the four increased gradually.

The last four-cylinder machines were built from 1923 to 1926.
1923 Overhead-valve chain-driven unit-construction singles were introduced. Side-valve and overhead-valve singles in capacities of 350cc, 500cc, and 600cc were the basis of the FN range until the 1950s. During the 1920s and 1930s FN entered many sports events creating several world records with René Milhoux. Lightweight two-strokes were made from 1933. A 1000cc flat twin was built briefly before World War II, and in the 1950s production centred on lightweight two-strokes of 50cc to 200cc.
1965 Motorcycle production ended.

FORTA
c.1931–32 A bicycle firm that made Sachs-engined mopeds.

FRABEL
1952 Built some machines with 125cc and 175cc Ilo engines.

GILLET-HERSTAL
1919 Founded by Léon Gillet, the firm began by building a 300cc two-stroke single, designed by Fernand Laguesse. It had a rear-facing exhaust port and the gearbox was mounted in front of the engine. Final drive was by belt. Capacity increased to 350cc before production stopped in 1927.
1926 Introduced its first four-stroke machine – an overhead-valve 498cc single. This engine formed the basis of all vertical Gillet-Herstal singles until 1959. Also in 1926 Robert Sexé rode around the world on a Gillet. The firm entered many sports events in the late 1920s and the 1930s.
1930 Introduced a new range of inclined singles. These were available in side-valve and overhead-valve form in capacities of 250cc to 600cc. After World War II, the firm returned to two-strokes with a range of lightweight machines of up to 250cc, as well as the big four-stroke single.
1955 The company merged with FN (see p.295) and Sarolea (see p.297). It was an unsuccessful attempt to stay afloat in the contracting European market. Production ceased in 1960.

GONTHIER
c.1919–20 Before founding CITA (see p.295), engineer Henri Gonthier of Streupas near Liège produced a limited number of four-cylinder 748cc overhead-valve chain-driven machines.

GRAINDORGE-CORNET
c.1900–03 Martin Graindorge-Cornet, bicycle maker in Engis, built some 2hp single-cylinder motorcycles.

HOUARD
1900–02 Houard built FN-engined motorcycles in Gent.

IMPERIA
1930 Automobile works based in Nessonvaux made a prototype motorcycle with a sleeve-valve engine. No production models were built.

JEECY-VEA
1920–27 Founded in Brussels by Jean Watelet, the firm's first motorcycles used Coventry-Victor engines. By 1926 the range included lightweight motorcycles of 250cc and 350cc.

KOPPEL
1903 Liège firm La Compagnie Belge de Vélocipedes built bicycles and some cars under the Koppel brand-name. Koppel was an engineer who, in 1903, designed a motorcycle with a three-cylinder engine in the rear wheel. It may not have gone into production.

LADY
1924 Founded by Lambert Van Ouwenwerk near Antwerp, Lady's first models had strange triangulated frames and Villiers engines of 150cc to 250cc.
1926 Orthodox-framed machines were introduced with various British engines such as Villiers 175cc to 350cc, and JAP 350cc and 500cc. During the 1920s and 1930s Lady entered many sports events.
1931 Some models were made available with rear suspension. During the 1930s Villiers, Blackburne, JAP, and Rudge engines were used.
1940 Production ended.

LAMOCO
c.1928 Engineer Fernand Laguesse left Gillet in 1927 and soon after founded the LAguesse MOtor COmpany in Liège. The firm built a revolutionary, 350cc shaft-driven flat-twin two-stroke with rotary valves. Due to lack of funds only a few prototypes were built.

LEGIA
c.1900–02 Made by Herstal bicycle manufacturer Deprez & Joassart, Legia motorcycles were equipped with DeDion Bouton or Kelecom engines.

LEVRIER
1951–52 Bicycle maker who also made Sachs- and Victoria-engined mopeds.

LINON
1902–05 André and Louis Linon founded a bicycle works in Ensival, near Verviers, that also built motor cars until 1914. Linon made a lot of motorcycles of between 1.75hp and 4.5hp.

LION RAPIDE
1938–57 Founded by Camille Steveninck in Aalst, this important bicycle works began building light motorcycles and mopeds in 1938 using 60cc to 100cc Sachs engines. After World War II the motorcycles used Villiers 125cc and 200cc

engines and some had rear suspension. In 1951 a bigger machine was introduced with a 350cc FN engine. From 1954 the popular models were named Salira and the more luxurious models were Lion Rapide. However, the following year all were named Salira and used Villiers and Ilo engines. The firm also produced an HMW-engined moped. The last year of production was 1957. Several thousand Lion Rapide and Salira units were made.

LION ROUGE
1953 Mopeds made in Kortrijk with Cucciolo engines.

MARCK
1904–08 Jean Marck's motorcycles had his own 499cc inlet-over-exhaust engines.

MECANIQUE ET MOTEURS
1903–05 Motor car builder of Liège that briefly made motorcycles. Some models were water cooled.

MEXICO
1932–35 Motorcycles built in Deurne near Antwerp using two- and four-stroke JAP and Villiers engines.

MIESSE
c.1901 Brussels-based car and truck maker that also made some motorcycles.

MIGNON
1921 A light 137cc chain-driven motorcycle made in Brussels by L. Gierts.

MINERVA
1900–09 Minerva was founded in Antwerp in 1897 by Sylvain de Jong to build bicycles. Its first motorcycle appeared in 1900. It was a Minerva cycle with an inclined-cylinder engine made under licence from ZL (Zürcher & Lüthi). In 1903 the engines were vertically mounted. The engines were of 1.75hp to 2.5hp and many of them were sold as proprietary units. Olieslagers won the Paris-Bordeaux race for Minerva in 1904. Later the firm's range increased to include 345cc singles and 580cc V-twins. Minerva's motorcycle production ended in 1909, after approximately 25,000 motorcycles and proprietary engines had been built. From 1953 to 1955 Minerva briefly resumed production of a 150cc scooter, built under licence from the Italian MV company.

MINEUR
c.1924–39 Previously a well-known engineer for Gillet and Sarolea, Paul Mineur founded his company in Herstal around 1924. The first model was an unsuccessful 500cc machine equipped with a Bradshaw engine. Later Mineur built models with JAP, MAG, and Rudge engines, as well as a light motorcycle with a Villiers engine. After World War II it built a prototype 500.

MLP
1951–52 MLP stands for Machine La Précision. It was built in Brussels with the company's own 118cc engine.

LA MONDIALE
1923–34 Brussels-based firm's first motorcycle had a pressed-steel frame with a 308cc two-stroke engine, friction transmission with five ratios, and final chain drive. The exhaust was in the foot boards and the petrol tank was under the rider's bucket seat. At the end of 1925 La Mondiale was bought out by Fondu of Vilvorde. Prior to World War I, Fondu made railway materials and motor cars and just after the war it built proprietary automobile engines. The firm then added new models to the range, also with pressed-steel frames, using various engines by Villiers, JAP, Blackburne, and Chaise. Jules Fondu won several races on La Mondiale bikes. Later the firm also made lightweight motorcycles with 147cc Villiers engines. The economic slump forced La Mondiale to cease motorcycle production in 1934.

MOTOCETTE
c.1925 Mopeds with 110cc engines built by the Carlier brothers in Tournai.

NOVY
c.1935–1960s Founded by Hilaire Lannoy in Kortrijk, Novy made light motorcycles with Villiers engines. After World War II it built 100cc to 225cc Villers-engined machines, some with rear suspension. A 250cc Ilo-engined motorcycle was produced from 1954 until the 1960s.

OMEGA
1951–55 Made lightweight motorcycles and the Sitta scooter under licence from the German Hummel marque (see p.241).

PA
c.1920–29 Founded by Jules Praillet and Gustave Antoine of Liège, PA was later sold to Dieudonné Hanlet, builder of Perfect sidecars in Herstal. Early models used Blackburne engines of 250cc, 350cc, and 500cc. In 1927 a new range of lightweight machines with 174cc Villiers engines was introduced, plus a Sports model with a 341cc overhead-valve engine. In 1929 the marque was sold to an industrialist from Antwerp who later sold it to Lady (see left).

LA PERLE
c.1949 Brief production of Sachs-engined mopeds.

PHENIX
c.1948–55 Ateliers Lenoble, a cycle firm from Charleroi, produced scooters and lightweight motorcycles with 98cc to 175cc Sachs engines and 250cc Ilo power units.

PIATTI

1955–58 Vincent Piatti designed the 49cc Trojan Mini-Motor before producing the Piatti scooter, which was made under licence in Belgium and the U.K. The Belgian licence was bought by D'Ieteren Frères, a famous Belgian coachmaker. It had a 123cc two-stroke engine in a pressed-steel chassis. Although exhibited for several years it never went into series production in Belgium.

PIEDBOEUF

1902–06 Single-cylinder motorcycles made in Liège. In 1906 Adrien Piedboeuf went on to create Imperia motor cars.

PIEPER

1902 Henry Pieper made single-cylinder belt-driven motorcycles.

RATLY

1951–c.1955 A bicycle maker from Brussels that made mopeds and light motorcycles with Sachs engines.

READY

1924 Founded in Kortrijk by Norbert Vanneste, Ready made 175cc to 500cc proprietary-engined machines. It broke many Belgian and world records.
1926 Ready was sold and production continued in Brussels.
1932 Lighter models, with 150cc and 200cc Villiers engines, were added to the range of 350cc to 600cc motorcycles.
1939 A large range of motorcycles with 100cc to 600cc engines was produced, as well as sidecars and tri-vans. Ready ceased production after World War II.

RED STAR

1902–c.1905 Brussels-based company that used BSA engines in its early machines, which were sold in the U.K. under the Gamage brand-name (see p.220). In 1903 Paul Kelecom designed a 2.5hp Red Star. The company won many sports events.

ROYAL JELLY

1956–58 J. H. Foucart of Brussels made 50cc mopeds and light motorcycles of 100cc and 175cc using Sachs engines.

ROYAL NORD

1932–1960s Brothers Jean and Achille Hufkens began production with 100cc to 175cc Gillet-engined mopeds and lightweights. After World War II, they built mopeds, motorized tandems, and lightweight motorcycles of up to 248cc using Gillet, Maico, and Ilo engines. In the 1960s the company made high-quality 49cc mopeds, using engines of its own design.

ROYAL STAR

1902–04 Made in Antwerp in 2hp, 2.75hp, and 3.5hp versions by a car manufacturer who later became SAVA.

RUHL

1901–03 Car manufacturer from Verviers that briefly made motorcycles.

RUSH

1921 Founded in Brussels by Omer Cravillon, Rush produced side-valve 3hp JAP-engined singles and V-twins of 5hp to 10hp. Belt drive was used. The company was sold to Brussels' engineer J. Van Geert in 1923.
1926 Started making its own 350cc to 550cc side-valve and overhead-valve single-cylinder engines. During the 1920s the company achieved some competition success.
1930 Introduced more economical frames made from steel channel. Production ended in 1934.

SALVATOR

1931–32 Bicycle maker that built mopeds with Gillet 1.75hp engines.

SAROLEA

1901 Founded by arms manufacturer Joseph Sarolea. Motorcycles were made from 1901. Early machines used single-cylinder and V-twin engines of up to 750cc, which were also supplied to other manufacturers. After 1918 side-valve and overhead-valve singles of up to 550cc were built. By the end of the 1920s approximately 50 motorcycles were being produced per day. The bikes often featured in sports events and in the 1930s the most famous sports bike was the Monotube.
1932 Introduced an utilitarian two-stroke. Prior to World War II, a sidecar outfit with 980cc side-valve flat-twin engine and a driven sidecar wheel was produced for the army. After World War II production of pre-war 350cc and 600cc four-strokes continued.
1950 Built 125cc two-stroke bikes and a powerful 498cc parallel twin was introduced.
1955 An agreement was made with FN and Gillet, and from 1956 a 50cc Ilo-engined moped was added to the range.
1960 Sarolea merged with Gillet and production stopped in 1963.

SCALDIS

1913–14 Bicycle maker from Antwerp that made single-cylinder and V-twin bikes with 2hp, 3hp, and 4hp engines. Later returned to bicycle production.

SOCOVEL

1941–59 Founded by Maurice and Albert de Limelette in Brussels. Under German occupation in World War II, Socovel built electric motorcycles. After the war it made conventional two-strokes with Villiers engines of 98cc to 197cc. These were followed by 250cc and 350cc Jawa-engined machines. From 1952 a *moto carénnée* with a CZ 150cc engine was produced. In 1954 Villiers engines were

A Minerva-engined bicycle, photographed in 1903

back in the range. Later models included a 200cc bike with a Maico engine and a 49cc Ilo-engined moped.

SOUPLEX

1939–48 Joseph Menko of Brussels began by making motorcycles with cast-alloy frames. From 1946, Souplex used Villiers 125cc engines and Coventry-Victor flat-twin 285cc and 350cc engines.

SPHINX

1923–29 Assembled in Liège with 346cc and 490cc JAP side-valve and overhead-valve engines.

SPRING

1910–24 Built two- and four-cylinder bikes, with front and rear suspension, mainly for sidecar use. Later built V-twins of 348cc to 998cc.

STABIL

1931–33 Made in Tienen with 98cc to 123cc Villiers engines.

STAR

1932–1960s Star built two-strokes equipped with 100cc Gillet and 175cc Gem engines. From the late 1930s it also offered 100cc Sachs-engined mopeds. After World War II it used Sachs 100cc to 175cc engines and from 1953 built 50cc Sachs-engined mopeds.

SULTAN

1952 Sachs-engined 150cc motorcycles.

SUPERIA

1957–1970s Prestigious bicycle maker that made Sachs-engined motorcycles and mopeds. Built mopeds with proprietary engines in the 1960s.

THOMPSON

1952 Sachs-engined 98cc and 150cc motorcycles by bicycle maker De Smet.

VAN HAUWAERT

c.1930–54 Champion cyclist Cyrille Van Hauwaert began making motorized tri-vans in 1930. Between 1932 and 1940 he built some light motorcycles with Gillet 125cc and Gem 175cc engines. Resumed production in 1952 with a 122cc Ardie-engined motorcycle. The Motoretta, a large-wheeled scooter with an Ilo engine, was produced in 1953. A moped with a Gasquy engine was added in 1954, but soon after Van Hauwaert closed down.

VERSCHAEVE & TRUFFAUT

c.1906 Limited production of belt-driven V-twins.

VOLTA

c.1932–33 Built in Brussels by Eycken & Gillot using Gillet 175cc engines. Also built the 100cc Voltanette moped.

Netherlands

AGS
1971–76 J. de Groot from Havelte produced specialized 125cc scramblers with two-stroke engines by Sachs, Puch, and Zündapp.

ALTENA
1900–06 The Haarlemse Automobiel-en Motorrijwielfabriek, formerly known as A. van Altena, Haarlem, was the first Dutch motorcycle manufacturer to make its own four-stroke engines, of 2hp and 3hp. From 1902 to 1906, the firm also built cars.

AMSTEL
1962–66 Motorcycle and moped importer R. S. Stokvis in Rotterdam produced mopeds combining frame parts from the RAP moped (see p.300) with the two-stroke Puch engine.

ARISTO
1953–56 Mopeds built by De Globe cycle factory at Leiden, using a French Vimer two-stroke engine. In 1955 it produced a model with an ingenious automatic three-speed gearbox of its own design, but the make did not last.

AVADA
1951–64 Established bicycle maker Avada Rijwielfabriek, in Alphen aan de Rijn, first produced autocycles with 38cc Victoria engines and later built mopeds with Victoria, HMW, FBM, and Sachs two-stroke engines.

AVAROS
1952–65 Using the Avaros trademark, the firm of A. VAn ROSsem in Dordrecht started with 40cc two-stroke Rex-engined autocycles and later built 49cc two-stroke mopeds under an agreement with the Belgian firm of A. Claeys, producer of Flandria mopeds. In 1965 Avaros and Claeys merged and the mopeds were named Flandria.

BAJ
1952–54 NV B. A. Jansen's Handelmaatschappij in Hertogenbosch built 38cc two-stroke Victoria-engined autocycles.

BAKKER
1973– Nico Bakker of Heerhugowaard started with special frames for racing motorcycles. Since the mid-1980s he has produced complete rolling chassis for sporting motorcycles, using proprietary engines.

BARZOI
1952–54 The firm of Is. Troostwijk in Zwolle built small numbers of 38cc two-stroke Victoria-engined autocycles.

BATAVUS
1932–76 The Rijwiel-en Motorenfabriek Batavus, Heerenveen, began selling bicycles in 1904, producing its own from 1914. In 1932 the first Batavus motorcycle, powered by a 98cc Villiers two-stroke engine, appeared. This was followed by Sachs- and Ilo-engined autocycles of 74cc and 98cc, and motorcycles of 100cc to 150cc with Ilo, Sachs, and Villiers engines. After World War II, models with 148cc and 200cc Ilo and Villiers engines appeared. From the 1950s the company concentrated on mopeds, but also built motocross and enduro bikes, usually with Sachs engines. In 1969 it acquired fellow moped maker Magneet, followed in 1970 by Phoenix, Fongers, and Germaan. Due to falling sales, moped production ended around 1976.

BEMA
1950–51 The Rotterdam motorcycle trader BEn MAltha built a 197cc two-stroke Villiers-engined scooter with a novel fibreglass "coachwork"; a second prototype with a commercial sidecar was used by the ANWB (the Dutch Automobile Association).

BERINI
1949–81 Moped maker that started production with a 49cc two-stroke rotary-valve clip-on engine that mounted above the front wheel, later followed by an extensive range of mopeds. In 1956 the trademark became the property of the Pluvier Motorenfabriek in Delft, who until then had produced the mopeds for sales organization Hart Nibbrig & Greeve. In 1964 Pluvier went broke and was bought by Anker Motoren Maatschappij, later Laura Motoren. In 1981 all production machinery was sold to Korea, but engine drawings also found their way to India.
1991– Rotterdam motorcycle importer Alblas, which owns the trademark, imports Indian mopeds with the old Berini M48 engine, marketing them under the Berini badge.

BITRI
1955–64 The Nederlandse Scooterfabriek NV in Dokkum built Bitri scooters with 147cc Ilo two-stroke engines, followed by models powered by Rotax engines of 148cc and 192cc.

BMI
1934–37 Autocycles built by the Bilthovensche Metaal Industrie had 80cc four-stroke engines with an automatic inlet valve. The cylinder, cylinder head, and crankcase were made in one piece.

BRICO
1954 Although plans existed to produce this scooter with a choice of 100cc, 125cc, or 150cc Ilo engine, only one model was actually built.

BURGERS-ENR
1896–52 In 1896 the Eerste Nederlandsche Rijwiel & Machinefabriek H. Burgers in Deventer produced its first motorcycles with Fafnir and Minerva engines. Later it built models with JAP V-twin engines and light two-strokes, using Vitesse engines. From 1930 to World War II it built autocycles with Ilo and Sachs engines of 60cc and 80cc. In 1950 Burgers entered the moped market, but without success, and from 1952 concentrated on bicycles again.

CAVALETTA
1953–1956 The Amsterdam firm of Mofaca produced a moped of its own construction with a two-stroke Cavaletta single-speed engine.

CEDE
1920 A former generator and carburettor maker in Ruinerwold, Cede tried to bring a motorcycle with a two-stroke engine of its own design onto the market. Only a few were built.

CENTRO
1954–61 Based in Schiedam, this firm entered the market with scooters of its own design, powered by Ilo and Lavalette two-stroke engines, but soon switched to producing mopeds using two-stroke HMW engines.

CUP
c.1903 Bicycle maker Johannes Cup in Maashees built a small number of motorcycles with clip-on engines of his own manufacture, but resembling those made by Minerva around that time.

CYRUS
1952–71 An established bicycle maker that from 1952 built mopeds using Victoria, Sachs, Zündapp, and, later, also FBM two-stroke engines. In 1961 Cyrus and the bicycle maker Empo in Vorden (see right) agreed that Cyrus could produce mopeds with the Empo trademark.

DISSELHOF
1956–57 In 1952 a Mr Disselhof in Zwolle developed a scooter with fibreglass panels over a frame constructed of tubing, and using a 150cc Ilo engine. In 1956 the scooter went on the market, but only about 15 machines were sold.

DMF
1940–57 The Driebergsche Motorrijwielen Fabriek made motorcycles with 125cc Villiers, Ilo, and Puch engines, later followed by 150cc, 175cc, 200cc, and 250cc models using Ilo engines. It also built the popular Nestor moped with a

49cc Ilo engine and, shortly after, a similar model with a Zündapp two-speed engine.

DOPPER
1904 J. Dopper, working for the Appingerdammer Bronsmotorenfabriek, built the first Dutch motorcycle powered by a diesel engine as an experiment.

DPP
1992– Custom specialist Diks Paints Products has built a series of chopper-type bikes using Harley-Davidson engines.

EENHOORN
1905–07 Bicycle producer Bingham & Co. of Rotterdam built four-strokes, using single-cylinder and V-twin engines of 3hp, 3.5hp, 4hp, and 6hp.

EFA–SPEEDWHEEL
See Wingwheel (p.300).

ELAND
1951–59 The Eland bicycle maker in Delft started with autocycles with 38cc Victoria two-stroke engines. It later built mopeds powered by two-stroke 49cc Gasquy, Junior, and Victoria engines.

EML
1983– In 1972 Hennie Winkelhuis in Neede started building scramble sidecars under the trademark Eigen MakeLij – "Home-Built". From 1983 EML built complete touring and sporting sidecar outfits with suspension and frames of its own design, using proprietary engines.

EMPO
1955 Under the name Empo-Carley the Empo bicycle factory in Vorden sold an ingenious ultra-light 49cc motorcycle designed by Joop Carley. Although intended as a moped, it had no pedals, so officially it was a motorcycle. Poor sales put an end to production.
1961–71 Empo sold mopeds, produced by Cyrus, under its own name.

ENTROP
c.1909 Entrop, a bicycle maker in Gravenmoer, built four tricycles with its own single-cylinder four-stroke engines.

ESMI
1955–56 Stein-based firm that made a few Ilo- and Gasquy-engined mopeds.

EYSINK
1901–56 In 1901 Eysink made its first complete motorcycles with engines of 1hp and 1.75hp. Among its several models in 1905 was a 453cc vertical twin. The marque developed into the foremost Dutch motorcycle producer with an international reputation. V-twins and flat twins were made before the company switched to using proprietary engines, starting with a 2hp Villiers-

A 1971 Batavus GS125 ISDT bike equipped with a 125cc Sachs engine

engined model in 1926. In the 1930s New Hudson, JAP, Python, Villiers, Ilo, and Sachs engines were used. After World War II Eysink built Villiers- and Ilo-engined lightweights, a scooter, and several mopeds, but the factory closed in 1956. Dick Eysink, grandson of the founder, continued with mopeds, first using the Renata trademark (see p.300), later under his own name.

FAIR LADY
1967–68 Name used on a Franco Morini-engined moped sold by moped and motorcycle importer R. S. Stokvis.

FAMA
1936–37 Willem Gerth & Zonen of Utrecht sold a 100cc Sachs-engined motorcycle, largely built by the German Rixe company, under the Fama name. It was followed by a similar model with a 122cc Villiers engine.
1952 The company tried again with a motorized bicycle with a Victoria engine.

FLYTE
1968–70 The Flyte name attached to a Sachs-powered moped sold by moped and motorcycle importer R. S. Stokvis.

FONGERS
c.1909 The Groninger Rijwielfabriek A. Fongers built a number of motorcycles with FN engines.

1956–c.1976 The company entered the moped market with a two-stroke 49.9cc Zündapp-engined machine. In 1966 it merged with Phoenix and Germaan, and was later bought by Batavus (see p.298).

GAZELLE
1903 The Gazelle Rijwielfabriek in Dieren introduced a motorcycle with a Belgian Sarolea engine.
1931–76 The company re-entered the field, with autocycles with Ilo engines of 60cc and 80cc, followed in 1934 by lightweight motorcycles with 148cc Villiers and 146cc Ilo engines. In 1956 motorcycle production was ended in favour of bicycle and moped production. For the latter, engines by FBM, Ilo, Sachs, and Anker-Laura were used.

GEDO
1954–57 The firm of F. GEerts in DOkkum built a few mopeds using two-stroke Victoria M51 engines.

GERMAAN
1935–69 Germaan built lightweight motorcycles using small-capacity Villiers, Ilo, and Sachs engines. After the war it also used Csepel power units. In the late 1950s, motorcycle production ended and the company concentrated on mopeds. From 1955 it built the German Achilles Capri moped under licence, using a Sachs engine, selling it as

Germaan Capri. In 1966 Germaan merged with Phoenix and Fongers and continued with Sachs-engined mopeds.

GMF
1952–1958 The Gelderse Motoren Fabriek in Varseveld, later Rijssen, began production with a moped using its own 45cc engine, but later used Zündapp power units.

HAM
1902–06 The Haarlemsche Automobiel- en Motorrijwielfabriek built motorcycles using 2hp Altena engines.

HERMES
1903 Bicycle maker J. Baakman in Assen advertised motorcycles under the Hermes trademark. They were probably Belgian Minerva or Sarolea machines.

HERVO
1962–63 Produced a few mopeds with Saxonette and Sachs 50cc engines.

HINDE
1899 Bicycle factory De Hinde in Amsterdam offered clip-on engines of 2hp on DeDion Bouton lines.
1936 The firm of G. C. Schultze in Amsterdam used the Hinde trademark for an autocycle and two lightweight motorcycles using Ilo engines of 60cc, 100cc, and 120cc.

HOENSON
1954–55 After building mopeds under the Ranger (see p.300) name, the firm Internationale Motoren-en Rijwielenfabriek of Schiedam, later Haarlem, built mopeds with Express and Myster engines, and German Express motorcycles with Ilo engines, under the trademark Hoenson.

HULSMANN
1939–55 Schiedam bicycle factory that produced a range of lightweights using 125cc and 200cc Villiers engines. The post-war models were unique in that the bottom frame tubes doubled as exhaust pipes and silencers.

JAMATHI
1969–71 Sporting mopeds and a few motorcycles, all with 47.6cc Minarelli engines, but with cylinders and cylinder heads of its own manufacture, were produced by the team that had built, and successfully raced, the 50cc Jamathi racing motorcycles.

JANSEN
1898–1903 The firm of B. A. Jansen in Hertogenbosch made tricycles powered by 1.75hp DeDion Bouton engines, and from 1901 to 1903, motorcycles with 1.5hp Minerva clip-on engines.

JONKER
1956–57 Jonker offered 197cc single-cylinder and 244cc two-cylinder two-strokes, both with Ilo engines.

JUNCKER
1932–35 Rotterdam bicycle company that built lightweight machines with 80cc, 98cc, 148cc, and 196cc Ilo and Villiers engines.
1961–63 The firm resumed production with 50cc Sachs-engined mopeds.

KAPTEIN-MOBYLETTE
1949–70 Through an agreement with the French Motobécane company, Kaptein built Mobylette mopeds under licence, including models of its own design, but using Mobylette engines.

KESTEIN
1935–36 Rotterdam bicycle company that made a 98cc Villiers-engined bike.

LIMO
1952–54 Limo offered an autocycle with a 40cc two-stroke Rex engine.

LLOYD
1930–31 Zutphen-based company Lloyd announced plans in 1930 for a new motorcycle factory where machines using DKW 198cc engines in pressed-steel frames were to be built. Around 700 machines were partly built before the company abandoned plans for full production early in 1931.

LOCOMOTIEF
1952–66 Amsterdam-based bicycle factory that began production with autocycles using a 32cc Berini engine, which mounted over the front wheel. Starting in 1956 it made mopeds with Sachs engines.

MAGNEET
1953–early 1970s Bicycle company from Weesp that began manufacturing mopeds with its own engines, but soon used HMW and Sachs engines.

MAXWELL
1951–60 Bicycle maker in Amsterdam, started with cyclemotors powered by a mini motor that mounted over the rear wheel; later it built HMW-engined mopeds.

METZ
c.1922–24 Amsterdam company that built motorized bicycles and produced a few complete motorcycles, probably from proprietary components.

MEYER
1908 The firm of J. W. Meyer built a prototype of a motorcycle with car-type steering wheel and luxury seat for the rider/driver. Plans for series production did not materialize.

MEYER
1931–36 The Amsterdam parts and accessories company Motormeyer sold motorcycles of 98cc to 500cc under the names New Rapid, Meyer, and None Better. The machines were re-badged imports made by Wolf, Sun, Dunelt, and AJW in Britain.

MM
1953 The Amsterdam company of Motormeyer showed a scooter, available with both 50cc and 70cc engines, at the RAI Show under the trademark of MM. It was listed as the "people's scooter". It never reached series production.

MUSTANG
1953–54 Short-lived company that assembled mopeds equipped with Rex power units.

MZ
1952–54 J. K. van der Molen's Automobielbedrijf in Zand produced a 43cc moped along scooter lines, based on frame parts and engine bought from the German firm of Varel. The moped had no pedals. Dutch law required pedals as of 1953, so MZ production ended that year. From 1953 MZ imported the German Varel scooter, selling it as the Varelli.

NEW RAPID See Meyer (above).

NONE BETTER See Meyer (above).

OTTEN
1901–1911 A small number of motorcycles, including a specific ladies' model, with engines of the firm's own manufacture, were made in Breda.

PELIKAAN
1952–54 The name of 38cc Victoria-engined autocycles produced by the firm of A. J. Wagelaar in Enschede.

PJK
1952–57 Victoria-engined autocycles, and later mopeds, built by bicycle producer P. J. Kruse & Zonen in Rotterdam.

PLUVIER
1956 After a rift with sales-organization Hart Nibbrig & Greeve, which sold the mopeds built by Pluvier under the Berini trademark, the company used its own name on its products. After a year the factory got the Berini trademark back.

PON-LOHMANN
1951–64 Cycle manufacturer from Amersfoort that built autocycles using Lohmann "diesel" engines. Later it also made a model with a Berini engine, followed by the Ponette mopeds, with two-stroke Mival and Pluvier engines.

PONETTE See Pon-Lohmann (above).

POST
1953 The Rubicon Rijwiel- en Motorfabriek in Apeldoorn showed a scooter of its own manufacture at the Amsterdam RAI of that year, to be powered by 49cc, 70cc, and 100cc two-stroke engines, but none of the models reached production.

PRIMARIUS
1953–c.1955 Small manufacturer of mopeds with Rex engines.

RANGER
1953–54 In 1953 the Internationale Motoren- en Rijwielenfabriek in Schiedam started production of a moped with a two-stroke engine of its own design. This was soon replaced by engines by Myster and Express. In 1954 the company moved to Haarlem and the name Ranger was dropped in favour of Hoenson (see p.299).

RAP
1952–c.1970 Mopeds built by motorcycle and moped importer and general trading firm R. S. Stokvis.

RENATA
1953–77 In 1952 Dick Eysink left the Eysink motorcycle factory (see p.298) in Amersfoort and started out on his own in the village of Soest. Early machines were motorized tandems powered by Victoria Vicky engines mounted

alongside the rear wheel. The rights on the name Eysink remained with the factory in Amersfoort, so Dick Eysink used the Renata trademark. In 1955 proper mopeds followed, using Victoria M50 engines. In 1958 Eysink won the right to use the family name on his products, and dropped the Renata trademark.

RIJWIELSOLEX
1948–69 The Van der Heem company in The Hague built the French VéloSolex under licence under the Rijwielsolex name, later simply Solex. Until 1966 the whole machine was produced in Holland, then only the engine, with the cycle parts imported from France.

ROLEMO
1955–56 In its short life this firm from Zwolle built light motorcycles and mopeds using its own engines.

ROND-SACHS
1971–77 Former scrambler Gerard Rond built motocross machines with 49cc and 123cc Sachs engines.

SIMPLEX
1902–68 Bicycle company that first used Minerva, Fafnir, and MAG engines in its machines. From the 1920s it built a range of machines of 98cc to 499cc with engines by Blackburne, Bradshaw, Villiers, and Sachs. After World War II, the company concentrated on mopeds.

SINAMEC
1950–51 The Mechaninca company of Delft developed a two-stroke hub engine of 38cc with a planetary transmission for mounting in the front wheel of a bicycle, which came on the market in 1950 as the Sinamec. When the financier died a year later, Sinamec production stopped.

SPARTA
1931– The Sparta bicycle company in Apeldoorn first offered an autocycle with a 100cc two-stroke Sachs engine, soon followed by lightweight motorcycles of 98cc and 198cc with Sachs, Villiers, and Ilo engines. After the war models with Victoria engines of up to 250cc were added to the range, but in 1961 motorcycle production ended. From 1952 Sparta also built mopeds, using Sachs engines. Although moped production stopped in 1982, soon afterwards Sparta presented the Spartamet, a bicycle with a 30cc two-stroke hub engine in the rear wheel (developed for Sparta by Sachs), which is still available.

SUCCESS
1904–c.1914 Under the trademark Success the firm of Klaas Baving in Zwolle built motorcycles of its own design with proprietary Fafnir engines.

TURNER
1952–54 A 38cc Victoria-engined autocycle built by bicycle manufacturer Meerkerk in Alkmaar.

TYPHOON
1952–68 Amersfoort-based firm of A. Knibbe started production with Mosquito engines in strengthened bicycle frames, followed by proper mopeds using, among others, Belgian Claeys engines. Later it imported an Italian Giulietta moped, selling it under the Typhoon trademark.

UNION
1951–57 The NV Union Rijwiel Fabriek in Den Hulst built autocycles using 38cc Victoria engines. From 1955 it produced the German Achilles Capri moped under licence as the Union Capri, using an Ilo engine, and later mopeds powered by two-stroke Sachs engines.

VELENZO
1955– Amsterdam cycle maker built mopeds with 1.8hp Myster engines.

VESTING
1955–59 Bicycle company of Haarlem, which built mopeds with HMW and Demm engines.

VIERKLEUR
1904–06 The bicycle maker Vierkleur in The Hague sold Altena motorcycles (see p.298) under its own name. When Altena folded, Vierkleur motorcycles also disappeared.

VULKAAN
1911–17 This bicycle maker in Venray produced a number of side-valve single-cylinder and V-twin motorcycles with Zedel engines. Production stopped when supplies of Zedel engines ended in World War I, and the company switched to the import of Dayton, Cleveland, and Cedos motorcycles.

WABO
1955–57 Amsterdam company WAgenBOuw produced a few scooters equipped with 98cc and 147cc Villiers engines. Some were exported to Britain.

WILHELMINA
1914 One of the oldest bicycle makers in Holland, this company produced a motorcycle with a 2.5hp single-cylinder Precision Junior engine. Manufacturing was stopped by World War I.

WINGWHEEL
1950–52 Developed and first presented as the Efa-Speedwheel by the Amsterdam company Efa-Produka in 1948, this 38cc two-stroke hub engine for mounting in the front wheel of a bicycle was later built by the Kromhout engine company and sold as the Wingwheel.

Czech Republic and Slovakia

ACHILLES
1906–12 A bicycle maker that built motorcycles with single-cylinder and V-twin proprietary engines. It relocated to Germany and briefly produced lightweights after World War II.

AEROS
1927–29 Built in Bohemia using 347cc and 497cc single-cylinder overhead-camshaft Küchen engines in BMW-inspired cradle frames with leaf-sprung trailing-link forks.

AZA
1924–26 These 147cc two-strokes were built in Prague.

BAF
1927–30 Built by B. A. Frisek in Prague using Bekamo two-stroke engines and single-cylinder four-strokes supplied by Kühne and Chaise.

BARRY
1932–39 First produced 250cc overhead-valve racing machines, then a simple 98cc two-stroke lightweight was introduced just prior to World War II.

BD
1927–29 Built by Breitfeld-Danek and designed by J. F. Koch, this was a 490cc unit-construction overhead-camshaft single. The company was taken over by Praga (see p.302) in 1929.

BEKAMO
1925–30 A branch of the German Bekamo works that continued production in Rumburg, Czechoslovakia, when manufacturing ended in Berlin. It produced advanced 173cc two-strokes with a pumping piston in the crankcase to increase engine efficiency.

BÖHMERLAND 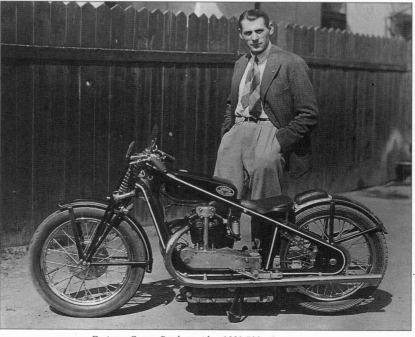 p.33
1925–39 The bizarre Böhmerland was designed and built by Albin Liebisch. It used a single-cylinder 598cc overhead-valve engine in a long-wheelbase frame. Slightly more conventional short-wheelbase sports models were also built. The design changed little during 14 years of production.

CAS
1921–24 CAS built lightweight motorcycles and a small-wheeled, tubular-framed scooter with the engine mounted above the back wheel. Two- and four-stroke engines were used.

CZ p.45
1932 Armaments company built its first motorized bicycles using a two-stroke engine mounted on the front forks. A more conventional 76cc machine appeared in 1933, followed by a range of 98cc to 496cc two-strokes. Post-war production restarted in 1946.
1949 CZ linked with Jawa (see below) within the nationalized bike industry. CZ models were small-capacity two-strokes of 125cc to 250cc. The 175cc Cezeta scooter appeared in 1959. From the late 1950s 125cc to 250cc overhead-camshaft road racers were built but CZ achieved greater success with motocross machines. These won 250cc and 500cc World Championships in the 1960s and were still competitive into the 1970s.
1993 Following political upheaval in Czechoslovakia the Italian Cagiva firm bought 51% of CZ.

EISLER
1920–26 Eisler made a 148cc clip-on bicycle engine, which was mounted over the rear wheel. Later, a complete motorcycle was built using this engine.

ESO p.57
1949–66 Founded by former racer, Jaroslav Simandl, to build competition machines. It produced unit-construction overhead-valve singles of 248cc to 499cc motocross and also 499cc engines for speedway. ESO was already state-owned when it was incorporated into Jawa.

GRIZZLY
1925–32 First built a conventional-looking tubular-framed 246cc two-stroke, later versions were offered with 350cc MAG four-stroke engines.

HURIKAN
1947–49 Very limited production of a 247cc overhead-camshaft single.

ITAR
1921–30 Built 706cc, and later746cc side-valve fore-and-aft flat twins intended for military use. Later machines also used 346cc and 490cc side-valve and overhead-valve JAP engines.

JAC
1929–32 Built by J. A. Cvách and obviously inspired by the Wanderer design (see p.250), the JAC had a 500cc engine in a pressed-steel frame with a leaf-sprung trailing-link fork.

JAWA p.111
1929 F. Janacek bought the rights to the Wanderer 498cc overhead-valve shaft-driven single when the German firm collapsed (see p.250). It was renamed the JAnacek-WAnderer, subsequently abbreviated to Jawa. This unsuccessful model was replaced by lightweight machines powered by 175cc Villiers two-stroke engines in 1932. Capacity of the two-stroke was increased to 250cc, and a 346cc four-stroke single was also built. A 98cc lightweight named the Robot appeared in 1937.
1945 The company was nationalized but new 250cc two-stroke singles and 350cc two-stroke twins soon appeared. In 1949 it became associated with CZ and in 1951 new 500cc overhead-camshaft twins were produced. Jawa continued to make four-strokes until 1966.
1966 ESO speedway machines were re-named Jawa. Involvement in speedway continues today. Road bike production is still concentrated on the 350cc two-stroke twin and mopeds.

JELINEK
1904–c.1907 Built in Prague, Jelinek machines had single and V-twin engines supplied by Minerva, Orion, and Fafnir.

JFK
1923–26 J. F. Koch built an advanced 348cc overhead-camshaft single. He later worked with BD, Praga, and CZ.

KILEAR
1924–26 Orthodox machine with a single-cylinder 250cc two-stroke engine.

KOHOUT
1904–06 Kohout installed Minerva and Fafnir engines in strengthened bicycle frames.

LAURIN & KLEMENT p.120
1899–1908 Located in the former Austro-Hungarian Empire, Laurin & Klement was a successful pioneer firm that made its own single-cylinder, V-twin, and in-line four-cylinder power units. Early machines had the engine positioned over the front wheel, later a variety of positions within the frame was used. They were possibly the first bikes to use a magneto ignition. The Republic and Slavia names were also used on some machines. The firm was the basis of the present Skoda car company.

LINSER
1902–12 Began production with quality machines under the Zeus name. Linser engines had mechanical valves with magneto ignition, a spray carburettor and cooling fins on the cylinder. Advanced V-twin engines followed.

MANET
1948–67 Part of the then nationalized Czechoslovakian motorcycle industry, Manet built an 89cc motorcycle with a split-single two-stroke engine before switching to scooter production.

MAT
1929–30 Limited production of a 498cc side-valve square-four machine with shaft drive. It was made in Prague by Milos Bondy who had earlier made MB machines.

MB
1927–28 A 500cc rotary-valve four-stroke single built in Prague by Milos Bondy who later built the MAT machine.

MC
1924–27 A 1000cc side-valve V-twin intended for use with sidecars.

METEOR
1909–26 Built 147cc to 169cc two-stroke single-cylinder clip-on engines in

Designer George Patchett with a 1931 500cc Jawa racer

Prague before making a complete machine with an open frame.

NECO
1923–27 NECO used JAP side- and overhead-valve single-cylinder engines.

NOVICUM
1904–08 Built in Prague using single-cylinder and V-twin engines supplied by Fafnir, Peugeot, Minerva, and others.

OGAR
1934–50 Machek & Spol of Prague built 198cc and 246cc two-stroke singles, which underwent continual improvement before World War II. Limited numbers of competition machines using overhead-valve single-cylinder engines were also built. In 1945 Ogar became part of the nationalized motorcycle industry and the name was briefly attached to a Jawa-designed 346cc two-stroke twin.

ORION
1902–33 Early single-cylinder and V-twin machines with its own engines were produced by Vilém Michl. These included racing machines with 90° V-twin engines. After World War II the company built two-strokes including a 594cc split-single. From 1927 it built 496cc and 598cc overhead-valve and side-valve singles.

PENTA
1992–94 Penta was started by the Janoska family. The company made a 125cc trail bike equipped with a water-cooled two-stroke engine but production was brief.

PERUN
1904–24 Built by F & J Zdarsky and also sold under the Vulkan trademark. Proprietary single-cylinder and V-twin engines were used, but few were built. After World War I Perun built clip-on bicycle engines.

POUSTKA
1924–34 Prague-built orthodox Villiers-engined machines.

PRAGA
1929–33 Car maker that took over production of the J. F. Koch-designed BD motorcycle. It was a clever double overhead-camshaft 499cc single. In 1932 a 346cc shaft-driven model with a pressed-steel frame appeared. Few were built before Praga stopped making motorcycles.

PREMIER
1913–33 The British Premier company established a subsidiary in Germany in 1910. It relocated to Czechoslovakia in 1913. The British branch left motorcycle production in 1915, while the Czech branch continued until 1933. The first machine was a 346cc side-valve single as built by the English company. The 269cc two-strokes inspired by the Triumph Junior followed. Later models used its own and JAP single-cylinder and V-twin four-stroke engines.

REPUBLIC
1899–1908 Provocative name used on some Laurin & Klement machines (see p.301). At this time Czechoslovakia was part of the Austro-Hungarian empire.

R&K
1924–26 Lightweight machines built in Prague using Villiers two-stroke engines.

RÖESSLER & JAUERNIG
1902–07 Bohemia-based company that used its own single-cylinder and V-twin engines in advanced sprung frames. By 1905 it used mechanical inlet valves and magneto ignition. It also built cars.

RULLIERS
1924–29 Orthodox Villiers-engined machines made in Prague.

SAGITTA
1928–30 Sagitta briefly built machines with 247cc Villiers engines.

SATAN
1929 Satan used its own 550cc sloping side-valve single-cylinder engines.

S-FORTIS
1929–31 Limited production of a 598cc single, equipped with a Sarolea engine.

SIROCCO
1925–28 Orthodox machines that used 147cc to 348cc Villiers engines.

SKO
1924–26 Prague-built 348cc two-strokes.

SLAVIA
1899–1908 Name used on some machines built by Laurin & Klement.

STADION
1958–66 Moped-making section of the state-owned industry.

TERROT
1933–35 French Terrot-designed 350cc side-valve model built under licence.

TORPEDO
1903–c.1912 Made single-cylinder and V-twin machines with its own inlet-over-exhaust engines of 3.5hp to 8hp.

TRIPOL
1925–26 Bicycle factory that briefly built motorcycles powered by 246cc Villiers engines.

VELAMOS
1927–30 Used its own 250cc to 500cc two-stroke engines. Built by Gustav Heinz, producer of the Sirocco.

VELOX
1923–26 Lightweight machines equipped with 123cc to 174cc Villiers and Bekamo two-stroke engines.

VULKAN See Perun (left).

WALTER
1900 Bicycle maker turned motorcycle manufacturer Josef Walter began making 346cc single-cylinder belt-driven atmospheric-inlet-valve machines. From 1905 there was also a 751cc V-twin. Chain drive followed in 1907.
1912 Production of cars halted motorcycle manufacture. Josef Walter subsequently sold the company. His son Jaroslav later built racing machines and worked as a designer for CZ.
c.1923 A 746cc overhead-valve transverse V-twin with chain drive was produced.
1927 Again car production halted the manufacturing of motorcycles.

WEBER & REICHMANN
1923–26 Built 142cc and 172cc machines with DKW engines.

ZEUS
1902–06 Marque name used on early Linser machines (see p.301).

Unconfirmed marques

Bezdez *1923–26*
Brilant-Alcyon *1932*
GH *1924–25*
Jules *1929–34*
Koch *1934–35*
Peta *1921–24*
Radvan *1924–26*
Wagner *1930–35*

A 1994 Penta Aqua Fifty with an Italian Franco Morini engine

Poland

JUNAK
1956–64 Single-cylinder overhead-valve machines of 247cc and 347cc produced by SFM (see below).

KOMAR
c.1958–68 Brand-name used on mopeds produced by ZZR (see right).

MOY
1937–40 These 172cc two-strokes had pressed-steel spine frames.

OSA
1958– Brand-name used on scooters produced by the nationalized Polish motorcycle industry. Osa used fan-cooled single-cylinder two-stroke engines of 123cc and 173cc. Trailing-link forks were concealed behind a bulbous bodywork. The competition versions of Osa's machines won gold medals in the ISDT.

PROMOT
c.1968–73 Off-road competition machines made in limited numbers and equipped with 123cc Puch engines.

PZI
1936–37 Limited production of 600cc singles and 1200cc V-twins.

SARENKA
c.1960s The WSK factory (see right) built these 125cc two-stroke machines.

SFM
1956–64 Stettinska Fabrika Motocyklova, based in the town of Stettin, was part of the nationalized Polish industry. Stettin was formerly part of Germany and was the location of Alba, Hermes, and other marques in the 1920s. SFM built 247cc and 347cc overhead-valve singles which were used successfully in off-road competition. It was also known by the Junak brand-name (see above).

SHL
1935– SHL was the only name from the pre-war Polish motorcycle industry that survived nationalization. Its machines were originally equipped with Villiers engines, but after the war they had the company's own two-stroke engines of 125cc and 175cc.

SM
1935 SM produced a limited number of 350cc overhead-valve shaft-driven single-cylinder motorcycles.

SOKOL
1936–39 Built V-twins inspired by Harley-Davidson machines, using 995cc side-valve engines and some British

components. Most of the bikes were supplied to the military.

WFM
1947– Typical East European 123cc to 173cc two-stroke motorcycles produced by the state-owned Warszawska Fabrika Motocyklova factory, which also made Osa scooters (see above).

WSK
1946– Eastern bloc two-strokes of between 123cc and 240cc that were inspired by DKW (see p.236).

ZZR
c.1960– ZZR, the moped-making section of the nationalized motorcycle industry, produced the Komar range of mopeds (see left).

Unconfirmed marque

LOT *1937*

Hungary

CSEPEL
1951–75 State-owned factory that built two-stroke scooters and motorcycles. A limited number of these machines was exported to the West. As with other East European factories, different brand-names were used at various times. These included Pannonia, Danuvia, Tünde, and Panni (see individual entries below).

DANUVIA
c.1955–63 These were 123cc two-stroke singles made in quantity by the nationalized Hungarian industry. See Csepel (above).

MATRA
c.1938–47 Built in Budapest using Sachs and Ilo 100cc and 200cc two-stroke engines.

MERAY
c.1921–44 Built in Budapest with a variety of proprietary engines including overhead-valve JAP singles. Later it also built its own engines.

PANNI
c.1959–62 These machines were 48cc scooters built by the nationalized Csepel factory (see above).

PANNONIA
1951–75 Two-stroke 250cc machines built by the nationalized Csepel factory (see above). The early machines were singles, but in 1967 a 246cc two-stroke twin was introduced.

TÜNDE
c.1959–72 The state-owned Csepel factory (see above) built these 174cc scooters.

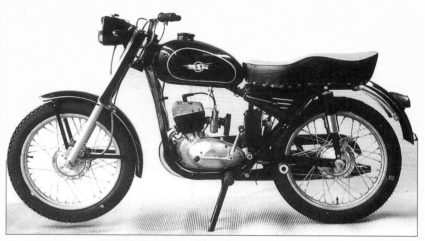
A 1967 WSK 125 derived from the pre-war DKW RT125

Unconfirmed marques

BMG *c.1939–44*
Dorman *c.1920–37*
Emmag *c.1924–27*
FP *c.1924–25*
Nova *c.1925–28*

Bulgaria

BALKAN
1958–71 First built 250cc two-strokes based on the Czechoslovakian Jawa. It also produced small-capacity mopeds and motorcycles. Production of mopeds continued for some time after Balkan stopped making motorcycles.

Romania

CARPATI
c.1960s Moped manufacturer.

Slovenia

TOMOS
1954– Tomos originally built Puch mopeds under licence. The company soon developed its own designs, but it remains primarily a moped maker, though there have also been 90cc and 175cc machines.

Unconfirmed marque

Ivo Lola Ribar *1956*

Ireland

FAGAN
c.1935–37 Conventional lightweight machines assembled in County Dublin with 122cc Villiers engines.

Sweden

ALBIN-MONARK
1939–44 Albin-Monarks were built for the Swedish military during World War II. They were assembled by Monark to a Husqvarna design. The 500cc single-cylinder overhead-valve engines were built by Albin, also from a Husqvarna design. These engines formed the basis of several post-war Swedish motocross bikes, including World Championship-winning Monarks, Husqvarnas, and Litos of the late 1950s and early 1960s.

APOLLO
1937–57 Apollo started motorcycle production at Värnamo with 98cc Sachs-engined lightweights. During World War II it used Husqvarna engines, and after the war Husqvarna, Zündapp, and Ilo two-stroke engines of 98cc to 198cc. Apollo was sold to NV (see right) in 1957 and it became part of the MCB group in 1960. Production of Apollo-badged mopeds continued for a few years.

COLIBRI
1919–23 Colibri began production with clip-on four-stroke engines for bicycles. It later developed a complete machine called a Furir. From 1921 it built a proper motorcycle with its own 250cc twin-cylinder engine.

CRESCENT
1937–60 The Crescent name was used on 98cc Sachs-engined lightweights built by Velociped AB Lindblads before World War II.
1955–60 The name was reintroduced by NV (see right) on two-stroke machines. An Albin-engined four-stroke motocross machine was also built. In 1960 the marque was bought by MCB.

DS
1922–27 The first machines built by David Senning were assembled from proprietary components, but from 1924 they had their own forged frames. The engines were mainly MAG V-twins.

EBE
1918–29 EBE's first motorcycle was a 184cc four-stroke, which was followed by 498cc to 598cc side-valve singles. A Villiers-engined machine was introduced in 1925. Its final model was a 172cc four-stroke with its own engine.

EIBER
1924–38 Eiber's first motorcycle was a Harley-Davidson-inspired prototype for the Swedish army. It also produced 193cc and 246cc four-strokes and supplied these engines to NV. In the 1930s it built 500cc to 650cc face-cam-engined competition bikes. Eiber died in 1938.

ESSE
1920–c.1925 Before adopting its more famous name, Monark built a simple lightweight called the Esse. It had a 172cc two-stroke engine.

HÄGGLUND
1972–74 Hägglund, suppliers of military vehicles, developed a machine for the Swedish army that had automatic transmission, single-sided suspension, and a box section frame. Rotax supplied the 345cc two-stroke engine. Only a few machines were built before the order was cancelled.

HEDLUND
1955–87 Nils Hedlund built the Albin engines used in the successful 500cc Swedish motocross bikes of the late 1950s and early 1960s. A few complete motocross bikes were produced as the NH. A V-twin engine for sidecar motocross was built from 1975.

HUSABERG
1988– Company founded by former Husqvarna employees after the transfer of Husqvarna production to Italy. It produces specialized and successful off-road competition machines. The engines are 350cc and 510cc four-stroke singles.

HUSQVARNA   pp.98–99
1903 Bicycle and arms company that put Moto-Rêve, NSU, and FN engines on its first machines before making its own 550cc side-valve V-twin engines from 1920. Sturmey-Archer and JAP 250cc to 500cc singles were also used, while the capacity of its own engines later grew to 1000cc. Racing versions were also built. Production of large-capacity machines, which was never great, ended in 1936.
1935 Built its first two-stroke, a 98cc two-speed machine that sold well. After World War II capacity of the two-strokes grew and Husqvarna began to develop off-road competition machines. The only four-strokes that it produced were successful Albin-engined motocross bikes. It won ten World Motocross titles between 1960 and 1970 and increasingly concentrated on building competition machines. Developments included automatic transmission, water cooling, and, in the 1980s, a reintroduction of four-stroke machines.
1986 The company was bought by Cagiva (see p.254). The last Swedish-built Husqvarnas were produced the following year. Thereafter the bikes were made in Italy. The two- and four-stroke motocross and enduro machines still win competitions.

LITO
1961–67 Lito built a limited number of high-quality 500cc motocross bikes based on the Albin-engined Monark machines. Other engines were used in

later bikes. The marque and its owner vanished at the appearance of inquisitive tax inspectors.

MCB
1960–75 Monark acquired the Apollo and Crescent brand-names when it bought Nymans (NV). The new group was renamed MCB – Monark Crescent Bolagen. See Monark below.

MONARK
1927 Monark built its first motorcycle in 1913. From 1920 lightweight machines were made under the Esse name (see left). The Monark name was used from 1927. Its first machines were 250cc to 600cc Blackburne-engined side-valve and overhead-valve singles.
1936 Production switched to lightweight machines with 98cc Ilo two-stroke engines. During World War II Husqvarna/Albin 500cc four-stroke engines were used in a machine for the Swedish army. Post-war models used two-stroke engines of 50cc to 250cc, mainly supplied by Ilo. By the early 1950s Monark was Sweden's largest manufacturer. A 500cc Monark-badged scrambler with an Albin engine won the World Motocross Championship in 1959 it was the only four-stroke Monark built after World War II.
1960 Monark took over NV (see below) to create MCB. Production machines of the 1960s and 1970s were Sachs- and Franco Morini-engined 50cc to 175cc two-stroke lightweights, including off-road competition machines. During the early 1970s, factory road-racing machines briefly appeared.
1975 Motorcycle production stopped.

NV
1926–60 Nymans Verkstäder built successful overhead-valve 246cc machines with Eiber engines until 1932, when production stopped. From 1936 it

began to use proprietary two-stroke engines of up to 123cc from Royal Enfield, Sachs, and DKW. It also developed a 1000cc V-twin for the military. After World War II the Royal Enfield 350cc Bullet was assembled in Sweden as an NV. It also controlled the Crescent and Apollo marques. Monark bought the company in 1960.

REX
1908–57 An established bicycle company that used Motosacoche engines in its first machines. Proper production began in 1923 using Villiers and SA two-stroke engines and JAP 350cc to 500cc four-stroke singles. During World War II a battery-powered commuter bike was produced. After the war Villiers and Sachs engines were used in lightweight machines.

SOK
1923–28 Built a small number of bikes that were based on the British OK machine – hence the name SOK, which stands for Svenksa OK. Most bikes had 350cc Blackburne engines.

SUECIA
1927–39 Suecia machines were built in the former Eiber factory using 250cc to 750cc engines supplied by MAG, Blackburne, and JAP in orthodox frames.

TYPHOON
1947–54 Until 1950 Typhoon built a 210cc two-stroke, designed by Folke Mannerstedt. Production resumed in 1951 using 198cc Zündapp engines.

UNION
1949–51 Union was a joint Swedish-Norwegian venture – hence the name. It had a 500cc single-cylinder overhead-valve Albin engine in a conventional plunger-sprung frame. Only 42 complete machines were built.

A 1936 Monark with an Ilo auxiliary engine mounted on a bicycle frame

Norway

STAFFETT
1953–63 Moped maker.

TEMPO
1949– Tempo built lightweight 49cc to 124cc bikes equipped with proprietary engines supplied by CZ, Ilo, Villiers, and Sachs. The company still distributes mopeds built by other manufacturers.

Denmark

ANGLO-DANE
c.1912–14 Assembled in Copenhagen using British components, including JAP and Villiers engines.

ELLEHAM
1904–09 An open-framed, scooter-style machine built in Copenhagen by Christian Ellehammer. A Peugeot engine was mounted vertically under the rider's seat and drove the rear wheel by belt.

JUERGENSEN
1904–14 Built under licence from Humber (see p.221).

NIMBUS 🏍 p.141
1919 Vacuum cleaner makers Fisker and Nielson began production of an advanced four-cylinder motorcycle. It used an inlet-over-exhaust four-cylinder engine of 750cc and had a three-speed gearbox and shaft drive. The engine was mounted onto a pressed-steel frame in which the fuel tank was incorporated into a large-diameter top tube.
1928 Increasing demand for vacuum cleaners halted motorcycle production.
1934 A new factory was completed to house the motorcycle division, and production of a new model was begun. The new machine was still a 750cc in-line four with shaft drive, but it now had an overhead camshaft and a different frame. It survived in this form, with only detail changes, for over 20 years.
1957 Demand for vacuum cleaners again stopped motorcycle production. It was not resumed.

Former U.S.S.R.

C-259
c.1961 The C-259 was a 250cc double overhead-camshaft twin-cylinder racing machine rarely seen outside the former Soviet Union. See also S354/555 (right).

COSSACK
c.1974– The Cossack name is used on some shaft-driven BMW-inspired flat twins in export markets. They are the products of the Kiev and Irbit factories.

DNEPR
c.1974– Dnepr is the export name used on some bikes built at the Kiev factory.

IRBIT
1940– Irbit is one of two factories in the former Soviet Union that builds 650cc overhead-valve shaft-driven BMW-inspired flat twins. The factory is based near the Ural mountains. The Ural name is used in some export markets.

IZH
1933– IZH is a state-owned factory at Izhevsk; which produces 350cc two-stroke singles and twins. The single-cylinder machine was introduced in 1946 and was originally based on the German DKW NZ350 design. The twin has been in production since 1961. Both are typical basic Eastern European designs. The model names Planeta (single) and Jupiter (twin) are used. Export to the West has been limited.

JUPITER See IZH (above).

KARPATY See L'vov (right).

KIEV
1954– The Kiev is another Soviet machine based on the BMW layout. Two versions of the shaft-driven flat twin have been produced. A 750cc side-valve model, available with reverse gear and a driven sidecar wheel, was built until 1983. A 650cc overhead-valve machine was introduced in 1968 and is still being produced. The machines are known by the Dnepr, Cossack, and Phoenix trademarks in Western markets.

KOVROV
1946– Early Kovrov machines were based on the DKW RT125, but the capacity of this Russian copy was soon increased to 175cc. From 1966 the factory also built the Voskhod machine. In 1965 a 250cc motocross machine was developed, but few were built.

KRASNY-OKTYABR
1931–43 Leningrad-based firm that built 300cc two-strokes, which were sometimes described under the model name L-300.

L'VOV
c.1970– Made 49cc motorcycles and mopeds in L'vov, near the Carpathian mountains and the Polish border.

MINSK
1946– Minsk builds 125cc two-stroke singles based on the much-copied DKW RT125 design. The design has been gradually updated and to date more than five million machines have been built.

PLANETA
1946– The name of the single produced at a factory in Izhevsk (see IZH, left).

PMZ
1932–39 Small company based at Podol'sk near Moscow. It produced a 750cc side-valve V-twin based on a Harley-Davidson and a 250cc single based on the BMW R22.

RIGA
c.1960– Maker of 49cc motorcycles and mopeds in Latvia.

S-354/555
c.1957–64 S-354/555 machines were 350cc and 500cc double overhead-camshaft twin-cylinder racers, which were built in very limited numbers. They were rarely raced outside the fomer Soviet Union.

TIZ-AM
1935–43 TIZ-AM built 600cc side-valve singles based on a 1931 BSA design. The company was located in Taganrog near the Ukraine.

TULA
1957– Tula produced a scooter copied from the design of the 197cc Ilo-engined German Goggo (see p.239). It also made commercial three-wheelers, and later an off-road motorcycle with fat tyres, which used the same 200cc two-stroke engine as the scooter.

URAL
c.1976– Brand-name used on some machines built at the Irbit factory.

VIATKA
1957–79 Viatka built copies of the Vespa scooter. It produced 150cc and later 175cc versions.

VOSKHOD
1966– Name used on 175cc two-stroke singles built at the Kovrov factory.

VOSTOC
c.1964–65 Limited production of a 350cc four-cylinder double overhead-camshaft racing machine. It was rarely seen outside the former Soviet Union.

A typical Russian sidecar outfit; the sidecar is hitched to an Irbit flat twin

India

ALLWYN
c.1972–88 The state-owned Andhra Pradesh Scooters company, which used the Allwyn badge, was one of several Indian concerns that made 125cc to 200cc Lambretta-designed scooters after the purchase of Innocenti (see Lambretta p.259) by the Indian government. In 1985 a 100cc Vespa scooter was introduced, but the company soon folded.

API LAMBRETTA
c.1965–88 Automobile Products of India joined forces with the Innocenti company (see Lambretta p.259) before it stopped making its Lambretta scooters, and 150cc and 175cc models were built. A three-wheeled autorickshaw is still made in limited numbers.

ATLAS
c.1975–90 Bicycle manufacturer that began producing the French VéloSolex under licence. This was replaced in 1984 by a more conventional 50cc moped, which was based on the French Mobylette (see p.281) design and called the Atlas Speedomatic.

AVANTI
1982–93 Refrigerator manufacturer Kelvinator India produced a range of mopeds and a 150cc scooter using technology acquired from the Italian Agrati-Garelli company (see p.252).

BAJAJ
1961– Originally an importer of Vespa scooters and three-wheelers into India, Bajaj soon established its own manufacturing facilities. Production began in 1961. Its main model was the Vespa 150GS. The association with Piaggio ended in 1971 and it later introduced its own scooter designs.

1980 A new 49cc two-stroke step-thru machine was introduced, and 80cc and 100cc versions were later offered.
1986 Collaboration with Kawasaki resulted in the introduction of the Bajaj-Kawasaki KB100; variations on this design were later produced. A Bajaj-designed moped was introduced in 1990. The scooter range was updated.
1995 Production of the Kawasaki ZZ-R 250 began. The double overhead-camshaft liquid-cooled twin is the flagship of the Bajaj range. Total production of Bajaj mopeds, scooters, and motorcycles exceeds one million units in 1995.

BOND See BSA (below).

BSA
c.1980–89 This Bangalore-based company was licenced to use the BSA brand-name, but it had no other British connection. The bikes were sporting 50cc machines with monoshock rear suspension and Italian Morini two-stroke engines. Competition versions proved successful. The company was taken over by the tea company Brooke Bond and later versions acquired the Bond name.

CADI
c.1984–90 Four-stroke mopeds produced by a pharmaceutical company.

CHAMUNDI
1984–89 Chamundi Mopeds produced a Peugeot moped under licence. It was too expensive to sell in large numbers.

ELECTRO-ANIL
1983–89 Produced the battery-powered Vidyut 24 moped.

ENFIELD p.57
1955– India's original motorcycle manufacturer continues to produce models based on the design of the Royal Enfield Bullet, which was introduced in

Britain in 1949. The 346cc and 499cc versions of the traditional overhead-valve single are now exported throughout the world. Smaller capacity two-stroke machines were introduced in the mid-1960s. These were originally powered by Villiers-designed engines but from 1982 Zündapp-derived power units were used. The smaller machines were never able to achieve the success of the Bullet.

ESCORTS See Rajdoot (right).

GIRNAR
1974–91 Originally established by the Gujarat state government to produce a Vespa-inspired scooter, the concern was taken over in 1984 and revised models were introduced. The introduction of the hideous Narmada Fuji model in 1990 probably influenced the closure of the company the following year.

HERO
1978– The largest bicycle manufacturer in the world, Hero began making Peugeot mopeds under licence. In 1985 it introduced a Honda-designed 98cc overhead-camshaft single. Over one million of these machines have now been produced. In 1986 Hero purchased some of the assets of the Austrian Puch concern and two years later introduced a Puch-derived 63cc two-stroke lightweight known as the Hero Puch. Other variations on this machine, including the Turbo Sport followed.

IDEAL JAWA
1960–80 Produced a popular, 250cc single-cylinder two-stroke motorcycle based on a Jawa design. In the late 1960s a 60cc step-thru was also made but was much less popular. From 1980 the Yezdi name (see right) was adopted although revised versions of the long-lived 250cc single, including the Monarch and the Road King, remain in production.

INDIA AUTOMOTIVES
c.1985– Limited production of machines assembled from proprietary components, including Enfield's Zündapp-based two-stroke engines.

KGP
c.1972–85 Located in Kolhapur, KGP built two-stroke mopeds based on designs acquired from the Innocenti company (see Lambretta p.259) in 1972.

KINETIC
1972– Kinetic Engineering Ltd produced the Vespa Ciao moped under licence using the Luna name. It was very popular. The company then introduced a range of mopeds and scooters using two-stroke engines inspired by Minarelli and Franco Morini power units. From 1986 it has also made 100cc Honda scooters under licence.

LML
1982– Joint venture between India Machines Ltd of Kaipur and the Italian scooter maker Piaggio (see p.264), which was keen to establish itself on the Indian scooter market. It produced a range of Vespa derivatives and is now an important scooter producer.

PEARL
c.1960–67 Textile machinery maker that built a 75cc two-stroke step-thru in association with Yamaha (see p.287).

RAJDOOT
1962– Produced by Escorts Ltd, the first machines were built with technology acquired from the Polish WFM company (see p.303). These were 175cc two-stroke singles based on the pre-war DKW RT125 design. Variations, including scooters, with the same power unit were also made. In 1983 it began building the air-cooled Yamaha RD350 two-stroke twin under licence; production continued until 1989. In 1985 a further tie-up with Yamaha resulted in Rajdoot producing the successful Yamaha RXS 100.

SAUND
c.1962–88 The Saund Zweirad Union was associated with the German Zweirad Union (see p.251) from which it acquired the rights to produce the Victoria Vicky moped.

SIL
1978– The Indian government bought the tooling and manufacturing rights to the Lambretta scooter when the Italian Innocenti company ended scooter production in 1971. Scooters India Ltd was one of several Indian concerns that made Lambrettas. SIL Lambrettas are exported throughout the world under the original Lambretta logo.

SUVEGA
c.1972–82 French Mobylette designs built by Mopeds India Ltd.

TVS
1976– Began making Batavus mopeds. From 1983 it became associated with Suzuki (originally under the Ind-Suzuki name) to make lightweight 98cc two-stroke motorcycles based on Suzuki designs. In 1993 a new all-Indian 60cc scooter, the TVS Scooty, was produced. TVS mopeds have been the Indian market leaders since 1992.

YEZDI
1980– New name for the Ideal Jawa marque. The 250cc single-cylinder Jawa two-stroke first produced in India in 1960 remains the company's staple product. Attempts to produce 175cc singles and a Jawa-based 350cc twin have been less successful.

A 1980s Yezdi 250 showing its Jawa ancestry

Canada

ALOUETTE
1973–74 Lightweight two-stroke Sachs-engined trail bikes sold by the Montreal-based snowmobile concern Featherweight Corp. The bikes were available in both 100cc and 125cc versions.

ALSPORT
1975 Trail bikes in road and off-road trim equipped with 80cc and 100cc two-stroke engines.

BOMBARDIER
1972–87 Bombardier invented the modern snowmobile and the group was also involved in manufacturing other transport-related products. It also owns the Austrian engine-making company Rotax. Bombardier-badged 50cc mopeds and motorcycles, including the Puch Maxi, were sold through its Ski-Doo dealers before developing a two-stroke Rotax-engined 250cc military motorcycle in 1977. Bombardier also produced Can-Am motorcycles (see below).

CAN-AM
1973–87 Off-road competition machines produced by Bombardier. Originally using 125cc and 175cc disc-valve two-stroke engines, later there were 250cc and 350cc two-strokes and finally 500cc and 560cc four-stroke singles. All engines were produced by Bombardier's Rotax subsidiary in Austria. Can-Am machines were highly successful in motocross and enduro competitions. A 500cc road-going water-cooled two-stroke twin was developed but restrictive U.S. emission legislation killed it before production began. An increased demand for Bombardier snowmobiles eventually put an end to Can-Am production.

CCM
1903–12 Canada Cycle and Motor of Weston, Ontario was a large bicycle-making concern. Its early motorcycles used 3.5hp Fafnir engines. By 1907 it was using the Swiss Motosacoche clip-on engine mounted on a sturdy bicycle with a spring fork.

EATON'S
c.1931 T. Eaton & Co. is a large Canadian department store chain. In the 1930s it sold the Glider clip-on engine for bicycles.
c.1955 Eaton's returned to the two-wheeler market with a CZ (see p.301) Cezeta scooter rebadged as the Eatonia Road King.

ESSEX
c.1914 A 1000cc transverse flat twin with hub-centre steering built in Windsor, Ontario, by J. H. Hill. It had an open tubular frame and chain final drive with an Eclipse hub-clutch. Total numbers built probably did not exceed five machines.

PRO-AM
1973 Two-stroke trail bikes of 70cc and 125cc were sold under the Pro-Am banner by Auto Ski of Levis, Quebec. The 125cc model used a Sachs engine.

QUEEN CITY
c.1903 A 3.5hp motorcycle and a 5.5hp tandem built in Toronto by the Queen City Cycle Co. The engine was mounted in the seat-post of the frame in the style of the Indian motorcycles (see p.271), and the engine casings were apparently supplied by the American Marsh firm.

Unconfirmed marques

Galt Flyer
Jordan

Argentina

LUJAN
1946– Producer of machines with the Puma, Lujancar, and Cucciolo brand-names. These are mostly small-capacity machines of up to 125cc. Some are built under licence from European manufacturers including Malaguti.

MOTO GELIS
c.1955–62 Italian-style lightweight machines powered by licence-built 125cc Sachs engines.

ZANELLA
1957– Maker of mopeds, scooters, and lightweight motorcycles. Early machines were built under licence from Ceccato in Italy. From 1960 Zanella produced its own complete machines. Linked with Yamaha in the 1990s, it produces the Yamaha DT175 in Argentina. Other models include modern air- and water-cooled two-strokes of up to 200cc to road and enduro specification. It also makes machines at factories in Brazil.

Unconfirmed marque

Tehuelche *1958–62*

Mexico

CARABELA
1964– Built a range of machines of between 50cc and 450cc. These included licence-built Jawa 350cc twins and Minarelli-engined 49cc and 172cc road and off-road machines. The company's motocross bikes were exported to the United States in the 1970s. Carabella also produced its own two-stroke engines.

ISLO
1958– Began making a 175cc hybrid scooter/motorcycle using imported Italian components including the two-stroke engine. This was soon followed by more conventional 49cc and 175cc machines. Local content has increased over the years and Sachs engines of 48cc to 248cc have been produced under licence. Islo motocross machines were sold in the United States under the Cooper brand-name in the 1970s.

Brazil

AMAZONAS
1978–90 The Brazilian marque Amazonas built massive machines powered by flat-four-cylinder 1600cc Volkswagen Beetle car engines. Other VW components included the disc brakes. The machines were produced in civilian, police, and military trim. The Amazonas had all the elegance and performance of a truck.

KAHENA
1992– Another Volkswagen-engined Brazilian-built machine, the Kahena is produced by a car accessory manufacturer. The bike's design is more compact and sophisticated than the earlier Amazonas (see above) and it includes a single-sided swingarm and twin-spar frame.

Unconfirmed marque

SACI *1959–mid-1960s*

Australia

AUSSI-ALSO
1919–22 Built a single-cylinder two-stroke with two-speed gearbox and shaft drive and also a more conventional overhead-valve V-twin in Carlton, Victoria. The two-stroke may only have been made in prototype form.

A 1976 Can-Am enduro machine with a 175cc two-stroke Rotax engine

ELLIOT
c.1913–24 Orthodox machines made in South Australia. JAP four-stroke and Villiers two-stroke engines were fitted.

GCS
1914–17 Diamond-framed bikes with JAP engines made by G. C. Stilwell.

GROWDEN
c.1904–07 G. Growden of Port Pirie made typical belt-driven machines.

HAVELOCK
c.1905–10 Built in Hobart, Tasmania, with single-cylinder and V-twin Sarolea engines and belt final drive.

HEALING
c.1903–18 Built in Melbourne, the first motorcycles were typical pioneer machines. After a break, diamond-framed belt-driven machines were built; some had Precision engines. The Peerless and Big 4 names were also used.

HERCULES
c.1920 Used a Coventry-Victor flat-twin engine. Hercules may have also produced machines with Precision and JAP engines.

KENT
1911–19 L. S. Eglington of Adelaide first built an engine with a patented exhaust-valve system. It mounted on the cylinder and opened at the bottom of the piston's power stroke. Complete bikes were also built; some used the Rova-Kent name.

LENNOX
c.1912–18 Built in Victoria with the company's own single-cylinder and V-twin engines. Production was minimal.

LEWIS
c.1900–19 An Adelaide bicycle maker, its first motorcycle had a vertical engine mounted behind the seat-post. Later it used single-cylinder and V-twin Minerva, Precision, and possibly its own engines. Some were water-cooled singles with the radiator behind the headstock.

LIBERTY
c.1903–16 Produced a variety of machines in Melbourne with engines supplied by Moser, Peco, and others.

MAGNET
1902–c.1906 The first Magnet machines had an inclined engine fitted near the steering head of a bicycle frame. Belt drive was used. Soon a loop frame with additional bracing struts appeared. The vertical engine drove to the rear wheel by chain. It was made in Melbourne.

MALVERN STAR
c.1938–52 These were autocycles powered by 98cc Villiers engines made in Malvern, Victoria.

MONA
c.1915 Made a 4.5hp side-valve flat twin with belt final drive, which was marketed by Quirk's Lighting and Engineering Co. of Melbourne.

PASCO
c.1919–22 Assembled in Melbourne using typical British components, including side-valve V-twin JAP engines.

QUIRKS See Mona (above).

ROVA-KENT See Kent (left).

SWASTIKA
c.1913–22 JAP-engined machines made in Adelaide.

TILBROOK
1947–56 Rex Tilbrook made spare parts and sidecars before constructing a 250cc two-stroke single from scratch in just 58 days. All the work was carried out on his stand at the Adelaide State Show in 1947. Production versions used 122cc and 197cc Villiers engines and leading-link forks but retained the welded tubular frame of the prototype. Just 60 complete machines were made including some successful racers.

VICTOR
c.1903–05 Made motorcycles with Minerva engines. Production may have continued later using JAP engines.

Unconfirmed marques

Empire *c.1906*
Jolly Yorketown, SA *1907–09*
Mallee
The Ren *c.1921*
Stevens *c.1915*
Trescowthick *1904*
Warren
Whiting
Woolston *c.1905*
Wyatt-JAP Adelaide *c.1917–20*

New Zealand

BRITTEN
1988– Advanced racing machines built in very small numbers by John Britten. The 986cc 60° V-twin engine has four valves per cylinder and fuel-injection. The engine forms part of the unorthodox chassis design, which also uses many carbonfibre components.

MAORI
1913–17 Developed by New Zealanders, but built in England. A 292cc JAP engine and a variable-ratio belt drive was used. A shipment of 20 bikes destined for New Zealand was sunk en route; the marque went down too.

MOUNTAIN GOAT
c.1963–72 Limited production of farm bikes. It used 80cc Suzuki and, later, 120cc Kawasaki engines.

N-ZETA
1960–63 These were Jawa and CZ machines assembled in New Zealand. Some carried the JNZ badge.

STEWART
1959–63 A simple scooter, early models had industrial engines but they later had Villiers power units.

South Africa

PATRIOT
1994– A 600cc Rotax-engined machine with a square tube-frame. Few have been built, but series production is planned.

China

DONGHAI
1978– Solid 745cc vertical twin built for sidecar use. See also Xingfu (right).

HONGDU
1965– Began making the 80cc Yamaha YG1 under licence. Two-stroke Yamaha-based lightweight production continues.

JIALING
c.1975– Small-capacity machines made in association with Honda.

MIG
1971– Makes designs licenced from Honda, Suzuki, and Kawasaki. Its largest model is a 250cc four-stroke single. Scooters and mopeds are also made.

QUIN-QI
c.1975– Small-capacity two-strokes made in association with Suzuki.

TIANJIN
1985– The German Zündapp company folded in 1984, and the entire operation was bought by the Chinese. Production of 80cc to 125cc two-strokes began in 1988.

XINGFU
1985– Builds a 125cc Honda-designed model and 250cc two-stroke singles. Also produces the 750cc Donghai vertical twin.

Unconfirmed marque

Lanying

South Korea

DAELIM
1962– Produced lightweight machines before linking with Honda in 1978. Later models were made under licence from Honda and some are of its own design.

Taiwan

GEMINI
c.1970– Gemini make lightweight two-strokes under licence from Yamaha including scooters and trail bikes.

PGO
1964– First made motorcycles as the Yeu Tyan Machinery Co. Licence-built Vespa scooters were introduced in 1972. Later there were also links with Peugeot. The PGO initials were adopted in 1978. Two-stroke scooters and the 125cc Kung Fu motorcycle are now built. An advanced 1600cc V-twin never reached production.

Unconfirmed marque

San Yang *c.1962*

Israel

ZWI
c.1952–55 Lightweight machines with 125cc Villiers and JAP two-stroke engines.

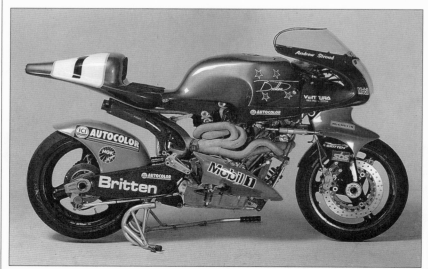

The Britten racer with a 986cc V-twin engine hidden behind the convoluted exhaust manifold

Glossary

Words in italic within an entry have their own entry in the glossary.

a.i.v. Atmospheric/automatic inlet valve. System used on early engines in which the inlet valve is held shut by a weak spring and opens by atmospheric pressure when the falling piston creates a vacuum in the cylinder.

alternator Electrical generator that makes alternating current by spinning a magnetic rotor inside a coil-wound stator.

autocycle A 98cc *moped*.

bash plate A protective plate fitted under the engines of off-road machines to prevent damage caused by grounding.

bathtub Bodywork resembling an upside-down bathtub used on rear of some Triumph motorcycles. It was introduced in 1957 and dropped in the early 1960s (see p.184).

bell mouth Bell-shaped air intake fitted to some *carburettors*.

bevel gears A pair of gears with faces cut at an angle of 45°, allowing drive to be turned through 90°.

b.d.c. Bottom dead centre. The point during *crankshaft* rotation at which the piston is in its lowest possible position.

bhp Brake horse power. A unit of measurement for engine power output.

big end The larger (*crankshaft*) end of the connecting rod.

bore The measurement of a cylinder's diameter (see also *stroke*).

cam An eccentrically shaped rotor that converts rotational movement into linear movement. Cams are used in the operation of valves, *contact breaker* points, and drum brakes.

camshaft A shaft with two or more *cams* used in the four-stroke engine to operate inlet and/or exhaust valves.

carburettor Device that mixes fuel and air into a combustible vapour.

chair Sidecar.

clincher rims Type of wheel rim used with early beaded-edge tyres.

clip-on engine An engine that attaches to a conventional bicycle frame.

clip-ons Low racing handlebars that clamp directly onto the fork legs.

compression ratio A measurement of the difference between cylinder volume at *t.d.c.* and *b.d.c.*

contact breaker The sprung switch in the low-tension ignition circuit that controls the timing of the spark in the high-tension circuit. Operated by a *cam*, contact brakers are sometimes called points.

contracting-band brake A brake in which a band is tightened around a rotating drum.

cradle frame Frame with two tubes passing under the engine (see also *open cradle frame*).

crankshaft The cranked shaft in an engine that changes the piston's linear motion into rotational motion.

cush drive A transmission shock absorber, usually a rubber cushion in the rear hub.

cylinder head A casting that caps the cylinder and contains the valves and combustion chamber.

damper Means of controlling speed of movement of the steering or suspension.

desmodromic Valve gear operation in which the *camshaft* actively closes as well as opens the valves.

d.o.h.c. Double overhead camshaft. Two *camshafts* fitted into the *cylinder head*.

diamond frame Tubular-frame design common until World War II and derived from the bicycle layout. The engine cases often form part of the structure. In profile it resembles a diamond shape.

distributor Device used in the ignition system of some multi-cylinder machines to send the high-tension spark to the correct cylinder.

dope Highly combustible alcohol/methanol-based fuel mixture.

Druid forks Side-sprung *girder forks*. Druid were the original makers.

duplex Double, having two parts. Applies to frames with two downtubes, and chains with double rows of rollers.

dynamo Electric generator that produces alternating current.

Earles forks Long leading-link forks, i.e. front suspension by pivoting fork controlled by twin shock absorbers.

Designed by Ernie Earles, they were used by many manufacturers in the 1950s.

enduro Off-road competition against the clock and usually over long distances.

epicyclic gear A gear that operates around the circumference of another.

face cam A *cam* system in which the eccentrics are situated on the face of a rotating disc.

fairing An enclosure fitted to improve the aerodynamic performance of the machine and/or rider comfort.

featherbed frame Famous Norton frame design by the McCandless brothers. It was introduced in 1950 and was given its name by factory rider Harold Daniell.

FIM Fédération Internationale Motocyclistes, the governing body of international motorcycle sport.

final drive Means of transmitting power to the driven wheel, usually by chain, shaft, or belt.

flat tank Fuel tank shape used on early motorcycles.

flat twin See *horizontally opposed*.

float bowl The fuel reservoir on a *carburettor* into which fuel flow is controlled by a valve operated by a float.

fore-and-aft flat twin A *flat-twin* engine mounted with the cylinders positioned in-line with the frame

forecar Early three-wheeled vehicle with two-front wheels fitted to a motorcycle-based frame. Passenger accommodation was sited above the front axle.

"garden gate" Nickname for the plunger-sprung frames used on Norton machines from the late 1930s.

gear cluster A set of gears.

gear ratio The ratio of the turning speeds of a driving and driven gear or the cumulative ratios of a series of gears.

girder forks Type of forks common on early machines, comprising rigid beams attached to the steering head by parallel links that allowed movement.

helical gear A gear with a spiral or semi-spiral meshing face.

horizontally opposed Type of engine layout in which the cylinders are placed at 180° to one another. It is also

described as a flat twin/four etc. or a boxer engine.

hub-centre steering Steering system in which the wheel pivots about its centre point; the axle is normally fixed.

ignition timing Point at which, relative to *crankshaft* rotation or piston position, the ignition spark occurs.

in-line Engine layout in which the cylinders are arranged in a row, and in-line with the wheels of the machine.

i.o.e. Inlet over exhaust. Valve layout used on some early machines in which the exhaust valve was mounted to the side of the engine and the mechanically operated inlet valve was positioned above the exhaust.

ISDT International Six Day Trial.

Isolastic Proprietary name for an engine/*swingarm* rubber mounting system used by Norton on its early Commando models.

JAP English engine manufacturer (see p.222). Founded in 1903 by John A. Prestwich, the company was bought by Villiers in 1957.

jockey wheel A wheel used to maintain tension in a chain or belt.

keystone frame An American term to describe a diamond-type frame in which the engine serves as part of the structure.

leading link Front suspension design in which the axle is mounted at the front end of two short links that pivot at the bottom of solid forks. The links are sprung to control movement. A long leading-link system has a complete fork that pivots behind the wheel.

leading shoe A brake shoe whose operating mechanism is adjacent to its leading edge. Twin leading-shoe brakes have two operating *cams*.

leaf spring A spring that comprises strips of spring steel clamped together. One end is fixed and the other is attached to the sprung component.

loop frame Early frame design in which the downtube curves underneath the engine cases to become the seat-post.

MAG Swiss engine makers, the initials stand for Motosacoche Accacias Geneva. The company also produced complete Motosacoche bikes (see p.293).

mag alloy Magnesium alloy, a strong lightweight metal used for many components, particularly wheels.

magneto A high-tension spark generator for the ignition system that does not require an external power source.

manifold A branched collection of pipes for inlet or exhaust gases.

marque Make or brand of motorcycle.

megaphone An outwardly tapered, high-performance exhaust.

monocoque Frame in which the structure is made as one unit from a sheet material (i.e. alloy or steel). It may also include bodywork or fuel containers in the structure. The Vespa *scooter* and the F750 Norton of c.1973 are among the rare examples in motorcycles.

moped A pedal-assisted motorcycle of less than 50cc.

motocross Off-road racing over a rough circuit. Formerly known as scrambling.

multi-plate clutch A clutch with several friction and drive plates. Its compact size makes it ideal for motorcycles.

MX See *motocross*.

nacelle A housing, usually for mounting instruments.

Neander-pattern Frame and fork design by Neander (see p.245) using pressed steel or Duralumin.

"new" Werner frame Frame design first used on the 1901 Werner (see p.195), the engine was fitted between the front downtube and the bottom bracket.

o.h.c. Overhead camshaft.

o.h.v. Overhead valve. Valves situated in the *cylinder head* above the combustion chamber. They are operated by pushrods controlled by a *camshaft* situated below the *cylinder head*.

open frame See *step-thru*.

open cradle frame Frame without tubes running under the engine. The engine unit bolts into place between the front downtube and the *swingarm* pivot area as a semi-stressed or *stressed member*.

over square An engine with a greater cylinder *bore* than piston *stroke*.

parallel twin A two-cylinder engine layout in which both cylinders are side by side and mounted across the frame.

pinion A small gear.

planetary gear A gear driven by a central sun gear or crownwheel.

plunger suspension A suspension system in which the vertical movement of the axle is controlled by springs mounted above and below the axle.

port Opening into a cylinder.

port timing In two-stroke engines the critical moment when ports are covered or uncovered by the piston.

pressed steel Sheet steel made into curved sections by press forming. It is often used in the construction of the frame and forks.

pre-unit An engine and gearbox that are not built together in the same casing. Pre-unit construction was common on earlier motorcycles.

primary drive The system of transferring power from the engine to the gearbox. Usually achieved by chain or gear.

privateers Racers who do not have the backing of a manufacturer.

proprietary Component supplied by an outside manufacturer.

pushrod Metal rod used to transmit linear motion, most often from *camshaft* to rocker arm on *o.h.v.* engines.

rear sets Racing-style footrests fitted towards the rear of the machine to allow the rider to adopt a racing crouch.

rectifier A component that converts alternating current into direct current.

rising rate A suspension system that becomes harder to compress the further it is compressed. This is usually achieved by a mechanical linkage with variable leverage ratio.

rocker arm Centrally pivoted arm acting as a lever to open valves.

rolling chassis The assembled frame, wheels, and suspension of the bike.

saddle tank A fuel tank that fits over the top tube of the frame.

scooter Small-wheeled utilitarian machine with a *step-thru* frame.

sender A sensor unit conveying information about an engine to a gauge, warning light, or other component.

servo Any system used to assist a mechanism to operate with greater force than that initially applied to it.

side valve Valves positioned at the side of a cylinder.

simplex Single, one of. Usually applied to frames with a single downtube.

skirt The part of a component that hangs down, particularly the area of a piston below the gudgeon pin.

snail-cam chain adjuster Axle-mounted helical cams that allow accurate chain adjustment.

s.o.h.c. Single overhead *camshaft*.

speedway Specialized sport run on short, oval dirt tracks with four riders from two teams in each race.

spine frame A frame with a single main structural member from which the engine is suspended.

split single A two-stroke engine with two pistons that share a single combustion chamber (see p.49).

step-thru A frame layout with a low structure between the seat and the steering head. On early machines it was commonly called an open frame.

stressed member A component that is an integral part of the whole structure.

stroke Measurement of length of piston travel in the *bore*, usually expressed in millimetres (see also *bore*).

subframe Any auxiliary framework attached to the main body of a vehicle. On a motorcycle this often refers to the rear section of the frame, which supports the seat etc.

supercharger Mechanically powered device that compresses the combustible charge into the cylinder, artificially increasing the compression ratio. When the "blower" is driven by exhaust gas, the device is called a turbocharger.

s.v. See *side valve*.

swept volume The volume displaced by a piston's travel.

swingarm Suspension member pivoted at one end and supporting the wheel at the other. In most cases the swingarm is more accurately described as a pivoted fork, as the wheel is supported at both sides.

t.d.c. Top dead centre. The point at which the *crankshaft* and piston are in their highest possible position.

telescopic forks Front suspension system with two fork legs, each with

sliding and fixed tubular members that telescope together to allow suspension movement.

timing Measurement of the moment at which valves open or close, or when the spark occurs. It is normally expressed in degrees or millimetres before *t.d.c.* (see *ignition timing* and *port timing*).

total loss Ignition or lubrication system in which electricity or oil is used without being generated or recirculated. The ignition system uses power from a battery, eventually running it flat. The lubrication system uses oil without returning it to a tank. Both systems were common on early motorcycles. Two-stroke engines use a total-loss lubrication system.

trail bike Dual purpose machine for use on or off-road.

trailing link Front suspension design similar to *leading link* except the layout is reversed: the links pivot forward of the axle.

trials Off-road competition in which the rider has to surmount obstacles. Points are deducted if the rider puts his feet on the ground, goes outside the marked course, or fails to clear an obstacle.

TT Tourist Trophy races held on the Isle of Man.

twin-spar frame Frame in which the steering head and the *swingarm* pivot are connected by two metal, usually alloy, members that wrap around the engine.

twin port A *cylinder head* design in which there are two exhaust ports.

unit construction Integrated unit consisting of the engine and gearbox within the same casings.

unsprung weight The weight of that part of the machine that is not sprung, i.e. wheels, brakes, tyres, and half of the suspension.

upside-down forks *Telescopic forks* in which the lower section, on which the wheel is mounted, telescopes into the fixed upper tube. They are sometimes called inverted telescopic forks on earlier bikes.

V-twin Two-cylinder engine layout in which the cylinders form a "V".

works racers Racing machines built and operated by the factory.

worm and pinion gear System for turning rotational movement through 90°, in which a pinion is turned by a spirally cut gear.

Useful Addresses

APRILIA
Aprilia SpA
Via G. Galilei 1
30033 Noale
(VE) Italy

Aprilia Moto U.K. Ltd
Gregory Way
South Reddish
Cheshire
SK5 7ST
England

BIMOTA
Bimota SpA
Via Giaccaglia 38
47037 Rimini
Italy

Galleria Bimota Ltd
Stocklund Square
Cranleigh
Surrey
GU6 8RG
England

BMW
BMW Motorrad GmbH & Co.
Triebstr. 32
80993 München
Germany

BMW G.B. Ltd
Ellesfield Avenue
Bracknell
Berkshire
RG12 8TA
England

BMW Australia Ltd
783 Springvale Road
Mulgrave 3170
Australia

BMW New Zealand Ltd
7 Pacific Rise
Mount Wellington
Auckland
New Zealand

BMW South Africa Pty Ltd
31 3rd Road
Randjespark Ext. 17
P.O. Box 29 55–Pretoria 0001
Midrand
Republic of South Africa

**CAGIVA/DUCATI/
HUSQVARNA/MORINI**
Cagiva Trading SpA
Via A Cavalieri Ducati 3
40132 Bologna
Italy

Three Cross Motorcycles Ltd
Woolsbridge Industrial Estate
6 Old Barn Farm Road
Wimborne
Dorset
BH21 6SP
England

Norm Fraser Imports
17–19 Parramata Road
Homebush
NSW 2140
Australia

Eurobike Wholesale Ltd
58 Leach Street
New Plymouth
New Zealand

Ducati SA
214 Main Street
Johannesburg
South Africa

ENFIELD
Royal Enfield Motors
P.O. Box 5284
Thiruvottiyur
Madras
600019
India

Bavanar Products Ltd
Unit 3
Therapia Trading Estate
Therapia Lane
Croydon
Surrey
CR0 3DH
England

HARLEY-DAVIDSON
Harley-Davidson Intl
3700 Juneau Avenue
Milwaukee
Wisconsin 54320
U.S.A.

Harley-Davidson Motor Co.
Royal Albert House
Sheet Street
Windsor
Berkshire
SL4 1BE
England

HONDA
4 Power Road
London
W4 5YT
England

Honda Australia Pty Ltd
Lot 95, Sharps Road
Tullamarine
Victoria 3043
Australia

Honda New Zealand Ltd
105 Wiri Station Road
Manakau City
New Zealand

JAWA-CZ
Jawa-CZ
Motokov UK Ltd
Bergen Way
North Lynn Industrial Estate
King's Lynn
Norfolk
PE30 2JH
England

KAWASAKI
Kawasaki Heavy Industries
1-1 Kawasaki-cho
P.O. Box 16
Akashi
Japan

Kawasaki Motors Pty Ltd
Unit Q, 10–16 South Street
Rydalmere
NSW 2116
Australia

Kawasaki Motorcycle Distributors
9 Moa Street
Otahuhu
Auckland
New Zealand

KMSA Distributors Pty Ltd
Kawasaki Building
4 Standartd Close
Strijdom Park Ext. 25
Randburg 2125
Republic of South Africa

KTM
Dual Sport Motorcycles Ltd
Worcester Road
Ledbury
Herefordshire
HR8 1PL
England

MZ
MuZ
Motorrad-und-Zweiradwerk GmbH
Postfach 70
Alte Mariengerger
Strasse 30–35
09401 Zschopau
Hohndorf
Germany

MZ Motorcycles G.B. Ltd
Speedwell House
West Quay Road
Southampton SO15 1GY
England

PIAGGIO
Piaggio Veicolo Europei SpA
Viale Rinaldo Piaggio 23
56025 Pontedera
Italy

Piaggio Ltd
Unit 8, Ravensquay Business Centre
Cray Avenue
Orpington
Kent BR5 4BQ
England

SUZUKI
Suzuki Motor Corporation
Hamamatsu-Nishi
P.O. Box 1 432–91
Hamamatsu
Japan

Suzuki Australia Pty Ltd
144 Hall Street
Newport 3015
Victoria
Australia

Suzuki G.B. PLC
46–62 Gatwick Road
Crawley
West Sussex
RH10 2XF
England

Suzuki New Zealand Ltd
1 Heads Road
Wanganui
New Zealand

TRIUMPH
Triumph Motorcycles Ltd
Jacknell Road
Hinckley
Leicestershire
LE10 3BS
England

Triumph Australia
399 Elizabeth Street
Melbourne 3000
Victoria
Australia

Northern Accessories
64 Atkinson Avenue
Otahuhu
Auckland
New Zealand

YAMAHA
Yamaha Motor Co. Ltd
2500 Shingai
Iwata-shi
Shizuoka-ken 438
Japan

Mitsui Machinery Sales U.K. Ltd
Sopwith Drive
Brooklands
Weybridge
Surrey
KT13 0UZ
England

Yamaha Motor Australia Pty Ltd
49 Bentley Street
Wetherill Park
2164 NSW
Australia

Yamaha Motorcycles
299 Great North Road
Grey Lynn
Auckland
New Zealand

Yamaha Motor Europe NV
P.O. Box 75033
117 ZN Schipol
The Netherlands

Yamaha Distributors
P.O. Box 2760
Pinetown 3600
South Africa

Bibliography

Raymond Ainscoe, *Gilera Road Racers,* Osprey, 1987

Ashby and Angier, *British Motorcycles,* Pentagon, 1950

Autoexport Round Up, V/O Autoexport, 1976

Hans Axelsson, *MC Fran Alla Tider,* Forlags AB Semic, 1981

Roy Bacon, *Military Motorcycles of World War II,* Osprey, 1985

Roy Bacon, *British Motorcycles of the 1930s,* Osprey, 1986

Roy Bacon, *British Motorcycles of the 1960s,* Osprey, 1986

Bourdache, *La Moto En France 1894–1914,* Edifree

G.H. Brooks, *Motoring History Book 4,* Sporting Car Club of South Australia

G.H. Brooks, *Motoring History Book 10,* Sporting Car Club of South Australia, 1990

Alan Cathcart, *Ducati Motorcycles,* Osprey, 1983

C.F. Caunter, *Motorcycles – A Historical Survey,* HMSO

Jeff Clew, *British Racing Motorcycles,* Foulis, 1976

Harold Connolly, *Motorcycle Story 1875–1905,* MCN, 1962

Robert Cordon Champ, *The Sunbeam Motorcycle,* Haynes, 1980

Piet Cornet, *De Nederlandse Motorhistorie,* c.1974

Robert M. Croucher, *The Observer Book of Motorcycles 1977–80,* Warne

Robert M. Croucher, *The Observer Book of Motorcycles 1988/89–1991,* Bloomsbury Books

Davey and May, *Lagonda – the History of the Marque,* David & Charles, 1978

Demaus/Tarring, *The Humber Story 1868–1932,* Alan Sutton, 1989

Nathalie Denis, *La Motocyclette En France 1894–1914,* La Vie de l'Auto, 1989

Hans van Dissel, *Motorfietsen 1900–1960,* 1989

Hans van Dissel, *Motoren 1980–1990,* 1994

Michael and Eric Dregni, *Illustrated Motor Scooter Buyer's Guide,* Motorbooks, 1993

David Dumble, *Veteran Motorcycles in Australia,* VMC (Victoria), 1974

Gert Ekström, *Svensk Motorcykelhistoria,* Hudiksvall, 1991

Gaspard, *Les Demoiselles de Herstal & Les Dames de la Basse-Meuse,* 1970s

Allan Girdler, *Illustrated Harley-Davidson Buyer's Guide,* Motorbooks, 1986

Glass' Motorcycle Checkbook 1969–78, Glass' Guide, 1978

Glass' Motorcycle Checkbook 1992– , Glass' Guide, 1992

Jean Gorbuzzi, *Bike Catalogue International,* Sonnen Verlag, 1984

Rozsa Gyorgy, *Motorkerekpar Tiposuk,* Muszaki Konyvkiado, 1965

Han Harmsze, *75 Jaar Motorleven in Nederland,* 1979

Jerry Hatfield, *American Racing Motorcycles,* Haynes, 1982

Jerry Hatfield, *The Illustrated Indian Buyers Guide,* Motorbooks, 1989

Jerry Hatfield, *Inside Harley-Davidson,* Motorbooks, 1990

The History of Honda, Honda Motor Co., 1989

T.A. Hodgson, *Motorcycling's Golden Age of Fours,* Bagnall, 1973

Bob Holliday, *Norton Story* (3rd edition), PSL, 1986

Hought/Setright, *A History of the World's Motorcycles,* Allen & Unwin, 1973

W.E. Hulme, *The Register of Machines of the VMCC* (3rd edition), VMCC, 1991

Peter Jones, *Historic Motorcycling,* Modern Magazines Holdings (NSW)

Kawasaki Model Recognition Manual, Kawasaki Heavy Ind., 1982

Jacques Kupélian and Jacques Sirtaine, *Motos Belgea,* 1983

Jan Leek, *MZ: The Racers,* 650 publications, 1991

Ernst Leverkus, *Faszination Motorräd,* Deutsches Zweirad-Museum, 1991

Brian Long, *The Marques Of Coventry,* Warwickshire Books, 1990

Abramo Luraschi, *Storia della Motocicletta,* Edisport, 1992

Colin MacKellar, *Yamaha Two-stroke Twins,* Osprey, 1985

Macauley and Butler, *The International Motorcycle File,* Pictorial Presentations Ltd, 1972

Margolius and Meisl, *Skoda Laurin & Klement,* Osprey, 1992

Denis N. Miler, *Source Book Of Motorcycles,* Ward Lock, 1977

Don Morley, *Classic British Trials Bikes,* Osprey, 1984

Don Morley, *Spanish Trials Bikes,* Osprey, 1986

Don Morley, *Classic British Scramblers,* Osprey, 1986

Ian Morrison, *Motorcycle Sport Fact Book,* Guiness, 1991

Motocyclo Catalogue 1957–58, SOSP, 1958

The Motorcycle Index 1913–24, Fletcher & Son

The Motorcycle Index 1925–36, Fletcher & Son

The Motorcycle Index 1928–39, Fletcher & Son

Mitsuru Nakaoki, *Autobiography: Japanese Bike History,* Sony Magazines

NSU - vom Hochrad zum Automobil (2nd edition), Stuttgart, 1992

On Two Wheels (8 volume Motorcycle Encyclopedia), Orbis, 1978

Dominique Pascal, *50 Ans de Motocyclettes Françaises,* EPA, 1979

Dominique Pascal, *Le Grand Dictionnaire des Motos Françaises,* Ch. Massin

Brigitte Podszun, *Die Deutschen Motorräder der Wirtschaftswunderzeit* (2nd edition), Stuttgart, 1977

Pol and Walig, *Veteraanmotoren in Nederland,* VMC, 1978

Barrie Price, *The Lea-Francis Story,* Batsford, 1978

George Rance, *Vintage Motorcycles Illustrated*

Thomas Reinwald, *Motorräder aus Nürnberg,* Erlangen, 1994

Claude Reynaud, *Le Mythe Des 4 Cylindres,* Claude Reynaud, 1991

Rudolph Santer, *Österreichische Motorräder und Beiwagen 1918–1960,* Weishaupt, 1994

Richard Henry Schultz, *Henderson: Those Elegant Machines,* Pine Hill Press, 1994

Ulrich Schwab, *Motorräder 1970 bis 1987,* Stuttgart, 1987

Andy Schweitzer, *Zweiradfahrzeuge aus Östdeutchland,* Schrader Verlag, 1994

Hans Seper, Helmut Krackowizer, and Alois Brusatti, *Österreichische Kraftfahrzeuge,* Verlag Welsermühl, 1982

James Sheldon, *Veteran & Vintage Motorcycles,* Transport Bookman, 1971

Harry V. Sucher, *The Iron Redskin,* Haynes, 1977

Erwin Tragatsch, *The World's Motorcycles 1894–1963,* Temple Press, 1964

Erwin Tragatsch, *Motorräder. Deutschland, Österreich, Tschechoslowakei,* Motorbuch Verlag, 1974

Erwin Tragatsch, *The New Illustrated Encyclopedia of Motorcycles,* Grange, 1992

Trelland, *Motorcycle Reference Guide,* Trelland, 1991

Bart H. Vanderveen, *Motorcycles to 1945,* Frederick Warne, 1975

Mick Walker, *Spanish Post-war Road and Racing Motorcycles,* Osprey, 1986

Mick Walker, *MV Agusta: Road and Racing Motorcycles,* Osprey, 1987

Mick Walker, *Moto Guzzi Singles,* Osprey, 1987

Mick Walker, *German Motorcycles,* Osprey, 1989

Mick Walker, *Classic German Racing Motorcycles,* Osprey, 1991

Mick Walker, *Italian Motorcycles,* Aston, 1991

C.O. Windecker, *Motorrädtypen 1951–52,* Verlagklasing, 1951

Brian Wooley, *The Directory of Classic Racing Motorcycles,* Aston, 1988

David K. Wright, *The Harley-Davidson Motor Company: An official 80 year history* (2nd edition), Motorbooks, 1987

A number of periodicals and magazines was also used for research, including

Bike Catalogue International
Car and Bike International
Classic Bike
The Classic Motorcycle
The Engelbert Magazine
De Fietsmotor
France Automobile
Het Gemotorjseerde Rijwiel
Klein Motorsport
LVM (La Vie de la Moto)
Moto 73
Motociclismo (1915–present)
Moto Légende
The Motor
The Motor Cycle
Motor Cycling
Motorcyclist
Moto-Revue
De Motorrijder
Het Motorrijwiel
Motorsport
Vie Automobile

Index

Acknowledgments

The author's acknowledgments

It is an honour to have worked with so many knowledgeable and talented individuals during the year it took to make this book. Without their efforts and attention *The Encyclopedia of the Motorcycle* would not have been possible.

Annice Collet, Marie Thièce, and Mike Budd at the National Motor Museum Library suggested, researched, checked, double-checked, and found masses of motorcycles we never knew existed. Doug Jackson found even more (and in the most unlikely places). Mike Jackson found fewer marques but more mistakes.

Mike Jackson (again), Prosper Keating, Sean Hawker, Mick Phillips, and Rosie Marston contributed words and facts for The A–Z of Motorcycles.

The Directory of Motorcycles was produced with the collaboration and assistance of many people. Among those who deserve thanks for sharing their knowledge, experience, and contacts are:

Jim Rogers and Ed Youngblood of the American Motorcycle Heritage Foundation; Mort Wood and Dick Winger of the Antique Motorcycle Club of America; Allan Johnson of the Canadian Vintage Motorcycle Group; Klaus Arth, Peter Kuhn and Friedhelm Raatz of the Deutsches Zweirad-Museum and NSU-Museum, Neckarsulm, Germany; Serge Garcia of *Moto Legende* magazine, France; Jan Leek (Germany); Jacques Kupélian (Belgium); Hans van Dissel (Holland); Alain Rochat, Eric Bezon, Daniel Tille, Pierre Muhlemann, Jacques Leu, and Walter Murri (Switzerland); Yuko Sugeta (Japan); Adil Jal Darukhanawala (India); Mario Colombo (Italy); Paul Millin and Grant Howard (New Zealand); Raymond Ainscoe (the Italian province of Yorkshire); *Moto* magazine; Elena Konovalova (Moscow). In many cases they called on the assistance of others.

Jo Evans, Julia Wilson, Peter Jones, Matthew Pardoe, and Flavia Sottocornola translated from French, German, and Italian.

Dave King and Jonathan Buckley took excellent photographs and went to considerable trouble to track down the elusive Friday Farago Mk4, a motorcycle so rare that we could not include it.

Most of the photographs in this book were taken at the following locations: National Motorcycle Museum, Birmingham, England; Deutsches Zweirad Museum, Neckarsulm, Germany; and American Motorcycle Heritage Foundation, Westerville, Ohio, United States. Many of the machines were from their collections, others were provided by individuals and private collections.

Without the editorial and design team at Dorling Kindersley there would be no book. Without Janice Lacock and Jo Evans it would not have happened in the time allowed. Without Dave Walton, Dave Williams, Claire Pegrum, Carla De Abreu, Jacky Jackson, Tracy Hambleton-Miles, Stephen Croucher, and Lol Henderson it would have been even more difficult. They did not deserve my appalling spelling.

Thank you all.

Dorling Kindersley would like to thank the following:

All those who allowed us to photograph their machines: Ian Abrams; Donald Accola; Raymond Ainscoe; American Suzuki; Larry and Leslie Anderson; Mike Arden; Howard Atkin; Bill Baird; George Beale; Gary and Lois Beeler; Galleria Bimota; BMW; Pete Bollenbach; Pete Booth; Clayton T. Brooks; Ron Bussey Restorations; Jim Carlton; Chris Childs; Dr William Cleveland; Peter Collins; John Comerford; Jeff Dean; Millie and Frank DeGenero; Richard Dieter; Lockwood Doench; Al and Pat Doerman; Jesse A. Dowler; Duckhams Oils; Arthur Farrow; Larry Feece; Simon Fenning; Robert Fergus; Brian Foot; Greg L. Georges; Richard Gerhold; Wilf Green; Ross Hansell; Greg Harrison; Ernest H. Hartman, Jr; Ernie Hartman, Sr; Thomas L. Hayden; Graham Head; Herman Herz; Hinds Kawasaki Yamaha; Jim Hollern; John Holliday; Günther Holweg; Honda of America; Dennis Howard; Roger Hull; Husky Sport U.K.; Don Irminger; Bill Jarski; Dave Jones; Peter Jones; Doug Kane; Helmut Kern; Ron Kuhlman; Steve La Belle; John Lawes; Mike Leach; Tom Lewandowsky; Kit Lewis; Bruce Lindsay; Richard and Scott Luzander; Cyril Malem; Loren Mariano; Mark Mederski; Mike and Van Mefford; Sammy Miller; Jim, Jeff, and Kevin Minnis; The Montagu Collection; MotorCycle City; Motorräd Museum, Schloß, Augustusburg; Bob Mounce; William A. Murar; Jeff Murphy; MuZ Ltd; Mrs G.M.I. Nash; Jim Nickerson, Jr; Joe O'Brien; Mike Olney; Paul Pearce; Bruce Penhall; Bill Quinn; Eldon Raasch; Hayden Racknell; Carl Redman; Renham Motorcycles; Art Ridgway; Al Roberts; Robert and Galia Saar; Anthony and Kathy Salyers; Francis Sheehan; Gerald Shipano, Jr; Gary Slurkanich; Beverly and Ted Smith; Phil Somerfield; Darrel Spinosi; Jerry Stageberg; John Surtees; Jerry Tamanini; Bruce Troxall; Merrill Vanderslice; Gregory Walden; Dick and Wanda Winger; Mort Wood; John Wynne; John and Mary York; Roger T. Young; Ed Youngblood.

Additional thanks goes to Tony Hodson and Michael Sharpe for supplying text; Jo Lyford and Philippa Colvin for editorial assistance; Mick Gillah for artwork; Mark Johnson-Davies, Tassy King, and Simon Murrell for design assistance; Ingrid Nilsson and Helen Stallion for picture research; Kay Wright for the index; and Jim Rogers for all his help.

Any additional information concerning any marques that we may not have included will be gratefully received and used in future editions of *The Encyclopedia of the Motorcycle*.

PICTURE CREDITS

t=top; c=centre; a=above; b=below; l=left; r=right

The Publisher would like to thank the following for their kind permission to reproduce their photographs:

Advertising Archives 113cl.
Aprilia Moto U.K. Ltd 16b, 17tl.
BMW AG 27tr, 29cr, 32cl, 33cla, tr.
Etienne Bol 193cr.
Britten 308bc.
Classic Bike Magazine/EMAP Nationals 37cr, 38cr, 79tr, 135cr, 145tr, 148cb, 149cr, 166cr, 172cr, 183t, 184cr, 237b, 239br, 250tr, 263tr, 271bl, 278tr, 279bl, 290bl.

Russell Frears 222b, 228t.
Robert Harding Picture Library 85cr.
Honda Motor Europe Ltd 95br.
The Hulton Deutsch Collection 18cr, 190cr.
Kawasaki 115br, 117tr.
Stewart McDiarmid 138cr.
Mrs O. Miller 225tl.
Mitsui Machinery Sales U.K. Limited/Yamaha 206t.
Don Morley 105tr, 291tr.
Motorcycle Heritage Museum, Westerville, Ohio, photo courtesy of Doug Strange 11cr.
The National Motor Museum, Beaulieu 10cr, 46cr, 111tr, 140cr, 146ca, 156cr, 212b, 213t, 214b, 216b, 217b, 218b, 219br, 220t, 223t, 225br, 227br, 229b, 230bl, 232tl, 241bl, 243br, 244br, 253tr, 255bl, 256tr, 260br, 269b, 270t, 272tl, 273b, 274b, 276b, 293bl, 297tr, 301br.
Ricardo Consulting Engineers Ltd 180br.
Suzuki GB Plc 178t.
Triumph Motorcycles 186, 187.
Mick Walker 240t.
The World's Motorcycles News Agency 40cr, 47tr, 54t, 61tr, 118cb, 120br, bl, t, 132tr, bl, 151tc, 235b, 238tr, 242t, 245bl, 246t, 247br, 248b, 249tr, 252bc, 258tl, 259br, 262br, 264t, 265b, 266tr, 267br, 277bc, 281tl, 282b, 283tr, 284b, 286bc, 287tc, 288bl, 289bl, 299tl, 301br, 302bl, 303tr, 304bl, 305br, 306bl, 307br.